D1034335

A HISTORY OF PUBLIC LIBRARIES IN GREAT BRITAIN
1845–1965

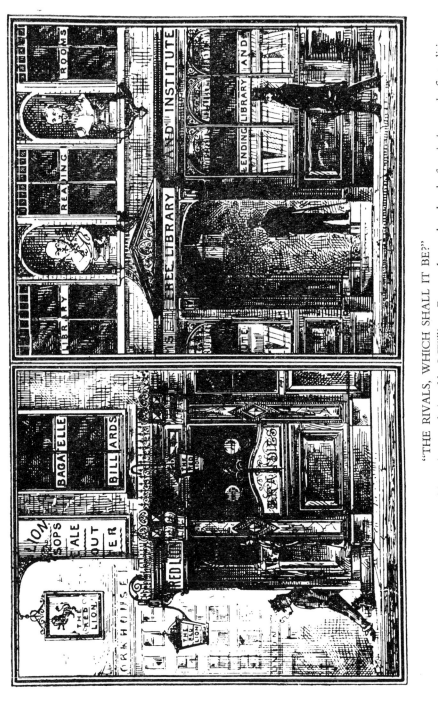

"THE RIVALS, WHICH SHALL IT BE?"

The most famous cartoon in English library history, designed by J. Williams Benn and reproduced as the frontispiece to the first edition of Thomas Greenwood's *Free Public Libraries*, 1886.

A HISTORY OF PUBLIC LIBRARIES IN GREAT BRITAIN

1845-1965

BY
THOMAS KELLY
Professor of Adult Education
in the University of Liverpool

THE LIBRARY ASSOCIATION
1973

"Librarianship, as we know it, can be fully apprehended only through an understanding of its historic origins."

—P. Butler, *An Introduction to Library Science* (1933).

© Thomas Kelly 1973
First published by The Library Association
7 Ridgmount Street, London, WC1E 7AE
ISBN: 0 85365 346 1

Printed and bound in England by
STAPLES PRINTERS LIMITED
at The Stanhope Press, Rochester, Kent.

PREFACE

IN this volume I have attempted to provide a fuller account than has hitherto been available of what seems to me one of the most important social and cultural developments of the nineteenth and twentieth centuries—the creation of the public library service. Forty years ago it was still customary to refer to "the public library movement", and rightly so, for until 1965 there was no compulsion on any local authority to make library provision: such provision was essentially a voluntary activity, requiring in its earlier phases the specific consent of the ratepayers. The heart of library history, therefore, is not to be found in its more general aspects, such as the growth of library legislation or the development of library techniques, important as these things are. Rather it is to be sought in the often highly individual history of the hundreds of individual libraries which together make up the library service. I have had this in mind throughout, and in the period prior to 1919 have been able to reinforce the general narrative with case-studies of selected libraries large and small. For the later period, because of the very large number of library authorities involved, this method has not been possible, but I have still sought to base the narrative firmly on the work and experience of individual libraries.

I cannot regard this as a final account, but I hope that, like my former work on *The History of Adult Education*, it will provide a framework within which further research can be carried on. I have tried throughout to tell the story in a way that will be of interest not only to the professional librarian but also to the social historian and the general reader. I have, in consequence, kept technical descriptions to a minimum. If, at times, I seem to have oversimplified, or to be labouring the obvious, I hope my librarian friends will forgive me.

I am very conscious that, as a non-librarian, I could never have attempted such a task without the constant encouragement and assistance given me by the Library Association and by librarians everywhere. Almost every chief librarian in the country has helped me in some way, and many have taken immense trouble in hunting out information for me and in supplying me with annual reports and other documents. Only in a small number of cases have I been able to acknowledge these obligations in the footnotes. To all the others I would like to express my very sincere thanks. I would particularly like to acknowledge my indebtedness for help at every stage of the work to Mr. Douglas Varley, Librarian of the University of Liverpool, and the staff of the Harold Cohen Library; to Mr. J. E. Vaughan, Librarian of the Liverpool University School of Education; to Mr. L. J. Taylor, Librarian of the Library Association, and his assistant Miss Andrea Polden; to Dr. George Chandler, City Librarian of Liverpool, and his staff; to Mr. Philip Hepworth, City Librarian of Norwich; and to Dr.W. A. Munford, Director- General of the National Library for the Blind. In the final stage I have incurred a fresh crop of obligations to all those librarians who have assisted with the loan of illustrative material.

I am also much indebted for information and assistance to Dr. William Aitken of the University Library School at Strathclyde; to Mr. A. C. Jones and Mr. P. H. Sewell of the Department of Education and Science; and to Dr. Alex

Law of the Scottish Education Department. I have also to express my particular gratitude to Mr. Frank Withers, formerly of the Department of Education and Science, and Mr. W. H. Snape, Head of the School of Librarianship at the Liverpool Polytechnic, who have read the entire work at the manuscript stage. I have profited much from their comments and suggestions, but they are, of course, in no way responsible for any errors that remain. Finally I must acknowledge, as always, the continuing help and support of my wife, who in the concluding stages has assisted in the preparation of the indexes.

July 1973   THOMAS KELLY

CONTENTS

BOOK I
THE FIRST PHASE, 1845–1886

BOOK II
FROM THE JUBILEE TO THE FIRST WORLD WAR, 1887–1918

BOOK III
BETWEEN THE WARS, 1919–1939

BOOK IV
THE SECOND WORLD WAR AND AFTER, 1939–1965

APPENDICES

LIST OF ILLUSTRATIONS

LIST OF ABBREVIATIONS
used in the footnotes

Adams Report	W. G. S. Adams, *A Report on Library Provision and Policy to the Carnegie United Kingdom Trustees* (Dunfermline 1915).
ASLIB	Association of Special Libraries and Information Bureaux.
Bourdillon Report	Ministry of Education, *Standards of Public Library Service in England and Wales* (1962).
Conference Transactions 1877	*Transactions and Proceedings of the Conference of Librarians ... 1877* (1878).
Dip. Lib.	Diploma in Librarianship.
1849 Report	Select Committee on Public Libraries, *Report* (1849).
F.L.A.	Fellow of the Library Association.
F.Y.W.L. 1951–55 (etc.)	P. H. Sewell (ed.), *Five Years' Work in Librarianship 1951–55* (etc.) (Library Association 1958 (etc.)).
Greenwood 1886 (etc.)	Thomas Greenwood, *Free Public Libraries* (1886, etc.). For details of the editions see Bibliography, No. 24.
Kenyon Report	Board of Education, Public Libraries Committee, *Report on Public Libraries in England and Wales* (Cmd. 2868, 1927).
L.A.	Library Association.
L.A. Conference Transactions, (Proceedings, Papers) 1878 (etc.)	Reports under various titles of the annual conferences of the Library Association, 1878–1962. For details see Bibliography, No. 93.
L.A.R.	*Library Association Record.*
L.Y.B. 1897 (etc.)	*Libraries, Museums and Art Galleries Year Book, 1897* (etc.). For details see Bibliography, Nos. 105-7.
McClelland Report	Scottish Education Department, Advisory Council on Education in Scotland, *Libraries, Museums and Art Galleries: a Report* (Cmd. 8229, Edinburgh 1951).
McColvin Report	L. R. McColvin, *The Public Library System of Great Britain* (1942).
Minto Report	C. S. Minto, *Public Library Services in the North of Scotland: a Report and Recommendations* (1948).
Mitchell Report	J. M. Mitchell, *The Public Library System of Great Britain and Ireland 1921–1923: a Report prepared for the Carnegie U.K. Trustees* (Dunfermline 1924).
P.L.A.E.C.	Public Libraries and Adult Education Committee for the North-West.
P.R. 1853 (etc.)	Parliamentary Returns of Public Libraries, 1853–1912. For details see Bibliography, Nos. 114-22.
Roberts Report	Ministry of Education, *The Structure of the Public Library Service in England and Wales* (Cmnd. 660, 1959).
Survey	L. R. McColvin (ed.), *A Survey of Libraries: Reports on a Survey made by the Library Association during 1936–37* (1938).
Y.W.L. 1928 (etc.)	(Various editors), *The Year's Work in Librarianship, 1928* (etc.) (Library Association 1929 (etc.)).

xiii

BOOK I
THE FIRST PHASE
1845–1886

CHAPTER I

The Origins of the First Public Libraries Act

Introductory

THE Public Libraries Act of 1850 was one of a whole series of reforming measures passed at a time when the country was just emerging from the worst horrors of the Industrial Revolution. In spite of the Chartist movement and the early efforts at trade union and co-operative organization, these measures were due more to the enlightened goodwill of a sector of the ruling classes than to revolutionary agitation from below. The Parliamentary Reform Act of 1832, the first Government grant for education in 1833, the Factory Act of 1833 and its successors of 1844, 1847, and 1850, the Poor Law Amendment Act of 1834, the Municipal Corporations Act of 1835, the Prisons Act of the same year, the Mines Act of 1842, and the Public Health Act of 1848, were successive milestones along the road to a more humane and more democratic society, and in every case the initiative came from above.

The Public Libraries Act, though it has attracted little attention in the history books, was not the least important of these reforms. Its background was more complex than has hitherto been supposed. It is generally treated as an event which came about rather suddenly, almost unexpectedly, as the result of the combined efforts of two members of Parliament, William Ewart and Joseph Brotherton, and a librarian, Edward Edwards. Edwards, in his old age, roundly declared that the 1850 Act and its successors "had their first inception, and origin" in his own labours during the years 1847–49, though he admitted the claim of Ewart to be regarded as their "*parliamentary* author".[1] New research, however, makes it possible to view the matter in a juster perspective, and to see the Act (as indeed we should expect) as the end product in a long process of historical development.

In an earlier volume I have described the immense variety of libraries which came into being, from the Middle Ages onwards, to meet the needs of the reading public.[2] In the first half of the nineteenth century they were mostly either institutional libraries, such as those attached to mechanics' institutes and literary and philosophical societies, or subscription libraries (private or commercial). At one time, especially in the seventeenth and eighteenth centuries, there had also been a great many libraries created by gift or endowment, but with a handful of exceptions these had now ceased to make effective provision.

Both the concept and the name of "public library" had long been familiar. The concept had evolved from the Guildhall Library in fifteenth-century London, catering for a public consisting almost exclusively of clergy and students, to the point where an endowed library such as Chetham's in Manchester could claim to be really and effectively open to all classes of the com-

---

[1] Preface to the second (and incomplete) edition of his *Memoirs of Libraries*, written in 1885 and published posthumously in 1901.
[2] T. Kelly, *Early Public Libraries* (1966).

munity. The name, which appeared first in its Latin form (*bibliotheca publica*) as a technical term to distinguish the general university libraries of Oxford and Cambridge from those of the colleges,[1] was frequently used in its more modern sense with reference to endowed libraries from the seventeenth century onwards, e.g. the parochial library at Totnes in 1634,[2] the Lewisham Grammar School Library in 1652,[3] Chetham's Library, Manchester, in 1653,[4] and the Norwich City Library in 1659.[5] In the late eighteenth and early nineteenth centuries, unfortunately, the term was frequently appropriated to proprietary subscription libraries, and it was to avoid the confusion resulting from this usage that so many of the early libraries formed under the Act of 1850 were called "free libraries", or "free public libraries".

Even the idea that a library might be supported from public funds was not without its precedents. Apart from the British Museum Library, which from its beginning in 1753 was maintained from national funds, we can count a score of old endowed libraries, from the fifteenth century onwards, which were at least in some degree assisted from municipal resources. The town library of Kirkwall in Orkney was even receiving contributions, in the mid-eighteenth century, from the rates of a parish ten miles away.[6] A late example of a municipally supported library was the new London Guildhall Library, created in 1828 as a repository for "all matters relating to this City", and maintained from the Corporation's Privy Purse.[7]

Early Proposals for a Public Library Service

Developments of this kind all helped to prepare the way. We can say with confidence, however, that at the opening of the nineteenth century the idea of a nation-wide, publicly supported library service, open to all classes of the community, was still undreamed of. Only John Evelyn had come within reach of such a conception, when in a letter to Samuel Pepys in 1689 he had called for the establishment of libraries for the clergy "by a public law and contribution

---

[1] E.g. at Cambridge in 1533, at Oxford in 1556. See C. Sayle, "Annals of Cambridge University Library," in *The Library*, 3rd Ser., Vol. VI (1915), p. 148; W. D. Macray, *Annals of the Bodleian Library* (Oxford 1890), p. 13.

[2] Central Council for the Care of Churches, *The Parochial Libraries of the Church of England* (1959), p. 102.

[3] W. H. Black, *Bibliothecae Colfanae Catalogus* (1831), p. xxxv.

[4] Kelly, *op. cit.*, pp. 77–99.   [5] *Op. cit.*, p. 74.   [6] *Op. cit.*, pp. 99–100.

[7] On the subsequent history of this library see below, p. 24.

The question may be asked at this point why, in view of the existence of municipally supported libraries from an early date, it was necessary in 1850 to pass an Act empowering local authorities to spend money on libraries. The answer is to be found in the Municipal Corporations Act of 1835, which swept away the old borough corporations, and placed the management of municipal affairs in the hands of elected town councils whose power to spend money from the rates was restricted to certain specified categories of expenditure, mainly in the first instance those connected with the maintenance of law and order. This Act was widely interpreted as abolishing the much wider powers which the corporations had formerly exercised, but Greenwood (1891), p. 432, cites an "authority on Public Library matters" for the view that these powers still subsisted, and that the penny rate limitation then operating could be removed by the simple expedient of repealing the Libraries Acts *in toto*.

in every county in England".[1] It was the nineteenth century, with its new emphasis on the provision of libraries for the working classes, and its new attitude to the powers and responsibilities of government, that first turned men's minds in the direction of a library service assisted from public funds.

As early as 1808 J. P. Malcolm, the topographer, suggested that circulating libraries "should be encouraged by the Legislature under proper regulations".[2] As far as present knowledge goes, however, the first precise proposal for a rate-aided public library service is to be found in a document discovered a few years ago in the Brougham Papers at University College, London. It is a letter endorsed "6 Feby. 1831", and addressed to the then Lord Chancellor, Henry Lord Brougham, the great champion of mechanics' institutes and other forms of popular education. It reads:

> "My dear Lord Chancellor,
> I send the notes relating to the bill for the establishing public libraries in towns. I think if you have time to look at them you will find the plan very simple. I have mentioned it to many, who think well of it: if made a law, it will be another step in the *grand March*.
> If you give the notes to Sir H. Parnell, and he approves, I will confer with him, if he will send to me, and I will bestow all necessary pains in drawing the bill. . . ."

The enclosure referred to is headed *Proposal for a bill to enable Towns of a given population to raise funds for the establishment of public reading and public lending libraries*. In some ways it anticipates, in some it goes beyond, the Act eventually passed in 1850. Its main features are:

(1) Towns, or districts having a certain population, to be empowered by resolution of the inhabitants at the vestry meeting, to raise money either from the rates or by borrowing, to provide a public library.

(2) The library to be open for reading to all inhabitants, and for borrowing to all ratepayers and to other parishioners on the guarantee of a ratepayer.

(3) The vestry to appoint a library committee and a librarian, and to build or hire suitable premises.

(4) The control of book selection to be in the hands of a Board of Commissioners in London, which would recommend an appropriate selection of books according to the amount of money available.

(5) Borrowers to pay a small charge (say $\frac{1}{2}$d.) for each volume borrowed, as a contribution to the running expenses.[3]

The writer of this letter, Charles Henry Bellenden Ker (1785?–1871), was a lawyer and a particularly close friend of Brougham, who in August, 1831, assigned to him a life annuity of £320.[4] In later life he made something of a name for himself in the field of law reform. Both he and Sir Henry Parnell (1776–1842), to whom he refers, were fellow-members with Brougham of Lincoln's Inn, and both were zealous members of the Society for the Diffusion

---

[1] *Diary and Correspondence of John Evelyn*, ed. W. Bray (new edn. 1902), Vol. III, p. 307.

[2] *Anecdotes of the Manners and Customs of London during the Eighteenth Century* (1808), p. 48.

[3] For details of these and related documents see below, App. I, where the Proposal is printed in full. It should be noted that this was before the Municipal Corporations Act of 1835: hence the proposal to use the vestry, i.e. the governing body of the parish, as the library authority.

[4] Indenture in Brougham Papers, University College, London.

of Useful Knowledge which Brougham had founded in 1826, under his own chairmanship, to carry out his ideas for the provision of cheap educational literature for the masses. Ker is described by Charles Knight, publisher to the Society, as "the most fertile in projects of any member of the committee", and it may well be that the scheme set out in the letter was of his own devising; but we cannot exclude the possibility that he was putting into shape an idea originally conceived by Brougham.

Be this as it may, the project was considered by the General Committee of the Society, inquiries were made through local correspondents regarding public library provision in various parts of the country, and on 29 March 1831, a sub-committee was appointed, including Ker, to consider the matter and make recommendations. Apparently, however, no recommendations were ever made: the last we hear of the proposal is a minute of September 1832, "that Mr. Ker be requested to return the accounts of libraries transmitted some time since to the Committee".[1] Only a few months earlier Thomas Carlyle, on his lonely farm at Craigenputtock, had confided to his journal:

> "What a sad want I am in of libraries, of books to gather facts from! Why is there not a Majesty's library in every county town? There is a Majesty's jail and gallows in every one."[2]

As far as can be ascertained, Ker's abortive proposal had no influence whatever on later developments, but these developments came surprisingly quickly. The general election which followed the Reform Act of 1832 brought into the House of Commons a whole crop of new members, many of them with reforming plans of their own. One of them was Benjamin Hawes, M.P. for Lambeth, who was interested enough in museums and libraries to call for a report on foreign museums and public libraries, which was duly made and circulated in October 1834.[3] Another was James Silk Buckingham, M.P. for Sheffield, who made the first attempt to secure Parliamentary sanction for the provision of public libraries from the rates—an attempt which, oddly enough, has hitherto escaped the notice of library historians.[4]

Buckingham is one of the more interesting minor figures of the early nineteenth century. Son of a Cornish farmer, he was born near Falmouth in 1786, went to sea before he was ten, educated himself largely by his own efforts, travelled all over the world, and eventually, after being expelled from India for criticizing British rule there, settled down in London in 1824 as a rather un-successful journalist. He served as member for Sheffield for only five years,

---

[1] For further details see below, App. I.

[2] J. A. Froude, *Thomas Carlyle: the First Forty Years of his Life* (1882), Vol. II, p. 281 (18 May 1832).

[3] Summarized in *Quarterly Journal of Education*, Vol. X (1835), pp. 284–306, and printed in full in *Parliamentary Papers* (1836), Vol. X. Hawes (1797–1862) was interested in a variety of reforms and inventions, and was responsible, among other things, for securing the opening of the British Museum on holidays. He was afterwards knighted, and ended his political career as Permanent Under-Secretary for War.

[4] Since this was written, E. R. Reid-Smith has drawn attention to Buckingham's work in *Parliament and Popular Culture in the Early Nineteenth Century* (Research in Librarianship, Oldham 1969), and it is also referred to in the 2nd edn. (1971), of W. J. Murison, *The Public Library: its Origins, Purpose and Significance*, pp. 31–33.

devoting the remainder of his life to foreign travel, popular lecturing, and the writing of travel books and pamphlets about temperance, of which he was a fervent advocate. A projected four-volume *Autobiography* remained only half completed at the time of his death in 1855.

In 1834 Buckingham secured, in spite of Government opposition, and much public ridicule, the appointment of a Select Committee under his own chairmanship to inquire into "the extent, causes, and consequences of the prevailing vice of intoxication among the labouring classes of the United Kingdom", and to consider possible remedies. In his speech moving the appointment of the Committee he urged the need not only for control of the liquor trade but also for more positive measures, amongst them "encouraging the establishment of parish libraries, and district reading-rooms".[1]

Benjamin Hawes was a member of this Committee; so also—significantly in view of later developments—was another new M.P., Joseph Brotherton of Salford. Brotherton (1783–1857) was a cotton manufacturer who retired at an early age to devote himself to public work. Parliamentary reformer, factory reformer, free trader, fundamentalist, total abstainer and vegetarian, he served for nearly forty years as pastor of the Bible Christian Church in Salford, and for twenty-five years, until his death, as M.P. for the borough.[2]

One of the best-informed witnesses to give evidence before the Committee was the veteran London working-class leader, Francis Place. Place was suspicious of the Committee, and sceptical about the effectiveness of legislative restrictions and regulations, but in answer to a direct question from Buckingham he agreed that "the establishment of parish libraries and district reading rooms, and popular lectures on subjects both entertaining and instructive to the community might draw off a number of those who now frequent public houses for the sole enjoyment they afford".[3] Other witnesses testified to the same effect, and in its report the Committee recommended, in addition to regulations for the control of public houses,

> "The establishment, by the joint aid of the government and the local authorities, and residents on the spot, of public walks and gardens, or open spaces for athletic and healthy exercises in the open air, in the immediate vicinity of every town, of an extent and character adapted to its population, and of district and parish libraries, museums and reading rooms, accessible at the lowest rate of charge."[4]

The significant feature of this recommendation is the proposal for assistance from the government and local authorities.

In accordance with the terms of the report, Buckingham sought leave in

[1] Hansard, *Parliamentary Debates*, 3rd Ser., Vol. XXIV (1834), cols. 118–119.

[2] Brotherton's contribution to the public library movement is assessed in J. S. Cowan, "Joseph Brotherton and the Public Library Movement," in *L.A.R.*, 4th Ser., Vol. XXIV (1957), pp. 157–158.

[3] Select Committee on Inquiry into Drunkenness, *Report* (1834), p. 173. In a letter to William Lovett, 21 Nov. 1834, Place denounced the report as "a most unjust false and cruel imputation upon the working classes, calculated to make them appear despicable miscreants"—Place Papers, Brit. Mus. Addit. MS. 35149, ff. 327v.–328v. This question is discussed in B. Harrison, "Two Roads to Social Reform: Francis Place and the 'Drunken Committee' of 1834", in *Historical Journal*, Vol. XI (Cambridge 1968), pp. 272–300.

[4] *Report*, p. viii. Rather similar recommendations regarding public walks had been made in the previous year by a Select Committee on Public Walks, chaired by Robert A. Slaney.

1835 to bring in three bills—one to regulate the drink trade, one to secure the provision in all towns of "Public Walks, Gardens, and Places of Recreation in the Open Air", and one "to authorize the erection of Public Institutions, to embrace the means of diffusing Literary and Scientific Information, and forming Libraries and Museums, in all Towns, for the use of the Inhabitants of the same".[1] Leave to bring in the first bill was refused, but the other two were proceeded with, and reached the committee stage before being abandoned.

The machinery proposed by the two bills was almost identical. In the case of the Public Institutions Bill the ratepayers of any city, borough or town were to be empowered to decide, by majority at a public meeting, on the establishment of institutions of the kind described above. In the event of such a decision, a Committee of Public Instruction, of twenty-one members, was to be elected to supervise the erection and management of the institutions. Any necessary funds might be borrowed, subject to repayment in twenty years, and a sixpenny rate might be levied for the repayment of the capital and interest.

The public institutions envisaged were specified in some detail: a spacious hall for social gatherings of the labouring classes; smaller rooms for committees and societies; a lecture-theatre; a library and reading rooms; and a museum and picture gallery. The great weakness of the scheme was its lack of adequate provision for upkeep. It was assumed that if only the capital charges could be covered from the rates, the cost of maintaining the institutions could be met by charges to the users, which were to be kept as low as possible, and by the subscriptions of the wealthier citizens.

It may be remarked that Buckingham's proposal, as far as libraries are concerned, bears more resemblance to the plan drafted by Bellenden Ker than to that adopted in 1850: indeed, the resemblance is sufficient to make it just possible that Ker's idea contributed one element to Buckingham's more grandiose project.[2]

A number of minor amendments were made in committee, including the replacement of the politically suspect title "Committee of Public Instruction" by "Committee of Public Institutions"; and a number of useful new clauses were added. One of these allowed the Committee to take over and adapt existing institutions where these were suitable; another permitted the establishment of branch institutions in large towns. It was, however, the clause giving power to levy a rate which brought about the defeat of the bill.[3]

Both bills were brought forward again in 1836, the Public Institutions Bill in its amended form, with a further additional clause enabling the new municipal corporations (established under the Act of 1835) to exercise the powers assigned to the Committees of Public Institutions. This time neither bill reached the committee stage, and the same fate befell a combined bill promoted by Buckingham in 1837. At the close of the session he ceased to be a member of Parliament.

His efforts, though apparently a failure, were not wasted. He undoubtedly drew attention to the need for better social and educational amenities in large towns, and by mid-century most of the objectives for which he had fought were at least within sight of achievement.[4] As far as public libraries were concerned

[1] *House of Commons Journal*, Vol. XC (1835), p. 452.

[2] For the text of the Bill see below, App. II.

[3] *House of Commons Journal*, Vol. XC (1835), pp. 561–562.

[4] See the Preface to Buckingham's *National Evils and Practical Remedies* (1849), p. xxii.

he performed a particularly valuable service by enlisting the interest not only of Joseph Brotherton, who was one of the sponsors of his 1837 bill, but also of William Ewart, who spoke in support of the amended Public Institutions Bill of 1835. Its provisions would, he thought, be better administered by the new municipal councils (the Municipal Corporations Act was at this time passing through the House of Lords), but "in the principle of the Bill he cordially agreed".[1]

The Museums Act of 1845

Ewart (1798–1869), a Liverpool man by birth and a Scot by descent, served in the House for more than forty years, chiefly for Liverpool (1830–37) and Dumfries (1841–68). Active in all liberal causes, he was responsible for many useful reforms, including measures to mitigate the horrors of capital punishment, which indeed he would have liked to see abolished altogether. Benjamin Haydon the artist, who knew him well, described him in a revealing phrase as "a keen little man".[2] He came to an interest in public libraries gradually, by way of an interest in industrial design. The Select Committee on Arts and Manufacturers, which he chaired in 1835–36, recommended *inter alia* the provision of public museums and galleries of art, but did not concern itself with public libraries.[3] In 1839, however, we find Ewart, in the House, linking the two types of institution together in much the same way as Buckingham had done, arguing that

> "The public libraries, the public galleries of art and science, and other public institutions for promoting knowledge, should be thrown open for the purpose of inducing men merely by the use of their outward senses to refine their habits and elevate their minds."[4]

In the same year the argument concerning public libraries was carried a step further by B. F. Duppa (another Lincoln's Inn man and friend of Brougham's) in a *Manual for Mechanics' Institutions* published by the Society for the Diffusion of Useful Knowledge. Duppa was impressed by the number of small and often inefficient libraries of various kinds then existing and was in favour of bringing together the libraries of each town into a single efficient collection. He wrote:

> "In this the government might greatly assist, by enabling corporations, both lay and ecclesiastical, to place the books and other documents in such a public repository; and by giving a collection of public documents or expensive standard books, and granting a sum towards the erection of a public building to hold the books. . . .; and by enabling municipalities to apply a portion of their borough rates to the maintenance of public libraries".[5]

Ewart continued to raise the matter in the House. In 1840 he suggested "the propriety of having public libraries in different parts of the metropolis".[6]

[1] Hansard, *Parliamentary Debates*, 3rd Ser., Vol. XXX (1835), col. 652.
[2] W. B. Pope (ed.), *The Diary of Benjamin Robert Haydon* (Harvard 1960–63), Vol. IV, p. 356. The best study of Ewart is W. A. Munford, *William Ewart, M.P.* (1960).
[3] Select Committee on Arts and Manufactures, *Report* (1836), p. v.
[4] Hansard, *Parliamentary Debates*, 3rd. Ser., Vol. XLVIII (1839), col. 91.
[5] [B. F. Duppa], *A Manual for Mechanics' Institutions* (1839), pp. 56–57.
[6] Hansard, *Parliamentary Debates*, 3rd. Ser., Vol. LIII (1840), col. 1186.

In 1844, casting his net wider, he urged "the formation of public libraries in the metropolis and provincial towns". Replying to this point the Prime Minister, Sir Robert Peel, said "He should be sorry to see the Government interfering in a matter which had much better be left to private exertion".[1]

In this same year 1844, however, an opportunity at last arose for Ewart to do something practical about museums. In 1840 Edward Edwards, at that time a junior assistant in the British Museum Library, had published an essay on *The Fine Arts in England*, in which he had taken up the proposal of Ewart's Select Committee for the establishment of public museums and galleries, and had suggested that this operation should be financed partly by government grant and partly from the rates.[2] In November, 1844, a public meeting in Manchester led to the more precise and practical suggestion that towns should be empowered not merely to establish museums but to support them by means of a penny rate. Brotherton, who was present, carried the proposal to Ewart, who immediately brought the matter before Parliament.[3] The result was the Museums Act of 1845,[4] which in due course was to serve as a model for the Public Libraries Act.

The Act empowered councils of boroughs with a population of at least 10 000 to levy, not a 1d. rate, but a $\frac{1}{2}$d. rate, for the establishment of public "museums of art and science", and to make an admission charge of not more than 1d. This Act passed through Parliament with the greatest of ease, being presented by Ewart as a contribution to improved standards of industrial design. It was, however, capable of wider interpretation, and three towns, Canterbury, Warrington and Salford, ingeniously took advantage of it to establish combined museums and libraries.

At Canterbury the Corporation purchased for public use, early in 1847, the museum and library of the Philosophical and Literary Institution. In accordance with the Act, members of the public were admitted at a charge of 1d., and they were also allowed, at least until 1853, to borrow books at 1d. per volume, but this privilege was subject in each case (and initially for each separate borrowing) to an order from a member of the Museum Committee.[5]

Warrington, in 1848, brought together in rented premises the museum presented by the Warrington Natural History Society (founded ten years previously), and the books of the moribund Warrington Subscription Library (founded in 1760). The library was open on Wednesdays and Saturdays from 10 a.m. to 4 p.m., and from 6 p.m. to 9.30 p.m., and the books were available to all for reference. For more than forty years, however, books could be borrowed only by subscribers. A full-time curator and librarian was appointed from the beginning. "We have a skilled naturalist," explained the Town Clerk

---

[1] *Op. cit.*, Vol. LXXVI, cols. 1075–1081.

[2] E. Edwards, *The Fine Arts in England* (1840), pp. 101, 107–113.

[3] *Manchester Guardian*, 4 Dec. 1844; "The Origin of the Free Libraries and Museums Act", in *The Library*, Vol. I (1889), pp. 341–345; and Greenwood, (1891), pp. 59–60.

[4] 8 and 9 Vict. c.43.

[5] J. J. Ogle, *The Free Library* (1897), p. 11. The details are set forth in the Minutes of the Council and of the Museum Committee, of which the present City Librarian, Mr. F. Higenbottam, has been kind enough to furnish me with extracts. On 2 Feb. 1853 the Council asked the Museum Committee to consider and report on "the restrictions relative to the loan of books from the library".

to the Select Committee of 1849, "who is competent to stuff and prepare specimens, and he and his family act also as librarians. . . . We pay the curator a salary, which secures the services of all his family".[1]

Salford, on Joseph Brotherton's initiative, followed the example of Warrington by taking power in 1849 to establish a museum and library in a building already available in the recently acquired Peel Park. The reference library and one room of the museum were opened in 1850.[2] These three libraries can therefore claim to be the first modern rate-aided libraries in the country.[3] Whether it was legitimate, as the Town Clerk of Warrington contended, to count a library as part of the contents of a museum, is an open question, for before it could be brought to the test, the Museums Act was superseded.

The Select Committee of 1849

It was while all these developments were taking place that Edward Edwards came forward as a powerful and informed advocate of public library provision. Edwards (1812–86) was another of those self-educated men of humble origin who contributed so much to the progress of social reform in the early nineteenth century. A regular habitué of the British Museum Reading Room, he attracted notice in 1836 with a pamphlet on the organization of the Library,[4] which led to his being called as a witness before the Select Committee then sitting on the affairs of the Museum, and ultimately to his appointment by Panizzi to a junior post on the Library staff (1839). Panizzi, however, was something of a martinet, Edwards was a very bad subordinate, and ill-feeling between the two ended in Edwards's dismissal in 1850. He was no more fortunate in his next post as first librarian of the Manchester Free Library, from which, as we shall see, he was dismissed in 1858.[5] His reputation today rests on his contribution to the Act of 1850, and on his voluminous writings on library history and organization, which though often diffuse and ill-organized reveal a scholarly knowledge of the past and a far-sighted appreciation of contemporary problems.[6]

In 1848 Ewart's attention was caught by a paper by Edwards entitled, "A Statistical View of the Principal Public Libraries in Europe and the United

---

[1] Select Committee on Public Libraries, *Report* (1849), pp. 107–111; J. P. Aspden (ed.), *Warrington Hundred* (Warrington 1947), pp. 95–99; G. A. Carter, "Warrington and the Public Library Movement", in *The Fortnightly* (Dec. 1950).

[2] B. H. Mullen, *The Royal Museum and Libraries, Salford* (Salford 1899), pp. 22–26; see also the article by Cowan, cited above, p. 7, note; and Select Committee on Public Libraries, *Report* (1849), pp. 246–247.

[3] Ogle's statement (*op. cit.*, p. 35) that at Leicester, where a museum was established in 1848, the Council resolved in the following year to levy an additional ½d. rate for a free library, is incorrect. This decision, which would have been *ultra vires* in 1849, was not taken until twenty years later. There was, however, from 1849, a small collection of reference works acquired along with the museum from the Literary and Philosophical Society.

[4] *A Letter to Benjamin Hawes: being strictures on the "Minutes of Evidence" taken before the Select Committee on the British Museum* (1836, 2nd edn. 1839).

[5] See below, p. 42.

[6] His major works were: *Memoirs of Libraries*, 2 v., 1859; *Libraries and Founders of Libraries*, 1864; *Free Town Libraries*, 1869; and *Lives of the Founders of the British Museum*, 1870. The best biography is W. A. Munford, *Edward Edwards, 1812–1886* (1963).

States".[1] It was one of three produced by Edwards about this time, all seeking to demonstrate how badly Great Britain compared with other countries in the provision of libraries freely open to the public. Ewart wrote to Edwards in August, 1848. After referring to his own efforts in the House on behalf of public libraries, he went on:

> "I was desirous (and still am) that the Government should make a grant (as they do in the case of Schools of Design) wherever a disposition is shewn by the inhabitants of a town to maintain a Library. A *small* annual grant would do considerable good."[2]

It would be possible, he pointed out, to proceed either by way of a resolution in the House of Commons or by a motion for a Select Committee. If the latter course were adopted, could sufficient evidence be supplied? Edwards's reply was an unhesitating affirmative, and in March, 1849, the Commons agreed to the appointment of a Committee, with Ewart as Chairman, "on the best means of extending the establishment of Libraries freely open to the Public, especially in large towns, in Great Britain and Ireland".[3]

This was the Committee which produced the well known 1849 Report.[4] From 1848 onwards Ewart and Edwards worked hand in hand to ensure that the Report was on the right lines. Ewart planned the general strategy, Edwards supplied the detailed material. Questions were carefully prepared, witnesses procured, statistics collected. Brotherton gave valiant support in committee. It would be too much to say that the Report was a "frame-up", but certainly no stone was left unturned to demonstrate, first, that the existing public library facilities in Great Britain were totally inadequate, and second, that facilities in other countries were much better. Where the evidence did not support this view, Ewart was reluctant to accept it. "Prince Albert's German Secretary, Dr. Meyer", he writes to Edwards, "told us today that the German Libraries are not freely accessible. I think he must be wrong".[5]

Edwards's own 495 questions and answers were prepared with special care. Appearing as the first witness, and reinforcing his evidence with statistical tables covering libraries both at home and abroad, he made a most valuable contribu-

---

[1] Statistical Society of London, *Journal*, Vol. XI (1848–49), pp. 250–281.

[2] W. A. Munford, *Edward Edwards* (1963), p. 56. The provincial schools of design received an annual government grant of about £150 to pay a master, subject to a similar contribution from local sources towards general maintenance—Q. Bell, *The Schools of Design* (1963), p. 102.

[3] Hansard, *Parliamentary Debates*, 3rd Ser., Vol. CIII (1849), col. 755. W. A. Munford, *William Ewart* (1960), pp. 184–185, thinks that Edwards misguided Ewart by advising a Select Committee and by pressing for local rate-aid, and that he should have advised him to concentrate first on obtaining government grant for library buildings. This seems a little unfair. Ewart offered Edwards the choice of a resolution in the Commons (which since he was a private member could not be a money resolution and could therefore be of little practical value) or a Select Committee which might lead to legislation. It is difficult to see how Edwards could have decided otherwise.

[4] The Committee was three times reappointed, and produced further Reports in 1850, 1851 and 1852, but these were mainly occupied with additional statistical material relating to foreign libraries.

[5] J. J. Ogle, "Edwards and Ewart and the Select Committee on Public Libraries of 1849", in *L.A.R.*, Vol. I (1899), p. 704.

tion to the Committee's knowledge, and set the tone of the whole proceedings, though some of his preconcerted exchanges with Ewart have a faintly comic air as we read them today.[1]

Both the 1849 Report and the Parliamentary debates on the Act of 1850 have been dwelt on in loving detail by earlier library historians. There is no need, therefore, to narrate the proceedings of the Committee at length here.[2] The Report is a fascinating document which throws much light not only on libraries but also on the educational and social conditions of the time, and it deserves to be much more widely known. The information available to the Committee was inevitably rather patchy: my own view is that the Report underestimates the extent to which books were generally available in this country,[3] and I suspect it overestimates the accessibility of libraries abroad. None the less it is, by and large, an extraordinarily comprehensive document, and the picture it gives is substantially true.

The Committee made a number of suggestions (not always very precisely worded) for securing the maximum use of existing resources, e.g. easier public access to the British Museum Library and other copyright libraries; the opening up of the university libraries to the public "under proper regulations"; increased facilities for readers at Dr. Williams's Library and the library at Sion College; the restoration of Archbishop Tenison's Library to form the nucleus of a local library for Westminster; the development of the use of the British Museum's duplicate copies to form a lending library and to strengthen provincial collections. They urged on landowners and clergy the need to provide libraries for their workpeople. They emphasized the importance of evening opening for all public libraries, even though this implied the use of artificial lighting; and equally the importance of facilities for borrowing, since "Many men, in order to derive the fullest advantage from books, must have them not only in their hands, but in their houses".[4] They pleaded for more international exchange of books, and for the removal of such impediments to the formation of libraries as the paper duty, the advertisement tax, and the duty on imported foreign books.[5]

Recommendations of this kind, however, were of little value unless steps were taken to increase the number of libraries. To this end the Committee proposed, first, government grants in aid of libraries, on the same principle as those already made for primary schools and schools of design; and second, an extension of the Museums Act of 1845 to enable municipal authorities to levy a small rate for the establishment and maintenance of a library. Optimistically, they believed that there was no need to subsidise the provision of books: given

---

[1] See for example Q. 296–301 at p. 21 of the *Report*.
[2] For a full summary see J. Minto, *A History of the Public Librray Movement* (1932), Chs. iii–iv. W. J. Murison, *The Public Library: its Origins, Purpose and Significance* (1955, 2nd edn. 1971), ch. ii, gives a particularly valuable analysis. A recent study is J. R. Allred, "The Purpose of the Public Library: the historical view", in *Library History*, Vol. II (1970–72), pp. 185–204.
[3] See T. Kelly, *Early Public Libraries* (1966), Ch. viii.
[4] Select Committee on Public Libraries, *Report* (1849), p. xii. (This *Report* is cited hereafter as 1849 *Report*).
[5] The paper duty was at this time 1½d. per lb; the advertisement tax 1s. 6d.; and the duty on foreign books averaged, according to Edwards (1849 *Report*, p. 31), 12 per cent *ad valorem*. The advertisement tax was abolished in 1853, and the paper duty in 1861.

a proper place of deposit under public control, they argued, "Donations will abundantly supply the books."[1] How mistaken they were on this latter point was soon to be proved.

The recommendation regarding government aid was curiously imprecise as to the type of aid required. The grants to elementary schools, made first by the Exchequer and then by the Committee of Council on Education from 1833 onwards, were for school buildings, though small sums were also made available from 1846 to promote the training of pupil-teachers. The grants to schools of design made by the Board of Trade were towards teaching costs.[2] As events turned out, however, this recommendation was, regrettably, never pursued: it was on the second recommendation, for local aid, that the Act of 1850 was based.

The Public Libraries Act

Ewart was given leave to introduce his Public Libraries Bill in February 1850, and it received the royal assent six months later. Unlike the Museums Act, however, it came under heavy fire from an opposition led by that crusted old Tory, the gallant and honourable member for Lincoln, Colonel Charles Sibthorp. On the second reading he is reported as follows:

> "COLONEL SIBTHORP thought this Bill nothing more nor less than an attempt to impose a general increase of taxation on Her Majesty's subjects; . . . He would be happy at any time to contribute his mite towards providing libraries and proper recreations for the humbler classes in large towns; but he thought that, however excellent food for the mind might be, food for the body was what was now most wanted for the people. He did not like reading at all, and he hated it when at Oxford; but he could not see how one halfpenny in the pound would be enough to enable town councils to carry into effect the immense powers they were to have by this Bill. . . . he would have been much more ready to support the hon. Gentleman if he had tried to encourage national industry by keeping out the foreigner. . . ."[3]

Sibthorp fought the bill relentlessly through every stage. On a later occasion he commented satirically

> ". . . . he supposed they would be thinking of supplying the working classes with quoits, peg-tops, and foot-ball. They should first teach the people to read and write. What would be the use of these libraries to those who could not read or write? He supposed that the hon. Member and his Friends would soon be thinking of introducing the performances of Punch for the amusement of the people. The Bill was wholly uncalled for. . ."[4]

These were, it must be confessed, not among the most intelligent utterances in these debates. There were, however, many besides Sibthorp to raise the cry of additional taxation—quite unjustifiably, since expenditure under the bill, on both libraries and museums, was limited to the $\frac{1}{2}$d. rate fixed in 1845 for museums alone. The member for Devonshire North, L. W. Buck, even contrived to find in the proposals a threat to the "agricultural interest." Taxation without consent was another objection that was raised, in spite of the fact that the town councils were now elected bodies.

---

[1] Op. cit., pp. x–xi.   [2] See above, p. 12, note 2, and below, App. I.
[3] Hansard, Parliamentary Debates, 3rd Ser., Vol. CIX (1850), col. 839.
[4] Op. cit., Vol. CXI (1850), cols. 1174–1175.

There were, of course, some who thought, as Peel had thought in 1841, that these matters were best left to private enterprise.[1] P. H. Howard (Carlisle), for example, feared that the bill "would tend to check the efforts of private enterprise in support of mechanics' institutions and the like."[2] In many cases, however, this view was clearly associated with a dislike of the results of popular education. From libraries, it was argued by several speakers, it was but a short step to lecture-rooms, "which might", declared Sir Robert Inglis (Oxford University) "give rise to an unhealthy agitation."[3] His colleague H. Goulburn (Cambridge University) viewed with alarm "an unrestricted presentation of all those publications emanating daily from the press, which certainly were not calculated to promote the preservation of either public order or public morals;"[4] and R. Spooner (Warwickshire) "almost feared that these libraries might be converted into normal schools of agitation."[5]

Ewart was not, however, without his supporters. The Whig Government of Lord John Russell was sympathetic if not enthusiastic, and Henry Labouchère (Taunton), President of the Board of Trade, came out strongly for the bill, stressing the importance of lending libraries.[6] Ewart's Radical colleagues, Joseph Brotherton (Salford), Joseph Hume (Montrose), John Bright (Manchester), and W. J. Fox (Oldham), also spoke up valiantly on his behalf, though Hume and Bright both asked that the adoption of the Act should be conditional on the approval of a majority of the ratepayers. Brotherton and some other speakers argued for the bill not only on educational grounds but as likely to lead to a diminution of crime: it would, declared Brotherton, "provide the cheapest police that could be established."[7]

In the end, to mollify his critics, Ewart had to agree to certain modifications in the terms of the bill as originally proposed. The Act as passed empowered municipal authorities with a population of 10 000 or more (not all municipal authorities as Ewart had wished) to spend a $\frac{1}{2}$d. rate on the provision of accommodation for a museum and/or library, and for the maintenance of the same, but did not permit any expenditure on books or specimens. Town councils wishing to adopt the Act had to conduct a special poll of the ratepayers, a majority of two-thirds of the votes cast being necessary to secure adoption.[8]

---

[1] See above, p. 10.

[2] Hansard, *Parliamentary Debates*, 3rd Ser., Vol. CIX (1850), col. 849.

[3] *Op. cit.*, col. 848. In the debate in this same year on W. J. Fox's Bill for National Education, Inglis declared that an extension of educational provision might make the people of this country as revolutionary as they had been on the Continent in 1848—R. E. and E. Garnett, *The Life of W. J. Fox* (1910), p. 303.

[4] Hansard, *Parliamentary Debates*, 3rd Ser., Vol. CIX (1850), col. 842.

[5] *Op. cit.*, col. 847.

[6] *Op. cit.*, cols. 844–845.

[7] *Op. cit.*, col. 841.

[8] Public Libraries Act, 13 and 14 Vict. c. 65.

CHAPTER II

The Foundation of the Municipal Library Service

The General Historical Background

IF we look at the long process of public library development from its humble beginnings at Canterbury in 1847 until the present day, it is difficult to perceive more than one or two clearly defined landmarks. One, which all students of library history would be disposed to accept, is the Public Libraries Act of 1919, which marked at once the end of the penny rate, and the beginning of the county library service. The Public Libraries Act of 1964, by which the Central Government for the first time assumed responsibility for the supervision of the library service, is probably another. But between 1847 and 1919 library history forms a continuum in which no single event stands out as making a significant change.

Change none the less there was: the libraries of the last decade of the nineteenth century, inadequate though many of them still were by modern standards, were far superior in numbers, size and organization to the pioneering efforts of earlier years. In almost every substantial urban centre the library was now an accepted part of public provision; endowments and benefactions were being received on an unprecedented scale; and within the libraries themselves revolutionary reforms in organization and techniques were under way.

It is necessary, therefore, to seek some dividing line, and the most convenient date for this purpose is probably 1887, the year of Victoria's Jubilee. It was about this time that the changes I have spoken of began to make themselves clearly felt, and the Jubilee itself, by the patriotic fervour it aroused, gave a notable impulse to the founding of new libraries. In 1886 the number of new libraries opened was seven, in 1887 it was thirteen. Taking the period 1847–86 as a whole, libraries were being established at the rate of three or four a year; for the period 1887–1900 the average was sixteen or seventeen a year. The Jubilee year can thus fairly be taken as symbolizing the opening of a new era of library development.

It is significant that 1886 saw the publication of the first edition of Thomas Greenwood's *Free Public Libraries*. Greenwood (1851–1908), the son of a yeoman-farmer near Stockport, began his working life as a clerk at a railway bookstall, served a brief spell (1871–73) as an assistant librarian in charge of Sheffield's Upperthorpe Branch, and ultimately made a successful career for himself as a publisher of technical literature. An ardent educationist and temperance reformer, he constituted himself the special champion of the public library movement. His book just mentioned was the first attempt to provide a detailed survey of public library history and organization, and the successive editions of this work, and of the *Library Year Book* which he launched in 1897, form an invaluable source of information on every aspect of library work. At his death he left £5000 to endow the library for librarians which he had established a few years before in the Manchester Public Library.[1]

What, then, from the point of view of library history, were the significant characteristics of the forty years from 1847 to 1886? In general it was, in spite of periodical commercial crises and industrial depressions, and in spite of the decline of agriculture in the later years, a time of increasing prosperity for the people of Great Britain, and especially for those engaged in industry and commerce. Population was growing fast, wealth even faster. Transport was improving, production was expanding, English exports led the world. Many individuals accumulated vast fortunes, and the mass of the working population benefited not only by an increase in real wages (more than 50 per cent between 1850 and 1886) but also in many cases by a substantial improvement in working conditions, as hours of labour were shortened and the Saturday half-holiday became more general.

"The tide of material progress", as a modern historian has remarked, "flowed up all sorts of creeks and inlets",[2] and one of these, undoubtedly, was the public library service, which profited alike from the modest improvement in the fortunes of the many and the spectacular improvement in the fortunes of the few. An important factor was that the increase of population (from under 20 millions in 1847 to over 31 millions in 1886) was concentrated chiefly in the urban areas. Some rural areas in Wales and Northern Scotland had a static or even a declining population, while by contrast many industrial towns of the North and Midlands doubled or even trebled their populations between 1851 and 1881, and the population of Cardiff jumped from 18000 to 83000. This increase brought, of course, new responsibilities for the public libraries, but it also meant that, in spite of the restriction of the penny rate, they could draw on a much larger rateable value.

From the point of view of political and social reform, the period falls into two almost equal halves. The years up to 1866 were dominated by Lord John Russell and Lord Palmerston, the last of the great Whig prime ministers. Both were born in the eighteenth century, and their government had about it something of the air of privilege and patronage which had been characteristic of the period before the Reform Act of 1832. It was during these years that the Crimean War was fought, and the emphasis throughout was on foreign policy. On the home front, apart from minor measures such as the Public Libraries Acts, there was virtual stagnation. "There is really nothing to be done,"

---

[1] See G. Carlton, *Spade-Work: the Story of Thomas Greenwood* [1949]; *The City Libraries of Sheffield, 1856–1956* (Sheffield 1956), pp. 16–17. Useful short accounts are to be found in J. Minto, *A History of the Public Library Movement* (1932), pp. 318–320; and J. L. Thornton (ed.), *Selected Readings in the History of Librarianship* (1966), pp. 225–226. E. A. Savage, *A Librarian's Memories, Portraits and Reflections* (1952), pp. 60–61, unjustifiably blames Greenwood for having prolonged the penny rate limitation.

A second edition of *Free Public Libraries* appeared in 1887, and third and fourth editions (completely re-written and under the new title *Public Libraries*) in 1890 and 1891. The 1891 edition was reprinted with additional material in 1894 as a revised 4th edition. For convenience all these works are cited henceforth simply under the name "Greenwood", with the date of publication. The *Year Books* edited by Greenwood were *Greenwood's Library Year Book* (1897) and the *British Library Year Book, 1900–1901* (1900).

[2] R. C. K. Ensor, *England, 1870–1914* (Oxford 1936), p. 135.

declared Palmerston. "We cannot go on adding to the Statute Book *ad infinitum*."[1] The later years were dominated by Disraeli and Gladstone, younger men, commoners both, and as different from Russell and Palmerston as they were from each other. With their advent to power we seem to enter on a more modern age, an era in which Britain was at peace, and in which the tide of domestic reform once more swept strongly forward.

The new era may be said to have begun in 1867, when Disraeli, Chancellor of the Exchequer in the Conservative Government of Lord Derby, stole the thunder of the Liberals by securing the passage of the Second Reform Bill, which almost doubled the electorate by enfranchising all male householders in the towns and reducing the property qualifications in the country districts. A similar bill for Scotland followed in 1868. The Ballot Act of 1872, and the Third Reform Act of 1884, which gave the vote to the rural worker, completed the basic structure of modern parliamentary democracy.

Other reforms of the same period vitally affected the life of the working people. The Public Health Act of 1875 codified the powers and responsibilities of the local authorities in this field, and in conjunction with the Housing Act of the same year (the first of a series of such Acts) enabled the municipalities to begin in earnest the task of clearing the slums inherited from the Industrial Revolution. In 1878 a new Factory Act consolidated and extended the legislation of earlier years, and among other things forbade the employment of children under ten years of age.

All these changes had their impact on library development, but no reform was so directly relevant as that which took place in the sphere of education. Throughout the first half of the nineteenth century, facilities for popular education proliferated with extraordinary rapidity. Elementary schools (sometimes endowed, mostly conducted by one or other of the religious denominations), evening schools, Sunday schools, adult schools, mechanics' institutes, private schools in infinite variety, combined to provide a network of institutions which enabled most people, at some time in their lives, to acquire at least a little schooling. By the time the first public libraries opened, most adult men and women (more men than women, however) were literate in the sense of being able to read, but many could do little more, and only a minority had any facility in the use of books. So far, although government grants on a small scale were being made in aid of elementary education and teacher-training, there was nothing approaching a national system of education.

The Newcastle Commission on the State of Popular Education, which reported in 1861, professed itself reasonably satisfied with a situation under which rather less than half the children between three and fifteen were enrolled in day schools, and a similar number in Sunday and evening schools, and concluded that "the difficulties and evils of any general measure of compulsion would outweigh any good results which could be expected from it."[2] The notorious Revised Code of 1862, introduced by Robert Lowe, Vice-President of the Education Department, was designed merely to render the existing system more efficient and to ensure that an adequate return was received

---

[1] A. D. Elliot, *The Life of George Joachim Goschen, First Viscount Goschen* (1911), Vol. I, p. 65.

[2] *Report of the Commissioners appointed to inquire into the State of Popular Education in England* (1861), Vol. I, p. 225.

for money spent: it established the principle of "payment by results", as tested in examinations.

In the great English cities, however, public opinion was becoming increasingly disturbed by the inadequacy of educational provision. In Manchester, where an Education Aid Society was founded in 1864, it was calculated that the position was worse than thirty years earlier. Similar societies were founded in Birmingham, Nottingham, and Liverpool. The victory of the North over the South in the American Civil War, and of the Prussians over the Austrians in the war of 1866, were used to point the moral that education was the foundation of military power, and the poor showing of British manufacturers at the Paris Exhibition of 1867 led to similar comparisons on the economic front.

The really decisive factor, however, was the 1867 Reform Act. Even Robert Lowe, who had bitterly opposed the extension of the franchise, saw its educational implications quite clearly: "it will", he said, "be absolutely necessary to compel our future masters to learn their letters."[1] A year later a general election swept the Liberals into power under Gladstone's leadership, with the Radical W. E. Forster as Vice-President of the Education Department. It was Forster who piloted through Parliament the epoch-making Education Act of 1870, which accepted the principle of universal elementary education and established local School Boards to fill the gaps left by the denominational schools. Under the corresponding Scottish Act (1872), the School Boards took over the denominational schools also, and attendance was made compulsory—a measure that was not adopted in England and Wales until 1876 and 1880. In 1891 (1893 in Scotland) elementary education was made free. The results may be measured by the fact that of nearly $2\frac{1}{2}$ million votes cast in the general election of 1886, less than 40000 were cast by illiterates.

It was unfortunate, from the point of view of public library development, that the great social reforms of the early and middle nineteenth century were not accompanied by the creation of an adequate system of local government. The Municipal Corporations Act of 1835 had indeed brought a measure of rationalization to the 178 boroughs in England and Wales recognized under the Act, and to others created subsequently, but in the rest of the country (including London, which had been excluded from the Act because of the opposition of the City), chaos still reigned supreme for another half-century. The only universal unit of administration was the parish, but the machinery of the parish vestry was quite inadequate for the purposes of modern government, and the 20000 parishes were consequently criss-crossed by a network of *ad hoc* bodies—improvement commissions, poor law unions, public health boards (from 1848), local government boards (from 1858), highway boards (from 1862), school boards (from 1870), and so forth. In London, in 1852, the functions of local government were shared out among at least 300 different bodies with a total membership of some 10000.

In Scotland the position in the rural areas was less complex, in that the parish functioned also as an authority for elementary education, and through a parochial board as an authority for poor relief and public health. The complicating factor in the Scottish situation was the number and variety of the

[1] A. P. Martin, *Life and Letters of the Right Honourable Robert Lowe Viscount Sherbrooke* (1893), Vol. II, p. 323.

burghs, many of them exceedingly small. There were royal burghs created by the Crown, burghs of barony or of regality created by feudal overlords, parliamentary burghs created by the Reform Act of 1832, and police burghs created under legislation of 1850 and 1862. The Municipal Corporations Act of 1835 did not apply to Scotland, but two years earlier a similar measure had placed the 84 royal and parliamentary burghs under the control of elected councils. The burghs of barony or regality were less important, and most of them, as the century wore on, either faded away or became police burghs, under the Acts of 1850 and 1862.

These Acts permitted the inhabitants of populous places to elect magistrates and commissioners to take control of police matters—a term which included drainage, paving, lighting and cleansing and in a minority of cases the establishment of a police force in the English sense. This new form of organization was intended to meet the needs of the mining and industrial towns which had sprung up as a result of the Industrial Revolution, but unfortunately the minimum population—fixed in 1862 at 800—was so low that many of the new burghs were no more than villages, or worse still, suburbs of large towns: Glasgow, for example, found itself before the end of the century almost surrounded by a ring of nine suburban police burghs. By this time the total number of police burghs was over a hundred.

This confusion in local government was not cleared up until the closing years of the century.

The Legislative Background

Library legislation, once begun, rapidly multiplied, no fewer than eighteen Acts being entered on the statute-book in the next half-century. Nine of these were passed in the years before 1887.

The Act of 1850, which was extended to the royal and parliamentary burghs of Scotland in 1853,[1] was valuable mainly as establishing a principle. In practice it was very unsatisfactory, because of the severe restrictions it imposed (a) on the kinds of authorities that might adopt it; (b) on the amount of money that could be spent; (c) on the ways in which that money could be spent; and (d) on the methods to be used for adoption. Subsequent development was directed largely to the removal of these limitations.

Substantial improvements were quickly made in Scotland, where in 1854 library authorities were empowered to raise a 1d. rate, and to spend money not only on library and museum buildings but also on books, maps and specimens.[2] The machinery of adoption by a poll of ratepayers was at the same time abandoned in favour of a two-thirds majority at a public meeting of £10 householders, though a poll might still be demanded by any five voters present.

Very similar amendments were embodied in the following year in a more comprehensive Act for England and Wales,[3] which included provision for the penny rate, power to purchase books, newspapers, maps and specimens, and adoption by a two-thirds majority at a public meeting of ratepayers. An

---

[1] Public Libraries (Ireland and Scotland) Act, 16 and 17 Vict. c. 101.
[2] Public Libraries (Scotland) Act, 17 and 18 Vict. c. 64.
[3] Public Libraries and Museums Act, 18 and 19 Vict. c. 70.

important change was the reduction of the population limit from 10000 to 5000 and the extension of the Act to areas outside the municipal boroughs. Another innovation, which however desirable in itself was not to the advantage of public libraries, was that library authorities were empowered (from the same rate income) to provide schools of science and art.

This Act, like that of 1850, had to be piloted through the Commons by Ewart in the face of considerable opposition, and he had to drop a proposal for adoption in municipal boroughs by simple resolution of the town council. In first presenting the bill in 1854, Ewart commented especially on the provision to purchase newspapers. He himself, he remarked, "had no objection to such powers being granted, but in such a case he thought the newspapers should be apart from the library, and the library consecrated to those objects to which it was more particularly devoted."[1] The Attorney-General, Sir Alexander Cockburn, provided the answer at a later stage, when the bill had been amended and had secured Government support. "However attractive general knowledge might be," he said, "nothing was so attractive as political knowledge, and if they shut out newspapers from libraries, they would deprive them of one of the principal attractions to be found in public houses."[2]

The confusion of local government authorities outside the corporate towns, which we have noted above, created difficulties in extending public library provision to the rural areas. The solution adopted in 1855 was to say that a library authority might be, subject to the minimum 5000 population, either a borough council, or an improvement board or commission, or a parish vestry or group of vestries. Improvement boards were bodies set up by local Act in many urban areas from the eighteenth century onwards, to take responsibility primarily for the paving, lighting, watching and cleaning of the streets, though in time many assumed wider functions. After 1835 their duties were gradually taken over in the reformed boroughs by the elected town councils, but in the urban areas outside the boroughs they continued, where they existed, to provide a rudimentary form of town government. Their use for library purposes avoided the creation of yet another *ad hoc* authority.

In 1866, an amending act, covering Scotland as well as England and Wales, removed the population limit altogether, substituted a simple majority for a two-thirds majority for the purposes of adoption, and permitted adjoining parishes to join forces with an existing or projected library authority.[3] An amending and consolidating Act for Scotland in the following year defined library authorities there as burghs (royal or parliamentary), districts (burghs of barony, burghs of regality, and police burghs), and parishes; and also prescribed the form of library committee which was henceforth to be characteristic of the Scottish burghs—not more than twenty members, of whom half were to be members of the council, and the other half chosen by the council from house-holders.[4]

These two Libraries Acts were the last to be promoted by Ewart, who

[1] Hansard, *Parliamentary Debates*, 3rd Ser., Vol. CXXXII (1854), col. 454.
[2] *Op. cit.*, Vol. CXXXVII, col. 219.
[3] Public Libraries (England and Scotland), Amendment Act, 29 and 30 Vict. c. 114.
[4] Public Libraries (Scotland) Act, 30 and 31 Vict. c. 37. In England the provision in the 1850 Act (carried forward into subsequent legislation) was simply that members of the committee of management need not be members of the council.

retired in 1868. The 1866 Act brought a well-earned tribute from his namesake William Ewart Gladstone, Chancellor of the Exchequer:

> "I cannot refrain from seizing this opportunity of congratulating my hon. Friend on having been permitted during a long and honourable Parliamentary life, to see the gradual development of the fruit of his labour, and to watch these institutions spread through the great centres of population where it is so desirable they should exist. My hon. Friend's name is associated with many achievements of public utility, but with this act of legislation, I think he may feel assured that his name will be associated, not only during his life, but after he is gone."[1]

The total removal of the population limit, making it possible for the smallest town or parish to establish a public library, must have seemed at the time the crowning triumph but, as W. A. Munford has pointed out, it was storing up trouble for the future by encouraging the growth of library authorities without adequate resources.[2]

The effect of the Acts so far described was substantially to remove two of the limitations inherent in the Act of 1850, namely those on the kinds of authorities that might adopt the Act and on the ways in which rate income might be spent. The amount of money available, however, was still limited to the product of a 1d. rate and the procedure for adoption by public meeting proved, in practice, no more satisfactory than adoption by poll.

The remaining four Libraries Acts of the period now under review did little towards resolving these difficulties. Acts passed for England and Wales and for Scotland in 1871[3] were concerned with relatively minor details of administration and finance: the former, keeping pace with changes in local government, permitted boards established under the Public Health Act of 1848 or the Local Government Act of 1858 to function as library authorities in the same way as improvement boards. A general Act of 1877, passed on the initiative of Glasgow Corporation, permitted adoption either by poll or by public meeting, but at the same time provided that the voters might, in deciding to adopt, stipulate for a lower rate of $\frac{1}{2}$d. or $\frac{3}{4}$d.[4] This was a retrograde step, which for some years proved troublesome to a number of authorities. Another general Act, passed in 1884, regularized the position of libraries conducting schools of science and art in connection with the Science and Art Department of the Committee of Council on Education by permitting such libraries to accept grant in aid.[5]

When the Jubilee year dawned, library legislation was still in a rather unsatisfactory state.

The Pattern of Growth

It has been customary for library historians to trace the development of the library service by recording the adoptions of the Libraries Acts by local authorities in successive periods. This is not entirely satisfactory because although in

[1] Hansard, *Parliamentary Debates*, 3rd Ser., Vol. CLXXXI (1866), cols. 1234–1355. W. E. Gladstone was named after his godfather, who was William Ewart's father.
[2] W. A. Munford, *William Ewart* (1960), p. 151.
[3] Public Libraries Amendment Act, 34 and 35 Vict. c. 71; and Public Libraries (Scotland) Amendment Act, 34 and 35 Vict. c. 59.
[4] Public Libraries Amendment Act, 40 and 41 Vict. c. 54.
[5] Public Libraries Act, 47 and 48 Vict. c. 37.

some places the establishment of the library followed almost immediately upon adoption, in others there was an interval of several years. Norwich adopted in 1850, but the library was not opened till 1857; Blackburn adopted in 1853, but did not open till 1862. In certain cases where library powers were taken by special local Act, designed primarily for other purposes, the interval was even longer.[1] It seems better, therefore, to think in terms of the dates at which libraries were actually opened.[2]

The pattern presented by a study of these dates is closely related to the general pattern of political, economic, and social development outlined in the first section of this chapter. In the Russell-Palmerston era, when domestic reform was muted, public library progress was very slow; in the Disraeli-Gladstone epoch, when reform was again in the air, progress was much more rapid. The first phase began with the three pioneering libraries established under the Museums Act—Canterbury in 1847, Warrington in 1848, and Salford in 1850. Twenty-three more libraries were opened in the years 1851–62: one in Wales, one in Scotland, and the remainder scattered over fifteen English counties. Then came a lull. During the next five years, 1863–67, only one new library is recorded, at Warwick in 1886. The initial impulse towards library foundation seemed to be petering out. It was in 1868, the year after the Second Reform Act, that revival began, at first slowly, but after the Education Act of 1870 with gathering momentum. Of the 125 libraries founded between 1847 and 1886, no fewer than 98 were established in the years 1868–86.

Fourteen of the 27 libraries opened before 1868 were in industrial and commercial centres, of which the most important were Liverpool (by special Act of 1852), Manchester (1852), and Birmingham (1861). London, as ever, showed itself backward in library provision, and the only library established there during this first phase was for the parishes of St. Margaret and St. John, Westminster (1857). Outside the major cities the largest of the industrial and commercial centres to establish a library was Sheffield (1856), with a population in 1851 of 135000; the smallest was the Lanarkshire mining town of Airdrie (1856) which, with a population in 1851 of only some 14000, had Scotland's first and for many years sole public library. The only Welsh library of this period, opened at Cardiff in 1862, also falls into this group, as do Warrington and Salford, created under the Museums Act, and Sunderland, formed in 1859 by an extension of the Museums Act which had originally been adopted there in 1846. The others were Bolton (1853), Birkenhead (1856), Walsall (1859), and Blackburn (1862).

By contrast the remaining thirteen libraries were established in pre-

---

[1] E.g. at Brighton and Oldham (see below, pp. 33–34).

[2] I have sought to establish in each case the date at which the library, or some part of it, was first made available for public use. It should be observed that the dates of adoption and opening given in many official reports (Adams, Mitchell, Kenyon) are often quite wrong. The most reliable information is to be found in the series of *Parliamentary Returns of Public Libraries* which appeared at intervals from 1853 to 1912. These are listed in the Bibliography, and are cited under the abbreviation *P.R.* and the date. Even here, however, there are curious discrepancies, and in most cases it has been necessary to check the information with the library concerned. The results of my inquiries are set out in Appendices III, IV and V.

dominantly rural areas. The county towns were early in the field: Canterbury led the way under the Museums Act, and Norwich was the first town in the country to adopt the Act of 1850. As we have noted, Norwich did not actually open its library until 1857. This was because of building delays. The honour of being the first town to open a library under the Public Libraries Act thus falls to Winchester, which adopted the Act in 1851 and opened its library in the same year. Other county towns which formed libraries during this period were Ipswich (1853), Oxford (1854), Cambridge (1855), Hertford (1856), Maidstone (1858), and Warwick (1866). Hertford, with a population in 1851 of 6600, was so far the only town to take advantage of the reduction of the population limit from 10000 to 5000 in the Act of 1855. The non-county towns which acquired libraries at this period were Kidderminster (1855), Leamington Spa (1857), Lichfield (1859) and Bridgwater (1860).

Significantly, in view of future developments, the only county with more than two libraries at the end of the first phase was Lancashire, which had six. More than a score of counties, including Cumberland and Westmorland, almost all the south-western counties, and more than half of the south-eastern counties, were still without libraries at all. The predominance of Lancashire is a pointer to the fact that the great strength of the library movement in the nineteenth century was to be in the industrial areas.

This became very clear in the second phase of development, from 1868 to 1886. The 98 libraries opened during these years did indeed include about a dozen in rural county and market towns such as Exeter (1870), Hereford (1871), Chester (1877), Reading (1883), Truro (1886), and in Wales Bangor (1871) and Aberystwyth (1874). A dozen more were to be found in residential centres such as Twickenham (1882), Ealing (1883), and Wimbledon (1886); in resorts such as Brighton (1873),[1] Southport (1876), Blackpool (1880), and Cheltenham (1884); in the tiny burgh and seaport of Thurso, on the northern coast of Scotland (1872); and in the rural parish of Tarves in Aberdeenshire (1884) – the first parish library in the country apart from that founded in Westminster in 1857.[2] The vast majority of the new libraries, however, were in the centres of industry and commerce.

London, it is true, still lagged behind: the pioneer library at Westminster long stood alone. The Guildhall library, set up, as we have seen, in 1828 as a repository for material relating to the City, was indeed provided with a new building (the present one) in 1872, and made available as a public reference library, but this was not a rate-aided library.[3] It was not until 1885 that a second rate-aided library was opened, at Wandsworth. Outside London, however, the accession of Leeds (1870), and Bristol (1876) to the public library movement meant that by the end of the period the only cities with a population of over 200000 at the 1881 census which were still without a public library were Edinburgh and Glasgow. Other large towns which opened libraries at this time

---

[1] By Special Act of 1850: see below, pp. 33–34.

[2] The only English rural parish to secure a library service at this time was Winnington in Cheshire, which from 1885 (apparently) attached itself for library purposes to its neighbour Northwich—*P.R. 1890*, pp. 2–3; *P.R. 1912*, p. 11.

[3] Limited public access (by ticket only) was permitted in 1856. The Acts were not adopted till 1921. C. Welsh, "The Guildhall Library and its Work", in *The Library*, Vol. I (1889), pp. 320–334, is a useful account to that date.

included Nottingham (1868), Dundee (1869), Leicester (1871),[1] Bradford (1872), Swansea (1875), Plymouth (1876), Newcastle upon Tyne (1880), Halifax (1882), Oldham (1883),[2] Portsmouth (1883) and Aberdeen (1885); and in the smaller industrial towns of the north and midlands libraries sprang up like mushrooms.

If we review the distribution of public libraries in 1886 we find that, of the total of 125 libraries, eighteen were in Lancashire and seventeen in Staffordshire. Yorkshire had seven, all in the West Riding; Cheshire also had seven, mostly in industrial towns; Durham and Warwickshire had five each; and twenty-six other English counties had a smaller number. Only eight English counties were still entirely without libraries. Five of these were in the East Midlands agricultural belt: Buckinghamshire, Bedfordshire, Huntingdonshire, Rutlandshire, and Lincolnshire; the others were Essex, Wiltshire, and Westmorland. The agricultural counties were, in general, very much underrepresented. The same was true of Wales and Scotland. The six Welsh libraries were all round the perimeter – on the coast or on the English border, leaving the central rural area untouched. The twelve Scottish libraries were mostly in the industrial towns of Central Scotland and the Central Lowlands: the whole of the South-West and almost the entire Highland zone were still unprovided for.

The Evolution of Public Opinion

The growth in the library service just described, patchy and uneven as it was, was not accomplished without a good deal of opposition. The need to secure the support of a majority of the ratepayers (a two-thirds majority of those voting until 1866) proved a real obstacle to the adoption of the Libraries Acts, and fifteen of the authorities which established libraries in the years 1850–86 did so only after previous attempts to secure adoption had failed: at Wolverhampton (1869) and Portsmouth (1876), it was only at the third attempt, and at Cheltenham (1883), only at the fourth attempt, that a library was established.[3] In 38 other centres, during this period, proposals for adoption were defeated, in many cases more than once.

The London parishes, populous and wealthy though many of them were, showed themselves especially reluctant to assume new responsibilities: in the City, Islington, St. Pancras and Camberwell the proposal for adoption was twice defeated. Hull rejected the proposition three times between 1857 and 1882. Up to 1886, however, the record for intransigence was held by the city of Bath, where the proposal for a public library had already been four times brought forward and as often rejected. After the second rejection, in 1872, the supporters of the cause secured a building and started a free library from their own resources, with close on 4000 books, but even the offer to transfer this valuable property free of charge failed to move the reluctant ratepayers, who

---

[1] By extension, under a Council resolution of 1869, of the Museums Act adopted there in 1848. (By the Public Libraries Amendment Act of 1866, an authority which had established a museum under an earlier Act was permitted to add a library without the usual machinery of adoption).

[2] Under Special Act of 1865: see below, pp. 33-34, note.

[3] The other twelve authorities were Birmingham, Sheffield, Cardiff, Exeter, Leeds, Thurso, Macclesfield, Newcastle upon Tyne, Reading, Worcester, Northwich, and Aberdeen.

preferred to see the building sold and the books either returned to their donors or given away.[1]

To appreciate the nature and extent of the opposition we must consider the state of public opinion. On this point a recent historian of the Scottish public libraries has commented:

> "There is an attractive and widely-held belief that public libraries were established as a result of public demand for them, but it has been shown on the contrary that the public library was largely the work of philanthropists and reformers who saw in it an ameliorating moral and educational force which they were devotedly willing to further."[2]

Though this is certainly true as far as the Public Libraries Act of 1850 was concerned, I think subsequent events demonstrate that in England at any rate there *was* a latent public demand, at various levels of society, for better library provision. In 1850, however, it was still inarticulate: it was to show itself only when public libraries appeared as a practical possibility. In the meantime, if we wish to discern the currents of opinion which were to make themselves felt in later years, we cannot do better than glance again at the columns of Hansard which record the debates on the 1850 Act.

Ewart himself presented the Bill primarily as a means for the economic betterment of the working classes: "the labouring population would be far more advanced," he argued, "if they had such opportunities as were afforded by means of public libraries to the working classes of other countries."[3] His ally, Brotherton, placed the main emphasis on social reform, seeing in public libraries a means for the prevention of crime.[4] On the opposing side the main argument was against increased taxation, but there were also fears that public provision would undermine voluntary effort, and that the new libraries would become centres of popular disaffection.[5]

Both sides, significantly, agreed that public libraries were for the working classes. The supporters of the Bill thought public libraries would make the workers more moral, sober, thrifty and industrious; its opponents looked on such institutions as an extravagance leading merely to idleness and discontent. It was an argument which had its parallels fifty years earlier, when Hannah and Martha More and other pioneers were teaching the working classes to read. The only M.P. who seemed to take a rather broader view of the purposes of public libraries was the Unitarian W. J. Fox, M.P. for Oldham, who true to the tradition of his sect considered that "the Bill would confer a most valuable boon upon the intelligent and studious among the middle and poorer classes."[6]

In the years that followed 1850, as in town after town the question of adoption was brought before public meetings, the arguments for and against public libraries were elaborated, and public opinion began to crystallize. The idea that public libraries were for the benefit of the working classes at once took a firm hold. The term "free library", which was so widely used for the new

---

[1] V. J. Kite, *Libraries in Bath, 1618–1964* (unpublished F.L.A. thesis 1966), pp. 184–210.

[2] W. R. Aitken, *A History of the Public Library Movement in Scotland to 1955* (Glasgow 1971), p. 74.

[3] Hansard, *Parliamentary Debates*, 3rd Ser., Vol. CVIII (1850), col. 760.

[4] *Op. cit.*, Vol. CX (1850), col. 156.

[5] See above, pp. 15.   [6] Hansard, *op. cit.*, col. 161.

institutions, and may still be seen carved in stone over some of our older library buildings, was probably used, as we have already observed, because the title "public library" had so often been pre-empted by proprietary subscription libraries, but it none the less served to foster the illusion that public libraries were on the same footing as soup-kitchens, baths and washhouses, and other charitable enterprises.

The working classes themselves, with that unselfconscious acceptance of the class structure which was characteristic of the period, were far from dissenting from the general view. In Manchester, when the Mayor, Sir John Potter, launched a subscription for a public library, more than 20 000 "hard-working clerks and artizans" contributed their shillings and pence towards the magnificent total of nearly £13 000 that was eventually raised.[1] At the brilliant inaugural ceremony in September, 1852, when the Earl of Shaftesbury, Sir Edward Bulwer Lytton, Charles Dickens, W. M. Thackeray, John Bright, and many lesser luminaries assembled to pay their tributes, Potter presented the library to the city, on behalf of the subscribers, as "a provision for the wants of the scholar and the student of every class,"[2] but in doing so he declared: "We have been animated solely by the desire to benefit our poorer fellow-creatures,"[3] and it was this theme which dominated the speeches of the distinguished guests. It found clear expression in the resolution moved by Dickens:

> "That as, in this institution, special provision has been made for the working classes, by means of a free lending library, this meeting cherishes the earnest hope that the books thus made available will prove a source of pleasure and improvement in the cottages, the garrets, and the cellars of the poorest of our people."[4]

Many such passages could be quoted from opening speeches in the early years. A few weeks after the Manchester ceremony came the opening of the Liverpool public library, at which the Mayor, Thomas Littledale, spoke of the need to spread knowledge "to the poorer orders."[5] At the foundation of the Brown Library in the same city in 1857, Rev. Hugh Stowell, an evangelical clergyman, summed up the current opinion with the remark: "although the free library is intended for the benefit of all, yet I take it that it is intended specially for the working people, men of all trades"[6]—a view that was confirmed at the official opening three years later, when addresses were presented to the founder, William Brown, by the literary and scientific societies of the city, by commercial and industrial organizations, and by "the working men of Liverpool." The working men presented also a clock and a silver salver, and their leader, Daniel Guile, made a speech which concluded:

> "But, my working friends, before we can attain the utmost amount of good derivable from this institution we have a great deal to learn. Self-denial must be exercised. The power of the mind must gain a complete victory over sensual appetites. Our leisure hours, instead of being spent in the taproom, the singing room and the dancing room, must be given to study, to thought, to perseverance and to

[1] E. Edwards, *Free Town Libraries* (1869), p. 71. [2] *Op. cit.*, p. 92.

[3] *Report of the Proceedings at . . . the Opening of the Free Library* (Manchester 1852, repr. 1903), p. 6.

[4] *Op. cit.*, p. 15.

[5] P. Cowell, *Liverpool Public Libraries: a History of Fifty Years* (Liverpool 1903), p. 39.

[6] *Op. cit.*, p. 65.

industry, ... my working friends, to-night let me beg of you to show the classes that move above us, as it is generally termed, to show our fellow men, that we can, that we do, that we will appreciate this great gift. . . ."[1]

For a further example of public attitudes at this time we may turn to Leeds, where in 1861 a group of citizens, among them Dr. Atlay, Vicar of Leeds, and other clergy, made an unsuccessful attempt to secure the adoption of the Acts. With the help of a number of working men who acted as canvassers, they secured signatures to a memorial to the Council representing:

> "That there are in Leeds vast numbers of working men who, for want of some place of proper resort after their day's labour, and in the absence of other available attractions, are compelled to seek for themselves amusements which are unfortunately but too often objectionable, much poverty and social distress being the necessary results. That a free library, where men of all grades might resort, and from which books of an instructive and elevating character could be circulated without charge, would greatly improve the social, moral and intellectual condition of the people of this populous and important borough."[2]

Ten years later, at the adoption meeting at Aberystwyth in 1871, Rev. E. O. Phillips declared that it would be "an act of morality" to adopt the Acts and to provide a library which would "keep the young men out of the more objectionable resorts."[3]

It is unnecessary to insist further upon this point, but it is of interest to note that at Norwich, when the public library committee was formed in 1856, the Council specifically included five representatives of the working classes, chosen at a special meeting. The first representatives were a printer, a weaver, a herbalist, a newsvendor, and a hairdresser, and the arrangement lasted until 1868[4].

As time went on more than one voice was raised in protest against this narrow class concept. One of the first was that of Edward Edwards, who wrote of public libraries in 1859:

> "Supported alike by the taxation of the wealthiest capitalist and of the humblest householder, they must be so formed, so augmented and so governed as to be alike useful to both. They must in no sense be 'professional libraries', or 'tradesmen's libraries', or 'working men's libraries', but 'town libraries.'"[5]

In Liverpool in 1875, James Picton, at the laying of the foundation stone of the great circular reading room named after him, expressed the same view: "It must be remembered that this institution is not for a class or a community. It is the common property of all, irrespective of rank, station or circumstances."[6] And in Birmingham in 1882, at the re-opening of the public library after the disastrous fire of 1879, Joseph Chamberlain, at that time President of the Board of Trade, declared: "in this provision there is no favour conferred; it is a right

---

[1] *Op. cit.*, pp. 71–72.

[2] T. W. Hand, "The Leeds Public Free Libraries" in *L.A.R.*, Vol. VI (1904), pp. 2–3.

[3] N. Roberts, "A Town and its Library", in *Ceredigion*, Vol. III, No. 2 (Aberystwyth 1956–59), pp. 163–164.

[4] G. A. Stephen, *Three Centuries of a City Library* (Norwich 1917), pp. 62–63; P. Hepworth and M. Alexander, *City of Norwich Libraries* (Norwich 1957), pp. 10, 12.

[5] E. Edwards, *Memoirs of Libraries* (1859), Vol. I, pp. 775–776.

[6] Cowell, *op. cit.*, p. 117.

which is enjoyed by all ... I have often thought that that is a kind of communism which the least revolutionary amongst us may be proud to advocate."[1]

These were noble sentiments, but the general view remained otherwise. Only a year before Chamberlain's speech at Birmingham the *Nottingham and Midland Counties Daily Express* had greeted the opening of the new College and Public Library buildings in the following terms:

> "We can now address the working men—and the working women, too—of this great borough, and pointing to the thousands of volumes of the best literature stored in the noble rooms in Sherwood Street, we can appeal to them to avail themselves of the privilege, in the matter of knowledge, of making themselves equal with the nobleman whose library has cost him £10000. Prepare to be presented at the court of royalty of intellect. Prepare to shake hands with nature's nobility. For you the great men of antiquity have lived, and still live, in their books—for you, philosophers and poets, heroes and demigods, await you to counsel with wisdom, to charm you with poesy, and to ennoble you by their example. Is it a small thing thus to be introduced within the sacred Pantheon of learning? Is it a trifle to be privileged to hold converse with the best minds of all ages, and to have, despite of intervening centuries, their more virtuous thoughts for your guidance?" (etc. etc.)[2]

The writer of this purple passage did at least emphasize the cultural value of the library to the working man, but the social reform motive was not lost sight of. Indeed, it reappears in a striking form in the very last year of the period with which we are now dealing, in the famous cartoon, *The Rivals*, which formed the frontispiece to the first edition of Thomas Greenwood's *Free Public Libraries* in 1886. Here we see on the one hand the Red Lion public-house, with its sinister offerings of Bagatelle, Billiards, and Brandies, and a couple of bibulous-looking characters hanging round the doorway; and on the other hand the Free Library, which is adorned by busts of Shakespeare and Bacon, and which is about to enjoy the patronage of two honest, upright citizens whom the Free Library has obviously improved into a state of considerable prosperity.[3]

Later in this narrative we shall have an opportunity to consider how far the readership of the new libraries corresponded to public expectations. For the present it will be sufficient to say that the users were, at this period, predominantly working-class. The library at Kidderminster summed up what must have been a common experience when it reported in 1856: "a large majority of the readers are young men from 14 to 30 years of age, chiefly belonging to the working classes."[4]

To the philanthropist and the social reformer the fact that the libraries appealed chiefly to the lower orders was their principal merit; but we can have no doubt that this same fact accounts for the fierce opposition to them in many places. This was not merely factious or obscurantist: it was the normal ratepayers' reaction to a proposal which involved, it seemed, taxing the rich for the benefit of the poor.

---

[1] J. J. Ogle, *The Free Library* (1897), p. 52.

[2] *Fifty Years: a Brief History of the Public Library Movement in Nottingham* (Nottingham 1918), pp. 23–24.

[3] The cartoon was dropped after the first edition of Greenwood's book. From the third edition (1890) he also dropped the word "Free" from the title, on the grounds that it savoured of charity. The title *Free Library*, however, was still used by J. J. Ogle as late as 1897.   [4] *P.R. 1856*, p. 5.

This is very obvious from the debate which took place in the Leeds Town Council when a memorial in favour of a public library was brought forward in 1861.[1] Councillor Newton, for example, complained that those who voted for the library would not be those who would pay for it, and that the additional tax would fall very heavily on the middle-class ratepayer. He went on to argue that the libraries already existing were decaying for lack of support, and that "the working classes should be taught to rely a little on themselves." Alderman Wilson was opposed to a compulsory contribution for educational purposes, and believed that "the working classes already had the opportunity of obtaining all the knowledge that was necessary to them." Mr. Yewdall said a 1d. rate would cost him 50s. a year, and he was not prepared to pay it. Councillor Stead added his impression that a public library was "merely a shelter for a lot of idle fellows to spend their time in."[2]

The argument that a free service would undermine the independence of the citizen—the standard argument against social reform of any kind—was very common. At Bristol in 1853 "a gentleman of influence" said

"the idea of a Free Library appeared to him to be futile one, for he thought if a person had not desire enough for his own improvement, to give a small annual contribution to carry on a Library, he ought not to have the advantage of it. He thought such an institution *would be extremely injurious to the public.*"[3]

These extracts are typical of what happened in many places where the proposal to adopt was defeated or delayed. The landlords and shopkeepers, because they were heavy ratepayers, were usually in the van of the opposition, often with vociferous support from publicans, booksellers, and proprietors of circulating libraries, all of whom feared, rightly or wrongly, that their vested interests would be affected. In Newcastle upon Tyne, where a motion for adoption was first passed at a public meeting in 1872, every conceivable manoeuvre was used to harass and delay the progress of the work, and it was not until 1880 that a temporary lending library was at last opened.[4] In Edinburgh, when the matter was raised for the second time in 1881, sandwich men were hired to parade the streets with bills bearing the legend:

RATEPAYERS!

Resist this Free Library Dodge,
And Save Yourselves from the Burden of £6000
of Additional Taxation.[5]

In London, about the same time, the Rev. De Kewer Williams, a Congregational parson, boasted that he had saved Hackney from "that dear luxury, a

[1] See above, pp. below, p. 49.
[2] T. W. Hand, "The Leeds Public Free Libraries," in *L.A.R.*, Vol. VI (1904), pp. 3–4.
[3] C. Tovey, *A Free Library for Bristol* (1855), pp. 6–7.
[4] B. Anderton, "The Struggle for a Public Library in Newcastle upon Tyne", in *L.A.R.*, Vol. VII (1905), pp. 259–271.
[5] J. J. Ogle, *The Free Library* (1897), p. 48.

Free Library."[1] This, however, was exceptional: in general the clergy and professional classes seem to have been in favour of the library movement. There were, too, it must be said, many worthy members of the merchant and manufacturing classes who were prepared to put their sense of public duty before all personal considerations. Some, who were wealthy, left their memorials in stone: such were, for example, William Brown of Liverpool, Edward Pease of Darlington, and William Gilstrap of Newark. But there were many others, whose names survive only in the yellowing pages of annual reports, who yet gave generously of both time and money in the library service.

From the late 'sixties, as a result of events described above—the Reform Act of 1867, the Paris Exhibition of the same year, the agitation for improved education, and so on—there was a marked shift of public opinion in relation to the libraries. The philanthropic aspect of the service, though it did not disappear, now sank into a subordinate place, and the libraries, like the mechanics' institutes before them, were seen as a part of a great forward movement in national education. Those who favoured the establishment of libraries could now counter the protests of disgruntled ratepayers with the argument that public libraries were not a gift but an investment, which would yield a rich return not only in the form of better citizenship but also in terms of industrial prosperity.

As early as 1867 Alderman J. V. Godwin of Bradford commented to James Hanson, Editor of the *Bradford Review*, that the difficulties that might have arisen in securing the adoption of the Libraries Acts in Bradford had been "much lessened by the greater unanimity which now prevails as to National Education."[2] From 1870 onwards it was hardly possible for a library to be formally opened without some reference to the Education Act of that year and its implications for the library service. A typical statement was that by Dr. Henry Newton, presiding at the opening of the Newcastle upon Tyne Reference Library by the Prince of Wales in 1884. Public Libraries, he declared, "would carry upward and onward the work of the public elementary schools."[3] The public libraries were now, in the modern phrase, on the educational "bandwaggon", and Greenwood, looking back in 1890, was able to say:

> "Although much good was accomplished during the first twenty years after Ewart's Act, the real impetus came with the passing of the Elementary Education Act of 1870".[4]

[1] Greenwood (1886), p. 248. Cf. G. Carlton, *Spade-Work: the Story of Thomas Greenwood* (1949), p. 84. In 1878 it was reported to the Library Association that householders in Hackney had been threatened with a large increase in rents unless they voted against adoption of the Acts—*Transactions and Proceedings of the First Annual Meeting of the Library Association . . . 1878* (1879), p. 14. The same kind of intimidation was reported four years later at Hull, where the landlords posted representatives outside the polling-booths— J. F. Hooton, *Libraries in Hull in the Nineteenth Century and the Struggle for the Adoption of the Public Libraries Acts* (unpublished F.L.A. thesis, 1967), p. 194.

[2] M. E. Hartley, "A Survey of the Public Library Movement in Bradford," in *L.A.R.*, Vol. VIII (1906), p. 423.

[3] *A Short History of the Newcastle upon Tyne Public Libraries* (Newcastle upon Tyne, 1950).

[4] Greenwood (1890), p. 275. Much valuable material relating to the development of public opinion on this subject has been assembled in W. J. Murison, *The Public Library: its Origins, Purpose and Significance* (1955, 2nd edn. 1971), espec. Chs. ii–iii. He cites (pp.62–64) a number of contemporary sources for the view that the Education Act of 1870 and its successors were slow to take effect, but by the late 'eighties, at any rate, the results were clearly visible in the statistics of new libraries founded (see above, p. 16).

Libraries on a Shoestring

The total of 125 libraries opened before 1887 sounds quite impressive, but it should be made plain that only a small proportion of these could be regarded by modern standards as in any way adequate or efficient. To see just how inadequate they were, we can turn to the statistical table appended to the second edition of Thomas Greenwood's *Free Public Libraries* in 1887. Greenwood's preface is dated April, 1887, and he evidently tried to secure, where possible, figures for 1886, but in a number of cases he had to fall back on figures for 1885. His statistics appear to be reasonably accurate, and read in conjunction with those given in the Parliamentary Returns for 1885 and 1890, offer a sufficient basis for some significant broad generalizations.

Taking Greenwood's figures, then, we note that even at this comparatively late date only four public libraries had a bookstock exceeding 100000 volumes: they were Manchester, which had 181000 volumes, and Birmingham, Leeds and Liverpool, which were between 135000 and 150000.[1] A long way behind came Salford and Sheffield, with 81000 volumes apiece, and there were four others—Bolton, Bristol, Newcastle upon Tyne, and Nottingham—with over 50000.[2] Nearly three-quarters of the total number, however, had fewer than 20000 volumes, and nearly half fewer than 10000 volumes, which is the size, in these days, of a very modest branch library.

The under-10000 group included, of course, a number of libraries recently formed which had not yet had time to build up a substantial stock, e.g. Gateshead, Loughborough, Shrewsbury, and Wandsworth, but it also included many libraries of older foundation, especially in the rural county and market towns, e.g. Canterbury (1847), Winchester (1851), Hertford (1856), Lichfield (1859) and Bridgwater (1860).[3] Three of the six libraries in Wales and Monmouthshire, and eight of the twelve Scottish libraries, were also in this group. In general the libraries in the manufacturing and commercial centres were better developed than those in the rural towns, but there were some quite sizeable industrial towns, e.g. Blackburn, Bradford and Leicester, with fewer than 50000 volumes; and no Welsh or Scottish library reached this figure. The largest Welsh library was at Swansea (29000 volumes), the largest Scottish library at Dundee (48000 volumes).

Inevitably many of the smaller libraries were unable to offer a complete service. The lending library and the newsrooms generally had first preference, and fewer than three-quarters of the libraries of which details are given in the Parliamentary Return of 1885 had reference sections amounting to more than 500 volumes. Kidderminster had 46 volumes, Aberystwyth 18, Bangor 60; Bridgwater reported "A few large volumes reserved for reading only in the

---

[1] For the purpose of comparison it may be mentioned that in March, 1965, Leeds held over 800000 volumes, and Manchester over 1¼ millions, while the stocks of Birmingham and Liverpool were approaching the 2 million mark. Of course these libraries now served substantially larger populations—in the case of Birmingham more than twice as large.

[2] Greenwood also shows Dundee with over 50000 volumes, but this is incorrect—see below, p. 65.

[3] Oxford (1854) is also shown by Greenwood as having under 10000 volumes, perhaps incorrectly. See below, pp. 57–58.

library".[1] Some libraries, mostly in Lancashire and Staffordshire, had no reference sections at all. Even the lending libraries, at a number of these places, were open only for a few hours a week.[2]

There were a few libraries which had reference books but no lending section. One of these was Wrexham, which was opened in 1879 but functioned mainly as a newsroom until, twenty years later, a gift of £390 from the surplus funds of the National Eisteddfod meeting there enabled it to be put on a proper footing.[3] The situation in 1885 is described in the Parliamentary Return:

> "The books in this library consist entirely of volumes given by various people, and the committee have not yet commenced a circulating library. There is no 'Reference Library', properly so called; but all the books (618 in number) are open to the public in a room adjoining the news room."[4]

At two other libraries in this category, Ipswich and Maidstone, the reason for the absence of a lending department was that the library was at this period subordinate to the museum. The Ipswich library and museum were opened in 1853. The museum was (and still is) a notable one, and the reference books were described in 1876 as "in Natural History, Biology, and General Science, to assist students and others at the Museum."[5] Eight years later the collection amounted to some 4500 volumes, including the remains of the old town library founded in 1599. It was tolerably well used, the total annual issues being returned as 20000.[6] Lending facilities were first made available in 1887 or 1888. At Maidstone the library and museum were opened in 1858 in the former residence of Dr. Thomas Charles, who had bequeathed his books, pictures and antiquities to the Corporation. By 1885 the library is said to have reached the then substantial figure of about 20000 volumes, but the number of readers was only about 20 a day.[7] The establishment of a lending library had to wait until 1890, when a memorial gift of £30000 by Samuel Bentlif, a local boot and shoe merchant, made possible the opening of a new wing.[8]

The position of Brighton and Oldham was rather similar. At Brighton the gift of two private libraries and the library of the Royal Literary and Scientific

---

[1] *P.R. 1885*, p. 14.

[2] Comprehensive information on hours of opening is not available for 1886, but the situation is unlikely to have been better than it was ten years later, when Bangor's lending library was open for 10 hours a week, Clitheroe's for 8 hours, Thurso's for 6 hours, and Brierley Hill's for 4 hours, and the village library of Tarves was content with 3 hours—*L.Y.B. 1897*, pp. 212 sqq. Cf. for the position in 1879, Library Association, *Transactions and Proceedings of the Second Annual Meeting . . 1879* (1880), table opp. p. 138.

[3] Wrexham Public Library, *Centenary Report, 1956–1957* (1957).   [4] *P.R. 1885*, p. 23.

[5] *P.R. 1876*, p. 39; cf. *P.R. 1885*, p. 19, "a library in connection with the museum collections."

[6] *P.R. 1885*, pp. 18–19; T. Kelly, *Early Public Libraries* (1966), pp. 71, 73, 254.

[7] *P.R. 1885*, p. 9. Greenwood (1887), repeats this figure of 20000, but it may have been an overestimate: *P.R. 1890*, p. 4, records only 12000 vols., and Greenwood in his 3rd edn. (1890), gives the same figure. In his 4th edn. (1891, p. 214) Greenwood remarks that most of the books were gifts from townspeople, which may explain the small number of readers.

[8] Greenwood (1891, p. 214) says the building was a memorial to Bentlif himself, but in fact it was given by him in memory of his brother George Amatt. Samuel survived until 1897—information from Mr. A. Joyce, Borough Librarian.

Institution led in 1873 to the establishment of a public library, under powers granted to the Corporation by the Pavilion Act of 1850, which permitted the levy of a 4d. rate for the upkeep of the Royal Pavilion Estate. The library was for reference only until 1889, when a public subscription of £2000 made possible the opening of a lending library.[1] At Oldham a special Act of 1865 gave power to establish a public library, museum, and schools of science and art, but it was not until 1885 that a central library was actually provided, and not until 1887 that, by public request, a lending department was opened there.[2] This was the first Act to give library powers without limiting the rate.[3]

Ipswich, Maidstone, Brighton and Oldham are examples of a considerable group of English towns in which the Acts were adopted, or special legislation secured, primarily for the purposes other than the formation of a library. Stockport adopted the Libraries Acts in 1861 for museum purposes; only in 1875, after an agitation by a Young Men's Committee, was a public library provided. It was in a room built over the market-hall, where the odour of the books mingled with the prevailing smell of cheese from the stalls below.[4] At Leicester, similarly, a museum was established in 1848, under the Museums Act, and a library was added only in 1871.[5]

At Lichfield both museum and library were opened in 1859, but the library long occupied a secondary position. Until 1874 it was a reference library only: by 1885 it appears to have been a combined reference and lending library, of some 4000 volumes.[6] At Exeter the library was opened in 1870 in the splendid Albert Memorial Buildings (afterwards Albert Memorial College) which had been erected by public subscription in memory of the Prince Consort. It was, we are told, originally "a small and unimportant appendage" to the museum and school of science and art,[7] but thanks to generous gifts it grew rapidly, and by 1885 was approaching the respectable total of some 13 000 volumes.[8] Other libraries in this group, of which we shall have more to say later, were Canterbury, Sunderland, Warrington and Winchester.[9]

Even where the library was the prime consideration, financial difficulties often stood in the way of satisfactory provision. The $\frac{1}{2}$d. rate granted under the original Act of 1850 was in most cases quite inadequate, as more than one library pointed out in the Parliamentary Return of 1853. Oxford, which had adopted the Act and was wondering how to implement it, commented: "£200 a year is not enough, and it has been suggested that power should be given to raise a

---

[1] H. D. Roberts, "The Brighton Public Library, Museums and Fine Art Galleries: a Retrospect", in L.A.R., Vol. X (1908), pp. 439–442.

[2] W. H. Berry, *Oldham Public Libraries, Art Gallery and Museum, 1883–1933* (Oldham 1933), pp. 16–19. A branch reference library was opened at North Moor in 1883, and lending facilities were made available there in 1886—*ibid.*, pp. 22.

[3] Three other authorities later secured by local Act total exemption from the rate limit. They were: St. Helens (1869), Huddersfield (1871), and Birmingham (1883).

[4] R. E. G. Smith, *The First Fifty Years of Public Libraries in Stockport* (unpublished F.L.A. essay 1950), pp. 13–27.

[5] Information from Mr. W. R. M. McClelland, City Librarian. Cf. above, p. 25 note 1.

[6] *P.R. 1885*, p. 16. Greenwood (1887) records only 3000 volumes, and says the library was open only twice a week, to change books.

[7] H. Tapley-Soper, "Exeter Public Library: an Historical Essay", in L.A.R., Vol. XIII (1911), p. 54.

[8] *P.R. 1885*, p. 4, so also Greenwood (1887).   [9] See below, Ch. iii.

sixpenny rate, but it is doubtful whether the burgesses would vote for this."[1] The 1d. rate allowed in Scotland from 1854 and in England from 1855 was at the outset regarded as adequate by the larger cities,[2] but became increasingly insufficient as libraries grew in size, especially where, as was the case with about one library in three, a museum or art gallery (or both) had to be financed from the same fund. In a few instances, e.g. Exeter, Watford, Wolverhampton and Cardiff, the elastic penny had to be stretched to cover also the provision of technical classes, but where accommodation was available this was less of a burden, since the work was grant-aided by the Science and Art Department.

For the smaller centres even the 1d. rate was inadequate from the start, and it is not surprising to find that in 1886 nearly half the libraries of fewer than 10000 volumes were in places with a population of less than 20000. More than a score of these places, indeed (nearly all the places with a population of less than 10000), had libraries of fewer than 5000 volumes. How could it be otherwise when, as at Tamworth and Thurso, a library had to be supported on a rate income of only £40 a year, or when as at Bangor a library and museum had to be supported on a rate income of £123 a year?[3] W. R. Credland, of Manchester, calculated in 1883 that the minimum annual income on which a library could be supported was £500, but he counted at that time over forty libraries whose income was below this figure, and nineteen with an income of under £200.[4]

The situation was made even more difficult by the fact that some libraries did not even have the benefit of the full library rate. Canterbury, Winchester, Bolton, Cambridge, Oxford, Sheffield, Leamington, Norwich, Sunderland, and Blackburn all had to be content, at least at times, with a ½d. or ¾d. rate in their earlier years, and quite a number of libraries still suffered under this limitation in 1886.[5] At St. Margaret and St. John's, Westminster, a ½d. rate might be excusable, since owing to the wealth of the two parishes it brought a yield of £1,425, but a ¾d. rate at Clitheroe, where the yield was only £75, could not be justified on any grounds.

In some cases the lower rate was due to a deliberate decision of the ratepayers at the time of adoption, under the Act of 1877.[6] More often it was due to the meanness of town councils which looked upon public libraries as an extravagance and viewed all library expenditure with deep suspicion. The library committee, which in England and Wales commonly and in Scotland always included some non-elected members,[7] saw the librarian's difficulties at first hand,

---

[1] *P.R. 1853*, p. 5.

[2] "Of the larger towns, few have yet levied for Free Libraries or Museums the whole sum that the Acts . . . permit them to levy"—E. Edwards, *Free Town Libraries* (1869), p. 34. At Manchester, from 1852 to 1869, library expenditure only once exceeded the rate yield, and then only by £2 (in 1855–56, when the ½d. rate was still in operation)—*P.R. 1870*, p. 18.

[3] Other library authorities with a population of under 10000 were Lichfield, Aberystwyth, Bideford, Tonbridge, Penrith and Tarves. Lichfield and Penrith also had museums. The highest rate income in this group was at Tonbridge (£135 per annum).

[4] W. R. Credland, "Starved Free Libraries", in Library Association, *Transactions and Proceedings of the . . . Sixth Annual Meeting, 1883* (1886), pp. 72–73.

[5] Greenwood (1886), Ch. xxii, lists Westminster, Leicester, Portsmouth, and Loughborough at ½d., and Clitheroe and Warwick at ¾d. Folkestone is recorded as levying a ½d. and 1d. rate in alternate years.

[6] See above, p. 22.   [7] See above, p. 21.

and could usually be relied on to be sympathetic, but within the council there was often a lack of understanding, if not downright opposition.

The modern historian of the Sheffield library writes of the situation there in the 1860s:

> "The Council were not in general unsympathetic to the library movement; many members frequently expressed themselves in favour of it, and the voting nearly always went in favour of any suggested improvement. But they seemed to think development did not need money, or, in the case of the Central Library, space."[1]

At this time the Sheffield Central Library (there were as yet no branches) occupied rented rooms in the Mechanics' Hall. In 1864 the Council generously increased the rate from $\frac{1}{2}$d. to $\frac{3}{4}$d. on condition that the increase should be used to acquire the whole premises. This was done, whereupon the Council promptly took over the most of the ground floor for its own use, and let the top floor to the Mechanics' Institute, leaving the library almost as badly off as before.[2]

In the less wealthy centres the cost of providing accommodation for the public library frequently had an inhibiting effect on development. As we shall see in a later section, the libraries of this period occupied premises of a most miscellaneous character, especially in their earlier years, but sooner or later most libraries sought to secure premises built for the purpose. A minority were fortunate in having libraries erected by public subscription, or by the generosity of a single benefactor, but others had to rely on public funds and, where building was undertaken on a substantial scale, the resulting interest and sinking fund charges were apt to be a heavy drain on the library's already exiguous income.

Norwich, the first authority to adopt the 1850 Act and the first to erect a library building from public funds, is a case in point. The building, when eventually completed in 1857, included a lecture room, a Museum, a School of Art, and accommodation for the Norwich Literary Institute (a private subscription library) as well as the public library. The space initially available to the library, therefore, was no more than a single room, but the total cost was nearly £7500, and for some years the loan charges took up such a large proportion of the rate income that there was no money at all to purchase books.[3] Similar stories could be told in the 'seventies and 'eighties of Birmingham, where municipal building was on a lavish scale,[4] of Rochdale, Bradford, Cardiff, and many others. At Bradford, following the opening in 1878 of a new library and art gallery built at a cost of £28 000, the library committee had to pay to the Corporation over £900 per annum in rent and rates—more than a quarter of the rate income.[5]

The expedients adopted by public libraries to surmount their financial difficulties were many and various. Appeals for public subscriptions were common form in the early years, and indeed throughout the period when some special objective such as a new building was in view, but by the middle 'seventies

---

[1] *The City Libraries of Sheffield, 1856–1956* (Sheffield 1956), p. 15.

[2] *Ibid.*

[3] G. A. Stephen, *Three Centuries of a City Library* (Norwich 1917), p. 65; P. Hepworth and M. Alexander, *City of Norwich Libraries* (1957), p. 13.

[4] See below, pp. 47-49.

[5] Greenwood (1891), p. 103; B. Wood, *A Brief Survey of the Bradford Public Libraries, 1872–1922* (Bradford 1922), p. 12; information from Mr. H. Bilton, City Librarian.

income from this source was negligible.[1] Appeals for books were more successful, and we shall have more to say on this subject later. At Oxford, in the opening phase, the newspapers and magazines for the reading room were provided by private subscriptions.[2] Oxford also drew some income at this time from lectures and concerts, which showed a profit of £43.16.0 in the first year. Wigan, having been presented in 1878 with a handsome library which it had difficulty in maintaining, appealed to the ratepayers for an additional voluntary rate of ½d.[3] Southport, in the following year, was levying an additional 1d. rate to clear off debts.[4] Richmond on Thames, in 1885, asked for an additional 1d. and we are told that more than one-fifth of the ratepayers responded.[5]

In an age when subscription libraries were still numerous and often flourishing, it was natural for hard-pressed library committees to wonder whether some contribution towards expenses could not be exacted from at least the wealthier users of the library. The Acts laid down that admission must be free, but some committees took the view that this obligation was sufficiently discharged by the provision of a free reading and reference room, and that a charge might legitimately be introduced for borrowers. In one or two of the smaller towns, Edwards tells us, this was done by making a charge for borrowers' tickets. "This, at best," he comments, "is an evasion of the intention of the Legislature, even if it be granted that it may, technically, be regarded as just escaping the precise censure due to the open violation of an Act of Parliament."[6] Oxford was one of the places which adopted this plan, and in 1867–68 the lending library was run entirely from "the scanty annual product of the sale of Catalogues, and of Borrowers' tickets."[7]

A common expedient for raising income, however, was either to place the lending library entirely on a subscription basis, or to run a subscription library alongside the free lending library. The former method was adopted at Warrington, where it will be recalled that the public library had its origins in a former subscription library, which was taken over by the local authority in 1848.[8] Here the arrangement in the early years was that the library was open to the public for reference only, on Mondays, Wednesdays and Saturdays; subscribers of half a guinea per annum, however, could use the library on any weekday, and they alone were entitled to borrow.[9] This subscription system persisted until 1887, when it was replaced by a charge of 1d. per book. Only in 1891, after a local Act had sanctioned a 1½d. rate, did the lending library become completely free.[10]

A more surprising case is that of Watford where, from the opening of the library in 1874 until 1887, borrowers had to pay 4d. a month, or 3s. per annum. This library, it may be remarked, was carrying out a very ambitious programme of activities, including lectures, science, art and music classes, a day school, and

[1] See the statements of income and expenditure in *P.R. 1876* and *P.R. 1877*.
[2] *Oxford City Libraries, 1854–1954* (Oxford 1954), p. 6.
[3] H. T. Folkard, *Wigan Free Public Library* (Wigan 1900), p. 3. Cf. below, p. 61.
[4] Library Association, *Transactions and Proceedings of the Second Annual Meeting . . . 1879* (1880), p. 93.
[5] Jubilee article by A. C. Piper in *Richmond on Thames Times*, 6 June 1931. This arrangement continued in force until 1894.
[6] E. Edwards, *Free Town Libraries* (1869), p. 58.
[7] *Op. cit.*, p. 174, citing *Oxford Annual Report, 1868*, p. 3.
[8] See above, p. 10.   [9] *P.R. 1856*, p. 13.   [10] J. J. Ogle, *The Free Library* (1897), p. 255.

even in the opening years a youth centre, on a rate income which rose from £80 in the year of opening to £240 in 1885. Until 1883 the work was done by honorary officers.[1]

Examples of subscription lending libraries operated alongside free lending libraries are found before 1886 at Bolton, Wigan,[2] Stockport,[3] Coventry,[4] Tynemouth,[5] Rochdale,[6] West Bromwich,[7] and Dundee.[8] At Dundee, where the subscription library was inaugurated in 1876 and lasted until 1943, the arrangement was that subscribers paid £1.1s. a year, the subscriptions being used to purchase books which for one year were available to subscribers only and then passed into the general library stock.[9] This fairly represents the principle on which libraries of this type were conducted at this period and later in the century. The outstanding example, however, is Bolton, where a subscription library was operated from the opening of the library in 1853 until 1908.[10] Initially there were three classes of borrowers: subscribers of £1.1s. a year, for whom books were reserved for twelve months; subscribers of ten shillings a year, for whom books were reserved for six months; and non-subscribers, who had to await their turn. Subscribers had the additional privilege of being able to borrow one volume at a time for home reading from the reference library.[11]

Edwards regarded subscription libraries as only a degree less objectionable than charges for borrowers' tickets, and was particularly critical of Bolton's three-fold "breeches'-pocket classification."

He commented:

> "The borrowing privileges of each class were made more or less ample, in proportion, exactly on the principle which gives to a First class railway traveller very soft cushions; to the Second class traveller very hard cushions; and to the Third class traveller no cushions at all."[12]

In an interesting statistical table Edwards was able to demonstrate that although the number of subscription issues rose from 6000 in 1853–54 to 33 000 in 1867–68, the number of non-subscription issues fell from 61 000 to 41 000 in the same period.[13]

J. Potter Briscoe, who was on the staff at Bolton before he became librarian

[1] J. Woolman, *Watford Public Library: its History and Development* (repr. from *Watford Observer*, 25 Jan. 1913.).

[2] H. T. Folkard, *Wigan Free Public Library* (Wigan 1900), p. 3.

[3] R. E. G. Smith, *The First Fifty Years of Public Libraries in Stockport* (unpublished F.L.A. essay 1950), pp. 79–81. The arrangement here lasted only about three years, from 1883 to about 1886.

[4] Library Association, *Transactions and Proceedings of the Second Annual Meeting . . . 1879* (1880), table opp. p. 138.

[5] *L.Y.B. 1900–01*, p. 217.

[6] R. P. Taylor (ed. E. E. Taylor), *Rochdale Retrospect* (Rochdale 1906), p. 132.

[7] The subscription library here was inaugurated in 1884 and lasted for fifty years—G. Hodges, *West Bromwich Public Library, 1874–1946* [West Bromwich 1946].

[8] Probably also at Chesterfield—Greenwood (1887), pp. 76–77.

[9] Dundee Free Public Library Committee, *Annual Reports, 1876*, p. 10; *1877*, p. 9. For a few years this library also paid a subscription to Mudie's Library—*Annual Report, 1872* p. 13.

[10] *Bolton Public Libraries, 1853–1953* (Bolton 1953), p. 7.

[11] E. Edwards, *Free Town Libraries* (1869), pp. 58–60.   [12] *Op. cit.*, p. 59.   [13] *Op. cit.*, p. 167.

at Nottingham in 1869, afterwards confirmed Edwards's view: a subscription library, he said, encroached on the time of the library staff, encouraged the municipal authorities to reduce their grant, and led to the acquisition by the library of "a mass of ephemeral literature, especially in the three-volume form."[1]

So far, in this section, we have given rather a dispiriting picture of public libraries in the period up to 1886. As we shall see shortly, there were libraries at this period which were both efficient and prosperous, but it would be wrong not to recognize that the service provided by most libraries was still very inadequate, and that the condition of many individual libraries, especially in the smaller centres of population, was deplorable. At Norwich, in 1865, a ratepayer complained that

> "the standard works of our language in fiction, history, travel, biography, and science, are, for the most part, in as dilapidated a condition as can well be imagined. . . I have seen many and many a time the librarian doing his best to preserve what was once a book, by the help of paste-pot and paper, but all his exertions have been of but little avail".[2]

The Cambridge library, at the same period, was so poor that it could not even spare old copies of *Punch* for the local workhouse.[3] Both these libraries had improved considerably by the end of the period, but many others were still in a parlous state in the 'eighties. At Oxford a newspaper correspondent described the library as in "a lamentable state of neglect and decay", and an editorial comment spoke of it as "an apology for a library."[4] The Hereford library was "rather crippled" by lack of funds;[5] at Cardiff the position was "desperate";[6] and at Northampton library and museum alike (housed at this time in the former County Gaol) were alleged to be "rotting in stagnation."[7]

We can hardly doubt that there were other libraries to which similar, if perhaps less opprobrious, comments could have been applied.

---

[1] J. P. Briscoe, "Subscription Libraries in Connexion with Free Public Libraries", in Library Association, *Transactions and Proceedings of the First Annual Meeting . . . 1878* (1879), pp. 19–21, reprinted in J. L. Thornton, *Selected Readings in the History of Librarianship* (1966), pp. 192–197. In the subsequent discussion (*Transactions*. pp. 123–124) the subscription library found defenders. The librarian himself, J. K. Waite, put the case in "A Subscription Library in Connection with a Public Library", in *The Library*, Vol. V (1893), pp. 40–47.

[2] P. Hepworth and M. Alexander, *City of Norwich Libraries* (1957), p. 13.

[3] W. A. Munford, *The Cambridge City Libraries, 1855–1955* (Cambridge 1955), p. 5

[4] *Oxford City Libraries, 1854–1954* (Oxford [1954]), p. 11.

[5] *P.R. 1885*, p. 7.

[6] J. Ballinger, *The Cardiff Free Libraries* (Cardiff 1895), p. 17.

[7] *Northampton Public Library, 1876–1926* (Northampton 1926), p. 4.

CHAPTER III

Some Case-Studies

A Note on Library Statistics

BEFORE attempting to generalize about matters of library organization and use, it will be useful to glance briefly at the history and development of the major libraries of this period, and of some of the smaller libraries which are for various reasons of special interest. This kind of treatment has its dangers, for local circumstances vary so much that the history of each library is in a real sense unique, but there are none the less certain common features and common problems which can be better appreciated in the context of the individual library.

First, however, a word about statistics. Libraries lend themselves peculiarly to the compilation of statistics. One can count the books, the issues, and the readers, and each of these headings can be almost endlessly subdivided. The books can be separated into reference books and lending books, and each of these can be classified under subjects; the issues can be similarly dealt with; and the readers can be categorized by age, sex and occupation. The early librarians, following the example set by Edwards at Manchester, tried to count everything, and the result is that the library historian has at his disposal a mass of statistical material such as can hardly be paralleled in the case of any other social institution. In a general narrative such as this I have tried to use statistics as sparingly as possible, but some statistics are essential if we are to form a clear idea of the size and character of the libraries of the period. For those interested in further detail, I have given in an appendix some key figures for each of the libraries dealt with for the year 1886.[1]

The non-professional reader should be warned that there are various factors which affect the calculation of stock and issues, and should be cautious in using the figures given, except in the most general way, for purposes of comparison between one library and another, or between nineteenth-century libraries and those of to-day. Just to give one example, the number of issues for home-reading depends very much on the period of the loan: a library which lends books for one week only will show a much higher total of annual issues than a library that lends for two weeks, though the total number of books read may be the same.[2]

The reader, can, however, fairly ask for some guidance as to how nineteenth-century library service compared with those of later periods, and for this purpose I have assembled some of the more significant statistics below.[3]

---

[1] See below, Appendix II.
[2] I have not used figures for numbers of readers at all for this period, because the variation in the period for which tickets were valid makes them quite meaningless.
[3] Apps. VI–IX. On the dangers of statistics see the last chapter in E. A. Savage, *A Librarian Looks at Readers* (1947, 2nd edn. 1950).

Manchester

We must begin with Manchester, which was regarded at the time and long afterwards as the first public library to be opened under the 1850 Act. We now know that Winchester, opened in 1851, has this distinction, but Manchester was certainly the first major library, and was looked to as an exemplar by libraries all over the country. We have already had occasion to notice the very successful efforts by the Mayor of Manchester, Sir John Potter, to raise funds for the library.[1] Of the total of nearly £13 000 subscribed, more than £7000 went to the purchase and adaptation of a building in Campfield, Deansgate, originally erected as an Owenite Hall of Science—"a building of ill-fame", Edward Edwards called it.[2] The subscription committee proceeded to appoint a librarian, to purchase books, and to make all other necessary arrangements. In August, 1852, the Public Libraries Act was adopted (by nearly 4000 votes to 40), and on 2nd September the completed library was formally handed over to the Council and opened to the public. Some of the speeches made on this occasion have already been referred to.[3] Strangely enough, in the circumstances, the provision made in the Libraries Act for the appointment of lay members to the library committee was ignored, and the library was placed under the control of a committee consisting exclusively of members of the Council. In this respect Manchester was exceptional.[4]

Edward Edwards, appointed librarian of Manchester in 1851, was one of the four early public librarians with substantial previous experience of library work. He afterwards expressed the view that Manchester had been mistaken in spending so much money, in the initial stages, on the Hall of Science building. Writing in 1868, he contrasted the position in Liverpool, where after a humble beginning the library now had a building sufficient for the probable require-ments for a century to come, with that at Manchester, where the library found itself saddled with a building badly situated and "worse than inadequate" to its present requirements.[5] In this matter he spoke more truly than he knew, for before long the weight of the growing library proved too much for the old building, so that in 1877 it had to be abruptly closed, and the books removed to the Old Town Hall.[6]

In the meantime, however, Edwards quickly set about putting the new library on a business footing. The nucleus of the collection was provided by some 18 000 carefully selected volumes purchased at a cost of over £4000 from the original public subscription. About 3 300 volumes were presented, and a few others begged from Government departments. By the time of the opening Edwards had managed to gather together more than 21 000 volumes, of which 16 000 were in the reference department and the remainder in the lending department.[7] In building up this library Edwards followed the advice he after-

---

[1] See above, p. 27.

[2] *P.R. 1853*, p. 5; E. Edwards, *Free Town Libraries* (1869), pp. 65–66: cf. his *Memoirs of Libraries* (1859), Vol. I, pp. 801–802.

[3] See above, p. 27. [4] See the table in *Free Town Libraries*, opp. p. 192.

[5] E. Edwards, *Free Town Libraries* (1869), pp. 39–40.

[6] W. R. Credland, *The Manchester Public Free Libraries* (Manchester 1899), pp. 116–117.

[7] E. Edwards, *Memoirs of Libraries* (1859), Vol. I, pp. 802–807; *Free Town Libraries* (1869), pp. 66–70.

wards gave to librarians to concentrate limited resources on acquiring really good collections in one or two chosen fields.[1] At Manchester he concentrated on history and the allied subjects of politics and commerce, with particular reference, as far as possible, to local interests; and the books under these headings comprised more than half his initial stock.

The response to the new library was good. The rooms were at once thronged with readers, and in 1856 the Town Clerk was able to report:

> "The working of the Libraries Act in Manchester has given unmingled satis-
> faction. . . . Persons of every class of society in the community have frequented the
> library, and the extent to which it has been used has steadily increased in every
> successive year since the opening. Out of an aggregate issue, considerably exceeding
> half a million of volumes, only 12 have been actually lost to the library, so far as has
> yet been ascertained."[2]

The only thing that worried Edwards, at this time, was the incurable preference of borrowers from the lending library for novels and "romances" rather than for more solid fare—a preference which he attributed, in his ponderous way, to "the utter insufficiency of that amount of command over the mere implements of education which is commonly imparted in popular schools."[3]

At this period the reference department was open every weekday from 10 a.m. to 9 p.m., and the lending department for nine hours on Saturdays and for five hours on other weekdays. The reference stock had now risen from 16000 to 22000 volumes, with 66000 issues per annum; and the lending library stock from 5000 to 10000 volumes, with 80000 issues per annum.[4] Considering that the library was not really centrally situated, the use reflected in these figures must be regarded as very satisfactory, though the total stock of 32000 volumes, for a town with about ten times that number of inhabitants, was by modern standards sadly inadequate.

The raising of the permissible maximum rate to 1d. in 1855 allowed the library committee to consider the establishment of the first branch libraries, which were opened in converted houses in two populous working-class areas, Hulme and Ancoats, in 1857. Three more branches were created in the 'sixties and 'seventies. All these functioned primarily as lending libraries, but in each case a reading and newsroom was attached, and the lending stock was available for reference purposes.

Edwards, during his term as librarian, saw only the opening of the first two branches. Just as in 1850 he had been dismissed from the British Museum Library for what Panizzi called "his rude and insolent manner", so now he was dismissed from his Manchester post after charges that he had been habitually "disrespectful" and "insubordinate".[5] He was indeed a difficult man to work with, but the fault was not entirely his. The Committee had treated him with scant respect, had constantly interfered with his work, had made him sign in and out of the library like any other "Servant of the Committee", had repeatedly

---

[1] *Memoirs*, Vol. II, pp. 574–575.
[2] *P.R. 1856*, p. 8.   [3] *Memoirs*, Vol. I, pp. 810–812.
[4] *P.R. 1856*, p. 7. By a clause in a local Act, Manchester obtained powers to purchase books from the rates prior to the Act of 1855—E. Edwards, *Free Town Libraries* (1869), p. 76 n.
[5] W. A. Munford, *Edward Edwards, 1812–1886* (1963), pp. 77, 130.

declined to increase his salary over the £200 per annum originally fixed—in short, had refused to treat him as a professional man.[1]

It was on 1 November, 1858, that Edwards inducted to the library his successor, R. W. Smiles.[2] A few days later he passed the final proofs of his monumental *Memoirs of Libraries*, which was published in January of the following year. In the penultimate chapter of his second volume he reproduces several of the documents used in the administration of the Manchester public libraries. They were documents which he had prepared, and which illustrate the care and thought he put into this pioneering work,[3] but the name they bear at the foot is "R. W. Smiles". Time, however, brought its revenge. R. W. Smiles is now forgotten, but Edwards's *Memoirs*, and his later volume, *Free Town Libraries*, are quoted by librarians to this day.

The new librarian, a brother of Samuel Smiles of *Self-Help* fame, served only until 1864. During these years he tackled seriously the question of the reference library catalogue—a subject on which Edwards and his committee had been unable to agree—but it was left to his successor, Dr. Andrea Crestadoro, to complete the work, which was published in 1864. It comprised an alphabetical index of authors and a subject index, and was criticized by Edwards for its "unsystematic, confused, and awkward construction."[4] But even an inferior catalogue was better than none. It was in Crestadoro's time, too, that the imminent collapse of the Hall of Science building led to the transfer of the reference library to the Old Town Hall, where it re-opened in 1878. This was a much more central position, and issues at once trebled.[5] The former central lending library later became the nucleus of a new branch (the sixth) opened in Deansgate in 1882.[6]

The year 1878 saw two other significant changes. One, carried after much public debate, was the opening of the reading rooms on Sundays. This was a controversial measure—Greenwood in 1886 could count only five or six libraries which practised Sunday opening—but it was very popular and, by the time Greenwood wrote, the average attendance each Sunday was nearly 5000.[7] To counter Sabbatarian criticism, the work was carried out by Jewish staff under the charge of a superintendent.[8] The other change was the introduction, at the Ancoats Branch, of a special reading room for boys. "The number of boys who assembled in the several reading-rooms in an evening," the Deputy Librarian reported, "caused so much inconvenience to grown-up readers as to suggest the desirability of fitting up rooms specially for them."[9] The Ancoats experiment was an immediate success, and was extended to other branches within the next few years. A description given by the same writer in 1895 is probably equally true of the earlier years, except for the reference to female assistants:

[1] *Op. cit.*, pp. 120–140.   [2] *Op. cit.*, p. 140.
[3] See below, p. 88.   [4] *Free Town Libraries* (1869), p. 96.
[5] W. R. Credland, *The Manchester Public Free Libraries* (Manchester 1899), p. 126.
[6] Manchester Public Free Libraries, *Annual Report, 1881–82*, p. 32.
[7] Greenwood (1886), pp. 54, 93. The arguments for and against Sunday opening are set out by Greenwood in a later edition of his work (1891), and are very similar to those later used in connection with the Sunday opening of cinemas.
[8] Greenwood (1887), p. 247.
[9] W. R. Credland, "Free Public Libraries of Manchester", in Library Association, *Transactions and Proceedings of the Second Annual Meeting . . . 1879* (1880), p. 123.

"The rooms are each provided with about 500 volumes, carefully chosen for
their suitability to the class of boys who are likely to use them, and a selection of
equally suitable periodicals is also supplied. It is quite true to say that during the
winter months they are, throughout the whole evening, crowded with lads busily
engaged in assimilating the literature provided for them. There can hardly be a
more pleasing and suggestive sight than is presented by any one of these rooms, with
its bright lighting, its busy and helpful female attendants, and its crowd of readers
eager for amusement or instruction. And the boys themselves are of that age and
class which it is most desirable to influence for good. They are for the most part
children of parents whose poverty draws them perilously near to the borderland of
crime, but they are still too young to have crossed that border themselves. It is just
such lads as these whom it is essential to detach from vicious companions, and to
surround with every possible influence that can tend to moral and social improvement, if they are to be made into useful men and good citizens, and rescued from
absorption into the pauper and criminal classes."[1]

Crestadoro died in 1879, and was succeeded by C. W. Sutton, who held
office until his death in 1920. Under his regime the library service continued its
steady development, and by 1886 he was able to report that the stock in the
Central Reference Library had reached over 80000 volumes, while the lending
stock (in the six branches) was approaching the 100000 mark.[2]

Liverpool

The second major civic library was that opened at Liverpool on 18 October
1852. It was created not under the terms of the Public Libraries Act but by
virtue of a special local Act of 1852 empowering the Corporation to levy a 1d.
rate for the establishment and maintenance of a public library, museum, and art
gallery.[3] The first step was the opening of a reference library in the former
Union Newsroom, a subscription establishment which had been purchased by
the Corporation for £2500.[4] Gifts of money and books provided an initial
stock of some 10000 volumes, and the library was an immediate success, issues
in the first year totalling 112000 exclusive of periodicals.[5] The first annual report
remarks:

"Works of amusement form about one-half of all the books read. Far from
regretting this result, the committee feel it their duty to render this portion of the
library more attractive still, being of opinion that the love of reading in any form
must tend to counteract the propensity to low and degrading pursuits, and that in
order to inspire a thirst for knowledge, the first step is to cultivate a taste for reading
in some direction. History, general literature, voyages and travels, and poetry, have

[1] Credland, *Free Library Movement in Manchester*, pp. 14–15. Separate provision for boys had
been made at the Central Library in 1862, but this was a temporary measure due to pressure
on accommodation caused by the Cotton Famine. See on the whole subject M. Barnes,
"Children's Libraries in Manchester: a History", in *Manchester Review*, Vol. XI (Winter
1966–67), pp. 80–89.

[2] For statistical details of the libraries dealt with in this chapter for the year 1886 see below,
App. IX.

[3] The special Act was sought because of the need to provide for a natural history collection
presented by the Earl of Derby.

[4] P. Cowell, *Liverpool Public Libraries: a History of Fifty Years* (Liverpool 1903), Ch. ii–iv.

[5] *Op. cit.*, p. 46. E. Edwards, *Free Town Libraries* (1869), pp. 118–119, gives rather higher
figures for both stock and issues.

been next in demand. The number of theological and philosophical works consulted being about 80 per week, or 4071 during the year, is somewhat remarkable, and indicates a higher class of general reading than might at first sight be expected."[1]

It is clear from this passage that the policy of the librarian, J. S. Dalton, and his committee differed radically from the policy pursued by Edwards in Manchester. This difference persisted for many years, and Edwards later condemned what he called an "overlarge provision of literature merely ephemeral." The Liverpool reference library, he pointed out, had ten times as many novel readers as the Manchester reference library, for the simple reason that ten times as many novels were provided.[2]

Liverpool was the first library in the country to develop a branch organization. When a public demand arose for borrowing facilities, these were provided not at the central library, but at two branch lending libraries—the North and South Branches as they were long called, in populous areas not far from the city centre. They were accommodated at first in schools, and subsequently in converted houses. R. W. Roulston, a member of the Lyceum Library staff, was appointed superintendent of these lending libraries, and is credited with having been the first to lend books for the blind—in 1857—and music—in 1859.[3] Both practices were widely adopted by later libraries.

In the Parliamentary Return of 1856, the librarian was able to report that the result of the opening of the library had been "satisfactory beyond all expectation." He went on to remark:

"Since the commencement in 1852, a marked improvement has been noticed in the habits and manners of the people who frequent the library; among other influences, this may perhaps be attributed in a trifling degree to the leading instructions to the assistants in the establishment, 'That all persons, however ragged or poor, shall be treated as gentlemen.' This has, no doubt, given that self-respect which has rendered the lavatories (i.e. washplaces) provided by the committee almost useless, and the silence and order in the reading-room strictly observed without any interference, even when 180 readers have been (frequently) present at one time, which is 30 or 40 beyond their comfortable accommodation. . . .

"The ready access, without any unpleasant restriction, to high-class works of art and science, hitherto (almost) beyond the reach of the artisan, will no doubt have a tendency to improve, and to raise new desires for intellectual enjoyment; this progress is shown in the increasing interest in the reference and lending libraries, and doubtless a new and beautiful tone of thought, of feeling, of refinement, and of happiness will arise from the diffusion of those innocent and elevating pleasures which such institutions are calculated to excite and to produce."[4]

As this report indicates, pressure on accommodation was now becoming acute. Fortunately at this point William Brown (afterwards Sir William Brown), a wealthy Liverpool-Irish merchant, reformer and philanthropist, came forward with an offer to build a new library and museum. The foundation stone was laid in 1857 on a site provided by the Corporation on Shaw's Brow (now William Brown Street) and the building was opened with much ceremony in 1860. The

---

[1] Cowell, *op. cit.*, pp. 46–47. [2] Edwards, *op. cit.*, pp. 122–123.
[3] Cowell, *op. cit.*, p. 52. J. J. Ogle, *The Free Library* (1897), p. 168, mentions the claim that Liverpool was also the first library to organize public lectures, but this is incorrect—see below, pp. 95–97.
[4] *P.R. 1856*, p. 6.

total cost was estimated at £40000 exclusive of the site. In addition to accommodation for the museum, the building included storage space for 100000
books; a large reading room to seat 450 people; a smaller students' room;
several classrooms; and a lecture-room to seat 400.[1] This was the first large-scale
individual benefaction to any English public library, and set an example which
was to be widely followed later in the century.

The handsome range of neo-classical buildings of which the Brown Library
and Museum form a part was completed by the opening in 1877 of the Walker
Art Gallery, erected at the expense of Alderman A. R. Walker (afterwards Sir
Andrew Walker); and in 1879 of the Picton Reading Room, erected by the
Library Committee from an unexpected windfall in rate income.[2] This great
circular reading room was named after J. A. Picton, Chairman of the Library
Committee and one of the earliest pioneers of public library work in the city
(he was knighted shortly after the opening). It was designed as a students' room,
to replace the overcrowded room at the Brown Library, and round its perimeter
had shelving for a further 60000 books. Below, in what had once been a cockpit,
was a lecture-hall with seating for 1200 people. This was the first public building
in Liverpool to be lighted by electricity; and the trial proved so successful that
before long arrangements were made for all the library buildings to be lighted
in this way, to avoid "the serious injury to the bindings of the books by the
fumes of the gas and the foul air poisoning the atmosphere."[3]

The emphasis on lecture-halls at Liverpool is interesting. The original
enabling Act of 1852 permitted the Corporation to provide public lectures on
science, and these were begun in the Brown Library in 1864–65. The scope of
the lectures was widened as time went on, and after some initial difficulties they
became very popular.[4] The classrooms were also used at times for science
classes, but these were not sponsored by the Library Committee.[5]

Throughout all these changes, and two changes of librarian,[6] the basic
structure of the Liverpool public library system remained the same, namely one
central reference library and two branch lending libraries. A notable feature was
that no current newspapers were provided for public reading. This omission
was remedied at the Brown Library in 1883, and in the following year five
evening reading rooms were opened in schools, providing current newspapers
and periodicals only.[7]

It would be fair to say, therefore, that Liverpool, in spite of, or perhaps
because of, its splendid buildings, had so far advanced on a fairly narrow front.
By 1886 its reference library, with 89000 volumes, was a little larger than

---

[1] Cowell, op. cit., pp. 102–104.

[2] Op. cit., pp. 113–114.

[3] Op. cit., p. 129; Greenwood (1886), p. 60; see also below, p. 72. The Picton Reading Room
is still in use, as a reference library. Its circular form, though it inevitably suggests the
Reading Room of the British Museum, was in fact conceived by Picton himself (no mean
architect), and provided an elegant solution to the problem of a rather difficult site.

[4] See below, pp. 96–97.   [5] Cowell, op. cit., p. 107.

[6] The original librarian, J. S. Dalton (formerly a schoolmaster), was followed in 1866 by his
deputy George Hudson, who in turn was succeeded in 1875 by Peter Cowell, the lending
librarian.

[7] Op. cit., pp. 136–139; P.R. 1885, p. 10. The distinction of providing no daily papers was
shared with the Paisley Public Library—Greenwood (1890), p. 243.

Manchester's, and its reference issues substantially larger; but its lending stock, at 46000 volumes, was less than half Manchester's, and its lending issues were not much more than half.[1]

Birmingham

Birmingham came rather later into the library field than either Manchester or Liverpool. A movement for the adoption of the Libraries Act in 1852 was defeated, and the first library was not opened until 1861, by which time Birmingham, though smaller than Liverpool and Manchester, was a city of nearly 300000 people. No great public benefactor came forward, as at Liverpool, nor was there at the outset, as at Manchester, any large public subscription. None the less, thanks to generous municipal expenditure, the movement got off to a good start.

Profiting by the experience of earlier libraries, the city was able to plan from the beginning for a comprehensive service including a central library (with museum and art gallery) and four district lending libraries with newsrooms attached. It is typical of the scale of library operations at this period that the estimate for the establishment of a lending library and its maintenance for the first year was £813.[2] The first building to be opened, in 1861, was in fact a lending library, in rented premises on Constitution Hill. A second branch was opened at Adderley Park in 1864. In the meantime work had begun on a special building for the central library. The central lending library was opened in 1865, the central reference library and a third branch library (at Deritend) in 1866, the Art Gallery in 1867, and the fourth branch library (at Gosta Green) in 1868.[3] Thus within seven years the entire scheme had been completed, at a total cost, for land and buildings, of £29000.[4] All this was borne either by the rates or from loans, and loan charges were consequently high—£1250 in 1868 out of a rate income of £4250.[5]

Nevertheless the libraries grew rapidly. The original lending library at Constitution Hill had begun with rather less than 4000 volumes.[6] By the close of 1868 the total stock exceeded 51000 volumes, of which 22000 were in the central reference library, and 12000 in the central lending library.[7] This very solid achievement is much to the credit of the Library Committee and the first chief librarian, J. D. Mullins, who was appointed in 1865 and held office until his retirement in 1898. Mullins came to the public library after seven years' service as librarian of the Birmingham (Subscription) Library, and proved himself a first-class administrator, a judicious book-buyer, and an erudite and skilful cataloguer. His catalogue of the Shakespeare Memorial Library,[8] published in 1876, was a remarkable achievement for one heavily engaged in the day-to-day routine of a large library.

With money scarce, the lending libraries seem to have been somewhat neglected in the 'seventies. It was the reference library, clearly, that was Mullins's special pride and joy. We cannot doubt that he had a hand in formulating the

---

[1] See below, App. IX.
[2] *Notes on the History of the Birmingham Public Libraries, 1861–1961* (Birmingham 1962), p. 3.
[3] *P.R. 1870*, p. 4. [4] E. Edwards, *Free Town Libraries* (1869), p. 156.
[5] *P.R. 1870*, p. 4. [6] Edwards, *op. cit.*, p. 139.
[7] *P.R. 1870*, p. 4. [8] See below, p. 48.

three principles laid down by the Library Committee to govern the selection of books for this library. These were:

> (1) That the library should, as far as practicable, represent every phase of human thought, and every variety of opinion.
> (2) That books of permanent value and of standard interest should form the principal portion of this library.
> (3) That it should contain those rare and costly works which are generally out of the reach of individual students and collectors and which are not usually found in provincial or private libraries.[1]

These principles evidently owed much to George Dawson, who gave the inaugural address at the opening of the library.[2] The third principle also seems to carry an echo of Panizzi's well-known statement regarding the British Museum Library in 1836.[3]

In the liberal provision made for expensive books, Birmingham's policy was similar to that of Liverpool, but Birmingham differed sharply from Liverpool in that it made in the reference library only "a very slender provision of ordinary novels and tales." The proper place for these, it was felt, was in the lending libraries.[4] It was unlike Liverpool, also, in its generous allotment for newspapers and periodicals: in the Parliamentary Return for 1876 periodicals account for 53 per cent of the reference issues.[5] Birmingham was, incidentally, one of the earliest reference libraries to open its doors on Sundays. The decision was taken in 1872, in spite of a good deal of opposition, and in spite of a deputation to the Council from the Lord's Day Defence Association.[6] By the early 'nineties the work was being carried out, as at Manchester, mainly by Jewish assistants.[7] Whether this was so from the beginning is not clear, but the arrangement continued until at least 1913.[8]

A notable feature of this library was the Shakespeare Memorial Library, the nucleus of which, comprising 1100 volumes, was presented by the local Shakespeare Club to mark the tercentenary of the poet's birth in 1864. By 1876, when the catalogue was printed, it had already grown to 6000 volumes.[9] There were also important collections on Cervantes (presented in 1873) and on the history and antiquities of Warwickshire (the Staunton Collection, purchased largely by public subscription in 1875).[10]

A tragic blow fell in January, 1879, during extensions to the central library building. A workman's blow-lamp set fire to some shavings, which in turn

---

[1] *Notes on the History of the Birmingham Public Libraries*, pp. 4–5. The same principles were afterwards adopted for the Mitchell Library at Glasgow.

[2] *Op. cit.*, p. 4. Dawson (1821–76) was the pastor of a Nonconformist congregation in Birmingham, and one of the best known and most gifted lecturers of his day. He had given evidence before the Select Committee in 1849. See the life by S. Timmins in *D.N.B.*

[3] T. Kelly, *Early Public Libraries* (1966), p. 162.

[4] Edwards, *op. cit.*, p. 142.

[5] *P.R. 1876*, p. 7.

[6] A. C. Shaw, "The Birmingham Free Libraries", in *L.A.R.*, Vol. IV (1902), pp. 499–500; A. C. Shaw, "Sunday Opening of Free Libraries", in *L.A.R.*, Vol. VIII (1906), pp. 79–88.

[7] Greenwood (1891), p. 469.

[8] Information from Mr. W. A. Taylor, City Librarian.

[9] *Notes on the History of the Birmingham Public Libraries*, pp. 7–8.

[10] *Op. cit.*, p. 5; J. J. Ogle, *The Free Library* (1897), p. 177.

ignited a wooden screen, and before long the whole building was ablaze. The lending library was saved, but of the reference library of nearly 50000 volumes only about 1000 volumes were rescued, the losses including almost the whole of the special collections. The *Birmingham Post* told how strong men wept as they watched their splendid library being reduced to smouldering ashes:

> "There was nothing of which Birmingham men of all classes and occupations were prouder than of their great library. Its extent, its richness, the completeness of its appointments, the stateliness of its home, the freedom of access to it, the sense that it was their own work—all contributed to make it a household word. The whole town suffers under a sense of severe, personal sorrow. . . ."[1]

Undaunted, the Library Committee at once set to work on plans for a new and larger central library, which was opened in 1882. The total cost was nearly £55000, of which over £15000 was raised by public subscription; and the resulting building was described by Greenwood, four years later, as *"par excellence* the finest building of its kind in the United Kingdom."[2] The consequent heavy burden of loan charges was provided for by a special local Act of 1883, which removed the 1d. rate limit for the library service. No new limit was fixed, but the rate did not in fact exceed 1½d. before the end of the century.[3]

By 1886, in spite of the disaster of the fire, Birmingham's total stock of 145000 volumes (88000 in the reference library, 57000 in the lending libraries) already exceeded that of Liverpool.

Leeds

The last of the big four civic libraries, Leeds, began its career only in 1870. As at Birmingham, an earlier move to secure adoption (in 1861) had been a failure,[4] but by 1868 the climate was more propitious, and at a public meeting the necessary resolution was passed by a rather narrow majority. James Yates, of the Bolton Public Library, was appointed librarian[5], and as a first step lending libraries and newsrooms were opened in rented accommodation in two suburban mechanics' institutes, Hunslet and New Wortley. In each case the library of the institute was acquired as nucleus for the public library. This emphasis on the suburbs was to be characteristic of the Leeds library service throughout the nineteenth century, and reflected the fact that Leeds was in 1871 a rather sprawling city of some 260000 people, incorporating many former villages and townships. There was also doubt at the outset whether the rateable income of £3000 per annum would support a large central library.[6]

This problem was eventually solved by renting the Old Infirmary, where a reference library of 14000 volumes was opened in 1871, and a lending library of 8000 volumes in the following year. Like many adapted buildings, it was very

---

[1] *Birmingham Post*, 13 Jan. 1879, quoted in *Notes on the History of the Birmingham Public Libraries*, p. 5.

[2] Greenwood (1886), p. 63.

[3] A. C. Shaw, *"The Birmingham Free Libraries"*, in *L.A.R.*, Vol. IV (1902), pp. 498–499.

[4] See above, p. 30.

[5] On Yates see R. D. Macleod, "Who was James Yates?" in *Library Review*, Vol. XVII (1959–60), pp. 250–257.

[6] T. W. Hand, *Leeds Public Libraries, 1870–1920* (Leeds 1920), pp. 4–6.

inconvenient: it was also badly lighted and ventilated.[1] The method of issue in
the lending library was by means of an "indicator"—a novel device at this time
but one which became standard practice later in the century.[2] In 1884 the central
library was transferred to a wing of the new Municipal Offices building. This
was larger, handsomer and better ventilated, but administratively it was as
inconvenient as ever, the lending and reference libraries being at the top of the
building, and the newsroom, reached by a separate entrance, on the first floor.[3]

The stock of the Central Reference Library grew steadily as the years went
by, though in 1886, with 37000 volumes, it was still less than half the size of
those at Manchester, Liverpool and Birmingham. It was the rapid growth of the
lending libraries which was the striking feature of the Leeds library, and enabled
it to compare in total stock with Liverpool and Birmingham. In 1885 these
libraries comprised 110000 volumes, of which one-third were in the Central
Lending Library and the remainder divided among no fewer than 25 branch
libraries. Yet the total cost of these operations—under £5000 per annum
according to the Parliamentary Return of 1885[4]—was substantially less than that
of any of the other three library systems mentioned.

The secret was that many of the branches were being provided on the
cheap, in the city's Board Schools. They were open for three hours on one, two,
three, or four evenings a week, and were staffed by the Board School teachers
at 1s.8d. an evening, plus 1s. for a porter and 1s. for a boy assistant if required.
This at any rate was the system as described by Greenwood in 1891, and there
seems no reason to suppose it was different in earlier years.[5] The average stock
per branch was not much more than 3000 volumes, and issues, less than five
times stock, were low compared with those from the central lending library,
which were eleven times stock. Greenwood thought other public libraries might
well make more use than they did of school premises, but that Leeds had "too
much of a good thing." "The aim of having a library within only a very few
minutes' walk from the door of every householder in Leeds", he commented,
"is not an unmixed good. It prevents that consolidation of work in large given
centres to the same extent as has been achieved in other towns, with their
specially constructed branch buildings."[6]

The system was, however, popular with Council members, and it lasted
until the retirement of James Yates in 1897, by which time a complete reorganization had become necessary. An interesting outcome of the system was
the creation of special collections of books for the use of the schoolchildren.
In this Leeds seems to have been a pioneer. A beginning was made in 1883, when
small libraries were provided for each of two schools, "the books to remain the
property of the Corporation, any damage thereto being made good by the
School Board, who would be responsible for the books under their charge."
These libraries were managed by the school staff, and were open one hour a
week for the issue of books to the scholars and to other children in the neigh-

---

[1] Greenwood (1891), p. 115.
[2] See below, pp. 90–91.
[3] Greenwood (1891), pp. 114–115; Hand, *op. cit.*, pp. 12–13.
[4] *P.R. 1885*, p. 21.
[5] Greenwood (1891), pp. 451–452. Greenwood is, however, in error in speaking of 33
branches.
[6] Greenwood (1891), p. 116.

Ia. THE OPENING OF THE BIRMINGHAM CENTRAL LIBRARY

Designed by William Martin and opened in 1865, this building was destroyed by fire in 1879. Note the height of the shelving.

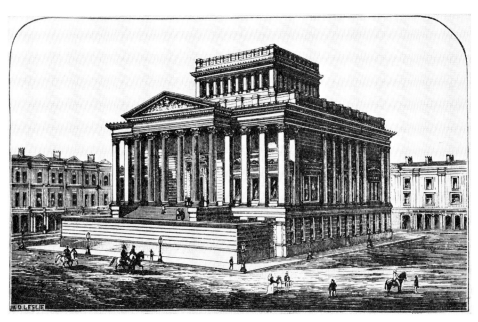

Ib. THE HARRIS LIBRARY, MUSEUM AND ART GALLERY AT PRESTON

A particularly fine example of the monumental style in late nineteenth-century civic architecture. Following a bequest by E. R. Harris the building was designed by James Hibbert and opened in 1892. It is still in use.

IIa. THE WILLIAM BROWN AND PICTON LIBRARIES, LIVERPOOL

This picture, from a water-colour by H. Magenis, 1884, shows the splendid range of classical buildings erected in Liverpool. The circular Picton Reading Room (by Cornelius Sherlock, 1879) is seen in the centre, with the William Brown Library and Museum (by Thomas Allom and John Weightman, 1860) on the left, and the Walker Art Gallery (by Sherlock and Vale, 1877) on the right. A corner of the St. George's Hall is glimpsed in the right foreground.

IIb. THE PASSMORE EDWARDS LIBRARY, HAMMERSMITH

This building, designed by Maurice B. Adams and opened in 1896, is a good example of the Romanesque style in late Victorian library architecture.

bourhood. A third school library was opened in 1885, and eventually there were 37 of them; but the cost of upkeep proved too great and after Yates's retirement the entire responsibility was transferred to the School Board.[1]

Salford

The Salford Public Library, which made an early start in 1850 under the Museums Act, was by 1886 larger than any except the "big four", but never attained the size or importance of its wealthier neighbour in Manchester. The creation of the library was due, as we have seen, to the enthusiasm of Joseph Brotherton, who was warmly supported by E. R. Langworthy, Mayor of Salford in 1849. Fortunately a building was ready to hand in the old hall in Peel Park, which had been acquired for public use, along with the estate, in 1846, and here a reading room and reference library of about 5000 volumes were opened in 1850. After extensions to the building (which also had to accommodate a museum), a lending library was opened, with 2500 books, in 1854. Langworthy contributed over £5000 to the costs of the institution in the opening years, and a further £2200 was raised by public subscription.[2] In 1878 a bequest of £10000 from Langworthy made possible the erection of a new wing and a considerable enlargement of the library accommodation, which now included a reading-room and newsroom for 150 readers.

In the meantime a beginning was made on branch organization. Branch lending libraries and reading-rooms were opened at Greengate in 1870 and Regent Road in 1873, in both cases in specially erected buildings; and in 1877 a third branch was opened in the former Pendleton Mechanics' Institute.[3] These branches seem to have been exceedingly popular from the beginning, issues greatly exceeding those at the central lending library. In 1875 the issues at the Regent Road branch represented almost 25 times the stock.[4]

The Parliamentary Return for 1856 gave a most enthusiastic account of the early success of the library, and added:

> "Another gratifying proof of the beneficial results will be found in the fact that the attention of the readers is being gradually and progressively drawn from light literature to historical and biographical works, general literature, and books of a more practical tendency."[5]

Figures are appended to show that in a sample of 3000 consecutive issues in each year since the library was opened, fiction accounted for nearly two-thirds of the issues in the first year (1850), but less than one-quarter in the latest year (1855). Alas for human hopes! In the Return for 1876 it appeared that fiction accounted for 45 per cent of the total lending library stock and 83 per cent of the issues (in the reference library fiction issues were only 5.4 per cent of the total, but this was because there was hardly any fiction in stock).[6] The most likely

---

[1] Hand, *op. cit.*, pp. 17–18.

[2] B. H. Mullen, *The Royal Museum and Libraries, Salford: their Inception and Development* (Salford 1899), pp. 22–29. The title "Royal" was adopted in 1849 when the Queen and Prince Albert agreed to become patrons.

[3] *Op. cit.*, pp. 29–38. [4] *P.R. 1876*, p. 62.

[5] *P.R. 1856*, p. 11. [6] *P.R. 1876*, pp. 62–63.

explanation of the figures given in 1856 is that the readers were turning to non-fiction because they had exhausted the available fiction.

Though not one of the outstanding libraries in the country, Salford by the end of the period with which we are concerned was well equipped with books and buildings, and was obviously doing solid and successful work. By 1886 the total stock was 81 000 volumes, of which 40 000 were available for lending, mainly in the branches.

Sheffield

Of Sheffield, the first public library in Yorkshire, something has already been said:[1] it was distinguished, at this period, chiefly by the niggardly spirit displayed by the Council, which for many years refused to levy the full 1d. rate. The central reference and lending libraries, begun in rented accommodation in the Mechanics' Hall in 1856, were overcrowded from the beginning, and remained so until nearly the end of the century. The opening of branch lending libraries—one for each of the four wards of the city—between 1869 and 1886, did indeed bring some relief, and went some way towards meeting the public need, but even this was achieved only with difficulty. In 1875–77, because the Council insisted on the rapid repayment of loans for branch buildings, the total amount available for the purchase of books for the central library and three branches was £36.3s.7d.[2] The central reference library was shamefully neglected, and in 1886 still comprised only 11 000 volumes. The central lending library, at this time, had 30 000 volumes, and there were 40 000 more in the branches.

Bolton, Nottingham, Bristol and Newcastle upon Tyne

These were the only four towns, other than the six already mentioned, which possessed in 1886 libraries exceeding 50 000 volumes.

In Bolton, though reference and lending libraries and a newsroom were opened in rented premises as early as 1853, the hard-headed business men who dominated the Council showed themselves in the opening years as unwilling as their opposite numbers in Sheffield to make any considerable sacrifice for the maintenance of the new institution. As late as 1869 the library rate was still only ½d. (£400 per annum), and growth was in consequence very slow. The initial stock, derived mainly from gifts and subscriptions, comprised some 12 000 volumes, of which one-quarter were in the lending library.[3] By 1868 the reference library stock had risen to 16 000, the lending library stock was approaching 9000,[4] but there had not been a corresponding increase in use. The subscription section of the lending library, started in 1853 with the idea of supplementing the supply of books,[5] had indeed steadily increased its issues, but the use of the free lending and reference libraries had fluctuated inversely with the state of trade. The Cotton Famine of the early 'sixties brought a boom in demand, followed by a slump as employment recovered to a normal level.[6] In

---

[1] See above, p. 36.
[2] *The City Libraries of Sheffield, 1856–1956* (Sheffield 1956), p. 20.
[3] *Centenary of the Bolton Public Libraries, 1853–1953* (Bolton 1953), p. 7.
[4] *P.R. 1870*, p. 5.   [5] See above, p. 38.
[6] *Centenary of the Bolton Public Libraries*, p. 11.

1867–68 the free lending library issues (41 000) were only two-thirds those of the opening year, and the reference library issues (39 000) only 50 per cent higher.[1] Edwards attributed this unsatisfactory result to the operation of the subscription library, and certainly the existence of this library must have tempted the librarian to postpone the purchase of new books in the hope that they would be provided by the subscribers.

In 1869 the former Mechanics' Institute was leased for the use of the lending library, and from this time there seems to have been some improvement. By 1874 a 1d. rate was being levied, and both issues and stocks had substantially increased.[2] In 1879 the first branch lending library was opened, in the former Little Bolton Town Hall.[3] By 1886 the reference library had grown to 29 000 volumes, with an annual issue of 89 000, and the lending stock to 28 000 volumes (nearly half of them at Little Bolton) with an annual issue of 87 000. The library was at last getting on to its feet.

At Nottingham a smoothly organized campaign led to the adoption of the Libraries Acts in 1867 with only a single dissentient. The library opened in the following year. It started off with the substantial stock of over 12 000 volumes— some of them purchased from the dissolving Artizans' Library—and within twenty years was, for a town of this size, one of the most successful libraries in the country. Its rapid development must have owed much to the professional care of John Potter Briscoe, formerly principal sub-librarian at Bolton, who was appointed as librarian in 1869 and served for 47 years; but it also reflected the rapid growth in the area, population and wealth of the town. In 1871 the population was 86 000, the income from a 1d. rate £1000 per annum: by 1885 the population was about 200 000, the 1d. rate income over £3000.

Within five years the bookstock had been doubled, and a reference library formed alongside the original lending library. The main difficulty lay in the exceedingly cramped accommodation in the old Artizans' Library building, which had been taken over for public library purposes in spite of the advice of the library committee.[4] This problem, however, was triumphantly overcome in 1881, when Prince Leopold opened a splendid new Gothic building to serve as a combined central library, natural history museum, and university college. Here the library had, as it seemed at the time, ample space—a large lending library and newsroom on the ground floor, a reference library and reading room on the first floor. The lending library at this time comprised 16 300 volumes, the reference library 8700 volumes, and the librarian had to set about a rapid build-up of stock to meet the greatly increased demand. By 1886 the total had reached 43 000 volumes, 24 000 of them in the lending library, and this central service was supported by eight branch reading rooms or lending libraries, and a separate children's lending library—said to be the first in the country—opened in 1882. The branch lending stock amounted to 14 000 volumes. With reference issues totalling 77 000, and lending issues approaching the 300 000 mark, the library was clearly in a flourishing condition.[5]

From the industrial north and midlands we turn to that ancient centre of commerce, Bristol, where the concept of a municipally controlled library had

[1] E. Edwards, *Free Town Libraries* (1869), p. 167.   [2] *P.R. 1876*, pp. 11–12.
[3] *Centenary of the Bolton Public Libraries*, p. 11.   [4] See below, p. 67.
[5] *Fifty Years: a Brief History of the Public Library Movement in Nottingham* (Nottingham 1918), pp. 3–29; *P.R. 1870*, p. 20; *P.R. 1876*, pp. 58–59; *P.R. 1885*, pp. 14–15.

been familiar for two and a half centuries. The old city library founded in
1615—some 1500 volumes of seventeenth and eighteenth century history and
theology—still existed in the pleasant building in King Street that had been
erected for it in 1740, but at the time of the passing of the first Public Libraries
Act books and building alike were in the care of a private subscription library
known as the Library Society, to which they had been handed over in 1773.[1]

Following the Act of 1850, Mr. Charles Tovey, a local councillor and wine
merchant, at once began a campaign to recover the old library as a nucleus for
a new public library service.[2] The first step was taken in 1855, when the Corporation resumed possession of the building and library, and began an annual
grant for book purchase. A city librarian was appointed, and from 1856 the
library, such as it was, was opened to the public. The legality of this arrangement
was apparently never questioned, and it was not until 1874 that the Libraries
Acts were formally adopted. A factor in bringing about the adoption was the
publication in 1871 of a pamphlet entitled *The Cry of the Poor*. This was a letter
from sixteen working men of Bristol to the sixteen city aldermen, and was a
plea for various amenities, including smoke abatement, parks, baths and
washhouses, and a free library:

> "We should be glad to be able to sit in our own room and read a bit out of an
> interesting book to our wives and families, or to get one of the children to read to us.
> Such a book would keep our boys from idling at street corners, where they learn no
> end of wickedness and mischief, and would, maybe, prevent many of them from
> going to the public-house, the dancing rooms, and to the bad."[3]

In 1876 a branch lending library was opened at St. Philip's, and the old city
library building became a rather inadequate central library, with reference and
lending departments and a newsroom.[4] From this point development was very
rapid. Two further branches were opened in 1877, and a fourth in 1885,[5] and
by the latter date the total stock already exceeded 60000 volumes, two-thirds
of them in the five lending libraries.[6] The main need at this point was for a
new central library, but this was not to come for another twenty years.

The first move towards a public library at Newcastle upon Tyne was taken
in 1854, but it was not until 1872 that the Acts were adopted (and only then
after two public meetings on the subject), and it was not until 1880 that a
temporary lending library was actually opened, in a room of the former
Mechanics' Institute.[7] The Institute was taken over by the Council, and incorporated in a new central library building which was opened in 1882. Two

---

[1] T. Kelly, *Early Public Libraries* (1966), pp. 75, 132–133.

[2] His pamphlet, *A Free Library for Bristol*, was published in 1855, along with *A History of the
City Library*, originally published two years earlier.

[3] Quoted Greenwood (1891), p. 221.

[4] S. M. Booth, *Three Hundred and Fifty Years of Public Libraries in Bristol* (Bristol 1963), p. 12.
For the inadequacies of the building see Greenwood (1886), p. 21.

[5] J. J. Ogle, *The Free Library* (1897), p. 199.

[6] These figures are from Greenwood (1886), p. 389. Mr. W. S. Haugh, City Librarian,
informs me that no figure is available for reference stock in 1886, but central lending stock
in that year comprised 27 600 volumes, and branch lending stock 38 500 volumes.

[7] Greenwood (1886), pp. 83–90, gives a full account of the early difficulties at Newcastle,
though oddly enough he omits to state until nearly the end of the narrative to which
town he is referring.

thousand volumes from the Institute library were also taken over. By this time the techniques of library organization were much better understood, and the first librarian, W. J. Haggerston, already had experience of the founding of a new library at South Shields (opened in 1873). As at Bristol, therefore, progress was rapid, and by 1885 the library could already boast a stock of 56000 volumes, almost equally divided between the reference and lending departments; no branches had yet been formed, but three evening newsrooms were opened in 1884.[1]

An interesting feature of this library was that whereas the lending department was operated by means of an indicator and a printed catalogue (now becoming standard practice), the reference library had a manuscript catalogue on cards.[2] The stock was selected with care and judgment, and the Parliamentary Return of 1885 was able to report:

> "The reference library is already exceedingly rich in the principal collections in history, science, and natural history, the mathematics, fine arts, and topography, the transactions of learned societies, collected works of authors, and complete sets of the chief serial publications."[3]

In 1885 the public library acquired a collection of over 4000 volumes which Dr. Robert Thomlinson, a local clergyman, had added in 1735–45 to the ancient parish library at St. Nicholas's Church. This had been formed in 1697, and had subsequently passed under the control of the Corporation.[4]

Some Smaller English Libraries

In the previous chapter we have already had glimpses of a number of the smaller libraries of this period. They are so numerous, and most of them are at present so ill-documented, that we cannot here do more than present brief accounts of a few which present features of special interest. It will be convenient to take them in order of opening.

Of the three libraries founded under the Museums Act only Salford, already described, became important at this period. At Canterbury (1847), the library remained an insignificant adjunct of the museum. Until at least 1853 loans were severely restricted, and there was a charge of 1d. per volume.[5] The issues that year (from 2430 volumes) were 171.[6] By 1870 the total stock was still only "about 2600 (some very old)": the books were little used for reference, and loans were about 14 a week.[7] There was no distinction between reference and lending stock. In 1884, 130 volumes were counted as constituting the reference library, and with 4200 volumes available for loan, issues had risen to nearly 100 a week.[8]

At Warrington (1848), as we have seen, the lending library was on a subscription basis,[9] and the total of 18700 loans in 1886, though it meant an

[1] *P.R. 1885*, p. 14.

[2] *A Short History of the Newcastle upon Tyne Public Libraries, 1854–1950* (Newcastle upon Tyne 1950).

[3] *P.R. 1885*, p. 15.

[4] T. Kelly, *Early Public Libraries* (1966), pp. 73–74, 96–97, 251. About 300 of the older books still remain at St. Nicholas's.

[5] See above, p. 10.   [6] *P.R. 1853*, p. 3.   [7] *P.R. 1870*, p. 7.   [8] *P.R. 1885*, pp. 6–7.

[9] See above, p. 37.

average of 32 borrowings for each of the 589 subscribers, represented a very poor turnover on a lending stock of some 11 000 volumes.[1] Nor can we say that the reference issues—21 000 against a stock of about 7500 volumes—offer any compensation, especially as the lending stock was also available for reference use by non-subscribers. Such a restricted service was obviously unsatisfactory, and the only agreeable feature which can be recorded of the library at this period is that it had the beginnings of a good collection of local history.

The Winchester library (1851) was, like that at Canterbury, subordinate to the museum, and the stock was even smaller: it was for this reason that Manchester was so long looked upon as the first library to be opened under the 1850 Act. The transfer of the Hampshire Museum to the city was regarded as an occasion for celebration: "the old Winchester bushel was filled with strong beer with part of which the parties assembled regaled, and the remainder distributed among the neighbouring poor."[2] When, however, the museum and library were re-opened in November, 1851, in the converted Governor's House of the old gaol in Jewry Street, the *Hampshire Chronicle* reported that the visitors

> "expressed themselves highly gratified with every arrangement, except that of the Library, which, stowed away in that high and remote part of the building, which our present Chief Magistrate once jocosely proposed should be a fever ward, appears for all the purposes of study to have been *studiously* made inaccessible."[3]

There was, in fact, only a handful of books available. The total stock numbered about 300 volumes in 1853,[4] and only ten times that number in 1886 (reference, 1300 volumes, lending, 1700 volumes).[5] Lending facilities were introduced in 1854, but issues were few—between eight and nine a week in 1855. At this time the library was open three days weekly from 10 a.m. to dusk, and the total cost of museum and library combined was less than £100 per annum.[6] In the 'seventies arrangements were made for the transfer of the library and museum to the new Guildhall, but though the museum was moved in 1873, the library had to languish for three years in inadequate quarters in the old Guildhall, and the lending service had to be suspended.[7] Even the accommodation in the new Guildhall, occupied in 1876, was by no means satisfactory. It is true that artificial light had now been provided, but it was reported that there was only one burner in the room, and that "as far from the reading table as it can be."[8] It was only in the 'eighties, with the raising of the rate from ½d. to 1d. in 1882, and the appointment of a new librarian in 1884, that a little progress began to be made.[9]

---

[1] Ten years earlier the number of loans per subscriber had been 53—*P.R. 1887*, p. 16.

[2] *A Hundred Years of Library Service, 1851–1951* (Winchester 1951), p. 3. The Winchester bushel was a measure of 64 pints said to date back to King Edgar in the 10th century. It was standardized as a national measure by Henry VII, and a bushel of this date was in the Museum.

[3] *Op. cit.*, p. 4.   [4] *P.R. 1853*, p. 8.

[5] This is Greenwood's figure. The present City Librarian, Mr. R. Helliwell, has no record of the reference stock in 1886, but estimates lending stock at 1600–1700.

[6] *P.R. 1856*, pp. 14–15.

[7] *P.R. 1877*, p. 19; and information from City Librarian.

[8] *A Hundred Years of Library Service*, p. 5.

[9] *Ibid.* Lending issues jumped from 9000 in 1885 to 27000 in 1886.

The two English university towns were quick off the mark. At Oxford a reference library and reading room were opened in the Old Town Hall in 1854, and a lending library was added in 1857. The first librarian was B. H. Blackwell, father of the founder of the famous bookselling firm of that name, but he died six months after appointment.[1] An excellent account of the operation of the library in its opening years is given by the Chairman of the Library Committee, C. J. Sadler, in the Parliamentary Return for 1856:

"The opening of this library has proved of the greatest benefit to the population of this city; during the two years since its establishment about 235000 persons have visited it. The greatest order, silence, and decorum has prevailed. Upwards of 4000 volumes have been given to the library. No complaints have been made. From the time of its being opened, public lectures and concerts in connection with the library have been given during the autumn and winter season, which have been attended by more than 500 persons, on an average; the cost of each lecture being less than threepence to those who take transferable tickets. We have also, in conjunction with the library, established a Working Man's Association; and lectures in the various departments of science, literature, and art, have been given by Graduates of the University and by many intelligent citizens to large classes in the various rooms attached to the City Buildings.

"We shall soon require a large room for our public library, or additional ones. Ten daily London papers are taken, and most of the reviews, magazines, and periodicals, and many local and county newspapers. These, and all the books, have hitherto been provided by voluntary contributions, but now that we have adopted a penny rate in lieu of an halfpenny one, we hope to defray the expenses without calling on the public for subscriptions. During the 40 years of my public life, I have pleasure in declaring that the establishment of the Free Public Library has, in my judgment, proved of more real benefit and rendered more solid advantages to the middle and working classes of this city than any other measure which has been adopted. Here the working man finds rest after a day of labour, and I affirm that a very large number of young men find an evening's amusement and instruction, which they were wont to spend on other and in a far less creditable manner [*sic*]. The library is open on Sunday evenings only, from 6 to 10 P.M. I believe no injury whatever has arisen therefrom. The newspapers are not allowed to be read on Sundays."[2]

To this statement, dated May, 1856, we can add that the library stock at this time was about 4000 volumes, apparently all given; and that on weekdays the library was open from 9 a.m. to 10 p.m. in winter, and from 9 a.m. to 11 p.m. in summer. Even at this period, when long hours were the custom, these hours were exceptional. The Chairman's reference to the adoption of a 1d. rate refers to the Act of 1855: as late as 1868 the rate actually levied at Oxford was still only $\frac{1}{2}$d.[3]

In the meantime, in 1865, the control of the library was transferred from Oxford Corporation to the Local Government Board, which seems to have neglected its responsibilities shamefully: hence that "lamentable state of neglect and decay" which has been commented on above.[4] This was in 1884, when it appears from such records as are available that the total stock was of the order of 10000 volumes or more, about one-third of them in the lending department.[5]

[1] *Oxford City Libraries, 1854–1954* (Oxford [1954]), pp. 4–6. [2] *P.R. 1856*, p. 9.
[3] E. Edwards, *Free Town Libraries* (1869), pp. 173–174. [4] See above, p. 39.
[5] *P.R. 1885*, p. 14, gives reference stock as "about 7000" and lending stock as "about 3100". Cf. above, p. 32, note 3.

Reference issues, estimated at 2500, compared with nearly 10000 in 1860, and lending issues, estimated at 12500, compared with nearly 20000 in 1860.[1] The library was, as the librarian reported in 1890, considerably "run down".[2]

The Cambridge story is a little more creditable. The library was begun in 1855 in the Friends' Meeting House in Jesus Lane (rented at £20 a year), and a lending department was opened in 1850, the gift of 1200 volumes from the Mechanics' Institute, then in process of dissolution, providing a welcome accession of stock. A permanent building, still in use to-day, was erected in 1861–62, and enlarged by an additional wing in 1883. In 1871, 600 volumes were set apart to form a Children's Library (a very early example of this kind of provision) and a small branch lending library and reading room was opened at Barnwell in 1875. The librarian throughout this period was John Pink, a former bookseller's assistant who was appointed at the age of 22 and served until his death in 1906—a period of 51 years.[3]

Shortage of money was always a difficulty. In the 'sixties the total income available was about £300 per annum, or about two-thirds of the penny rate,[4] and the library committee was driven to petty economies on heating and lighting, such as stopping up some of the jets in the gas-burners.[5] From 1874–75 a 1d. rate was levied, but the heavy expense involved in the extension of the library in 1883 made even the enlarged income inadequate and reduced the book-fund to £50 in 1885.[6] The Cambridge library was, however, fortunate in receiving a steady stream of gifts, and in spite of the exiguous funds available stocks slowly but steadily increased. The total for 1886 was over 31000 volumes —8700 in the reference library, 18500 in the central lending library, and 4200 at Barnwell. Lending issues totalled 82000. These figures compare very favourably with the corresponding figures at Oxford; indeed it would seem that Cambridge, with a population of about 35000, had at this time almost the highest ratio of books to population in the country.[7]

A particularly interesting feature at Cambridge is that from a very early period readers had free access to a small library of reference volumes—550 in 1870, about 800 in 1876—which was kept in the reading room. This is the first substantial example of what later became known as "open access."[8]

Birkenhead, in 1856, was the first unincorporated town in the country to adopt the Acts, and shows what could be done by a small but determined authority. With a population of about 25000, and a 1d. rate yielding £325 per annum, the improvement Commissioners went boldly ahead, borrowed £1000, and before the end of the year had made a start with a lending library of some 3000 volumes and a few volumes for reference. The library was at once so

---

[1] *P.R. 1885*, p. 15; *Oxford City Libraries, 1854–1954*, p. 25. There are no figures available for 1886.

[2] *Oxford City Libraries, 1854–1954*, p. 11.

[3] W. A. Munford, *The Cambridge City Libraries, 1855–1955* (Cambridge 1955), pp. 4, 10; J. Pink, "After Fifty Years: a Retrospect", in *L.A.R.*, Vol. VII (1905), provides a brief historical sketch.

[4] Not one-third of a penny as stated by E. Edwards, *Free Town Libraries* (1869), p. 174. Edwards was working on a mistaken figure for the 1d. rate. See *P.R. 1870*, p. 7.

[5] Munford, *op. cit.*, p. 5. Cf. above, p. 39.   [6] *Op. cit.*, pp. 7–9.

[7] Its record is matched only by Thurso, with a population of 3800 and a bookstock of 3500 volumes (Greenwood's figures).   [8] *P.R. 1870*, p. 7; *P.R. 1876*, p. 23.

overcrowded that within a few months a move had to be made to more spacious premises, and in 1864 a substantial new building was opened in a central position in the town. Here it became possible to develop the reference library service more fully, and a special juvenile section was also established. The incorporation of the borough in 1877, and the expansion of its boundaries, brought an enlarged income (nearly £1500) and new responsibilities. In 1886, with a total stock of 37000 volumes (29000 of them in the lending library), for a population of about 87000, Birkenhead was making more effective provision than many larger towns. Lending issues, at 4.7 times stock, were reasonably good, and reference issues, at 11.6 times stock, were particularly high.[1]

Another and considerably smaller unincorporated town, Leamington Spa (population in 1851, 16000), anticipated later legislation by opening a lending library in 1857 under the auspices of the Board of Health.[2] Here the enterprise was on a less ambitious scale: a ½d. rate only operated until at least 1876; there was no reference library until 1873; and total stocks in 1886 were under 12000 volumes—3300 in the reference library and 8300 in the lending library. The Parliamentary Return for 1876 notes: "The playing of chess and draughts has recently been introduced; the Room containing the Reference Library being used for the purpose."[3]

The progress of the public library at Norwich, which also opened in 1857, was very disappointing in view of the eagerness shown to adopt the Act in 1850. The difficulties there, arising partly from heavy building costs and partly from the parsimony of the Council, have already been referred to:[4] it was not until 1881 that the practice of levying a full 1d. rate was firmly established, and not until 1886 that the capital debt was at last paid off. George Easter, a woodcarver who was appointed librarian in 1877, did, however, succeed in making substantial improvements: by 1886 he had more than trebled the lending library stock (from 3500 volumes to 11200), doubled the number of borrowers, nearly trebled the number of loans, laid the foundation for a separate children's library, and built up from practically nothing a reference library of over 3000 volumes, including the beginnings of a valuable local collection.[5]

The old Norwich city library, numbering about 2000 volumes, which had been founded in 1608, and as at Bristol had been placed in the custody of a private subscription library, was transferred to the new public library in 1862.[6]

Yet another library opened in 1857 was that conducted by the united vestries of St. Margaret and St. John in Westminster—the first of the London libraries. The 1d. rate here yielded over £4000 per annum, so that a ¼d. rate sufficed at the outset, and ½d. rate from 1868 onwards.[7] The library began in a modest way by acquiring for £480 the library and fittings of the former

---

[1] The story is briefly told in *Birkenhead Public Libraries Centenary 1856–1956* (Birkenhead 1956), pp. 3–7, and more fully in A. H. Roberts, *Growth of the Provision of Public Facilities for Leisure-Time Occupations by Local Authorities of Merseyside* (unpublished M.A. thesis, Liverpool University 1933), pp. 32–38. See also *P.R. 1856*, p. 2; *P.R. 1885*, pp. 2–3.
[2] Cf. above, p. 22.   [3] *P.R. 1876*, p. 42.   [4] See above, p. 36.
[5] G. A. Stephen, *Three Centuries of a City Library* (Norwich 1917), pp. 66–67; cf. P. Hepworth and M. Alexander, *City of Norwich Libraries* (Norwich 1957), p. 14.
[6] Stephen, *op. cit.*, p. 17; Hepworth and Alexander, *op. cit.*, p. 12. Cf. T. Kelly, *Early Public Libraries* (1966), pp. 74–75, 126.
[7] E. Edwards, *Free Town Libraries* (1869), table opp. p. 192.

Literary Scientific and Mechanics' Institute in Great Smith Street, and a lease of
the premises. Here were established a small reference library (shortly made
available also for borrowing), a newsroom, and reading rooms, including a
separate Youths' Reading Room. A branch lending library, in two converted
Georgian cottages, was opened in 1859 for the hamlet of Knightsbridge. The
funds available for the purchase of books rarely exceeded £100 per annum
before 1880, but by 1886, with the help of gifts and bequests, the total stock had
reached over 19000 volumes, of which 2600 were at Knightsbridge. Reference
books in the strict sense were few,[1] but as at many early libraries the lending
stock was available also for reference purposes.[2]

At Sunderland a public library was decided on in 1858, by extension of the
Museums Act which had been adopted twelve years earlier. The Mechanics'
Institute handed over its collection of five or six hundred volumes, and a reading
room was opened in a hired room in the Athenaeum in January 1859. Later in
the year the gift of the Bishopwearmouth Mechanics' Institute library of some
three hundred volumes made possible a branch reading room there. In 1860 the
generosity of a member of the Council led to the acquisition of the Literary and
Philosophical Society's library of 4500 volumes. A librarian was appointed;
library regulations based on those of Manchester were adopted; and a $\frac{1}{2}$d. rate
was levied instead of the previous $\frac{1}{4}$d. rate.

There was, however, an opposition party which challenged the legality of
the procedure under the Museums Act. A public meeting failed to settle the
issue, and ended in uproar after declining to confirm the Council's action. The
Town Clerk insisted that the action was legal, but the opposition continued,
and more than one attempt was made to get rid of the library. In May, 1862, the
books were reported to be spoiling by damp and mildew, and the librarian was
instructed "to light the fires and open the windows in the library and place the
books in rotation to dry in the evenings." In 1863 it was actually agreed that all
the books except those belonging to the museum should be lent to the Co-operative Society. The Mechanics' Institute protested, and demanded the return of its
books, and in the end the decision was rescinded.

In 1865 the library was at length opened to the public in the evenings, the
Chief Constable being asked to arrange for a police officer to be in attendance.[3]
In 1866 the library was opened for lending.[4] Twenty years later the total stock
had reached 12500, nearly all in the lending department, and with about
100000 issues a year the library was evidently being extensively used.

Bradford resembled Nottingham in that it was growing rapidly and was

[1] *P.R. 1885*, pp. 12–13, records only 732 volumes in the reference library—presumably
encyclopaedias and other large works unsuitable for lending.

[2] For the details of this account I am indebted to *Great Smith Street Public Library, 1857–1957*
(Westminster 1957); the *Reports* of the Public Libraries Committee for 1950 and 1965;
and information from the City Librarian, Mr. K. C. Harrison.

[3] Not a few of the early public libraries were at first nervous about the consequences of
admitting the working classes. The help of the police was also sought, for example, at
Manchester (*P.R. 1853*, p. 5) and Norwich (P. Hepworth and M. Alexander, *City of
Norwich Libraries* (Norwich 1957), p. 11).

[4] The information on which this account is based (extracted from the Library Committee
Minutes and the columns of the *Sunderland Herald*) has kindly been made available to me
by the Director, Mr. J. T. Shaw.

therefore able to draw on increasing rate income. Its population, 146000 in 1871 when the Acts were adopted, was over 200000 by 1884, and the rate income in the latter year was approaching £4000. Such a town had the resources to build up a library quickly. Bradford, which began in 1872, at once purchased for £700 a private library of 13000 volumes belonging to the late Alderman Samuel Smith; and to this in 1875 was added a library of 2800 volumes belonging to the late William Houlbrook, Vicar of Wyke. This latter collection included many rare works on local topography, and provided a nucleus for what became in time an outstanding local collection.

In respect of branch organization Bradford followed the same plan as Leeds, by making use of Board Schools to house evening lending libraries. Six of these were established between 1875 and 1882, and the first full branch, at Manningham, was opened only in 1883.[1] In the meantime the growing needs of the central library had been met by the erection of a new public library and art gallery in 1878. The heavy rent which the library was called upon to pay for this[2] was a limiting feature on book purchases, but in spite of this difficulty Bradford had achieved, by 1886, a library system almost comparable in size and scope with that of Nottingham.[3]

Of most of the libraries opened in the smaller centres in the 'seventies and 'eighties, it is not possible to say a great deal at this point, because they had not time, within the period with which we are now concerned, to achieve any substantial development. In a few places, however, progress was speeded by handsome gifts of books and buildings. Thus at Derby, where the library opened in 1871, Michael Thomas Bass, local brewer and M.P., presented in 1879 a new library and museum building at a cost of £8000. This was one of the first important individual benefactions after William Brown's much larger gift to Liverpool in 1860. The only fault Greenwood could find with it was that

> ".... among all the costly fittings, the ornamental iron screens, the stained glass, the oriel windows, and the polished granite, the light is defective. Half the rooms are in a state of perpetual gloom, and unless the reader should have the nocturnal sight of the owl or the bat, it is almost impossible to decipher print."[4]

Wigan, most fortunate of the smaller libraries, was not only able to open in 1878 in a building erected at a cost of £12000 by a local cotton manufacturer, Thomas Taylor, but had a similar sum available for the purchase of books from an earlier bequest by a local doctor, J. T. Winnard.[5] At Newark, in 1883, the great benefactor was William Gilstrap (later Sir William Gilstrap of Fornham),

---

[1] Leeds had a slight priority in the use of Board Schools as branches, the first such branch (at Burley) being opened at midsummer, 1875 (Leeds Public Libraries, *Annual Report, 1873–4*, p. 16). The first Board School branch at Bradford (Whitley Lane) was opened in August of the same year.

[2] See above, p. 36.

[3] M. E. Hartley, "A Survey of the Public Library Movement in Bradford", in *L.A.R.*, Vol. VIII (1906), pp. 423–443; B. Wood, *A Brief Survey of the Bradford Public Libraries, 1872–1922* (Bradford 1922), pp. 8–12, 19–21. Total stock in 1886 was 48000, of which one-third was in the reference library.

[4] Greenwood (1890), p. 160. Since the above passage was written the early history of this library has been described in *Derby Borough Libraries, 1871–1971* (Derby 1971).

[5] H. T. Folkard, *Wigan Free Public Library* (Wigan 1900), p. 1.

who provided a well-planned though not impressive-looking building and added for good measure an endowment for the salary of the librarian. The total value of the gift was nearly £11 000, and further substantial endowments followed.[1] Unfortunately Newark, with a population at this time of some 14 000 and a 1d. rate income of £200 a year, lacked the resources to match this splendid gift, and even at the end of the century the bookstock was still very small.[2]

At Darlington the adoption of the Acts was long delayed by fears that a public library would be injurious to the existing Subscription Library and the library of the Mechanics' Institute. Edward Pease was one of the most earnest advocates of adoption, and what he could not achieve during his lifetime he achieved after his death. In his will he left £10 000 for the provision of a public library or a similar object, and with this offer before them the citizens of Darlington at last took the plunge. The new library was opened in 1885, and by the end of the first year had a stock of nearly 13 000 volumes, of which 8000 were gifts, including, it is satisfactory to note, 3500 from the Darlington Subscription Library. The main emphasis at this stage was on the lending department, which achieved the splendid total of 112 000 issues in the first year. The reference department was still in an embryonic stage.[3]

In contrast with the position of libraries such as these, we must consider the plight of many small libraries struggling along with no endowments and little income. In most cases we know little about them, but the story of one of them, Brierley Hill in Staffordshire, has recently been told, and provides an insight into the sort of thing that must have been going on.

This small industrial town, with a population of about 11 000 and a yield of £100 or so from the 1d. rate, adopted the Acts in 1875 and opened its library in the following year in two rooms in the offices of the Local Board, rented at £10 a year. For the equipment of the reading room, linoleum was purchased at 3s. 9d. a yard, and "three tables with Honduras mahogany tops which would last for generations." Seven daily papers, five weekly papers, and ten periodicals were ordered, and the reading room was open from 9 a.m. to 10 p.m. daily. A lending library was added in 1877, with an initial stock of 537 volumes of which 124 came from the tattered remnants of the former Mechanics' Institute Library, and the rest were standard works bought for £72. Thomas Price, a solicitor's clerk, was appointed librarian at £10 a year (later increased to £15), with the duty of attending the library on two evenings a week from 7.30 to 9 p.m. to issue books. Who looked after the reading room during the rest of the day is not clear—presumably the Local Board caretaker.

At the opening of the lending library Ebenezer Grove, Chairman of the Local Board, expressed the hope that it "would be the means of reforming the conversation and dealings of the working classes," but in this matter the

---

[1] William Gilstrap (1816–96), a local malt-manufacturer and landowner, was a generous giver to a variety of educational and philanthropic institutions. The endowment still produces a revenue of nearly £400.

[2] A. Smith, *The Gilstrap Public Library, Newark* (Newark [1933]), pp. 3–5. Cf. Greenwood (1891), pp. 181–182; J. J. Ogle, *The Free Library* (1897), pp. 261–262.

[3] *Edward Pease Public Library: Fifty Years' Progress, 1885–1935* (Darlington 1935), pp. 3–7. Pease (1834–80) came of a Quaker Family well known in the North-East for its prominent part in railway development. His father Joseph was the first Quaker M.P.

librarian did not set a very good example. Though a married man with two children, he ran off in 1883 with the 19-year old daughter of a local publican, and was subsequently brought before the assizes for threatening the girl's father with a loaded pistol. He was acquitted, but the library committee was not pleased, and a new librarian was appointed in 1884.[1]

Greenwood reports that the better-class people stood aloof from the library, and that during the first twelve years "the enormous sum of £10 has been contributed by a supine public".[2] At 25 March 1884, the library was reported to contain 1277 volumes and to have 720 borrowers.[3]

Some Welsh and Scottish Libraries

Of the six libraries of Wales and Monmouthshire only Cardiff and Swansea attained any substantial size at this period. Swansea was the larger of the two,[4] but Cardiff, founded in 1862, is the better documented.

The first proposal for adoption at Cardiff, in 1860, was defeated by 32 votes to 31, but the advocates of a public library at once set to work to organize their own reading room, which was maintained by subscriptions until adoption was agreed in 1862. The lending library and newsroom were at the outset the most important feature, though as early as 1863 a small collection comprising a Moon Bible, a few books, and "other lumber which could not possibly be offered to Lending Library readers," was dignified by the name of reference library.[5] A museum was added in that year, and science and art classes were begun in 1865. The total income at this time was very small—about £500 per annum, of which £100 went in rent to the Y.M.C.A.[6] The full 1d. rate was not accorded until the 1890s. By 1876 the total bookstock, for a town of over 70 000 people, was 8300 volumes, with annual issues of 26 000. This was not a very impressive figure.

In 1882 a new building was erected at a cost of £11 000. A bequest of 2000 volumes by Judge Falconer[7] provided a welcome accession to stock, and in 1886 the library was able to record a reference stock of 8700 volumes as well as a lending library of 11 600 volumes, and loans had risen to 109 000. Until 1885, however, the position was pretty desperate. After this things gradually improved: rateable value increased with the growth of the town, and the transfer of the museum and school of science and art to separate accounts also provided a welcome relief.[8] By the end of the period the library was at last beginning to establish itself as a force in the community.

At Aberystwyth, to choose a contrasting Welsh example, the adoption of

[1] Article in *County Express* (Stourbridge), 16 April 1966. Brierley Hill was absorbed by Dudley in 1966.

[2] Greenwood (1890), p. 146.

[3] *P.R. 1885*, pp. 16–17. Greenwood (1887) gives the same figure.

[4] See above, p. 32.

[5] J. Ballinger, *The Cardiff Free Libraries* (Cardiff 1895), p. 9.

[6] *P.R. 1870*, p. 25; Ballinger, *op. cit.*, p. 12.

[7] Thomas Falconer, of Usk (1805–82), county court judge and legal writer, bequeathed his library to be divided between the towns of Newport, Cardiff, and Swansea—Ballinger, *op. cit.*, p. 15, and information from Mr. J. E. Thomas, City Librarian.

[8] Ballinger, *op. cit.*, pp. 17–19.

the Acts in 1871 was undertaken primarily to enable the town to provide a gallery for a collection of paintings offered by G. E. J. Powell of Nanteos—a gentleman poet and scholar best known as the friend and intimate of Swinburne. The formation of a library was an afterthought first mooted at the adoption meeting by Rev. E. O. Phillips,[1] but the proposal was readily accepted. The town's 1d. rate, however, produced at this time an income of only £15 a year. This was insufficient to rent a suitable room for the pictures, and because of the unsatisfactory condition of the town's finances the Treasury refused permission to borrow funds for building. After eleven months of argument and procrastination, Powell's offer was withdrawn, but the Council now found itself, somewhat ironically, committed to the establishment of a library which it had at the outset never envisaged.

Once again the argument began as to whether to rent or build. By 1873 public impatience was being reflected in the columns of the *Cambrian News*, where it was argued that a public library was a necessary attraction to visitors. In October, 1874, nearly three years after this question was first brought forward, a Free Reading Room was at last opened in rented premises in the town centre. From the beginning the emphasis was on the lending section, but lack of funds was long a limiting factor. In 1886 the total stock was still only about 3000 volumes (nearly all in the lending department) and total issues were only about 2000 per annum.[2]

Of the twelve Scottish libraries of this period we can choose for brief comment only three—Airdrie, which was the first, Dundee, the second and also the largest, and Tarves, the smallest and almost the last.

Airdrie adopted the Scottish Public Libraries Act of 1853 almost as soon as it was passed, and proceeded to buy the library of the Mechanics' Institute as a starting-point. There was difficulty about accommodation, however, and it was only in 1856, after a memorial from the Institute, that a temporary library was provided in the Town Hall. In 1860 a move was made to a room in the market buildings, but on its limited income the library committee found it difficult to secure adequate premises, and there were several changes before Andrew Carnegie at last solved the problem in 1894. An attempt was made in 1871 to form a reference library, but this does not seem to have gone much beyond the purchase of an *Encyclopaedia Britannica*, and throughout this period the library was virtually a lending library only.

In the 'seventies, when the rate income was still less than £100 per annum, William Paterson, a local schoolmaster, was appointed to act as cleaner and caretaker at 12s. per week. At this time the library was open only in the evenings, but from 1878 onwards the profits from a series of concerts made it possible to arrange daytime opening. By 1886 the stock was at most 7000 volumes.[3]

The Dundee public library was established in 1869 in the Albert Institute, a memorial building erected by public subscription at a cost of some £27000, and subsequently transferred to the Corporation at a nominal charge.[4] The building

---

[1] See for his comments on this occasion above, p. 28.

[2] This account is based on the article by N. Roberts, "A Town and its Library", in *Ceredigion*, Vol. III (Aberystwyth 1956–59) pp. 161–181.

[3] [W. Scobbie], *A Century of Reading* (Airdrie 1953), pp. 4–8. See note to table below, App. IX.

[4] Dundee Free Library, *Annual Report, 1879*, pp. 5–6.

ultimately included an art gallery and museum as well as a library, and was described by Greenwood as "the high water mark of Public Library and Museum progress in Scotland."[1] The building of the art gallery and museum wing, however, involved the library committee in a debt of nearly £10000, which was a serious drain on the funds until happily cleared off by a Jubilee gift from John Keiller of Morven (a wealthy local jam manufacturer) in 1887.[2] After some early fluctuations the library was reported in 1875 to be very successful, and the substantial initial stock of 21 000 volumes was more than doubled by 1886. The subscription library inaugurated in 1876, which has already been mentioned,[3] does not seem to have had any adverse effect, for the figures for 1886 show an extensive use—78 000 issues for the reference library of 14 000 volumes, and 217 000 issues for the lending library of 34 000 volumes. On the whole, Dundee had every reason to be proud of its library.

Tarves, in Aberdeenshire, which opened in 1884, is interesting as the only rural parish library in the country at this time. It was a straggling parish whose scattered homesteads housed, in 1881, 2389 inhabitants. The library had its origins in a subscription library founded in 1878 with money and books bequeathed by a parish schoolmaster. When maintenance became difficult it was decided to adopt the Libraries Acts. Since a building and books already existed, it was felt that an income of £20 a year from the rates would be quite sufficient, and this was provided for by a rate of $\frac{2}{3}$d. The library was, of course, operated on a part-time basis,[4] probably by a voluntary librarian, so that expenses were minimal. We have no details of its bookstock in 1886, but in 1890 it is recorded as 2000—a very high figure in relation to the population.[5]

---

[1] Greenwood (1890), p. 229.
[2] *P.R. 1876*, p. 87; *Annual Report, 1887*, pp. 5–6.
[3] See above, p. 35.
[4] Three hours a week in 1897—see above, p. 33 notes.
[5] Greenwood (1890), pp. 245–246.

CHAPTER IV

Library Organization and Use

Buildings

ONLY a minority of public libraries at this period were so fortunate as to occupy premises specially erected for library purposes. At the outset, when library requirements in the way of buildings were little understood, the first thought of most local authorities was to provide accommodation as cheaply as possible, usually in a converted building; and even towards the close of the period shortage of funds often rendered a new building out of the question. The most economical arrangement was obviously to find room for the library in some existing public building—in a corner of the town hall, for example, as at Blackburn (1862),[1] or better still in a disused town hall, as at Oxford (1854).[2] Bristol, when it established its public library in 1876, already had available the building erected for the old city library in the eighteenth century.[3] At Winchester (1851) the library found its first home in the former prison governor's residence, at Doncaster (1869) and Shrewsbury (1883) in the old grammar school, at Leeds (1870), first in the old infirmary, and later in the new municipal buildings.[4] The Northampton library, after twelve years in the town hall, was lodged from 1884 to 1889 in a converted county gaol. Usually, it seems, accommodation in buildings under municipal control was provided rent free, but in some cases a charge was made: Brierley Hill in 1876 was paying £10 a year, out of its meagre rate income of under £100, for accommodation in the Town Hall.[5]

Where public buildings were not available, there was often a mechanics' institute, subscription library, or similar institution willing to surrender its premises, either free or at a modest charge, on the understanding that the service it had formerly provided for its members would now become a public responsibility. Several examples of this kind of thing have been noticed in the previous chapter,[6] and there are others. Wolverhampton (1869) took over the local Athenaeum,[7] and Willenhall (1875) the Literary Institute;[8] South Shields

---

[1] R. Ashton, *The Free Library, Museum and Art Gallery* (Blackburn 1906), p. 3. Other similar examples are Brierley Hill and Northampton (1876), Aston Manor (1878), Wrexham (1879), and Ashton-under-Lyne (1881). See above, p. 36.

[2] See above, p. 57. Other similar examples are Plymouth (1876), and Great Yarmouth and Hanley (1886).   [3] See above, p. 54.

[4] For Winchester and Leeds see above, pp. 49–50, 56; for Doncaster, Greenwood (1890), p. 100; for Shrewsbury, J. L. Hobbs, "Shrewsbury Public Library", in *Open Access*, Vol. IX, N.S. No. 1 (Shrewsbury 1960).

[5] See above, p. 62.

[6] E.g. at Westminster, Nottingham, Newcastle upon Tyne, Sheffield and Bolton (mechanics' institutes or similar bodies), Liverpool and Tarves (subscription libraries).

[7] J. J. Ogle, *The Free Library* (1897), p. 225.

[8] Information from Mr. F. H. Lamb, Librarian.

(1873), Ealing (1883), and Aberdeen (1885), acquired the buildings of the local mechanics' institutes;[1] and the libraries at Coventry (1868), St. Helens (1872), Smethwick (1877), Tamworth (1882), and Halifax (1883), all began in the premises of former subscription libraries.[2]

In default of public buildings, mechanics' institutes and the like, library committees often had to resort to rented premises of various kinds, though in a few instances, as notably at Manchester (1852),[3] public subscriptions made possible an outright purchase.

Most public libraries, therefore, had to be content at least in their early stages with makeshift accommodation, often overcrowded, ill-lighted, ill-ventilated, and generally inconvenient. In some cases these drawbacks became obvious only when the library came into use and the extent of the public demand was realized; but in other cases the inadequacy of the premises was clear from the beginning. At Nottingham, for example, the library committee in 1867 reported that the former Artizans' Library was "quite unfitted for the purposes of a Free Library," but the town council insisted that it must be used, and it had to serve as the central library for thirteen years.[4]

The first public libraries to have buildings designed for the purpose were Warrington and Norwich, in 1857. Warrington made a beginning in rented rooms in 1848, but at once launched a public subscription for a permanent building, and raised a sum of nearly £1800.[5] Norwich, having adopted the Act in 1850, waited seven years for a building to be completed. Both these buildings combined accommodation for library and museum, and the Norwich building served other purposes as well.[6] Cambridge, Birkenhead and Birmingham, which like Warrington rented accommodation to begin with, all erected special buildings in the 'sixties,[7] and Blackburn's library and museum were moved from the town hall to a permanent building in 1874.[8] As time went on, library authorities became more and more convinced of the importance of securing purpose-built premises, but in 1886 only about one-third had actually achieved this ambition.

The great age of library benefactions was not yet come, but already, and

[1] Greenwood (1890), p. 133 (on South Shields); Ealing Public Libraries, *Respice-Prospice 1883–1964* (Ealing 1964), p. 1; A. W. Robertson, *Aberdeen Public Library: Manual for Readers* (Aberdeen 1892), p. 3.

[2] Greenwood (1891), pp. 165–166 (on Coventry); St. Helens Public Libraries and Museum, *72nd Report, 1949–50*, p. 4; *Smethwick Public Library, 1877–1927* (Smethwick 1928), pp. 7–9; H. Wood, *Borough by Prescription* (Tamworth 1958), p. 93; *The Halifax Reader*, Vol. 4, No. 1 (July 1950), p. 2. For a lively description of the Halifax Library at the time of its opening, see L. S. Jast, "A Public Library in the 'Eighties," in *Librarian and Book World*, Vol. XXIV (1935), pp. 131–135.

[3] See above, p. 41.

[4] *Fifty Years: a Brief History of the Public Library Movement in Nottingham* (Nottingham 1918), p. 7.

[5] J. P. Aspden (ed.), *Warrington Hundred* (Warrington 1947), p. 95; *P.R. 1870*, p. 24; cf. *P.R. 1877*, which shows £1700 still outstanding.

[6] See above, p. 36.

[7] W. A. Munford, *Cambridge City Libraries, 1855–1955* (Cambridge 1955), p. 5; *Birkenhead Public Libraries Centenary, 1856–1956* (Birkenhead 1956), pp. 5–7; *Notes on the History of the Birmingham Public Libraries, 1861–1961* (Birmingham 1962), p. 4.

[8] R. Ashton, *The Free Library, Museum and Art Gallery* (Blackburn 1906), pp. 3–4.

increasingly as the period neared its close, private generosity was stepping in to compensate for public poverty. We have already seen instances of this in the case-studies in the previous chapter, in the gifts by Sir William Brown at Liverpool in 1860, by Michael Thomas Bass at Derby in 1875, by Thomas Taylor at Wigan in 1878, by Sir William Gilstrap at Newark in 1883, and by Edward Pease at Darlington in 1885. There were other benefactors, too, who have not been named, e.g. Sir Peter Coats, the thread manufacturer, at Paisley (1871); David Chadwick, M.P. and social reformer, at Macclesfield (1876); William Atkinson, a cotton manufacturer, at Southport (1878); and Sir John Brunner, founder of what later became Imperial Chemical Industries, at Northwich (1885). The most significant name in the list, however, is that of Andrew Carnegie, who in 1883 bestowed a library building, at a cost of £8000, on his native town of Dunfermline. It was a modest beginning to what was to become a gigantic enterprise.

Because of the variations in the size of libraries, and the variety of the buildings that had to be pressed into service, it is difficult to generalize about library interiors. There was, however, general agreement that the basic essentials for a developed service were a reference library, a lending library, and a reading room. Birmingham, Cardiff, and Manchester, from an early stage, provided separate newsrooms for newspapers and the lighter periodicals—a practice which Edwards regarded as desirable in order to check "frivolous resort to, and occasional needless crowding of, the principal Reading Room, by facilitating a practical and unobjectionable classification of readers."[1] At Liverpool, which as we have seen declined to admit newspapers until 1883, the Picton Reading Room was reserved for students.[2] The boys' reading rooms pioneered by Manchester from 1878 onwards were in the branch libraries only,[3] but a number of libraries included a special juvenile library in their central buildings, and in some cases, e.g. at Westminster from 1857, this involved a separate room.[4] Nottingham, as we have seen, had a separate building for the purpose.[5] Ladies' reading rooms were by 1886 fairly common, and were being provided in most new buildings. Rochdale's new library, completed in 1884, had a ladies' room which was used as a boys' room during the evening.

Greenwood, in 1886, strongly commended separate reading rooms for boys, and regarded ladies' reading rooms as indispensable.[6] On both points, it is interesting to note, he soon changed his mind. By 1890 he was writing:

> "Where there is one good-sized room, say of oblong shape, the tables for boys should be at the end nearest the assistant or caretaker. This would ensure the boys keeping quiet—a difficult thing to achieve sometimes when a separate room is allotted to their use[7] . . . . The tables for the ladies might be placed at the extreme end of the room, and their presence in a large room aids the general decorum, and gives an appearance of cheerfulness and brightness to a news and reading room. To say that frivolities are likely to go on by the sexes being in the same room in this way, would be an assertion only made by those who have never been in a large room where this

---

[1] E. Edwards, *Free Town Libraries* (1869), pp. 148–149.
[2] See above, p. 46.   [3] See above, p. 43.   [4] See above, p. 60.   [5] See above, p. 53.
[6] Greenwood (1886), p. 164.
[7] The *Annual Report* of the Dundee Free Library for 1881 records that it had been found necessary to adopt just such an arrangement.

plan is in operation. . . . A separate ladies' room means very often a good deal of gossip, and sometimes it is from these rooms that fashion-sheets and plates from the monthlies are most missed."[1]

A lecture-hall was generally regarded as desirable, though only a minority of libraries possessed one. A few libraries endeavoured, without much success, to create something of the social atmosphere characteristic of the mechanics' institutes. Thus among the many activities associated with the Watford Public Library there was at the outset (in 1874), a "youths' institute"—presumably a kind of youth club and reading room. It was abandoned five years later as incompatible with serious work.[2] Leamington Spa, in 1876, allowed chess and draughts to be played in the reference library.[3] Tamworth, when it began in 1882, had a special reading room for smokers;[4] and Wandsworth at its opening in 1885 provided a recreation room, with chess, draughts, and backgammon, but "a few boys took possession of the room, and made themselves a nuisance by unruly behaviour and gambling," so the experiment was abandoned.[5]

Edward Edwards, in his *Memoirs of Libraries* (1859), and his *Free Town Libraries* (1869), was the first to tackle the problems of library management from the point of view of the public library. Following the practice of earlier writers, he adopted for this subject the term "library economy"—an archaic and ill-omened name which unfortunately gained wide currency and has persisted to our own day. From 1877, when the librarians began to meet in annual conference, the whole range of problems involved in the organization of public libraries came under repeated discussion, in the light of experience not only in this country but abroad, and especially in the United States.

In an age when fire-fighting was less efficient than it is now, libraries were regarded as particularly vulnerable, and in his recommendations regarding library buildings Edwards insisted first and foremost that

> "The building should be fireproof; walls, floors, and roof should be exclusively formed of brick, stone, iron and slate. If the Reading Room or any other special apartment have a wooden floor, it should be embedded in stucco upon a stone flagging, or upon brick arches."[6]

He even went so far as to suggest that the bookcases might be made "wholly uninflammable" by being constructed of iron, with shelves of enamelled slate.[7] This, however, was a counsel of perfection that was universally ignored.

Since it was at this time an article of faith with public librarians that the public should not have access to the shelves, Edwards naturally recommended that the reading room or rooms should be quite separate from the rooms in which the books were kept. The lending library, he thought, should be a distinct department, as remote from the reading room as possible. He also made the important point that, even in a small library, provision must be made for admin-

---

[1] Greenwood (1890), p. 357.

[2] J. Woolman, *Watford Public Library* (repr. from *Watford Observer*, 25 Jan. 1913).

[3] See above, p. 59.

[4] H. Wood, *Borough by Prescription* (Tamworth 1958), p. 94.

[5] *1st Annual Report, 1885-86*, p. 6.

[6] E. Edwards, *Memoirs of Libraries* (1859), Vol. II, p. 730; cf. *Free Town Libraries* (1869), p. 41.

[7] *Memoirs*, Vol. II, p. 736.

istration—not only a room for the librarian, but accommodation for "the reception, registering, stamping, and cataloguing, of books."[1] This was a consideration too often neglected.

Edwards seems to have thought almost exclusively in terms of wall-shelving, with galleries every seven feet so that all the books were within reach without the need for ladders: thus in a room 35 feet high there would be four tiers of galleries all round the room.[2] Wall shelving was, in fact, characteristic of this period of library history, but since few public libraries had space to carry out the policy of separation Edwards recommended, the general tendency was to combine this type of shelving with the use of the central area for readers, the lower shelves being guarded by a rail or other barrier. In this way a single large room could be made to serve as a combined reference library and reading room; while another provided a newsroom with a lending library behind a counter at one end. In many small libraries a single room had to serve all purposes.

Good examples of the combination of reading room and reference library are seen in the Picton Reading Room at Liverpool, opened in 1879; and in the rebuilt Birmingham library of 1881, where a gallery is provided but the height of the shelves is such that ladders also have to be used. At Wigan in 1878 (illustrated opposite p. 306), the plan was attractively varied by the introduction of bookshelves at right angles to the walls so as to form alcoves, after the fashion first developed at Trinity College, Cambridge, in the seventeenth century.[3]

Edward's caution regarding the need for galleries may have derived from his experience of the first Manchester library, where the shelves, as seen in a picture of the opening, appear to go up to a terrifying height, with no sign of any gallery. At Leicester the assistants in the lending library had to race up and down ladders for books stacked to a height of 20–24 feet, without a gallery. Greenwood comments:

"There can be no wonder that a serious accident should have occurred a few months ago, when the ladder fell while an assistant was upon it, and who was so injured that he had to be taken to the hospital. The ladder in its fall struck another assistant upon the head, causing a very serious wound. It is almost criminal to place the shelving so high as this in any public library."[4]

To overcome the difficulty of high shelving there was invented a device known as the "long-reacher", of which a specimen still survives in the Norwich Central Library. It was like a pair of long-handled pruning shears, with rubber jaws in place of the cutters, and cannot have been very satisfactory to use.[5]

At the first Conference of Librarians, held in London in 1877, the whole principle of wall-shelving came under heavy attack from American delegates, who described the alternative system then being developed in the United

---

[1] *Free Town Libraries*, p. 42.   [2] *Memoirs*, Vol. II, p. 731.

[3] T. Kelly, *Early Public Libraries* (1966), p. 53.

[4] Greenwood (1890), p. 171. The reference is to the first central library, opened in 1871. It has recently been attractively reconstructed to serve as the central lending library. Another bad example of high shelving, still in use till 1967, was in the Newcastle upon Tyne reference library of 1884.

[5] "Cotgreave's long-reacher" was exhibited at the Library Association Conference of 1883 (*Transactions*, p. 183).

States, which was in all essentials similar to that used in libraries to-day, i.e. low-ceilinged stackrooms with rows of bookshelves a few feet apart occupying the entire floor space, and every book within reach without the use of ladders. W. F. Poole, Public Librarian of Chicago (the originator of Poole's *Index to Periodicals*), declared:

> "Our library buildings seem to have been constructed chiefly for show and architectural decoration, and with little reference to the preservation of the books and the convenient administration of the library. Nothing can be more absurd for a circulating library than the conventional arrangement which has been mentioned. The librarian and attendants are travelling for books the outside of a parallelogram, when they might save their steps by working from a centre outwards. They are climbing ladders and ascending into galleries, when by a better arrangement they might have all their books within reach on the ground floor."[1]

The argument was clinched in a paper given at the Library Association Conference of 1881 by William Archer, Librarian of the National Library of Ireland, who demonstrated that a reference library and reading room visited by delegates the previous day, which accommodated 25000 volumes on the walls, could be made by the new method to accommodate 230000 volumes, while still providing adequate space for readers.[2] From this time there was really no excuse for building in the traditional style, but it was a style attractive to architects, and change came only slowly.

Heating and lighting were the subject of much experiment in the libraries of this period. For heating, Edwards as late as 1869 still had a lingering preference for open fires, provided they were properly guarded,[3] and in some institutions this method of heating evidently persisted almost until the end of the century. Even in 1897 J. W. Hart, a heating engineer, was finding it difficult to convince people that the open fireplace "is not at all suitable for Public Libraries, on account of its wastefulness, and the tendency of a selfish few to monopolize the whole of the comfort and cheerfulness, and effectually screen others from it."[4] In the majority of public libraries, however, central heating by hot water or steam was the rule.

Since public libraries were intended particularly for the use of working people, they could not, as the British Museum and many other libraries did, close at dusk.[5] They had to be open in the evenings, and artificial lighting was therefore vital. Gas was commonly used but, as the incandescent mantle had not yet been invented, the quality of illumination was poor.[6] Gas was, moreover, a constant worry to librarians, not only because of the fire risk, but because the fumes and the heat were believed to be injurious to the books, rendering both paper and binding brittle and liable to crack. It was for this reason that it was never

---

[1] *Transactions and Proceedings of the Conference of Librarians ... 1877* (1878), p. 148. This volume (cited hereafter as *Conference Transactions 1877*) and the similar volumes of *Transactions and Proceedings* of the first seven Library Association Conferences, 1878–84 (cited hereafter as *L.A. Conference Transactions, 1878*, etc.) form a valuable record of professional opinion at this period.

[2] *L.A. Conference Transactions, 1881*, p. 55.

[3] E. Edwards, *Free Town Libraries*, p. 42 and note.

[4] *L.Y.B. 1897*, p. 39.

[5] Winchester, which did not have artificial light till 1876, was exceptional—see above, p. 56.

[6] The first commercial incandescent mantle was patented by Auer von Welsbach in 1885.

used in the British Museum Library. Edwards, who in 1859 recognized that gas might be used with perfect safety,[1] recommended ten years later that it should be wholly excluded from library interiors. If gas were used at all, he said, it should be "applied externally", i.e. by lights shining through the windows—a system which had been successfully used at University College, London, and elsewhere.[2] It does not appear, however, that this advice was often taken.

Only those of an older generation can appreciate the astonishing transformation brought about in library work, both for the readers and for the staff, by the introduction of electric lighting, which was brought into use in the British Museum Library in 1879, and in the Picton Reading Room at Liverpool in 1881. Peter Cowell, the Liverpool librarian, described the system to his fellow-librarians at Cambridge in 1882. The light used, he explained, consisted of three Serrin arc-lamps, grouped together in a large opal shade or screen, something in shape like an inverted umbrella (the incandescent electric lamp now in familiar use had at that time only just been invented). Some readers had complained of the brilliance of the new light, and one had complained that it gave him neuralgia, but such complaints had been short-lived. The staff not only appreciated the better light but also, because of the marked reduction in the temperature of the galleries, experienced "a wonderful freedom from that feeling of weariness and lassitude which invariably more or less oppresses us when working by gas in other parts of the library."[3]

Cowell's address evidently impressed his fellow-delegates,[4] but in 1886 Liverpool was still the only rate-aided public library in which electric light was in use.

Concerning branch library buildings it is not necessary to say much. Branches were comparatively few at this period—less than a hundred in all in 1886, of which a quarter were in Leeds. The buildings were as miscellaneous as those used for central libraries. Liverpool's two earliest branches, the first in the country, began in 1853 in the North and South Corporation Schools, with school teachers acting as librarians, but were transferred after about a year to rented houses, under the charge of a branch librarian.[5] Manchester's first branches, at Hulme and Ancoats in 1857, were in converted houses.[6] Leeds made a beginning in 1870 with branches in the Hunslet and New Wortley Mechanics' Institutes, but later as we have seen, made extensive use of the board schools which began to be established at this time.[7] Bradford did the same,[8] and

---

[1] *Memoirs*, Vol. II, pp. 733–734.

[2] *Free Town Libraries*, p. 41. Cf. the evidence of Edwards's friend John Imray, in *Report from the Select Committee on Public Libraries* (1849), pp. 205–206.

[3] *L.A. Conference Transactions, 1881–1882*, p. 156.

[4] See the discussion, *op. cit.*, pp. 211–213.

[5] P. Cowell, *Liverpool Public Libraries: a History of Fifty Years* (Liverpool 1903), pp. 48–49.

[6] E. Edwards, *Free Town Libraries* (1869), p. 84.

[7] T. W. Hand, *A Brief Account of the Public Libraries of the City of Leeds, 1870–1920* (Leeds 1920), pp. 5–6. Cf. above, p. 50 W. H. K. Wright, Librarian of Plymouth, in 1879 commended the use of board schools for evening reading rooms, "with if possible a small lending library attached", but his colleagues do not seem to have been enthusiastic—*L.A. Conference Transactions, 1879*, pp. 38–41, 96. Cf. J. L. Thornton, *Select Readings in the History of Librarianship* (1966), pp. 182–184.

[8] See above, p. 61.

Liverpool in 1884 opened five branch reading rooms in schools.[1] Sheffield's first branch, opened at Upperthorpe in 1869, was in a Congregational school-room.[2]

The provision in a branch library was usually restricted to a lending library and reading room. A particularly well equipped branch might have a separate newsroom, or a ladies' reading room. The expense of erecting a special building, therefore, was not great, especially as the site was usually at some distance from the town centre; but most libraries were so hard pressed financially that they just could not afford purpose-built branch libraries. The first was opened in Rochdale Road, Manchester, in 1860; it comprised a lending library, reading room, and newsroom, and cost about £1000 to build, about £450 to equip, and about £400 a year to run.[3] A handful of others were built in various places—Sheffield, to its credit, built three in 1872–76—but in 1886 there were probably not more than a dozen in the whole country.

Those who are specially interested in the architectural details of the libraries of this period can find full accounts of the newer buildings in the various editions of Greenwood's *Free Public Libraries*. To repeat them here would be tedious. Externally the buildings were in every conceivable style from classical to Tudor. Internally, with their high ceilings, dark walls and heavy furniture, they had that solid and gloomy grandeur characteristic of Victorian public buildings. The most significant differences between mid-Victorian libraries and the libraries of to-day were, first, the relatively large amount of space devoted to reading rooms, which was a reflection of the poverty and poor home conditions of so many of the users; and second, the shutting off of the books from the readers, either in separate rooms or on guarded wall-shelving.

Two brief descriptions must suffice as examples. The first, from the columns of the *Courier* at Leamington Spa, illustrates the kind of accommodation that must have been occupied by many small town libraries throughout this period. The rooms originally assigned to the Leamington library in the Town Hall in 1857 quickly proved inadequate, and in the following year it was transferred to new premises in Bath Street. Here four rooms were available:

"Two on the ground floor, and one on the first floor, are used for reading rooms . . . the books are kept in a room upstairs. . . . The furnishing also reflects great credit on the Committee. The tables, benches and chairs are of a useful and substantial character, and the floors of the reading rooms are covered with cocoa matting [sic] . . . The gas fittings impart an elegant appearance to the rooms. One great drawback, however, is the lack of ventilation."[4]

The other description is of the new library at Leeds, part of a large new block of civic buildings opened in 1884:

"The most imposing portion of the entire building is devoted to the library. It consists of a reading-room, a lending library, and reference library, with a small

---

[1] Cowell, *op. cit.*, p. 137.

[2] *The City Libraries of Sheffield, 1856–1956* (Sheffield 1956), p. 16. This was the branch at which Greenwood served his brief library apprenticeship—see above, p. 16.

[3] E. Edwards, *op. cit.*, pp. 82–85.

[4] *Courier*, 27 Nov. 1858. I am indebted for this quotation to the Librarian, Mr. H. S. Tallamy.

museum. The reading-room is 80 feet long by 40 feet wide, divided into a broad nave and aisles by six arches upon pillars of polished granite. These support vaults of mosaic work in hexagonal bricks of many colours, set off by golden bosses. The walls are tiled throughout the lower portion, forming a dado in rich dark colours, above which is a richly figured and embossed diaper of grey-green, finished by a band of brighter hue, with gilded panels. Above this are medallion busts of Shakespeare, Homer, Dante, Milton, Goethe, Scott, and others, the work of Mr. Creswick, a native of Leeds. The general character of the design and ornamentation of this room is Romanesque. On the floor above is the lending library, and here terra cotta takes the place of granite, the effect being different in character and more subdued than that of the room below. Above this is the reference library, which is 35 feet high, with a gallery running round and several compartments for readers. The tesselated floors, tiled walls, carved round arches, richly coloured ceilings, and stained-glass windows have a beautiful effect. The rooms are lofty and well lighted, so that everything is seen to advantage."[1]

Books

The belief expressed by the Select Committee on Public Libraries in 1849 that if libraries were once established books would be abundantly supplied by donations was quickly proved false, but many of the early libraries did in fact receive liberal donations of books, both from institutions and from private individuals, and for some small libraries such donations long continued to be the main source of supply. From a list prepared for the Library Association Conference in 1879 we see, for example, that at Brighton the entire stock of 22 000 volumes had been acquired by donations; at Cambridge two-thirds of the library had been presented; Coventry had received 9000 volumes from a local subscription library; at Doncaster nearly two-thirds of the stock had come from the mechanics' institute and a subscription library; at Maidstone the entire library had been bequeathed by Dr. Thomas Charles; at Stoke nearly all the books had come from the Athenaeum; and at Tynemouth more than half the stock had been presented by the mechanics' institute and the literary and philosophical society.[2]

This list, which is not complete, also reveals the extent to which the new public libraries were taking over the functions of the old mechanics' institute and subscription libraries and the like. In many cases these libraries were handed over, or sold for a nominal sum, at the outset; in other cases they passed into the possession of the public library at a later date. At Manchester for example, the 17 000 volumes acquired by gift between 1852 and 1868 included the Miles Platting Mechanics' Institute library (over 2000 volumes, 1861–62), the Phoenix and Wellington Mills Library (1712 volumes, 1866–67) and the Pin Mill Library (1044 volumes, 1866–67).[3]

A few public libraries, e.g. Bristol, Norwich, and Newcastle upon Tyne, also inherited books from old civic or parochial libraries, but as these consisted mainly of seventeenth- and eighteenth-century theology, often in Latin, they were not of much immediate value. More useful were the current publications, presented to some of the larger libraries by such bodies as the Record Commis-

[1] Greenwood (1887), pp. 71–72.
[2] L.A. Conference Transactions, 1879, table opp. p. 136.
[3] P.R. 1870, p. 17.

sioners and the Patent Commissioners, and the occasional distribution of dupli-cate copies by the British Museum.[1]

The free distribution of patent specifications and other Patent Office publications began in 1854, and thanks to the enthusiasm of Bennet Woodcroft, Superintendent of Specifications, was conducted on a generous scale. Most of the recipients, at this stage, were mechanics' institutes, learned societies, or similar bodies, but the needs of the newly emerging public libraries were not overlooked, and already in 1856 the Commissioners were claiming that "This gift has in most cases laid the foundation of public free libraries where none previously existed."[2] By 1875 more than 300 complete or partial sets were being distributed to repositories in the United Kingdom, including between thirty and forty public libraries.[3] These publications were in some places much in demand, but they also created a considerable storage problem, a complete set amounting to over 3000 volumes.[4]

Public libraries have always been indebted, and it is to be hoped will continue to be indebted, to private donors for many valuable gifts, often of rare books which they could not afford to purchase from their own funds. But dependence on gifts to the extent here indicated obviously had serious dangers. At best such dependence meant that the book collection was unbalanced and perhaps in important respects unsuited to its readers; at worst the library was made a dumping-ground for all kinds of unwanted rubbish. As Edward Edwards remarked:

> "Too often, the books that are given to libraries (otherwise than by bequest) are the mere weedings of private collections. Sometimes, they are even such weedings as might bring to the mind of a close observer an inscription which, in these days, often meets the eye in the purlieus of our watering-places: 'Rubbish may be shot here.'"[5]

As Edwards pointed out, the only satisfactory way of building up a balanced and useful collection was by systematic purchase on the basis of carefully prepared lists.[6] The most fortunate libraries, therefore, were those which received gifts in the form of money. Wigan, with its £12000 bequest from J. T. Winnard for the purchase of books, was in a peculiarly happy position and was at great pains to spend the money wisely:

---

[1] On efforts to secure a more generous distribution of Government publications see T. W. Hand, *A Brief Account of the Public Libraries in the City of Leeds, 1870–1920* (Leeds 1920), pp. 9–10.

[2] *Commissioners of Patents' Journal*, 8 Aug. 1856, p. 809.

[3] Patent Office, *List of Works printed by order of the Commissioner of Patents for Inventions* (1875), pp. 9–15.

[4] *Ibid.*; cf. *P.R. 1876*, p. 15. I am indebted for this information to Mr. D. R. Jamieson, Assistant Keeper of the Patent Office Library (recently renamed the National Library of Science and Invention). The free distribution continued on an increasing scale till 1900, but during the present century has gradually been concentrated in the major provincial public libraries, which in 1967 accounted for 21 of the 23 sets maintained for reference outside the Patent Office itself. For Bennet Woodcroft see the useful short sketch by C. W. Sutton in *Dictionary of National Biography*.

[5] E. Edwards, *Free Town Libraries* (1869), p. 153.

[6] *Op. cit.*, pp. 45–47.

"Prior to the purchase of the books, specialists in the various departments of knowledge were asked to draw up lists of the best works in each of them, thus Mr. Gerard B. Finch, M.A., may be specially fathered with the mathematical, astronomical and kindred divisions, Dr. W. E. A. Axon with the books relating to Lancashire and Cheshire, your librarian (H. T. Folkard) selected the works relating to the various branches of the fine arts, and the numerous other divisions were advised upon by experts, great care being taken to include only works of high merit."[1]

Few libraries, however, had the resources to set about the business in this systematic way. The results of a mixture of gifts and purchases can be studied in the Parliamentary Returns of Public Libraries of 1876 and 1877, which give for most libraries details of subject holdings. The classification used for this purpose varies from library to library, and more will be said about this later. In the meantime it will be sufficient to remark that most libraries, in these pre-Dewey days, were content to classify their books numerically under broad subject headings, e.g. Theology and Philosophy; Arts and Sciences; History and Biography; Classical Literature. In the 1877 Return an attempt is made to bring together the information provided by individual libraries, and these summary tables, imperfect though they are in many ways, do provide a valuable conspectus of library holdings about the year 1875.[2]

The total stocks were not large. Out of Great Britain's total population (at the 1871 census) of 26 millions, the library authorities which completed the returns catered for only some 4.2 millions, and the book-stock for these 4.2 millions was 1.06 millions—just about one book for every four persons. The lending stocks (including the branches) were on the whole larger than the reference stocks—605 000 volumes compared with 457 000. In the lending libraries the groups in which the largest stocks were held were: Fiction and Juvenile (25.3 per cent); Geography, History, Travels, and Biography (24.5 per cent); and Literature, Poetry, Drama and Miscellaneous (20.5 per cent). In the reference libraries the lead was taken by Geography, History, etc. (23.5 per cent), followed by Literature, Poetry, etc. (21.9 per cent), and Fiction and Juvenile (17.2 per cent).[3]

The picture presented by these figures should be taken as representing only a very rough approximation. In some respects total library stocks are exaggerated, since in a number of the smaller libraries the books in the lending library served also for purposes of reference, and accordingly figure under both headings.[4] On the other hand a close examination of the figures reveals a number of errors and omissions calling for correction in the opposite direction. And of course there were a number of libraries that made no return. It must be pointed out, too, that the heading "Fiction and Juvenile" is very unsatisfactory. Few libraries had any separate heading for juvenile books, and when they did the number was usually small,[5] so we may take it that most of the volumes listed

[1] H. T. Folkard, *Wigan Free Public Library: its Rise and Progress* (Wigan 1900), p. 2.

[2] *P.R. 1877*, pp. 20–31.

[3] For further details see below, Apps. VI–VIII. Note that in each case a proportion of books was unclassified.

[4] E.g. Canterbury, *P.R. 1876*, p. 24; Westminster, *ibid.*, p. 81; Warrington, *P.R. 1877*, pp. 16–17.

[5] Coventry, with 9 per cent of "Books for the Young" in its lending library, is rather exceptional—*P.R. 1876*, p. 27.

under this joint heading were in fact fiction. Many libraries, however, had no separate heading for fiction either, even in their lending sections. In these libraries fiction was classified under Literature. The proportion of fiction in lending library stocks was therefore probably nearer 33 per cent than 25 per cent[1], and some upward adjustment should also be made in respect of reference libraries. These facts have an important bearing on the question of fiction issues, which will be referred to shortly.

The same kind of criticism can be levelled at certain other headings used in the summary return. Such headings as Books of Reference, Foreign Books, Patents, and Books for the Blind do not record the total holdings in these categories, but merely the holdings of those libraries which classified such works separately.

One important feature of many libraries that does not appear from the statistical tables is the formation of local collections. This was discussed by the Select Committee of 1849, which recommended that in all the chief provincial towns there should be topographical libraries, "where history may find a faithful portraiture of local events, local literature, and local manners; and art and science a collection of all objects illustrative of the soil, climate and resources of the surrounding country"; and also that in appropriate localities there should be special libraries "illustrative of the peculiar trade, manufactures, and agriculture of the place, and greatly favourable to the practical development of the science of political economy."[2] Edward Edwards reinforced the point in 1869, when he wrote of the need for

"a thorough collection of all printed information about the history, the antiquities, the trade, the statistics, the special products, the special pursuits, and the special interests, of the Town and of the County in which it stands."[3]

The idea was one which appealed strongly to most librarians and library committees as being of immediate local interest and potential practical value; and such collections, once initiated, readily attracted local donations. It is not surprising, therefore, that many libraries from an early stage turned their attention in this direction. At first the various elements in the collection were not clearly differentiated, but by 1886 the larger libraries had grasped the distinction made in the 1849 Report between books illustrating local history, topography and literature, and books concerned with local trade, industry and agriculture.

From the latter section developed, in due course, our technical and commercial libraries, but at this period these were merely embryonic. Manchester, it is true, had already in 1879 a collection of seven or eight hundred works (begun by Edwards) on cotton manufacture; Rochdale had a small collection on woollen manufacture; and the recently opened library at Wigan had the beginnings of what was to be an important collection on mining.[4] As late as 1883, however, a speaker at a Library Association Conference complained of the paucity of technical books in public libraries, and reported that in the Leeds

[1] Where separate figures are given for fiction they range from under one-fifth at Manchester to over half at Bolton and Stockport, with an average of about one-third.
[2] *1849 Report*, pp. xi, 84.
[3] E. Edwards, *Free Town Libraries* (1869), p. 37.
[4] *L.A. Conference Transactions, 1879*, pp. 55–56.

Catalogue on Art, Science, and Technology not a single book was to be found under the headings of Cloth Manufacture, Weaving, or Spinning.[1]

Local historical, topographical, and literary collections grew more rapidly. W. H. K. Wright, City Librarian of Plymouth, commended such collections to his fellow-librarians in 1878 as the necessary complement of local museum collections, instancing not only his own incipient Devon and Cornwall Library at Plymouth but also the achievements of Manchester, Liverpool, Rochdale, Leicester, Bristol, and more especially Birmingham, with its splendid Shakespeare Library and its Staunton Library of books on Warwickshire—both, alas, shortly to be destroyed by fire.[2] He might have added, had he known of them, Blackburn, Bolton, Warrington, Bradford, Derby, Norwich, Dundee, and the small but important Welsh collection (part of the Rowland Williams Library) at Swansea—not to mention the London Guildhall library, which was a repository of local material from the start.

Liverpool, as Wright noted, collected not only books about local history but maps, drawings and engravings. The nucleus here was provided by the splendid collection, in twenty-six large folio volumes, assembled by Thomas Binns, a local antiquary, and purchased from his executors at the opening of the library in 1852.[3] In this matter the Library Committee showed great wisdom and foresight. It not only took every opportunity of adding to the collection, but engaged an artist to sketch streets and buildings about to be demolished. This practice is still continued at the present day, and the result is a quite unique record of the city's growth.

Children's libraries were just beginning to take shape. The provision made for young readers in the early years took various forms. There were, for example, the reading rooms for boys established in the Manchester branch libraries from 1878 onwards.[4] The youths' reading room provided at the opening of the Westminster library in 1857 was an earlier experiment in the same direction, which lasted at least eleven years, in spite of complaints from older readers regarding noise.[5] In both these instances the reading rooms were designed for older children: at Westminster the age limits seem to have been 13 to 18.

More usual was the provision of juvenile books as part of the lending library. Here again it was as a rule only the older children who benefited, since the majority of libraries had a minimum age limit, commonly 14 in the lending library, but occasionally 12 or 13.[6] A few libraries, however, made a special effort to cater for younger readers. Birmingham, from its commencement in 1861, had a juvenile section in every lending library, and in 1875 nearly a quarter of its borrowers were under 14.[7] Birkenhead created a juvenile section

[1] L.A. Conference Transactions, 1883, pp. 82–83.

[2] L.A. Conference Transactions, 1878, pp. 44–50. Reprinted in part in J. L. Thornton, Selected Readings in the History of Librarianship (1966), pp. 179–182.

[3] P. Cowell, Liverpool Public Libraries: a History of Fifty Years (Liverpool 1903), p. 47.

[4] See above, pp. 43–44.

[5] See above, pp. 59–60.

[6] For details see the table in L.A. Conference Transactions, 1879, opp. p. 138 (col. 22); and for discussion of the principle Conference Transactions, 1877, pp. 169–171.

[7] Notes on the History of the Birmingham Public Libraries, 1861–1961 (Birmingham 1962), p. 17; P.R. 1876, p. 7. Cf. below, p. 84.

in 1865, Wigan and Plymouth by 1879, and Newcastle upon Tyne in 1880.[1] In 1880–81 Birkenhead went further and made a separate children's library, which seems to have had its own room, and in the following year was provided with its own catalogue, priced at 1d.[2]

The best documented early example, however, was at Cambridge, where a separate juvenile branch was opened (within the main library), in 1872. It was established on the personal initiative of the Librarian, John Pink, and the committee agreed only on the understanding that it should be maintained entirely by voluntary contributions. It had its own rules and its own catalogue, and was open daily (except Sundays) from 11 a.m. to 2 p.m., and from 6 to 9 p.m. In a letter to the *Cambridge Independent Press*, Pink appealed to parents who could afford to buy books for their children not to use it. After eight years' experience it was incorporated in 1879–80 with the main lending library.[3]

In spite of these earlier precedents, it was Nottingham that was regarded as the pioneer in children's libraries. The Library for Boys and Girls in Shakespeare Street was opened in 1882, and was the result of a gift of £500 from Samuel Morley, the millionaire hosiery manufacturer and philanthropist, who afterwards gave his name to Morley College. Morley noted that "everywhere in our large towns the working classes are deluged and poisoned with cheap, noxious fiction of the most objectionable kind", and he thought it important that wholesome literature should be supplied to children too young to be admitted to the main library.[4] A paper on the subject given by J. Potter Briscoe, Librarian of Nottingham, to the Library Association Conference at Plymouth in 1885, encouraged other librarians to follow suit.

The paper is devoted mainly to considering the principles that should govern the organization of children's libraries. Such a library, Briscoe thought, should be in a room by itself, so that children did not have to mix with adults, "often to the inconvenience of both." Preferably it should be in the same building as the adult library, though Nottingham had been obliged to use a separate building. There should be shelving for two or three thousand volumes, and everything should be done to make the room as attractive as possible. Coloured illustrations from *The Graphic* and other similar papers should adorn the walls, and be changed from time to time.

The books should be carefully selected to suit the varying ages of the borrowers—at Nottingham from seven to fourteen. There should be plenty of variety; books should be morally sound but not goody-goody; they should be attractively written, printed and illustrated; and they should not be in very small type. School books should be excluded. The classification should be on the same system as that used for the adult library, but the emphasis would be different: about fifty per cent stories, ten per cent magazines and annuals, and the rest mainly history, biography, travels, and popular science, with a little poetry and fine arts. A cheap and simple author catalogue should be prepared

[1] *L.A. Conference Transactions, 1879*, pp. 40, 98; Greenwood (1890), pp. 121–122.

[2] *Annual Reports, 1881–82*. The former librarian, Mr. Stratton, informed me that to his personal knowledge the building in use at this time had a separate Children's Room.

[3] *Annual Reports, 1871*, p. 5; *1880*, p. 7; *Cambridge Independent Press*, letter dated 25 Jan. 1872. I am indebted for these references to Mr. E. Cave, City Librarian.

[4] *Fifty Years: a Brief History of the Public Library Movement in Nottingham* (Nottingham 1918), p. 27.

for the use of both children and parents, so that they could use it as a reading list.
    Briscoe stressed the importance of the children's librarian:

> "A person holding this position ought to have, in addition to the ordinary
> qualifications of a library assistant, a love for children, and to be accustomed to
> their management. Ex-pupil teachers of both sexes are admirably adapted for this
> position."

The expense, he concluded, need not be great: the Nottingham children's
library, with nearly 3000 books, had cost about £300 to establish and annual
upkeep was about £100 per annum, including £26 for the salary of the young
lady assistant who took charge.[1]

To us at the present day these ideas seem commonplace enough: in the
'eighties they were enlightened and forward-looking.

As we have mentioned above, Leeds in 1883 made a quite new approach to
this question by the provision of children's libraries (initially of 1000 volumes
each) in schools. This scheme, an interesting anticipation of more modern
developments, seems to have been within its limits very successful, and continued until nearly the end of the century.[2]

The provision of books for the blind seems to have begun at Liverpool in
1857, on the initiative of R. W. Roulston, Superintendent of the Lending
Libraries.[3] Manchester followed suit in 1863.[4] The books in use at this period
were in the Moon type, based on embossed letters: the widespread use of the
now familiar Braille type, based on a system of dots, came only later, as a result
of the advocacy of the British and Foreign Blind Association, founded in 1868.
Other libraries shown in the Returns of 1876-77 as possessing books for the
blind are Rochdale, Tynemouth, Birmingham, Cardiff, and Newport, Mon.
The largest number was at Liverpool (342), the smallest at Newport (17). In
every case the books were available on loan, though in Manchester they are also
included in the reference figures.[5]

Roulston was also the pioneer of the lending of music, introduced in
Liverpool in 1859.[6] Music stocks are not recorded in the Returns of 1876-77,
but we know from other sources that Manchester made similar provision, and
had by 1877 a liberal selection of music on loan.[7] A more surprising instance is
the library at Handsworth (now part of Birmingham), which was opened in
1880 and began a music department two years later.[8] The music library at
Nottingham, which was afterwards to attain considerable proportions, was in
1886 still embryonic.[9]

---

[1] J. P. Briscoe, "Libraries for the Young", in *Library Chronicle*, Vol. III (1886), pp. 45-48.
[2] See above, p. 50-51.
[3] P. Cowell, *Liverpool Public Libraries: a History of Fifty Years* (Liverpool 1903), p. 52.
[4] E. Edwards, *Free Town Libraries* (1869), p. 95; Greenwood (1890), p. 114.
[5] *P.R. 1876*, pp. 48, 52. The same number of volumes for the blind (142) is shown in both
    cases: the presumption is that they were the same books. Nottingham does not figure in
    these returns, but had over 200 volumes by 1886—information from Mr. D. E. Gerard,
    City Librarian.
[6] Cowell, *loc. cit.*
[7] W. E. A. Axon, *Handbook of the Public Libraries of Manchester and Salford* (Manchester
    1877), p. 114.
[8] Greenwood (1890), p. 162.
[9] The Catalogue of 1885 shows 58 volumes only. See below, p. 190.

Newsrooms were so important a part of library provision that they deserve a word here, even though as a rule the only books they contained were bound volumes of periodicals, which had to be asked for over the counter. In spite of the abolition of the newspaper tax in 1855, newspapers were still 1d. or 2d., which in those days was dear for the working man; the halfpenny press began only in 1896. This is not, however, the sole explanation of the enormous popularity of the newsroom, which continued well into the twentieth century: it is only in our own time that it has ceased to be a major element in the library service.

The larger libraries made very extensive provision at this period, including some foreign newspapers and periodicals and a wide range of professional journals. Even a medium-sized library such as Newcastle upon Tyne was providing, in 1886, 30 weekly or bi-weekly papers, 67 weeklies and fortnightlies, 72 monthlies, and 14 quarterlies, besides 3 colonial papers. All libraries seem to have relied a good deal on gifts, either from the publishers or from readers. Many of the professional journals especially were acquired in this way, and so were many periodicals of a propagandist character (health and temperance magazines, for example) which were evidently thought by librarians, or their committees, to be desirable reading. More than one-third of the items listed at Newcastle were presented.[1]

Lists of periodicals available in newsrooms and reading rooms are a regular feature of library annual reports, and make interesting reading. They are too long, unfortunately, to reproduce here, but we can catch something of their flavour from the list published in 1880 at Leicester (quite a small library at that time). The newspapers taken include all the principal London dailies (*Times, Daily News, Telegraph*, etc.), a selection of provincial papers (Birmingham, Dublin, Liverpool, Leeds, Manchester, Edinburgh), and a considerable number of local papers, together with oddments such as the *Brighton Herald* (presented). Periodicals of general interest include many familiar names (*All the Year Round, Argosy, Blackwood's Magazine, Chambers's Journal, Cornhill Magazine, Edinburgh Review, Fortnightly Review, Good Words, Graphic, Illustrated London News, Punch*, etc.). Periodicals presented include many professional journals (*Accountant, Architect, Boot and Shoe Maker, Building World, Furniture Gazette, Insurance Agent*, etc.), and also the *Atlantic News* and the *Watchword* (temperance journals), the *Dietetic Reformer*, and (on the ladies' table), the *Women's Suffrage Journal*.[2] The presence of this last item is intriguing, as just at this time women's suffrage was the subject of acute controversy.

Readers

There was, as we have seen, a general consensus of opinion that public libraries were primarily for the working classes. Librarians, however, were constantly proclaiming that they were (and ought to be) used by all classes of society. The truth of these statements can easily be tested from the actual records of the occupations of library users, which survive in vast quantities and formidable detail in parliamentary returns and library annual reports. No one,

[1] *Annual Report, 1886*, pp. 26–27.
[2] *Annual Report, 1880*, pp. 12–13.

as far as I know, has attempted to make use of this material, which though daunting is full of human interest.

For a serious examination of the subject the most convenient source is to be found in the Parliamentary Returns for 1876 and 1877, which give occupational analyses for the lending departments, and sometimes the reference departments, of 37 libraries. Unfortunately, each library was left to devise its own classification, so that the tables do not easily lend themselves to statistical comparisons. None the less much can be learnt.

A sample of consecutive entries from some of the longer lists reveals at once the great variety of readers' occupations and the great numerical predominance of the working class. Here are examples from five such lists, covering the lending departments of two large libraries and three smaller ones. It should be noted that the total number of readers recorded is no indication of comparative use, being dependent on the period for which readers' tickets were valid.

Birmingham (total 7499):[1]

Bakers and confectioners	44	Bookbinders	35
Bagmakers	2	Booksellers & stationers	16
Bandmaker	1	Boot & shoe trade	65
Barmaids, etc.	10	Bottler	1
Basketmakers	6	Box & casemakers	16
Bedsteadmakers	22	Bracemakers	4
Bellhangers	4	Brass trade, etc.	159
Bellowsmakers	6	Bricklayers	18
Billposter	1	Brushmakers	32
Billiardmarkers	4	Builders	20
Birdcagemakers	4	Burnishers, polishers, etc.	70
Blacksmiths	15	Butchers	14
Blindmakers	5	Buttonmakers	27
Boatbuilder	1		

Manchester (total 33 026):[2]

Labourers	216	Lecturers	3
Lacecutters	5	Lettercutter	1
Lamplighters	13	Letter sorters	4
Lampmakers	2	Librarians	6
Lathmakers	5	Linguists	9
Laundress	1	Livery dealer	1
Leatherdressers	13	Looking-glass makers	5

Heywood (total 15 037):[3]

Sawyers	2	Smiths	2
Scholars, boys and girls	80	Stonemasons	6
Schoolmasters	11	Surgeons	5
Schoolmistresses	15	Surveyors	2

Newport, Mon. (total 1188):[4]

Captains (master mariners)	2	Clerks, junior	33
Carpenters and joiners	21	Coachbuilders	3
Clerks	107	Compositors	18

---

[1] *P.R. 1876*, p. 8.   [2] *Op. cit.*, p. 50.   [3] *Op. cit.*, p. 38.   [4] *Op. cit.*, p. 57.

IIIa. BIRKENHEAD CENTRAL LIBRARY

A pleasing building in the Georgian style, designed by Messrs. Gray, Evans and Crossley. Opened in 1934, it replaced an earlier Carnegie library which after a brief existence had been demolished to make way for the entrance to the first Mersey Tunnel. The new building was notable for its spacious lending library.

IIIb. MANCHESTER CENTRAL LIBRARY

The best known of all the inter-war library buildings, opened like the Birkenhead library in 1934. It was designed by E. Vincent Harris, its principal interior feature being the great circular reference library at first floor level, surmounting and supported by a central core of bookstacks rising from basement level.

IVa. CHORLTON-CUM-HARDY BRANCH, MANCHESTER
A typical Carnegie branch library, designed by Henry Price and opened in 1914.

IVb. SOUTHFIELDS BRANCH, LEICESTER
A branch library in a more modern idiom, designed by Messrs. Symington, Prince and Pike and opened in 1939. Its central feature is the lofty circular lending library.

Paisley (total 3310):[1]

Tailors	42	Tobacconists	4
Tanners	3	Tobacco spinners	5
Teachers	41	Toll-keepers	1
Thatchers	1	Town chamberlain	1
Thread manufacturers	3	Town clerk	1
Thread workers	36	Town's officers	2
Tinsmiths	11	Twisters	3

Everywhere the picture is much the same. Everywhere labourers, artisans, clerks, and shop assistants, i.e. the working and lower middle classes, are recorded in considerable numbers and infinite variety; but everywhere there is at least a sprinkling, and often substantially more than a sprinkling, of readers from the higher classes. The Manchester lending library list which has been quoted, for example includes, in its total of 33 026 readers, 86 accountants, 111 architects, 2 authors, 1 banker, 2 barristers, 139 clergymen, 4 editors, 40 gentlemen, 3 lecturers, 6 librarians, 56 medical men, 39 military men, 35 missionaries, 2 professors, 1 publisher, 108 schoolmasters, 20 schoolmistresses, and 18 solicitors. In all, these amount to about 2 per cent of the total, but there are no doubt others whose status is less readily identifiable. Leeds returns for its lending library 81 per cent working class, 19 per cent professional and middle class.[2]

Occupation lists for the reference department, where given, are similar. Blackburn, which gives no list for this department, comments interestingly that the readers are "All classes, but principally the industrial working men as readers; others, for research and reference".[3] At Leeds manufacturers, merchants and professional men accounted for 15 per cent of reference library users.[4]

When we consider evidence of this kind it is easy to see how public opinion could be firmly convinced that the libraries were working-class institutions, while the libraries claimed with equal conviction that they were frequented by all classes of society. As John Pink, the Cambridge Librarian, romantically put it in 1883: "In the Free Library may be seen sitting side by side the M.A. and the mechanic, the Undergraduate and the Schoolboy, men in broadcloth and boys in fustian."[5] Both sides were right. Bearing in mind the numerical preponderance of the working classes, the extent of use by other classes is surprisingly high, but the majority of users were unquestionably drawn from the working classes. In particular it is plain that public libraries, just because they were free, were much more successful than the old mechanics' institutes had been in attracting the lower ranks of the workers.

This conclusion can be illustrated from the fact that in the industrial centres library use varied according to the state of trade. We have seen this at Manchester and Bolton, where the Cotton Famine brought a boom in library use, and full employment a slump.

The Report of the Birkenhead Library for the years 1882–86 tells the same story:

"Satisfactory as these figures may seem . . . . the Committee regret that much of this extended use is without doubt due to the stagnation and depression

[1] *Op. cit.*, p. 91. [2] *P.R. 1876*, p. 43. [3] *P.R. 1877*, p. 5.
[4] *P.R. 1876*, p. 44. I have excluded 53 "females" of unstated occupation.
[5] *L.A. Conference Transactions, 1882*, p. 241.

of the town and neighbourhood."[1] Credland, at Manchester, summed the matter up succinctly; "when work is good attendance at the library slackens, when bad it increases."[2]

Only a minority of libraries in the Returns of 1876 and 1877 give specific information about the age and sex of their readers, but those that do confirm the impression given by library annual reports throughout this period that young men and boys made up a substantial proportion of library users. The number of young readers was astonishing, especially where, as at Birmingham, the library had a juvenile section:

Birmingham (Lending):	Under 14, 23%; 14–20, 40%; 21–25, 13%
(Reference):	14–20, 32%; 21–25, 18%
Blackburn (Lending):	14–20, 45%; 20–25, 17%
South Shields (Lending):	14–20; 35%; 21–30, 27%
(Reference):	16–20, 34%; 21–30, 24%[3]

A random sample from other libraries and other years shows that these figures are very representative, and that it was common at this period for readers under 21 to account for between thirty and forty per cent of the total.

The public libraries were still very much under male domination. The staff were almost invariably male,[4] and so were most of the readers. None the less in many libraries, and especially in many lending libraries, women and girls already formed a quite substantial minority: 15 per cent at Bolton, 17 per cent at Bradford, 22 per cent at Leeds, 29 per cent at Newport, Mon.[5] In other libraries included in the 1876–77 returns, though the total number of female readers is not given, a similar position is revealed by the presence in the occupational returns of "wives and daughters" or "unoccupied females"—the useful term "housewives" had not, it seems, come into use.

In the reference departments female readers seem to have been less numerous. At South Shields they accounted for 25 per cent of the total in the lending section, but only 7 per cent in the reference section;[6] and at Dundee, where a combined figure of 15 per cent is given for both departments, the annual report for 1875, on which the figures are based, shows that nearly all the female readers were in the lending department.[7] It should, however, be borne in mind that periodicals used in the reading rooms did not normally figure in the statistical returns, and the existence in so many libraries of ladies' reading rooms bears witness to the popularity of this kind of reading.

Fact or Fiction?

In considering what books people actually read, we have to bear in mind that reading was to a large extent conditioned by what happened to be available. This is amusingly illustrated by the case of Stockport, where the Library Committee was alarmed to find that fiction constituted 73 per cent of the issues in the first year (1875–76), rising to 80 per cent by the third year. In 1878 the

[1] *Report, 1882–86*, p. 4.
[2] W. R. Credland, *The Manchester Public Free Library* (Manchester 1899), p. 100.
[3] *P.R. 1876*, pp. 7, 9, 70–71; *P.R. 1877*, p. 4.   [4] See below, p. 103.
[5] *P.R. 1876*, pp. 12, 14–15, 43, 57.   [6] *P.R. 1876*, pp. 70–71.
[7] *Op. cit.*, pp. 88; cf. *Annual Report, 1875*, pp. 12–13.

Committee therefore determined to provide "literature of a more substantial character for the future"; and in the next two annual reports (1879–80) they were able to congratulate themselves on the fact that "the reading of fiction is on the decline."[1] The same process is found operating in the reverse direction at Liverpool.[2]

Nevertheless the information available from library reports and other sources is comprehensive enough to enable us to speak with some confidence of reading tastes at this period. The two examples just cited illustrate the fact that the main demand then, as now, was for fiction. This stands out very clearly from the Returns of 1876 and 1877. In a sample of thirteen lending libraries, including all the larger libraries and a selection of smaller ones, there were only two in which the fiction issues formed less than 50 per cent of total loans. These were Sheffield (30 per cent) and Manchester (48 per cent). In the remainder the range was between 57 per cent at Birmingham and 83 per cent at Bradford and Salford. A similar sample compiled in 1883 shows a range between 55 per cent at Plymouth and 78 per cent at Nottingham: in this list Manchester has risen to 57 per cent and Sheffield to 63 per cent.[3]

It is indeed clear that in lending libraries everywhere, throughout the period, fiction was overwhelmingly the first choice. The second place was disputed between, on the one hand, History, Biography and Travel and, on the other, what was often classified as "Miscellaneous Literature"—a heading which commonly included periodicals. Arts and Sciences frequently occupied the fourth place. This order of priorities is remarkably uniform in the 1876–77 Returns, but where there was a strong juvenile section, as at Leeds, Birmingham, and Cambridge, Juvenile Books took third place.

In reference libraries it was not usually the policy to provide a large amount of fiction, and here pride of place in the issues generally went to Miscellaneous Literature (including periodicals), while History, Biography and Travel disputed the second place with Arts and Sciences. Only at Liverpool did fiction top the list, with 37 per cent of reference issues; but at Bolton Illustrated Literature (an unusual category) came first, Fiction second, and History, Biography and Travel third.

The unchallengeable predominance of fiction was most disturbing to Library Committees, which could not reconcile themselves to the fact that working people (and middle-class people, too) desired to be entertained after the day's labours rather than instructed. Such a situation seemed to be a negation of the educational purpose for which libraries had been founded. We have noted above the concern felt on this subject in the early years of the Manchester and Salford libraries,[4] and we have seen that Liverpool was disposed to defend a liberal provision of fiction on the ground that any kind of reading was better than none, and that the reading of fiction might lead on to better things.

By 1869 Edward Edwards, though still unhappy about the Liverpool situation, was prepared to concede that "those who begin with the less nutritive sort of mental food will, not infrequently, acquire by-and-bye an appetite for

[1] R. E. G. Smith, *The First Fifty Years of Public Libraries in Stockport* (unpublished F.L.A. essay 1950), p. 79.
[2] See above, pp. 44–45. [3] *L.A. Conference Transactions, 1883*, pp. 65–66.
[4] See above, pp. 42, 51–52.

the more substantial and wholesome kinds."[1] The Manchester Library Committee, by that time, was justifying a generous provision of light literature on the grounds that it had a duty as a public body to meet all proper public demands.[2] Eight years later, however, at the first Conference of Librarians, no less a person than Peter Cowell, Librarian of Liverpool, was casting doubt on what may be called the "improvement theory". Such improvement as he had observed, he commented sadly, was "microscopic."[3]

As increasing emphasis came to be placed on the educational function of the libraries, the pangs of conscience in this matter became more acute, and a considerable controversy arose which continued well into the present century, and of which indeed the echoes have still not entirely died down. It would be possible to quote endlessly (and entertainingly) from the literature on the subject but, for the present, one representative from each side must suffice. J. Taylor Kay, Librarian of Owens College, Manchester, was one of those who thought that in no circumstances was a public institution justified in making free provision of novels. He declared in 1878:

> "For many years a remarkable fact has been before my notice, and continually confirmed by a long experience in the Manchester Free libraries, that school-boys or students who took to novel-reading to any extent never made much progress in after life. . . .
>
> "Novel-reading has become a disease, a dissipation; and this dissipation, most librarians of circulating libraries will allow from their experience, is as enchanting and quite as hard to be rid of as other dissipations, and quite as weakening mentally."[4]

On the other hand we have John Lovell, of the *Liverpool Mercury*, not only arguing, as had been argued at Manchester earlier, that "it is no part of the function of the Managers of Free Libraries to decide what kinds of literature the public shall or shall not read," but also defending the novel in its own right:

> "Thus we may learn that though a work of fiction may be fictitious in form, though its sequences and its circumstantialities may be pure inventions, it may nevertheless be most veracious in its substance. It may enlarge the reader's knowledge, supply him with food for thought, furnish him with rules of conduct, help to form his character, and give him a wider and more intelligent outlook upon life than he ever had before."[5]

The preparation of lists showing the order of popularity of particular books seems to have been a favourite occupation of librarians at this period. A few examples only can be cited. The second Annual Report of the Liverpool Library Committee (1853–54) emphasises the high seriousness of some working-class readers:

> "A labouring man in the north district has read since the library opened, Gibbon's 'Rome', 'Universal History,' Macaulay's 'England,' and is now going through Lingard, as he says he wishes to know both sides of the question. Another in the same district has read Macaulay, the 'Universal History,' and is now reading Alison. At the south, two working men have read Moore's and Scott's 'Poetical

---

[1] E. Edwards, *Free Town Libraries* (1869), p. 46; cf. pp. 78–91.
[2] *Op. cit.*, p. 143. [3] *Conference Transactions, 1877*, p. 62.
[4] *L.A. Conference Transactions, 1878*, pp. 43, 45.
[5] *L.A. Conference Transactions, 1883*, p. 61.

Works,' and one Byron. Another has read Rollin's 'Ancient History', and is at present going through Alison; while a poor man at the extremity of Toxteth Park has, ever since the library opened, been reading the *Mirror*, he has now reached the 33rd volume."[1]

At Wolverhampton, in 1875, the books most frequently called for in the reference library were (with the number of issues):

Art Journal volumes	254	Shaw's *History of Staffordshire*	30
Dictionaries	63	Ure's *Dictionary of Arts, Science*	
Illustrated London News (1851)	61	*and Manufacture*	26
Cassell's Popular Educator	57	Gillray's *Works*	24
Encyclopaedia Britannica	49	*English Mechanic*	22
Phonetic Journal volumes	49	Richardson's *Ornamental*	
Pictorial Gallery of Art	36	*Designs*	21
Wolverhampton Chronicle	33	Maunder's *Treasury of Science,*	
Times volumes	31	*Natural History*	21
Owen Jones, *Grammar of*		Chambers's *Encyclopaedia*	20
Ornament	30	Knight's *Old England*	20[2]

Turning to the end of the period, we have in the Annual Report for Portsmouth in 1887 an interesting study of books read during the previous year by readers of various occupations. We can select only four:

A Civil Engineer
Fortunes made in Business, 2 vols.
Draper's *Intellectual Development of Europe*, 2 vols.
Ganot's *Physics*
Sport in Many Lands
Life of Henry Fawcett
Spiritual Wives, by Dixon
Wonders in Living Nature
United, a Novel, by Sinnett
A Look round Literature
Army Society, by Winter
The whole of Rider Haggard's *Works*
Animal Anecdotes, by Page

A Schoolmaster
Sweet Sleep and how to Promote it
A Diary of Two Parliaments, by Lucy
History of Crime in England, 2 vols.
Biographical Essays
Wonderful Characters
Froude, *Short Studies on Great Subjects*, 3 vols.
By Celia's Arbour
Golden Butterfly
Ready Money Mortiboy
She and *Dawn*, by Haggard
Society in London
Essays from the Spectator
For Cash Only
Mirk Abbey
History of English Literature, 4 vols. by Taine

A Labourer
Green's *Short History of the English People*
Greenwood's *Little Ragamuffins*
The Graphic and *Illustrated London News*
Dombey and Son
Old Curiosity Shop
Tale of Two Cities

A Domestic Servant
East Lynne, by Wood
The History and Life of Bishop Hannington
Lady Audley's Secret
Look before you Leap, by Alexander
Canadian Pictures, by Marquis of Lorne
Girl of the Period, by Linton
She, by Haggard

[1] P. Cowell, *Liverpool Public Libraries* (1903), p. 50.
[2] *P.R. 1876*, p. 85. Cf. pp. 79, 81, for similar lists for South Shields.

All Sorts and Conditions of Men	*Dishes and Drinks, or Philosophy in*
By Celia's Arbour	*the Kitchen*
Ireland, its Scenery, Character, etc.,	*Life of Harriet Martineau*
3 vols.	*Mill on the Floss*
Tales from Blackwood	*Her World against a Lie,*
Reminiscences of Abraham Lincoln	by Marryat[1]
Harry Richmond, by Meredith	

Mutatis mutandis, the selections are not so very different from what we would expect of similar readers to-day.

Library Administration

Many of the details of library routine at this period are of no particular interest or significance, but it is worth while drawing attention to a number of features which differed from modern practice.

One such feature, which owed much to the idealism of Edward Edwards, was the inordinate amount of time devoted to the keeping of records. This was partly because the records themselves were more elaborate than is considered necessary nowadays, and partly because the methods of keeping them were so cumbersome. The first point is illustrated by the kind of information that was asked for, and in most cases supplied, in the Parliamentary Returns of 1876 and 1877. This included tables showing, separately for the reference and lending libraries:

> The number of volumes in the library under each subject heading
> The number of volumes issued under each subject heading during the previous year
> The number of borrowers, classified under occupations
> The number of volumes issued to each occupational group during the previous year.

In addition librarians were called upon to calculate, for example, the "average number of times that each volume in each class has been issued during the year," and the "percentage of the total issues of each class of books to the total number of volumes issued during the year." Some librarians, as we have seen, even went beyond their brief and supplied a breakdown of library users by age and sex, or details regarding the issues of particular books, and this kind of information regularly figures in annual reports.

All these records, it must be remembered, had to be kept by hand, without the help of typewriters or other modern contrivances. The cumbersome nature of the procedure involved is shown by a consideration of the Issue Register used at the Hulme Branch Lending Library, Manchester, in the year 1858. The issue of a book at a lending library is now a simple matter, which usually involves stamping a date in the book and filing the book ticket along with the reader's ticket. In those days each loan involved the entry on the day's list of issues of the following particulars: No. of daily issue; Title of book; No. of vol.; Catalogue class and no.; Days allowed for perusal; Date of return; Name of borrower; No. of borrower's card; and in case the librarian had time to spare there was a final column for Remarks.[2]

---

[1] Portsmouth Public Library, *Annual Report*, 1887, pp. 12–13.
[2] E. Edwards, *Memoirs of Libraries* (1859), Vol. II, p. 1057.

How the libraries, ill staffed as they were, coped with all this drudgery is difficult to understand, but this "ledger system" persisted a long time, in many cases till the end of the century. At Birmingham it lasted, in a somewhat simplified form, till 1902, and is thus described by A. C. Shaw, the Librarian:

> "Until last June the system of issue in all the lending libraries was the old ledger system. This involved keeping a register in which the numbers of both the book and the borrower's ticket were entered at the time of issue, marking off the books when returned, and keeping a Posting Book, in which the date of issue was posted to the work issued."[1]

The substitution of cards for ledgers began at least as early as the 1870s, but made its way only slowly. The system familiar in modern lending libraries, in which the issue of a book is recorded by transferring a card from a pocket in the book to a pocket in the borrower's ticket, and filing the ticket under the appropriate date, was invented by Mr. C. G. Virgo, Librarian of Bradford, in 1873.[2]

Another distinguishing feature of libraries of this period arose from the conviction, already referred to, that the reader should not have direct access to the books except perhaps for a few works of common reference such as dictionaries and directories. As late as 1891 James Duff Brown, who was afterwards to be a recognised authority on library management, and who was shortly to be pioneer of the modern "open access" system in his own library in Clerkenwell, was proclaiming the "vital necessity to have the books cut off from personal contact with readers."[3]

The most notable exception to the general rule at this time was Cambridge, which as early as 1870 had begun to make standard works of reference available on open access in the reading room, and had a collection of over 1000 volumes available by 1882.[4] A successful though more limited experiment by Wigan from 1878 onwards does not seem to have been so generally known.[5] The idea was discussed with much misgiving at early meetings of librarians,[6] and Brown thought the success of Cambridge could be attributed only to some special virtue on the part of the Cambridge readers.[7]

Under the system commonly in use, which is often referred to as "closed access" but could more properly be termed "indirect access", the reader could secure a book only by looking it up in a catalogue and asking for it over the counter. This system, of course, is still in use in reference libraries except for those books which are on open shelves, but at this period it was universally applied in lending libraries also. In some it survived until quite recently, and

---

[1] A. C. Shaw, "The Birmingham Free Libraries," in *L.A.R.*, Vol. IV (1902), p. 513.

[2] J. D. Brown, *Manual of Library Economy* (1903), p. 395.

[3] Greenwood (1891), p. 390.

[4] *P.R. 1870*, p. 7; *P.R. 1876*, p. 23; *L.A. Conference Transactions, 1882*, p. 241.

[5] Greenwood (1890), p. 141. In a few other libraries an open access system was used in the very early days, before they were fully organized. This was the case, for example, at Sheffield's Upperthorpe Branch when Greenwood worked there in the 'seventies—G. Carlton, *Spade-Work: the Story of Thomas Greenwood* (1949), p. 31.

[6] See especially *Conference Transactions, 1877*, pp. 172–174.

[7] Greenwood (1891), p. 391. No one seems to have appreciated that the Patent Office Library (a national rather than a local library, but none the less open to the public) was on the open access system from its commencement in 1855. See below, p. 317.

many older readers will remember how it operated: first the search through the rather grubby printed catalogue, then the request for book after book until at length one of the books asked for proved to be available. It was a process frustrating to the readers, and exhausting to the library assistants who had to run backwards and forwards between the counter and the stacks. In the days we are now talking of, they frequently had to climb ladders as well. Not surprisingly, therefore, readers were usually required to submit a list of ten or a dozen alternatives.

It was to save the time of both reader and assistant that there was invented a piece of apparatus known as the "indicator", the purpose of which was to show at a glance whether the desired book was in or out. There were several different types of indicator, but in each case the basic structure was the same—a wooden frame fitted with rows of small slots or pigeon-holes each of which represented a book. The frame was erected at the edge of the lending counter nearest to the borrower, the pigeon-holes being protected by glass at the front, but accessible to the library staff from the back.[1]

From an early stage very simple indicators were devised in some libraries for the use of the staff. Manchester and Birmingham, for example, used an indicator board bearing the numbers of the books, with a reversible peg attached to each number. The first indicator for the use of the public was invented by Charles Dyall, Branch Librarian at Hulme, Manchester, in 1863. On this indicator each slot carried a moveable wooden block bearing the number of the book at front and back. When a book was taken out, the appropriate block was moved to one side so that the number was obscured.

More widely used was the Elliot indicator, which was invented in 1870 by John Elliot, librarian of Wolverhampton, and incorporated the results of earlier experiments at Aston Manor and Birmingham. It provided, in a frame three feet square, slots for 1000 books in ten vertical columns of 100 each. The number of the book was shown on the wooden upright beside each slot; when a book was taken out its number and the date were entered on the borrower's card and the card was deposited in the slot. John Kennedy, a member of the library committee at Dundee, devised a modified and more compact version in 1875, and a very similar model, by W. Morgan of the Birmingham Central Library, was patented and produced commercially as the Morgan Indicator in the following year.[2] Some librarians thought the compactness of this type of indicator a disadvantage when the library was crowded with would-be borrowers.

Most popular of all was the Cotgreave Indicator, designed in 1877 by Alfred Cotgreave, then in his first senior post as Librarian of Wednesbury.[3] It was somewhat more economical of space than the Elliot Indicator (4000 volumes in a width of 5 feet), but the main difference was that each slot held a

---

[1] For the details that follow see J. Yates, "Indicators", in *L.A. Conference Transactions, 1878*, pp. 76–78, and the discussion at pp. 132–133; A. Cotgreave, "An Indicator Book," in *Transactions, 1879*, pp. 71–72; "Report of the Indicator Committee", in *Transactions, 1880*, pp. 10–11; and J. D. Brown, *Manual of Library Economy* (1903), pp. 160–176.

[2] Kennedy was very indignant about this alleged piracy of an invention which he had deliberately refrained from patenting—Dundee, *Annual Report, 1878*, p. 6.

[3] He was afterwards librarian successively at Richmond, Wandsworth, Guille-Allès (Guernsey), and finally (1891) at West Ham.

small metal case containing a miniature ledger or "indicator-book", one inch wide by three inches long, ruled with columns for the recording of issues. The number of the book was shown at both ends of the metal case, usually in blue at one end and red at the other. When the book was in, the blue end was shown; when it was taken out, the borrower's name and/or number and the date of issue were marked in the ledger, and the case reversed to show the red end. "Blue in, red out" was the familiar rule.

As time went on, these indicators were elaborated and improved in various ways, for example by the use of coloured slides to show the week of issue and thus identify overdue volumes, and some librarians found it possible to dispense with any other record of issues than that provided by the indicator.[1] An Indicator Committee appointed by the Library Association in 1879, however, thought it was safer to use a simple indicator in conjunction with the normal entry in a ledger or on cards.

By 1886 indicators of one kind or another were becoming fairly common, though by no means universal. Their use was restricted to lending libraries, and sometimes to fiction only. Sometimes a "Key to the Indicator" was provided in the form of a list of indicator numbers with titles attached, so that the reader could first find out from the indicator which numbers were available, and then from the key which books they represented. The great advantage of indicators was that they enabled readers to be served in about one-third of the time previously taken. Their great disadvantage was the amount of space they required, which ruled out their use in the largest libraries. Darlington, opening its library in 1885, was equipped with 55 feet of indicators to provide for 24000 volumes.[2] It was this difficulty which eventually led to their discontinuance, independently of the introduction of open access.

One of the features of the indirect access system was that it was impossible for a reader to use the library without consulting the catalogue. Until almost the close of this period this was invariably a printed catalogue, and the preparation and revision of the catalogue was one of the librarian's constant preoccupations. It is not surprising to find, therefore, that the problem of what kind of catalogue to produce, and the associated problem of what kind of classification to use, occupied a very large part of the proceedings at the first conference of librarians in 1877, and remained a matter of controversy until the Dewey system came into general use.

The systems of classification used at this time were generally, as will have been gathered, very simple, being based on broad subject-divisions, and the main differences between one system and another lay in the extent of the subject-breakdown. If we look once more at the Returns for 1876 and 1877 a striking feature is the apparent contrast between Manchester and Liverpool—the earliest of the major civic libraries. Manchester uses the minimum number of headings:

Theology and Philosophy	Science and Arts
History, Travels, etc.	Literature and Polygraphy
Politics and Commerce	Fiction[3]

[1] Some of the main types are illustrated in A. Cotgreave, *Library Indicators* (1902).

[2] Greenwood (1890), p. 98.

[3] *P.R. 1876*, p. 9. I have omitted special headings for patent specifications and books for the blind, which are outside the usual run of classification.

Liverpool preferred a more elaborate system:

Theology, Morals, etc.	Jurisprudence, Law and Politics
Natural Philosophy, Astronomy, etc.	Commerce, Political Economy and
Science and the Arts	Statistics
History and Biography	Education and Language
Topography and Antiquities	Poetry and Dramatic Literature
Voyages and Travels	Prose Fiction
Miscellaneous Literature	Latin and Greek Classics and Translations
(principally collected works,	Heraldry, Encyclopaedias, and
magazines, etc.)	Works of Reference[1]

This contrast is, however, misleading. Edward Edwards was always particularly interested in classification, and the scheme he worked out for Manchester, which continued in use till the end of the century, was a very detailed one, of which the headings given in the 1876 Return represent merely the main categories. Its character may be judged from his published plan for the classification of a town library, in which History alone has 78 headings and sub-headings. This plan, incidentally, also includes the little used term "polygraphy", covering works such as encyclopaedias which extended over more than one subject category.[2]

The returns from other libraries nearly all follow broadly either the Manchester plan, with about half-a-dozen main headings, or the Liverpool plan, with some twelve to sixteen headings. Some of the libraries which used the Manchester scheme also adopted some of Edward's sub-classes and sub-headings, but none, it appears, in such detail.[3] The smaller libraries, we may be sure, whichever system they employed, limited themselves to main headings only. One small library, Hertford, had no subject classification at all, ordering its thousand volumes entirely by number: under this arrangement, the Town Clerk reported, "the management is much more simple, and books can be added to the existing catalogue with much greater facility than if the volumes were classified."[4]

It is interesting to observe that nearly all the classifications begin with theology. This represents a very ancient tradition, going back to the libraries of the mediaeval monasteries,[5] and indeed in many ways the public libraries, both in their classification and in their cataloguing, were merely continuing a system which had been handed down to them through the subscription libraries and the libraries of mechanics' institutes and similar bodies.

It should be added that the Dewey decimal system, which is now the standard public library classification, and of which more will be said later, was

---

[1] P.R. 1877, p. 9. Both this list and the Manchester one are for the reference library, but the lending library classification was not essentially different. Both lists follow closely the original classification of 1852, as shown in Liverpool's first Catalogue (1852) and Manchester's first Annual Report (1853), p. 27.

[2] E. Edwards, Memoirs of Libraries (1859), Vol. II, pp. 815–831; J. D. Brown, Manual of Library Classification (1898), pp. 51–52; information from Mr. S. Horrocks, formerly of the Manchester City Library.

[3] J. D. Brown, loc. cit.

[4] P.R. 1876, p. 37.

[5] T. Kelly, Early Public Libraries (1966), pp. 16–17.

known in England before the end of this period. It was devised by Melvil Dewey, then assistant librarian at Amherst College, during the years 1873–76, and was described by him in 1877 at the first conference of librarians in this country.[1] In the discussion it met with a certain amount of approval, but as far as I am aware the only library actually to adopt it at this time was that at Ashton under Lyne, which was opened in 1881 and published a catalogue based on the Dewey classification in 1883.[2]

Methods of shelving are seldom expressly indicated, but were usually simple. Edwards, influenced in this as in so many others matter by his British Museum experience, recommended that each book should have, in addition to its accession number, a press-mark indicating quite precisely the press (i.e. bookcase), shelf, and position on the shelf where it was located, e.g. XXI. A. 10. To allow for expansion there should be a gap in the numbering of the presses at the end of each subject-class.[3] As far as can be ascertained, however, he does not seem to have employed any such system at Manchester. Most libraries, in fact, were content to give each volume an accession number and a class number, and to shelve the books in classes in order of accession.[4]

In cataloguing, too, the average librarian found it necessary to ignore Edwards's advice, which was strongly in favour of a classified subject catalogue: the worst possible subject catalogue, he contended, was better than an author catalogue. Few early public librarians, however, had either the time or the skill for such a laborious compilation, which must be repeated at frequent intervals as new books were added; nor was it really necessary when, as was often the case, the catalogue of the entire library could be comprehended in a volume of a hundred pages or so, sold to the public at sixpence. When subject catalogues were compiled in the early years, they were usually mere class-lists, in alphabetical order of authors, following the main subject-divisions. The first reference library catalogues at Liverpool, the first lending library catalogue at Sheffield, and the first reference library catalogue at Leeds were of this kind, and so indeed, was Edwards's own first lending library catalogue at Manchester in 1854. Edwards did commence a detailed classified catalogue for the reference library, but this was never completed. Under his successor R. W. Smiles, the Library Committee abandoned the project as too slow and too costly, and called in the help of Andrea Crestadoro (afterwards Librarian) who in the astonishingly short space of two years (1862–64) produced a completely new catalogue—an author catalogue with author and subject index.

For the branch lending libraries Crestadoro invented a simpler catalogue known as an Index Catalogue, in which authors, titles and subjects were combined in a single alphabet. This was, in a rather crude form, the type of catalogue which, under the name of index or dictionary catalogue, soon became the most popular of all in English public libraries. It seems to have been first

[1] *Conference Transactions, 1877*, pp. 164–167. Dewey was by this time Editor of the *American Library Journal*.

[2] E. A. Savage, *A Librarian's Memories, Portraits, and Reflections* (1952), p. 104, gives the credit for the first public library catalogue based on Dewey to the young L. Stanley Jast at Peterborough in 1893. "The horror from Ashton-under-Lyne", he adds, "is too bad to count".

[3] E. Edwards, *Free Town Libraries* (1869), pp. 49–50.

[4] For further details see Greenwood (1890), pp. 374–375.

used at the Hulme Branch in 1867.[1] J. D. Mullins's catalogue of the Birmingham Reference Library in 1869 was a more elaborate example of the same method, which was also adopted at Liverpool in 1872, at Rochdale in 1873, and at Plymouth and Westminster in 1877.

The index catalogue of the Newcastle upon Tyne Central Lending Library, completed by W. J. Haggerston and published in 1880, was highly regarded at the time, and represents this type of catalogue in its fully developed form. It included subject entries on a generous scale, e.g. A. R. Wallace's volume on *Australasia* in Stanford's *Compendiums of Geography and Travel* was indexed under Stanford, Wallace, Geography, Ethnology, and each of the countries described. When the title of a book was not sufficiently descriptive, an indication was given of the contents; and the entries for periodicals included a list of the principal articles in each volume.

Not all index or dictionary catalogues, however, attained this degree of excellence. In spite of the guidance available from 1876 in the *Rules for a Printed Dictionary Catalogue* prepared by the distinguished American Librarian, C. A. Cutter,[2] a great many librarians were content to list authors and titles and to interpolate such subject entries as suggested themselves, without any attempt at consistency or comprehensiveness. Searching for a given subject in the average library catalogue was thus liable to be a rather chancy business.

The origin of the now familiar card catalogue is impossible to state with precision. It was a technique adopted from business practice, and was introduced into this country from the United States: Cutter recommended its use at the first conference of librarians in 1877,[3] and the Newcastle upon Tyne reference library, opened in 1884, was entirely catalogued by this method.[4] Its advantages over the printed catalogue, with its endless supplements, were indeed sufficiently obvious. The main doubts in the minds of librarians were two: first, would the public be able to use it? and second, would a single catalogue suffice when, as often happened under the indirect access system, a crowd of people wished to examine it at the same time?

Extension Activities

The term "library extension", covering a great variety of educational and cultural activities supplementary to the provision of books, is a modern one, but the concept it expresses goes back to the beginning of public library history.

[1] A specimen page is printed in E. Edwards, *Free Town Libraries* (1869), in the table opp. p. 193. For guidance through the early Manchester catalogues I am much indebted to Mr. Sidney Horrocks, formerly of the Central Reference Library. I have also profited by G. E. Haslam's article on "The Catalogues of the Manchester Reference Library", in *Manchester Review*, Vol. V (1949–50) pp. 358–61.

[2] Cutter was Librarian of the Boston Athenaeum. His *Rules* were published as Part II of *Public Libraries in the United States* (U.S. Bureau of Education, Washington 1876).

[3] *Conference Transactions, 1877*, pp. 155–156.

[4] *A Short History of the Newcastle upon Tyne Public Library 1854–1950* (Newcastle upon Tyne 1950). Card catalogues used at Liverpool were exhibited before the Library Association in 1883 (*L.A. Conference Transactions, 1883*, p. 184), but it seems unlikely that these were for public use. For early French precedents see R. B. Prosser, "The Origin of the Card Catalogue", in *L.A.R.*, Vol. II (1900), p. 661; W. C. B. Sayers and J. D. Stewart, "The Card Catalogue", in *Library World*, Vol. XIV (1911–12), pp. 162–165.

In part it was a carry over from the mechanics' institutes and literary societies whose traditions the public libraries to some extent inherited; in part it arose from the conviction that public libraries were part of the educational system, and therefore bound to do whatever lay in their power to promote educational work.

The full extent of such provision at this period will not be known until the records of individual libraries have been carefully examined, but it seems clear that it was not as great as it came to be later in the century—probably because in many cases suitable accommodation was not available. None the less quite a few libraries here and there, especially towards the end of the period, were providing public lectures, organising science and art classes, and encouraging the activities of local cultural societies.

A number of libraries organised lectures in their early years, but afterwards abandoned them. At Norwich, for example, the library committee arranged public lectures, admission 3d., as early as 1851 (six years before the library opened), and continued them into the 'sixties; they were not revived until 1888. Manchester arranged a few free lectures in its first year (1852–53), but again made no further provision until 1888. Oxford, when it opened in 1854, took over from the Oxford City Public Lectures Committee (a private body) the arrangement each year of a miscellaneous series of lectures, readings and music recitals (admission 1s., season tickets 3s. 6d.) which was continued until 1860.

The Oxford Library Committee, however, was not satisfied to purvey mere entertainment, and in January 1856 (it would seem) it launched a very unusual experiment, in the form of the Oxford Working Men's Educational Association—a kind of mechanics' institute under library auspices. The programme included not only a variety of Saturday evening lectures but also a considerable range of classes. By the end of March classes had been started in chemistry, botany, anatomy, mathematics, English composition, English and Latin grammar, French, elementary drawing, and advanced drawing, with an average student enrolment of about thirty; and an adult school was planned for the teaching of spelling and the three Rs. Membership was fixed at 1s., with an additional 1s. per term, sometimes more, for each class. The lecturers and teachers, many of whom were members of the University, gave their services free of charge.

The first response was encouraging, but, as so often happened with ventures of this kind, the Committee was disappointed in the number of working-class members:

> "Let no man think himself too poor, or too ignorant, to attend; the only qualification required is a desire to learn; neither is a suit of broadcloth necessary. Mechanics with their assistants, and Labouring Men in their plain clothes, will be most cordially welcomed, and the Committee will spare no pains to adapt the teaching of the Institution to their wants, and will endeavour to form classes in any subject which they may desire to study."[1]

It is sad to record that we have no further information concerning this interesting enterprise, which must be presumed to have died an early death.

---

[1] Prospectus of the Oxford Working Men's Institution, Bodleian Library, G. A. Oxon. 6113(87). I am indebted for this reference to the City Librarian, Mr. J. Wells. Cf. above, p. 57.

At certain other libraries we hear of lectures towards the end of the period—at Wolverhampton from 1874,[1] at Dundee by 1875,[2] at Aston from 1883, at Birmingham from 1884, and at Handsworth from 1886.[3] Only at one library, Liverpool, were lectures arranged continuously and systematically over a long period of years. The local Act under which this library was established included the unique provision that the Corporation should be empowered to organise lectures on scientific subjects, either free or at an appropriate charge, and the opening of the Brown Library in 1860, with a lecture-hall capable of seating 400 people, offered an opportunity to implement this provision. The work began during the winter of 1864–65, and has continued, in one form or another, until the present day.[4]

For the first few years substantial courses, mostly ten or twelve lectures each, were organised every winter in such subjects as Natural History, Chemistry, Geology or Mineralogy, and Art. The results were such as might have been anticipated by anyone familiar with the attempt to provide systematic science courses in the early mechanics' institutes. The initial response was very satisfactory, but attendances soon fell away and by 1871 the only ten-lecture course left was that on Art: all the rest had shrunk to four or six lectures. Dramatic readings now began to be introduced, and single lectures on a miscellany of topics, including not only science but literature, music, history and antiquities. This kind of programme proved much more attractive, and a French class "gratuitously conducted by Professor D. Gaillard", was carried on successfully for three years (1874–76). The introduction of the "oxy-hydrogen lantern", first referred to in 1879, was also a great help in stimulating attendance:

> "Hitherto the public appreciation of lectures was not very pronounced, but the pictorial illustrations, often artistically coloured, with which lectures now began to be made effective and attractive, gave the lecture a position in public estimation it had never before possessed. Previously the working man had been more conspicuous by his absence than his presence at the lectures, but since then mechanics and labouring men form the greater and by no means least attentive and appreciative portion of the lecture audiences."[5]

By this time the regular lecture programme had come to consist almost entirely of single lectures (41 of them in 1879, with an average attendance of 363) but, to counteract this tendency to superficiality, the Committee had begun in 1878 to arrange free University Extension courses in collaboration with the University of Cambridge. The inauguration of Extension work at Cambridge in 1873 marked a new and potentially very fruitful phase of public library activity, for the movement was quickly taken up by London, Oxford, and some of the Scottish universities, and in due course by the new provincial universities.[6] Through this system first-class university scholars, skilled in lecturing to popular

---

[1] See below, p. 98.

[2] *Annual Report, 1875*, p. 10.

[3] R. K. Dent, "Free Lectures in Connection with Free Public Libraries", in *The Library*, Vol. VI (1894), pp. 356–357; see also Greenwood (1886), pp. 359–367; (1890), p. 162.

[4] P. Cowell, *Liverpool Public Libraries: a History of Fifty Years* (Liverpool 1903), pp. 108–109.

[5] *Op. cit.*, p. 109.

[6] T. Kelly, *A History of Adult Education in Great Britain* (Liverpool 1962, 2nd edn. 1970), pp. 222–223.

audiences, were made available throughout the length and breadth of the country. The Cambridge courses were usually in units of twelve lectures, with a discussion class before or after each lecture, and an examination and certificate at the end for those specially interested. Other universities offered shorter courses.

Three courses were organised successively in the years 1878–80—two on Political Economy, and one on English Literature. The average attendance in each case was over 300, with some fifty or sixty people taking the examination and gaining certificates. A further course in English Literature was planned for 1881, but as Cambridge was unable to supply a suitable lecturer the course was given by T. Hall Caine, afterwards famous as a popular novelist. On this occasion the Library Committee itself arranged for an examination to be held and certificates awarded on the Cambridge pattern, and the same plan was adopted in 1884 with a particularly successful course on Astronomy by Father S. J. Perry of Stonyhurst College. The average attendance at this course was 1211.

By the end of the period the Liverpool Library's extension programme had thus attained astonishing proportions. It embraced a substantial programme of single lectures, occasional long courses such as those just described, and a number of shorter courses on a variety of subjects. The new Picton Lecture Hall was now available for the purpose, and attendances regularly numbered over 1000. Nor was this all. The library was also providing accommodation for local societies such as the Photographic Society, the Numismatic Society, and the Entomological Society, and for a School of Science organised by an independent committee. This School had been meeting in the library since its beginnings in 1861. Sometimes its courses are referred to in the library reports: in 1875–76 they included Geometry, Machine Construction and Drawing, Biology and Physiology, Navigation and Astronomy, and Geology and Mineralogy.[1]

We have mentioned above that library committees were, in fact, empowered to conduct schools of science and art (the precursors of our modern technical and art colleges) under the Act of 1855, and that a later Act, of 1884, made it clear that they were also entitled to receive grant on schools and classes of this kind from the Science and Art Department at South Kensington.[2] We have also noted that at Exeter, where the public library opened in 1870, the school of science and art was initially a much more important part of the institution.[3] There were, however, other cases in which activities of this kind occupied a large part of the attention of the library committee.

One of the earliest examples was Cardiff. In this busy and growing seaport, provision for technical education was an obvious necessity. By the time the public library was established in 1862 the facilities which had at one time been offered by the Mechanics' Institute had come to an end, and the library stepped

---

[1] A general account of all this is given in Cowell, *op. cit.*, Ch. ix. The details are from the Annual Reports, 1865–86; the *Free Lectures Statistics Books*; and the *Minutes of the Lectures Sub-Committee*. For details of the origin and management of the School of Science, see the printed circular, *Scheme for Establishing and Conducting a School of Science in Liverpool in connexion with the Free Library and Museum* (Jan. 1861) preserved in the Liverpool Record Office.

[2] See above, pp. 21–22.

[3] See above, p. 34.

in to fill the gap. Science and art classes began to be provided in January 1866, on the top floor of the library building, desks being improvised by means of planks placed across two barrels. By the winter of 1866–67 there were already about 70 pupils studying geometry, machine drawing, building construction, mathematics, and art, and the record of examination successes was impressive. Soon it was necessary to move to rented accommodation elsewhere, and here the classes remained until a new and larger library building was erected in 1872. Only in 1890, as a consequence of the Technical Instruction Act, did the School of Science and Art pass from the control of the Library Committee to that of the newly established Technical Instruction Committee, and it was not until 1892 that the last classes left the library building.[1]

Wolverhampton and Watford ran particularly enterprising programmes in which science and art classes formed a central feature. In the former town the library opened in 1869, and it appears that the librarian, John Elliot, was keen from the beginning to establish evening classes. This became possible in 1873, when larger premises were secured, and more than a score of classes, with nearly 350 pupils, were at once commenced. The range of subjects was broader than usual, including not only mathematics, science, and art, but also English language and literature, French, German, Italian, and Spanish, and shorthand. Within a few years other activities were added: Saturday evening lectures; a Naturalists' and Archaeological Department, which collected a museum and ran Saturday afternoon excursions; a Debating Society; an annual Essay Prize competition; and an annual "Celebration" for the students. The classes continued under library control until 1902.[2]

The Watford Library, opened in 1874, had to exist initially on a rate income of only £80 a year, and was conducted for the first nine years entirely by honorary officers. It had, however, the great advantage of a substantial building erected by public subscription at a cost of some £3000, and this quickly became the home of educational activities of all kinds: a School of Art, with day and evening classes; evening classes in science; evening lectures, under University Extension auspices from 1884; a Naturalists' Society; a Musical Society from which grew in 1880 a School of Music; and even an endowed day school. In 1885, by which time a full-time librarian had been appointed, the work was consolidated under the name of the Watford Public Library and College of Science, Art, Music, and Literature, with Sir John Lubbock, archaeologist and scientist, as the first President. Unfortunately it has to be said that the library itself suffered from all this welter of supplementary activities, but the connection between the public library and the educational institutions of the town continued, in spite of various administrative changes, until as late as 1919. The present Watford College of Technology and School of Music are the direct decsendants of the work originally begun under library auspices.[3]

---

[1] A. Harvey, *1866–1966: One Hundred Years of Technical Education* [Cardiff 1966] pp. 12–15; and information from Mr. J. E. Thomas, City Librarian.

[2] Information from Mr. F. Mason, Chief Librarian. F. Turner, "The Place of the Public Library in Relation to Elementary, Secondary, and Higher Education", in *The Library*, Vol. VI (1894), describes the early years.

[3] J. Woolman, *Watford Public Library* (reprinted from *Watford Observer*, 25 Jan. 1913), and information from the late Mr. R. C. Sayell, Borough Librarian.

Librarians and Librarianship

In 1850 the qualities and qualifications required of a public librarian were still unknown. Even in 1869 Edwards could only recommend library committees to look for a man with "(1) A genuine love of books; (2) An indomitable passion for order." Given these qualities, he thought, the person appointed would be "pretty sure to learn all the technicalities of his calling speedily." Edwards did indeed foresee a time when professional training would be available. "The day will come, "he declared, "when in Britain we shall have courses of bibliography and bibliothecal-economy for the training of librarians."[1] At this time, however, this was still very much in the future.

The earliest librarians, therefore, came from many different walks of life. Edwards at Manchester, exceptionally, was from the British Museum, and J. D. Mullins at Birmingham came from the Birmingham Subscription Library, but most had no previous library experience of any kind. Liverpool appointed as its first librarian a schoolmaster, J. S. Dalton; Oxford a bookseller, B. H. Blackwell; Cambridge a 22-year old bookseller's assistant, John Pink; Sheffield a 20-year old silverplater's apprentice, Walter Parsonson. At Cambridge the runner-up for the appointment was a retired stage-coachman, who was defeated only by the casting vote of the chairman.

Many of these amateur public librarians did very well. J. D. Mullins, especially, though pernickety in his administration (his Daily Routine Book for the reference library alone listed over a hundred items for the attention of the staff[2]) won during his thirty-three years' service at Birmingham (1865-98) a great reputation both as librarian and as bibliographer. Edwards, the best qualified, was in some ways less successful than some who approached the work with more modest pretensions.

For in the early years librarianship was indeed a humble task. The hours were long (often twelve hours a day or more), the working conditions unhealthy, the salary poor, the status lowly. Nowhere was the librarian regarded as a professional man: he was merely the servant of the library committee. "From the Committee minutes," writes the present Librarian of Leamington Spa, "it is apparent that initiative and planning was expected to arise from the Chairman and Committee and that it was the librarian's place to carry out instructions to the letter."[3] Even at Manchester, as we have seen, this attitude prevailed.[4] As to salaries, Manchester in the 1850s was paying £200 a year, Liverpool £180, and Sheffield £100, but the usual figure was £50 or £60, sometimes with a boy at 5s. a week or so to assist. At Oxford it was announced in 1854 that

> "A Librarian and an assistant have been appointed, whose duty it will be to be in attendance at all times, during the week-days, from 9 in the Morning till 11 in the Evening in Summer, and from 9 till 10 in Winter, and from 6 in the Evening till 10 on Sundays."

The salary of the librarian (Blackwell) was £60 a year, and the assistant, a

[1] E. Edwards, *Free Town Libraries* (1869), p. 30. Cf. his *Memoirs of Libraries* (1859), Vol. II, pp. 934-935.
[2] A. C. Shaw, "The Birmingham Free Libraries," in *L.A.R.*, Vol. IV (1902), pp. 515-516.
[3] Mr. H. S. Tallamy to the author.   [4] See above, p. 42-43.

boy, was paid 7d. a week.[1] At Kidderminster the hours were a little less exacting
—10 a.m. to 9 p.m. daily, except Sundays—but the first librarian was appointed
(in 1855), at a salary of £30 a year, "it being a condition that he should employ
and pay a proper person to assist him in his duties."[2]

These salaries (about the same as those paid to librarians of subscription
libraries) were low even by mid-nineteenth century standards, the customary
figure of £50–£60 being rather less than the salary of an uncertificated male
teacher in an elementary school.[3] The comparison is revealing.

The astonishing thing is that many librarians seemed to thrive on these
hard conditions. The outstanding example was John Pink at Cambridge, who
was librarian for fifty-one years (his successor W. A. Fenton served a further
thirty-nine years, so that this library had only two librarians in ninety years).
J. P. Briscoe's forty-seven years' service at Nottingham affords another very
striking example.[4]

By the 'seventies a great change was beginning to be evident. The first
generation of librarians had now not only learnt the job, but in the larger
libraries had trained up a body of assistants from whom future librarians could
be chosen. Thus Briscoe, appointed to Nottingham in 1869, came from the
Bolton Library, as did James Yates, who in 1870 became first librarian of Leeds.
W. J. Haggerston, of the Newcastle upon Tyne library, went to be librarian at
South Shields in 1872, then back again to Newcastle as librarian in 1879. One
could go on multiplying examples. It was still possible, in 1874, for Dundee to
appoint as its second librarian John Maclauchlan, librarian of the Perth
Mechanics' Institute[5]; and in 1877 for Norwich to appoint as its fifth librarian
George Easter, a woodcarver; and as late as 1890 advertisements for librarians
still brought applications from "soldiers, sailors, pensioners, clerks, teachers,
booksellers, and from every class and section of Society."[6] Increasingly, however, chief librarians were recruited from those trained and experienced in the
public library service.

Hence there began to arise, over the years, a measure of professional
expertise and a sense of professional solidarity. Both of these received a great
stimulus from the foundation, in October, 1877, of the Library Association of
the United Kingdom, "to unite all persons engaged in or interested in library
work, for the purpose of promoting the best possible administration of existing
libraries, and the formation of new ones where desirable", and also to encourage
"bibliographical research."[7]

This is not the place to recount the history of the Association, though we

[1] *Oxford City Libraries, 1854–1954* (Oxford [1954]), pp. 4–5.

[2] *P.R. 1856*, p. 5; *Centenary Festival of the Public Library and Music Hall* (Kidderminster
1955), p. 11.

[3] A. Tropp, *The School Teachers* (1957), p. 39 n. The average salary of male teachers in this
category in 1861 was £62 per annum.

[4] C. Walford, a lay member of the Library Association, commented "On the Longevity
of Librarians" in *Library Journal*, Vol. V (1880), pp. 67–71. On Pink see W. A. Munford,
"John Pink: Portrait of a Victorian Librarian", in *L.A.R.*, Vol. LVI (1954), pp. 289–294.

[5] This is one of the few instances I have come across at this period of the appointment of the
librarian of a mechanics' institute to a public library; later, as we shall see, it was not
uncommon.

[6] Greenwood (1890), p. 482.   [7] *Conference Transactions, 1877*, p. 179.

shall frequently have occasion to refer to its activities.[1] It is important to note, however, that it was not, and never has been concerned only with the rate-aided public libraries. At the outset, indeed, its proceedings were dominated by the librarians of non-rate-aided institutions—the British Museum, the university libraries, and the big private libraries of the metropolis. The impetus to the establishment of the Association came from the example of the U.S.A., where a conference of librarians held in 1876 resulted in the creation of the American Library Association. E. W. B. Nicholson, Librarian of the London Institution and later Bodley's Librarian, present at the Philadelphia conference (though not himself), took the initiative in organising, in London in 1877, the international conference of librarians which led directly to the formation of the United Kingdom Association. When the first officers and council came to be chosen, John Winter Jones, Principal Librarian of the British Museum, was elected president, Nicholson and H. R. Tedder, Librarian of the Athenaeum, were joint secretaries; and the council of twelve included only four public librarians— Cowell of Liverpool, Crestadoro of Manchester, Mullins of Birmingham, and Yates of Leeds.

It is also interesting to observe that the Association has never been a purely professional body. Membership has been open, subject to due process of election, to anyone interested in the objects the Association was formed to promote, and over the years a great many laymen—scholars, professional men, members of library committees, and the like—have participated in its work.[2] None the less its professional value was very great. The papers read at the early annual meetings dealt, inter alia, with such topics as local collections, subscription libraries in connection with public libraries, library legislation, the extension of public libraries to rural areas, and the duties, qualifications, and training of librarians; and there were also more technical contributions dealing with cataloguing, indicators, stockbooks, binding, and other aspects of library management. Much valuable information was collected regarding the operation of existing public libraries. Committees were set up to encourage the establishment of public libraries in the metropolis; to consider the compilation of a general catalogue of English literature; to arrange for the coverage of English material in Poole's *Index to Periodical Literature*[3]; and for various other purposes. A set of cataloguing rules was prepared and published (1881).

The important thing was that librarians were now able for the first time to meet together, to compare notes, and to pool their experience. For the first seven years the transactions and proceedings of their annual conferences were printed almost *verbatim*, in the volumes to which we have already frequently made reference; and, when this was no longer possible, the most important proceedings were printed in a series of professional journals published by or in

[1] Brief accounts of the history of the Association are given in J. Minto, *A History of the Public Library Movement* (1932), Ch. xii; and W. A. Munford, *Penny Rate* (1951), Ch. xv; and further details may be found in W. A. Munford (ed.), *Annals of the Library Association* (1965).

[2] By a recent decision non-professional members joining after 1966 do not have a vote. See below, p. 419.

[3] W. F. Poole was one of the great American librarians of the nineteenth century. His well-known *Index*, the foundation of all later work of this kind, was first published in 1848: a 3rd edition appeared in 1882.

collaboration with the Association. Since 1899 (following its incorporation by royal charter in the previous year) the Association has published its own journal, the *Library Association Record*.[1]

By 1880 we can already detect some amelioration in the librarian's hard lot. The hours of opening, as recorded in 1879, were indeed still very long.[2] No library, even Oxford, now kept its doors open beyond 10 p.m., but in the smaller libraries especially the staff were still expected to be on duty for twelve hours a day or even longer. The growth of staff in the larger libraries, however, did open up the possibility of a rota system to permit the assistants a reasonable amount of time off. At Sheffield, even in the 'sixties, the assistants were allowed one half day a week off, but this arrangement was stopped when the Council got to hear of it.[3] Dundee, however, was enlightened enough to introduce an eight-hour day for its library assistants in 1872,[4] and some similar, though probably less generous, arrangement may have operated in other libraries. Sunday opening, which was still confined to Birmingham, Manchester, and a handful of other libraries, was not yet an important factor, especially as extra staff were sometimes employed for this purpose.[5]

In the matter of salaries there was still constant complaint: one speaker at the first Library Association conference calculated that, taking into account the amount of work librarians performed, they were paid rather less than shoeblacks.[6] None the less the figures collected in 1879 show a quite marked improvement in this respect.[7] These figures, though not quite complete, show that the salary of £50–£60 a year which had been almost standard in small libraries in the 1850s had now given place to £80–£100 a year, and in fact most full-time chief librarians were now earning £100 a year or more. Figures between £100 and £200 are common—sometimes, as at Derby, Hereford, Maidstone, Warrington and Westminster, with free accommodation in addition to salary. Salaries over £200 included Dundee (£210), Bristol (£350), and Birmingham (£400).

This was, of course, a time when prices were falling, and both money wages and real wages were rising: average real wages rose by 51 per cent in the years 1850–86.[8] None the less the figures quoted above suggest that the increase in librarians' salaries was above the average, and that their status was improving in relation to other members of the community.[9]

The information we have for the salaries of library staff other than the chief librarian is not very meaningful, because the range of figures is so wide, e.g. in

---

[1] The earlier periodicals were the *Library Journal* (formerly the *American Library Journal*, published jointly under its new title by the two Library Associations 1877–82); *Monthly Notes of the Library Association* (1880–83); *The Library Chronicle* (1884–88); and *The Library* (by arrangement with the proprietor, 1889–98).

[2] *L.A. Conference Transactions, 1879*, table opp. p. 138, col. 9.

[3] *The City Libraries of Sheffield, 1856–1956* (Sheffield 1956), pp. 14–15.

[4] *Annual Report*, 1872.   [5] See above, pp. 43, 48.

[6] *L.A. Conference Transactions, 1878*, pp. 90–95.

[7] *L.A. Conference Transactions, 1879*, table opp. p. 138, col. 15.

[8] R. B. Mitchell and P. Deane, *Abstract of British Historical Statistics* (Cambridge 1962), pp. 343–344.

[9] Cf. the figures for teachers' salaries in A. Tropp, *The School Teachers* (1957), App. B, p. 272.

the table just cited Birmingham reports salaries of £20–£150 a year, Bolton £17–£90, Manchester £26–£150. The fact is that, whereas some small libraries, e.g. Kidderminster, still managed with the traditional "man and a boy", the larger libraries had now developed a considerable hierarchy of assistants. At the bottom were the boys, who were still found useful for fetching and carrying, and might be paid as little as 5s. a week.[1] In the best libraries they were treated as apprentices and trained for more responsible work. Above this were the library assistants or assistant librarians, whose salary varied according to age, experience and status. Those at the lowest level, engaged on purely routine duties, would be rewarded with about 10s.–20s. a week, but a post involving special responsibility, e.g. as a branch librarian or as superintendent of a reference library, might carry a salary of £100 or even £150 a year.

The employment of women assistants seems to have begun in 1871 at Manchester, where the expedient was adopted to overcome the shortage of suitable young men. The experiment was a great success: the young women proved "regular in their attendance, attentive to their duties, uniformly courteous to borrowers, and contented with their employment and position, evincing no disposition to leave" (except to get married). They were also cheaper, and by 1879 Manchester was employing thirty-one women assistants at 10s. to 18s. a week.[2]

In view of the very important part that women now play in public library work, this new development must be regarded as of momentous importance, and it is clearly linked with the growing movement at this time for the emancipation of women. Other libraries, however, were slow to follow Manchester's example: as late as 1898 it was only with much misgiving that women assistants were introduced into the public library at Leeds.[3] By 1879 seven other libraries only were employing women: they were Birmingham, Bradford, Bristol, Derby, Newcastle upon Tyne, Paisley, and Smethwick.[4] Only Bristol, however, employed any considerable number—eleven at this date. The librarian, commented Greenwood, "is a great believer in the humanizing power of the gentler sex in library work."[5]

As the larger library systems were gradually articulated, and opportunities for converse among librarians multiplied, the nature of a librarian's duties and the qualifications required of him became increasingly well defined, and the possibility of formal training in librarianship came into view. The need for it had long been felt, especially by the larger libraries. Mullins of Birmingham told the Library Association in 1879:

> "As a rule the librarian has to educate his own assistants; in other professions it is possible to obtain trained help, but the rapid growth of the library movement has so

---

[1] Birkenhead, in the 'sixties, was also using girls in a similar capacity, but this seems to have been exceptional (*Annual Report, 1862*).

[2] *L.A. Conference Transactions, 1879*, pp. 32–33.

The first woman chief librarian appears to have been a Mrs. Elliot who served as librarian of Hawick from 1879 to 1894. She was closely followed by Mrs. H. Eteson at Blackpool (1880–91), whose successor was also a woman, Miss Kate Lewtas (1891–1902). Cf. *L.Y.B. 1900–01*; *L.A.R.*, Vol. XXI (1919), p. 281.

[3] T. W. Hand, *A Brief Account of the Public Libraries of the City of Leeds, 1870–1920* (Leeds 1920), pp. 25–26.

[4] *L.A. Conference Transactions, 1879*, table opp. p. 138, col. 16. [5] Greenwood (1890), p. 112.

quickly promoted juniors into principals, that the librarian of to-day has to be to a certain degree the trainer for tomorrow."[1]

At the next annual conference a committee was appointed to consider the training of library assistants. The 1881 conference received the report of the committee but declined to adopt it, but at the 1882 conference, following an address by H. R. Tedder, the report was approved. The proposals provided for three certificates based on examination:

> (1) A Preliminary Certificate, to be taken before entry to library work, requiring competence in arithmetic, English grammar and composition, English history, geography, English literature, and at least one foreign language.
> (2) A Second Class Certificate, to be given after not less than one year's library work, and requiring a knowledge of English literature, one other European literature, the principles of classification, the elements of bibliography and cataloguing, library management, and a cataloguing knowledge of at least two foreign languages.
> (3) A First Class Certificate, available to assistants of at least two years' standing, requiring a more advanced knowledge of the subjects studied for the Second Class Certificate, with a paper on general literary history. At this stage a cataloguing knowledge of at least three foreign languages was required.[2]

The first examinations under the new scheme were organised by the Library Association at London and Nottingham in 1885, one of the first two candidates to secure the Second Class Certificate being J. J. Ogle of Nottingham, afterwards well known as librarian of Bootle.[3]

The paper by H. R. Tedder which immediately preceded the adoption of this scheme was on "Librarianship as a Profession," and we may suitably close this long chapter by quoting his views on the qualifications required of a librarian. He still stressed, as Edwards had done thirteen years earlier, the need for a librarian to have a love of books and a passion for order, but he placed much more emphasis than Edwards on technical qualifications:

> "Without going into particulars, . . . one may expect the ordinary librarian to be a man of refinement, of liberal education, and especially endowed with sympathy with books and reading. But a general taste for literature is not all that is required. . . . To be thoroughly qualified a librarian should have had the practical experience of library work which it is impossible to obtain from any amount of book-reading, and if without experience he must possess the faculty of teaching himself. He should be a man of business habits and a good administrator; above all, he must be willing to devote his whole life to the study of his profession, for a librarian should never consider that he has finished his education. These requirements imply qualifications of a somewhat higher character than may perhaps be needed in all libraries, but some knowledge of languages and literatures, of bibliography, bibliology, and general library management, must be possessed by any person holding the chief position in the administration of a library, however small this may be."[4]

[1] L.A. Conference Transactions, 1879, p. 72.
[2] L.A. Conference Transactions, 1882, pp. 7–8.
[3] J. Minto, A History of the Public Library Movement (1932), p. 211.
[4] L.A. Conference Transactions, 1881–82, p. 164. Reprinted in J. L. Thornton, Selected Readings in the History of Librarianship (1966), pp. 212–224.

BOOK II
FROM THE JUBILEE TO THE
FIRST WORLD WAR
1887–1918

CHAPTER V

The Age of Carnegie

The General Historical Background

THE years 1887–1918, which we have marked off as constituting the second epoch in public library history, were years which saw the disintegration of Victorianism and the emergence of what it was hoped would be a freer and juster society. Such remnants of Victorian ideas and ideals as still lingered in 1914 were burnt up in the holocaust of the first World War.

These tendencies, naturally, were not as clear to contemporaries as they appear in the light of subsequent history. In the closing years of Victoria's reign especially, between the first Jubilee in 1887 and the old Queen's death in 1901, the country was for the most part under the Conservative government of Lord Salisbury. Gladstone, a far greater man, was in the political wilderness, and after a brief return to office retired altogether in 1894. At this time it must have seemed to most people that Britain was as secure and prosperous as ever. Agriculture, it is true, continued to sink into decay under the stress of foreign competition, and industry and commerce continued to be disrupted from time to time by slumps of which economists vainly sought to divine the cause. In general, however, Britain remained a rich and powerful country, whose trade, wealth and imperial possessions increased year by year. Individual entrepreneurs continued to make immense fortunes, and the growing prosperity of humbler individuals is attested by the steady rise in real wages.

It is only when we compare the position of Britain with that of other countries, and especially Germany and the U.S.A. that we see the beginnings of decline. By 1900 Britain had fallen back to second place in the production of coal, and third place in the production of steel. At the same time her exports of manufactured goods, such as cotton, were tending to fall off, while her exports of machinery, railway equipment, and coal, which were arming her competitors against her, showed a substantial increase.

More serious still, however, were the signs that foreshadowed the collapse of the Victorian social order. The religious faith that had been the prop and sanction of that order was losing its power, church-going was on the wane, the Sabbath was becoming a day for cheap railway excursions. In 1889 Charles Booth shocked the conscience of the well-to-do, and knocked the bottom out of the much-vaunted Victorian idea of progress, by his revelation that close on one-third of the inhabitants of London lived below the poverty-line; and in the very same year the strike in the capital for the "dockers' tanner" demonstrated the determination of the skilled workers to assist their poorer brethren in the struggle against oppression.

The more articulate members of the working class were indeed no longer willing to accept, as the working men of the 'fifties had accepted, the theory of their natural subordination to "the higher classes." With the parliamentary vote and the right to education already achieved, they were organizing themselves

both economically and politically for further advances—economically through
the trade unions, and politically through the Independent Labour Party
(founded in 1893) and the Labour Representation Committee (founded in 1900).
Their hands were greatly strengthened by the local government reforms of 1888
and 1894, of which more shortly.

Women, the other oppressed class of Victorian times, had not yet reached
the stage of violent public protest against their exclusion from political power,
though there was a good deal of decorous propaganda and from time to time
unsuccessful attempts were made to secure favourable legislation. In the meantime the spread of the practice of birth-control, which by 1891 was already
slowing down the increase in population, was at last releasing women from the
drudgery of bearing and rearing unnecessarily large families, and paving the
way for a fuller participation in social, intellectual, and working life.

The Salisbury era was not notable for domestic reform, but it did bring an
important development in the structure of local government. As we have seen,
the reforming legislation of the 'thirties had made no provision for the rural
areas, or even for the administration of London.[1] These omissions were now
remedied. In England and Wales the Local Government Acts of 1888 and 1894
created the divisions to which we are now accustomed—counties, county and
non-county boroughs, urban districts, rural districts, and parishes, with at each
level an elected council in control. In 1899 the London Government Act created
the metropolitan borough councils to govern the area outside the City. In
Scotland county councils, with subordinate district committees, were established
in 1889, and parish councils took the place of the old parochial boards in 1894.
Under the Act of 1889, only the largest burghs retained complete independence:
the others, including all police burghs, came in varying degrees under county
control.

Closely associated with these local government changes, and equally
significant for the public library service, were certain changes in the educational
structure. The Technical Instruction Act of 1889 was the starting-point, in
England and Wales, for a wide development of technical education under the
auspices of the new county and non-county boroughs, which were empowered
to appoint special technical instruction committees and levy a 1d. rate for the
purpose. From 1890 to 1902 rate income for this purpose was usefully supplemented by the "whisky money"—a fund derived from a tax originally
intended to finance the closure of redundant public-houses.

There were now in England and Wales two publicly assisted systems of
education operated through local authorities: elementary education, under the
school boards, was the responsibility of the Education Department; and
technical and art education, largely but not exclusively under the technical
instruction committees, was the responsibility of the Science and Art Department.[2] The system was unified at the central level in 1899, when the two
Departments were brought together to form the Board of Education; and at the
local level by the Education Act of 1902, under which local councils were
constituted as education authorities for their areas. County borough councils
were made responsible for all publicly maintained elementary, secondary, and

[1] See above, p. 19.
[2] This Department also made grants to schools and pupil-teacher centres as well as to
institutions not under local authority control, e.g. mechanics' institutes.

technical education; and county councils were given similar powers, except that the larger non-county borough and urban district councils were permitted to exercise full responsibility for elementary education only.

In Scotland the position was different. Here, by an Act of 1887, technical education developed under the aegis of the school boards, which maintained their existence till 1918. The English Act of 1902 had therefore no exact Scottish equivalent.

The economic tendencies which had manifested themselves in the closing decades of the nineteenth century were accentuated in the opening decades of the twentieth. Once more there was no general consciousness of decline. Agriculture, so long in decay, showed some recovery; and new industries such as electrical engineering and motor-car manufacture were beginning to take their place in an economy which, in the immediate pre-war years, showed every outward sign of prosperity. In the race with Germany and the United States, however, Britain was falling further and further behind, and the rise in the prices of imported foodstuffs and raw materials, though it gave encouragement to the British farmer, brought to a halt the steady rise in real wages which, with minor fluctuations, had been continuous since the 'sixties. The falling birthrate too, however welcome it might be from some points of view, was economically a source of weakness. The first World War, when it came, made things worse: the normal channels of foreign trade were suddenly blocked, and production was distorted to meet overriding wartime needs, so that by 1919 the country faced a difficult period of adjustment and reorganization.

The social and political changes of the period were even more marked than the economic. The death of Queen Victoria in 1901 really did mark a break with the past. The new age was that of Shaw, Wells, Galsworthy and the Webbs, a sceptical and iconoclastic age utterly remote, in spirit if not in time, from that of Dickens and Thackeray, Tennyson and Browning. It was in this new atmosphere that the Labour party began to become a force in politics; that the power of the House of Lords was brought under control; that the women's suffrage movement erupted into violence and at length achieved, in 1918, a measure of success. The ten years of Liberal rule which began in 1905, first under Campbell-Bannerman and then under Asquith, produced a spate of social reform such as had not been seen since the 1870s. The Miners' Eight Hours Act, the Trade Boards Act, the Shops Act, the Miners' Minimum Wage Act—all these were paternalist measures after the Victorian model, designed to protect the worker against exploitation. But free meals in schools, the school medical service, old age pensions, labour exchanges, and national insurance against sickness and unemployment—these were reforms of a new kind, the first positive steps towards the welfare state.

In 1918, as the war came to a close, new Education Acts were passed both for England and Wales and for Scotland. The English Act, though designed by H. A. L. Fisher on bold and imaginative lines, never became fully operative, and is remarkable now chiefly for having effectively raised the minimum school leaving age to 14. The Scottish Act brought a dramatic change in administration, re-placing close on a thousand school boards by less than forty county and burgh education authorities; it also, almost incidentally, authorized the county educa-tion committees to provide a public library service. This clause, as we shall see in a later chapter, was to be of very great importance in Scottish library history.

The Legislative Background

In an earlier chapter we have traced the development of library legislation
to the end of the year 1886.[1] At that date the principal Act for England and
Wales was still that of 1855, and for Scotland that of 1867, but there had been a
number of amending acts and the time was ripe for consolidation. It came first
in Scotland, where an Act of 1887 replaced all previous legislation.[2] This Act
retained the alternative of public meeting or poll as the method of adoption only
in the case of very small authorities: in burghs of more than 3000 householders
the issue of voting papers was essential.

This Scottish Act also kept the form of library government which had been
prescribed by the previous consolidating Act of 1867, and it is worth noting
that the Scottish burgh library committee established under this legislation
enjoyed a much greater degree of independence than its English counterpart.
Consisting half of councillors and half of ratepayers chosen by the Council, it
had power to make its own regulations, and with the approval of the council
and sheriff, its own bylaws; and though it did not actually levy the library rate,
and was not empowered to borrow money, the burgh council was obliged to
levy whatever rate the library required up to the legal 1d. limit.

In England and Wales the confusion due to successive amendments continued for a few years longer. The Attorney-General even expressed doubt, in
1887, whether a library authority was empowered to lend books.[3] To remove
obscurity, a further amending Act of the same year enabled small authorities to
provide a lending library service without providing a building.[4] Still more
amendments followed in 1889 and 1890, the first concerned merely with details
of financial arrangements,[5] the second prescribing adoption by poll and excluding the alternative of a public meeting.[6]

The Public Libraries Act of 1892,[7] which at last consolidated the legislation
for England and Wales, was drafted with the advice and assistance of the
Library Association, which for some years had been pressing for reform.[8] It was
sponsored in the Commons by Sir John Lubbock, the Liberal Unionist

---

[1] See above, pp. 20–22.
[2] Public Libraries (Scotland) Consolidation Act, 50 and 51 Vict. c. 42.
[3] Greenwood (1891), p. 433. In Scotland this power was specifically stated in the amending
Act of 1871.
[4] Public Libraries Amendment Act, 50 and 51 Vict. c. 22. This Act, incidentally, transferred
to the Local Government Board (constituted in 1871) the powers previously exercised
by the Treasury in respect of library loans.
[5] Public Libraries Amendment Act, 52 and 53 Vict. c. 9.
[6] Public Libraries Amendment Act, 53 and 54 Vict. 68.
[7] Public Libraries Act, 55 and 56 Vict. c. 53.
[8] In 1889 J. Y. MacAlister (afterwards Sir John MacAlister), Hon. Secretary of the Association, offered a prize for the best draft of a Public Libraries Bill. The winning entry, which
provided the starting-point for the Act of 1892, was by J. J. Ogle, Librarian of Bootle,
and his colleague H. W. Fovargue, Assistant Town Clerk. It was printed in 1889, and a
copy is preserved at the Bootle Public Library. Ogle (1858–1909), afterwards Director of
Technical Instruction in Bootle, played an important part in public library development
at this period, and wrote an admirable volume on *The Free Library* (1897). See the sketch
in J. Minto, *A History of the Public Library Movement* (1932), pp. 332–334, and T. Landau
(ed.), *Encyclopaedia of Librarianship* (1958, 3rd edn. 1966), *s.v.*

M.P., who had now taken William Ewart's place as the leading Parliamentary champion of public library interests.[1] This Act, which was not repealed till 1964, simplified the confusion of terminology regarding library authorities by providing that "every urban district and every parish ... which is not within an urban district shall be a library district," the phrase "urban district" covering both the county boroughs recognized under the Local Government Act of 1888 and other urban authorities. Parishes adopting the Act were required, as they had been since 1855, to appoint Commissioners for Public Libraries and Museums to carry it into effect, and neighbouring parishes might combine for this purpose. In London the library authority might be the City, a district board, or a parish. Adoption was to be by a simple majority in a poll of ratepayers.

These English and Scottish consolidating Acts left two matters still in an unsatisfactory state. One was the procedure for adoption, which was cumbersome, expensive, and uncertain in its results. This was quickly put right, as far as the English urban authorities were concerned, by an amending Act of the following year, which permitted adoption, subject to due notice, by "a resolution ... passed at a meeting of the urban authority."[2] The same Act, incidentally, permitted neighbouring urban authorities to combine in the same way as parishes. The procedure for adoption by resolution was extended in 1894 to the burghs of Scotland,[3] and power for neighbouring authorities in Scotland to combine was given in 1899.[4] In the rural parishes, however, the decision to adopt still had to be by a majority of householders.[5]

The other and more serious problem was that of the rate limitation. A measure of relief was indeed afforded in some instances by the Technical Instruction Act of 1889, which permitted the levying of a separate 1d. rate for technical education, and the Museums and Gymnasiums Act of 1891 which permitted the levying of a separate $\frac{1}{2}$d. rate for the maintenance of a museum. The provision of 1877 regarding a library rate lower than 1d.,[6] though not repealed, lost much of its force in urban districts when the power to adopt was transferred to the council. From 1893–94, therefore, there was nothing to prevent an urban authority from having the full 1d. rate available exclusively for library purposes. The trouble was that 1d. was just not enough.

The only public libraries Act before the end of the century which has not already been mentioned was a minor one of 1898 providing a fine of up to 40s. for disorderly behaviour.[7] This was, no doubt, a sufficiently severe penalty for those times, but it seems mild compared with the penalty for destroying or

---

[1] Lubbock became 1st Baron Avebury in 1900. He died in 1913.

[2] Public Libraries Amendment Act, 56 Vict. c. 11. This Act did not apply to London, where a poll continued to be necessary.

[3] Public Libraries (Scotland) Act, 57 and 58 Vict. c. 20.

[4] Public Libraries (Scotland) Act, 62 Vict. c. 5.

[5] H. W. Fovargue, "How to adopt the Acts in Rural Parishes", in *The Library*, Vol. VIII (1896), pp. 105–107, records a decision by the Local Government Board that the Local Government Act of 1894 should be interpreted to mean that in a rural parish the Public Libraries Acts might be adopted by resolution of the parish meeting only, unless a poll should be demanded before the close of the meeting. It does not appear that any parallel decision was taken in Scotland.

[6] See above, p. 22.

[7] Libraries Offences Act, 61 and 62 Vict. c. 53.

damaging books or manuscripts prescribed by an Act of 1861, namely imprison-
ment up to six months, with or without hard labour, and in the case of a male
offender with or without whipping![1]

When the new century dawned the removal of the rate limitation was still
not in sight, yet apart from another minor Act of 1901[2] there was to be no
further library legislation until after the first World War.

Changing Attitudes

The years from the Jubilee to the first World War, and especially the
twenty years 1899–1909, were, as we shall shortly see, a time of tremendously
rapid development in public library provision. The number of library authorities
grew (in spite of some amalgamations) from 125 in 1886 to 549 in 1918, and the
proportion of the population covered grew from about a quarter to about
two-thirds.[3] This dramatic expansion is in a way surprising, for although with
the new emphasis on the educational needs of the nation public opinion was
already by the beginning of the period better disposed than it had formerly been
towards public library development,[4] attitudes were still by no means uniformly
favourable.

Greenwood, in 1891, declared that "The task of advocating and defending
these institutions becomes lighter with each succeeding year,"[5] but he still
found it necessary to rehearse in detail the arguments for public libraries and the
principal objections raised against them. He argues in favour of libraries, first,
on economic grounds—"knowledge is power"; secondly, on cultural grounds—
"knowledge, like virtue, is its own true reward", and thirdly, on social grounds,
because want of amusement drives men to vice and crime. Of the arguments
against, he names first the basic objection to additional taxation, especially to
provide for the needs of others, but he lists also a variety of other objections:
that public libraries are socialistic institutions, and nurseries of socialism; that
they disrupt family life; that they spread infectious diseases; that they injure the
interests of mechanics' institutes, subscription libraries, and the book trade; and
not least that they are the haunt of idlers and readers of trashy novels.[6]

These now familiar arguments could be illustrated endlessly from the press
and from platform utterances throughout the 'nineties. We have space only for
a few further illustrations. At Willesden, in 1891, the committee organizing the
campaign for a public library argued, moderately enough, that

> "The immense benefit conferred by public libraries is now universally
> recognized. They provide the means of self-instruction for those who wish to learn;
> of recreation to the weary worker, and the opportunity of research to the studious.
> They furnish a place of safe and healthful resort to young people and they develop
> intelligence, sobriety and self-respect in both young and old."[7]

---

[1] Malicious Injury to Property Act, 24 and 25 Vict. c. 97.
[2] Public Libraries (England and Ireland) Act, 1 Edw. VII, c. 19. This Act further strengthened
the disciplinary powers of library authorities, and also provided that authorities must
notify the adoption of the Acts to the Local Government Board.
[3] 23% in 1884, 60% in 1914—see below, App. VI.
[4] See above, p. 31.
[5] Greenwood (1891), p. 2.   [6] Op. cit., pp. 17–34.
[7] Willesden Public Libraries, The Willesden Library Service 1894 to 1954 (1954), p. 6.

The *Middlesex Courier* declared, more dramatically:

"The public-house is the ante-room of the gaol, while the library is the doorway of the knowledge which is power—power for success, for prosperity, and for honour. The public-house is the high-road to perdition; the library the wicket of truth."[1]

Sir John Lubbock, who has already been mentioned for his part in library legislation, was a firm believer in the social value of public libraries. In 1890, at the opening of the Rotherhithe Free Library, he developed in detail the argument that "A great part, at any rate, of what we spend on books we save in prisons and police."[2] Eight years later, at the opening of the Hoxton Branch Library at Shoreditch, he abandoned this prosaic approach to proclaim that

"A Library was a true fairyland, a very palace of delight, a haven of repose, where amusement, comfort and consolation would be found by everyone who brought to it the right frame of mind.[3]

From the opposing side perhaps the most startling statement is that attributed (in the correspondence columns of *The Standard*, 1891) to a visitor to the Public Library at Brighton, who is alleged to have declared "that no greater curse existed than these libraries, and that he had rather see a young man hanging about a public-house than spending his time in these places."[4] This statement, incidentally, bears a curious resemblance to the remark attributed to a gentleman of Bermondsey in 1827 in connection with the mechanics' institute there: "I had rather," he said, "see my servants dead drunk than I would see them going to the Mechanics' Institution."[5] Public attitudes to public libraries and to mechanics' institutes were, indeed, remarkably similar.

The argument that library users were just loafers and novel-readers was common currency. "What would become of their errand boys," demanded a speaker at Lowestoft in 1891, "when sent out on messages when the library was established? They would loaf about the place and the people might wait for their meat and fish!"[6] A writer in *Blackwood's Magazine* for 1895 complained that a legacy originally intended to provide flannel petticoats for the poor had been diverted to library uses "in order that a number of louts may have a nice warm room to read the worst novels and the sporting news in the papers and neglect their natural work."[7] At Islington in 1900, when the question of adoption was under consideration, a ratepayer inquired in the columns of the *Islington Gazette* why he should have to pay eight shillings a year for "lazy people that have nothing else to do but lounge about at home or in a library reading books." Another gentleman described a library as a place "where you can arrange to meet your young lady instead of waiting about in the street and catching a cold."[8]

[1] Greenwood (1891), p. 350.
[2] J. J. Ogle, *The Free Library* (1897), pp. 89–91.
[3] J. J. Macdonald, *Passmore Edwards Institutions* (1900), p. 17.
[4] Quoted Greenwood (1891), p. 82.
[5] *New London Mechanics' Register*, Vol. I (1827), p. 106.
[6] Greenwood (1891), p. 213.
[7] *Blackwood's Magazine*, Vol. CLVII (1895), pp. 153–154. Quoted W. J. Murison, *The Public Library: its Origins, Purpose, and Significance* (1955, 2nd. edn. 1971), p. 228.
[8] *Islington Public Libraries: Golden Jubilee, 1906–1956* [1956], p. 3.

There was just sufficient truth in allegations of this kind to give them a colouring of credibility. Poor people certainly did go into libraries to keep warm, and their presence created problems for librarians;[1] the prevalent interest in fiction was also a cause of concern. We can have little doubt, however, that in most cases such arguments were merely rationalisations of deeper prejudices deriving from vested interests, among which those of the property owners and the brewers figured most prominently.

Until the power of adoption was transferred to town councils in 1893 (1894 in Scotland), these vested interests continued to use every possible device to discredit the idea of public libraries and prevent adoption. "I do not wish to influence you in any view you may have respecting a free library", wrote a Hull landlord to his tenants in 1888, "but I presume if it is adopted, you will have no objection to my adding the library rate to the rental."[2] We hear of similar threats at Lowestoft, Peterborough and Taunton.[3] At Peterborough the local press pointed out that on a house rented at 4s. per week the library rate would amount to $\frac{1}{2}$d. per month, but we can hardly doubt that some voters here and elsewhere were influenced by fear of victimization. At Taunton it was alleged that "unscrupulous opponents had frightened the poorer people into the belief that their rents would be raised by the adoption of the Libraries Acts to such a fabulous amount that they would be unable to pay them, and the workhouse would be the only place of refuge from the library rate."[4]

The most notable provincial centres which declined to adopt the Acts during the years 1887 to 1893 were Hull and Glasgow. Hull turned the proposal down a fourth time in 1888 before finally deciding to adopt in 1892. Glasgow, in 1888, was rejecting the Acts for the third time, and in fact never adopted them, the procedure being eventually circumvented by a private Act in 1899.[5] In London, where the Act of 1893 did not apply, many districts continued to refuse every proposal for a public library right up to the end of the century, when the establishment of the metropolitan boroughs at last brought to an end the cumbersome procedure of the public poll. Before this happened Paddington and St. Pancras had rejected the Acts three times, Deptford and Marylebone four times, and Islington five times.

The abolition of polling did not, of course, necessarily put an end to opposition and controversy. At Malvern, for example, the battles which preceded the Council's decision to adopt in 1902 were by no means unlike those which had raged elsewhere in the 'seventies and 'eighties, and in fact involved many of the same arguments.[6] By this time, however, the opposition was in general dying down, and the idea was coming to be accepted that a public library was a necessary amenity of a civilized community.

This gradual change was due to a number of factors. The abolition of public polling was certainly one, for it was easier to secure a hearing for reasoned

---

[1] Greenwood (1891), pp. 36–37, advises that people should not be allowed to sleep or write letters.

[2] J. F. Hooton, *Libraries in Hull in the Nineteenth Century and the Struggle for the Adoption of the Public Libraries Acts* (unpublished F.L.A. thesis, 1967), p. 205. On Hull see further below, pp. 150–151.

[3] Greenwood (1891), pp. 191–192, 213, 429–430.

[4] *Op. cit.*, pp. 429–430.   [6] See below, pp. 161–162.

[5] See below, p. 142.

argument in the council chamber than on the public hustings. Another was the growing sense of civic responsibility which resulted from the local government reforms of 1888–94. Yet another, which has been little appreciated, was the steady rise in the rate income of local authorities. This rise must be attributed to population growth and the increase in industrial and commercial activity. Coupled as it was, almost to the end of the century, with falling prices, it placed the authorities in a much more favourable position than would otherwise have been the case for assuming the burdens of a library service. The overall increase in rate income in England and Wales was from £25.7 millions in 1885 to £40.7 millions in 1900 and £75.4 millions in 1918. The sharp increase in government grants also brought indirect benefits to the library service.[1]

Unquestionably, however, the largest single factor in persuading local authorities to undertake the burden of library provision was the availability of substantial grants in aid—not, as originally suggested by the 1849 Report, from the government, but from private funds, and above all from Andrew Carnegie.

Carnegie and Other Benefactors

Carnegie's career, so typical of that of the self-made industrial magnate of the nineteenth century, is too well known to need more than a brief reference here. Born in Dunfermline in 1835, he was the son of William Carnegie, a Chartist handloom weaver who in 1848, finding his employment gone, emigrated with his family to America. Andrew, at the age of twelve, began work as a bobbin-boy in a cotton mill in Allegheny (now part of Pittsburgh); when he retired in 1901 he was master of the largest iron and steel combine in the world, and his personal fortune was reckoned in hundreds of millions of dollars.

By this time he had already given away substantial sums. These gifts were sometimes objected to at the time, and have been sneered at since, as the "conscience-money" of one who had amassed his wealth by ruthless exploitation. A Gainsborough town councillor used the term "blood money".[2] This view has its origins in the notorious strike at the Carnegie Steel Company's Homestead Mills in 1892, in which a considerable number of lives were lost. It is fair to say, however, that at this date Carnegie had retired from active management of the concern. He was out of the country at the time, and there is evidence that he disapproved of the way the matter was handled.[3] His own attitude to his employees, though it may have been old-fashioned, had not been by the standards of the time inhumane or illiberal, and in the disposal of what some considered his ill-gotten gains he showed a deep sense of social responsibility. In an article on "Wealth" published in the *North American Review* in 1889 (afterwards reprinted by the *Pall Mall Gazette* under the title "The Gospel of Wealth"), he argued that the private capitalist alone could provide the energy, enterprise and leadership that modern industry needed. He admitted that the

[1] R. B. Mitchell and P. Deane, *Abstract of British Historical Statistics* (Cambridge 1962), pp. 414–415.
[2] Information from the Borough Librarian, Mr. J. S. English.
[3] The whole story is graphically told in B. J. Hendrick, *The Life of Andrew Carnegie* (1933), Ch. xx.

reward accruing to the successful capitalist was excessive, but the remedy for this, in his view, was for the capitalist himself to devote the same talents that had amassed his great fortune to the task of using it for the public good. It was wrong for such a man to leave his wealth unused: "The man who dies thus rich dies disgraced."[1]

Carnegie's philanthropy embraced the United States, Canada, the British Isles, Australia, New Zealand, almost the entire English-speaking world. He sedulously avoided any kind of poor relief, preferring to invest his money in universities, libraries, museums, parks, and other institutions which would yield a long-term benefit in improving the condition of the people. To public libraries he always accorded a special priority, and when in 1913 he established the Carnegie United Kingdom Trust, with a capital of £2 millions, to take over his philanthropic work in this country, he declared in the preamble to the trust deed that "Libraries are entitled to a first place as instruments for the elevation of the masses of the people."[2] In his article on "The Gospel of Wealth" he had explained the origin of this conviction:

> "It is no doubt possible that my own personal experience may have led me to value a free library beyond all other forms of beneficence. When I was a boy in Pittsburg, Colonel Anderson of Allegheny—a name I can never speak without feelings of devotional gratitude—opened his little library of four hundred books to boys. Every Saturday afternoon he was in attendance at his house to exchange books. No one but he who has felt it can know that intense longing with which the arrival of Saturday was awaited, that a new book might be had. My brother and Mr. Phipps, who have been my principal business partners through life, shared with me Colonel Anderson's precious generosity; and it was when revelling in these treasures which he opened to us that I resolved, if ever wealth came to me, that it should be used to establish free libraries, that other poor boys might receive opportunities similar to those for which we were indebted to that noble man."[3]

At the time the United Kingdom Trust was created, Carnegie had already made grants amounting to £1¾ millions in aid of public libraries in the United Kingdom. Promises already made carried the total almost to £2 millions.[4] His grants began in a modest way in 1879 with an offer of £8000 for a public library in his native town of Dunfermline. The offer was accepted and the library duly opened in 1883. Other Scottish gifts followed, notably £50000 to Edinburgh in 1886, and £10000 to Ayr in 1890.[5] It was not until after 1897, when the business of library-giving was put, as Carnegie sometimes said, on a wholesale as distinct from a retail basis, that his bounty was extended to other parts of the United Kingdom, the first grant in England being to Keighley in 1899.[6]

---

[1] The article is reprinted in Carnegie's book, *The Gospel of Wealth and other Timely Essays* (New York 1900, English edn. 1901), and is summarized in Hendrick, *op. cit.*, Ch. xvii.
[2] The deed is printed in the *First Annual Report* of the Trust, for 1913–14 (Edinburgh 1915), pp. 20 sqq.
[3] A. Carnegie, *op. cit.*, pp. 27–28.
[4] Carnegie U.K. Trust, *First Annual Report, 1913–14*, p. 9.
[5] Lesser gifts were received during the 'eighties and 'nineties by Aberdeen, Airdrie, Arbroath, Elgin, Grangemouth, Inverness, Kirkwall, Peterhead, Tarves, Thurso and Wick.
[6] *The Public Library Service in Keighley, 1904–1954* (Keighley 1954). Carnegie gave £10000 towards the cost of a central library, which was opened in 1904.

It was now necessary to formalize the procedure, and responsibility was placed in the hands of Carnegie's secretary, James Bertram. The rules were clear and simple. Except in a very few instances, grants were not made for books but solely for library buildings and equipment, the local authority being required to provide a site free of encumbrance, to adopt the Libraries Acts, and to levy at least a 1d. rate for maintenance. Plans and estimates had to be submitted for approval, and if the promised grant were exceeded the excess must be borne by the authority.[1]

It was on such principles that Carnegie proceeded to give away, in various parts of the world, more than 2800 public libraries.[2] "I am now giving away libraries at the rate of two or three a day", he wrote to his friends.[3] When he died in 1919 it was said more than half the library authorities in Great Britain—213 out of 437 in England and Wales, and 50 out of 77 in Scotland—had received grants in aid, and in the United Kingdom as a whole 380 library buildings were associated with his name.[4]

In making these gifts Carnegie congratulated himself that he was forcing the municipalities which received them to do, in the long run, even more. "America's conscript fathers," writes his biographer, "stolid and balky in the face of growing public opinion, suddenly found that Carnegie, by proposing so palpable an argument as money on the popular side, had lighted fires beneath them."[5] The same was true in this country: in Edinburgh, for example, proposals for a public library had twice been rejected before Carnegie's offer of £50000 persuaded the citizens to change their minds.[6] At Ayr the library committee wrote to Carnegie after receiving his offer:

> "Your generous offer of assistance towards a library building was very much appreciated.... The chances of the adoption of the Free Libraries Act were fully discussed. The overwhelming defeat of the former attempt was in the minds of all the members, and I daresay none of us, before the receipt of yours of the 3rd, had any thought of making another attempt. This letter, however, put a different complexion upon the matter, and with your proffered help, we have resolved to do all in our power towards effecting so desirable an end."[7]

Another attempt *was* made, and this time the public vote was overwhelmingly in favour. Indeed we can safely say that the majority of library authorities established in Scotland during this period owed their existence in the first place to the promise or the hope of a Carnegie grant. In England and Wales

---

[1] W. G. S. Adams, *A Report on Library Provision and Policy to the Carnegie United Kingdom Trustees* (Edinburgh 1915), pp. 11–12.

[2] Carnegie Endowment for International Peace, *A Manual of the Public Benefactions of Andrew Carnegie* (Washington 1919), p. 317.

[3] Hendrick, *op. cit.*, p. 554.

[4] A. L. Hetherington, "The Late Andrew Carnegie", in *L.A.R.*, Vol. XXI (1919), p. 284. Hetherington seems to have underestimated the number of library authorities at this time. My own total for 1918 is 549 compared with his 514 (below, p. 123). His total of 380 Carnegie buildings in the U.K. also seems below the mark compared with the 660, given *or* promised, recorded in the *Manual of Benefactions* just cited.

[5] Hendrick, *op. cit.*, p. 552.

[6] See above, p. 30.

[7] Carnegie Public Library, Ayr, *Address by Andrew Carnegie ... 1892* (Edinburgh 1892), pp. 7–9.

a higher proportion of the grants than in Scotland went to assist libraries already established, but here too, where new libraries were under consideration, a Carnegie grant was often the decisive factor. At Maidenhead, for example, the movement for a public library began in 1891, but in spite of guarantees amounting to more than £1000 it was not until Carnegie came forward, in 1902, with an offer of £5000 that the Council agreed to adopt the Acts.[1] At Torquay a similar decision taken in 1903, following an offer from Carnegie of £1500, brought to an end an agitation of which the beginnings can be traced back to 1857.[2] And at Islington in 1904, it was Carnegie's munificent offer of £40000 for a central library and four branch libraries which eventually overcame the stubborn opposition of the ratepayers, who had rejected proposals for a public library five times between 1870 and 1897, and had even turned down, on the last occasion, an offer of £10000 from John Passmore Edwards.[3]

There were, indeed, some local authorities which were strong-minded enough, or as some thought reactionary enough, to resist Carnegie's blandishments. Paddington, which turned down a £15000 offer in 1903, was a notable example, and there were others, but they were exceptional.[4] Where the will was present, Carnegie's money often provided the way.

One of the first things the Carnegie United Kingdom Trustees did was to commission Professor W. G. S. Adams of Oxford (afterwards Warden of All Souls) to prepare a special report on *Library Provision and Policy*. This report paid generous tribute to the Carnegie benefactions, "which have had," it declared, "a far-reaching influence on the library movement in the United Kingdom, and have made possible at many centres a development which would not otherwise have come into existence." There was, it was stressed, "still wide scope for development in the system of town libraries", but the special attention of the Trustees was directed to what Adams considered was now the most urgent problem, that of library provision in the rural areas.[5] With what alacrity the Trustees took up this new task we shall see in a later section, but grants for new buildings in urban libraries were henceforth on a smaller scale, and were discontinued altogether, apart from outstanding commitments, in 1917.[6]

The Trustees did, however, agree at an early stage to consider grants in aid of libraries which had incurred heavy loan charges by building without Carnegie's help, and which were consequently unable to maintain an adequate service. These grants were usually made on the understanding that matching grants would be made from local sources (other than the rates) and it was a

[1] Maidenhead Public Library, *First Annual Report, 1906*, pp. 3–6.
[2] *Torquay Public Library: Fifty Years of Service, 1907–1957* [Torquay 1957].
[3] *Islington Public Libraries Golden Jubilee, 1906–1956* [1956], pp. 2–3.
[4] For Paddington see below, p. 134. Dartford rejected a Carnegie grant in the same year, but accepted later, the Acts being adopted in 1912—Borough of Dartford, *National Library Week: Dartford Public Libraries and Museums Jubilee, 1916–1966* ([Dartford] 1966), p. 5.
[5] W. G. S. Adams, *A Report on Library Provision and Policy to the Carnegie United Kingdom Trustees* (Edinburgh 1915), pp. 13–15. This report is cited hereafter as *Adams Report*.
[6] Carnegie U.K. Trustees, *First Annual Report, 1913–14*, p. 11; *Fourth Annual Report, 1917*, pp. 17–18; *Fifth Annual Report, 1918*, p. 14. Some promised grants, however, remained unclaimed for many years: the last to be paid was for the Merthyr Tydfil Central Library in 1935.

condition that the additional income thus made available should be used for current library expenditure. About a score of libraries were assisted in this way during the years 1915–18.[1]

Even if Carnegie had never existed, the years from about 1880 to the onset of the first World War would still count as a great age of library benefactions. Small-scale gifts and bequests of books or money were common, and there were many more substantial donations to provide for buildings also. The most notable of these was the gift of £105 000 by the trustees of Edmund Robert Harris, a wealthy local solicitor, for the erection of a public library, museum, and art gallery at Preston. The Corporation provided a central site worth a further £30 000, and the splendid classical building which still houses the public library was opened in 1892.[2] It need hardly be said that it is now very over-crowded: this is the trouble with monumental buildings of this kind. At the time, however, it made Preston "as to a public library far and away the best endowed place of the size in England."[3]

Scotland, which in the 'eighties and 'nineties was already profiting from Carnegie's generosity, received at the same period other important gifts. In the 'eighties John Thompson Paton of Norwood, a wealthy and enterprising woollen manufacturer, provided a town hall and library for Alloa at a cost of some £30 000: the library, complete with over 7000 books, was opened in 1889.[4] In the 'nineties a bequest of £50 000 from Michael Beveridge made similar provision for the town of Kirkcaldy, of which he had once been provost;[5] and Archibald Sandeman, a former professor of mathematics at Owens College, Manchester, bequeathed £30 000 to provide a library for Perth.[6] No public library, however, was so fortunate in this respect as Glasgow, which over a period of some thirty years received gifts and bequests to the value of over £200 000.[7]

In England the most fortunate authority, apart from Preston, was Lambeth, which commenced its library service in 1888 and within ten years had accumulated gifts to the value of close on £43 000. Frederick Nettlefold, nut and bolt manufacturer, gave the site for the first building, a branch at West Norwood. Henry Tate (afterwards Sir Henry), sugar magnate and founder of the Tate Gallery, gave the central library at Brixton and a branch library in South

[1] Carnegie U.K. Trustees, *Second Annual Report, 1915*, pp. 22–23. For details see the financial statements appended to this and later Reports.

[2] E. R. Harris (1804–77), son of Robert Harris, a Church of England clergyman and schoolmaster, was partner with his brother in an old established firm of solicitors, and for some years protonotary for the County Palatine of Lancaster. A man of reserved temperament, almost a recluse in his old age, he died a bachelor, leaving a fortune of over £300 000 to found institutions in Preston in memory of his father. The facts concerning him have been assembled in an article in the *Lancashire Daily Post* for 6 Mar. 1933.

[3] J. J. Ogle, *The Free Library* (1897), p. 228.

[4] On Paton see J. Archibald, *Alloa Sixty Years Ago* (Alloa 1911), pp. 23–24, 52–57, 133–136. The library continued in this building till merged with the Clackmannan County Service in 1936.

[5] P. K. Livingstone, *Kirkcaldy and its Libraries* (Kirkcaldy 1950), pp. 15–21.

[6] The Sandeman family, noted for their connection with the port and sherry trade, had long established links with Perth. For the origins of the Sandeman Library see *Library World*, Vol. I (1898–99), pp. 93–95; and *L.A.R.*, Vol. XIII (1911), pp. 322–329.

[7] See below, pp. 142–144.

Lambeth, and a Miss J. Durning Smith gave another branch. Tate also gave a library to the nearby parish of Streatham, where he lived, and subsequently the site for a branch library at Balham: his total public library benefactions were well in excess of £30 000.[1] Among lesser but still substantial gifts we may mention the provision, in the 'nineties, of technical institutes and libraries for two Lancashire towns: at St. Helens by Colonel David Gamble,[2] and at Ashton under Lyne by the trustees of George Heginbottom, to whose earlier bequest the library owed its origin ten years before.[3] In Yorkshire at the same period the energy and generosity of Charles Harvey, a local linen-draper, converted a bankrupt public hall into a library for Barnsley;[4] and we shall see how James Reckitt shamed Hull into adopting the Libraries Acts by building and maintaining a free library for part of the town at his own expense.[5] At the other end of England, in 1893, Octavius Allen Ferris left an estate of £10 000 to his native town of Truro and other Cornish towns for public library purposes.[6]

It was, however, another Cornishman, John Passmore Edwards, who came nearest to Carnegie in the wholesale character of his library benefactions. Born in the little village of Blackwater, in the derelict mining area between Truro and Redruth, in 1823, Edwards got such education as he could from the village school and his own reading. Like Carnegie he owed his interest in public libraries to his boyhood experience. In his autobiography he writes:

> "My father rather discouraged than encouraged reading, and particularly in the daytime. On winter evenings the room in which the family mostly lived was lighted by a single candle similar to what miners used underground. Such candles in those days required frequent snuffing, but they rarely got it. I, however, by the aid of such light, managed to read whilst others were talking or moving about; and hundreds and hundreds of times I pressed my thumbs firmly on my ears until they ached, in order to read with as little distraction as possible. In this way I managed to frequently entertain myself and pick up fragments of knowledge. These recollections of early days, fresh and vivid as those of yesterday, have encouraged me in after years to promote the public library movement...."[7]

---

[1] See Greenwood (1891), pp. 318–323, and for Tate, R. H. Blackburn, *Sir Henry Tate: his Contributions to Art and Learning* (Chorley [1940]); and the entertaining address on *Sir Henry Tate as a Benefactor of Libraries* given by K. Povey to the North-West Branch of the Library Association in 1957 (duplicated for private circulation by Lambeth Public Libraries).

[2] St. Helens Public Libraries and Museum, *72nd Report, 1949–50*, p. 5. Gamble (knighted in 1897) was a leading figure both in the local chemical industry and in civic affairs.

[3] George Heginbottom, a cotton spinning manufacturer, is briefly characterized in H. Heginbottom, *Thomas Heginbottom: a few slight impressions of his life and times* (Hyde 1913), pp. 24–27. The present librarian, Mr. Trevor Bolton, has pointed out to me that the elaborate Victorian Gothic building was a mixed blessing. It cost over £20 000 towards which the Heginbottom trustees gave only £10 000, leaving the library with a load of debt which inhibited its development for forty years.

[4] Greenwood (1894), p. 93. The hall, rechristened the Harvey Institute, continued to provide accommodation for public meetings.

[5] See below, pp. 150–151.

[6] J. J. Ogle, *The Free Library* (1897), pp. 69, 264.

[7] J. P. Edwards, *A Few Footprints* (1905), p. 6.

It was a story about John Hunter the anatomist, in the *Penny Magazine*, which inspired in him the ambition "to become known and useful in some way myself".[1] He became a journalist, first in Manchester, then in London, and was active in societies for the abolition of capital punishment, war, taxes on knowledge, the opium trade, flogging in H.M. Forces, and so forth. A first attempt as a publisher of periodicals ended in bankruptcy, but eventually he not only established himself in this line of business but made a substantial fortune. Among the journals he owned was the *Echo*, London's first ½d. daily newspaper, which he controlled for about twenty years before selling it off to a syndicate in 1896. He was Liberal M.P. for Salisbury for a time (1880–85) but found it a frustrating experience.

Edwards died in 1911, having twice declined a knighthood. He used his accumulated fortune to found not only libraries but also hospitals, convalescent homes, and other charitable institutions, to a total of about seventy, mostly in or around London or in his native Cornwall. In his library benefactions he began, about 1890, with gifts of books, and went on to give buildings. By the time he came to write his autobiography in 1905, he had provided fifteen public libraries in and around London (most of them in the poorer, central areas of the city) eight in Cornwall (including Truro) and one in Devon.[2] During the same period he had also presented some 70000 volumes to public libraries and other institutions.

We may aptly bring this section to a close by quoting the last three stanzas of what can only be called a "hymn to a library benefactor." It was composed and sung in Fleetwood, Lancashire, on the occasion of the opening of the Fielden Public Library there in 1887. The eponymous benefactor, Samuel Fielden, was a well known Todmorden cotton manufacturer with property interests in Fleetwood, who had been persuaded to purchase and present to the town a building for a public library. The hymn, which we quote because it is so typical of the atmosphere of such occasions, concludes as follows:

> "We thank our benefactors
>   With willing hearts and kind,
> Who nobly make provision
>   To feed the hungry mind,
> Who use their wealth and influence,
>   And throw a cheering ray
> To lighten life's rough journey
>   And cheer man on his way.
>   *Chorus*
> "Come, raise aloud your voices
>   In one harmonious lay,
> Let not harsh word or discord
>   Be heard in town to-day.

---

[1] *Op. cit.*, pp. 5–6.

[2] See list below, App. X. Cf. J. P. Edwards, *op. cit.*, pp. 40, 53–54; J. J. Macdonald, *Passmore Edwards Institutions* (1900). There is an interesting essay on Edwards in D. Owen, *English Philanthropy, 1660–1960* (1965), pp. 428–434. Cf. E. Harcourt Burrage, *J. Passmore Edwards, Philanthropist* (1902). The collaboration between Edwards and S. A. Barnett in the east end of London is illustrated in H. Barnett, *Canon Barnett and his Friends* (1919), Vol. II, pp. 10–11.

> "The daring deeds of warriors
> We sing in deathless lays,
> And surely acts of kindness
> Deserve our warmest praise.
> The well known name of Fielden
> Shall shine on history's page
> When wall, and roof, and rafters,
> Are crumbling down with age.
> *Chorus*
> "Come, raise aloud your voices, *etc.*
>
> "Yes, acts so kind and gracious,
> Shall be remembered long,
> And handed down for ages
> In story and in song.
> God bless our benefactor
> God bless his worthy wife
> May heaven be pleased to grant them
> A long and happy life.
> *Chorus*
> "Come, raise aloud your voices, *etc.*"

The hymn was sung to the air of *God bless the Prince of Wales*. Samuel Fielden himself, with modesty and commendable foresight, chose to absent himself, leaving his wife to declare the library open and to hand over his cheque for £100 for books.[1]

The Pattern of Growth

Against this background we can survey in a little more detail the manner in which the country's library service developed. In 1887 the service was still exceedingly patchy. It was, as we have seen, almost entirely restricted to the urban areas, and the Parliamentary Return of 1885 shows it as covering only about 23 per cent of the total population—25 per cent in England, 15 per cent in Wales, and 8 per cent in Scotland. By 1914 the overall percentage had risen to 60, and though England continued to lead the way with 62 per cent, both Scotland, with 50 per cent, and Wales, with 46 per cent, showed remarkable increases.[2] The periods of most rapid growth were 1892–96, with nearly twenty new library authorities commencing service each year, and 1905–07, with more than one hundred new library authorities in three years. After 1909 there was a sudden falling off, not, it may fairly be supposed, because of any failure of enthusiasm, but simply because practically every local authority which could afford to run a library on a 1d. rate had now got one.

Even during the war years, however, a few new library authorities came into existence, and by the close of 1918 the number of authorities which had commenced service had risen to 584. A comparison with the figures for the close of 1886 is very striking:

	England	Wales	Scotland	Total
1886	107	6	12	125
1918	438	63	83	584

[1] Information from Mr. D. B. Timms, Borough Librarian.
[2] *Adams Report*, p. 7.

It should be noted that in 1918 the process of amalgamation of library authorities, which was to be so marked a feature of the period following the first World War, had already begun, especially in London and the larger English cities, so that the number of authorities actually operating in 1918 was not 584 but 549, including 406 in England, 61 in Wales, and 82 in Scotland.

The most notable growth areas of this second period of library history were London and the home counties where, as we have seen, development in earlier years had been very slow. The change was due in large measure to the bene-factions of Passmore Edwards, Carnegie and others. In the area which is now Inner London there were in 1886 only three library authorities in operation—St. Margaret and St. John at Westminster, Wandsworth, and the City. Within the next few years, however, progress was rapid: Battersea, Chelsea, and Fulham in 1887; Clerkenwell, Kensington, Lambeth and Putney in 1888; Christchurch, Clapham, Hammersmith, and St. Martin in the Fields in 1889; and so on. By the end of the century there were 34 authorities operating, embracing more than half of the city's parishes. The London Government Act which came into force in 1900 reduced the number to 20, leaving only Bethnal Green, Deptford, Greenwich, Hackney, Islington, Paddington, St. Marylebone, and St. Pancras entirely without library service.[1] Most of these metropolitan boroughs adopted the Acts and inaugurated a library service within the next few years, but Bethnal Green, Paddington and St. Marylebone resisted the tide of public opinion until the 'twenties.

In the region which is now Outer London, the growth was almost as rapid. To the little cluster of libraries which had sprung up on the western fringe of London in the early 'eighties—Wimbledon, Kingston, Twickenham, Richmond, and Ealing—there were added by 1908 twenty-five more. Barking in 1889, Brentford and Croydon in 1890, Chiswick in 1891, Penge, Tottenham, West Ham and Wood Green in 1892, Edmonton and Leyton in 1893, Bromley, Enfield, Walthamstow and Willesden in 1894, were the first of what soon became a ring of libraries round the entire city.

Elsewhere in the country the main growing points continued to be, as in the earlier period, the populous industrial areas of the North and Midlands—Lancashire, with no fewer than 51 new library authorities established during these years, Cheshire with 15, the West Riding with 37, Staffordshire with 11. The industrial area of South Wales also came into the picture at this time, with 13 new library authorities in Glamorganshire to make a total of 15 for the county. In Scotland there was no comparable development: it was not industrial and heavily populated Lanarkshire, with a mere seven library authorities, but mainly rural Aberdeenshire, with nine, that topped the list of Scottish counties at the end of the period.

With the establishment of libraries in Southampton (1889), Edinburgh (1890), Hull (1893) and finally Glasgow (1899), the coverage of the major urban centres was by the end of the century almost complete. Apart from the metro-politan boroughs referred to above, there was now not a single town of more than 100000 population without a library; and even if we count the towns of

---

[1] For details of these changes see *L.Y.B. 1900–01*, pp. xv–xvi, and *Library World*, Vol. II (1899–1900), pp. 85–88, which has a useful map. The development of library authorities before 1900 is studied in P. M. Whiteman, *The Establishment of Public Libraries and the Unit of Local Government in London to 1900* (unpublished M.A. thesis, Belfast, 1969).

between 50000 and 100000 population, we can find only a handful unprovided for. By the close of 1918 this handful had shrunk to two—Leith and Rhondda.[1] Most towns of over 20000 inhabitants now had a library service, and a considerable number of smaller towns, and even rural parishes.[2] No English county was now entirely without library authorities; in Wales only Pembrokeshire had this melancholy distinction, in Scotland only Berwickshire, Bute, Wigtownshire and Zetland.

It must, however, be emphasized that even in 1918 the library service was still predominantly urban in character. An estimate made in 1913 indicated that 79 per cent of the urban population had access to public library facilities, compared with 2.4 per cent of the rural population.[3] There were at this time close on a hundred parish library authorities in rural districts, but only about three-quarters of the number had actually implemented the Acts, and many even of these were not giving a full service. The Adams Report comments on these figures:

> "But when further it is remembered that a very considerable number of the libraries in the small towns and parishes are little more than libraries in name, it is plain to how slight an extent the public library movement has reached the smaller towns and the country districts."[4]

This comment is borne out by the fact that between 1887 and 1909 more than fifty authorities adopted the Acts but were never in a position to commence a library service. A few of these were urban or suburban areas overtaken by amalgamation before they could establish a service; but a great many were rural areas in which the penny rate just did not yield enough to support a library.[5] Many of them, no doubt, were hoping for a Carnegie grant.

We are fortunate to have in the Adams Report a detailed picture of public library provision as it was near the end of our period, in 1913–14. As in many centres the library service was curtailed during the war, a later date would indeed have been less satisfactory. It is illuminating to compare the figures regarding the size of libraries which can be calculated from this report with those previously calculated for the year 1886.[6]

In the latter year there were only four libraries with a bookstock of more than 100000 volumes—Manchester, Birmingham, Leeds and Liverpool. All these now exceeded the 300000 mark—Birmingham and Manchester the 400000 mark—and they had been joined by a new major library which overtopped them all—Glasgow with 468000 volumes. No fewer than a dozen other libraries now counted more than 100000 volumes, though none more than 200000: the lead in this group was taken by Cardiff with 193000 volumes,

---

[1] Leith was incorporated in Edinburgh in 1920; Rhondda inaugurated its public library only in 1939. The other towns in this group were Merthyr Tydfil (opened 1900), Bury, Lancs. (1901), Greenock (1902), Southend (1906), and Burnley (1914).

[2] *Adams Report*, pp. 7–8. The figures given by Adams include Ireland and refer to the year 1913–14.

[3] J. McKillop, "The Rural Library Problem", in *L.A.R.*, Vol. XVI (1914), p. 48.

[4] *Adams Report*, p. 8. Here again the figures include Ireland and refer to the year 1913–14. In Great Britain 62 parish authorities had implemented the Acts—28 in England, 18 in Wales and 16 in Scotland.

[5] See the list in Appendix V below.   [6] See above, p. 32.

Edinburgh (another newcomer) with 188000 volumes, and Sheffield with 187000 volumes. Some three dozen libraries, compared with six in the earlier period, now had between 50000 and 100000 volumes. Total bookstocks also showed an impressive increase—from about 2 million volumes in 1886 to 11.4 millions in 1913–14 for a total population about half as large again.[1]

At the other end of the scale, however, there were still three-quarters of the total number of libraries with fewer than 20000 volumes, and substantially more than half with fewer than 10000 volumes. The enormous growth of the years since 1887 had been, in fact, mainly a growth of small libraries. This was particularly true of Wales, where all but a handful of libraries were under 10000 volumes, and most were under 5000 volumes. Even in England, however, it is possible to count, outside the county boroughs and metropolitan boroughs, less than thirty libraries of more than 20000 volumes, and in Scotland there were only about a dozen such libraries altogether.

The basic weakness, as has been pointed out above, lay in the 1d. rate limitation, which pressed all the more hardly as libraries grew older and stocks accumulated. For a time the pressure was relieved, for some authorities, by the legislation of 1889–91 which permitted the levying of separate rates for the maintenance of technical classes and museums.[2] Falling prices may also have helped: by the mid-'nineties the overall index of agricultural and industrial products had fallen to three-quarters of what it had been in 1882–83.[3] An attempt in 1892 to make public library property liable to income tax was success-fully resisted by Manchester, which with the help of other library authorities carried the case to the House of Lords and eventually secured a judgement that public libraries were literary institutions and thus exempt from tax under the Income Tax Act of 1842. This judgement had the incidental effect of making it possible for public libraries to apply, under another Act of 1843, for exemption from the local rates to which many of them were liable, but this long remained a contentious issue, and the position of the libraries was weakened by an adverse judgment in respect of the Liverpool Public Libraries in 1905. The Adams Report shows that most libraries were paying something, and some very considerable sums, under the heading of "rates and taxes".[4]

The device of running a subscription library or book club under public library auspices as a means of procuring books cheaply persisted into this period, and even later. In addition to Bolton, Dundee, and Tynemouth, which we have already had occasion to notice[5], we can count from various sources more than a dozen libraries making use of this arrangement.[6] The Darlington book club,

---

[1] *Adams Report*, p. 68. Cf. below, Appendix VI.   [2] See above, p. 111.
[3] Rousseaux Price Indices, in B. R. Mitchell and P. Deane, *Abstract of British Historical Statistics* (Cambridge 1962), pp. 472–473.
[4] See on these questions Greenwood (1891), pp. 366–368; the chapter by W. R. Credland in *L.Y.B. 1897*, pp. 44–51; J. D. Brown, *Manual of Library Economy* (1903), pp. 46–48; H. W. Fovargue, "The Exemption of Public Libraries and Museums from Rates and Taxes," in *L.A.R.*, Vol. X (1908), pp. 103–104; and Board of Education, Public Libraries Committee, *Report on Public Libraries in England and Wales* [Kenyon Report] (1927), pp. 55–56.
[5] See above, p. 111.
[6] Accrington, Alloa, Chesterfield, Darlington, Dewsbury, Dumfries, Elgin, Hawick, King's Lynn, Leek, South Shields, Wednesbury, Willesden and Workington.

begun in 1893, continued in operation until 1911, and added over 4000 volumes to the general library stock.[1]

As the twentieth century advanced it became increasingly difficult either to establish or to maintain an adequate library service on the 1d. rate. Short of general legislation the most satisfactory though also the most expensive solution was to secure by special Act permission to raise a higher rate, and by 1914 more than fifty places had in fact done this. The list included nearly all the large provincial towns—in England: Birmingham, Bradford, Bristol, Leeds, Liverpool, Manchester, Newcastle upon Tyne, Nottingham, Salford, and Sheffield; in Wales: Cardiff and Swansea; in Scotland: Dundee and Glasgow (but not Edinburgh). Lancashire was particularly notable for its enterprise in this direction, no fewer than seventeen county and municipal boroughs having secured additional rating powers. Bury and Oldham were actually levying a 3d. rate, the highest in the country, but this had to cover the art gallery and museum as well as the library. In general, even where special rating powers were held, the rate actually levied rarely exceeded 2d. Huddersfield, operating under a local Act which imposed no set limitation at all, still levied only 1d.[2]

The great majority of libraries still had to work within the limit of a 1d. rate, and at least a score had to manage with less—$\frac{3}{4}$d., $\frac{1}{2}$d., even in one or two cases $\frac{1}{4}$d.[3] Professor Adams found 55 libraries in England, and 44 in Wales and Scotland, with annual incomes in 1910–11 of less than £100, and well over half the total had incomes under £500. In some instances a 1d. rate—even at Bath a $\frac{1}{2}$d. rate—had to maintain a museum as well as a library. After necessary deductions for salaries, maintenance charges, and possibly loan charges, the amount left for books and periodicals was often derisory—in many cases less than £10 a year. Many poor libraries actually spent more on periodicals than on books, and this fact indicates very clearly the character of the service provided.[4]

Even the gift of a building, though it relieved the library authority of rent or loan charges, was not always an unqualified benefit. Adams mentioned that the major criticism of Carnegie grants might be summed up in the word "over-building".

> "Libraries have, in a number of cases, been provided, involving a scale of expenditure on upkeep which left no sufficient means for the main purpose and object of the library. . . . Buildings in several instances costing £10000 or even larger sums have been erected, the upkeep of which absorbed the greater part of the income from the 1d. rate, leaving a mere pittance, and in some cases not even that, for the purchase of books. In certain instances, where there had previously been a

[1] *Edward Pease Public Library: Fifty Years Progress, 1885–1935* (Darlington 1935), p. 7.

[2] *Adams Report*, p. 10 and tables; cf. Library Association, *Public Libraries: their Development and Future Organisation* (1917), pp. 107–111.

[3] The tables in Adams show one parish (Shirebrook in Derbyshire) and one urban district (Ross on Wye) with $\frac{1}{4}$d rate. Three metropolitan boroughs (Holborn, Kensington, and Westminster) and two county boroughs (Bath and Burton upon Trent) levied varying amounts under 1d.

[4] *Adams Report*, pp. 9, 13; Carnegie U.K. Trust, *Statistics relating to Public Libraries in the United Kingdom compiled from the Returns contained in Professor Adams' Report on Library Provision and Policy* (1916, reprinted from the Trust's *Second Annual Report*), pp. 3–6; Library Association, *Public Libraries: their Development and Future Organisation* (1917), App. I.

library on smaller premises, the gift of the larger building has ultimately involved a reduction in the expenditure on books. In many cases there is not an adequate income to provide a librarian worthy of the building and competent to create the true library."[1]

In an appendix Adams cites several examples of overbuilding, including one library (with a £10000 building) which in 1914 could only afford £1 for books.[2] Another example, which we may surmise to be Hawick, is recorded as follows:

"In 1902 Mr. Carnegie gave £10000 for a library building—the penny in the pound produces £300. The gift was too great in proportion both to the size of the town (16887 pop.) and to the yield of rate. Salary of librarian is £100; and in 1914, £11.17s.5d. was spent on books. Local effort has started a book-club, which transfers the books, bought by subscription, to the public library after one year.

The former librarian writes, that previously the library had 'accommodation in the Municipal Buildings, and out of a revenue of £300 spent £80 on books. Grant of £10000 obtained, and the cost of maintenance swallowed up the whole income, and nothing was left for purchase of books. In this case a Carnegie grant seriously crippled a prosperous library.'"[3]

Twenty-five years later Stanley Jast, City Librarian of Manchester, referred "to the buildings which Mr. Carnegie, infinitely well-meaning but infinitely ill-advised, showered on library authorities whose funds were exhausted in the effort to keep them up".[4]

This kind of problem, of course, did not arise only with Carnegie libraries: it was a danger inherent in every major benefaction which was not accompanied by a continuing endowment.[5] To do Carnegie justice, it was precisely for this reason that he insisted that his gifts must be accompanied by adoption of the Libraries Acts.

It was, of course, the small town and village libraries which had the hardest struggle. Some, very wisely, did not attempt to provide an independent service but joined forces with a neighbouring town.[6] The difficulties of those which did operate independently are revealed in the details given in the Adams Report and the Parliamentary Return of 1912. Very often they were no more than reading rooms with a few hundred books for lending or reference. "Collection of books in Reading Room" is the description attached to the library of Letcombe Regis, a small parish in Berkshire, which had 439 inhabitants, and a total library income of £6 per annum, none of which in 1913–14 was devoted to books or periodicals.[7] This was one extreme case, but there were quite a few

---

[1] *Adams Report*, p. 14. [2] *Op. cit.*, p. 94.

[3] *Ibid.* Cf. W. R. Aitken, *A History of the Public Library Movement in Scotland to 1955* (Glasgow 1971), p. 78.

[4] L. Stanley Jast, *The Library and the Community* (1939), p. 43.

[5] J. D. Brown, *Manual of Library Economy* (1903), p. 13, draws attention to the absurdity of "a huge library building without books, like some of those erected in Cornwall by Mr. Passmore Edwards." For further details see his article "Some Cornish Libraries", in *Library World*, Vol. III (1900–01), pp. 57–62.

[6] Ashton on Mersey (with Sale), Audenshaw, Hurst, and Waterloo (with Ashton under Lyne), Bowdon (with Altrincham), Chesterton (with Cambridge), Ince in Makerfield (with Wigan), Papcastle (with Cockermouth), Stainburn (with Workington), Winnington (with Northwich).

[7] *Adams Report*, pp. 26–27.

parish libraries, especially in Wales and rural England, which were not much better off. Cratfield, in Suffolk, had 200 volumes "kept in the Parish Council office", which suggests that there was not even a reading-room: the issues were about one a week.[1] Great Wyrley, in Staffordshire, had 500 volumes available through three delivery stations.[2] Burwell, in Cambridgeshire, hired its books from a book club;[3] the small Lancashire town of Padiham paid a guinea a year to the Union of Lancashire and Cheshire Institutes for a supply of books changed once a quarter.[4] And, of course, many of these small libraries were unable to open for more than a few hours a week.[5]

By 1914 there was general agreement in informed circles on the urgent need for reform, in order to increase the financial resources available to public libraries and to provide more adequately for the rural areas. Then came the war, and all possibility of new legislation vanished till victory was won. In the meantime prices were rising steeply, and despairing librarians saw their services becoming less adequate with every year that passed. They were not assisted in their plight by the government, which clearly regarded public libraries as expendable. In August, 1915, a circular from the Local Government Board grouped together "parks, recreation grounds, libraries, street lighting, and watering", as forms of expenditure requiring "careful investigation with a view to possible economies".[6] At Birmingham four branches were actually closed for the duration of the war, one of them never to reopen.[7] Other closures were threatened, and the Carnegie Trustees made it known that they "would view with the greatest displeasure the closing of a library which Mr. Carnegie had been instrumental in providing".[8]

In some libraries closure was brought about just as effectively by the taking over of premises for war-time purposes. The reference library at Torquay became a Red Cross hospital;[9] at Darlington it became the Food Control Office—and the librarian became Assistant Food Controller.[10] The York City library was for a time under military occupation.[11] At Islington all the three branch libraries were taken over;[12] and at Westminster by the end of the war only one of the city's four library buildings continued, with restricted hours, to provide a library service.[13] Other libraries had to contend with cuts in the library grant: at Camborne in Cornwall, for example, "on the declaration of

---

[1] *P.R. 1912*, p. 29.   [2] *Adams Report*, pp. 44–45.

[3] *P.R. 1912*, p. 10.   [4] *P.R. 1912*, p. 19.

[5] See also, on these libraries, J. J. Ogle, *The Free Library* (1897), Ch. xii.

[6] The relevant passage of the circular is printed in G. T. Shaw, "War Finance and Public Libraries", in *L.A.R.*, Vol. XVIII (1916), pp. 139–140.

[7] *Notes on the History of the Birmingham Public Libraries, 1861–1961* (Birmingham 1962), p. 9.

[8] Library Association, *Public Libraries: their Development and Future Organisation* (1917), p. 24.

[9] *Torquay Public Library: Fifty Years of Service 1907–1957* [Torquay 1957].

[10] *Edward Pease Public Library: Fifty Years Progress, 1885–1935* (Darlington, 1935), p. 9.

[11] See below, p. 160.

[12] *Islington Public Libraries: Golden Jubilee 1906–1956* [1956], pp. 3–4. The South-East Branch, which had been completed in 1916 and immediately requisitioned for war purposes, was seized in 1920 by unemployed and ex-servicemen as headquarters for a "General Co-operative Trading Store", and did not become available for library use until 1921.

[13] See below, p. 152.

war with Germany the Urban Authority decided to reduce its Library grant by £30 per annum for the duration of the War."[1]

It is not surprising to find that when the figures came to be added up immediately after the war the growth of municipal library stocks during the war years was only of the order of $1\frac{1}{2}$ per cent per annum, and the growth in annual issues only of the order of 1 per cent per annum.[2] The only ray of comfort in this dismal war-time scene is to be found in the efforts of the Carnegie Trust to lay the foundations for a library service by the county authorities. These efforts we shall describe later, by way of prologue to the 1919 Act.

The Deprived Areas

At the start of the period with which we are now concerned, something like three-quarters of the population of Great Britain was, as we have seen, without the benefit of a public library service. In 1913–14, in spite of the rapid progress that had been made, the proportion still stood at two-fifths. The deprived areas were for the most part rural, but they also included important urban areas, such as the metropolitan boroughs of Bethnal Green, Paddington and St. Marylebone. It would be quite wrong, however, to suppose that these areas were entirely without library provision: on the contrary most of the urban areas had, as in the first half of the nineteenth century, a considerable variety of endowed, subscription and institutional libraries at their disposal; and even rural areas often had small collections of one kind or another.[3]

When the city of Carlisle was called upon in 1869 for a return of public libraries, it listed the Carlisle Library (an eighteenth-century subscription library) with 10 000 volumes or more; the Carlisle Mechanics' Institute with 6000 volumes, the Caldewgate Working Men's Reading Room with 2000 volumes, and some other institutions, including two adult schools, two working men's reading rooms, and a church reading room, all with smaller collections. The total amounted to 21 850 volumes—more than many municipal libraries of the time.[4]

Most towns without a public library could have drawn up a comparable list at any time in the nineteenth century, though the types of libraries varied somewhat from place to place.[5] Indeed, the Carlisle list is by no means exhaustive: it clearly includes only those libraries which its compilers regarded as in some sense 'public'. It makes no mention, for example, of commercial circulating libraries, or of libraries attached to Sunday schools, or co-operative

---

[1] See below, p. 162–163.

[2] These percentages are calculated from a comparison of the figures for Great Britain given in the Adams Report for 1913–14 (see below, App. VI) with the figures for 1919 given in G. E. Roebuck, "Public Libraries of the United Kingdom: Statistical Return, 1919", in *L.A.R.* Vol. XXI (1919), pp. 161–165.

[3] See, for example, B. Wood, 'Yorkshire Village Libraries', in *The Library*, Vol. VI (1894), pp. 37–41.

[4] *P.R. 1869*, p. 8.

[5] See for example J. Shelley, "Notes on the Public Libraries of Plymouth, Devonport, and Stonehouse," in *Library Chronicle*, Vol. III (1886), pp. 1–8; *Lancaster Public Library Service Diamond Jubilee, 1893–1953* (Lancaster 1953), pp. 2–3; V. J. Kite, *Libraries in Bath, 1618–1964* (unpublished F.L.A. thesis 1966), pp. 226 sqq.; J. S. English, "Books and Libraries in Gainsborough", in *L.A.R.*, Vol. LXX (1968), pp. 62–65.

societies, or political clubs, or large firms, though libraries of this kind certainly existed, and in many towns were numerous.[1] If, however, one were asked to list the main agencies of book provision in the urban areas, one would have to say: first, private subscription libraries; second, the libraries of mechanics' institutes, literary institutes, and the like; third (in the industrial areas), co-opera- tive society libraries; and finally commercial circulating libraries. The other types of library mentioned, though numerous, were usually much smaller. The inclusion in the Carlisle list of three working men's reading rooms, as well as several other institutions of a similar character, is of interest as illustrating a trend which seems to have been common from mid-century onwards. These institutions, sometimes under the auspices of churches, employers, or political societies, existed primarily to provide newspapers and periodicals: they seldom had more than a few hundred books. Those at Carlisle had all been established between 1846 and 1868, and the subscription in each case was 1d. per week.

In the mining areas of South Wales, working men's libraries and reading rooms became especially common during the 'nineties. Evan Owen, secretary of the Miners' Provident Society, explained to the annual conference of the Library Association, at Cardiff in 1895, that this development was stimulated by the 'Free Education Act' of 1891:

> "Before the former measure became law, it was the custom in the majority of our colliery districts, to provide for the maintenance of our elementary schools by the deduction of a certain amount from the wages of the workmen. This deduction, which was termed 'poundage', amounted as a rule to about a penny in the pound of wages earned, and, with the grant made by Government, was applied for the maintenance of elementary schools. When Parliament provided for the sole main- tenance of schools by the system which is paradoxically termed 'Free Education', this 'poundage' was no longer required for education in this particular form, but to the credit of the workmen be it said, in several of the collieries the 'poundage' has been continued by them, and has, in most areas, been applied for the maintenance of colliery libraries and reading rooms."[2]

Owen goes on to describe more than a score of libraries and reading rooms in the colliery towns and villages, many of them founded or enlarged in the 'nineties. Two quotations will illustrate the character of these institutions:

> "A magnificent library and institute exists at Blaenavon. It was originally estab- lished in 1883, and in 1895 was removed to the present buildings, which cost nearly £70000. It contains 1600 volumes, and the principal newspapers and periodicals are

---

[1] Huddersfield in 1881 had fifty libraries, with a total of over 21000 volumes attached to Nonconformist Sunday schools alone—*Public Library Handbook: History of the Library Movement in Huddersfield* (Huddersfield [1946]), p. 3. Greenwood, *Sunday School and Village Libraries* (1882), urged that Sunday school libraries should be reorganized and their contents refurbished to meet the needs of a literate age. Cf. E. A. Savage, *A Librarian's Memories, Portraits and Reflections* (1952), pp. 11–13, for a colourful but depressing descrip- tion of a Sunday school library at Croydon in the 'eighties. J. R. Clynes, afterwards Home Secretary, paid tribute at the Rural Library Conference in 1920 to the important part played in his education by the library of his local cooperative association (at Oldham, Lancs.)—J. M. Mitchell (ed.), *Rural Library Handbook: the Proceedings of the Carnegie Rural Library Conference . . . 1920* (Dunfermline 1921), pp. 65–68.

[2] E. Owen, "Workmen's Libraries in Glamorganshire and Monmouthshire", in *The Library*, Vol. VIII (1896), p. 2.

taken in. It is maintained by a contribution of 1d. per week from the workmen, and a subscription of 6s. per annum from outsiders. The management is vested in a committee of workmen."[1]

"The Cwmaman Library containing 1400 volumes was established in 1879. A new building, including a public hall, was erected in 1892. Cost £1800. It is maintained by a contribution of ½d. in the £ from the workmen. The leading periodicals, and Welsh and English papers are taken in. Billiards, chess, draughts, etc. are provided. A notable feature in connection with this library is a reading room for boys under sixteen years of age. This room contains 200 books, and suitable games are also provided, in addition to which the Committee provide a magic lantern, and subscribe £5 for a teacher of arithmetic for evening classes."[2]

Very similar, in many ways, were the libraries and reading rooms maintained by many co-operative societies. The most famous of them, that of the Rochdale Pioneers, was still flourishing in 1877, five years after the opening of the town's public library. In that year the Society had a central lending library of 12000 volumes, a central reference library of 650 volumes, a central newsroom stocked with a wide variety of newspapers and periodicals, and thirteen branch newsrooms, in various parts of the town, each with a small collection of books for reference. Fiction accounted for one-sixth of the lending stock and one-third of the 37000 annual issues.[3]

In some places libraries created by private gift or endowment, or attached to institutions similarly formed, continued to play an important role. These included a few old foundations such as Chetham's Library in Manchester (which from mid-century began to concentrate increasingly on material related to local history and antiquities[4]) and a surprising number of new foundations. The most substantial of these was the Mitchell Library at Glasgow, which was opened in 1877 and was to become in due course the foundation of the public library: it will be described in a later chapter.[5]

At the other end of the scale we may select as an example the Mayer Library at Bebington in Wirral, which owed its origin to Joseph Mayer, a Liverpool jeweller who settled in Bebington in 1864 and proceeded to dispose of the accumulations of a lifetime. To the Liverpool City Museum he gave a splendid collection of Egyptian, Saxon and other antiquities, valued at £80000; and to the village of Bebington (as it then was) he presented a little collection of 1500 books as the nucleus of a public library. This was in 1866, and he went on adding to the library until his death twenty years later. When the first house he had rented for its accommodation became too small, he purchased and converted a farmhouse which still served as the central library a century later. It

[1] Op. cit., p. 9.

[2] Op. cit., p. 10. For miners' institute libraries in Fife in the early twentieth century see A. Anderson, The Old Libraries of Fife (Fife Co. Library 1953), p. 21. The Cornish institutes performed a similar service.

[3] A. Greenwood, The Educational Department of the Rochdale Equitable Pioneers Society (Manchester 1877), pp. 9–13. By 1884 co-operative societies had a total of 77 lending libraries, 82 reference libraries, and 225 newsrooms. The majority of these institutions were in North-West England—H. J. Twigg, An Outline of Co-operative Education (Manchester 1924), p. 62.

[4] Chetham's Hospital and Library (Manchester 1956), pp. 24–27. By 1900 the library comprised some 50000 volumes besides important MS. collections.

[5] See below, p. 142.

was opened in 1870, with a stock of some 10000 volumes. The village school-master served as honorary librarian with a team of voluntary helpers, and in this first year there were 33000 issues. A reference room and newspaper room were added in 1873.

From 1878 the library was administered by a trust which included the churchwardens and representatives of the local authority. After Mayer's death, however, the funds at the disposal of the trust proved inadequate to maintain an efficient library service and from 1894 it was assisted by an annual grant from the local authority. In 1930 the urban district council took over complete control in order to be able to cater more effectively for what was now a populous town.[1]

Many other such benefactions can be recorded from the second half of the nineteenth century, rather fewer in the twentieth century. Among those which were libraries only we may mention the Stanley Library at King's Lynn (1854)[2], the Macfarlane Library at Stirling (1855)[3], the Ogilvy Library at Alyth in Perthshire (1870)[4], the Griffits Library at High Wycombe (then known as Chepping Wycombe), (1874),[5] the Anderson Library at Woodside, Aberdeen (1882),[6] the Rylands Library at Stretford (1883),[7] the Elder Library at Govan (1900),[8] and the Bingham Library at Cirencester (1905).[9] Listed like this they can be no more than names, but they are names which bear witness to the lives and achievements of men honoured in their generation. The same is true of certain libraries of a more specialist character, such as the William Salt Library at Stafford (a local collection established in 1874), and the John Rylands Library at

---

[1] Greenwood (1891), pp. 446–447; J. J. Ogle, *The Free Library* (1897), pp. 293–296; *Bebington Public Libraries: a Century of the Public Library Service, 1866–1966* (Bebington 1966). For Mayer himself see also the article by C. W. Sutton in *Dictionary of National Biography*. A new central library was opened in 1971.

[2] Mr. R. Wilson, Borough Librarian, has kindly drawn my attention to an account of this rather unusual library by H. J. Hillen in the *Lynn News* for 6 Feb. 1897. Founded by Lord Stanley (afterwards fifteenth Earl of Derby), it was a subscription library assisted by the Corporation.

[3] *Monthly Notes of the Library Association*, Vol. III (1882), p. 112. Amalgamated 1882 with the Smith Institute.

[4] Founded by William Ogilvy of Loyal, who in his deed of bequest of 7 Feb. 1870 directed that it should be known as the Loyal Alyth Public Library.

[5] Greenwood (1891), p. 506; *The High Wycombe Free Library: its Origin, Donation and Foundation* (High Wycombe, n.d.).

[6] Founded by Sir John Anderson, an ordnance engineer and a native of Woodside. The present Librarian of Aberdeen, Mr. M. K. Milne, has kindly drawn my attention to the lengthy MS., still preserved, in which Anderson gave detailed instructions for the manage-ment of the library. Although the endowment provided an income of only £100 per annum, he prescribed that the librarian should be a married man and if possible a total abstainer; that he should have a passion for books and a thorough knowledge of libraries and bibliography; and that he should be able to read fluently in Latin, Greek, German, French and Italian. The library was transferred to the City in 1929, and is now the Anderson Branch. Cf. A. W. Robertson, "The Public Libraries of Aberdeen", in *The Library*, Vol. VI (1894), p. 11.

[7] *Public Libraries and Art Galleries in Stretford* (Stretford 1946).

[8] *Glasgow Public Libraries, 1874–1966* (Glasgow 1966), p. 46.

[9] Originally a free library, though placed on a subscription basis after the first World War because of a decline in the value of the endowment. See G. P. Jackson, *The Bingham Public Library Golden Jubilee*, repr. from *Wilts. and Gloucestershire Standard*, 17 Sept. 1955.

Manchester (a scholar's library, famous for early printed works, opened in 1900).[1]

In many private foundations the library formed part of an institute which also served other purposes, including, usually, technical education. Examples of such foundations are the Chambers Institute at Peebles (1859),[2] the Hartley Institute at Southampton (1862),[3] the Brassey Institute at Hastings (1881),[4] and the Storey Institute at Lancaster (1887).[5] In this group, too, we must reckon two important institutes in the City of London—the Bishopsgate Institute (1891) and the Cripplegate Institute (1896)—both established by the Charity Commissioners from funds at their disposal. Both were educational institutions, but they also had substantial libraries, which by the end of the century were providing what was virtually a public library service for the population of the City. In 1910 the Bishopsgate Institute was recorded as possessing a library of 43000 volumes; while the Cripplegate Institute had 29000 volumes, and 26000 more in three branch institutes[6].

Many of these endowed libraries (though not the two City institutes just mentioned) ultimately became public libraries, and indeed it was often the intention of the founders that this should happen. In some cases, however, the existence of the endowed library operated to delay the creation of a public service. High Wycombe, which did not adopt the Libraries Acts until 1920, and Hastings, which did not adopt until 1927, are obvious examples. Elsewhere the delay was caused by other types of libraries. At Chelmsford, for example, it was the closure of the Literary and Mechanics' Institute in 1899 which led to a demand for a public library and so to adoption in 1902[7]. At Burnley, where a public library was established only in 1914, the difficulty lay in the existence of a number of rival libraries, notably those of the Mechanics' Institute and the Co-operative Society.[8] At Hitchin a number of successful subscription libraries stood in the way.[9]

It is of interest to note that in towns where a proposal to adopt the Libraries Acts was defeated an attempt was often made to provide a public library, or the equivalent of a public library, without rate aid. Greenwood in 1891 gives several examples of this kind of development, of which on the whole he disapproved as likely to retard rather than help in the adoption of the Acts.[10]

---

[1] E. Robertson, *The John Rylands Library, Manchester* (Manchester 1955), pp. 7–9. For the early history of this important institution (now linked with Manchester University) see M. Tyson, "The First Forty Years of the John Rylands Library", in *Bulletin of the John Rylands Library*, Vol. XXV (1941), pp. 46–66.

[2] The origin of this is described in W. Chambers, *Memoir of William and Robert Chambers* (Edinburgh 1872, rev. edn. n.d.), pp. 321–322.

[3] The fantastic story of the origin of this institution, and its eccentric founder, is related in A. T. Patterson, *The University of Southampton* (Southampton 1962), Ch. ii.

[4] A. Belt (ed.), *Hastings: a Survey of Times Past and Present* (Hastings 1937), pp. 85–87.

[5] This Institute became the home of the public library in 1893—*Lancaster Public Library Service Diamond Jubilee, 1893–1953* (Lancaster 1953), pp. 3–4.

[6] *L.Y.B. 1910–11*, pp. 172, 175.

[7] *Chelmsford Public Library Diamond Jubilee, 1906–1966* (Chelmsford 1967), pp. 5–6.

[8] R. Caulfield, "How we got our Public Libraries", in *Burnley Express and News*, 26 and 30 August 1950.

[9] R. F. Ashby, *A Small Town's Libraries in the Early Nineteenth Century* (unpublished F.L.A. essay 1949).   [10] Greenwood (1891), p. 504.

He is particularly sarcastic about the Bethnal Green "Public Library", which was established in 1876 and maintained by public subscription. He points out that the total expenditure for 1888–89 was £837.14s.8d, out of which only £16.15s.8d was spent on books, magazines and newspapers. "There never was", he concludes, "in the entire history of libraries, so much cry and so little wool."[1]

Greenwood is critical also of a similar library which opened at Paddington in 1888 with donations of books to the number of about 3550. "If, however," he comments acidly, "the books in the Paddington Library represent the high-water mark of Paddington book-giving, the sooner the Acts are adopted and a good selection of books bought the better."[2] For the corresponding institution at St. Marylebone, on the other hand, he has a word of praise:

> "Immediately the plan was launched subscriptions were promised, and a suitable habitation was found in a block of modern buildings situated in Lisson Grove. These were opened on August 12, 1889, by a quiet ceremony, and there is no question about the library and reading-room being largely used by the people. A branch was opened in Mortimer Street about twelve months ago, and is greatly appreciated by the people of that district. Between 500 and 700 people visit the two libraries daily, and in the evening both places present an air and appearance of business. The reading-stands and the tables are well occupied, and not infrequently there are over 100 readers in the rooms at one time. A good selection of newspapers and magazines is provided. In the lending section there are 6703 volumes of thoroughly good and readable literature. Every class of literature is represented, and greater care and discretion could not have been exercised in the selection of materials for the reading tastes of Marylebone. The nucleus of a reference library has been formed, and already there are about 1000 books in this section."[3]

Basically similar arrangements were made at Ayr, where in 1870 the provost, magistrates and sheriff were formed into a body of trustees to administer a "public library" created by bringing together existing libraries, especially the Mechanics' Institute Library and a subscription library of long standing,[4] and at Stroud, where in 1888 £3500 was subscribed to convert the old grammar school and endow it as a library.[5] At Kensington the cost of setting up a specimen public library was borne by a private individual, James Heywood,[6] and the same service was later performed by James Reckitt at Hull.[7] At Reading the library of the local temperance society served for some years (from 1875) as a free public library.[8] At Falkirk after the rejection of the Acts in 1887, the Y.M.C.A. took the initiative in organizing a library, using as a starting-point the sum of £1000 granted for that purpose by a returned emigrant, Robert Dollar of Michigan.[9] At Arbroath, in 1873, an old established subscription library endeavoured to meet the need by reducing its annual subscription to

---

[1] Op. cit., p. 505. A more favourable view is to be found in G. F. Hilcken, "An East End Free Library", in The Library, Vol. II (1890), pp. 174–177.

[2] Op. cit., p. 512.

[3] Op. cit., p. 511.

[4] Carnegie Public Library, Ayr, Address by Andrew Carnegie ... 1892 (Edinburgh 1892) pp. 5–6.

[5] Greenwood (1891), pp. 513–14.

[6] See below, p. 154.   [7] See below, pp. 150–151.

[8] Greenwood (1891), pp. 216–217; information from Borough Librarian.

[9] Greenwood (1891), p. 263.

2s. 6d.[1] In Edinburgh an attempt was made, from 1881, to establish cheap
subscription libraries on a district basis.[2] At Malvern, in the 'nineties, while the
question of adoption hung fire, a group of residents pooled their books to
provide a library of 10000 volumes,[3] and a similar arrangement was inaugurated,
in 1915, in the garden city of Letchworth, where adoption was still ten years
away.[4]

Nearly all these examples of what we may call substitute libraries relate to
urban areas. The rural areas were in much worse plight, for few of them had
benefactors as generous as Joseph Mayer at Bebington. Even where parish
councils adopted the Acts they were, as we have seen, quite unable to provide
an adequate service.[5] Some rural inhabitants were able to subscribe to a nearby
town library,[6] but the majority either had no library provision at all, or had to
be content with some kind of village library and reading room whose meagre
stock of books and periodicals was provided mainly by the contributions of
the well-to-do.

Examples of this type of library are common from the early nineteenth
century onwards, though like all voluntary enterprises of this kind they tended
to be short-lived.[7] Rev. F. W. Naylor, who established one about 1844 in his
parish in Upton, Nottinghamshire, wrote a book called *Popular Libraries in Rural
Districts*, which was published in 1855. After arguing, as it was then necessary
to do, the case for the freer diffusion of knowledge among the lower orders, he
draws attention to the inadequacy of the village libraries already existing:

> "Stores of books selected exclusively from the publications of a particular
> society,[8] and placed under the custody of the clergyman or the schoolmaster;
> libraries furnished at the sole expense of the wealthy, for the use of their poor
> neighbours, limited in their object and varied in their duration; donation libraries,
> proceeding from the liberality or bequest of some well meaning individual, but
> usually impeded in their operation by the stringency of their conditions; public stock
> libraries, hastily got together, and into which the generously disposed are invited to
> pour the refuse of their shelves, however unsuitable or heterogeneous its nature; and
> religious libraries, established only with a religious object, or promoted and sup-
> ported for the purpose of giving expression to the sentiments of a particular
> modification of the outward church: all these exist, and are found for the most part,
> to fail of accomplishing any object of general utility."[9]

[1] W. R. Aitken, *A History of the Public Library Movement in Scotland to 1955* (Glasgow 1971),
pp. 67–68.
[2] *Monthly Notes of the Library Association*, Vol. III (1887), p. 36. The first such library was
established in a disused Presbyterian Church at Morningside.
[3] See below pp. 161–162.
[4] Letchworth National Library Week Committee, *A Town Built on a Book* (Letchworth
1966), p. 7. For two unsuccessful attempts to found a public library from private
resources at Bath (1864–80) see V. J. Kite, *Libraries in Bath, 1618–1964* (unpublished
F.L.A. thesis 1966) pp. 173–209.
[5] See above, pp. 127–128.
[6] The tables in the *Adams Report* show that by that time it was common for public libraries
to permit use by out-district residents in return for an annual subscription of a few
shillings.
[7] T. Kelly, *Early Public Libraries* (1966), pp. 199–200.
[8] i.e. the S.P.C.K. or the Religious Tract Society—see Kelly, *op. cit.*, pp. 202–203.
[9] F. W. Naylor, *Popular Libraries in Rural Districts* [1855], pp. 34–35.

After explaining the reasons for this failure—resentment of charity, suspicion of religious propaganda, unsuitable books, lack of popular control—Naylor propounds his own plan for "district village libraries" to be formed by the "educated middle classes", "for the improvement and entertainment of themselves and their neighbours." The libraries were to be supported by a subscription of 2s. a year from members and ½d. per volume from non-members.[1] The Upton Rural Library, formed on this basis, had after eleven years 120 members and 450 volumes. It covered an extensive area, and had five outlying distribution centres.[2]

The kind of upper-class patronage which Naylor deplored is well represented in a series of articles in *The Queen* by Lady John Manners, whose husband, a leading Conservative politician, was shortly to be Duke of Rutland. The articles, reprinted in book form in 1885–86, were concerned to expound the advantages of reading and recreation rooms and free libraries. Among the many examples cited by the authoress is a reading room at Oakham in Rutlandshire provided by Mrs. John Pochin of Edmundthorpe. It was open three times a week, and supplied not only newspapers and a few books, but also games for the men, coffee, biscuits, tobacco, "occasionally apples and sometimes peppermint drops."[3] A similar reading room at Allington, near Grantham, was provided in 1881 by Mrs. John Welby, of whom we are told:

> "She has studied the men's comfort in every way, and provided cushions for the seats. The men find the cushions delightfully comfortable after their hard day's work."[4]

Lady John Manners lists a great many examples of village libraries and reading rooms, especially in Leicestershire and adjoining counties, though she also mentions that they were to be found in many villages in Lancashire.[5] Other examples could be quoted from many different sources, but one more must suffice, illustrating at a somewhat earlier date a similar provision in the neighbourhood of Cyfarthfa, near Merthyr Tydfil. Mrs. Rose Mary Crawshay, of Cyfarthfa Castle, wrote to *The Times* in 1872 to report that:

> "Five free cottage libraries have been opened every Sunday for four years with a yearly increasing number of readers . . . newspapers are the chief attraction in that room, people usually taking the books home. The librarian is in every case a workman, who get £3 per annum if open on a Sunday; and £5 per annum if open on weekdays as well. All are furnished with maps and chairs and tables and the weekday ones with draughtboards, some of which have had to be replaced owing to use . . . I would respectfully suggest this policy to everyone desirous of conferring such a boon on his or her neighbourhood."[6]

---

[1] *Op. cit.*, pp. 42–44.

[2] *Op. cit.*, Preface. Naylor's volume was elaborated in a later book, *Continuous Education* (1858), on which see T. Kelly, "Continuous Education: a Nineteenth Century Pioneer", in *Journal of Librarianship*, Vol. I (1969), pp. 62–67.

[3] Lady John Manners, *Encouraging Experiences of Reading and Recreation Rooms* (1886), p. 4.

[4] *Op. cit.*, p. 7.

[5] Lady John Manners, *Some of the Advantages of Easily Accessible Reading and Recreation Rooms and Free Libraries* (1885), p. 26.

[6] *The Times*, 2 Aug. 1872. I am indebted for this reference to Mr. T. Evans of Ferryside, Carms. The writer's husband, R. T. Crawshay, was manager of the great Cyfarthfa ironworks shortly to be closed as a result of industrial unrest—*Dictionary of National Biography*, *s.v.*

In the North of England the various unions of mechanics' institutes—the Union of Lancashire and Cheshire Institutes, the Yorkshire Union, and the Northern Union—provided a service of bookboxes modelled on the itinerating libraries of Haddington earlier in the century. The best known of these was the Yorkshire Village Library, which had its beginnings in the Itinerating Library of the Yorkshire Union established on the initiative of James Hole of Leeds, in 1852.[1] The Castle Howard United Villages Itinerating Library was formed in the North Riding later in the year, and the East Riding Library Mission in 1853. The three were united in 1856, and according to Greenwood the joint library was still flourishing nearly forty years later:

> "Boxes with fifty or a hundred books are sent out periodically to mechanics' institutes and working men's clubs, and the books find their way into every part of that great county; and the weaver, the ploughman, the collier, and the fisherman are all reached by that association."[2]

The problem of rural library provision became a matter of increasing concern towards the close of the century as the contrast between urban and rural areas became obvious. The case for an improved rural service was strongly put in the 'nineties by Greenwood, J. J. Ogle (librarian of Bootle), J. D. Brown (at that time librarian of Clerkenwell), and many others, and a number of practical suggestions were canvassed. The success of the Yorkshire Village Library naturally suggested the use of bookboxes distributed from a central store; and the more modern form of travelling library, e.g. the library van, was also proposed. Other ideas included the exchange of bookstocks between neighbouring libraries; co-operative cataloguing; and the use of post offices as delivery stations.[3] The real answer, of course—already envisaged by forward looking librarians—was the development of a county library service. The origins of this service fall within the period now under review, but it will be convenient to postpone our account of them to a later chapter.

---

[1] J. F. C. Harrison, *Social Reform in Victorian Leeds: the Work of James Hole* (Leeds 1954), pp. 30–41; Carnegie U.K. Trust, *Second Annual Report, 1915*, p. 62. Cf. *Union of Lancashire and Cheshire Institutes, 1839–1939* (Manchester 1939), p. 17; R. E. Grimshaw, *The Northern Union of Literary, Scientific and Mechanical Institutions* (unpublished F.L.A. essay 1951), pp. 15–17.

[2] T. Greenwood, *Sunday School and Village Libraries* (1892), p. 56.

[3] For suggestions of this kind see especially T. Greenwood, *op. cit.*, pp. 45–50; the same author's *Public Libraries* (1891), ch. xxii; articles by J. D. Brown and J. J. Ogle in *The Library*, Vol. VI (1894), pp. 42–44, 98–105; and by E. A. Baker in *The Library*, Vol. VIII (1896), pp. 298–303; J. J. Ogle, *The Extension of the Free Libraries Acts to Small Places* (1887); and the same author's *The Free Library* (1897), pp. 281–284. For the idea of the library van see further below, pp. 174–175.

CHAPTER VI

Some Further Case-Studies

BECAUSE the necessary research into the history of individual libraries has not yet been done, it is not possible to offer as representative a selection of case-studies for this period as in the chapter dealing with the period ending in 1886. Quite a number of libraries have histories written round about the turn of the century, but with a few exceptions, e.g. Sheffield and Norwich, nothing of substance has been written about developments in the present century. Statistics, of course, we have in plenty, but raw statistics are not in themselves very helpful without some clue as to the circumstances and policies lying behind them.

In spite of the difficulties, however, it is worth while to try to gain, from such scattered and imperfect sources as are at present available, some impression of how individual libraries were developing in different parts of the country and the kind of difficulties they had to contend with.

Leading English Libraries

We may begin with the four major English libraries. Taking the figures for 1913–14 in the Adams Report as our measuring rod, these were still, as in the earlier period, Manchester, Leeds, Birmingham and Liverpool, but the order had changed somewhat. The two great giants now were Birmingham, with a total stock of 446 000 volumes, and annual issues of 2 128 000; and Manchester, with 434 000 volumes and 2 765 000 issues. Liverpool, with 350 000 volumes, and Leeds, with 313 000 volumes, lagged slightly behind.[1]

Birmingham's achievement is all the more remarkable in view of the almost total destruction of the library in the fire of 1879. Much was due to the generosity of the public and of the civic authorities, who as early as 1883, as we have seen, had secured local legislation to remove the 1d. rate limit.[2] In 1890, when the Corporation made successful application for permission to borrow £63 690 for library purposes, it was actually claimed that library expenditure was "the most popular which the Corporation made".[3] It does not appear that such a claim was ever made for Manchester, but Manchester did in 1891 secure permission to levy a 2d. rate, and in fact the history of the public libraries in the two cities ran closely parallel.

At Manchester the librarian throughout this period was C. W. Sutton, who succeeded Crestadoro in 1879 and remained in office until his death in 1920. At Birmingham the veteran J. D. Mullins reigned until 1898, and was succeeded on his retirement by his sub-librarian A. Capel Shaw, who continued in the same tradition. In both libraries, therefore, the administration tended to be

---

[1] For fuller statistics, including the relative population figures, see Appendix XI.
[2] See above, p. 49. [3] Greenwood (1891), p. 156.

cautious and conservative, and innovations were embarked on only after much deliberation. It was not until Walter Powell succeeded Shaw at Birmingham in 1912, and L. Stanley Jast became deputy librarian at Manchester in 1915, that the wind of change began to blow.

In both cities the central reference library was the main focus of interest. Enriched not only by purchase but also by generous gifts, it attained in each case a total approaching a quarter of a million volumes by 1913–14. At Birmingham this figure included the restored Shakespeare and Cervantes Collections, as well as a number of other special collections. At Manchester items of interest included a notable Gypsy Collection purchased in 1895, the Henry Watson Music Library, which was presented in 1900 and of which more will be said later,[1] and the Thomas Greenwood Library on librarianship and allied subjects, presented in 1904.[2] In both cases special attention was devoted to building up the local history section, and impressive collections of local material were accumulated.

Growth on this scale inevitably created problems of accommodation. At Birmingham these were solved for the time being by the construction of a basement store for 100000 volumes, but Manchester was less fortunate. The old Town Hall, which had housed the central library since 1878, was demolished in 1912, and pending the erection of a new art gallery and central library the library was accommodated in a group of wooden huts. Unfortunately, owing to the first World War and other difficulties, this temporary accommodation had to serve for twenty-two years.

The development of branch library services (mainly for lending) was by no means neglected. In each city an inner ring of branches had been established in the early years, and in each case a second ring of five new branches became necessary in the 'nineties to provide for new suburban demand and the incorporation of new areas. The early twentieth century brought a further round of boundary extensions, in Manchester gradually, between 1903 and 1909, in Birmingham in a single operation in 1911, and these extensions inevitably involved further library provision by the two cities. Some of these successive expansions involved the takeover of areas which were already library authorities: this was particularly the case at Birmingham, where the absorption in 1911 of Aston Manor, Handsworth, Erdington, and King's Norton added at a stroke twelve new branches to the Birmingham library network. On the eve of the first World War Birmingham thus had a total of twenty-one branches (four of them, in the innermost ring, destined to be closed during the war on grounds of economy). Manchester, at the same period, had twenty-three branches, besides eight branch reading rooms which provided newspapers, periodicals and a few books and served also as delivery stations to which books could be supplied on request.

Neither Birmingham nor Manchester was in a hurry to introduce the new "open access" system which began to make headway in the 'nineties. At Manchester, after tentative experiments, the system was introduced into most of the branch libraries during the years 1912–15, but at Birmingham only one branch was converted during this period. This was the Northfield Branch, a

[1] See below, p. 190.
[2] Greenwood also bequeathed £5000 for the maintenance of this library. He had previously presented (1902) a small library of works relating to Edward Edwards.

Carnegie library which was built in 1906 and destroyed by fire, supposedly by suffragettes, in 1914. The new librarian, Walter Powell, took advantage of this opportunity to reorganize the branch on open access lines, but other branches had to wait until after the war.

Birmingham was even more conservative in the matter of classification and cataloguing: the work of modernising these was not undertaken until after the war. At Manchester, on the other hand, Sutton was a pioneer in the use of the Dewey classification. He was, indeed, the first librarian of a major library to reclassify on this system. The work was begun in 1894 and took many years to complete.[1]

"Liverpool," wrote Ogle in 1897, "is chiefly interesting to the student of popular libraries for the long concentration of effort on the reference collections."[2] This concentration represented the deliberate policy of the first Chairman of the Library Committee, Sir James Picton, whose "aim and absorbing idea", the librarian tells us, "was to build up a great reference library, not in number of volumes merely, but great in its literary and scientific importance."[3] He undoubtedly succeeded, and by the time of his death in 1889 (after nearly forty years' service) the collection of nearly 100000 volumes was exceeded in size only by that at Birmingham. The local history material was particularly fine. Eleven years later came the magnificent bequest from H. F. Hornby of Wavertree, of a lifetime's collection which included 7200 volumes on art and over 3000 etchings and engravings. With the bequest came the sum of £10000 to provide a suitable building, which was duly erected as part of the central library complex.

Contemporary writers pointed with pride to Liverpool's two central reading rooms—the Brown Reading Room, which by its liberal supply of fiction and periodicals attracted large numbers of working people; and the great circular Picton Reading Room, which supplied only serious literature and was mostly patronized by students and professional people. The availability of popular literature in the Brown Reading Room came under some criticism, but was defended by the Committee on the ground that under the new social conditions it was essential to provide intellectual entertainment for the masses.[4]

Peter Cowell, who was librarian from 1875 to 1909, attributes Liverpool's backwardness in the matter of lending library provision to financial reasons, pointing out that Manchester, for example, had a 2d. rate for library purposes alone, while Liverpool had to support a library, an art gallery, and till 1895 a museum, out of a 1d. rate only. It was not until 1899 that Liverpool secured permission to increase the rate, and even then only to 1½d.[5] There is some truth

---

[1] For Birmingham see A. C. Shaw, "The Birmingham Free Libraries", in L.A.R., Vol. IV (1902), pp. 492–499 (also published in book form, Aberdeen [1902]); and Notes on the History of the Birmingham Public Libraries, 1861–1961 (Birmingham 1962); for Manchester, W. R. Credland, The Free Library Movement in Manchester (Manchester 1895); the same author's The Manchester Public Free Libraries (Manchester 1899); obituary of C. W. Sutton by W. E. A. Axon in L.A.R., Vol. XXII (1920) pp. 207–208; and G. C. Paterson, A Short History of the Manchester Public Libraries, 1852–1948 (unpublished F.L.A. essay 1949).

[2] J. J. Ogle, The Free Library (1897), p. 169.

[3] P. Cowell, Liverpool Public Libraries: a History of Fifty Years (Liverpool 1903), p. 137.

[4] Greenwood (1891), pp. 117–120; Ogle, op. cit., pp. 170–172; Cowell, op. cit., pp. 132–134.

[5] Cowell, op. cit., p. 169.

in this, but it is also clear that as long as Picton lived he was unwilling to see money spent on lending libraries if this expenditure threatened the high standard of the reference library. Apart from a few reading rooms in board schools opened in 1884, and never very successful, the public had to be content with the branch facilities available at the original North and South Branches.[1]

After Picton's death a change in policy immediately made itself evident. A third branch, the East Branch, was opened at Kensington in 1890; a central lending library was created in the basement of the Brown Library in 1895; the old North Branch was replaced by a new branch at Everton in 1896; the old South Library was replaced by a new branch at Toxteth in 1902; and provision was made for a number of new areas—Wavertree, Walton, South Toxteth, and West Derby—incorporated in the city under an Act of 1895.[2] With the help of Carnegie, who paid for six branches opened between 1905 and 1913, the total number of branches had risen by the latter date to eleven, but Liverpool in this respect still lagged considerably behind Manchester and Birmingham.[3]

George T. Shaw, who succeeded Cowell in 1909 and served as librarian for twenty years, continued the policy of improving the branch service, and took an early opportunity of introducing open access. This was at the Sefton Park Branch in 1911, but the process of conversion was not completed until after the war. The Dewey classification seems to have been introduced at the same time.[4]

In the matter of branch development Leeds was as we have seen at the opposite pole from Liverpool, the first librarian James Yates having made a special feature of cheap branch libraries in Board Schools.[5] T. W. Hand, who took over in 1898, found himself obliged to undertake a considerable overhaul of stock and organization. He dealt first with the central libraries. The reference library was enlarged, reorganized, partly restocked, reclassified according to Dewey, and recatalogued on cards. The lending library was provided with a new printed dictionary catalogue.

Next he turned to the branch organization. Here one of his first concerns was to replace the part-time libraries in schools, wherever possible, by full-time branches. Between 1900 and 1904, when financial difficulties called a halt to the programme, he secured the erection of seven new branches, three of these combined, for reasons of economy, with police stations, and a fourth with public baths. By 1914 there were fourteen full-time branches and nine evening branches (still mostly in schools). In 1916 the Carnegie United Kingdom Trust offered funds to provide four additional branch buildings, but it was not until after the war that this offer was taken up.

Finance continued to be a problem, and shortage of funds was one of the reasons that lay behind the decision, in 1898, to employ women assistants. The proposal was looked on with some misgiving at first, but was so successful that by 1904, when powers were taken to levy a 2d. rate, women occupied all except the senior administrative posts. From 1912 open access and the Dewey classifica-

---

[1] See above, p. 45.

[2] Cowell, *op. cit.*, pp. 137, 145, 154, 159, 168, 193–194.

[3] For details of the branches see *Liverpool Public Libraries Centenary, 1850–1950* (Liverpool 1950).

[4] G. T. Shaw, "Open Access: an Experiment," in *L.A.R.*, Vol. XV (1913), pp. 13–21; and information from Dr. G. Chandler, City Librarian.

[5] See above, p. 50.

tion began to be introduced into the branches, and the same year saw one of Hand's most successful innovations, the "story half-hour" for children. This was another job for women staff, and proved so popular at the Armley Branch where it was first introduced, that it had to be extended in the following year to four other branches.[1]

Glasgow

Alongside the four leading English libraries we may place, from 1899, the public library of Glasgow. In that year the stubborn opposition of the citizens, who between 1876 and 1888 had thrice rejected proposals to adopt the Libraries Acts, was at length circumvented by a special clause in a local Act known as the Glasgow Corporation (Tramways, Libraries, etc.) Act. Having taken this belated step, however, the Corporation at once found itself in possession of a splendid central reference library in the form of the Mitchell Library, established in 1877 from a bequest by Stephen Mitchell, tobacco manufacturer, who died three years earlier.

Under the terms of the bequest, a sum of £70000 had been made available to the Corporation for the establishment of "a large public reference library". This library was placed under the direction of a committee of the Lord Provost, magistrates and councillors of the city. F. T. Barrett was appointed first librarian, and, with his experience as sub-librarian at Birmingham to guide him, quickly built up a large and valuable collection.[2] "The Mitchell" became well known not only in Glasgow but throughout the West of Scotland, and began to attract important gifts and legacies. By 1889, when the bookstock had reached 89000 volumes, it was necessary to deplete the capital fund to acquire new premises, and from this time onwards the Corporation provided an annual subsidy towards the cost of maintenance. Since this could not be taken from the rates, it was procured in the first two years by raiding the profits of the Gas Trust, and for the next seventeen years (1891–1908) from the "whisky money" accruing to the Corporation under the Act of 1890. By 1899 the library numbered 136000 volumes.

There were at this time, it should be noted, two other non-rate-aided public libraries in Glasgow. The original Stirling's Library, bequeathed to the Corporation in 1791, was amalgamated in 1871 with a subscription library known as the Glasgow Public Library, but it still remained freely open to the public for reference purposes. The combined library numbered about 50000 volumes at the end of the century.[3] Baillie's Institution Library, opened in 1887, owed its origin to George Baillie, procurator, who in 1863 placed £18000 in the hands of trustees with instructions that, after the lapse of twenty-one years, the capital and accumulated interest should be used to form a library and a school. When the time came, the trustees judged that schools were sufficiently provided for,

[1] L.Y.B. 1914, pp. 283–284; Adams Report, pp. 48–49; T. W. Hand, A Brief Account of the Public Libraries of the City of Leeds, 1870–1920 (Leeds 1920), pp. 23–40.
[2] Cf. above, pp. 47–48.
[3] L.Y.B. 1900–01, p. 291. For the early history of this library, and details of Stirling's benefaction, see T. Mason, Public and Private Libraries of Glasgow (Glasgow 1885); and the Account of Stirling's and Glasgow Public Library reprinted from the General Catalogue (Glasgow 1888).

and devoted all the money to a library. This was first in Miller Street, and later in a converted church near Blythswood Square, where it remained till 1952. Its object was defined in the trust deed as

> "To aid the self-culture of the operative classes, from youth to manhood and old age, by furnishing them with warm, well lighted, and every-way comfortable accommodation at all seasons, for reading useful and interesting books. . . ."[1]

In 1900 this library was recorded as possessing 17000 volumes,[2] and it seems to have been well used and well managed.

Under the terms of the 1899 Act the Corporation took power, not merely to establish and maintain public libraries, but specifically to hold and maintain the Mitchell Library, and to enter into agreement for the transfer to the Corporation of Stirling's Library or any other library within the city. A scheme drawn up by Barrett for the erection of branch libraries throughout the city was at once adopted, and a start was made on a branch in Gorbals, over the public baths. At this point (1901), Carnegie came forward with the offer of no less than £100000, which was promptly used to create a further dozen branches, opened at various dates between 1904 and 1907. Thereupon Carnegie gave £15000 more, for the erection of two additional branches. Only one of these was completed before the first World War, but another Carnegie library came into Glasgow's possession in 1905 through the annexation of Kinning Park. A further boundary extension in 1912 brought within the Corporation's scope two privately founded libraries—the Elder Park Library at Govan and the Couper Institute Library at Cathcart. By 1914 there were in all sixteen full branches and one branch reading room. The final Carnegie library, at Langside, was opened in 1915.

The Mitchell Library, now the central reference library, continued under fostering care of F. T. Barrett (librarian till 1914) to accumulate gifts and bequests, notably the Jeffrey Reference Library, comprising more than 4000 valuable works on natural history, antiquities, and fine arts, bequeathed in 1902. By this time the Mitchell had long since outgrown its second home, and a third building—the present Mitchell Library—was opened in November 1911. This change provided the opportunity to complete the library system: in January, 1911, Stirling's library was taken over by the Libraries Committee and transferred to the former Mitchell building, which in 1913 was re-opened as the central lending library.[3] It was in connection with this change that the Corporation in 1912 secured powers to levy a $1\frac{1}{2}$d. rate.

Thus in a few short years Glasgow had acquired a library service which could challenge comparison with any in the country, and which in the size of its bookstock (468000 volumes in 1914) exceeded them all. It also distinguished itself by forming the first separate Commercial Library in the country. The manner in which this came about is thus described:

> "The removal of the Mitchell [in 1911] deprived the business centre of the city of an important and convenient source of information. As a partial remedy, when the vacated building was utilized for the housing of Stirling's library, most of the

---

[1] *Handbook to Baillie's Institution Free Public Reference Library* (2nd edn. Glasgow 1909), p. 8.
[2] *L.Y.B. 1900–01*, pp. 288–289.
[3] Baillie's Institution Library remained, and still remains, independent. In recent years it has focussed its attention (like Chetham's Library, Manchester) on local history.

directories, guides, and other volumes required by persons engaged in business were placed in a prominent and easily accessible position on the ground floor. The regular and growing use of this provision demanded increased facilities, and, in 1916, a room on the first floor was more fully equipped and opened as a Commercial Library. Arrangements had been made for extension if required, and in 1918, such extension having become imperative, the whole of the floor—doubling the accommodation— was furnished and devoted to the needs of the department."[1]

Cardiff and Edinburgh

We have already had occasion to notice that apart from the big five just described, there were at this time no public libraries in Great Britain with more than 200000 volumes, of the dozen with bookstocks of between 100000 and 200000, the largest, according to the Adams Report figures for 1913–14, were Cardiff (with 193000 volumes) and Edinburgh (with 188000 volumes).

In 1886, at the end of the earlier period of library history, the Cardiff library was, as we have seen, only just beginning to establish itself. Its rapid growth during the next thirty years was greatly assisted by the transfer of the science and art schools to the Technical Instruction Committee in 1890 and the transfer of the museum to a separate Committee in 1893. Much was due, also, to the energetic leadership of J. Ballinger (afterwards Sir John Ballinger), who was librarian from 1884 to 1908. After the considerable extension completed in 1896 the library building provided accommodation for a reference library, lending library, reading room, news and magazine room, and ladies' room, besides a special room for the important and growing Welsh collections— recently enriched by the purchase of the Rees collection. The reading room had accommodation for 466 readers—more than three times as many as before.

The remarkable growth of the town about this time (from 83000 to 129000 inhabitants between 1881 and 1891), made it necessary to develop also a branch organization. At first finance made this difficult, and it was only with voluntary help that five branch reading rooms were opened between 1889 and 1891. By 1893, however, the library committee was able to assume full responsibility, and a further reading room was opened in the following year. These branch reading rooms contained newspapers and periodicals and a few hundred reference books, in most cases on open access. Ballinger reported that this system was popular, but that, as expected, it had "met with some abuse from systematic book thieves."[2] The first full branch, with lending facilities, was opened at Splotlands in 1900: by 1908, when Ballinger resigned to become first librarian of the National Library of Wales, there were five such branches, two of them (Cathays and Canton) recently built with the help of grants from Carnegie.

---

[1] *Descriptive Account of the Corporation Public Libraries of the City of Glasgow* (Glasgow 1924), p. 35. For the history of the library at this period see also "Notes on Glasgow Libraries", in *L.A.R.*, Vol. IX (1907), pp. 549–567; *Glasgow Public Libraries, 1874–1966* (Glasgow 1966); and for Barrett and the Mitchell Library, J. Minto, *A History of the Public Library Movement* (1932), pp. 302–303; and W. A. Munford, *James Duff Brown, 1862–1914* (1968), pp. 6–8.

[2] J. Ballinger, *The Cardiff Free Libraries* (Cardiff 1895), p. 25.

Ogle, in 1897, describes Cardiff's recent progress as "a triumphal advance", and its newly enlarged central library as a "people's palace"; and he refers especially to the magnificence of its Welsh collections.[1] Very shortly the city was to become famous also for its school libraries. Ballinger was particularly concerned about children's reading, and he saw the school library, organized by the library staff, paid for by the School Board, and administered by the teachers, as the first step in a ladder leading to full membership of the adult library. In 1899 he was able to secure the establishment of a library in every elementary and secondary school in the city, and by 1905 the scheme had been extended to include infant schools, a school for the deaf, and the voluntary schools. We shall have occasion to consider this matter again.[2]

We have already observed that the citizens of Edinburgh were as obstinate as the Glaswegians in refusing to put their hands in their pockets for a library rate. In 1886, however, Carnegie's offer of £50000 overcame their reluctance, and four years later the new library on George IV Bridge was opened amid considerable popular enthusiasm. With its reference library, lending library, newsroom, ladies' room and juvenile room, its Ionic columns and faience tiles, its electric lighting and steam heating, the building was regarded in its day as the last word in library architecture.[3]

Unlike Glasgow, Edinburgh had to start its library service from scratch. Under Dr. Hew Morrison, the first librarian, steady progress was made with the central library, but the provision of branch libraries soon languished for lack of funds. Five branches were indeed established between 1897 and 1905, three of these in recreation halls erected by the trustees of Thomas Nelson, the publisher, but after this there was no major branch development until the 'twenties.[4] At the outbreak of the first World War the total bookstock was still less than half that of Glasgow. Both lending and reference stock were classified by Dewey, but a wall of indicators still separated the readers from the books. It was still there in 1922, when E. A. Savage succeeded Hew Morrison as librarian. The library was, he says in his usual picturesque style, 'a museum piece . . . it felt like an impiety to lay a finger on a survival so perfect.'[5]

Other Large Libraries

Apart from the four major libraries already referred to—Birmingham, Manchester, Liverpool, and Leeds—the largest English libraries during this period were Sheffield, Bristol, Bradford and Newcastle upon Tyne, each of which was reported by Adams as possessing a total stock of between 150000 and 200000 volumes.

Sheffield, which by 1911 had overtaken Leeds in population, ought not really to have been in this second group at all, but it still suffered under the same

[1] J. J. Ogle, *The Free Library* (1897), pp. 230–234.
[2] See below, p. 198, For the Cardiff Public Libraries at this period see, in addition to the works already cited, *Cardiff Public Libraries 50th Anniversary Celebration* (Cardiff 1932).
[3] For a description see Greenwood (1891) pp. 250–251.
[4] *Edinburgh Public Libraries and City Museums: Historical Guide and Handbook to the Libraries* (Edinburgh 1958), p. 7.
[5] E. A. Savage, *A Librarian's Memories, Portraits and Reflections* (1952), p. 96.

parsimonious civic administration that had hampered its early development.[1]
Samuel Smith, who came from Worcester Public Library to be Sheffield's
second chief librarian, was not the man to fight against the prevailing spirit of
philistinism, and his chairman, Alderman W. H. Brittain, does not appear to
have given him the support he needed. In 1889 a local Act empowered the city
to levy a 2d. rate for library purposes, but in 1914 the rate actually levied was
still less than 1½d. The library's official historian has described the period of the
joint rule of Smith and Brittain (1894–1920) as "The Stagnant Years".

There were, of course, some improvements. The appalling congestion in
the central reference library was relieved when in 1896 the town council moved
to a new civic building and thus made the whole of the old Mechanics' Hall
available for library purposes; and the turn of the central lending library came
with the purchase and conversion in 1909 of an adjoining building, the Music
Hall. The reference library was classified according to Dewey, and along with
one of the newer branches was converted to open access in 1913–14. The
reference collection of 32000 volumes at this time, however, remained inadequate for a library of this size, lending issues were falling, library administration
was old-fashioned and inefficient, and branch development lagged far behind
the growth of the city. The four new branches acquired between 1903 and 1912,
and the eight delivery stations, to which books were sent out daily by handcart,
were quite insufficient to meet the needs of a population which increased by
almost sixty per cent between 1881 and 1911, and in 1908 the library was
resorting to the pitiable expedient of subscribing to W. H. Smith's for a supply
of new books.[2]

At Bristol also there was a problem of accommodation for the central
library. The eighteenth-century building in King Street, with its elaborate
wood-carving, its ancient oak presses, and its Grinling Gibbons chimneypiece,
was, as the librarian remarked to the Library Association when it met in Bristol
in 1900, "quaint and interesting, but painfully inconvenient",[3] especially as
Bristol was growing even faster than Sheffield. In this case the answer was found
in an entirely new central library, provided from a bequest of £50000 by
V. Stuckey Lean, a local banker, and opened in 1906.

It is interesting to read, by contrast with the situation in Sheffield, that in
this new library the reference department occupied pride of place: the lending
department, still fenced round with indicators until after the war, occupied only
a small section of the ground floor.[4] In 1914, in fact, the reference works (classified
by Dewey) accounted for almost half the total stock of 177000 volumes.
Ironically enough a major factor in the building up of the reference collection
was the taking over in 1892 of the Museum Library, successor to the Library
Society which had once occupied the King Street building.[5] When it was
incorporated in the reference library in 1905 in preparation for the opening of

[1] See above, pp. 36, 52.
[2] *The City Libraries of Sheffield, 1856–1956* (Sheffield 1956), pp. 20–30; *L.Y.B. 1910–11* and
    1914; S. Smith, "A Brief Note on an Experiment in Connection with a Subscription
    Library", in *L.A.R.*, Vol. X (1908), pp. 19–23.
[3] E. R. N. Mathews, *A Survey of the Bristol Public Libraries* (Bristol 1900), p. 13.
[4] S. M. Booth, *Three Hundred and Fifty Years of Public Libraries in Bristol, 1613–1963* (Bristol
    1963), p. 13.
[5] See above, p. 54.

the new building, the Museum Library's stock amounted to some 45 000 volumes, though it appears from the available figures that the net increase in reference stock was substantially less.

The most significant development during these years, however, was the articulation of the branch system. Two new city branches were opened during this period,[1] three of the other branches were rehoused,[2] and four branches were established to cater for newly incorporated areas. These last were St. George's (1898), Fishponds (1900), Shirehampton (1904), and Westbury-on-Trim (1906).[3] Unlike Sheffield, Bristol did not have to resort to the doubtful expedient of delivery stations. Bearing in mind that even in 1914 Bristol's library rate was still only 1¼d., this record of service was very creditable.[4]

Bradford continued the rapid progress which had characterized the library in the earlier period[5], and in 1913–14, with 174000 books for its 289000 inhabitants, was relatively better provided for than some larger places. As at Cardiff, the financial situation eased considerably after 1890. The first relief came in 1890–91 with a grant of £500 from the profits of the Gas Department; in the following year annual grants began to be made available from the "whisky money" for the purchase of scientific and technical books; in 1892 the adoption of the Museums Act made it possible to levy an additional rate for museum purposes; and following an extension of the city boundaries in 1899 a private Act was secured authorising a 2d. library rate (though it was not till 1904–05 that an extra rate was actually levied).[6]

The central library benefited in 1895 by the gift of a private library of 12000 volumes, formerly the property of James Hanson, newspaper proprietor and library pioneer; and the local collection, always a strong feature, was enriched in 1909 by the purchase for £120 of the Federer Collection of 10000 books and pamphlets about Yorkshire or by Yorkshire authors. By this time the accommodation for the central library had been greatly improved by the removal of the museum, which originally occupied the entire top floor, to new premises in 1905. As part of the reorganization the central library was reclassified on the Dewey system, a dictionary catalogue being retained for fiction, poetry, and general literature in the lending library.[7]

The main weakness of the library lay in its branch organization. Following the Leeds tradition of "taking the library to the doors of the people", Bradford

---

[1] Hotwells (1888) and Avonmouth (1896). The former was closed in 1905 owing to its proximity to the new central library.

[2] St. Philip's (1896), North District (1901), and Bedminster (1914).

[3] The St. George's building was presented by Sir William H. Wills, the tobacco merchant (afterwards Lord Winterstoke); the Shirehampton building was erected with funds provided by Carnegie prior to incorporation.

[4] I am indebted to Mr. W. S. Haugh, City Librarian, for information on branch development and on the Museum Library. See, in addition to the works already cited, E. R. N. Mathews, "History of the Public Library Movement in Bristol", in The Library, Vol. VIII (1896), pp. 198–205; and the account of the Bristol library in Library World, Vol. XII (1909–10), pp. 217–224.

[5] See above, pp. 60–61.

[6] B. Wood, A Brief Survey of the Bradford Public Libraries, 1872–1922 (Bradford 1922), pp. 10–11.

[7] M. E. Hartley, "A Survey of the Public Library Movement in Bradford", in L.A.R., Vol. VIII (1906), pp. 434–435, 442.

had created a large number of small branches—mostly part-time branches of a few thousand books providing an evening service only, in schools, Sunday schools, mechanics' institutes, public baths, and the like. From 1902 onwards the authority began to make use also of centres to which the books were supplied by travelling libraries. This kind of provision was cheap and easy, but it sacrificed quality for quantity. In 1913–14 Adams recorded twelve branches and ten travelling libraries, but only four of the branches were full-time, and only two of these—Manningham and Great Horton—had purpose-built premises. It was at the Great Horton Branch, opened in 1912, that the first experiment was made in the use of the open access system.

The library at Newcastle upon Tyne offers an interesting contrast. The population it served (267000 in 1911) was not much smaller than that of Bradford, and its bookstock of 172000 volumes was proportionately a little larger, but its policy towards branch development was quite different. Under its first librarian, W. J. Haggerston, who died in 1894, there were no branches at all, and even under his successor Basil Anderton, who held office until 1935, progress in this direction was slow. The difficulty was in part financial, for although the library rate no longer had to support the science and art classes (which had been transferred to the Technical Instruction Committee in 1889), it did have to support, from 1904, the Laing Art Gallery. The maximum rate was raised by local Act to $1\frac{1}{2}$d. in 1898 and 2d. in 1906, but even the latter figure left little margin, and there were years when virtually no books could be purchased.

It is not surprising, therefore, to learn that all the four branches which came into existence before the first World War were gifts. Three of them—at Elswick in 1896, at Heaton in 1899, and at Walker in 1909—were presented by Sir William Stephenson,[1] and the fourth, at Benwell in 1909, by Andrew Carnegie. It should, however, be noted that these were all full-time, purpose-built libraries, each of them carrying a substantial stock: in the Parliamentary Return of 1912 the four branches are shown as holding a total stock of 50000 volumes, compared with 77000 in the twenty-three branches at that time operated by Bradford.

It can also be said that the Newcastle library did its utmost to maximize the use of its resources by careful attention to cataloguing. Haggerston's work in this field has already been noted: under his successor Anderton, a special feature was the production of special class-lists as a guide both to the student and to the general reader. Conversion to the Dewey system was undertaken about 1900. Open access was still a thing of the future, but on the production of a new consolidated printed catalogue in 1908 the indicators were abandoned and modern issue methods were introduced. Book exhibitions were arranged from time to time, and public lectures in the lecture-room at the new Benwell branch. On the whole, the library was doing a useful if somewhat unspectacular job.[2]

---

[1] William Haswell Stephenson, industrial magnate, ardent Methodist, four times Mayor and three times Lord Mayor of Newcastle, dominated the public life of the city from 1870 until his death, at the age of 92, in 1918. His many public benefactions included three Methodist chapels and the three branch libraries, here referred to, which looked like Methodist chapels—information from Mr. A. Wallace, City Librarian.

[2] See J. J. Ogle, *The Free Library* (1897), pp. 212–215; *A Short History of the Newcastle upon Tyne Public Libraries* (Newcastle upon Tyne 1950).

The only other authority in this group was Dundee, which with an income from a 2d. rate of £7600 in 1913–14 was supporting not only the third largest library in Scotland, with six branches and a total bookstock of 151 000 volumes, but also a museum and art gallery.[1] Ogle, writing in 1897, commented on the many generous gifts of money and books received by this library; on the exhibitions, art classes, and public lectures; on the generous accommodation provided for the cultural societies of the town; and on the exceptionally high quality of the catalogues produced for the lending library (1891) and the Lochee branch:

> "The subject entries are particularly well done, and journalists and literary men would find the Dundee catalogue unlock new stores of knowledge even to the best informed. Whether the thoroughness of the work is best explained by the generosity of the people, . . . it is perhaps difficult to say; but certain it is that such work implies both men and means."[2]

Some Medium-sized Libraries

If we take a bookstock of between 50 000 and 150 000 volumes as representing, at the time of the Adams Report, a medium-sized library, we find ourselves with a group of forty-three libraries of which only six had more than 100 000 volumes. Two of these six, Nottingham and Bolton, were old-established libraries; two, Lambeth and Hull, were new; and the others, Westminster and Wandsworth, though their origins went back before 1887, were also virtually new.

Of Nottingham we need say little more than that the service continued to develop under the direction of J. Potter Briscoe, who retired from the post of librarian only in 1916 (to be succeeded by his son W. A. Briscoe). It was in 1890 that he launched his series of half-hour talks on books and writers, designed to help library users in their choice of reading, and this very successful venture became well known and was widely imitated.[3] He also retained his special interest in provision for children: Cotgreave commented in 1901 that "the perfect arrangements made for juvenile readers" were a special feature of the Nottingham library service.[4]

As at Bradford the branch organization was a weakness, for the early branches, though numerous, were little more than reading-rooms, supplemented in some instances by delivery stations at which books could be supplied on request. Before the first World War a beginning was made in the provision of full-scale branches, and Carnegie undertook to provide four at a total cost of £15 000, but the war prevented these plans from being carried out. Adams in 1913–14 recorded six branch libraries and six reading rooms. By 1918 the system included seven branch lending libraries, ten branch reading rooms, and

---

[1] By way of comparison we may note that Bradford's income in 1913–14 was £12 700, Newcastle upon Tyne's £10 600—*Adams Report*. Carnegie provided £37 000 for three branch libraries and two reading rooms—*Library World*, Vol. XII (1909–10), p. 306.

[2] Ogle, *op. cit.*, p. 239.

[3] Ogle, *op. cit.*, p. 211; see also the sketch of Briscoe in J. Minto, *History of the Public Library Movement* (1932), pp. 304–306.

[4] A. Cotgreave, *Views and Memoranda of Public Libraries* (1901), p. 9.

one delivery station, three of the branches having been converted during the war to open access.[1]

Bolton, after its initial difficulties, also made creditable progress.[2] Thanks in part to the generosity of Bolton citizens, two additional branches were opened in 1888 and 1891 respectively, and following the large extension of the borough boundaries in 1898 three more were added, one in 1900 at Astley Bridge, and two more in 1910 at Great Lever and Halliwell. The last two were provided at the expense of Carnegie, who at the same time gave money to provide a new building for Astley Bridge.[3] A seventh branch was added in temporary premises at Tonge Moor in 1918. What was still lacking was reasonable accommodation for the Central Library, which was located, it may be remembered, in the old Mechanics' Institute building, and which, as the town grew, became increasingly overcrowded. A new building for the lending department in 1893 gave only temporary relief, and by 1919 the central services were divided among four different buildings. This was a situation that was not remedied until the new civic centre was built in 1938.[4]

It is interesting to observe, once more, how a change of librarianship brought a modernization of the administration. J. K. Waite was the librarian from 1870 to 1904. His photograph in the official history shows a grey-bearded gentleman of venerable aspect, and one is not surprised to read in the *Library Year Book* for 1897 that he still used "Edwards' fixed location by press, shelf and number." He was succeeded by Archibald Sparke, a fierce-looking man with a waxed moustache, and if we look at the *Year Book* for 1910 we note that the classification has been completely reorganized, with Brown's Adjustable Classification in the lending library and Dewey in the reference library; that the reference library now has a card catalogue; that the use of the indicator has been abandoned except for fiction; and that the open access system is about to be introduced at one of the branches.[5]

The library at Hull, opened in 1893, is interesting chiefly because of its origins. After the fourth failure, in 1888, to secure the adoption of the Public Libraries Acts, James Reckitt, a Quaker, a Liberal, a teetotaler, and co-chairman of the well-known firm of Reckitt and Sons Limited, decided to bring pressure to bear by setting up a model public library for East Hull (the section of the town east of the river). He erected a special building, complete with reference library, lending library, and reading room, endowed it with over 8000 books, and from his own pocket subscribed for its maintenance the equivalent of a 1d. rate for that part of the town (about £500). The library was opened to the public in 1889, and recorded over 100000 issues from the lending department in the first year. When the question of adoption again came before the public in 1892,

---

[1] *Fifty Years: a Brief History of the Public Library Movement in Nottingham* (Nottingham 1918), pp. 35, 43. The Central Boys' and Girls' Library was also on open access.

[2] Cf. above, pp. 52–53.

[3] *Library World*, Vol. XII (1909–10), pp. 312–315, has excellent illustrations of these three Carnegie branches.

[4] *Bolton Public Libraries, 1853–1953* (Bolton 1953), pp. 11–13.

[5] *Op. cit.*, p. 9; *L.Y.B. 1897*, p. 126; *L.Y.B. 1910–11*, p. 80. For the details of this revolution see the account of the Bolton Public Library in *Library World*, Vol. XI (1908–09), pp. 139–143. In the closing days of 1970, while this book was still being written, came the news of Archibald Sparke's death, at his Southport home, at the age of 99.

the proposal was carried, but only by a small margin. This victory can almost certainly be attributed to the example set by the library in East Hull, which was now handed over to become a branch library. By 1914 four other branches had come into existence—one of them provided by Carnegie.[1] The Central Library, after a period in temporary accommodation, was rehoused in 1907 in a new building which included also a public hall and a technical college.

W. F. Lawton, formerly sub-librarian at Leeds, served as librarian from 1893 until his death in 1918. The history of the library during his term of office was not specially distinguished, but by 1913–14, with 792 000 issues per annum from a bookstock of 114 000 volumes, it was being more extensively used than many larger libraries.[2]

The large and populous parish of Lambeth, which inaugurated its public library service in 1888 and became a metropolitan borough in 1900, had by 1913–14 the largest bookstock of any of the London boroughs (though it was Islington, under J. D. Brown, which headed the list for number of issues[3]). The people of Lambeth, it must be confessed, had not at the outset been particularly keen to adopt the Act. In 1886 they had reluctantly agreed to a $\frac{1}{2}$d. rate, but in 1889 they had actually rejected an offer of £10 000 for the erection of a central library on condition that the rate should be raised to 1d. Over against this defeat for the library cause, however, we must place the extraordinary story related by Greenwood of how, when in that same year 1889 the first branch library at West Norwood was re-opened after a week's closure for cleaning, the road outside "was blocked by an expectant throng of three or four hundred people, long before the library was opened".[4]

Lambeth, was moreover, blest by benefactors who were both numerous and persistent, notable among them being, as we have seen, the wealthy industrialist Henry Tate.[5] A parish six miles long by a mile or two broad was not easy to cater for, but before the close of 1891 it had already been equipped with four branch libraries; the 1d. rate had been agreed on; and plans for the Tate Central Library in Brixton were under way (it was opened in 1893). A fifth branch was established in 1906, and the Lambeth Authority also shared responsibility for two branch libraries on its borders. The Minet Library, presented by a Mr. W. Minet in 1890, and situated in an outlying part of Camberwell, was administered by a joint committee of Camberwell and Lambeth; and the Upper Norwood (Gipsy Hill) branch, opened in 1900 at the extreme southern end of Lambeth, was administered by a joint committee of Croydon and Lambeth. These two rather exceptional arrangements persisted

---

[1] *L.Y.B. 1914*, p. 264.

[2] See on all this J. F. Hooton, *Libraries in Hull in the Nineteenth Century and the Struggle for the Adoption of the Public Libraries Acts* (unpublished F.L.A. thesis, 1967); and the same author's article on "The James Reckitt Public Library, Kingston upon Hull", in *Library History*, Vol. I (1967–69), pp. 184–191.

[3] For Lambeth see below, App. XI. For Islington (opened in 1906) Adams records a bookstock of 81 000 volumes and total issues of 943 000. The borough had a population of 327 000 compared with Lambeth's 298 000.

[4] Greenwood (1891), p. 319.

[5] See above pp. 119–120.

into our own times.[1] The Minet Library became a centre for material relating to the County of Surrey.[2]

The city and metropolitan borough of Westminster faced on its establishment in 1900 some of the problems of amalgamation which have recurred in our own day as a result of the creation of the London boroughs in 1965. It brought together three pre-existing library systems: one whose origins have already been described, serving since 1857 the parishes of St. Margaret and St. John;[3] another inaugurated in 1889, serving the parish of St. Martin in the Fields (and also by arrangement since 1893 the adjoining parish of St. Paul, Covent Garden); and a third inaugurated in 1894, serving the wealthy parish of St. George, Hanover Square. These three systems had a total of five libraries—one in St. Martin's parish and two each in the others. In 1900 the Libraries Acts were at once adopted for those parts of the new borough which had not previously adopted, and the five existing libraries were brought under common regulations and thrown open to all the inhabitants.

For the time being the three librarians continued to administer their own libraries, and even issue separate annual reports, but when two of them retired in 1904 the third, Frank Pacy of St. George's, became the first chief librarian, and his headquarters library in Buckingham Palace Road became the first central library. It was to serve in this capacity until 1948, in spite of repeated schemes for its replacement. Fortunately it was in the first instance built on a generous scale and by the standards of the time sumptuously fitted up.[4]

The creation of a chief librarian and a central library, however, did little to solve the fundamental problems. As late as 1925–26 the amalgamation of the three systems was still imperfect, and it was reported that "the inheritance of buildings, books and methods differently inspired, differently acquired, has always hampered and restricted a real constructive and progressive policy".[5]

The administration prior to the first World War does not seem to have been particularly enterprising. The bookstock was improved, but not much increased, and the number of issues rose only slowly. When the war came one of the branch libraries and all the news and magazine rooms were closed; the opening hours of the remaining departments were reduced; and the buildings, one by one, were taken over for war purposes, until by 1918 only the central library remained in service. It was a dismal and unjustifiable record.[6]

The difficulties of divided administration were to be seen also at Wandsworth. Here the metropolitan borough created in 1900 included not only Wandsworth itself, which had opened a library as early as 1885, but also Putney (1888), Clapham (1889), and Streatham (1891). The last named had at the time of the take-over a branch at Balham (1898), and another was subsequently established for the parish of Tooting (1902). As at Westminster, however, the various libraries long continued to function separately under their own libra-

[1] The Minet Library was eventually taken over by Lambeth in 1956; the library at Upper Norwood remains under joint control.
[2] There is no published history, but see, in addition to the official reports and year books, Greenwood (1891), pp. 318–323; and J. J. Ogle, *The Free Library* (1897), pp. 144–145.
[3] See above, pp. 59–60.   [4] Ogle, *op. cit.*, pp. 150–152.
[5] City of Westminster, *Report of the Public Libraries Committee, 1949–1950*, p. 5.
[6] See in addition to the report just cited, City of Westminster, *Public Library Service, 1900–1965: Report of the Public Libraries Committee, February 1965*.

rians. It was not until 1920 that Thomas Everatt, librarian at Streatham since its opening nearly thirty years earlier, was appointed first principal librarian.[1]

Of the remaining thirty-six libraries in this group, i.e. those with book-stocks of between 50000 and 100000, more than half traced their origins back before 1887. The earlier history of some of these—Salford, Birkenhead, Cambridge, Warrington and Sunderland—has already been sketched above. To find Salford here is rather surprising, for in 1886 it had been the fifth largest library in the country. The work of the branches, of which there were six by 1913–14, was still popular, and issues were high. In 1897 it was recorded that chess and draughts were provided in some branches, and one branch reading room had a smoking room. A considerable sum was also spent on newspapers and periodicals, but the amount spent on books was quite inadequate, and the total stock increased only from 81000 to 96000 between 1886 and 1913–14.[2]

Birkenhead, Cambridge and Warrington all grew much more rapidly. Birkenhead, described in 1891 as "among the live libraries of the country",[3] managed to stretch its 1d. rate to provide, in 1894, branch libraries to meet the needs of new areas north and south of the town; and in 1908–09, with the help of Carnegie grants of £20000, the central library and the branches were all rebuilt.[4] Cambridge, with an income in 1913–14 of £1843, was supporting a central library, a branch library, and two reading rooms, with a total staff of eleven and a total bookstock of 59000 volumes for the town's 52000 inhabitants.[5] At Warrington, which had given very poor service in the earlier period, the position was transformed when in 1891 all charges for the use of the lending library were at last abolished.[6] Issues jumped from 19000 in 1885–86 to 52000 in 1891–92 and 110000 in 1913–14—still not an impressive figure compared with a bookstock of 58000, but vastly better than before.

Sunderland, in spite of its early difficulties, was now tolerably prosperous. Equipped in 1879 with a central building which housed also a museum, art gallery, and conservatory, and was regarded at the time as handsome, it had since acquired, with Carnegie's help, three branch libraries. Between 1886 and 1913–14 it had more than quadrupled its bookstock, and by the latter date all the books had been reclassified on the Dewey system and (with the exception of certain reserved categories in the reference library) were available to members on open access. As was not uncommon in towns with a large working-class population, the main emphasis was on the lending libraries, which accounted for some 45000 of the total stock of 51000 volumes, and the bulk of the 352000 issues during the year.[7]

Features of special interest in some of the other older libraries will be

[1] Information from Mr. E. V. Corbett, Librarian of the present London Borough of Wandsworth. As will be seen from Appendix III, this borough includes only part of the former metropolitan borough, Clapham and Streatham having been transferred to Lambeth. For Tate's benefactions to Streatham see above, p. 120.

[2] *L.Y.B. 1897*, p. 193; *Adams Report*, pp. 34–35. A 1½d. rate was available by local Act of 1890, and an additional ½d. for the museum from 1894.

[3] Greenwood (1891), pp. 154–155.

[4] *Birkenhead Public Libraries Centenary, 1856–1956* (Birkenhead 1956), pp. 7–9.

[5] *L.Y.B. 1914*, p. 172; *Adams Report*, pp. 26–27. The rate was still only 1 1/16 d., though a 2d. rate had been sanctioned since 1894.   [6] See above, p. 37.

[7] Greenwood (1891), pp. 144–146; *L.Y.B. 1914*, pp. 433–434; *Adams Report*, pp. 30–31; information from Mr. J. T. Shaw, Director.

commented on in their due place in the chapter dealing with library organization. The one Welsh library in the group—Swansea—and the one Scottish
library—Aberdeen—are noticed below.[1] Of the sixteen new libraries which at
this period attained a bookstock of between 50 000 and 100 000 volumes, it is not
surprising to note that twelve were London metropolitan boroughs,[2] and three
more—Croydon, West Ham and Willesden—were places within what is now
the Outer London area; the other one was Bournemouth. Because of their
substantial populations and high rateable value, most of the London boroughs
had both the incentive and the resources to develop a library service quickly.
The one notable exception was Paddington, which with a population of 16 000
in 1911 and an income from a 1d. rate of £240 was clearly not equipped to
start a library service, and in fact did not adopt until 1920.[3]

It will be of interest to take a closer look at four of these libraries—Kensington, Willesden, West Ham and Bournemouth.

Kensington, though with a population of 172 000 in 1911 it was by no
means the largest of the metropolitan boroughs, was second in wealth only to
Westminster. In 1913–14 it was still managing with a $\frac{1}{4}$d. rate, but this $\frac{1}{4}$d. rate
brought in over £6000 per annum, more than a 1d. rate in most of the metro-
politan boroughs. As at Hull, however, it was only when private initiative had
set the example that the citizens could be persuaded to adopt the Libraries Acts.
In this case the lead came from James Heywood, a wealthy Manchester banker
and philanthropist who had settled in Kensington and who for fourteen years
(1874–88) maintained a public library at his own expense in a converted shop in
Notting Hill Gate. He offered to present the library to the parish authorities free
of charge if they would undertake to maintain a public service, but it was not
until 1887 that this proposal was accepted, and not until 1888 that the Heywood
Library was formally handed over to the library commissioners.

The commissioners set to work energetically to develop the new service.
The Heywood collection of about 4000 volumes became the nucleus of the
North Kensington Branch, which was provided with new and purpose-built
premises in 1891. In the meantime a second branch had been established at
Brompton in 1888, and a central library in the St. Mary Abbot's Vestry Hall in
1889. This central library was from the beginning too small, but even as late as
1905 an attempt to increase the rate by $\frac{1}{10}$d. in order to provide a new library
had to be withdrawn in the face of violent public opposition. With relatively
minor additions and alterations, the old building had to serve until 1960. There
was a similar struggle with the ratepayers over the first children's library, which
was established in a basement of the North Kensington Branch in 1912.

The use of the libraries expanded rapidly at first, to reach a peak approaching 300 000 issues per annum in 1894, but fell away to about half this
figure by 1900, and thereafter climbed only slowly and spasmodically. It was

---

[1] The others are, in order of size of bookstock: Portsmouth (88 000), Brighton (82 000),
Leicester (78 000), Wigan (76 000), Coventry (75 000), Exeter (71 000), Preston (71 000)
Plymouth (69 000), Rochdale (63 000), Worcester (55 000), Reading (54 000), Oldham
(52 000), and Halifax (50 000).

[2] Battersea, Camberwell, Chelsea, Hackney, Hampstead, Islington, Kensington, Lewisham,
Shoreditch, Southwark, Stepney, and Woolwich.

[3] For the pattern of growth in the London area see above, p. 123. From 1901 Paddington
did in fact have a library in the Queen's Park Ward, taken over in that year from Chelsea.

not until the early 'twenties that the 1894 figure was overtaken. The historian of the Kensington libraries attributes this poor record partly to cramped and inadequate premises, partly to shortage of money to provide new books (the figure for books and binding in 1913–14 was £1100), and partly to the continued use of the old-fashioned indicator system long after the open access system was in use elsewhere.[1]

Willesden (since 1965 part of the London Borough of Brent) was growing rapidly in the late nineteenth century, the population increasing from 16000 in 1871 to 61000 twenty years later. After a vigorous campaign the motion for the adoption of the Acts was carried by a two to one majority in 1891, and since the community consisted of three more or less isolated townships—Harlesden, Kilburn, and Willesden Green, it was decided to establish not one library but three. Sites were acquired, buildings erected, and all three duly opened in 1894. In response to local demand a fourth library developed at Kensal Rise, beginning with a reading room in 1900.

Except that Kensal Rise was under the control of the librarian at Willesden Green, the four libraries were virtually independent, with their own committees, their own allocations from the 1d. rate, their own library procedures. With such an organization, any impartial observer could have predicted disaster, but surprisingly it did not happen. Public interest was keen, and the libraries were from the first well supported. The population continued to increase rapidly, rising to 159000 in 1911, and rateable value rose correspondingly. Between 1904 and 1910 Carnegie provided funds for an extension of all four libraries to meet growing demand. By 1913–14, therefore, the libraries could be regarded as reasonably flourishing, but they still functioned almost independently of one another; their individual bookstocks were small—from 12000 to 19000 volumes apiece; and the income available to each library was less than £1000 per annum. It is not surprising, therefore, that when the first World War came to an end the problem of co-ordinating the library service was high on the agenda.[2]

West Ham (since 1965 joined with East Ham in the London Borough of Newham) was another rapidly growing area, described by Ogle in 1897 as "the forest of homes continuous with our great capital on its Essex side". Its population in 1911 had already reached 289000. In library history it has a special interest because it appointed as its first librarian, in 1891, Alfred Cotgreave of indicator fame. A Cheshire man, Cotgreave had had library experience in Manchester and Birmingham before becoming librarian successively at Wednesbury, Richmond, Wandsworth, the Guille-Allès Library in Guernsey, and finally, at the age of 42, at West Ham, where he served until his retirement on health grounds in 1905. He was a man of great industry and of an inventive turn of mind, his inventions including not only several indicators, but also a variety of magazine racks, shelf fittings, magazine covers, and other gadgets. His *Views and Memoranda of Public Libraries* (1901) provided a useful guide to library buildings, and his laboriously compiled *Contents Subject-Index to General and Periodical Literature* (1900) was a pioneering reference tool. Unfortunately, in exploiting the commercial possibilities of his inventions, he found it difficult

[1] H. G. Massey, *Kensington Libraries Service* (duplicated, Kensington Public Libraries 1950), pp. 1–9.
[2] Willesden Public Libraries, *The Willesden Library Service 1894 to 1954: a Jubilee History and Annual Report, 1953–54* (1954), pp. 1–12.

at times to distinguish private advantage from public benefit, and in his battle for the indicator against the new system of open access, he showed himself none too scrupulous.[1]

The library system built up under Cotgreave included a central library at Stratford and three branch libraries. The central library opened in temporary premises in 1892 and was transferred in 1898 to a new building, erected at a total cost of £80000, which included also a museum, art gallery and technical college. The earliest branch, at Canning Town, was opened in 1893 by Passmore Edwards, who celebrated the occasion with a gift of a thousand volumes. Ten years later Edwards presented a building for a second branch at Plaistow, and the third branch (Custom House) was given by Carnegie in 1905. In spite of Cotgreave's preference for the indicator (which it must be remembered was still in widespread use), everything possible was done by careful cataloguing, periodical lists of new accessions, and supplementary readers' tickets, to en-courage maximum library use.

Unfortunately, when Cotgreave resigned in 1905 he recommended that no chief librarian should be appointed to succeed him but that the librarians in charge at the central library and the three branches should be made separately responsible to the library committee. This disastrous advice was adopted and the four libraries continued until 1933 to operate as separate units, with their own budgets, their own catalogues, and their own library procedures.[2]

In strong contrast to West Ham was the quiet but prosperous seaside resort of Bournemouth, with a population in 1911 of 79000. The story here was, at this period, mainly one of improvisation. Following the adoption of the Acts in 1893 a temporary central library was opened in 1895, to be replaced by a second temporary library in 1901, and by a permanent building only in 1913. Two temporary newsrooms were opened in 1897, supplemented in the fol-lowing year by a lending service from travelling libraries. In 1899 these ar-rangements were superseded by three temporary branch libraries, which in turn were eventually replaced (1907–16) by four permanent libraries provided with the help of a £10000 grant from Carnegie. This improved accommoda-tion led to a big increase in the use of the libraries in the years leading up to the first World War.

The librarian, at any rate, was not temporary. He was Charles Riddle, a Tynesider who was appointed to Bournemouth in 1894 after six years' experi-ence at Clerkenwell, and served until 1934. At Clerkenwell he had served under J. D. Brown and had stayed just long enough to see the pioneer open access lending library open its doors.[3] It was this experience, we may be sure, that led Riddle to recommend open access at Bournemouth from the very beginning. The recommendation was accepted, and Bournemouth thus became the second library in the country to adopt the new system, and the first to adopt it on opening.[4]

---

[1] See below, pp. 178–180.

[2] Ogle, *op. cit.*, pp. 202–204; *L.Y.B. 1897, 1900–01, 1910–11* and *1914*; A. Cotgreave, *Views and Memoranda of Public Libraries* (1901), pp. 1–2; *L.A.R.*, Vol. VII (1905), pp. 190–191.   [3] See below, pp. 178–179.

[4] Bournemouth Public Libraries, *Report for the Year 1931–1932, with a Brief Survey of the History of the Library Movement in Bournemouth* (1932), pp. 8–9, 12–14; see also *L.Y.B. 1897*, p. 127; *Library World*, Vol. XI (1908–09), pp. 463–466.

Some Smaller English Libraries

Nearly nine-tenths of the public libraries existing in 1913–14, including all the municipal borough libraries except Cambridge and of course all the urban district and parish libraries, had bookstocks less than 50000. In selecting from among more than three hundred English libraries we may begin with a brief reference to some of the older libraries whose origins have been referred to above.[1] There are six of them: Winchester, Canterbury, Oxford, Leamington, Darlington and Norwich. In size they ranged in 1886 from about 3000 volumes at Winchester to about 14000 at Norwich; in 1913–14 the relative order was the same, but the stocks ranged from about 10000 volumes at Winchester to about 41000 at Norwich.

Winchester, to begin with the smallest, was in 1913–14 still very backward. J. T. Burchett, librarian from 1884 to 1914, had a 1d. rate to help him instead of the ½d. rate which had to suffice until 1882, but in his last year the total annual income was still only £505, of which £250 went to pay the librarian and five other staff. Of the rest, £40 went on books and binding, and £55 on periodicals —a fact which sufficiently illustrates the order of priorities. The modern history of the library begins only with the appointment in 1914 of a qualified librarian, A. C. Piper, who in his seven years in office reorganized the entire library: he secured an extension of the building, reclassified and recatalogued the stock, and made the books available for the first time on open access.[2]

Of Canterbury, England's oldest rate-aided public library, Greenwood has an interesting story:

> "In the early part of 1889 an offer was received from an old Canterbury resident, Dr. Beaney of Melbourne, to build new premises for the Public Library, and to include in it a working-men's institute. In March, 1889, when the question was discussed in the Town Council, it was determined that a letter should be sent to Dr. Beaney suggesting that, as there was no need for another institute in Canterbury, the city would be much benefited, and his name brought into permanent connection with the place of his birth, if he would give them a new Town Hall . . . the offer was withdrawn, as it deserved to be."[3]

Shortly afterwards Beaney died, bequeathing to the Corporation £10000 for the provision of a working men's library and reading room. It was the public library, in the end, which benefited most from this bequest, and in 1900 it was able to re-open in the Beaney Institute. There are signs that at this time, under a new librarian, H. T. Mead, the library underwent a certain amount of modernization and reorganization, but with a bookstock in 1913–14 of less than 13000 volumes, and annual issues of less than 50000, it remained an exceedingly modest collection.

The public library at Oxford, with 24000 volumes and annual issues in excess of 100000, stood higher in the scale, but was still very inadequate. It had, of course, been shamefully neglected in the earlier years,[4] and it was not until the new county borough council took over from the local government board

---

[1] Ch. iv.

[2] *Adams Report*, pp. 44–45; City of Winchester, *A Hundred Years of Library Service, 1851–1951* (Winchester, 1951). Piper left to go to Richmond.

[3] Greenwood (1891), p. 206. The reference is to James George Beaney, M.D.

[4] See above, pp. 57–58.

in 1889 that things took a turn for the better. In 1895–96 the library moved
from the old town hall to what was regarded at the time as handsome accommodation in the new town hall. Handsome it may have been, but it did not
include accommodation for the librarian and his four assistants, or even a
retiring room. By 1911 it was described as "overcrowded in almost every
department, and . . . ill adapted for the purpose of a modern public library."[1]
A small branch at Summertown (1894) gave little relief.

In spite of acute difficulties of accommodation successive librarians did
their utmost to improve the service. Space was somehow found for a children's
reading room and lending library (in the basement) and for a bulky collection
of Braille books provided by a special trust. In 1913 open access was introduced,
and the stock reclassified according to Dewey. To make this possible the library
had to be entirely replanned, and the building was closed for three weeks.[2]

The record of Leamington Spa is not impressive. This was not a rapidly
growing industrial town: its population of 23 000 in 1881 grew only to 27 000
in 1911, and its library did not grow much faster. Under a conservative administration total stocks rose slowly from 11 000 volumes in 1886 to 25 000 in
1913–14, issues from 45 000 per annum to 60 000. The first clear indication of
progress came in 1902, when the library rooms in the town hall, long overcrowded, gave place to a new library, with a school above and behind it (the
present central library building). Ten years later Leamington got its first qualified librarian in William Ewart Owen, who at once introduced a measure of
open access and set about reclassifying the library according to Dewey. The
possibilities of improvement remained limited, however, for even with a 1½d.
rate the library's annual income in 1913–14 was only £1100.[3]

The Adams Report shows that with the exception of a few village libraries
all the public libraries of Co. Durham were particularly well used.[4] Darlington
was no exception. Thanks to the generosity of Edward Pease and other benefactors it had, as we have seen, got off to a good start at its opening in 1885,[5]
and by 1913–14 it appears to have been a tolerably flourishing little library, with
a combined reference and lending stock of 29 000 volumes and 183 000 annual
issues. As in so many places, a recently appointed qualified librarian, William
Wilson, was busily occupied reclassifying the stock (this time according to the
Brown subject classification, not Dewey), following the introduction of open
access. This latter change had been carried through in 1911, the year before
Wilson's appointment, on the initiative of the Chairman of the Library Committee, Major B. G. D. Biggs, and had involved a considerable reconstruction
of the building. The compilation of the new 'sheaf' catalogue was not completed
till 1918.[6]

A similar pattern, though with variations, can be discerned at Norwich.
Under George Easter, librarian from 1887 to 1900, the lending library, though
still on a small scale, became popular and successful (a Cotgreave indicator had

---

[1] *Oxford City Libraries 1854–1954* (Oxford [1954]), pp. 12–13.   [2] *Op. cit.*, p. 15.
[3] Greenwood (1891), p. 177; *Library Year Books, 1897–1914, s.v.; Adams Report*, pp. 46–47.
[4] *Adams Report*, pp. 30–31. Cf. Sunderland, above, p. 153.
[5] See above, p. 62.
[6] *Edward Pease Public Library: Fifty Years' Progress, 1885–1935* (Darlington 1935), pp. 7–9.
For the subscription book club operated in connection with this library from 1893 to 1911
see above, pp. 125–126, and for difficulties during the first World War, p. 128.

to be introduced in 1896); the reference library was established in 1894 as a separate department (though for five years without a catalogue); experiments were made in the provision of books to schools; and provision was made for University Extension lectures, Gilchrist Trust lectures, and Home Reading Circles. Unfortunately neither J. G. Tennant, the elderly deputy who was unwisely appointed to succeed Easter in 1900, nor L. R. Haggerston, who displaced Tennant in 1908, had the ability needed for the job, and in spite of the best endeavours of the Committee the affairs of the library fell into complete confusion.

It was in 1911 that G. A. Stephen, chief assistant librarian at St. Pancras, was brought in to repair the damage. He held office until his death in 1934, and wrought a complete transformation. When he arrived he found that the only really valuable part of the library was the local collection, which had been enriched by many benefactors, and especially by the generosity of a local antiquary, Walter Rye. The reference library was "quite inadequate to meet the requirements of students and business men", and the lending library was a mere random collection in which most of the fiction volumes were so filthy as to be a menace to health. For years the new librarian, with the able assistance from 1913 of his sub-librarian Charles Nowell (afterwards chief librarian at Manchester), devoted himself to the task of sorting, discarding, rebinding, replacing, reclassifying, recataloguing. A periodical *Readers' Guide* provided revised sectional catalogues as they were completed, gave notice of new accessions, and provided booklists on a variety of special topics. Book purchase, bookbinding, and finance were put on a proper footing. The library rooms were redecorated and in some degree reconstructed. Schemes for staff training were introduced. The local collection was strengthened not only by further gifts but by the inauguration of a press-cuttings record and a photographic survey of Norfolk and Norwich. By 1920 the Norwich public library had become one of the foremost in the country.[1]

Among other libraries in this group whose origins went back before 1887 we have space to mention only two, Stockport and Stoke. At Stockport a new librarian, Richard Hargreaves, took office in 1902, and fought a gallant and eventually successful battle to improve the service. With help from the Greg family he was able in 1908 to establish a modern open access branch in the newly incorporated district of Reddish; and four years later, thanks to a £10 000 grant from the Carnegie Trustees, he was at last able to secure a modern central library to replace the unsatisfactory old premises over the market hall.[2]

Stoke-on-Trent, which commenced its library service in 1878, is of interest because in 1910 it became a county borough, amalgamating for this purpose with five other towns—Burslem, Fenton, Hanley, Longton and Tunstall—which already had their own library services begun at various dates between 1869 and 1906. The situation was thus similar to that in the London metropolitan boroughs after the mergers of 1900. Hanley eventually became the central library, but for a long time, as in some metropolitan boroughs, the previously

[1] Stephen's own account is given in his *Three Centuries of a City Library* (Norwich 1917), Pt. ii; see also Ogle, *op. cit.*, pp. 215–217; and P. Hepworth and M. Alexander, *City of Norwich Libraries* (Norwich 1957), Chs. iii–v.

[2] R. E. G. Smith, *The First Fifty Years of Public Libraries in Stockport* (unpublished F.L.A. essay 1950), pp. 27 sqq. Cf. above, p. 34.

existing libraries remained in some degree separate. They had separate librarians, had their own allocation of funds, and were responsible to six separate sub-committees. It was not until 1915 that a chief librarian was appointed, and it was not until 1921 that the separate sub-committees were abolished and a start made in replacing the federal system by a single library service.[1] The total book-stock recorded in the Adams Report was 34000 volumes, but should probably be at least 50000, for a total population of 235000.[2]

The libraries founded after 1886 ranged, in 1913–14, from metropolitan boroughs to rural parishes. Among the provincial English town libraries the story of York is not untypical. After a long struggle, well documented in the library records, the Acts were adopted here in 1891, and the library was opened in 1893 in the former Mechanics' Institute building. This handsome building, only recently erected, was acquired along with the stock of about 4000 volumes on payment of the Institute's debts of £4100, and the Institute's secretary, A. H. Furnish, was appointed first public librarian. He held office for thirty-six years, and saw before his retirement the opening (in 1927) of a new central library building. Prior to 1919, however, he had a hard struggle.

The annual sum available for the purchase of books was under £200 and, had it not been for financial assistance from supporters of the library, the stock would have grown very slowly indeed. An offer of £5000 from Carnegie for two branch libraries had to be refused because money was not available for their upkeep. By 1913–14, however, in spite of all the difficulties, total stock had risen to the respectable total of 38000 volumes, about two-thirds of them in the lending library. As was appropriate in such a historic city, special attention was paid to local material and both the general library and the local collection were enriched by the purchase in 1917 of the old York Subscription Library, founded in 1794.

Many public libraries suffered during the first World War from the taking over of premises for war purposes, but few suffered, as York did, from actual military occupation. Here, we are told,

> "a company of soldiers was quartered in the basement and on the staircases leading from it. The smell of cooking pervaded the air at all hours of the day, and at un-expected times a brass band would strike up, usually with the strains of 'Poet and Peasant'. After a time the soldiers left, but heavy machinery was installed, and the building rumbled and shook from morning to night, until one felt that 'Poet and Peasant' would have been a relief."[3]

Two other historic towns which opened libraries about this time were Lincoln and Bath, both of which commenced service in 1895. The library at Lincoln, like that at York, began in the former Mechanics' Institute, a rather

---

[1] City and County Borough of Stoke on Trent, *Jubilee Report of the City Librarian, 1960*, pp. 22–30.

[2] The Adams Report lists only Stoke, Hanley and Fenton. Mr. K. D. Miller, City Librarian, advises me that there is no record of total stock at this period, but issues for the six town-ships combined in 1914 were 299000 (compared with 202000 in Adams). *P.R. 1912*, p.7, gives total stock 61663 vols., annual issues 344927.

[3] *City of York Public Libraries, 1893–1943* (York 1943), p. 5. For the history of the library see, in addition to the account given in this pamphlet, A. Cotgreave, *Views and Memoranda of Public Libraries* (1901), p. 68; *L.Y.B. 1914*, p. 470; *Adams Report*, pp. 48–49.

delightful building which had originally been an eighteenth-century assembly room. A letter signed "Henry Harris, Science Teacher", published in the *Lincoln Gazette* on the day the library was opened, is worth quoting. It gives instructions for obtaining a book from the library. The first step, says Mr. Harris, is to secure a guarantee form from the librarian and have it signed by "two citizen householders who are willing to be bondsmen for the return of a book in good condition, and for the payment of fines should any be incurred". The next step is to exchange this form for a borrower's card.

> "The third step to take is to purchase a shilling catalogue and to ask for a form in which to enter a 'Written Request' for the book the reader prefers, with its letter, number and title, from the catalogue. Before handing in the form the borrower must ascertain from a stand on the counter named 'The Indicator', that the book is in the library at the time".[1]

It is satisfactory to note that the new Carnegie library opened in 1914 was available to the readers on open access.

At Bath, as we have seen, public resistance to the adoption of the Libraries Acts was particularly obstinate, and the proposal was four times rejected between 1869 and 1880.[2] After 1893 the power of decision lay with the town council, but mindful of the powerful interests aligned against the public library movement they were content, at first, to bring together in a remote upper room in their new Guildhall three libraries which had at various times come into the Corporation's possession: a seventeenth-century parochial library, a small local history collection, and a theological library bequeathed by a local clergyman. These volumes, about 2500 in all, were constituted in 1895 into a public library, and Joseph Davis, a second-hand bookseller, was engaged as librarian and cataloguer at 15s. a week (increased to 25s. when the library was opened full-time in 1898).

In 1900 the library was transferred to a new Art Gallery built from a legacy (a proposal to use part of the legacy for a new library building was defeated at a stormy public meeting). Now at last the Acts were adopted, but a $\frac{1}{2}$d. rate only was levied, and until 1924 the library was for reference only. In 1905, after yet another contentious meeting, and a public poll, an offer of £13 000 by Carnegie for an extension of the library was rejected. With only £100 per annum available for books between 1906 and 1914, and even less during the first World War, it is not surprising to learn that the library was little used at this period, though it is reported that the librarian's daughter found the long library tables very useful for dressmaking.[3]

In defence of Bath it can be said that this was for the city a period of decline: in the second half of the century every decade saw a fall in the population, and the figure for 1911 (51 000) was still below that for 1851. Much, however, was also due to the innate conservatism characteristic of the smaller country towns remote from the centres of industry and commerce. The same attitude can be seen in the story of Malvern. Here in the mid-'nineties, in the absence of a public library, a group of thirty-two citizens pooled their libraries to form a

[1] *Lincoln City Libraries, 1914–1964* [Lincoln 1964], p. 2.

[2] See above, p. 25–26.

[3] On all this see V. J. Kite, *Libraries in Bath 1618–1964* (unpublished F.L.A. thesis 1966), espec. pp. 213 sqq.

collection of some 10 000 volumes for their mutual benefit. This arrangement lasted till 1902, the year in which the adoption of the Libraries Acts was eventually decided upon. The struggle that preceded the adoption, however, recalled the battles in other towns a generation earlier.

The opponents of the scheme argued that it would encourage idleness, gossip, and novel-reading; the supporters denied these charges and urged that even novels were better than comic papers or the sickly storyettes available to young women. At the Council meeting at which the decision to adopt was taken (October 1902), the supporters of the resolution "eloquently outlined some of the uses of a public library, as a comprehensive source of instruction, elevation, relaxation, information and general improvement calculated to amply repay to all classes the slight incidence of rate". The opposition argued that the district was too scattered to make library provision practicable; that the expense would be prohibitive; and that the implementation of the scheme would lead to the "socialisation" of Malvern.

When the library was actually opened in temporary premises in July 1903, and an offer of £5000 for a new building was received from Carnegie, the Vicar of Holy Trinity organized a petition urging the Council to reject the offer, and was supported by the Headmaster and several of the staff of Malvern College; but this move was countered by a public deputation to the Council in which Church of England and Nonconformist clergy spoke on behalf of their respective denominations, Mr. W. Vernall spoke on behalf of the working men of Malvern, Mr. T. Jones on behalf of the stonemasons, Mr. Bert Williams on behalf of the carpenters, and Mr. W. Davis on behalf of the temperance movement. It was all very nineteenth-century, but it ended in a victory for the library cause by eight votes to four.

With the help of further gifts a pleasant library building was erected in a pleasant setting, and was opened in 1906 with an initial stock of 6000 volumes. In spite of a very small income (£190 a year had to pay for a librarian, a male assistant, two female assistants, and a part-time caretaker) the collection grew fairly rapidly, and by 1913-14 it had reached close on 15 000 volumes, all available on open access.[1]

Camborne, a small Cornish mining town, was an example of that not uncommon phenomenon at this time, a povery-stricken library with a fine building. The building, provided by Passmore Edwards, and furnished and stocked from the Ferris bequest,[2] was opened in 1895. At that time the lending library had 2900 volumes ready for issue, and the reference library was reported to have, in addition, "a valuable collection of books mainly provided by gifts from private libraries",[3] but in practice this valuable collection amounted to about 100 volumes.[4] The lending library was popular and well used, and absorbed practically all the money that could be spared from the library's annual income of about £200: by 1913-14 the original stock had doubled. The reference library, on the other hand, languished for lack of sustenance, and in 1901 the room was rented to the Urban District Council for office accommodation.

[1] For the narrative see J. W. Lucas, *Malvern Public Library* (Malvern 1940), pp. 7-28; and for the statistics *Adams Report*, pp. 48-49, and *L.Y.B. 1914*, p. 355.
[2] Cf. above, p. 120.
[3] J. F. Odgers, *Camborne Public (Free) Library, 1895-1963* (Camborne 1963), p. 12.
[4] Cf. *L.Y.B. 1897*, p. 132.

When war came in 1914 the Council promptly reduced the library grant, and in spite of gifts from various quarters the library did not make any real progress until 1927, when the Carnegie Trustees came to the rescue with a series of annual grants.[1]

The little hosiery town of Hinckley, in Leicestershire, was in a similar plight. The public library here originated in a small reading room and lending library which was established on private initiative in 1874, and maintained partly by public subscription and partly from the income of a small legacy. A new building was provided in 1888 as a memorial to Arthur Atkins who had been for some years the library's treasurer, and a bequest of £500 provided a new stock of books. It was only after the new building had been completed and opened that it was handed over to the Local Board (forerunner of the Urban District Council). The Libraries Acts were adopted, but the managing committee undertook to meet all expenses for the first five years.

The library building was described in 1891 as "a pretty structure in a species of Flemish architecture".[2] It included both a reading room and a lending library, and as in the original library of 1874 there were facilities for chess and draughts. What was lacking, as at Camborne, was books. Hinckley's rate income of £130 in 1913–14 was, indeed, even less than Camborne's. From the figures for that year we note that the sum of £65 had to suffice for the salaries of the librarian and his assistant; and even more significantly, that £45 was spent on newspapers, periodicals, but only £5 on books and binding.[3] Again as at Camborne, it was only when Carnegie grants became available in the 'twenties that a real library service began to be possible.

The public library of the little mining town of Whitehaven, in Cumberland, resembled that of York in that it originated (in 1888) in the gift to the town of the Mechanics' Institute and a collection of 4000 books, and also in that it had as its first librarian a former member of the Institute, John Simpson, who held office for a very long time—in fact until his death in 1933.[4] He proved an autocratic but devoted librarian, who did wonders in the collection and storage of local material, but in the matter of finance he was much worse off than his colleague in York. The 1d. rate in Whitehaven, though it yielded more than in Camborne or Hinckley, was still not enough to provide an adequate and continuing stock, and the number of readers fell away until 1906, when a new building provided from a Carnegie grant of £5000 gave a fillip to library use. In 1913–14 the stock comprised 12000 volumes for a population of 19000.[5]

The smallest libraries of all, of course, were those under the auspices of parish councils. The difficulties such libraries had to contend with have been referred to above, and are interestingly illustrated in a recent study of the library of Oakley in Buckinghamshire.[6] In this parish of some four hundred

---

[1] On all this see Odgers, *op. cit.*, pp. 8–21, and on the reduction of grant, above, pp. 128–129.   [2] Greenwood (1891), p. 174.
[3] H. F. Warren, *A History of the Hinckley Public Library, 1888–1938* (Hinckley 1938), pp. 3–20.   [4] For York see above, p. 160.
[5] Whitehaven Public Library and Museum, *Annual Report, 1951*, pp. 3–7; and *Annual Report, 1964*, pp. 3–5.
[6] Now provided for by the county. See L. Lisher, "Oakley, or the Life and Death of a Public Library," in *Buccaneer* (Bucks. Co. Lib. June 1968), pp. 5–8. I am indebted also for information concerning this library to Miss Gwenda Jones, County Librarian.

souls, the Libraries Acts were adopted, on the initiative of the local vicar, at a parish meeting held in December, 1905, and it was agreed to levy a 1d. rate, which produced £5.9s. Mr. and Mrs. Bevan gave £5 each and 26 books; Sir Edmund and Lady Verney gave 70 books; Mrs. Bevan promised a plot of land for a building, and a letter was sent to Andrew Carnegie appealing for his assistance. The schoolmaster agreed to act as honorary librarian, a temporary home was found for the books in the school, and by the spring of 1906 the library had begun work.

Carnegie proved less helpful than had been hoped. After first declining to help on the ground that Oakley's rate income was insufficient, he eventually offered £150 on condition that the parish raised a similar sum, but this proved impossible. In 1909 the Council resolved to purchase and erect a railway hut at a cost of £87.10s. Lady Verney furnished one room as a reading room in memory of her husband, and another room appears to have served as a games room. The building was officially opened with due ceremony in 1911. It now had a few hundred books, and the reading room was supplied with newspapers. Even these modest services, however, were seriously curtailed by the war, and from 1919 until the county took over responsibility in 1936 the building was used mainly for social purposes, the 1d. rate and income from letting going to pay the caretaker and to provide coal and oil.

Some Welsh Libraries

Apart from Cardiff, already described,[1] the only libraries of any size in Wales were Swansea, with 62000 volumes in 1913–14, Newport, Mon., with 36000, and Aberdare, with 30000 Merthyr Tydfil had 14000 volumes, Llanelli and Wrexham 12000 volumes each, Barry 11000; no other Welsh library reached a figure of 10000. It is significant that four of the places here mentioned —Cardiff, Swansea, Aberdare and Barry—are all in the industrial county of Glamorgan.

Swansea, to which we have not hitherto made more than brief reference, adopted the Acts in 1870 and commenced service five years later with the opening of three branch reading rooms. The central library was opened in hired premises in 1876, and in the jubilee year 1887 was transferred to splendid new premises which housed also, on the upper floors, a museum, art gallery, and science and art classes. A 2d. rate secured by a local Act of 1889 provided for all these activities except the science and art classes, which were covered by a special annual grant from the town council.[2] The building also provided accommodation for extension activities such as free Saturday evening lectures and the meetings of the National Home Reading Union and of the local Cymmrodorion Society.[3]

From this time the library grew steadily and appears to have been well used. A special feature was the attention paid to the reference collection, which was early enriched by important gifts and by 1913–14 accounted for close on

---

[1] See above, pp. 144–145.

[2] J. J. Ogle, *The Free Library* (1897), p. 236. Presumably this grant was under the Technical Instruction Act, which Swansea had adopted.

[3] Ogle, *loc. cit.*

half the total stock. J. Deffett Francis, who by his gifts and his labours virtually created the art gallery, presented a library of some 3700 volumes on the fine arts, increased by later gifts to about 7700 volumes; Rev. Rowland Williams bequeathed a library of some 800 volumes of theology and Welsh history, which likewise grew by later additions to about 3300 volumes; T. J. Margrave of Llangennech gave over 1200 volumes of French, German, Italian and Spanish literature; and the librarian S. E. Thompson, who held office throughout this period (1880–1919), devoted himself assiduously to the collection of local material. On the whole, Swansea had every reason to feel modestly proud of its library.

All the other Welsh libraries fall into the category which in dealing with England we have referred to as "smaller public libraries". Aberdare's library celebrated its jubilee in 1954, and from the booklet published at that time we learn something of its earlier history. After two abortive attempts to secure adoption of the Acts in the nineteenth century, the crucial decision was taken by the urban district in 1900, but it was not until 1904 that a library was actually opened, in temporary premises in a church club. It moved to further temporary premises (a converted shop) in 1917, and did not in fact acquire a permanent building until 1963. Throughout the period with which we are now concerned it remained small and poverty-stricken, though the raising of the rate to 2d. on the move to new premises in 1917 promised better things.[1]

In 1917–18 the total stock is recorded as just under 15000 volumes, of which nearly one-third were for reference; lending issues were at the rate of about 40000 a year. These figures are at first sight in contradiction to those in the Adams Report, which record for 1913–14 a total stock of 30000 volumes, with over 63000 issues. The discrepancy may arise from the fact that the Adams Report shows the existence of three "branches". Strictly speaking this is not correct, but several of the mining villages which made up the urban district of Aberdare had workmen's institutes, and by an arrangement legalized under a local Act of 1912 the libraries of some of these institutes functioned as branch libraries, being opened to the public in return for grants towards administration and the cost of books and periodicals.[2]

The library at Aberystwyth, which we have seen came into existence in 1874 almost by accident as the result of a move really intended to establish an art gallery, remained throughout this period insignificant, though thanks to a Carnegie grant of £3700 it did secure a new building in 1906. Aberystwyth was, after all, a very small town, with only 8400 inhabitants in 1911, and a correspondingly small rateable value, and short of legislation to remove the rate limit the accumulation of a library was bound to be a slow business. The emphasis continued to be on the lending library, and of the 8000 volumes recorded by Adams only about 1000 were in the reference section. Miss Mary Ann Jenkins, who succeeded her father as librarian in 1894, was one of the twenty-five women chief librarians recorded in 1900.[3]

---

[1] *Aberdare Central Public Library Golden Jubilee, 1904–1954* (Aberdare 1955).

[2] Information from the Librarian, Mr. G. I. John. One of the institutes, whose earlier history is referred to above, was that at Cwmaman (see p. 131).

[3] *L.Y.B. 1900–01*, pp. 68, 263; *L.Y.B. 1914*, p. 125; *Adams Report*, pp. 50–51. Miss Jenkins probably served at least until her marriage in 1909, perhaps until 1918, when a male librarian, W. R. Hall, is known to have been appointed.

Some Scottish Libraries

We are hardly better informed about the Scottish libraries than about the Welsh ones. The Scottish libraries were more numerous (Adams lists 77 compared with 62 in Wales), and rather larger (there were 13 libraries of 20000 volumes or more compared with 4 in Wales), but the great majority were still tiny by modern standards. Three of the thirteen, Glasgow, Edinburgh and Dundee, all with bookstocks in excess of 150000 volumes, have already been described. A long way behind came Aberdeen, with 79000 volumes. The remaining nine, which in the Scottish context could be regarded as medium-sized libraries, had bookstocks ranging from 45000 volumes at Paisley to 20000 at Arbroath: the others were Greenock, Perth, Hawick, Dunfermline, Ayr, Kilmarnock, and Kirkcaldy.

Aberdeen was in those days the fourth city in Scotland. Its population in the 'eighties, however, was not much in excess of 100000, and its rate income was well under £2000 a year. The creation of a substantial public library, therefore, was a considerable achievement. The central library opened its doors in 1885 in the former Mechanics' Institute, which had been taken over, along with its library of some 17000 volumes, on payment of debts of about £2500. Unfortunately one-third of the books thus acquired were useless, and most of the remainder were in rather poor condition, but by a great effort a collection of nearly 15000 volumes was made available for the opening of the lending library. The public response was so great that it quickly became obvious that a new and larger building would soon be needed. By 1892 it was erected and ready for opening, at a cost of over £10000. Nearly all this sum was raised, within a few years, by public subscription, Carnegie and his wife giving £1000 each. The building comprised three storeys, with a large reading room on the ground floor, a lending library on the first floor, and a reference library on the second.[1]

The lending and reference rooms each had accommodation for 75000 volumes, so that in 1913–14 the library was still not much more than half full. In point of fact the stock was at this time just about equally divided between lending and reference, and this makes the recorded figure for annual issues (337000) quite impressive. Greenwood observed that in the early years the proportion of fiction read was relatively low, even though all juvenile works and all poetical works were austerely classed as fiction.[2]

The first librarian, H. W. Robertson, distinguished himself by inventing a new kind of indicator, known as the Duplex, which showed not only book numbers but also author and title. It never became popular, because it not only took up a considerable amount of space but also required the use of a subsidiary indicator for storing readers' tickets. The published plan of the library, indeed, shows the lending stacks almost completely walled in by indicators, to a total length of about seventy feet.[3]

---

[1] The ground floor is sometimes referred to as the basement, the library being built on a sloping site.

[2] Greenwood (1891), p. 237.

[3] F. J. Burgoyne, *Library Construction, Architecture, Fittings and Furniture* (1897), pp. 80–82, 143. Cf. below, pp. 180–182.

In the matter of branch development Aberdeen lagged behind Glasgow, Edinburgh and Dundee. All of these accepted Carnegie grants for the purpose, but Aberdeen feared the additional rate burden. Robertson did, however, establish one branch reading room, and his successor, G. M. Fraser, who took office in 1900, and was to be the real architect of the modern library system (he died in harness in 1938), established at this time three more, and also three delivery stations. The Council did agree, also, to accept a Carnegie grant of £10,500 for the extension of the central library. The money was used to provide a new reading room, thus releasing space for the establishment of an excellent juvenile library, which unlike the adult library above was on open access. The present City Librarian, Mr. W. Critchley, tells me that he was himself a constant reader there, and remains "grateful for the pleasure this rather dark but spacious room gave me".

Two special collections enriched the library during these early years. One was the Walker Music Collection, a library of over 400 musical works presented by James Walker, a local merchant, in 1891. It was especially rich in the vocal and instrumental music of Scotland. The other was the Croom Robertson Collection—over 1800 volumes of philosophy, psychology, and general literature formerly belonging to Professor G. C. Robertson of University College, London. The Collection was presented to the city library by his brother Charles in 1893.[1]

Scotland's oldest public library, at Airdrie, developed considerably during this period under the direction of John Gardiner, a former grocer's assistant who was librarian from 1892 to 1931. The bookstock indeed continued small—it was still only about 10000 volumes in 1913–14—but it was well used and the library was, moreover, the centre of a vigorous cultural life. A new library building erected in 1894 at a cost of £3000 (of which Carnegie gave £1000) provided accommodation not only for the usual reading room, lending library, reference library and ladies' room, but also for a combined lecture room and museum. This was quickly brought into use as a meeting place for classes in photography, and for lectures in connection with the photographic society, the naturalists' society, the literary society, and other cultural organizations. There was even an observatory, established in 1896. All this was somehow managed on the 1d. rate. Naturally it was not long before there were demands for an even larger building, but this was not to come until after the war.[2]

Greenwood pointed out in 1891 that Tarves, Scotland's first rural parish library, with a rate of $\frac{2}{5}$d. yielding an income of about £20, was providing four volumes for every five of the population, whereas the city of Aberdeen, twenty miles to the south, was providing only one.[3] In 1897 the library was still to all appearances flourishing. It now possessed 3250 volumes, and was growing at

---

[1] For these brief paragraphs I have drawn on a variety of sources, including a *Manual for Readers* prepared by A. W. Robertson (Aberdeen 1892); a duplicated account by G. M. Fraser, *Public Library Service in Twenty-five Years* (1934); and a *Memorandum of Information* published by the Corporation (1964). I have also, as indicated, had the benefit of assistance from the present City Librarian.

[2] [W. Scobbie], *A Century of Reading: Airdrie Public Library 1853–1953* (Airdrie 1953), pp. 9–16. See also above, p. 64.

[3] Greenwood (1891), p. 261.

the rate of 100 volumes a year. Most of the books were in the hamlet of Kirk-town, which with its 150 inhabitants was the most important centre of popula-tion in this widely scattered parish. Here, with the help of a gift of £100 from Carnegie, a room had been built which housed the library and provided accommodation also for a local literary society. The library was open for the exchange of books for three hours every Saturday, and the librarian, John Young, who had been librarian of the original subscription library, received £3 a year for his services. There was also a small branch about five miles away: here about 450 books were deposited, and were looked after by members of the library committee who lived in the neighbourhood. Altogether there were 252 borrowers, who had the use of a printed dictionary catalogue and were able to borrow books for a month. Ogle reports that the most popular authors were Matthew Arnold, J. A. Froude, Samuel Smiles, S. R. Crockett, "Rolph Boldre-wood", and Annie S. Swan.[1]

The position does not seem to have changed much in the years preceding the first World War. When the returns were drawn up for the Adams Report in 1913–14 John Young, now in his 'eighties, was still acting as librarian, but now had an assistant; the number of volumes in stock had risen to 6000; and although the population was shrinking (it was just over 2000 in 1911), the number of borrowers had risen to 450. A new printed author catalogue was available, and issues for the year were nearly 3000. For its revenue the library still depended on a rate of $\frac{2}{5}$d., yielding £30 a year of which £20 was spent on books. The figure for issues was low, and one suspects that by this time a good deal of the stock must have been in need of renewal.[2]

We conclude this section with a brief reference to the Ewart Library at Dumfries, so called (at Carnegie's suggestion) to commemorate William Ewart's service as M.P. for Dumfries from 1841 to 1868. Actually the library served not only Dumfries but the neighbouring town of Maxwelltown in Kirkcudbrightshire, which is divided from Dumfries only by the River Nith. A special Act of 1899 permitted the two towns to combine for library purposes, a local citizen gave a site, and Carnegie gave £10000 for a building. G. W. Shirley was appointed librarian and in 1903 the new library opened its doors to the public.

This was a typical example of what the Adams Report called overbuilding, for at the outset, although "the outward shell of a library unquestionably existed in all its columned splendour . . . there was not a single book on the shelves nor a single penny in the bank with which to buy one".[3] A loan of £1000 provided an initial stock of 8000 volumes for lending and 4000 volumes for reference, and at first these were well used, the issue figure of 83000 for the opening year representing nearly four per head of population. But the ensuing years were "penurious to an unbelievable degree".

---

[1] J. J. Ogle, *The Free Library* (1897), pp. 279–280; *L.Y.B. 1897*, p. 199. " Rolf Boldrewood" was the pen-name of T. A. Browne, a writer of Australian adventure stories.

[2] *L.Y.B. 1914*, p. 436; *Adams Report*, pp. 56–57. It should be noted that there is a considerable discrepancy between the stock figures given by these two sources. *L.Y.B.* gives (for 1913), a total of 3634 vols; *Adams* gives (for 1913–14), a total of 6020 vols. The issue figures (*L.Y.B.*, 2639, *Adams*, 2960) do not differ so widely.

[3] M. D. McLean, *Fifty Years A-Growing: the Ewart Library Attains its Jubilee* (repr. from *Dumfries and Galloway Standard*, 8 Sept 1954).

By 1918 the annual expenditure on books had fallen to 2s.11d., and the annual issues to one per head of population.[1] It was not until additional funds became available in the 1920s that it was possible to create a library worthy of the building that had been erected for it.

[1] *Ibid.* There was a Book Club associated with the library until about 1927, and *L.Y.B. 1910–11* and *L.Y.B. 1914* misleadingly show the income from this Club as though it were library income. The Club was in fact run as a separate unit, though its books did eventually find their way into the library.

CHAPTER VII

Library Organization and Use

Buildings and Equipment

MOST of what needs to be said about buildings and finance at this period has already been said in the previous chapter. The big change was that, thanks largely to Carnegie and other donors, far more libraries now had purpose-built premises, even if sometimes they lacked the funds to stock and maintain them. Externally these buildings, as in the earlier period, followed no uniform pattern. Some of them looked like Greek temples, others like Renaissance palaces, Dissenting chapels, or Tudor mansions, or a mixture of several of these. Of the new library at Montrose the *Library World* observed: "The style is what may be termed Free Renaissance and Scots Baronial."[1]

Library interiors varied according to the size and position of the building, but the basic needs were agreed. They were, according to Frank Burgoyne, Librarian of Lambeth, "a reference department, a lending department, a reading-room or rooms for newspapers and magazines, and the necessary working rooms for the librarian and his staff." Even the smallest library sought to provide these, even if they all had to be crowded into a single room. In large libraries additional rooms might be provided: "separate reading-rooms for boys, girls, and women; an inner reading-room for students; lecture hall; museum and art gallery; residences for the librarian and the caretakers; strongroom for the safe keeping of MSS. and incunabula, or local collections; and rooms for binding and repairing."[2]

Less usual features were a games room (at Hucknall and Oakley), a smoking room (at Hucknall, Chorley, Salford and Peterhead) a recreation room (at Fleetwood, Peterhead and Wick) an observatory (at Airdrie),[3] and a roof garden (at Hove). This last, rightly described at the time as "a novelty in the United Kingdom", was on a semi-circular flat roof above the lending library in the new Carnegie building:

> "Grown in boxes, and trained along the supports and rafters of a pergola, are jessamine, rose, wistaria, honeysuckle, clematis and other climbing plants. Three daily newspapers and a number of chairs are provided, and smoking and conversation are permitted. In the summer months it is highly appreciated."[4]

[1] *Library World*, Vol. XII (1909–10), p. 179. A malicious description of library buildings of this period (and later) is to be found in R.G.C. Desmond, "Some Unquiet Thoughts on Public Library Architecture", in *L.A.R.*, Vol. LIX (1957), pp. 79–88.

[2] F. J. Burgoyne, *Library Construction, Architecture, Fittings and Furniture* (1897), p. 8. See also, for a comprehensive professional treatment of this subject, A. L. Champneys, *Public Libraries: a Treatise on their Design, Construction and Fittings* (1907).

[3] On all these see *L.Y.B. 1900–01*, p. 271, and for Peterhead, *Peterhead Free Library Demonstration* (repr. from *Peterhead Sentinel*, 1891).

[4] *Library World*, Vol. XI (1908–09), p. 425. The garden was roofed over in 1912. The Passmore Edwards branch library at Haggerston, Shoreditch (now Hackney), opened in 1893, had in a garden behind the building an open-air covered shelter for newspaper reading—J. J. Macdonald, *Passmore Edwards Institutions* (1900), pp. 2–3, 14–15.

J. D. Brown, who was greatly impressed by the evils of overbuilding, and was acutely conscious of the financial difficulties faced by the smaller library authorities, argued strongly in the first edition of his *Manual* in favour of keeping accommodation as simple as possible, pointing out that every extra department meant extra staff and extra expense. He could not see any justification for special rooms for women, or for students, or for children except those under twelve, who were liable to be a nuisance to their elders.

A librarian's residence as part of the library premises (a not uncommon arrangement at this time) he thought a dubious advantage. He was opposed to the provision of refreshment rooms, and even, except perhaps on a very limited scale, lavatory accommodation for readers. A lecture room, he was prepared to admit, was a useful addition where funds permitted, but accommodation for museums, art galleries, classes, clubs, and recreation rooms should not be provided at the expense of the library rate.[1]

The design of branch libraries, and indeed all small libraries, was greatly influenced by a Carnegie Corporation leaflet, *Notes on the Erection of Library Buildings*, orginally published in 1911. The purpose of these notes was to assist library committees "to obtain for the money the utmost amount of effectiv accommodation, consistent with good taste in bilding".[2] They recommended a simple rectangular plan with all the library rooms on a single floor, divided as necessary by moveable bookstacks. This provided maximum economy in roofing, lighting and heating, permitted re-arrangement of rooms at discretion, and enabled the entire library to be supervised from a central delivery desk. The vestibule and entrance hall were reduced to a minimum, and a semi-basement provided a lecture room, staff room, and workrooms. The effect of these recommendations was seen in simpler and more functional designs, and the elimination of much superfluous ornament.

Methods of heating, lighting, and ventilation were still the subject of much experiment. By the end of the century low-pressure hot water heating was coming to be fairly standard; and the superiority of electric lighting was generally agreed, though the fact that it cost about half as much again as gas often prevented its use. With both forms of lighting there were problems of how the actual lighting points could best be distributed for different purposes, e.g. in reading rooms or in bookstacks. The introduction of open access brought a new range of problems of this kind. On the subject of ventilation there was no general agreement, nearly every method appearing to have its drawbacks.[3]

A good deal of ingenuity was now expended on the provision of specialized library equipment, of which a varied and increasingly sophisticated range was made available by commercial agencies such as the Library Supply Company. Much of this equipment, for example the rather elaborate apparatus of clips and locks found necessary for the display and protection of newspapers and periodicals, was of a kind now obsolete or obsolescent, but the invention of simple and effective methods of shelf adjustment proved a permanent boon. It

---

[1] J. D. Brown, *Manual of Library Economy*, (1903), Ch. x.

[2] See for the text and full discussion J. L. Wheeler and A. M. Githens, *The American Public Library Building* (New York 1941), pp. 216–225. The spelling reflects Carnegie's interest in the movement for spelling reform, which he saw as a means of spreading the influence of the English language.

[3] Burgoyne, *op. cit.*, ch. ii; Brown, *op. cit.*, ch. ix.

is interesting to find Brown, in 1903, recommending the installation of speaking tubes, or better still a telephone, which "should be provided for every large public library", and "ought to be connected with the municipal offices, the telephone exchange and its own branches".[1] He also recommends the acquisition of a typewriter, for which, he says, many uses will be found in a large library.[2]

The first public library to have a telephone linkage seems to have been Croydon. L. Stanley Jast, formerly librarian at Peterborough, took charge at Croydon in 1898, and one of his first steps was to instal a telephone service to ensure a rapid interchange of books between the centre and the four branches. The books ordered in this way were despatched by tram.[3]

General Organization

The reading room or rooms for newspapers and periodicals still occupied the dominant place in all except the largest libraries, though some librarians were already beginning to be sceptical of the value of newspaper provision. Brown argued that "the habitual newspaper reader is a man who rarely reads anything else,"[4] and both he and E. A. Savage believed that newsrooms attracted an undesirable type of reader:

> "We knew that the poor could buy newspapers. We knew that all the verminous old soaks, in the days of cheap potent booze, sang in the pubs and streets and police cells when they had money, and when it was gone, crept to the newsrooms whence they had to be carried out with the tongs. . . . We knew that in the cramped buildings of those days the smell from tramps and outcasts was keeping readers from our books, yet we recoiled from the trouble that would follow any attempt to turn their shelters into newspaperless periodical and book-reading rooms where people could sit without itching."[5]

Another librarian noted that the tramp "waiting till he can get his ticket for the workhouse" was one of the factors that brought the newsroom into disrepute, and described how on a wet night a man "who can barely pick his way through a race-card" may be seen "struggling with an article in the *Contemporary* on 'Peculiarities in the Greek Root'."[6]

The same writer's reference to "the bookmaker—bedizened, ringed and horsey", who slyly tore off the margin of the paper to copy down the betting odds,[7] illustrates another problem of this period, which some libraries met by blacking out the betting news. This was a practice which seems to have begun at Aston Manor, Birmingham, in 1893, and was for a time widely adopted, especially by library authorities in the Midlands and in and near London. Brown reported in 1903 that the practice had been largely abandoned, but it

[1] Brown, *op. cit.*, p. 133.
[2] *Op. cit.*, p. 199. The recommendation regarding the telephone is carried forward to the 1907 edition, but that concerning the typewriter is dropped.
[3] *L.Y.B. 1900–01*, p. 111; *Library World*, Vol. XI (1908–09), p. 225.
[4] *Op. cit.*, p. 428.
[5] E. A. Savage, *A Librarian's Memories, Portraits and Reflections* (1952), p. 168.
[6] L. Huntley, "The Burden of Newsrooms," in *Library World*, Vol. VII (1904–05), pp. 121–122. The author was first librarian of Beverley, 1906–33.
[7] *Ibid.*

was still in use in nearly forty libraries in 1910.[1] Brown, when he became first librarian of Islington in 1905, persuaded his committee to restrict the supply of newspapers and dispense with a newsroom, but for a long time he had few imitators.[2]

Rivalling the reading room in importance and popularity was the lending department, of which we shall have more to say shortly. The reference department, except in the largest libraries, was apt to be neglected, and was sometimes a mere dumping ground for unwanted books, such as sets of old magazines or books too large to be suitable for lending.[3] Brown adduces three reasons for this neglect: first, lack of careful selection; second, inadequate catalogues and cumbersome form-filling procedures; and third, inefficient staff. "There are," he wrote, "plenty of municipal reference libraries at the present time, whose service is in the hands and at the mercy of the frivolous small boy or helpless girl."[4] Savage called the reference library "the municipal library's most expensive and least useful department."[5]

The extent and efficiency of branch organization varied a great deal. We have seen in the previous chapter that some of the larger authorities, to meet the needs of their rapidly expanding populations, were by the end of the period engaged in their second or even their third round of branch provision, and that many smaller authorities were just beginning to make such provision for the first time. In 1905 it was argued that no reader should be obliged to go much more than three-quarters of a mile to his public library, and that there should be a branch for every 25–30000 inhabitants.[6] By 1913–14 the 533 library authorities in Great Britain listed in the Adams Report had a total of 345 branches, each with at least a lending library and a newsroom. This compares with about five times the number of full-time branches to-day.[7] It should be remembered, of course, that there were in those days no county libraries, and that many libraries which would now be branches were then independent. On the other hand not all the branches recorded by Adams were full-time.

As to-day, there was in fact a hierarchy of branch and other service points. At the top of the scale was the full-time branch offering a full library service comparable with, or superior to, that offered by a small independent library. Such, for example, was the Westcotes Branch at Leicester, of which nearly half was occupied by a newsroom 50 feet by 24 feet and the remainder (not counting

[1] J. Elliot, "The Extinction of the Betting Evil in Public News Rooms", in *The Library*, Vol. V (1893), pp. 193–194; R. K. Dent, "Introduction to a Discussion on the Blacking-out of Sporting News in Free Libraries", in *The Library*, Vol. VI (1894), pp. 127–129; *L.Y.B. 1897*, pp. 4–5; Brown, *op. cit.*, pp. 429–430; "The Obliteration of Betting News", in *L.A.R.*, Vol. IX (1907), pp. 24–29; *L.Y.B. 1910–11*, p. 282.

[2] Introduction by W. C. B. Sayers to the 3rd edn. of J. D. Brown, *Manual of Library Economy* (1920), pp. 6–7; W. A. Munford, *James Duff Brown, 1862–1914* (1968), p. 68. The matter was discussed from time to time in the columns of the *Library Association Record* from 1905 onwards.

[3] F. Pacy (Librarian of St. George's, Westminster), "The Reference *versus* the Lending Department", in *L.A.R.*, Vol III (1901), p. 596; Brown, *op. cit.*, p. 418.

[4] Brown, *op. cit.*, p. 424.

[5] *L.A.R.*, Vol. VII (1905), pp. 429–31.

[6] M. B. Adams, "Public Libraries, their Buildings and Equipment", in *L.A.R.*, Vol. VII (1905), pp. 171, 220.

[7] *Adams Report*, App. I.

the entrance hall) was divided between the lending library, reference library, and ladies' reading room. This was regarded at the time of its opening in 1889 as "a model of what a small Public Library should be."[1] By the end of the century such a branch would be most likely to have a juvenile library instead of a ladies' room.

At a slightly less ambitious level, but still full-time, was the branch which concentrated on reading room and lending library provision, with perhaps a shelf or two of dictionaries and encyclopaedias to meet the need for ready reference. Below this again were a variety of part-time branches, e.g. branch reading rooms such as figured prominently in the early days of the Nottingham libraries, or branch lending libraries in schools as at Leeds and Bradford. Adams lists, in addition to the branches mentioned above, 33 branch reading rooms, all but four of them in England.

Finally there were service-points that carried no permanent stock. These were either "delivery stations" or "travelling libraries." Ogle records in 1897 that delivery stations, "much after the American plan", have recently been organized in several large towns,[2] and J. D. Brown, in the *Library Year Book* of the same date, describes the system as follows:

> "These stations are generally shops, and the proprietor undertakes to receive lists of wants from enrolled borrowers, and issue the books when sent from the central Library. The common plan is for a borrower to leave a list of wants at the delivery station, and return for a book on the next or some succeeding day. . . ."[3]

Delivery stations were also established in connection with branch reading rooms. At Nottingham, indeed, a weekly delivery of books was arranged at the Bulwell Branch Reading Room as early as 1879, and when delivery stations became popular in the 'nineties the authority arranged for periodical deliveries at most of its reading rooms.[4] Brown regarded the system as a makeshift, and it seems to have declined in popularity after the turn of the century, but in some libraries it persisted into the 'sixties.[5]

Brown's own preference was for travelling libraries, i.e. boxes of books deposited at a centre and periodically exchanged. Such a system, he pointed out in 1903, though little developed in this country, was extensively used in the U.S.A., and he foresaw the time when, with the extension of the Libraries Acts to the counties and the removal of the rate limitation, libraries "will not only be able to deal adequately with outlying districts, but will be in a position to make door-to-door deliveries of books in towns by means of actual travelling libraries on wheels."[6]

---

[1] Greenwood (1891), p. 180. A plan is given at p. 179.

[2] J. J. Ogle, *The Free Library* (1897), p. 102.   [3] *L.Y.B. 1897*, p. 88.

[4] Ogle, *op. cit.*, p. 211. See also the same author's pamphlet, *The Extension of the Free Libraries to Small Places* (1887), pp. 4–5.

[5] *L.Y.B. 1900–01*, p. 258, lists 83 delivery stations at 21 libraries, Darwen and Plymouth having 20 each. Adams lists only 35 (8 each at Blackburn, Halifax, Sheffield and Warrington, and 3 at Great Wyrley), but it appears from *L.Y.B. 1914* that these figures are incomplete: they omit, for example, Oldham (10 stations) and Rawtenstall (3 stations). Bootle, also, from 1906 had a delivery station at Johnson's Dyeworks (A. H. Roberts, *Growth of the Provision of Public Facilities for Leisure-time Occupations by Local Authorities of Merseyside*, unpublished M.A. thesis, Liverpool University 1933), p. 51.

[6] Brown, *op. cit.*, p. 410.

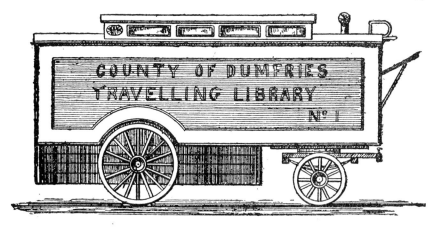

PROPOSAL FOR A TRAVELLING LIBRARY

This sketch of an imaginary travelling library appeared in James Duff Brown's article on "The Village Library Problem" in 1894.

Brown is here suggesting what we now call mobile libraries, a scheme for which he had propounded as early as 1894.[1] Travelling libraries in this sense were to come only in the 'twenties, but travelling libraries in the older sense were brought into use in connection with the Carnegie schemes for county libraries which preceded the 1919 Act.[2] They were also used briefly, from 1898 to 1899, at Bournemouth,[3] and from 1902 onwards at Bradford, where the transition from branches in schools to full-time branches was accompanied by the creation of a considerable number of travelling library centres, open in the evenings, to serve outlying villages. We can hardly doubt that the model here was the Yorkshire Village Library.[4] At Wick, in the far north of Scotland, bookboxes were carried fortnightly by mailcoach to remote parts of the parish.[5]

The Open Access Revolution

The closing years of the century saw the beginning of two closely related revolutions in library practice—the open access revolution and the Dewey decimal revolution. We have seen that a measure of open access to reference works was introduced at Cambridge and elsewhere as early as the 1870s. This practice gradually extended as the years went by, on the whole with great success, though thefts were, of course, not unknown.[6]

[1] "The Village Library Problem", in *The Library*, Vol. VI (1894), pp. 99–105. Cf. above, p. 137.
[2] See below, ch. viii.   [3] See above, p. 156.
[4] M. E. Hartley, "A Survey of the Public Library Movement in Bradford", in *L.A.R.*, Vol. VIII (1906), p. 446; *Library World*, Vol. XIII (1910–11), p. 80; B. Wood, *A Brief Survey of the Bradford Public Libraries, 1872–1922* (Bradford 1922), p. 27. Cf. above p. 137.
[5] Greenwood (1891), p. 262.
[6] For thefts at Cardiff see above, p. 144. For other examples see A. C. Shaw, "The Birmingham Free Libraries", in *L.A.R.*, Vol. IV (1902), p. 506; and B. Wood, "Three Special Features of Library Work", in *The Library*, Vol. IV (1892), pp. 105–108.

Prior to 1892, however, no one seems to have seriously suggested the application of open access to a large public lending library. Here the reader still had to select books from a printed catalogue and ask for them over the counter, with the dubious assistance, in many libraries, of the indicator. Savage's description of his early days at the Croydon Central Lending Library (then housed in a shop) vividly illustrates the weariness and frustration of both readers and staff:

"During the hot summer of 1890, on four evenings of the week from six to nine, and nearly all day on Saturdays, the tiny room before the indicator was jammed with a crowd of lurching, overheated readers lusting for books. . . . In its first full year that shop, one small branch, and five evening libraries, served 8601 readers, with one ticket each, with 2564 volumes, and did it for £162 194 a year. 17670 books were in stock. And the people wanted more. . . .

"For every book borrowed we wrote, illegibly for the most part, the reader's number and the issue date in the fiddling ledger stuck to the indicator slide, and then on the book's issue-label. The numbers of all books issued were recorded in a fat account book. Three numbers and two dates for each issue, besides handling the slide and fetching the book, perhaps up and down a ladder. . . . Except for brief spells at meals we were on our feet from eight in the morning until near ten at night; no wonder we were strong and agile. . . .

"At first a happily expectant reader would buy a catalogue, find in it the novel he wanted, and refer to the indicator. Out, out, out—for ever out! After shoving other people aside and goosing his neck for half an hour or so he'd had enough. We assistants besought him to bring long lists of novels, and he did, but alas! often he got through his numbers and was still bookless."[1]

It was James Duff Brown, first librarian of Clerkenwell, who more than anyone else was responsible for introducing open access in public lending libraries. This small, delicate, brown-bearded Scot, who had received his earlier training at the Mitchell Library in Glasgow, became an outstandingly successful library administrator, and the most influential public librarian of his generation. He served at Clerkenwell till 1905, after which until his death in 1914 he was in charge of the newly established library at Islington. Besides introducing revolutionary changes in library management, he founded and edited the *Library World* (1898), and his *Manual of Library Economy* (first edition 1903) was long a standard work. Though quiet to the point of taciturnity in his personal dealings, he proved himself in writing a lively and vigorous controversialist. Amid all this press of activity he found time also to write on musical biography.[2]

As late as 1891, in the fourth edition of Greenwood's *Public Libraries*, Brown was still expressing his conviction that to give readers direct access to the shelves "would be productive of no good results,"[3] but a year later, in an anonymous article in *The Library*, he was pleading the cause of the reader, and putting forward detailed proposals for the system afterwards widely adopted under the name of "safeguarded open access" (and still extensively used). Under

[1] E. A. Savage, *A Librarian's Memories, Portraits and Reflections* (1952), pp. 64–67.
[2] See the Memoir prefixed by W. C. Berwick Sayers to his 3rd edition of Brown's *Manual of Library Economy* (1920); E. A. Savage, "James Duff Brown after Fifty Years", in *Library Review*, Vol. XVII (1959–60), pp. 489–495; W. A. Munford, *James Duff Brown, 1862–1914* (1968); and W. G. Fry and W. A. Munford, *Louis Stanley Jast: a Biographical Sketch* (1966), which has many references to the collaboration of the two men.
[3] Greenwood (1891), p. 391. Cf. above, p. 89.

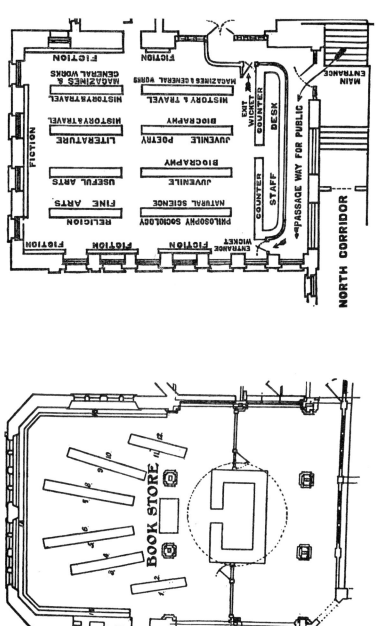

EARLY LAYOUTS FOR OPEN ACCESS LENDING LIBRARIES

Left: a wasteful layout at Montrose, with radial stacks to ensure adequate supervision from a single point.

Right: a much neater and more economical layout at Croydon, with supervision from a long counter.

this plan the reader entered the library through a controlled wicket-gate, selected his own book, and passed out through another wicket where his loan, if any, was recorded. Brown's outline sketch showed fiction arranged under authors on wall shelves, and non-fiction in classified order in island stacks.[1]

In 1893 a visit to the United States, where free access to reference books was almost universal, confirmed Brown in his view, and on his return he discussed the whole question with his committee at Clerkenwell. The result, in October 1893, was a decision to try open access in the lending library. After due preparation the experiment was launched in May of the following year, and it was made known to Brown's fellow-librarians in a paper at the Library Association Conference at Belfast in September, 1894.[2] Broadly speaking, the plan adopted was that described by Brown in 1892. One of the difficulties was that the bookshelves, though altered, were still too high, so that stools had to be used to reach the top shelves.

J. Y. W. MacAlister, Honorary Secretary of the Library Association, welcomed this innovation as "The Dawn of a New Epoch," and wrote:

> "A hundred years hence the authorities of the greater municipal London ... will pass a resolution ordering a tablet to be fixed to the wall of a quaint three-cornered building in Clerkenwell, to commemorate the fact that here, in 1894, the revolution had begun which in a few years had changed the entire system of public libraries throughout the land."[3]

Not everyone agreed. Many librarians were genuinely alarmed for the safety of their books and the good order of their libraries, and others had a vested interest in preserving the existing system. Greenwood declared pointedly that the protests came not from librarians of standing, but "almost solely from an individual who had pecuniary interest in a library indicator."[4] The reference here is to Alfred Cotgreave, who at this period was librarian of West Ham. A bitter controversy was carried on in a journal called *London* (predecessor of the *Municipal Journal*), and in 1895 an anonymous pamphlet, *The Truth about giving Readers Free Access to the Books in a Public Lending Library*, by One who has tried the system in two large Libraries, summarized the argument against open access.

Brown himself, in 1897, summed up the main objections as "1, Likelihood of extensive thefts; 2, disorder and misplacements among the books; 3, wear and tear among books; 4, crowding and rowdyism among the borrowers; 5, reduction of storage space for books; 6, practical uselessness of the system to a large majority of the borrowers, because they know nothing about books." He thought the last argument was absurd, and contended that experience had already shown the first four to be without substance, but he admitted that lack of space might be a real obstacle in the older libraries.[5]

---

[1] "'A Plea for Liberty' for Readers to Help Themselves," in *The Library*, Vol. IV (1892), pp. 302–305. The quotation in the title is a reference to a volume of essays edited by T. MacKay (1891), on which see below, p. 193.

[2] J. D. Brown and H. W. Fincham, "The Clerkenwell Open Lending Library," in *The Library*, Vol. VI (1894), pp. 344–353. Fincham was a member of the library committee.

[3] *The Library*, Vol. VI (1894), p. 212.

[4] *L.Y.B. 1897*, pp. 5–6.

[5] *Op. cit.*, p. 80.

Va. HAMPSTEAD CENTRAL LIBRARY

Designed by Sir Basil Spence and opened in 1964, the Hampstead Central Library is one of the most striking civic library buildings of the period since the second World War. In this picture it appears in the foreground, with the Civic Centre in the rear.

Vb. KENT COUNTY LIBRARY HEADQUARTERS, MAIDSTONE

Another striking post-war building, also dating from 1964, and designed by E. T. Ashley Smith. The main buildings, including the elegant tower block, provide for storage and administration, and there is also an attractive decagonal Students' Library, here seen in the foreground.

(a) James Silk Buckingham, M.P.

(b) William Ewart, M.P.

(c) Andrew Carnegie.

(d) John Passmore Edwards.

VI. SOME LIBRARY PIONEERS

Berwick Sayers, recalling the early years of open access in the third edition of Brown's *Manual*, writes:

> "So sharp were the divisions the simple suggestion created that the municipal library profession went into two armed camps, and friendship and good-feeling were frequently destroyed by it. It is difficult for younger librarians to realize the courage and confidence that were needed to champion open access twenty-five years ago against the active antagonism of 90 per cent of the profession."[1]

CHAOS IN THE LENDING LIBRARY

Frontispiece to the anonymous pamphlet, *The Truth about giving Readers Free Access to the Books in a Public Lending Library*, 1895.

Sayers (afterwards Chief Librarian of Croydon) began his training in 1896 at Bournemouth, a new library which had opened on 1st January of the previous year. Its librarian, Charles Riddle, had been one of Brown's assistants at Clerkenwell, and this was the second open access public lending library in the country. The third, opened in June 1895, was Darwen in Lancashire, which was not a new library but had just acquired a new building; and the fourth, in August 1895, was Kingston upon Thames, where the change marked the advent of a new librarian. Thus one way or another the movement slowly spread, and by 1900 there were at least sixteen library authorities which had adopted safeguarded open access, besides eight small libraries which granted access without the safeguards Brown prescribed. A substantially larger number of libraries had partial or complete open access in their reference sections.[2]

[1] J. D. Brown, *Manual of Library Economy*, (3rd edn., ed. W. C. B. Sayers, 1920), p. 3.
[2] *L.Y.B. 1897*, p. 81; *L.Y.B. 1900–01*, pp. 267–268.

By 1899 sufficient experience had been gained for a pamphlet to be published by twelve libraries actually using the new system.[1] This rebutted in detail the various objections commonly raised against open access. On the subject of theft, for example, it was able to demonstrate that the loss of books in open access libraries amounted to one volume (value 2s. od.) for each 27547 issues. None the less progress towards the adoption of open access continued to be slow. This was not so much, it would appear, because of the arguments of Cotgreave, who maintained a stubborn rearguard action until his death in 1911,[2] as because of the high cost of conversion in the older libraries. In 1910 there were still fewer than 70 libraries in Great Britain which had adopted full open access, and it was not until the rate limit was removed in 1919 that the new system became general.[3]

A few libraries which hesitated to adopt open access went half-way by allowing readers to see the backs of the books. Birkenhead adopted this plan for one of its branch libraries:

> "Cases with wire-mesh fronts are displayed on counters, in which the books are arranged so that their backs can be examined by readers. When the borrower has made up his mind which book he fancies best, either by its title or binding, he pushes it back with his finger so that the assistant can see it from the inside."[4]

A similar system was adopted at St. George's in the East, Stepney. Here the borrowers were allowed access to the bookcases but the books were protected by locked grilles.[5]

Elsewhere indicators continued to be extensively (though by no means universally) used, especially for fiction. Of the many new varieties of indicator developed at this time (more than a score were in use in the early years of the century) we need mention only two, the Chivers and the Adjustable.[6] The

---

[1] *Account of the Safeguarded Open-Access System in Public Lending Libraries.* Prepared and circulated by the Librarians in Charge of English Open-Access Public Libraries (1899).

[2] See, for example, his letter in *Library World*, Vol. XIII (1910–11), pp. 255–256. Cotgreave does not always seem to have been too scrupulous in his use of evidence. In his *Views and Memoranda of Public Libraries* (1901), for example, he states that at Chester "Open access has been tried in Lending and Reference Departments, but abolished after a fair trial" (p. 190). Actually all that happened here was that in 1896 a new librarian was given permission, as an experiment, to admit borrowers behind the counter to select their own books at quiet periods. A year later the librarian left under something of a cloud and under his successor the experiment seems to have been abandoned (information from Mr. P. Pocklington, City Librarian).

[3] *L.Y.B. 1910–11*, p. 279, lists 61 open access libraries in England, four in Wales (Aberystwyth, Barry, Cardiff, and Holyhead), and only one in Scotland (Montrose, which adopted the new system on opening in 1905). In addition eight English libraries are shown as having partial open access.
For a general account of the open access controversy see *L.Y.B. 1897*, pp. 79–87; J. D. Brown, *Manual of Library Economy* (1903), Ch. xxxiii; W. A. Munford, *James Duff Brown, 1862–1914* (1968), pp. 24–38, 41–44; G. Carlton, *Spade-Work: the Story of Thomas Greenwood* [1949], pp. 123–126. The implications of the new method are explored in J. D. Brown (ed.), *Open Access Libraries: their Planning, Equipment and Organisation* (1915).

[4] *L.Y.B. 1897*, p. 93, where references are cited to earlier plans of this kind.

[5] *L.Y.B. 1900–01*, p. 195.

[6] For the Duplex indicator invented by the librarian of Aberdeen see above, p. 166.

Chivers indicator, introduced in 1894 by Cedric Chivers who ran a Library Bureau in Bloomsbury Street, was connected with a change in the method of recording book-issues. The tedious method of recording issues in a ledger ("ledger-charging", to use the technical term) was now increasingly giving way to the system under which a card extracted from the book was filed along with the borrower's card until the book was returned ("card-charging"). The origins of this system have been described above.[1] There were a number of variants but essentially the method was the same as that employed in most lending libraries to-day.

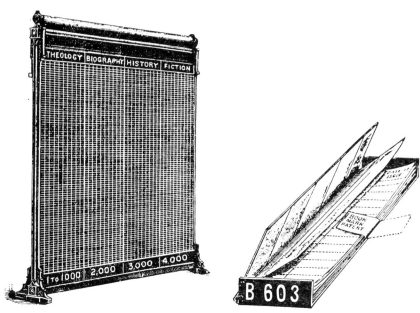

THE COTGREAVE INDICATOR

Though it had many rivals, the Cotgreave Indicator was always the most popular and continued in use in some libraries till after the second World War. The accompanying drawing shows, on a much larger scale, the drawer and the miniature ledger which were provided for each book.

The most popular indicator, the Cotgreave, was designed to fit in with the ledger system, and indeed each of the numbered cases which made up this indicator contained its miniature ledger.[2] The Chivers indicator was designed for use with card-charging. Each book was represented by a numbered wooden block, with a slot underneath to hold the book card. When the book was in, the edge of the card thus had the effect of underlining the number; when the book was out the card was removed and filed with the borrower's card.[3]

The Adjustable indicator was proposed, rather surprisingly, by J. D. Brown in 1895, and was so called because it showed only the numbers of books actually

[1] See above, p. 89.   [2] See above, pp. 90–91.

[3] Described in "A New Indicator", by a Public Librarian, in *The Library*, Vol. VII (1895), pp. 318–321.

in use, and was thus much more economical of space.[1] It does not appear to have attracted much attention, but it was an attempt to deal with the serious problem created by the constant growth of indicators to match the growth of library stocks. In a facetious testimonial to another indicator also proposed by him Brown hit the problem off very well:

> "Dear Sir,
> Your indicator is a —— fraud. After filling up the Library, the new Town Hall and the old Parish Churchyard, it has now overflowed into the County Cricket Ground and the Racecourse. Please take it away before it overwhelms the town."[2]

It may be mentioned that the immense simplification involved in the introduction of open access stimulated the further simplification which could be achieved by card-charging, though the two changes were not inevitably associated. The full rigour of the old-style ledger charging was now gradually being abandoned almost everywhere, giving place to some system of indicator or card-charging, or a combination of the two. Librarians were reluctant to give up their records, and until the first World War most of them still kept a permanent record, either on the book-card or in an indicator ledger, of the date of each loan and the borrower's number.[3]

The Dewey Decimal Revolution

The open access movement brought many consequences in its train. Merely to construct wicket-gates instead of counters was not enough. If the readers were to be allowed to move freely among the books it was first necessary to reorganize the shelving. Nearly always this meant reducing the height of the shelving: often it meant substituting island stacks for lofty wall shelving, and where this was done the stacks had to be so situated as to make possible a reasonable measure of supervision. Heating, lighting and ventilation had all to be reconsidered. And when all this was done there remained the all-important problem of helping the reader to find the books he needed.

The problems of lay-out are illustrated by the plans (page 177). For ease of supervision a radial arrangement was often adopted, so that an assistant at the counter could have a clear view between the stacks. This was convenient for Clerkenwell, which happened to have a triangular site; it was appropriate also for a semi-circular room such as that at North Islington; but when it was applied to a rectangular room it could be exceedingly wasteful, as in the example shown from Montrose. The Croydon plan shows a much more economical lay-out which still allows for adequate visual supervision.

The problems of reader guidance were new and complex. So long as the public did not have access to the shelves, the arrangement of the catalogue was the all-important thing, and it did not really matter in what order the books were arranged on the shelves, provided only that each book had a number

---

[1] J. D. Brown, "Suggestions for a New Form of Library Indicator," in *The Library*, Vol. VIII (1896), pp. 96–100.
[2] A. Cotgreave, *Library Indicators* (1902), p. 15.
[3] For the various charging systems at this period see W. Pollitt, "The Principles of Book-Charging", in *Library World*, Vol. XV (1912–13), pp. 340–343.

which enabled the assistant to find it.[1] In practice, as we have seen, the usual plan was to shelve the books in order of accession within broad subject groups. Brown, always intemperate in his denunciation of what seemed to him out of date, compared this "unorganized confusion" to "the heterogeneous contents of a dustbin or a marine store".[2]

Once the public was admitted, the position was different. It was now clearly necessary to arrange the books in such a way that the reader could find his own way about, without constant reference either to the catalogue or to an assistant. This meant smaller subject groups, combined with "shelf-guiding", i.e. labels on the shelves to indicate the topics covered. Brown and other advocates of open access therefore constantly insisted that "close classification" was a necessary corollary of the new system.

At Clerkenwell, at the outset, Brown retained the traditional broad divisions, but "subdivided as may be necessary, each main class and subdivision being indicated by means of boldly printed guides fastened to the bookcases and shelves so as clearly to describe the contents of each".[3] Thus under the division "Natural and Mathematical Sciences", he had sub-divisions for "Botany, Chemistry, Geology, Zoology, Astronomy, Mathematics, etc. This is an immense advantage to the student, and has been appreciated and greatly taken advantage of wherever introduced".[4]

This arrangement was initially accompanied by a most elaborate system of labelling to ensure that books were not misplaced. Each book on each shelf bore on its spine a label of a particular shape (round, square, oblong, etc.), a particular colour (red, green, yellow, etc.) and affixed at a particular height ($1''$, $1\frac{1}{2}''$, $2''$ etc.) from the base. By ringing the changes on all these shapes, colours and heights it was possible to ensure that any book accidentally misplaced was easily discovered.[5] Apart from the enormous labour involved, this system had the great disadvantage of involving a fixed shelf-location for each book. Fortunately these elaborate precautions to prevent misplacement proved unnecessary and were soon abandoned.

Brown formalized his system of classification in what was known first as the Quinn-Brown classification (1894),[6] then as the Adjustable Classification (1898),[7] and finally in its fully developed form as the Subject Classification (1906).[8] Like all classifiers he seeks to arrange the various branches of knowledge in some kind of logical order. The order he chooses is a rather unusual one, based on a concept of historical evolution. Matter and force are assumed to come first in the history of the universe, then life, then mind, and finally

---

[1] Cf. L. S. Jast, *Whom do ye Serve?* (Newark 1933): "When books were known, like convicts, simply by their numbers, it didn't matter how they were arranged. . .".

[2] J. D. Brown, *Manual of Library Economy* (1903), p. 245.

[3] *L.Y.B. 1897*, p. 81.   [4] *Op. cit.*, p. 83.

[5] *Op. cit.*, pp. 83–84.

[6] Compiled in collaboration with J. H. Quinn, Librarian of Chelsea, and published as "Classification of Books for Libraries in which Readers are allowed Access to the Shelves", in *The Library*, Vol. VII (1895), pp. 75–82.

[7] J. D. Brown, *Manual of Library Classification and Shelf Arrangement* (1898), Ch. vi; also published separately as *Adjustable Classification for Libraries, with Index* (1898).

[8] J. D. Brown, *Subject Classification* (1906, 2nd edn. 1914, 3rd edn. 1939). The second and third editions were prepared by Brown's nephew, James D. Stewart.

record. His main subject-groups, distinguished by capital letters, are arranged in this order, as follows:

A.	Generalia
Matter and Force	
B–D	Physical Science
Life	
E–F	Biological Science
G–N	Ethnology, Medicine
I	Economic Biology
Mind	
J–K	Philosophy and Religion
L	Social and Political Science
Record	
M	Language and Literature
N	Literary Forms, Fiction, Poetry
O–W	History and Geography
X	Biography

Under the heading Generalia were included subjects which "qualify or pervade" other branches of knowledge, e.g. education, logic, mathematics, general science, and the graphic and plastic arts.

Under each main heading sub-groups were represented by numbers, and each of these sub-groups was further divisible into 100 topics. Thus in the main class B, representing Physical Science, B0 was Physics and Dynamics, B1 Mechanical Engineering, B2 Civil Engineering, B3 Architecture, and so on. Under the sub-group Architecture B300 represented General Architecture, B305 Building Construction, B329 Roofs. In addition Brown supplied lists of numbers to represent categories of literature within each subject. These numbers were always used after a point, e.g. .1 represented bibliography, .2 dictionaries, .7 periodicals, .10 history, and so on. A work on the history of building construction, therefore, would figure as 305.10. There were other elaborations, too, which need not be gone into here.

It is easy to criticize Brown's scheme as arbitrary and illogical: the Generalia class was especially vulnerable to criticism. The fact is, however, that this was a scheme which was specially devised for English libraries. Its main classes were not so dissimilar to those in common use as to make its adoption difficult, and yet it offered the possibility, within these main classes, of systematic sub-division to any degree that might seem desirable. Not surprisingly, therefore, it was in the early years of the century quite popular.

The *Libraries Year Book* for 1910–11 shows only three classification systems in extensive use in public libraries, namely, Brown's Adjustable (49 libraries), Brown's Subject (59 libraries), and the Dewey Decimal (117 libraries).[1] It is, however, significant that it was on the whole the smaller libraries that favoured the Brown classifications: the Subject classification, for example, was especially popular in Scotland. Most of the larger municipal libraries figured in the Dewey list,[2] and it was with this system that the future lay. An inquiry made in 1937

---

[1] *L.Y.B. 1910–11*, pp. 280–281. The only other system listed is C. A. Cutter's Expansive Classification (an American system published in 1891–93), in use at Aberdeen, Bootle, and Chelmsford.

[2] Aberdeen, Bradford, Bristol, Cardiff, Edinburgh, Glasgow, Leeds, Manchester, Newcastle upon Tyne, Nottingham, Salford and a score of libraries in or near London.

showed 380 public libraries in Great Britain using Dewey or modifications of Dewey, and only 34 using the Adjustable or Subject classification.[1] To-day Dewey is almost universal.[2]

Most regular library users have at least some acquaintance with this system, but few who are not professionally concerned know the scope of the entire scheme. Basically it is very simple. The starting-point, as set out in the first edition of Dewey's classification (1876), is the division of the books into ten classes. One of these is for general works, the other nine represent subject divisions. Each of these classes is denoted by a three-figure number, thus:

000	General works
100	Philosophy
200	Theology
300	Sociology
400	Philology
500	Natural Science
600	Useful Arts
700	Fine Arts
800	Literature
900	History

Each of these classes has nine divisions, and each division nine sections. The class 600, Useful Arts, for example, has nine divisions ranging from 610, Medicine, and 620, Engineering, to 690, Building: and the division 620, Engineering, has nine sections ranging from 621, Mechanical Engineering, and 622, Mining Engineering, to 629, Other Branches of Engineering. If a more detailed breakdown is needed, further sub-sections can be created as desired by the use of additional figures after the decimal point, so that we get an orderly sequence of subjects as follows:

600	USEFUL ARTS
620	Engineering
621	Mechanical Engineering
621.1	Steam Engineering
621.11	Mechanism of Steam Engineering

Dewey's subject groupings are not random, but are based ultimately on a theory of knowledge. Some scholars have traced them back to Bacon's *Advancement of Learning*, while others detect the influence of Hegel.[3] For Dewey, however, philosophic theory had to yield in the last resort to practical usefulness, and the neat numerical basis of the classes, divisions, sections and sub-sections is obviously artificial and contrived. Even at the outset the scheme was not without its anomalies, e.g. the inclusion of Amusements under Fine Arts, and Medicine under Useful Arts, and these anomalies have been multiplied in the period of nearly a century that has passed since it was devised. The astonishing thing is that

[1] J. L. Thornton, "Classification in Great Britain: a Brief Survey" in *Library World*, Vol. XL (1937–38), pp. 155–157.

[2] As these words are written, a letter in *L.A.R.*, Vol. 71 (1969), p. 311, laments the passing of the Brown classification at Bournemouth, where it had been introduced by Brown's disciple Charles Riddle.

[3] The subject is interestingly discussed in E. E. Graziano, "Hegel's Philosophy as Basis for the Dewey Classification Schedule", in *Libri*, Vol. IX (1959), pp. 49–52.

it has lasted so long. Even to-day Dewey's main classes remain substantially as they were in the first edition, and, although various elaborations and refinements have been introduced over the years, it is only since the 15th edition (1951) that a serious attempt has been made to reallocate the subordinate classes to cope with the growth of knowledge.

The virtues of the system from the point of view of the early open access libraries were many: it offered a simple, coherent, and easily intelligible scheme for library classification; its numerical notation was easier to follow, both for readers and library staff, than the usual mixture of letters and numbers; the classification could be as broad or as detailed as the librarian found convenient; by the addition of a single number a new sub-section could be inserted at any point without disturbing the general arrangement; and above all, provided the sections were kept reasonably small, and the books were arranged in alphabetical order of authors in each section, there was never any doubt as to where a particular book should be placed in relation to its fellow. Without any kind of press-marking the old problem of how to keep the books in perfect order in an expanding library was solved at last.[1]

One young librarian to whom the Dewey system came with the force of a new revelation was Louis Stanley Jast, who in 1892 moved from a post as assistant at Halifax to be the first librarian at Peterborough. Jast, son of a Polish refugee (his name at this time was Jastrzebski) was a man of many interests and many talents, at once librarian, poet, playwright and ardent theosophist. He was afterwards to be chief librarian at Croydon (1898–1905), deputy librarian at Manchester (1915–20) and finally chief librarian at Manchester (1920–31). It was soon after his arrival at Peterborough that he first saw a copy of the Dewey decimal classification. He wrote afterwards:

> "The D.C. was like the opening of a new world. For the first time librarianship seemed to me a science and an art, even a fine art . . . I had never looked at librarianship like that, and my enthusiasm rose to the highest pitch. Greatly daring, I made up my mind to apply it to the library I was to bring into being. I did so, relating the decimal marks to the indicator numbers. Not only this, but I based my catalogue on the system."[2]

In reviewing this catalogue (the second in the country based on Dewey) *The Library* pointed out with some justice that the inclusion of both the indicator number and the classification number was likely to be more confusing to the reader than helpful, and it was, of course, not until open access was introduced, and the indicator abolished, that the Dewey system came into its own.[3] Jast continued to be its fervent advocate, for although he became a great friend of J. D. Brown, and his warm supporter in the advocacy of open access and close classification, he continued to regard the Dewey classification as preferable to Brown's.

---

[1] For a recent assessment of Dewey see B. A. Custer, "Dewey Decimal Classification: Past, Present, Future", in R. L. Collison (ed.), *Progress in Library Science, 1966* (1966).

[2] W. G. Fry and W. A. Munford, *Louis Stanley Jast: a Biographical Sketch* (1966), p. 8, quoting "Recollections of Melvil Dewey", in *Library Review*, Vol. IV (1933–34), pp. 285–286.

[3] *The Library*, Vol. V (1893), p. 156. The first Dewey catalogue was at Ashton under Lyne (see above p. 93).

Another matter in which Jast allied himself with Brown was the reform of library catalogues. The dictionary catalogue was now firmly established as the favourite form, and remained so throughout this period.[1] At its best it was remarkably effective, but it was quickly out of date, and because of the large number of entries required was becoming increasingly difficult to maintain as library stocks expanded. Already by 1900 some London library catalogues were up to 600 pages long, and were costing 2s. or 3s. a copy to print, though they had to be sold at 6d. or 1s.[2] Where open access was introduced, the demand for catalogues dropped sharply, and the net loss became even greater.

Brown thought the dictionary catalogue was wrong in principle, and in his usual dogmatic way, denounced Haggerston's Newcastle catalogue of 1880, one of the most admirable examples of the art, as "undoubtedly the most colossal piece of pretentious ineptitude ever produced".[3] His own prescription was threefold:

(1) A complete and fully annotated MS catalogue in every department of the library.
(2) Printed class-lists, published class by class or in groups of classes, e.g. Science and Arts, History and Biography, Fiction and Poetry, in alphabetical order of authors in each class, with annotations, where necessary, to indicate the precise subject-matter.
(3) Periodical bulletins including lists of recent accessions (Brown's own *Guide for Readers*, first published in 1894, and sold at a penny, was a pioneer in this field, and was widely imitated).

In the "battle of the catalogues" which began in the 'nineties, Brown and Jast argued that class-lists were more scientific, quicker and cheaper to produce, and lent themselves to easy and frequent revision, but many of their colleagues still clung to their belief in the dictionary catalogue, at least for the general reader. The class-list, of course, was impossible unless the library was adequately classified.

Card catalogues were now coming increasingly into use, and were recommended by Brown for the complete MS. catalogue referred to above. Writing in 1903, he still finds it necessary to describe the principles on which a card catalogue works, but the catalogue cabinet he illustrates differs only in detail from those in use today. A minority of libraries preferred, and still prefer, what is called a sheaf catalogue, in which the entries are made on slips of stout paper rather longer than the ordinary catalogue card, and bound into bundles in loose-leaf binders. This method is more economical of space and enables more readers to have access to the catalogue at the same time.[4]

[1] J. D. Brown, *Manual of Library Economy* (3rd edition by W. C. B. Sayers, 1920), p. 242.
[2] *L.Y.B. 1900–01*, pp. 38–39.
[3] *L.Y.B. 1897*, p. 89.
[4] On these developments see *L.Y.B. 1897*, pp. 88–92; J. D. Brown, *Manual of Library Economy* (1903), Chs. xxi–xxii; W. A. Munford, *James Duff Brown, 1862–1904* (1968), pp. 45–47. Brown later argued ("The Tyranny of the Catalogue", in *Library World*, Vol. XI, 1908–09, pp. 1–6) that if a printed catalogue was necessary at all a catalogue of the more important works only would satisfy most readers; and in 1910 he actually produced such a *Select Catalogue and Guide* for the Islington libraries, to which he had moved from Clerkenwell in 1905.

A cataloguing oddity of the 'nineties was the "wheel" or "panoramic" catalogue, in which the catalogue entries (or columns of entries) were mounted on a continuous belt. This device appears to have been invented by Thomas Mason when he was librarian of Stirling's Library, Glasgow, and when he moved to St. Martin in the Fields as first librarian in 1888 he used it to display the titles of new accessions. "This invention of the librarian," says Ogle, "is placed beneath glazed portions of the counter, and by means of a lever is made to revolve and bring successively into view a long list of book-titles arranged on the circumference of the wheel". A more elaborate device illustrated by Brown in 1903, and known as the Rudolph Continuous Indexer, had 600 columns revolving round two hexagonal drums in a continuous chain, and could accommodate 40000 double-line entries.[1]

Books and Readers

It must be constantly borne in mind that the majority of public libraries at this period were still relatively new. More than one-third of the libraries existing at the outbreak of the first World War had come into being since 1900, and more than two-thirds since 1890. Shortage of books, therefore, was the most serious problem that libraries had to face. Even among the older libraries only a handful could boast anything like adequate stocks; and among the newer libraries only a few, for example some of the wealthier London boroughs, had anything like the resources needed to build up stocks quickly. As in the earlier period, books acquired from defunct mechanics' institutes, subscription libraries, and the like, often provided a start, but thereafter many libraries continued to be heavily dependent on gifts and legacies. The results were, inevitably, unsatisfactory. As Brown pointed out:

> "Gifts of modern scientific books, or works of travel, or batches of the best current fiction are just the kind that are seldom or never made. But piles of unbound and ragged periodicals, old guide-books, calf-bound theology of the eighteenth century, prayer-books and useless lumber of the same sort seem to exist in untold quantities, and are the usual donations thought suitable for public libraries."[2]

A few years later the same writer calculated that 15 per cent of public library books came by way of donation, and no less than 41 per cent of periodicals.[3]

Brown also provides us with an estimate of the percentage of books on various subjects held by public libraries in 1907. His figures are printed below, and it is interesting to try to compare them with those in the Parliamentary Returns of 1876–77. The categories unfortunately are by no means the same, but if we look at some of the major groupings it would appear that in 1907 there was more emphasis upon "science", "useful arts", "fine arts", and "social science" at the expense of literature. These four headings account in all for 30 per cent of total stock, whereas the equivalent headings in 1876–77, namely "law, politics, commerce, statistics", and "art, science, education,

[1] J. J. Ogle, *The Free Library* (1897), pp. 154–155; Brown, *op. cit.*, pp. 312–314; Munford, *op. cit.*, pp. 45–46.

[2] J. D. Brown, *Manual of Library Economy*, (1903), p. 221.

[3] The same, 2nd edn. (1907), p. 413.

natural history, geology" account for only 17 per cent of total stock. History, biography and geography remain much the same (23 per cent in 1907, 23.5 per cent in 1876–77). Fiction, we note, represents 20 per cent of the total in 1907, compared with 17 per cent for "fiction and juvenile" in 1876–77, but the 1907 heading probably includes works which in 1876–77 are classed as "literature".[1]

The creation of separate subject departments had not yet made any serious headway, but special collections were common. Practically every library of any size made it one of its first tasks to build up a local history collection, which often included prints and photographs as well as books, pamphlets and manuscripts. Other special collections often related to local literary figures, e.g. Shakespeare at Birmingham or Tennyson at Lincoln, or to local industries, e.g. shipbuilding at Poplar, furniture-making at Shoreditch, cotton manufacture at Stalybridge, mining at Redruth. Yet other special collections had no special relevance to the library in which they were housed, e.g. Chinese books at Manchester, oriental and Indian books at Newcastle upon Tyne, a collection on fishes at Cheltenham, and a collection on tobacco at Todmorden.[2] Many such collections, no doubt, had their origins in bequests or donations.

As we noted earlier, the collections of books relating to local crafts and industries provided a starting-point for technical libraries. Some libraries were helped in building up their stocks of technical works in the 'nineties by regular or occasional grants from the so-called "whisky money".[3]

The public demand was not only for technical education but also for commercial and industrial information, for example on banking, insurance, company law, and trading conditions overseas. In the City of London the reading room at the Guildhall Library had long been available to supply information on subjects such as these, and Croydon had an information bureau at least as early as 1910.[4] Wartime developments stimulated the demand for a comparable service in other great commercial and industrial centres. Glasgow was a pioneer in this field, opening a separate Commercial Library in November 1916. Liverpool followed suit in 1917, Bradford in 1918, and in the latter year Leeds established a separate Commercial and Technical Library.[5] In general, however, the creation of separate commercial and technical departments was a development of the inter-war years.[6]

[1] See below, Apps. VIII and XII.

[2] For these and other examples see *L.Y.B. 1900–01, s.v.*

[3] *L.Y.B. 1900–01*, p. 268, lists over thirty libraries in receipt of such grants. Cf. J. D. Brown, *Manual of Library Economy* (1903), p. 441.

[4] H. Krauss, "Information Bureaux in Libraries", in *L.A.R.*, Vol. XII (1910), pp. 14–22.

[5] For Glasgow see above, pp. 143–144, for Liverpool F. Hope, *A History of the Liverpool Public Libraries, 1852–1952* (unpublished F.L.A. essay 1954), p. 23; for Leeds I am indebted to information provided by Mr. A. B. Craven, City Librarian. In 1897 the Colonial Office suggested the establishment of a Commercial Department at the Hull Public Library, but the proposal was turned down on the ground that there was no demand for such a service—J. F. Hooton, *Libraries in Hull in the Nineteenth Century and the Struggle for the Adoption of the Public Libraries Acts* (unpublished F.L.A. thesis 1967), p. 261. *The City Libraries of Sheffield, 1856–1956* (Sheffield 1956), p. 26, mentions that a very small collection of books was designated as a Commercial and Technical Library in 1916, but adds: "Recorded complaints of readers show that this 'library' little deserved the name." For a brief general history see J. P. Lamb, *Commercial and Technical Libraries* (1955), Ch. i.

[6] See below, pp. 243–244, 290–292.

By 1900 most of the main libraries, and many smaller ones, had collections of music available both for reference and for loan. The possibility of borrowing music was greatly appreciated by the choral and orchestral societies that flourished so greatly at this epoch. Nottingham, for example, had in 1891 a collection of "anthems, ballads, fugues, glees, masses, operas, songs and symphonies"—250 volumes in cheap editions half-bound in hogskin—which were in constant demand.[1] Other libraries active in catering for the needs of music-lovers were Birmingham, Bournemouth, Brighton, Cardiff, and in the London area Finsbury, Islington, and St. George's, Hanover Square.[2]

Manchester was particularly fortunate in acquiring, in 1900, the Henry Watson Music Library of 16700 volumes, which Dr. Watson deposited in the library to be available for reference and in certain cases for borrowing. The collection remained the donor's property until his death in 1911, by which time it had grown to more than 30000 volumes, and was rightly described in the annual report for that year as "unquestionably the finest collection of its kind in the United Kingdom". At the present day it is one of the largest in the world.[3]

Manchester also had the distinction of possessing the largest collection of foreign works to be found in any public library. This was originally a subscription library, founded in 1830, and its stock of 14000 volumes was taken over by the city library in 1902 on payment of outstanding liabilities of £65.[4]

The provision of books for the blind was a matter of concern in many places. Most libraries provided and issued the books themselves, but some preferred to assist local institutes for the blind. Bradford, for example, established in 1912 a branch for the blind in the Royal National Institute for the Blind, which transferred its own stock to the library's control.[5] Manchester, which at one stage employed two or three blind copyists continuously in the making of Braille texts, eventually transferred its library to the Manchester Blind Aid Society and agreed to subsidize the Society's work. In 1918 the Society was reconstituted as the Northern Branch of the National Library for the Blind, and it was this latter body, founded as a voluntary association in 1882, which gradually assumed the major responsibility for the supply and distribution of books for blind readers.[6]

[1] Greenwood (1891), p. 191.
[2] C. Riddle, "Music in Public Libraries", in *L.A.R.*, Vol. XVI (1914), pp. 3–10. For the J. B. M. Camm Music Library at Bournemouth see the same author's article on "The Library Movement in Bournemouth", *ibid.*, p. 115.
[3] G. C. Paterson, *A Short History of the Manchester Public Libraries, 1852–1948* (unpublished F.L.A. essay 1949), pp. 21–23. On music libraries generally see E. R. N. Mathews, "Libraries and Music", in *The Library*, Vol. V (1893), pp. 190–192; J. D. Brown, *Manual of Library Economy* (1903), p. 218; "Orchestral Music in Libraries", in *Library World*, Vol. VII (1904–05), pp. 36–37.
[4] The subscription library is described in W. E. A. Axon, *Handbook of the Public Libraries of Manchester and Salford* (Manchester 1877), pp. 132–133.
[5] B. Wood, *A Brief Survey of the Bradford Public Libraries, 1872–1922* (Bradford 1922), p. 25.
[6] See W. A. Munford, *A Short History of the National Library for the Blind, 1882–1970* (2nd. edn. 1971), and the article by the same author in T. Landau (ed.), *Encyclopaedia of Librarianship* (1958, 3rd edn. 1966), pp. 251–252. For a fuller and earlier account see E. W. Austin, "The National Library for the Blind", in *L.A.R.*, Vol. XII (1910), pp. 304–313. For developments at Manchester see W. E. A. Axon's obituary of C. W. Sutton in *L.A.R.*, Vol. XXII (1920), p. 207.

For a picture of the public library's clientèle during the early part of this period we can turn to a paper given by G. H. Elliott, Librarian of Belfast, at a Library Association meeting there in 1894. Elliott was trained on Tyneside and was thus familiar with English conditions. Speaking of the users of the lending library he said:

> "Our readers, or borrowers as they are more correctly called, represent nearly every section of the community. As in most of the other public libraries in England and elsewhere so it is here—the class most largely represented is that of book-keepers or clerks, and not mechanics or factory workers as some suppose. Next come students, schoolboys and apprentices, then engineers and mechanics, labourers, porters, packers and messengers. The other occupations chiefly represented are as follows: warehousemen and salesmen, linen business, teachers and monitors, joiners and carpenters. Among the learned professions, solicitors and apprentices head the list, clergymen and medical men follow. The total number of borrowers last year (1892–3, both sexes) was 7152, of this number about one half were between 14 and 20 years of age, and a fourth of them were aged from 21 to 30."[1]

This account of library readership does not differ very markedly from that we have given above in respect of the 'seventies,[2] and the statistics gathered by Brown, from a survey of annual library reports, for the second edition of his *Manual* in 1907, do not suggest any fundamental change. These figures also relate only to the users of lending libraries, whom Brown reckoned at this date as six per cent of the total population of library towns. They had at their disposal about three books each, and made about thirty borrowings per annum. Nearly half of them were under twenty years of age, nearly three-quarters under forty. Their occupations are estimated as follows:

Domestic	7%
Professional	7%
Students and Scholars	20%
Industrial (trades)	20%
Commercial	29%
Unstated	17%

The only figure given by Brown which is significantly different is that for the proportion of female readers, which he puts at the very high average of 41 per cent.[3]

The greater facilities now available for the education and training of women were no doubt mainly responsible for this change, and the increasing number of women staff in the libraries themselves must have helped to overcome the initial timidity of women readers. This timidity is illustrated by the fact that at Bradford, about 1896, a special portion of the counter at the central lending library was partitioned off for use by ladies, with the consequence that issues to women readers trebled in six months.[4] This was unusual, but separate ladies' reading rooms were provided in a great many libraries. Brown attacked the practice, especially in the 1907 edition of his *Manual*, where he declared:

[1] *The Library*, Vol. VII (1895), p. 276.
[2] See above, pp. 81–84.
[3] J. D. Brown, *Manual of Library Economy* (2nd edn. 1907), pp. 413–414. For the earlier period see above, p. 84.
[4] J. J. Ogle, *The Free Library* (1897), p. 209.

"The sentimental idea that women are delicate creatures requiring seclusion in glass cases is resented no more strongly than by the ladies themselves, and the mere fact that they do use general reading rooms without complaint or hesitation in places where separate accommodation is not provided is quite enough to demonstrate that such rooms are not essential."[1]

This comment was called forth, however, by the fact that "about eighty" libraries were still providing separate ladies' rooms.[2]

These ladies' rooms were of a piece with the restrictive atmosphere of the older libraries, which still bore the marks of their working-class origin, and had about them something of that same spirit which in the early days had led to the posting of policemen at the doors. Greenwood in 1897 complained about unnecessary and obsolete restrictions, and Brown in 1903 elaborated the theme in his usual picturesque fashion:

"The whole tone of these rules was fraught with suspicion and distrust, and throughout their long course they were nothing but prohibitions against doing all sorts of things, from spitting on the floor to criticizing the librarian. . . .

To judge by some of the rules that have been published one would imagine that a public library was a kind of private trust or benefaction to which the citizens had the privilege of entry, subject to the caprice or good nature of a committee of owners, who had drawn up certain drastic rules to protect their personal property from the onslaughts and unwelcome attentions of a horde of goths and vandals."[3]

As the older generation of librarians died out, this attitude was now fast disappearing, and the revolutionary notion was gaining ground that the purpose of library regulations was not to restrict the reader's access to the books but to assist him to make the fullest possible use of them. The spirit that had inspired the open access movement was spreading to other aspects of library administration.[4]

On what people actually read there are statistics in plenty, and it must suffice to quote a few. In the paper already referred to given by G. H. Elliott in 1894 he provides the following comparative table for lending library issues at Birmingham, Liverpool and Manchester:

Subject	Birmingham	Liverpool	Manchester
Prose fiction	64.21%	79.79%	78.45%
Science and arts and natural history	7.66%	7.00%	5.22%
History, biography, voyages, travels	6.10%	5.00%	5.72%
Miscellaneous literature	3.90%	5.00%	9.00%
Theology, morals and metaphysics	1.67%	1.32%	1.08%

[1] J. D. Brown, *Manual of Library Economy* (2nd edn. 1907), p. 387.

[2] *Ibid.* This figure of "about eighty" is a little suspect. It is carried forward from the 1903 edition, p. 119, and perhaps derives ultimately from the list in *L.Y.B. 1900–01*, p. 269.

[3] J. D. Brown, *Manual of Library Economy* (1903), pp. 349–350. Cf. *L.Y.B. 1897*, p. 14.

[4] Among the restrictions of which Greenwood and Brown complained were: requiring that every borrower should be guaranteed by two ratepayers; refusing to lend books for more than seven days at a time; refusing to renew by post; refusing to issue books on the day on which they were returned to the library; and charging heavy fines (up to 1d. a day) on books overdue.

Subject	Birmingham	Liverpool	Manchester
Poetry and drama	1.50%	0.66%	—
Commerce, political			
economy, law and politics	0.30%	0.75%	0.50%
Juvenile literature	9.97%	—	— [1]

Ogle, eschewing percentages, sought information about the most popular authors. He was not able to secure details regarding the largest libraries, but the returns from twelve medium-sized towns and fifteen smaller ones showed that in fiction sixteen libraries counted Mrs. Henry Wood as their most popular author; eleven Marie Corelli; four Charles Dickens; and the same number Mary Elizabeth Braddon, the now unknown author of *Lady Audley's Secret* and seventy-four other novels. In non-fiction Carlyle and Ruskin headed the list, and others much in demand were J. A. Froude, J. R. Green, T. B. Macaulay, and Shakespeare.[2]

Brown, reverting to statistics, provides us in 1907 with the following table, which is of special value and interest because it includes reference issues as well as lending issues:

Subject	Lending	Reference	Total
Fiction	63.95%	0.26%	54%
Juvenile	15.57%	—	15%
Science and arts	6.17%	20.36%	8%
History and biography	6.12%	34.39%	10%
Religion	1.58%	6.29%	2%
Poetry	0.99%	4.68%	1%
Social science	0.55%	4.86%	1%
Magazines	2.53%	14.87%	5%
General	2.54%	14.29%	4% [3]

The controversy over what Greenwood called "The Great Fiction Question",[4] and a later writer called "The Great Fiction Bore",[5] continued to rage throughout the 'nineties and well into the twentieth century—indeed it is by no means dead even today. One of the best documented attacks on the supply of fiction by public libraries was in a paper by M. D. O'Brien, who produced statistics to show that in twenty-three public lending libraries, in the year 1887–88 or 1888–89, the percentage of fiction issued varied between 49 per cent (at Barrow in Furness) and 88 per cent (at Chester) with an average of 69 per cent. This attack appeared in a volume of anti-socialist essays edited by Thomas Mackay, with a preface by Herbert Spencer.[6] The author not only disapproved of fiction in public libraries: he disapproved of public libraries altogether, and referred nostalgically to "country districts where no socialistic collection of unjustly gotten books exists to hinder the development of personal thrift, or poison the springs of spontaneous generosity."[7]

[1] At Liverpool and Manchester juvenile literature is presumably classed for the most part with fiction.
[2] J. J. Ogle, *The Free Library* (1897), pp. 195–196, 243–244.
[3] J. D. Brown, *Manual of Library Economy* (2nd edn. 1907), p. 415.
[4] *L.Y.B. 1897*, pp. 107–116.
[5] *Library World*, Vol. XI (1908–09), pp. 127–133.
[6] T. Mackay (ed.), *A Plea for Liberty* (1891, 3rd edn. 1892), Ch. ix.
[7] *Op. cit.*, p. 264.

O'Brien was not alone in this view. As late as 1897 Passmore Edwards was being accused by a London newspaper of "going about offering public libraries to be upheld at the expense of ratepapers for lazy fiction-reading people".[1] There were, however, other more moderate critics, including some librarians, who while fully accepting the need for public libraries were concerned that they were being diverted from their primary educational function to become mere purveyors of fiction. A speaker at the Library Association Conference in 1894, for example, thought this was one reason why the London authorities had been slow in adopting the Acts.[2]

The answers were all given by Greenwood in the 1891 edition of his *Public Libraries*. They were as follows:

> First, that good fiction has great moral and intellectual value;
> Second, that even fiction of no great literary merit has a recreative value;
> Third, that such reading may be the starting-point for better things;
> Fourth, that figures for the reading of fiction are exaggerated because several novels may be read in the time required for the study of a more serious work; and
> Fifth, that the phenomenon is in any case a temporary one, since in all the leading libraries fiction is on the decline.[3]

Greenwood's second and third points, regarding the recreational value of ordinary fiction, and its importance as a starting-point for more serious study, were emphasized in the same year by no less a person than Carnegie, at the opening of the Peterhead Free Library. "They who begin with fiction", he confidently declared, "generally end with solid literature."[4]

J. Y. W. MacAlister, in 1897, pleaded for a frank recognition of the recreational function of the library service;[5] and eleven years later L. S. Jast, opening a discussion at the Library Association Conference at Brighton, defended the provision of lighter and more ephemeral fiction to attract readers who would not otherwise enter the building.[6]

The discussion to which Jast contributed arose on a paper by A. O. Jennings, Chairman of the Brighton Library Committee, on "Fiction in the Public Library". By this date the long-heralded decline in fiction issues was at last beginning to show itself, though as we see from Brown's table above the percentage of such issues in lending libraries was still nearly 64. This decline was

---

[1] J. J. Macdonald, *Passmore Edwards Institutions* (1900), p. 51.

[2] C. Welsh, "The Public Library Movement in London", in *The Library*, Vol. VII (1895), pp. 97–109.

[3] Greenwood (1891), pp. 32–33. These arguments are elaborated in *L.Y.B. 1897*, pp. 107–116.

[4] *Peterhead Free Library Demonstration* (Peterhead 1891), p. 34.

[5] W. J. Murison, *The Public Library: its Origins Purpose and Significance* (1955, 2nd edn. 1971), pp. 182–183, quoting *Transactions and Proceedings of the Second International Library Conference, held in London . . . 1897*, p. 11.

[6] W. G. Fry and W. A. Munford, *Louis Stanley Jast: a Biographical Sketch* (1966), p. 23, quoting *L.A.R.*, Vol. X (1908), pp. 325–335. Jast, like Cowell before him (see above, p. 86) afterwards became somewhat disillusioned on this score, and in an address delivered at Newark in 1933 entitled "Whom do ye Serve?" he referred sadly to "this assumption, which we should all like to believe, but for which I am afraid there is very little basis of fact, that the reader who begins on rubbish will be led gradually to better stuff".

almost certainly due, not to any real reduction in fiction reading, but to the device of providing readers with an additional ticket for non-fiction. This was suggested by MacAlister in 1893, and was quickly adopted in a great many libraries (over sixty by the end of the century).[1]

Dr. E. A. Baker, librarian of the Midland Railway Institute at Derby, very sensibly pleaded in 1907 for a distinction to be drawn between worthwhile fiction and "ephemeral fiction",[2] and this distinction provided a basis for a series of resolutions adopted at the Brighton Conference following Jennings's paper. These resolutions were:

> "(1) That the function of a Public Lending Library is to provide good literature, and the same test must be applied to works of fiction as to books in other departments—they must have literary or educational value.
>
> (2) That every library should be amply supplied with fiction that has attained the position of classical literature; and
>
> (3) That the purchase of mere ephemeral fiction of no literary or moral value, even if without offence, is not within their proper province."

These resolutions did not end the long controversy, but they did much to reduce its virulence and put it on a more rational plane. Though they did not actually change the situation in any way they provided libraries with a reasoned defence for the supply of fiction, and with a code of practice that was all the more acceptable because its interpretation was so entirely subjective.

Services for Children

Encouraged by the example of Nottingham and other pioneers,[3] many library authorities sought in the late 'eighties and 'nineties to make more effective provision for children. In studying this development we have to keep clear the basic distinction between provision made within the framework of the library service itself, and provision made in association with the schools. The former involved children's lending libraries, children's reading rooms, and combinations of these two; the latter included various arrangements for the supply of books either by the public library, or by the education authorities, or by both together.

The original Nottingham children's library was a lending library, and formed, as we have seen, a separate branch. This remained a rather exceptional arrangement, but it became increasingly common for children's books in central and branch lending libraries to be set apart in some way so as to constitute a "children's" or "juvenile" library.

Separate children's reading rooms were much less common, and in big cities seem to have been established partly for reasons of social welfare. This was the case at Manchester when a reading room for boys was opened at the time of the cotton famine in 1862; and in 1895 "moral and social improvement" was

---

[1] J. Y. W. MacAlister, "New Ways of Keeping Down the Issues of Fiction", in *The Library*, Vol. VI (1894), pp. 236–237. For a list of libraries issuing "students' extra tickets" see *L.Y.B. 1900–01*, pp. 270–271.

[2] E. A. Baker, "The Standard of Fiction in Public Libraries", in *L.A.R.*, Vol. IX (1907), pp. 70–80.

[3] See above, pp. 79–80.

still a leading motive in the establishment of boys' reading rooms in the city.[1] Two years later Greenwood was urging that "large district reading rooms" should be provided for the juvenile population of London, "and especially for little waifs between the ages of six and twelve, who most need the shelter and educational influence of such rooms".[2] John Ballinger of Cardiff made the same point in recommending "children's reading halls",[3] and at Birmingham the success of the special boys' reading room opened in the central library on Sundays is described as follows:

> "... here on Sundays may be seen a rather extraordinary spectacle, every chair occupied and rows of boys sitting on the floor in every conceivable spot, each occupied in looking at the pictures in the papers that are abundantly provided for them. It is not contended that they are doing much reading, as a rule probably they are not reading at all; they are of a class who are more interested in the illustrations than in the printed page, but even though this be the case the work that is being done is by no means to be despised."[4]

J. J. Ogle of Bootle, in a survey published in 1898, recorded a total of 107 public libraries in England and Wales which were making special provision for children, but only six of these are shown as having special reading rooms.[5] One that he omits from his list is Wigan, where the Powell Boys' Reading Room and Library, presented by Sir Francis Powell, M.P., was opened in 1893. This functioned as a separate branch, and was, as far as I know, the first children's library which combined a reading room with a lending collection. It had 1120 volumes by 1900.[6] At Stockport the success of a children's reading room and lending library at the new Reddish branch in 1908 led to similar and much more extensive provision in the new central library in 1913.[7]

J. D. Brown included open shelves for juvenile books in his first open access library at Clerkenwell in 1894. Later he created a special juvenile room, and when he moved to Islington in 1905 he introduced, both at the central library and in the branches, a children's service which sought to parallel the facilities offered to adults:

> "The whole department was in a large room. In the centre of the room were tables on which were children's periodicals; along the walls were desks equipped with pens and ink where they could write; and in proximity to these were a few of the best reference books for their use—dictionaries, atlases, encyclopaedias and similar works. About one-third of the room, near the entrance, was screened off by a glass partition, making a small room. This was an open access lending library."[8]

---

[1] See above, pp. 43–44. Girls began to be admitted in the 'nineties, and from 1901 the term "children's room" began to replace "boys' room".   [2] *L.Y.B. 1897*, p. 13.

[3] J. Ballinger, "Children's Reading Halls", in *L.A.R.*, Vol. V (1903), pp. 557–558.

[4] A. C. Shaw, "The Birmingham Free Libraries", in *L.A.R.*, Vol. IV (1902), p. 510.

[5] Hammersmith, St. Leonard (Shoreditch), Manchester, Reading, St. Helens, and Tottenham.—J. J. Ogle, "The Connection between the Public Library and the Public Elementary School," in Education Department, *Special Reports on Educational Subjects*, Vol. II (1898), p. 247. *L.Y.B. 1900–01*, p. 269, lists 39 libraries with juvenile rooms.

[6] H. T. Folkard, *Wigan Free Public Library: its Rise and Progress* (Wigan 1900), p. 1; *L.Y.B. 1900–01*, p. 227.

[7] R. E. G. Smith, *The First Fifty Years of Public Libraries in Stockport* (unpublished F.L.A. essay 1950), pp. 97–99.

[8] W. C. B. Sayers, *A Manual of Children's Libraries* (1932), p. 125.

In general, however, open access remained the exception. Hull, at its Western Branch opened in 1895, shelved the children's books against a glass screen so that the children could read the titles on the spines and point to the ones they wanted,[1] and at children's rooms at Stepney and Chelsea, a little later, the books were visible through an iron grille;[2] but most children had to struggle with catalogues and indicators. At Aberdeen open access was introduced in the juvenile library in 1911, at a time when the adult library was still on indirect access, and the results are interestingly described in the annual report for that year:

> "The most picturesque feature in connection with the new Juvenile Department was the fact that it was arranged and has been worked on the 'Open Access' system, the children being allowed free access to the shelves and the stock of 6,000 volumes or thereabouts to choose their books for themselves. So far as the mere working of the arrangement is concerned . . . there is nothing but perfect order and smoothness. There is quite clearly to be a considerable amount of additional repairs necessary from the more frequent handling of the books, but that was foreseen."

Oddly enough this first year of open access brought a slight fall in issues. This was attributed partly to the fact that "a good many adult Borrowers fond of reading from the Juvenile stock, were debarred from using the new Juvenile Department".[3]

Inadequate stocks and lack of open access must have discouraged many of the very children who, because of their poor home background, needed the library service most. Many libraries sought to overcome these difficulties by arranging lantern lectures, story half-hours, visits by parties of school children, and similar devices, but there were others who believed that the only effective way to reach the majority of children was through the schools themselves. The story of the Leeds experiment in the provision of school libraries, begun in 1883 and terminated on the grounds of cost in 1898, has been told above.[4] The School Board now took over the provision of school libraries, and the public library began in 1902 to provide children's reading rooms.[5] Norwich had a similar experience: a scheme for school libraries was launched in 1889, and met with considerable success, but the cost of renewals proved so great that after ten years the plan was abandoned, and the books were handed over to the School Board, which established a juvenile library of its own.[6]

At Bootle, in 1894, J. J. Ogle devised an alternative scheme under which the elementary schools acted as delivery stations. Once a fortnight "a neat covered handcart" brought the books requested by the scholars, and collected their requests for the next delivery. The scholars chose their books from a printed catalogue, and were provided on each delivery day with a special "book

[1] J. F. Hooton, *Libraries in Hull in the Nineteenth Century and the Struggle for the Adoption of the Public Libraries Acts* (unpublished F.L.A. thesis 1967), p. 238.

[2] Sayers, *op. cit.*, p. 103.

[3] I am indebted to Mr. W. Critchley, City Librarian, for these quotations.

[4] See above, pp. 50–51.

[5] G. Rees, *Libraries for Children* (1924), pp. 23–24.

[6] Greenwood (1891), pp. 214–215; G. A. Stephen, *Three Centuries of a City Library* (Norwich 1917), pp. 67–68.

card" on which they were required to enter the numbers of not less than ten books wanted.[1] The scheme operated successfully for many years.

The trouble about all arrangements of this kind was that most libraries just could not afford, within the limits of the library rate, to provide an adequate service to schools as well as to the general public. In some places, notably in London, the School Boards took on the responsibility of providing school libraries, but under this arrangement there was, of course, no direct link between the scholars and the public libraries. The solution to the problem was obvious, namely that the public libraries should provide the service, and the education authorities meet the cost, and development on these lines was facilitated by the 1902 Education Act, which empowered authorities to spend money for this purpose. In the meantime, John Ballinger of Cardiff had already made extensive use of this system from 1899 onwards:

> ". . . there is a library in every school department. The Education authority pays for the books, renewals, and book-binding, the library authority finds the service for organisation and supervision, while the teachers take charge of the books in the school and do all the work of lending, advising, and guiding the reading of the children."[2]

These libraries were quite small. Initially they were about 125 volumes per school, and the aim was to build up to a total of about 8000 volumes in all, i.e. one for every pupil in the fourth standard or over. The grant at this stage was £300 per annum. In Ballinger's view this modest provision was of crucial importance. Reinforced as it was by organized visits of school children to the public library, and later (1907) by children's "reading halls" at the Cathays and Canton branches, it was the first step towards regular use of the library in adult life.[3]

Ballinger had a number of imitators, among others L. Stanley Jast, Librarian at Croydon 1898–1915. In 1900 Jast was inclined to think that children were receiving too much attention. "As for the juvenile reader", he wrote, "he is just now the little tin god of the library movement".[4] A visit to the U.S.A. in 1904, however, seems to have made him more favourably disposed, and with the help of his deputy W. C. Berwick Sayers he soon developed a quite elaborate provision for children, including nearly sixty school libraries on the Cardiff plan[5].

By 1914 the idea of special provision for children was widely accepted. A considerable proportion of libraries had children's rooms, and a smaller number provided libraries for schools. Special lectures for children, and organized visits by school parties, were not uncommon. Undoubtedly much more would have been done if more money had been available. The inadequacies of the situation

[1] Ogle, op. cit., pp. 237–240.

[2] J. Ballinger, "Work with Children", in Library Association, Public Libraries: their Development and Future Organisation (1917), p. 30.

[3] L.Y.B. 1900–01, pp. 49–50; Cardiff Public Libraries 50th Anniversary Celebration (1932), pp. 14–15. Cf. above, p. 145.

[4] L.Y.B. 1900–01, p. 22. J. D. Brown, Manual of Library Economy (1903), p. 438, expresses similar doubts.

[5] W. G. Fry and W. A. Munford, Louis Stanley Jast: a Biographical Sketch (1966), p. 29; Library World, Vol. XI (1908–09), p. 226. Cf. L.Y.B. 1910–11, p. 107. Sayers's little volume on The Children's Library (1912) was a pioneering work. For a general account of all these developments see E. Green, in L.A.R., Vol. XII (1910), pp. 227–241.

as it was in 1917 were plainly stated in a discussion at the Library Association Conference of that year in London, at which Jast and others complained that children's reading rooms were still thought of too much in terms of social welfare; that their atmosphere was that of the schoolroom rather than the library; and insufficient attention was given to the all-important business of training special children's librarians. The resolution passed by the Conference expressed the members' conviction that "library work with children ought to be the basis of all other library work", and that "reading rooms should be provided in all public libraries, where children may read books in attractive surroundings, with the sympathetic and tactful help of trained children's librarians".[1]

Extension Activities

By 1900 technical classes were ceasing to be an important branch of public library activity. The *Year Book* for that year was able to record only twenty-two libraries organizing classes,[2] and many of these very soon handed over the task to the local technical instruction committee, or after 1902, the local education authority. Among these was Bootle, whose librarian, J. J. Ogle, has often been cited in these pages. Ogle was particularly interested in this kind of provision, and from 1891 acted as organizing secretary for technical instruction as well as librarian and curator. In 1900, however, the Bootle Technical School was established and Ogle had to choose. To the regret of the library world he chose to be Director of Technical Instruction.[3] At Watford the connection between technical education continued until 1919,[4] at Oswestry as late as 1921,[5] but these were exceptional cases.

As the classes dwindled, lectures at first increased in popularity and more than fifty authorities were sponsoring them by 1900.[6] A review of lecture provision in various libraries in the *Library World* about this time begins:

"Most librarians are agreed as to the desirability of having courses of lectures in connection with Public Libraries. They are generally recognised, not only as valuable aids in making known the contents of the library on particular subjects, but as tending to foster a closer relationship between the institution and its frequenters."[7]

[1] Library Association, *Public Libraries: their Development and Future Organisation* (1917), pp. 29–47.
The most readable general account of children's libraries at this period is still to be found in G. Rees, *Children's Libraries* (1924), pp. 13–59, but much useful information is also assembled in A. Ellis, *Library Services for Young People in England and Wales, 1830–1970* (1971), Chs. ii–iii.
[2] *L.Y.B. 1900–01*, p. 268.
[3] J. J. Ogle, *The Free Library* (1897), pp. 256–260; J. J. Ogle, *Educational Work in Bootle, 1884–1900, in connection with the Free Library, Museum and Technical School* (Bootle 1900), espec. pp. 21 sqq.; J. Minto, *The Public Library Movement* (1932), p. 332.
[4] For Watford and Wolverhampton see above, p. 98.
[5] H. Jones, *A History of the Oswestry Public Library to 1963* [Oswestry 1963] (duplicated), p. 6.
[6] *L.Y.B. 1900–01*, p. 269.
[7] "Library Extension Work: Lectures", in *Library World*, Vol. I (1898–99), p. 121. See for a more cautious view W. J. Willcock, "Library Lectures: a Retrospect and Suggestion", in *L.A.R.*, Vol. IV (1902), pp. 394–400.

A minority of libraries, mostly the larger ones, themselves organized popular lectures. These were generally of a miscellaneous character, illustrated wherever possible by lantern slides, and sometimes varied by an occasional concert, literary reading or play-reading. Courses of a more continuous character, however, were provided in many centres through collaboration with the University Extension authorities or educational trusts such as the Gilchrist Trust, which from 1878 onwards was active in promoting short courses of popular lectures, especially on science. Even where such courses could not be accommodated on library premises, the libraries nearly always gave their support and assisted in the provision of books.

The attendance at lectures and courses of this kind was often phenomenally high. At Liverpool, in 1903, it was reported that the attendance at nearly 2000 lectures, over a period of 37 years, had averaged over 700 per lecture;[1] and in neighbouring Bootle, where "popular lectures" began in 1887, attendances by the end of the century were ranging between 300 and 1000 per lecture.[2] In London, when Passmore Edwards in 1900 endowed six series of London University Extension lectures on modern English history, to be given in public libraries, the lecture halls were in many cases full before the lectures began;[3] and at Bethnal Green, according to Cotgreave, "Upwards of 27 000 persons attended the course of six Gilchrist lectures—thus quite 'beating the record' in the history of the movement".[4]

One difficulty about library sponsored lectures was that the Public Libraries Acts nowhere gave library authorities power to spend money on lectures; and in the London metropolitan area at least it was known for such expenditure to be disallowed by the district auditor.[5] This did not, of course, apply to the provision of University Extension courses. On these a Library Association Committee reported in 1905:

> "There appears to be a very general desire on the part of Committees and Librarians to help forward the work of the centres. Lectures are advertised, book-lists prepared and posted, and the recommended books not in stock obtained. Several librarians act as local secretaries, others undertake the distribution of tickets, syllabuses, etc., from the libraries. Libraries having lecture or other suitable rooms lend them to the centres free, or charge only a small fee to cover expenses."[6]

[1] P. Cowell, Liverpool Public Libraries: a History of Fifty Years (Liverpool 1903), p. 111.

[2] J. J. Ogle, Educational Work in Bootle, 1884–1900, in connection with the Free Library, Museum and Technical School (Bootle 1900), pp. 20–21.

[3] J. P. Edwards, A Few Footprints (1905), pp. 79–80. Cf. C. W. Kimmins, "Lectures under the Public Libraries Acts", in L.A.R., Vol. III (1901), p. 11.

[4] A. Cotgreave, Views and Memoranda of Public Libraries (1901), p. 23. Mr. H. Ward, the present Librarian of Tower Hamlets, tells me that this almost incredible figure is confirmed by the Annual Report for 1893. The lectures were on "Other Worlds than Ours" and were illustrated by lantern slides. They were held in the Great Assembly Hall in the Mile End Road, which seats 5000 people, and at the second lecture "the hall was packed from floor to roof with an appreciative audience of working people."
Among numerous articles on library lectures in professional journals of this period one may note especially R. Haxby, "The History, Organisation and Educational Value of Municipal Library Lectures", in L.A.R., Vol. XIII (1911), pp. 123–132.

[5] C. F. Newcombe, "The Raison d'Etre of Library Lectures", in L.A.R., Vol. VIII (1906), pp. 241–242; "Library Lectures", in Library World, Vol. XIII (1910–11), p. 113.

[6] Library Association, Report of the Committee on Public Education and Public Libraries (1905), p. 5.

University Extension centres were provided in connection with 78 library authorities, and the Committee recommended:

"That the principal text-books and auxiliaries recommended by various teaching bodies, including those directing technical studies as well as University Extension Centres, the National Home Reading Union, etc., be provided and kept up to date in the public library."[1]

Other extension activities included readings, story-hours, half-hour talks about books, exhibitions and concerts. At Stalybridge in Cheshire, soon after the library opened in 1889, a reading class was opened on the lines of a mutual improvement class:

"The course consists of an opening lecture on the value of books by some eminent man; followed on other nights by a person reading a criticism of the work or works of a certain author, showing the style, merits, language, etc., and a public discussion follows."[2]

In 1890, as we have seen, Potter Briscoe at Nottingham introduced a plan of half-hour talks about books and authors which proved very popular and was imitated elsewhere. At Nottingham in the first year, we are told, the talks were "highly appreciated by the working men, who were busily occupied with pencil and note-book during the delivery".[3] Rather similar in purpose was the encouragement given by some libraries, about the same period, to study-circles formed under the auspices of the National Home Reading Union—an organization founded in 1889 which devoted itself mainly to publishing courses of guided reading at various levels.[4] At Norwich, where a branch of the Union was formed in 1891, the library bought the books needed for the course.[5] Other librarians encouraged the work of literary societies and other cultural organizations.

All this activity earned the disapproval of J. D. Brown, who took a more austere view of a library's functions. Referring to "this never-ending and futile talk about libraries and education", he wrote:

"The real connecting points between popular education and Public Libraries are obvious to everyone who is not blinded by the craze for magic-lantern entertainments, lecturettes, reading-circles, and so forth. The endeavour should be to unify the educational work of both agencies for the benefit of the whole community, and not for such select portions of it as entomological clubs, photographic societies, school children, teachers, or debating societies. The libraries must be run on the broadest democratic lines, and not run for the prime satisfaction of university extensionists, or other select educational cliques."[6]

---

[1] *Op. cit.*, p. 3. *A Preliminary Report* (1904), pp. 4–5, makes more detailed recommendations.
[2] Greenwood (1891), p. 143. [3] *Op. cit.*, p. 473. Cf. above, p. 149.
[4] T. Kelly, *A History of Adult Education in Great Britain* (Liverpool 1962, 2nd edn. 1970) pp. 238–239. For examples of library-sponsored reading circles at Darwen and Bromley respectively see J. Pomfret, "Reading Circles" in *Library World*, Vol. XIII (1910–11), pp. 289–294, and W. J. Harris, "The Organisation and Conduct of Reading Circles", in *Library World*, Vol. XVII (1914–15), pp. 69–72. On the alliance between the public libraries and the Union see also "New Developments of the National Home Reading Union", in *L.A.R.*, Vol. X (1908), pp. 485–497.
[5] P. Hepworth and M. Alexander, *City of Norwich Libraries* (1957), p. 15.
[6] Unsigned article in *Library World*, Vol. VI (1903–04), p. 76.

Brown's friend Jast at Croydon, however, took a different view. In 1908, at a time when Croydon was recognized as one of the leading library systems in the country, its extension activities were summarized as follows:

> "Library Talks to Adults (two series at Central and Branch Libraries, each fortnightly); Library Talks to Children (every Friday). Library Readings (plays, selections from authors, or of types of literature). Book, picture and print Exhibitions. Exhibitions of Holiday Literature. Reading Circles in connection with the National Home Reading Union, and the University Extension Courses. Object lessons to school children in the use of the Libraries."[1]

A smaller library, but one which offered an interesting range of activities, was that at Bromley in Kent. In 1909 it was able to report that its free popular lectures were attended by large and appreciative audiences; its Adult Reading Circle, under the leadership of the librarian, W. J. Harris, was meeting fortnightly, alternating dramatic readings with readings of other literature; its Reading Circle for Girls, meeting weekly under the leadership of the librarian's wife, was in its fourth year; lectures for children were arranged monthly during the winter, and parties from fifteen elementary schools regularly visited the library to receive instruction in its use; a Literary and Debating Society established in connection with the library was continuing its successful career; a local botany teacher was responsible for a Wild Flower Stand in the entrance hall, with a constantly changing exhibition of flowers; and two very successful Local Exhibitions had been held.[2]

One has the impression, though the evidence still needs to be examined in detail, that during the war years extension activities reached a very low ebb in most libraries. If this impression is correct, one can hardly doubt that the main reason was financial, for prices were now rising sharply and the 1d. rate limitation was becoming ever more pressing. In these circumstances it is not surprising if many public libraries tended to shrink back into their shells, and concentrate their limited resources on "service to readers".

Librarians and Librarianship

Throughout this period librarianship was struggling, with a fair degree of success, to establish itself as a recognized profession. The subject is one on which it is difficult to generalize, for even in 1914 many libraries were still very small, and conditions in some of these small libraries, partly through poverty and partly because of the ignorance of managing committees, were unbelievably bad. If we look at the *Library Year Book* for 1900–01, for example, we find that at Brechin the single librarian worked a 66-hour week for £52 a year; that at Hertford, with a 40-hour week, the librarian received £50 a year and had to pay his own assistant; and that at Holyhead, with a 46½-hour week, the woman librarian was paid £30 a year and her woman assistant £7.10s. a year. Even at Hull the caretaker, with £78 a year, was earning 10s. a week more than the reference librarian,[3] and this kind of situation was not uncommon. In 1908 Bolton

---

[1] *Library World*, Vol. XI (1908–09), p. 224.
[2] *Library World*, Vol. XII (1909–10), pp. 351–352.
[3] J. F. Hooton, *Libraries in Hull in the Nineteenth Century and the Struggle for the Adoption of the Public Libraries Acts* (unpublished F.L.A. thesis 1967), p. 244.

upon Dearne invited applicants "for the combined duties of Caretaker for the Council Offices and Carnegie Library and Librarian", at a salary of 30s. a week with a free house.[1]

It was conditions such as these that led Greenwood in 1891 to declare that librarians as a body were "shockingly paid",[2] and Brown in 1903 to denounce the scale of remuneration outside London and the largest provincial cities as "miserably inadequate".[3] In 1911 the Library Assistants' Association was still commenting on "the decidedly inadequate remuneration of the majority of library officials". The report in which this comment is made, however,[4] does provide precise details not only regarding salaries but also regarding hours and conditions of service generally, and enables us to see that if there were many bad libraries there were also some good ones.

The report tabulates salaries according to the rate income of the authority, without identifying particular authorities. The range of chief librarian's salaries is very remarkable, from £70 a year (in an authority with rate income of under £1000 a year) to £700 a year (in an authority with rate income of over £10000 a year). The commonest figure, for medium-sized authorities, is somewhere between £200 and £300 a year, compared with £100–£200 in 1879. This is a fairly sizeable increase, and suggests that chief librarians were more than keeping up with the general rise in the standard of living.[5] In 1914 the average salary of a male certificated head teacher in an elementary school was £177.[6]

Library assistants, however, had a very raw deal at this time. The report draws attention especially to the enormous and unjustifiable differences between chief librarians and their second officers, citing cases in which, for example, the chief librarian earned £500 a year and the second officer £175, or the chief librarian £250 and the second officer £52. If we take as representative the salaries of assistants employed by authorities with a rate income of £2000–£3000, we have the following average figures: sub-librarian, £92–£122; branch librarian, £78–£106; chief assistants, £84–£93; male senior assistants, £47–£72; female senior assistants, £39–£57; male junior assistants, £20–£45; and female junior assistants, £15–£27.[7] These figures are important, for the Adams Report lists more than eighty libraries with ten or more staff, and in some of the larger libraries the staff now ran into three figures—Glasgow with 270 and Manchester with 234 were the largest.

Salaries apart, however, conditions were beginning to improve. By 1911 the number of hours worked by assistants, which at the beginning of the century had usually been 48 or more per week, had fallen to an average of just over 45, and there was a tendency in many large libraries to move towards a

---

[1] *Library World*, Vol. XI (1908–09), p. 232.

[2] Greenwood (1891), p. 356.

[3] J. D. Brown, *Manual of Library Economy* (1903), p. 10.

[4] Library Assistants' Association, *Report on the Hours, Salaries, Training and Conditions of Service of Assistants in British Municipal Libraries* (1911).

[5] See above, p. 102. Bowley has calculated that the money wage index rose from 72 in 1880 to 95 in 1911—B. R. Mitchell and P. Deane, *Abstract of British Historical Statistics* (Cambridge 1962), pp. 344–345.

[6] A. Tropp, *The Teachers* (1957), p. 272.

[7] In a few libraries the most junior assistants were actually apprenticed, and required to work for a certain initial period without wages.

42-hour week. Sunday opening, too, was beginning to fade out (in many places it disappeared during the war of 1914–18) and an increasing number of libraries allowed their staff a weekly half-holiday. Annual leave varied from one week for junior assistants to a month or more for chief librarians. The main complaint of the assistants was in respect of spreadover hours: with $1\frac{1}{2}$ hours for dinner and up to $1\frac{1}{4}$ hours for tea they could, without actually working excessive hours, be kept going from morning to night, with little or no time for recreation or outside interests.

As in the earlier period, many librarians held office for long periods—often, in the absence of any regular superannuation arrangements, to an advanced age. Charles Madeley of Warrington (librarian 1874–1920), S. E. Thompson of Swansea (1880–1919), and G. M. Fraser of Aberdeen (1900–38) all served until they were in their 'seventies, and Richard Gough of Wrexham (1879–1930) until he was nearly ninety.

The prejudice against women staff died hard. In 1897 J. D. Brown reported that except for Manchester, Bradford, Bristol and Aberdeen, hardly any large town employed them, and that London was practically closed to them.[1] Leeds joined the list of exceptions in the following year, but only, as we have seen, with serious misgivings.[2] The smaller libraries, probably for reasons of economy, were much readier to employ women, and from the *Library Year Book* for 1900–01 we note that 25 libraries in Great Britain had women chief librarians, and 46 employed women assistants. The total of women employees was 293, or about 12 per cent of the total number of library staff (in the U.S.A., at this time, nearly 95 per cent of staff were women.)[3] By 1910, however, there had been a fairly sharp increase: the number of women chief librarians had risen to 33, and the number of libraries employing women assistants to 132, new additions including Glasgow, Liverpool, Newcastle upon Tyne, and ten London boroughs.[4] In this as in other spheres, however, it was the first World War which really gave women their chance, and pointed the way to the predominance of women staff which became characteristic of the post-war period.

In the early part of this period some of the newer and smaller library authorities were still making rather odd appointments to librarianships. The appointment of the librarian or some other official of the local mechanics' institute was not uncommon, and perhaps forgivable when the institute was being taken over as the nucleus of the public library;[5] but we also hear of the appointment of a solicitor (at Worthing), a second-hand bookseller (at Bath), a grocer's assistant (at Airdrie), and even a former engine-driver (at Corwen).[6] In defence of the solicitor at Worthing, it must be said that his post was honorary and unpaid. The *Library Year Book* for 1900–01 reports of him that he had "learned what he does know of librarianship from library literature", and with these modest qualifications, and the help of two women assistants and a care-

[1] *L.Y.B. 1897*, p. 94.

[2] See above, p. 103.

[3] *L.Y.B. 1900–01*, p. 263, J. B. Brown, *Manual of Library Economy* (1903), p. 87.

[4] *L.Y.B. 1910–11*, p. 277.

[5] For examples see above, pp. 160 (York) and 163 (Whitehaven). Later instances are to be found at Kirkby Lonsdale (1903), Keighley (1904), and Farnworth (1911).

[6] All these were in the 'nineties. For Bath and Airdrie see above, pp. 161, 167; for Worthing and Corwen *L.Y.B. 1900–01*, *s.v.*

taker, he contrived to manage a lending and reference library open for 42 hours a week, and a reading room open for 78 hours.

In 1903 Brown was still warning library committees against "the blunder of appointing chief librarians from the ranks of stickit ministers, unlucky schoolmasters, returned soldiers, minor journalists, unsuccessful booksellers, dilettante town councillors, or such-like remnants of the failures or super-annuated in other walks of life".[1] He himself prescribed a long list of necessary qualifications, including a wide knowledge of English and foreign bibliography and literature, a sufficient acquaintance with foreign languages, and a sound understanding of classification, cataloguing, and other aspects of library routine. At this date, however, there was no regular system of training, and no recognized professional qualification. The necessary knowledge and experience, therefore, could be gained only by library service, and for this reason Brown laid down, as the first essential qualification for a chief librarian, "Previous training for at least three years in a library which is classified according to some scientific and exact system".

The Library Association had for some years been doing its best to establish a regular training system, but up to this time without much success. Neither the certificate scheme launched in 1885,[2] nor the revised schemes begun in 1891 and 1894, brought much response, and it was not until a new syllabus was brought into operation in 1904 that any considerable number of candidates was forth-coming.

The 1904 scheme provided for examinations in six subjects: literary history; bibliography; classification; cataloguing; library history and organiza-tion; and library administration. An essay was also required on some aspect of each subject. Separate certificates were awarded for each subject; and a librarian who secured all six certificates, and had three years' satisfactory library ex-perience, was entitled to the Diploma of the Library Association. In 1907 further hurdles were erected: candidates for the Diploma had also to submit a thesis showing original thought or research and a certificate of competence in Latin and a modern foreign language. It is not surprising to learn that few librarians completed this long and arduous course: ten years later only twelve diplomas had been awarded. At the certificate level, however, the examinations proved more popular, and the number of candidates rose from 39 in 1904 to 313 in 1914.

One of the difficulties was lack of teaching. To expect overworked and underpaid library assistants to work for examinations on their own, with no more guidance or assistance than some friendly superior might be willing to provide, was really asking too much. The Library Association did its best to meet the need, and from 1893 onwards a variety of summer schools, classes, and correspondence courses became available, first in London and later in provincial cities such as Birmingham and Liverpool. The Library Assistants' Association, founded in 1895, also helped by arranging meetings and study circles, forming a library, and publishing its own journal, the *Library Assistant*. From 1902 courses in librarianship were provided in London in collaboration with the

---

[1] J. D. Brown, *Manual of Library Economy* (1903), p. 55. The warning is carried forward into the 2nd edn. of 1907.

[2] See above, p. 104.

London School of Economics, but it was not until 1919 that, with the help of a five-year grant from the Carnegie Trust, the first full-time School of Librarianship was established at University College, London.[1]

One way or another, in the years before the war, a new race of librarians was emerging, and in the previous chapter we have seen several instances of the often dramatic effect of the arrival of one of these new men in a library still dominated by the outmoded techniques of the nineteenth century.[2] In 1909 the Library Association, which had been chartered since 1898, at last took the decision to establish an official register of librarians, comprising fellows, honorary fellows, members, associate members, and student members. The main professional grades were fellowship (F.L.A.) and membership (M.L.A.). Broadly speaking the former was restricted to chief librarians and other senior officers and to holders of the Association's Diploma; and the latter to experienced and qualified librarians not eligible for the fellowship. The category of associate membership catered for other members of library staffs and non-librarians; and the category of student membership for those under 25.[3]

---

[1] For the details of all this see J. Minto, *A History of the Public Library Movement* (1932), Chs. xii–xiii. J. Macfarlane, *Library Administration* (1898), Ch. i, gives details of the position at that date, with syllabuses and specimen papers.

[2] Those readers specially interested in this transitional period may like to know of the special *Report on the Luton Public Library* which was prepared in 1908, at the request of the town council, by L. Stanley Jast of Croydon. This report, of which a copy is available at Luton, highlights the differences between the old school of librarians, represented by the then incumbent David Wootton (formerly librarian of the Luton Subscription Library) and the new generation represented by Jast.

[3] For the details see *L.Y.B. 1910–11*, pp. 11–12.

BOOK III
BETWEEN THE WARS
1919 — 1939

CHAPTER VIII

The Birth of the County Libraries

LIBRARY history from the close of the first World War until 1965 was dominated by a single Public Libraries Act, that of 1919. By abolishing the 1d. rate limitation that Act made possible the extension of the urban library service to meet new and growing needs; and by giving library powers to the counties it also made possible a complementary provision in the rural areas. In Scotland the development, though accomplished within a different and somewhat more restrictive legislative framework, was basically similar in character. The whole period thus has, from the library point of view, a certain unity. It is, none the less, a very long period, and in view of the complexity of the developments to be described, and the enormous changes in the political, economic and social background, it seems best to break it up for the purposes of this narrative into smaller and more manageable sections. We begin with the origins of the 1919 Act, and with the years immediately following the Act, leading up to the Kenyon Report of 1927. These years were not a time of spectacular library growth, but they saw the county libraries struggling into existence, and the urban libraries beginning to catch up with the arrears that had accumulated during the war.

The Genesis of the Act of 1919

By the close of the nineteenth century the conviction was rapidly gaining ground among all concerned with public libraries that new legislation was urgently needed to bring about two changes: first, to abolish the rate limitation, and second, to empower county councils to act as library authorities. Both these proposals had long been under discussion. The proposal to abolish the rate limitation had been put forward in forthright terms by W. E. A. Axon, a member of the Salford Library Committee, at a Library Association meeting as early as 1881;[1] and the idea of county libraries was the subject of a paper by John Maclauchlan, Librarian of Dundee, in the Association's meeting in the previous year.[2]

This was, of course, before the passage of the Local Government Act of 1888, and Maclauchlan suggested a library board for each county, with power to levy a 2d. rate and to make library provision for every parish. His plan was a very simple one, envisaging the use of schools as lending libraries, open in the

---

[1] *L.A. Conference Transactions, 1881,* pp. 31–33.

[2] *L.A. Conference Transactions, 1880,* pp. 58–66. At the outset Machlauchlan mentions a Bill to extend the library service to the county areas which had been promoted three or four years earlier. This must have been the Bill to facilitate the Establishment of Free Libraries and Museums, introduced by A. J. Mundella and others on 9 February 1876. It was not printed and no details of its contents have survived—see *Journals of the House of Commons,* Vol. CXXXI (1876), pp. 13, 15.

evenings as and when necessary. At a small extra expense these branches could be fitted up as reading rooms, with newspapers, magazines, and a few standard reference works. All book purchasing, cataloguing, and the like would be centralized in a special headquarters building. Even this modest proposal, however, was described by John Plant, Librarian of Salford, as "adapted to the millennium".[1]

Thomas Greenwood, in 1890, proposed central government aid for village libraries established under the Acts, in the form of a grant of say £10 to £25 per annum from the Consolidated Fund. Gladstone, opening the St. Martin-in-the-Fields library the following year, sharply rejected this proposal, preferring to rely for a solution of the problem on "the liberality and enlightened judgement" of the great landed proprietors.[2] By 1897 J. D. Brown was already proposing that the county councils should be given power to adopt the Libraries Acts,[3] and by the time he came to publish the first edition of his *Manual of Library Economy* in 1903, this solution was widely accepted.[4]

In 1902 the Library Association, following a paper at its Birmingham Conference by J. B. Ballinger (afterwards Sir John Ballinger), Librarian of Cardiff, instructed the executive to take immediate steps to secure the removal of the rate limit. Unfortunately during these years the Association, riven by dissensions between the municipal and the "learned" librarians, and labouring under the influence of a conservative treasurer, H. R. Tedder, was in no position to exert effective authority.[5] A draft Bill was, however, prepared, and from 1904 onwards repeated but vain attempts were made to secure its passage through Parliament. In 1913 and again in 1914 the Bill was amended to increase the library rate to twopence only, and at the same time a clause was added to give library powers to the counties; but whatever hopes there may have been for the passage of this revised Bill were destroyed by the outbreak of the first World War. For the time being all prospect of new legislation was at an end.

During all these years the financial position of the established libraries became more and more acute, and the new libraries which until 1909 continued to be opened in considerable numbers found it difficult to make much headway. As to the rural areas, when they had any service at all they had still to be content with improvised schemes, usually under private auspices and based on the periodical exchange of bookboxes. In addition to such organizations as the Yorkshire Village Library, which still continued,[6] we note the emergence of new institutions to meet the needs of areas not hitherto provided for.

[1] *L.A. Conference Transactions, 1880*, p. 127.

[2] Greenwood (1890), p. 330; Greenwood (1891), pp. xix–xxi, 441; and the same author's *Sunday School and Village Libraries* (1892), pp. 43–47.

[3] J. D. Brown, "The Village Library Problem", in *The Library*, Vol. VI (1894), pp. 99–105.

[4] *Manual*, p. 6. Cf. Greenwood in *L.Y.B. 1897*, p. 9; W. R. Credland, "County Councils and Village Libraries", in *L.A.R.*, Vol. I (1899), pp. 763–769.

[5] Tedder, one of the first Joint Secretaries of the Association (see above, p. 101), was Hon. Treasurer almost continuously from 1889 until his death in 1924. For his baneful influence on the affairs of the Association see E. A. Savage, *A Librarian's Memories, Portraits and Reflections* (1952), pp. 129–132, who quotes Tedder himself as saying that he "detested town libraries".

[6] See above, p. 137; and J. Daykin, "Village Libraries", in *L.A.R.*, Vol. VIII (1906), p.p. 365–374.

(a) John D. Mullins,
    Librarian of Birmingham 1865–98.

(b) James Duff Brown,
    Librarian of Clerkenwell 1888–1905,
    and Islington 1905–14.

(c) Alfred Cotgreave,
    Librarian of Wednesbury 1877–80,
    Wandsworth 1880–84, Guille-Allès,
    Guernsey 1887–90, West Ham 1891–1905.

(d) Miss Kate Lewtas,
    Librarian of Blackpool 1891–1902, and
    one of Britain's first women chief
    librarians.

VII. SOME NINETEENTH-CENTURY LIBRARIANS

(a) Sir John Ballinger,
    Librarian of Doncaster 1880–84, Cardiff
    1884–1909, National Library of Wales
    1909–30.

(b) L. Stanley Jast,
    Librarian of Peterborough 1892–98,
    Croydon 1898–1915, Manchester 1920–31.

(c) E. A. Savage,
    Librarian of Bromley 1904-06, Wallasey
    1906–15, Coventry 1915–22, Edinburgh
    1922–42.

(d) Miss A. S. Cooke,
    County Librarian of Gloucester 1918–21,
    and of Kent 1921–43.

VIII. SOME EARLY TWENTIETH-CENTURY LIBRARIANS

In 1904 Sir Charles Seely of Brook, Isle of Wight (a Nottinghamshire colliery owner), founded what can properly be called the first county library. He gave £5000, more than ten thousand books, and an endowment of £100 per annum, to establish in Newport a lending library, reading room, and chess-room available to all the residents of the island, and he also arranged for small collections to circulate among the villages. The distinctive feature of this scheme was that from the first it was placed under the management of the County Education Committee. The present County Seely Library is its direct descendant.[1]

Elsewhere similar arrangements were made under private auspices. As early as 1892 Suffolk had a Village Clubs Association which was hiring out books to village libraries.[2] In 1906 a liberal-minded Bishop of Hereford, Dr. John Percival, secured a grant of £1600 from Carnegie to launch a system of circulating libraries for the county, based on the town of Hereford. For a subscription of £1 a year a village could receive a box of fifty books, exchangeable three times yearly.[3] In Dorset in 1908 Sir Henry Peto, a former High Sheriff of the County, established the Dorset Schools and Villages Booklending Association "to foster a love of reading and circulate good literature among the Schools and Villages". This was a less ambitious scheme, with an initial capital of only £250, of which Carnegie gave £60. The method of organization was the same as in Herefordshire, but the boxes contained only 30 books, and were in fact mainly used by schools.[4]

More traditional in character was the provision for rural areas in Scotland made by James Coats of Paisley. This was by far the most extensive scheme of its kind in the country and was based on the old pattern of the fixed village library. The Coats benefactions began in 1901 with a gift of books to the lighthouse keepers on Ailsa Craig. Thereafter, every New Year's Day until his death in 1912, Coats sent books to every lighthouse in Scotland, together with two pipes and 2 lbs. of tobacco. He also distributed during these years small collections of books, complete with lock-up bookcases, to hundreds of rural parishes throughout Scotland, and especially in the Highlands and Islands. W. G. S. Adams, in 1914, was able to identify 150 of these libraries in the islands, and 186 on the mainland, but it seems likely that there were many more which he did not hear about. G. H. Coats, writing in 1920, put the total at about 4000.[5]

[1] Mr. F. S. Green, to whom I am indebted for this information, was the second County Librarian since 1904.

[2] T. Greenwood, *Sunday School and Village Libraries* (1892), p. 51. Mr. E. F. Terry, East Suffolk County Librarian, tells me that the village of Shotley was hiring books from this source from 1896 onwards.

[3] W. Temple, *Life of Bishop Percival* (1920), pp. 289–291; Board of Education, Public Libraries Committee, *Report on Public Libraries in England and Wales* (Cmd. 2868, 1927), pp. 96–97. This report is cited hereafter as *Kenyon Report*.

[4] *Ibid.* Some of the details given are taken from the *Minutes* of the County Education Committee for 18 December 1918, which have kindly been communicated by the present County Librarian, Mr. K. Carter.

[5] *Adams Report*, pp. 17–20; G. H. Coats, *Rambling Recollections* (privately published, Paisley 1920), pp. 182–184; A. Anderson, *The Old Libraries of Fife* (duplicated, Fife Co. Library, Kirkcaldy 1953), p. 20; W. R. Aitken, *A History of the Public Library Movement in Scotland to 1955* (Glasgow 1971), pp. 93–94. James Coats was a nephew of the Sir Peter Coats referred to above, p. 68.

Adams sent out a questionnaire to all the surviving libraries he was able to locate, and reported to the Carnegie Trustees:

"More than half of the answers indicate that the library is housed in the school; in several places the books are in the parish hall or parish council offices, others are in a room in connection with the church or in the manse, a few in a village recreation room and institute, and here and there the library is in the village shop. In one or two places, such as Montrose, where there was already a public library, the Coats grants of books were housed there. One library was given to the soldiers' barracks formerly at Dingwall, now at Fort George.

"Regarding the number of books given, most places received about 300 or 400 volumes, but in some cases altogether 600 to 700 volumes were given. Several places have also added fresh books to their libraries at their own charge by means of grants raised locally."[1]

This last sentence hints at the main weakness of the Coats libraries. It was the same weakness that had already brought about the decay of hundreds of parish libraries founded by individual benefactors from the sixteenth century onwards, namely the lack of any continuing endowment for the maintenance and renewal of stocks. This appears also in many of the very interesting comments quoted by Adams in respect of particular libraries:

"The gift was highly appreciated by the parishioners, and for about seven years after the opening of the library in February, 1905, an exchange of books on a large scale took place every fortnight. During the last two years there has been a large decline in the number of those availing themselves of the privileges of the library. This decline I attribute mainly to the lack of funds to meet ordinary expenses, and to secure from time to time a fresh infusion of books of a popular character. The population of the parish consists almost exclusively of crofters and labourers, and numbers of the books represent a type of literature somewhat heavy for the average man to tackle after the exhaustion of a laborious day's work."[2]

"My experience with the Coats Library has been that the readers found the selection so restricted that they soon exhausted the books they cared to read, and the result was that in the course of three or four seasons our regular reading list had almost disappeared. The difficulty with a library of this sort seems to lie in the lack of a fresh supply of books."[3]

"Good books—like those of Scott, Dickens, etc., are *clean*; the demand is for trashy stuff like A. S. Swan's.

"I have patched, gummed and glued till some books are scarcely recognisable, and about 200, more or less, ought to be scrapped."[4]

The Carnegie Trustees readily accepted the recommendation of the Adams Report that a limited number of experiments should be launched in the supply of books to rural areas, with in each case a central collection, available for circulation over a wide area and using village schools, as far as possible, as distributing centres.[5] This decision was implemented, over the next few years, partly by grant-aiding existing schemes and partly by promoting entirely new schemes. In the former category were the Yorkshire Village Library and the Dorset Booklending Association. Both these were assisted to extend their operations and improve the quality of their service, the Yorkshire Library being

---

[1] *Adams Report*, p. 18.   [2] *Op. cit.*, p. 102.
[3] *Op. cit.*, p. 101.   [4] *Ibid.*
[5] Carnegie U.K. Trust, *First Annual Report, 1913–14*, p. 11.

provided in 1916 with a new headquarters building.[1] In Westmorland, where under an arrangement made in 1903 the Kendal Public Library had been providing bookboxes, at the cost of the County Education Committee, for schools throughout the county, the Trustees provided extra funds to enable the scheme to be extended to adults.[2]

A scheme very close to the hearts of the Trustees was that for the North of Scotland, which, following up a suggestion from Adams, was intended to reinforce the existing Coats libraries by regular supplies of fresh books.[3] Beginning in 1915, boxes of about 75 books, exchangeable every six months, were provided for more than a hundred centres in Orkney, Shetland and Lewis. A local committee—the Coats Library Committee whenever possible—was appointed to take charge of each centre, and there was a central committee for each of the three areas. Additional books, including some reference works, were also given to the existing public libraries at Kirkwall, Stromness, and Stornoway, and to a reading room at Lerwick. The work of distribution was carried out from a central repository at Dunfermline, where the Trust had its headquarters.

The development of this North of Scotland scheme is chronicled in detail in successive annual reports of the Trust. The story they had to tell was on the whole one of success, in spite of wartime difficulties of transport and the absence of so many of the menfolk of the islands in the armed forces or on other essential service. A schoolmaster at Foula in Shetland, in 1918, described the 52 rural libraries there as "a silent yet most powerful factor for lasting good".[4] A pleasant detail recorded in the first report on the scheme is that a non-returnable supply of magazines and illustrated papers was included in each box, to be lent at the librarian's discretion without a record being kept.[5] Here also we read that:

> "For readers in the so-called 'black houses' of the Lews [i.e. Lewis and Harris] cheap cloth-bound editions are being provided, the cost of replacement of which will not be a heavy item. In the 'black houses' the ventilation is very poor, and books read in the peat smoke atmosphere soon have to be destroyed."[6]

The new schemes sponsored by the Carnegie trustees, as distinct from those built on pre-existing schemes, were of two kinds, both seeking to make use of powers available under existing legislation. One, known as the Worksop scheme because first put into practice there in 1916, was based on the powers given to neighbouring authorities, under the Libraries Acts, to combine for library purposes, and involved the grouping of a number of rural parishes round an urban library which would act as a centre for the distribution of books. The Trust undertook to bear the cost for the first five years, but thereafter every

[1] Carnegie U.K. Trust, *Third Annual Report, 1916*, pp. 43–44. The Dorset scheme was taken over by the County Education Committee in June, 1919—*Seventh Annual Report, 1920*, p. 23. The Yorkshire Village Library was wound up only in 1925, following the adoption of the 1919 Act by all three Ridings—*Eleventh Annual Report, 1924*, p. 30.
[2] Carnegie U.K. Trust, *Second Annual Report, 1915*, pp. 61–62; for the origins of the scheme see J. W. Brown, "Village Libraries: the Westmorland Scheme", in *L.A.R.*, Vol. X (1908), pp. 644–648.
[3] *Adams Report*, pp. 19–20.
[4] Carnegie U.K. Trust, *Fifth Annual Report, 1918*, p. 30.
[5] Carnegie U.K. Trust, *Second Annual Report, 1915*, p. 49.
[6] *Op. cit.*, p. 48.

parish in membership would be expected to adopt the Acts and levy a rate in support of the service. By 1918 Worksop was supplying 25 neighbouring villages in North Nottinghamshire and South Yorkshire, and seven of them had already adopted the Acts.[1]

It will be noted that this scheme was not dissimilar in its general arrangements to that described above operated in conjunction with the Kendal Public Library. Area schemes based on Montrose and Perth were inaugurated in 1916 and 1918 respectively, and plans were made for a similar development at Grantham.[2]

The other type of Carnegie scheme, known as the Staffordshire scheme because first introduced in that county in 1916, was based not on library legislation but on an enlargement of the powers exercised by the county education committees in respect of elementary schools. Article 20 of the Elementary School Code of 1907 charged the authorities with the duty of providing suitable books for the scholars, and added:

> "In cases where the school does not possess a school library, arrangements should be made to supply the want of one, if possible, in other ways, such as by co-operation with organisations existing for the purpose."[3]

In Staffordshire the Trust agreed to finance, for five years, the distribution of bookboxes under the management of the County Education Committee to all schools in the county's rural areas, the books being intended to provide suitable reading "principally for the children in attendance at the schools, and also for other inhabitants in the villages".[4] The great advantage of this plan was that it was related to the entire administrative county; one disadvantage was that it did not apply to Scotland, where elementary education was outside the purview of the county education committees.

This Staffordshire scheme, ably administered by the Director of Education, Sir Graham Balfour, quickly became popular, and by the close of 1918 similar schemes had been approved for five other English counties—Warwickshire, Wiltshire, Gloucestershire, Somerset and Buckinghamshire—and four Welsh counties—Caernarvonshire, Cardiganshire, Montgomeryshire and Breconshire.[5]

All these experimental schemes achieved a degree of success, but it should be realized that they were on a very small scale. The total cost, in 1918, of the thirteen rural schemes approved by the Trust which had commenced operations up to that time was less than £6000.[6] The total issues for Staffordshire for the year were 48000 (42000 to schools); for Worksop 46000 (16000 to schools); for the North of Scotland 19000 (10000 to schools). It had been supposed at

---

[1] *Op. cit.*, pp. 13–14, 56–59; *Fourth Annual Report, 1917*, p. 59.

[2] Carnegie U.K. Trust, *Third Annual Report, 1916*, p. 12; *Fourth Annual Report, 1917*, p. 19; *Fifth Annual Report, 1918*, pp. 9–10. The Grantham scheme was launched in 1920— *Eighth Annual Report, 1921*, p. 43. Details of the Perth scheme are given in W. R. Aitken, *A History of the Public Library Movement in Scotland to 1955* (Glasgow 1971), App. II, pp. 316–320.

[3] Board of Education, *Code of Regulations for Public Elementary Schools in England* (1907), p. 11.

[4] Carnegie U.K. Trust, *Second Annual Report, 1915*, p. 12.

[5] Carnegie U.K. Trust, *Fifth Annual Report, 1918*, p. 5; K. A. Stockham (ed.), *British County Libraries: 1919–1969* (1969), p. 28.

[6] *Op. cit.*, p. 40.

the outset that rural readers would be avid for books about country life and rural economy, but this illusion was quickly shattered, and as in the town libraries fiction easily topped the list. In the Kendal area, where the Trust scheme catered for adults only, fiction issues reached 93 per cent.[1] In the North of Scotland, in 1917, the most popular authors were Marie Corelli, Ethel M. Dell, Rider Haggard, W. W. Jacobs, Jack London and Baroness Orczy.[2]

The most valuable service these early Carnegie schemes rendered, indeed, was to demonstrate the need for a full county library system. The Worksop plan, though its results were at first very encouraging, was in the last resort at the mercy of individual parish councils, which might or might not be disposed to co-operate. The Staffordshire plan made for "more rapid development and smoother working".[3] In 1918, in fact, the Worksop scheme was wound up, to give way early in the next year to a scheme for the whole of Nottingham county.[4]

In Scotland, the year 1918 brought an important change. A short but significant clause in the Education (Scotland) Act read as follows:

> "It shall be lawful for the education authority of a county, as an ancillary means of promoting education, to make such provision of books by purchase or otherwise as they may think desirable, and to make the same available not only to children and young persons attending schools or continuation classes in the county, but also to the adult population resident therein.
>
> "For the purpose of this section an education authority may enter into arrangements with public libraries, and all expenses incurred by an education authority for those purposes shall be chargeable to the county education fund . . ."[5]

This was a clear mandate, and was the foundation upon which the county library service of Scotland was built during the next ten years. The clause, which came into effect in May, 1919, was all the more satisfactory in that it imposed no financial limit on the operation.

The corresponding English Education Act, unfortunately, contained no such clause. Throughout the war, agitation for reform had necessarily been suspended, but as the war neared its close the libraries could contain themselves no longer. In conference after conference, meeting after meeting, they imperatively demanded, as a first priority, the removal of the rate limitation. The Carnegie Trust supported this demand very strongly, and also pressed, in view of its own special interests, the case for the county library.

In the summer of 1919 there appeared the Third Interim Report of the Adult Education Committee of the Ministry of Reconstruction. This Committee, under the chairmanship of A. L. Smith, Master of Balliol, included such distinguished adult educationists as Albert Mansbridge and R. H. Tawney. Its Final Report, produced later in the year, was a classic statement which pro-

---

[1] *Op. cit.*, pp. 21–22.

[2] Carnegie U.K. Trust, *Fourth Annual Report, 1917*, p. 49.   [3] *Op. cit.*, p. 20.

[4] Carnegie U.K. Trust, *Fifth Annual Report, 1918*, pp. 8–9; *Sixth Annual Report, 1919*, p. 9. For a general review of these early Carnegie Trust schemes see F. A. Keyse, "The Birth of County Libraries: C.U.K.T. Experiments 1915–19", in *Journal of Librarianship*, Vol. I (1969), pp. 183–190.

[5] 8 and 9 Geo. V, c. 48, §5. The remainder of the clause is concerned to ensure that a burgh or parish which already levies a rate under the Libraries Act should be liable only for the difference between its own rate and that levied for library purposes by the county.

foundly affected the development of adult education in this country and which is still quoted wherever English is spoken. The Third Interim Report, a much more modest affair, was concerned with Libraries and Museums. It recommended not only the abolition of the rate limitation and the extension of library powers to counties, but also the transfer of public libraries and museums in England and Wales to the control of education authorities, and the transfer of the powers in respect of public libraries hitherto exercised by the Local Government Board to the Board of Education.[1]

The Library Association welcomed the first two of these proposals, but strongly opposed the other two, which undoubtedly reflected the adult education bias of the committee. These latter proposals, indeed, were not persisted with. The result of the combined pressure of the Library Association, the Carnegie Trust, and the Adult Education Committee, however, was that in November 1919, a short Government Bill was at last introduced to amend the Public Libraries Acts in relation to England and Wales. Its basic clauses were two: the removal of the rate limitation and the extension of library powers to county authorities. The Bill was fought step by step by that uncompromising Tory, Sir Frederick Banbury (afterwards the first Lord Banbury), who had successfully blocked new library legislation before the war. In a speech which reminds one irresistibly of Colonel Sibthorp seventy years earlier he declared:

> "My experience is that Public Libraries are places where, if the weather is cold, people go in and sit down and get warm, while other people go in to read novels. I do not believe, speaking generally, that Public Libraries have done any good. On the contrary, they have done a great deal of harm, because the books read, as far as my information goes, are chiefly sensational novels, which do no good to anybody."[2]

This time, however, the feeling of the House was against him, and before the end of the year the Act was passed.[3]

In moving the second reading Herbert Lewis, Parliamentary Secretary to the Board of Education, put the case in words which recorded the desperate state of many libraries:

> "The Board of Education have been receiving most urgent representations by deputation and otherwise from all parts of the country from library authorities who complain that owing to the limitation of the penny rate they are wholly unable to pay any war bonuses to their staff. There are many of them who are actually unable to buy any new books. There are some who do not know how to meet the expenses of the coming year, and I know of cases in which branch libraries have had to be closed . . . .There is also the further point that the Carnegie Trustees have been establishing libraries in rural areas at their own expense, but they are only able to carry on for a term of years, and their work is brought to a standstill owing to the fact that under the existing law it is doubtful whether any county authority can undertake to carry on the work."[4]

---

[1] For the details see pp. 18–19 of the Report (Cd. 9237, 1919).
[2] Hansard, *Parliamentary Debates*, 5th Ser., Vol. CXXII, col. 369.
[3] Public Libraries Act, 1919, 10 Geo V, c. 93.
[4] Hansard, *loc. cit.* This passage is quoted in J. Minto, *A History of the Public Library Movement* (1932), p. 139. Ch. ix of this work describes in detail the events leading to the passage of the Act. See also the bitter passage from E. A. Savage, *A Librarian's Memories, Portraits and Reflections* (below, p. 233) on the condition of the libraries at this time.

The passage of the Act left one group of library authorities in Great Britain still labouring under the limitation of the penny rate, namely the non-county authorities of Scotland—the Scottish counties, as we have seen, could operate without limit under the Education Act of 1918. The anomaly was only partly removed by the Public Libraries (Scotland) Act of 1920, which did indeed abolish the penny rate limit, but in deference to the views expressed by the Convention of Royal Burghs earlier in the year retained a limit of 3d.[1] An escape clause permitting the rate limit to be increased to sixpence subject to the approval of the Secretary of State for Scotland or the Scottish Board of Health was deleted in the House of Lords.

The 1919 Act was so important in subsequent library history that its main provisions are worth noting. These were:

(1) A county council might adopt the Public Libraries Acts by resolution for such part of the county as it thought fit, excluding county boroughs and existing public library districts (i.e. areas in which the Acts had been adopted and expenditure incurred under the Acts during the last financial year, or in which a public library was maintained under a local Act).

(2) Existing library authorities (other than county boroughs) might relinquish their library powers to the county.

(3) The county might with the agreement of the Board of Education relinquish its powers in respect of any part of its library area to permit the establishment of an independent library service.

(4) All county library matters, other than the raising of the rate and the borrowing of money, must stand referred to the county education committee, which might, however, delegate its powers to a sub-committee which need not consist wholly of members of the main committee.[2]

This last provision reflected the influence of the Adult Education Committee. It placed the English county libraries, like those of Scotland, firmly within the ambit of the education service, and thereby marked them off sharply from their urban counterparts.

The Post-War Years

The county libraries could hardly have been born in less auspicious circumstances, for the years immediately following the 1919 Act were years of political instability, economic depression and industrial strife. By 1921 the brief post-war boom had already given way to depression, and ruthless economy was the order of the day. By 1925 conditions were a little better, but unemployment still remained at a high level, and the general strike of the following year was a warning against easy optimism. In the meantime Lloyd George's coalition government, which had survived the war, had collapsed on the withdrawal of Conservative support in 1922. A Conservative government followed, first under

---

[1] 10 and 11 Geo. V. c. 45. Cf. W. R. Aitken, *A History of the Public Library Movement in Scotland to 1955* (Glasgow 1971), pp. 83–88.

[2] As a concession to what we may call the education lobby, the Act did *permit* county boroughs to refer library business to the education committee if they so chose, but only county boroughs which were not library authorities at the time of the passing of the Act were compelled to do so.

Bonar Law and then under Stanley Baldwin, but Baldwin gave way in January 1924 to Ramsay MacDonald at the head of Britain's first Labour government, and Ramsay MacDonald in turn made way for Baldwin before the year was out.

All this uncertainty created a very unfavourable atmosphere for any considerable extension of the public library service, and indeed had it not been for the consistent support and propaganda of the Carnegie United Kingdom Trust it seems doubtful whether the county service could have been launched at all at this time. Fortunately in more than a score of counties Carnegie funds had already enabled a start to be made.

There was, too, one encouraging feature, namely the widespread conviction that something must be done towards the rehabilitation of the countryside. The basic factor in the situation, of course, was the decline in Britain's agriculture. This was a long-term trend, only temporarily halted by the extension of cultivation during the war. The resulting low wages, coupled with geographical isolation, poor housing, and an almost complete lack of social and educational facilities, led to a constant drift of population from the villages into the towns. For the decline of agriculture, there was no easy cure, but the advent of the motor-car and the motor-bus (coming rapidly into use in the early 'twenties) and the radio (still at the "cat's whisker" stage and generally known as "the wireless") did much to break down the sense of isolation, and a number of organizations, from different angles, were trying to improve social and educational amenities.

The Women's Institutes, which began in England and Wales in 1915 and in Scotland two years later, were an immensely powerful influence, bringing new facilities for education and recreation as well as much practical advice on housekeeping and local government. In some parts of the country Y.M.C.A. huts erected for the use of the troops were converted after the war into Y.M.C.A. clubs; and the creation of village clubs was financially assisted by the Treasury. From the Treasury also, through the Development Commissioners, came from 1925 onwards grants towards the cost of village halls. In the mining areas a special fund created under the Mining Industry Act of 1920 provided Miners' Institutes for welfare and recreational purposes. In England, following the pioneering work begun by Grace Hadow in Oxfordshire in 1919, the Carnegie Trust from 1921 onwards began to make grants towards the establishment of Rural Community Councils to coordinate the activities of voluntary bodies and statutory authorities. By 1926 there were 14 such Councils in England, one in Wales and one in Scotland.[1]

The county library service thus came into being as part of a general movement for rural rehabilitation, and this fact contributed in no small measure to its success in spite of the many difficulties it had to contend with in its early years.

The Beginnings of the County Service

Before the 1919 Act was passed, rural library schemes supported by the Carnegie Trust were already operating or about to commence, in the following areas:

---

[1] On this subject see especially W. Robertson, *Welfare in Trust: a History of the Carnegie United Kingdom Trust, 1913–1963* (Dunfermline 1964), Ch. iv.

England
- Buckinghamshire
- Dorset
- Gloucestershire
- Lincolnshire—Kesteven
    - (Grantham and District)
- Nottinghamshire
- Somerset
- Staffordshire
- Warwickshire (begun 1920)
- Westmorland
- Wiltshire
- Yorkshire (Village Libraries)

Wales
- Brecon and Radnor (begun 1920)
- Caernarvonshire
- Cardiganshire
- Denbighshire (begun 1921)
- Montgomeryshire (begun 1920)

Scotland
- Forfar (Angus) and Kincardineshire
    - (Montrose and District)
- Orkney, Shetland and Isle of Lewis
    - (North of Scotland Scheme)
- Perthshire
    - (Perth and District)

These schemes were not immediately wound up, but for the most part continued until the expiry of the period for which the Carnegie grant had been made—customarily five years. To help things along the Trust adjusted its grant policy to meet the new conditions. In Scotland, where the 1918 Education Act came into force in May 1919, the Trust offered to each county education authority establishing a library service a grant in aid of capital costs; and in the case of the poorer northern counties it also expressed its willingness to consider a maintenance grant for a limited period.[1] Following the 1919 Public Libraries Act, policy was further defined. Maintenance grants were henceforth excluded (since the money for this purpose could now be found from public funds); building grants were excluded (because experience had shown that special buildings were unnecessary); and grants were in future to be restricted to capital cost in respect of books (calculated on the basis of one book for five children at school), bookboxes, shelving and other accessories.[2] It was anticipated that such an initial grant would cover capital costs for four or five years.

In Scotland the first rate-aided county library to operate under the terms of the 1918 Act was Perthshire, which in 1919 took over and extended the scheme formerly based on the Sandeman Library at Perth.[3] In the following year a joint scheme by the counties of Forfar (now Angus) and Kincardineshire took over the service formerly based on Montrose. The counties of Renfrew, Berwick, Peebles and Midlothian also commenced operations in 1920, and Caithness began to provide a service with the help of a five-year maintenance grant from the Carnegie Trust. The arrangement here was interesting and unusual, being based on the existing public libraries at Thurso and Wick. Thurso acted as distributing centre for the north of the county, Wick for the centre and south. In each case a room was provided for the use of the county, and the local librarian was paid to act as librarian for the county scheme.[4]

---

[1] Carnegie U.K. Trust, *Sixth Annual Report, 1919*, p. 10.
[2] Carnegie U.K. Trust, *Seventh Annual Report, 1920*, p. 8.
[3] Carnegie U.K. Trust, *Sixth Annual Report, 1919*, p. 11.
[4] *Op. cit.*, p. 10; *Seventh Annual Report, 1920*, pp. 22–23. The library service of Thurso and Wick was by 1930 completely unified in practice with that of the County, but the two burghs remained technically independent until at least 1931—see Carnegie U.K. Trust and Scottish Library Association, *Proceedings of the Scottish Library Conference ... 1931* [Dunfermline 1931], p. 15; Carnegie U.K. Trust, *Eighteenth Annual Report, 1931*, p. 16.

In England and Wales Cheshire, Cumberland, Kent, Middlesex, Pembroke-shire, Warwickshire and Worcestershire all adopted the new Act in 1920, and a number of other counties negotiated for Carnegie grants without at this stage adopting. During the next year or two progress was slowed by economic difficulties, but by 1923 the forward movement had been resumed, and by the end of 1927 the only areas which had not commenced service under the 1919 Act were, in England, the Isle of Wight and Westmorland (which continued their pre-1919 arrangements), Holland (Lincolnshire), Rutland, and the Scilly Isles; in Wales, Carmarthenshire; and in Scotland, Argyll.

The scale of provision was, however, pitifully inadequate. The original aim of the Carnegie Trustees was simply a bookbox service for the rural areas, and county education committees tended to think in terms of a rate of $\frac{1}{10}$d. Sir William Robertson, Vice-Chairman of the Rural Libraries Conference sponsored by the Trustees in 1920, referred to this low level of expenditure with satisfaction:

> ". . . you have already heard that in quite exceptional cases the rate might amount to $\frac{1}{2}$d. in the pound; in average cases it runs anywhere from $\frac{1}{16}$ of a penny to $\frac{1}{4}$d. in the pound."[1]

From the Report of the same Conference we note that Gloucestershire was serving 303 centres on a $\frac{1}{8}$d. rate, and Staffordshire was serving 206 centres on a $\frac{1}{18}$d. rate.[2] Even in 1925, 35 out of 40 counties in England and Wales were levying a rate of less than $\frac{1}{4}$d., and the highest rate, in Cardiganshire, was only 0.88d. The average annual expenditure per head of population served (excluding county libraries in their first year) was 0.9d., compared with 1s. in non-county libraries.[3]

Initially no attempt was made to cater for the urban centres within the jurisdiction of the counties; and indeed many counties, e.g. Nottingham, Northumberland, Staffordshire, and Glamorgan, deliberately excluded such centres from the area for which the Acts were adopted. Altogether 13 municipal boroughs (including Swindon, Crewe and Wallsend), and 48 urban districts (including Rhondda, Mountain Ash, and Finchley) found themselves excluded in this way. If we add three small parishes adjoining the city of Worcester, and the county borough of Hastings, which had still not adopted, there remained in 1925 nearly 1 400 000 people in areas without a library authority.[4]

Even for the rural areas the provision was less than generous, usually a box of 50–100 books for each village, deposited in the local school and with the schoolteacher acting as voluntary librarian. In a typical box the books might be half adult fiction, one-quarter juvenile fiction, and the rest non-fiction. The books were usually exchanged three times a year, the boxes being

---

[1] Carnegie U.K. Trust, *Rural Library Handbook: the Proceedings of the Carnegie Rural Library Conference . . . 1920* (Dunfermline 1921), p. 14. This report is cited hereafter as *Rural Library Conference Proceedings, 1920*.

[2] *Op. cit.*, p. 69.

[3] *Kenyon Report*, p. 105.

[4] *Op. cit.*, pp. 99, 230–234. In Nottinghamshire the excluded areas were brought within the county orbit in 1929, and in Staffordshire in 1931, but in some cases the process of absorption was very slow. In Glamorganshire the urban districts of Rhondda and Mountain Ash remained without a library service until 1939 and 1964 respectively.

transported by rail and carrier or any other method of transport that might be available. In Sutherland, because of the long distances involved, the boxes had to do the round of several libraries before returning to headquarters for checking and overhaul, but this was generally considered undesirable.[1] In Orkney and Shetland distribution often had to be by boat, and the first box sent to St. Kilda, in 1920, went by trawler from Fleetwood[2]. The Carnegie report which records this fact enshrines also a charming illustration of the difficulties of transport in a rural area in the North of Scotland. Here, as frequently elsewhere, the children were used as agents of distribution:

> "A schoolmaster describes how he has through the winter carried the books for the children until they fell in with the sheepdogs who were sent to meet them and bring them safely over the last part of the track. The books were then slung round the dogs' backs and so transported to the lonely croft."[3]

Headquarters accommodation was of the simplest. "The idea has gone abroad," wrote R. D. MacLeod in 1923, "that any old barn or classroom may be made to serve as the home of the county library".[4] Wiltshire County Library, at this time, was housed in a former army hut;[5] Surrey County Library, two years later, commenced operations in converted stables.[6] Denbighshire began in 1920 in an inn, and moved in 1927 to a former prison; Anglesey, in 1925, established its headquarters in a billiard room.[7]

Provided there was an office for the librarian, and shelving for the few thousand books not actually in circulation, all was thought to be well. The librarian, at this early period, often had to work entirely on his own: at best he would have the help of a clerk. The Carnegie Trust insisted, as a condition of grant, that a librarian in charge of a hundred of more centres must have a salary of at least £300 a year, but the question whether an assistant was needed, and if so at what level, was left open.[8] In Pembrokeshire the work was undertaken on a half-time basis by the Deputy Director of Education.[9]

After a few years, however, the scale of operations gradually expanded. In the rural areas the number of centres was increased, and in order to overcome the persistent belief that the libraries were intended for schoolchildren there was an increasing tendency to establish centres in buildings other than schools, e.g. in village halls, women's institutes, Y.M.C.A. clubs, and miners' welfare institutes. In this way the county libraries tied in with other aspects of the rural rehabilitation movement.

By 1927 about one-third of all the centres were in places other than schools, and in some English counties, notably Hertfordshire, Oxfordshire, Surrey and

---

[1] Carnegie U.K. Trust, *County Libraries in Great Britain and Ireland: Reports 1925* (Dunfermline 1925), p. 34.
[2] Carnegie U.K. Trust, *Seventh Annual Report, 1920*, p. 21.   [3] *Op. cit.*, p. 22.
[4] R. D. Macleod, *County Rural Libraries* (1923), p. 120.   [5] *Op. cit.*, p. 121.
[6] R. G. Bird, *A Short History of the Surrey County Library* (unpublished F.L.A. essay 1950), p. 6.
[7] J. Roe, *The Public Library in Wales* (unpublished M.A. thesis, Belfast University 1970), pp. 90–92, 98–99.
[8] Carnegie U.K. Trust, *Seventh Annual Report, 1920*, p. 9; *Rural Library Conference Proceedings, 1920*, p. 22.
[9] Roe, *op. cit.*, p. 95. A full-time librarian was not appointed till 1951.

the West Riding, non-school centres were in a majority.[1] In many instances old village subscription libraries were taken over as centres. "It is particularly satisfactory," reported the Carnegie Trust in 1922, "that many derelict local libraries have voluntarily offered the hospitality of their shelves and rooms, and in many cases handed over their entire stock to the County Library".[2]

From an early stage it was the custom in some counties to establish village committees to support and assist the local librarian, and this practice was warmly commended in the Kenyon Report.[3]

One factor in the improvement of service to the centres was better transport. Increasingly the slow and cumbersome combination of train and carrier was replaced or supplemented by hired motor transport, and a few venturesome authorities actually acquired their own book vans. These were at this stage of two types. One, known as an exhibition van, was built on a 20 cwt. or 30 cwt. chassis and had shelf accommodation for 1000–2000 volumes. Its great advantage was that it enabled the local librarian, and such readers as might be available, to make their own selection on the spot instead of having the "carefully balanced selection" made up at headquarters. This form of book van was first introduced in Perthshire in 1921. In England Kent was the pioneer, and within the next few years was followed by Norfolk, Northumberland, and the East Riding. In all these vans the shelves were arranged in alcoves, with access from outside. Lindsey, in 1925, was the first to introduce an interior access van, which accommodated fewer books but gave protection from the weather. Aberdeenshire and Denbighshire had exhibition vans by 1927.

The other type of book van, favoured at this period by Surrey, West Sussex, Wiltshire, and Middlesex, was simply a delivery van. It was commonly used for the carriage of bookboxes, but Middlesex in 1927 introduced the more convenient method of book-trays fitting into racks in the van. The relative merits of the various methods of carriage were discussed in annual reports and conferences in great detail and with great earnestness, and it is interesting to find a speaker in 1926 strongly recommending that vehicles should be fitted with headlamps, a self-starter, and a mileage recorder.[4]

A difficulty was that because of the shortage of staff the librarian often had to drive the van himself. This was the position in the first year or two in Lindsey, and when it was decided to engage a chauffeur the committee prudently provided also a folding table and a portable typewriter, so that the librarian could deal with correspondence *en route*. "There is something heroic", com-

---

[1] Carnegie U.K. Trust, *County Libraries in Great Britain and Ireland: Report, 1927–28* (Dunfermline 1928), p. 13. Cf. the corresponding *Report* for 1926–27, p. 16.

[2] Carnegie U.K. Trust, *Ninth Annual Report, 1922*, p. 17. For good examples from Cambridgeshire see Carnegie U.K. Trust, *County Libraries in Great Britain and Ireland: Reports 1924* (Dunfermline 1925), p. 19.

[3] *Kenyon Report*, p. 122.

[4] On all this see especially the two papers on "Transport Problems" in *Rural Library Conference Proceedings, 1920*, pp. 36–51, and Carnegie U.K. Trust, *County Libraries in Great Britain and Ireland: Report 1926–27* (Dunfermline 1927), App. I, pp. 46–52. Library vans for county areas were first suggested by Cornelius Walford in 1880—see *L.A. Conference Transactions, 1880*, p. 127. A plan for an interior access van was described and illustrated by J. D. Brown in 1894—See above, pp. 174–175.

ments the Carnegie report, "in the picture of a librarian typing his letters and memoranda in a van doing thirty to forty miles an hour, even on the relatively level roads of Lincolnshire."[1]

Books and Readers

On the whole the efforts of the new county libraries were well received. Occasionally, indeed, we hear of apathy, and even downright hostility, but this is only in the more backward rural areas.[2] Elsewhere the success of the work is attested by the fact that the scale of book supply laid down by the Carnegie Trust, which was, as we have seen, one volume per five of the school population, soon proved quite inadequate to meet the public demand. Fortunately the £192 000 allocated by the Trust for the establishment of county libraries during the quinquennium 1921–25 proved an over-estimate, and from 1923 it was possible to make supplementary grants for book supplies to those counties where the need seemed most pressing. At the close of 1925, when the offer of grant for the establishment of county libraries was withdrawn, these supplementary grants were continued, and a total of £72 000 was disbursed to eighty-two libraries in Great Britain during the quinquennium 1926–30.[3]

By 1927 the recently established County Libraries Section of the Library Association was recommending a minimum stock of 25 volumes per 100 population, and a number of established libraries held stocks considerably in excess of this figure.[4] Even so, it not infrequently happened that there were more readers than books, and the report from the West Riding in 1925 is not untypical:

"A widespread difficulty is the insufficient supply of books, the librarians frequently having to face borrowers—some of whom come from a distance— with the statement, 'no books left'. Again, borrowers frequently wait until some other borrower turns up with a book."[5]

Fiction was still the main staple of provision. In 1927 Middlesex, which had the largest and probably one of the best balanced of the county collections (close on 100 000 volumes) was still supplying 22 volumes of fiction to 10 of non-fiction per 100 of the population.[6] Operating as the county libraries were, however, under the aegis of the county education committees, they were always acutely conscious of their educational mission, and the most strenuous efforts were made to supply the needs of teachers, students and other serious readers. A very striking example is the circular posted at all distribution centres in Cumberland "that any applicant having a special interest in the non-fiction

---

[1] Carnegie U.K. Trust, *County Libraries in Great Britain and Ireland: Reports 1927–28* (Dunfermline 1928), p. 41n.

[2] Examples are reported in 1924 from Denbighshire and Co. Durham—*County Libraries Reports, 1924*, p. 39; *County Library Conference Proceedings, 1924*, p. 33.

[3] Carnegie U.K. Trust, *Seventeenth Annual Report, 1930*, p. 5.

[4] *County Libraries Reports, 1927–28*, p. 48.

[5] *County Libraries Reports, 1925*, p. 48.

[6] *County Libraries Reports, 1927–28*, p. 48. Cf. *County Libraries Reports, 1925*, pp. 40–41, where the high proportion of fiction is justified on the usual grounds.

side . . . may have sent, immediately on application, through his local librarian a book, a set of books, or a series of books dealing with his particular interest."[1]

Special attention was paid to the needs of teachers: indeed in quite a number of counties a small teachers' library already existed, under the auspices of the education committee, before the county library was created. In some cases, e.g. Durham, Essex, Fife, Nottinghamshire and Oxfordshire, this library continued for some years to be separately financed and administered, but in others, e.g. Kent and Surrey, it was handed over at an early stage to the care of the county library. In general the trend was for the service to be developed under library auspices, and for libraries restricted to teachers to be broadened into students' libraries available to all serious readers. This provision was, however, quite separate from the service to the centres: the books were kept at county library headquarters (or sometimes in the Education Offices), and were available either to personal borrowers or by post.[2] Some county libraries, e.g. Kent, made an important feature of individual postal loans, which they regarded as compensating in some degree for the lack of a reference service.

The provision of libraries for schools was still rudimentary, and no clear pattern had as yet emerged, but here again the tendency was for this branch of the library service to be administered by the county library. This was, of course, additional to the normal provision of juvenile literature through the library centres—a provision which, as the Oxfordshire report of 1924 remarked, was "limited only by the Trust's desire that the expenditure on children's books should not exceed one-fifth of the whole."[3]

Most county libraries also took special pains to provide books for adult classes. The demand came chiefly from University Extension and W.E.A. classes, and annual reports of the period repeatedly refer to arrangements made for these classes. The West Riding, in 1924, created a special Adult Class Library of over 2000 volumes.[4] Miss A. S. Cooke, the distinguished county librarian of Kent, observed in 1924:

> "The W.E.A. is, at the moment, probably doing more than any other movement to awaken an interest in education among adults, and it is impossible to do too much to help its ventures."[5]

Some county libraries, however, sought also to arouse the interest of classes in evening institutes and technical schools. Pembrokeshire, for example, provided special boxes of books for classes in mining, agriculture, horticulture, dairying and poultry-keeping: these were taken to the classes by the teachers, and issued by them to the students.[6]

From the beginning, in fact, the provision made by the county libraries for adult classes was much more generous than that made by most non-county

---

[1] *County Libraries Reports, 1925*, p. 28. The effect is a little spoilt by the list of non-fiction topics suggested, namely "bee-keeping, polar exploration, chess, rugby football, wood-turning, foreign agriculture, and so forth".

[2] Pembrokeshire's teachers' library was available through twelve local centres as well as at headquarters—*County Libraries Reports, 1925*, p. 106.

[3] *County Libraries Reports, 1924*, p. 32.

[4] *Op. cit.*, p. 36.

[5] *County Library Conference Proceedings, 1924*, p. 66.

[6] *County Libraries Reports, 1925*, p. 106.

libraries. Partly this was due to the keen interest in adult education shown by the Carnegie trustees; and partly it arose from the nature of the county service. For a municipal library individual loans for short periods were the normal practice, and any other arrangement was difficult, whereas the county library was specially organized to provide bulk loans for long periods.[1]

The possibilities opened up by the new county service were developed in an article by Robert Macleod, formerly librarian to the Carnegie Trust, who saw the county library as the essential connecting link in rural culture between organized education and the voluntary adult education associations, and the county librarian as the chief liaison officer. He proposed that both the library service and adult education should be placed under a single county adult education committee, chosen half from the education committee and half from the voluntary associations[2].

In a few counties the income from the library rate was supplemented by special grants from the Education Committee in respect of educational services. Kent was perhaps the most fortunate county in this respect, receiving in 1926 special grants from the Elementary and Secondary Education Sub-Committees in respect of services to schools, and from the Further Education Sub-Committee in respect of services to adult classes.[3] The Kenyon Report of 1927 approved of this kind of arrangement, and recommended that it should be generally applied, and the Carnegie Trust, needless to say, warmly supported this proposal.[4]

An element of growing importance in the supply of books to students and educational organizations was the Central Library for Students, which had its origins in a small Central Library for Tutorial Classes founded in 1912 by the Workers' Educational Association in collaboration with Toynbee Hall. Recognizing the wider possibilities of this library, the Carnegie Trust provided funds in 1916 for its transformation into an independent organization under the title Central Library for Students, and it was ultimately to become, in 1930, the National Central Library.

In the 1920s the Central Library was still operating on quite a small scale, but by the end of 1927 it had acquired a stock of 37 000 volumes and was making 50 000 issues a year from its Bloomsbury headquarters. Of these 20 000 were going to county libraries, 15 000 to non-county libraries, 2000 to other libraries, 11 000 direct to adult classes, and 2000 direct to individual borrowers. Apart from its own stock, the Central Library was now able to draw on the resources of over forty "outlier libraries", including many specialized collections.

There was also a Scottish Central Library for Students, established by the Carnegie Trust in 1921 in Dunfermline. In 1927 it was responsible for over 12 000 loans, nearly 7000 of them to county libraries. The help given by these two Central Libraries, limited as it was, was immensely useful

---

[1] For useful general surveys of all these educational activities, see the *County Libraries Reports* for 1926–27 (Ch. vi) and for 1927–28 (Ch. viii).

[2] R. D. Macleod, *Rural Libraries and Rural Education*, originally published in *Library World*, Jan.-Feb. 1921, and reprinted first as a pamphlet (1921), and then in Macleod's *County Rural Libraries* (1923), Ch. iii.

[3] *County Libraries Reports, 1926–27*, p. 27.

[4] *Ibid.*, and for Kenyon Report below, p. 245.

in supplementing the meagre resources of the new county authorities, and especially in providing scarce and expensive books.[1]

Many of the more enterprising libraries also sought to extend their range and their readership by creating special collections of various kinds. As early as 1923 Kent had a collection of plays for loan to literary and dramatic societies, a collection on beekeeping, and a library of 6000 lantern slides; while Warwickshire and Perthshire had collections of musical scores. Later other counties followed this lead. Drama and music collections became very popular, and we hear also of special collections on agriculture, and on local history and topography.[2]

One of the problems for the county library was how to acquaint the serious student with the library's resources. Some counties produced a printed catalogue, but this was expensive and quickly out of date; and card and sheaf catalogues could not readily be circulated among a multitude of small centres.[3] Many libraries found the solution in the practice long familiar in non-county libraries, i.e. in the issue of subject lists, often in association with lectures. The comment of the Denbigh librarian in 1925—"I am firmly convinced that a lecture scheme should form part of the organisation of every library"—reflects a common opinion.[4] In that same year it was reported from Cumberland:

> "The number of new readers created by lecture-courses, or single lectures given in the rural areas, has greatly swelled the number of students using the library. The most remote villages have been reached during the winter by the Director and his colleagues, and lectures on forestry, hydro-electric power development, humorous verse, aeroplane photography, etc., have been given with a view to stimulating the study of questions so pertinent to rural development and to the awakening of literary interest."[5]

Cambridgeshire, at the same time, was circulating special booklists on beekeeping, home crafts, horticulture, and divinity;[6] while Leicestershire was planning lectures (with appropriate consignments of books) by the staff of Loughborough College and of the County Agricultural Committee.[7] By 1927,

---

[1] Carnegie U.K. Trust, *Fourteenth Annual Report, 1927*, pp. 78–82. A good account of both these Central Libraries is given in *County Library Conference Proceedings, 1926*, p. 92–105.

[2] Carnegie U.K. Trust, *Tenth Annual Report, 1923*, pp. 55–56; *County Library Conference Proceedings, 1924*, p. 37; *County Libraries Reports, 1926–27*, pp. 35–36, 45.

[3] Among the counties which produced printed catalogues were Gloucestershire (1920), Kent (1924) and Perthshire (1925). Fife published in 1928 a massive dictionary catalogue (462 pp.) which had taken ten years to produce (G. H. Ballantyne, *Comparative Studies in Scottish County Library Organisation and Administration*, unpublished F.L.A. thesis 1965, pp. 285–286). An attempt by Middlesex to maintain a complete MS. catalogue at each centre was a failure, and was replaced by subject lists (*County Libraries Reports, 1925*, p. 45; D. H. Harmer, *The Foundation and Growth of County Library Services around London, with special reference to Middlesex*, unpublished F.L.A. essay 1964, pp. 11–12). North Riding had much success in its first year with a typewritten non-fiction catalogue circulated to the centres a month before an exchange of books was due (*County Libraries Reports, 1925*, p. 97).

[4] *County Libraries Reports, 1925*, p. 28.

[5] *Op. cit.*, p. 60.

[6] *Op. cit.*, p. 63.

[7] *Op. cit.*, p. 69

some county libraries were preparing booklists in connection with the B.B.C.'s new "wireless discussion groups", and some such groups were actually meeting on library premises.[1]

The Problem of the Populous Areas

We should, indeed, be astonished not so much at the modest scale on which the county libraries operated at this time, but rather at the number of things they were able to do, or attempted to do, on such slender funds.[2] Their achievement is even more remarkable when we take into account the efforts of some counties to deal with what was generally called "the problem of the populous areas".

These included small market towns, industrial and mining villages, and suburban areas of county boroughs or other independent library authorities. The Carnegie Report for 1924 records as the salient fact of the year "the steady evolution of a simple system, originally designed to supply villages only, into a comprehensive machinery serving populous areas also, and in direct contact with independent urban libraries."[3]

To attempt to provide for such areas merely by multiplying small centres of the rural type was of course quite inadequate.[4] What was needed was a branch system on the model of that developed by the urban libraries. The problem was to finance such a development, and the answer generally agreed, at this period, was that the locality concerned must bear the additional cost involved. The Kenyon Report, in 1927, was emphatic on the point:

> "The provision of libraries in the ordinary sense, that is to say places to which persons can resort to read as well as to borrow books, is no part of the primary idea of the county scheme . . . the provision of such a library should, so far as finance is concerned, be the business of the locality."[5]

One way of providing the money was for the local authority to agree to the levying of a special rate over and above the normal county library rate. For this arrangement, known as differential rating, legal authority was found in England and Wales by a somewhat strained interpretation of a passage in the 1919 Act.[6] The earliest example was at Kenilworth, where in 1922 the Urban District Council agreed to an additional ¼d. rate for the maintenance of a reading room and a small collection of books. Some 400 to 500 volumes came from an old parochial library and formed the nucleus of a permanent local library; in addition the Warwickshire County Library provided about 650 volumes which were periodically exchanged. The library was open on

---

[1] *County Libraries Reports, 1927–28*, p. 36.
[2] Interesting personal recollections of these early years are given in the symposium entitled "As it was in the Beginning", in *L.A. Conference Proceedings, 1950*, pp. 79–87; and in *Library World*, Vol. LXX (1968–69) pp. 287–290, 296–299.
[3] Carnegie U.K. Trust, *Eleventh Annual Report, 1924*, p. 23.
[4] See on this *County Library Conference Proceedings, 1924*, pp. 41–42.
[5] *Kenyon Report* (1927), p. 102.
[6] Section 4, sub-section 2. The discussion in E. J. Carnell, *County Libraries* (1938), pp. 47–51, shows clearly that this clause was really intended for quite a different purpose.

two days a week and was looked after by a part-time library assistant, the arrangement being supervised by a local committee.[1]

This proved, in hard times, a useful device, and within a few years began to be fairly widely adopted, often on a scale rather more elaborate than at Kenilworth. An agreement reached in 1925 between Lindsey County Library and the Urban District of Cleethorpes provided for the establishment of a lending and reference library in the Cleethorpes Technical Institute. The books for the lending library were to be supplied by the county, those for the reference library were expected to be supplied by gifts. The library was to be open on five days a week for a total of eighteen hours, and a part-time librarian was appointed at £130 per annum.[2] By 1927–28 the differential rating system was in use in at least a dozen English counties. The recently inaugurated Lancashire County service had already reached agreements for the establishment of branches on this basis in eleven urban areas; and the scheme was also popular in Cheshire, the West Riding, Durham, and Kent.[3]

Some rural counties were content with a less formal arrangement under which, without a special rate, the local council undertook to provide accommodation, heating, lighting, a team of voluntary helpers, and a management committee. By 1924 Buckinghamshire had created branches on this basis in eight urban areas, and Wiltshire had a comparable record.[4] Kent adopted this plan for Sandgate and Sheerness.[5]

In Scotland, too, where there was no legal provision for a differential rate, Renfrewshire secured the help of local councils in the establishment of branches in the larger centres of population.[6] The Midlothian librarian, Alfred Ogilvie, rejected this kind of makeshift arrangement, and boldly pleaded for direct county provision to the populous areas under section 5 of the 1918 Education Act. His library authority accepted the argument, and in 1925, with the help of a special £300 grant from the Carnegie Trust, he was able to open his first urban branch at Musselburgh, which with 18 000 inhabitants was the most populous centre in the county area. It had accommodation for 4000 volumes and was intended to be open on three hours a week, but the public demand was so overwhelming that from January, 1926, the branch had to be put on a full-time basis.[7]

Musselburgh has the distinction of being the first purpose-built county branch in Great Britain, but it was, of course, on an exceedingly modest scale. "It had been proposed," explains Ogilvie, "to erect a small dwelling-house for the caretaker of the principal school of the burgh, and, killing two birds with one stone, we planned a composite building which would house a

[1] Carnegie U.K. Trust, *Ninth Annual Report, 1922*, pp. 37–38; *Twelfth Annual Report, 1925*, pp. 23–24; information from Mr. H. D. Budge, County Librarian of Warwickshire.

[2] *County Libraries Reports, 1925*, pp. 86–89.

[3] *County Libraries Reports, 1927–28*, pp. 17–19; *Kenyon Report*, p. 113; for the Lancashire arrangements see *County Libraries Reports, 1926–27*, pp. 37–38.

[4] *County Libraries Reports, 1924*, pp. 14–15; *County Library Conference Proceedings, 1924*, pp. 43–44.

[5] *County Libraries Reports, 1925*, p. 34.

[6] *Op. cit.*, p. 18.

[7] *County Library Conference Proceedings, 1924*, pp. 46–50; *County Libraries Reports, 1925*, p. 58; *County Library Conference Proceedings, 1926*, pp. 70–74.

small library on the ground floor and provide the dwelling-house on the upper."[1]

The first building erected exclusively for the purposes of a county branch library appears to have been that opened at Ashford in Kent in 1927. This was built under a differential rate agreement between the county and the urban district. The county agreed to provide and maintain a collection of books, periodically changed, initially at the rate of about one book per ten of the population; while the urban district agreed to an additional rate to cover the cost of accommodation, the formation of a reference library and newsroom and if thought fit permanent lending stock, and the salary of a librarian. The management of the library was in the hands of a sub-committee of the urban district council with two representatives from the county. A similar agreement was reached with Broadstairs.[2]

Of course many populous areas, and indeed some rural parishes, were already independent library authorities, and the relationship between these and the new county libraries presented special problems. Those authorities which had never exercised their powers, or had ceased to exercise them, fell automatically under county jurisdiction, and a few others voluntarily surrendered their powers,[3] but on the whole there was at this stage little disposition to give up the advantage of a permanent local collection, however inadequate, in favour of the still scanty and spasmodic provision made by the counties. In Scotland, however, there were a number of special arrangements. In Caithness, from the commencement of the county service in 1920, a close relationship was, as we have seen, established with the existing libraries at Wick and Thurso.[4] In Midlothian the county in 1921 took over responsibility for the lending department of the library at Bonnyrigg. In Kirkcudbrightshire the Castle Douglas burgh library became the county headquarters, the burgh receiving free service in return for the maintenance of the building.[5]

Elsewhere the majority of the independent libraries continued on their way without any attempt to develop a special relationship with the county, but there were many instances of assistance by the larger urban libraries to the nascent county service, and as time went on an increasing number of small libraries found it advantageous to supplement their stock from county resources. The *County Libraries Reports* for 1926–27 list five county towns—Gloucester, Hertford, Leicester, Norwich, and Ipswich—which were lending books on a limited scale to their respective county libraries; and nine smaller urban libraries, among many, which were borrowing from their county libraries.[6] The largest operation of this latter kind was in Middlesex, where the boroughs

---

[1] *County Library Conference Proceedings, 1926*, p. 72.

[2] *County Libraries Reports, 1925*, pp. xix, 34; *County Libraries Reports, 1927–28*, p. 19.

[3] The confusing negotiations on these matters are documented in the Public Record Office (Further Education—Public Library Files, 1919–1935 [Ed. 64]). The earliest urban authorities to surrender library powers to the county seem to have been Audenshaw in Lancashire in 1926 and Bridgend in Glamorganshire in 1927 (the Bridgend agreement was negotiated in 1926 but did not take effect till the following year).

[4] See above, p. 219.

[5] Carnegie U.K. Trust and Scottish Library Association, *Proceedings of the Scottish Library Conference . . . 1931* [Dunfermline 1931], pp. 15, 21.

[6] *County Libraries Reports, 1926–27*, pp. 39–43.

of Hounslow and Hanwell were each borrowing from the county 1000 volumes a year at a charge of £50.[1] This plan, which provided also for the borrowing of non-fiction books by the county for the use of individual readers, was widely imitated elsewhere.[2]

The Mitchell Report of 1923 argued strongly for co-operation,[3] so that arrangements of this kind had the warm support of the Carnegie Trustees, and sometimes in the initial stages a measure of financial assistance. The Trustees were particularly delighted with the comprehensive scheme of co-operation developed in Leicestershire between 1923 and 1926. The headquarters of the county library were at this time at Loughborough College, and two members of the staff there, William Birrell and G. K. Grierson, voluntarily shared the duties of county librarian (a full-time appointment was not made until 1927). The chief features of the plan Birrell and Grierson worked out were:

(a) Leicester City Library supplied books needed by students in the county area, calling on help from the Central Library for Students. The charge for this service was £7.10s. per annum plus 2d. per volume. The City Library also lent to the County Library 1000 volumes a year for use in seven villages near Leicester, at a charge of £50 per annum.

(b) The County Library exchanged about 500 volumes twice a year with Loughborough Borough Library.

(c) The County Library supplied or assisted the six smaller independent libraries in the county, i.e. the parish libraries of Bottesford, Ibstock, and Shepshed, and the urban district libraries of Hinckley, Melton Mowbray, and Oadby.

Loughborough College and the Mining Institute at Coalville were also brought into the scheme, and there were various useful arrangements about interavailability of tickets.[4]

The *County Libraries Reports* produced by the Carnegie Trustees for 1926–27 show that at that date there were in all 84 county library authorities— 43 in England, 9 in Wales, and 32 in Scotland. Returns from 80 of these authorities showed a total circulating bookstock of 1 326 000 (about 16 500 volumes per authority), besides in some cases small stationary stocks. The largest stocks were those held by Middlesex (83 000 volumes) and Kent

---

[1] For the Hounslow scheme, begun in 1924, see *County Library Conference Proceedings, 1924,* pp. 97–99; for that at Hanwell, begun in the following year, see *County Libraries Reports, 1925,* p. 37.

[2] Other counties mentioned in the reports of this period as providing a service to the smaller independent libraries are Buckinghamshire, Cheshire, Cumberland, Lancashire, Leicestershire, Norfolk, Denbighshire, Aberdeenshire, Angus and Kincardineshire, Dumfriesshire, and Fife. In Denbighshire, the town of Denbigh, acting on the advice of the county, adopted the Acts in 1922 and levied its own rate in order to pay the county for providing a library service—*County Library Conference Proceedings, 1926,* pp. 10–11.

[3] Carnegie U.K. Trustees, *A Report on the Public Library System of Great Britain and Ireland (1921–1923)* (Dunfermline 1924), pp. 11–21.

[4] *County Libraries Reports, 1925,* p. 70; Carnegie U.K. Trust, *Twelfth Annual Report, 1925,* p. 26; *County Library Conference Proceedings, 1926,* pp. 16–20. Bottesford, by prior arrangement, drew book supplies from Grantham—see below, App. III. For an attempt at a comprehensive scheme for Cornwall see the Trust's *Fourteenth Annual Report, 1927,* pp. 16–17.

(68 000 volumes). Cardiganshire was unusual in having 16 000 volumes in stationary collections compared with only 10 000 in its circulating stock. The number of centres served was 10 342, and the average rate .285d.[1]

It is interesting to set alongside these figures a statement prepared by the Trustees in 1926 of the main defects of the county service as they then saw it. These were: inadequate stocks (almost universal); inadequate staff (common); poor headquarters accommodation (not infrequent); lack of service to populous areas; lack of co-operation with municipal libraries; inadequate provision for students; undue emphasis on provision for children; inadequate status of the librarian and his committee.[2]

[1] Figures calculated from *County Libraries Reports, 1926–27*, Appendix.
[2] *Op. cit.*, p. 7.

CHAPTER IX

The Mitchell and Kenyon Reports

General Progress of the Non-County Libraries

The political and economic uncertainties that overshadowed the nascent county libraries inevitably had their impact also on the non-county libraries, and progress during these years was exceedingly slow. The three remaining metropolitan boroughs which had not yet commenced service now came into line—Paddington in 1920, Bethnal Green in 1922, and St. Marylebone in 1923—but Paddington, which had adopted solely to avoid a takeover by the London County Council, provided only a minimum service until 1930.[1] The pattern of county borough provision was not completed until 1927, when Hastings adopted the Acts in order to levy a rate for the maintenance of the library at the Brassey Institute (hitherto maintained from general borough funds).[2]

Other communities of more than 20 000 population which commenced service at this period were the municipal boroughs of High Wycombe (1920), Tunbridge Wells (1921), Margate (1923), Bexhill and Guildford (1924), and Bridlington (1926), and the urban district of Cannock (1925). Guildford, like Paddington, adopted to avoid a takeover, and for many years did no more than maintain a small reference library in the local mechanics' institute, leaving the institute to provide a lending library service.[3] A score of smaller places also adopted for various reasons, e.g. to provide rate support for an existing library, as at Letchworth;[4] or to pay for an improved county service, as at Denbigh;[5] or on the other hand to avoid county taxation, as initially at Bottesford.[6] Developments such as these, however, interesting as they are, seem merely the dotting of i's and crossing of t's when we compare them with the developments of pre-war years.

It might be supposed that in the established libraries, following the removal of the rate limit, progress would be rapid, but this was not so. Most libraries were so accustomed to their fetters that they found it difficult to strike them off, and even where the rate was raised the increase was generally swallowed up in higher prices, especially in the immediate post-war years. By 1924 the overall price index had fallen back to 139 compared with 251 in

---

[1] A. C. Jones, *Paddington Public Libraries: a Short History* (1965), pp. 8–10.

[2] See above, p. 133.

[3] Information from Miss M. D. Liggett, Borough Librarian. A full library service was not provided until 1942.

[4] Letchworth National Library Week Committee, *Letchworth: a Town built on a Book* (Letchworth 1966), p. 10.

[5] See above, p. 230, note.

[6] Information from Mr. G. E. Smith, Leicester County Librarian. As we have seen (above p. 230) Bottesford later accepted county assistance, and in 1929 it surrendered its independent powers.

1920 and 85 before the war,[1] but 333 out of 482 library authorities in England and Wales were still levying a rate of 2d. or less, and 169 less than 1d.[2] Savage counted the whole period 1915 to 1930 as "our black period":

> "From 1914 Government raked up all our money to wage war, prices rose steeply, our income was slashed. By the time the relief Act was passed in 1919 all town libraries had dirty leavings of bookstocks in their lending rooms. Stores were choked with books to bind or replace. Buildings were in shabby disrepair, some hardly weather-tight. Librarians, never without gold coins in their pockets in 1914, were near the bread-and-soup line. And the long-awaited relief did not come at once; instead, ever-mounting prices, the brutal Geddes axe . . . . About 1926 the outlook became rather brighter. After a rude check when the Government muddled the national finances in 1931, we had a little summer of prosperity before 1939."[3]

This situation is reflected in the record of library building as given in the annual reports of the Carnegie Trust. In spite of many long-standing promises, only two Carnegie libraries were completed during the years 1918–23. One of these was at Barrow, and represented the completion of work begun in the early years of the war; the other was at Bethnal Green, and was a conversion from a disused lunatic asylum. Both were completed in 1922.[4] In that year the Trust announced that promises not claimed by the end of 1925 would lapse, and that meantime no new claims for building grants would be considered.[5] With this stimulus, and with a general easing of the economic position, the laggard authorities began to bestir themselves. Three new Carnegie libraries were opened in 1924, and two in 1925, and by the close of the latter year a dozen more libraries had either begun building or secured approval for their plans. Most of these were built within the next two years, but a few were delayed by site difficulties and the like, and the last, the central library at Merthyr Tydfil, was not opened till 1935.[6]

The Carnegie trustees had by 1925 reached the firm conclusion that further grants in respect of buildings were both unnecessary and unwise—unnecessary because the cost could now be charged to the rates, and unwise because there were so many cases in which the cost of maintaining buildings was absorbing an undue proportion of library income. Grants towards the extinction of

---

[1] B. R. Mitchell and P. Deane, *Abstract of British Historical Statistics* (Cambridge 1962), pp. 474–475.

[2] *Kenyon Report*, p. 256.

[3] E. A. Savage, *A Librarian's Memories, Portraits and Reflections* (1952), p. 73. The Geddes here referred to is Sir Eric Geddes, chairman of a committee which in 1922 recommended drastic reductions in public spending. The recommendations were in large measure implemented by Lloyd George's government.

[4] Carnegie U.K. Trust, *Ninth Annual Report, 1922*, p. 10.

[5] *Op. cit.*, p. 11.

[6] Major commitments by the Trust were in respect of central libraries at Ipswich (opened 1924), Gateshead (1926), York (1927), Burnley (1930) and Exeter (1930), but substantial grants were also made for branch developments at Leeds and Nottingham. The only substantial grants outside England were to Airdrie (1925), and Llanelli (1926). Negotiations for a Carnegie grant in aid of a new central library at Huddersfield eventually broke down, and this and four other intended grants lapsed.

building loan charges were brought to an end at the same time, the last payment under this heading being to Leamington in 1926.[1]

The new Carnegie policy was to make grants not for bricks and mortar but for books, and of this we shall have more to say shortly. In the meantime we may note that, although the final Carnegie building grants marked the start of what was to prove a notable era in library building, the position in 1927 was still very uneven, with some libraries, such as Battersea, Gateshead and Ipswich, enjoying the luxury of splendid new buildings, while others languished in Victorian accommodation which was now becoming increasingly congested. At Manchester the wooden huts temporarily assigned to the central library in 1912 were still in use.[2]

Comparative Statistics

For a comparative study of the non-county libraries during these years we can turn to the two major reports of the period—the Mitchell Report of 1924 and the Kenyon Report of 1927. The Mitchell Report was prepared for the Carnegie Trust by its secretary, Lieut. Colonel J. M. Mitchell. Designed as a sequel to the Adams Report, it covered the whole of the United Kingdom and focussed attention particularly on the development of the new county service and on problems of library co-ordination. An appendix gave valuable statistical tables.[3] The Kenyon Report was prepared by a Departmental Committee appointed by the Board of Education in 1924, its terms of reference being:

> "to enquire into the adequacy of the library provision already made under the Public Libraries Acts, and the means of extending and completing such provision throughout England and Wales . . ."

The Committee's chairman was Sir Frederic Kenyon, Director and Principal Librarian of the British Museum, its secretary was C. O. G. Douie of the Board, and its members included, besides officials: John Ballinger, Librarian of the National Library of Wales; S. A. Pitt, City Librarian of Glasgow; Frank Pacy, Honorary Secretary of the Library Association and City Librarian of Westminster; Albert Mansbridge, founder of the Workers' Educational Association and of the Central Library for Students; J. M. Mitchell of the Carnegie Trust; E. Salter Davies, Director of Education for Kent; and Lady Mabel Smith, a West Riding County Councillor. The Committee's report provides a very comprehensive and well documented survey of the library service in England and Wales, and though its recommendations were

---

[1] Carnegie U.K. Trust, *Twelfth Annual Report, 1925*, p. 20; *Thirteenth Annual Report, 1926*, p. 17. Building loan grants, introduced in 1915 to assist libraries which had incurred loans before Carnegie building grants became available, were never an important feature of the Trust's work. Cf. above, pp. 118–119.

[2] Cf. above, p. 139.

[3] J. M. Mitchell, *The Public Library System of Great Britain and Ireland, 1921–23: a Report prepared for the Carnegie United Kingdom Trustees* (Dunfermline 1924). A valuable analysis of the figures in the Report, by Captain R. Wright, County Librarian of Middlesex, is printed in *County Library Conference Proceedings, 1924*, pp. 83–97.

not followed by legislation they had a considerable impact upon future library development.[1]

The Kenyon Report noted with satisfaction that 96.3 per cent of the population of England and Wales were now within the area of library authorities, but it noted also that the coverage was by no means uniform. In the county areas, which accounted for one-third of the total population, half the inhabitants were still without a library service; 49 non-county areas had adopted the Acts but were apparently providing no service; and the quality of the service in the remaining non-county areas varied greatly.

When the statistics of these non-county libraries (the urban libraries as the Kenyon Report calls them) are presented in relation to the populations served, they show more uniformity than might be expected. The great majority of libraries, serving populations between 20 000 and 50 000, were spending 10d.–1s. per head per annum, held a stock of about 50 volumes per 100 of population and had 10 or 11 borrowers per 100. The major variations in pattern were at the upper end of the scale, where the three authorities serving populations over 500 000 returned an average expenditure per head of 1s. 6d., an average bookstock of 62 per 100 of population, and 12.5 borrowers per 100. At the other end of the scale authorities serving populations under 20 000 showed lower than average figures for expenditure and number of borrowers, but bookstocks in relation to population tended to be larger. The implications for the quality of the bookstock in these libraries are even more pointed when we note that these small authorities were spending a relatively large amount on newspapers and periodicals.[2]

These figures, of course, are all averages based on size of population. If we look at the situation in more detail we see that by this date (1923–24) three English libraries, Manchester, Birmingham and Liverpool, were quite outstanding. Manchester, with a total bookstock of 570 000, 78 volumes per 100 of population, 14.7 borrowers per 100 of population, a rate of 2.6d., and an annual expenditure of 1s. 11d. per head, led the way in every respect; Birmingham came second, and Liverpool third. In all Great Britain only Glasgow, with a bookstock at this time of over 580 000, exceeded these three.

If we list all the libraries with bookstocks of 100 000 or more we find that the relationship of stocks to population is by no means as regular as the averages cited above would suggest (see following page).

This list of the larger libraries includes many old friends, but there are also many newcomers, particularly from among the London boroughs. The presence of Brighton, too, is something of a surprise: it had been building up its stocks steadily since 1913–14, when the Adams Report recorded a total of 82 000 volumes.[3] For size of stock in relation to population, however,

---

[1] Board of Education, Public Libraries Committee, *Report on Public Libraries in England and Wales*, Cmd. 2868 (1927). It should be noted that the statistics in the Report refer mainly to the year 1923–24.

[2] *Kenyon Report*, pp. 264–265. J. Roe, *The Public Library in Wales* (unpublished M. A. thesis, Belfast University 1970), p. 116, points out that 84 per cent of Welsh non-county libraries at this time were serving populations under 20 000, and 65 per cent populations under 10 000.

[3] *Adams Report* (1919), pp. 47–48.

Authority	Bookstock (000s)	Population (000s)	Volumes per 100 population
Manchester	570	730	78.0
Birmingham	550	919	59.9
Liverpool	411	803	51.1
Leeds	359	458	78.3
Cardiff	301	200	150.4
Bradford	234	286	81.9
Bristol	209	377	55.4
City of London	206	364	56.6
Newcastle upon Tyne	197	275	71.7
Nottingham	164	263	62.3
Hull	158	287	54.8
Lambeth	149	303	49.1
Wandsworth	147	328	44.7
Sheffield	143	491	29.2
Bolton	133	179	74.2
Brighton	117	142	82.0
Southwark	112	184	60.5
Westminster	110	142	77.8
Islington	107	331	32.4
Croydon	104	191	54.3[1]
Scottish libraries falling within this group are:			
Glasgow	581	1,034	56.2
Dundee	195	168	116.1
Edinburgh	184	420	43.8[2]

Cardiff is seen to be quite outstanding. Others which are well above the average are Leeds, Newcastle upon Tyne, Bolton and Westminster. Sheffield's poor showing is due in part to the fact that it was still in the throes of a massive reorganization begun by R. J. Gordon in 1921.[3]

The weaker libraries among those serving populations of 100 000 or more were, in addition to Sheffield: Camberwell (26.3 volumes per 100 population), St. Marylebone (newly opened—19.4 volumes), St. Pancras (14.8 volumes) and bottom of the list Paddington (9.9 volumes) which as we have seen was not really trying.[4] In Scotland there were no other libraries serving populations of this size.

[1] *Kenyon Report*, pp. 266 sqq. The City of London figures are based on the day population for 1911—see Kenyon p. 301 note (p).

[2] Figures of stock at Dundee and Edinburgh kindly supplied by the respective librarians. Those for Dundee show stock at 31 July, 1924; those for Edinburgh are for 1923. The former Edinburgh librarian, Mr. C. S. Minto, who joined the staff in that year (the year after the appointment of E. A. Savage) tells me that owing to years of poverty the library service was at a very low ebb, and this is borne out by the figures. The figures for Glasgow are from *L.Y.B. 1923–24*, and may understate the position.

[3] See below, pp. 284–289.

[4] See above, p. 154.

The Problem of the Small Authorities

The most depressing feature of the non-county library situation was the large number of small authorities, many of them so small as to be quite uneconomic. Both the Mitchell and the Kenyon Reports stress this, and draw attention to the heroic but unavailing efforts of some such authorities to provide an adequate service. Richard Wright, in his analysis of the Mitchell figures, pointed out that only 23 libraries out of the 491 making returns had a stock of over 100 000 volumes (these are the 23 we have just listed), and that 123 had a stock of less than 5000 volumes. Only 19 authorities had an income of £2000 or more for expenditure on books, and 219 had less than £100.[1]

Both reports make special mention of the group of four small parish authorities in the county of Buckinghamshire: East and Botolph Claydon, Middle Claydon, Steeple Claydon, and Oakley. The Kenyon Report's figures for these authorities are as follows:

Steeple Claydon: population 741, bookstock 4761 (642.5 vols. per 100); rate 2.5d. (2s. 8d. per head); expenditure on books nil, on newspapers and periodicals £6, on wages and salaries £24.

East and Botolph Claydon: population 311, bookstock 3790 (1218.6 vols. per 100); rate 3d. (2s. 7d. per head); total expenditure £40 (no details).

Middle Claydon: population 195, bookstock 4472 (2293.3 vols. per 100); rate 1d.; expenditure on books £3, on newspapers and periodicals nil, on wages and salaries £6.

Oakley: population 327, bookstock 680 (208 vols. per 100); rate 1d. (5d. per head); expenditure on books, newspapers and periodicals nil, on wages and salaries £4.

Mitchell pointed out how much better off these libraries would be if they contributed to the Buckinghamshire County rate (at that time about $\frac{1}{10}$d.) and reinforced their stock by loan collections changed three or four times a year; and by the time the Kenyon Report was published an arrangement of this kind had in fact been made.[2]

This was, of course, an extreme example, but there were many others. The Kenyon Committee took the view that in general a community of less than 20 000 population could not support an efficient library, and recommended that existing authorities in this group, if they did not choose to surrender their powers to the county, should enter into co-operative arrangements either with the county or with one of the larger urban libraries. It also recommended that the counties be at once established as library authorities for any areas for which the Acts had still not been adopted (excepting only the county borough of Hastings, which as we have seen adopted in the year the Report was published).[3]

Mitchell and Kenyon both recognized that the final goal must be a national system. As the Kenyon Report put it:

[1] *County Library Conference Proceedings, 1924*, pp. 84–86.
[2] *Mitchell Report*, pp. 13–15; *Kenyon Report*, pp. 34, 286–287; *County Libraries Reports, 1925*, p. 4.
[3] *Kenyon Report*, pp. 30–33, 203–204.

"Co-operation, while a vital necessity to small towns and villages, is desirable throughout the library service, even in the largest centres of population. A fully adequate service is clearly not within the reach of any locality, even the greatest city, entirely out of its own resources."[1]

The Mitchell Report thought primarily in terms of voluntary co-operation on a county basis,[2] and this idea found much favour, as might be expected, at the County Libraries Conference of 1924, where Richard Wright of Middlesex and F. N. Cook of the West Riding both propounded schemes on these lines. Wright thought that in general only communities with populations of 40 000 and more had the resources to provide adequate bookstocks.[3] At the same conference, however, Berwick Sayers, Librarian of Croydon, emphasized the need to bring the resources of the great urban libraries into play to reinforce and improve the service available from the counties to villages and small towns.[4] The Kenyon Report envisaged a system of which the basis consisted of

"(i) voluntary co-operation, on financial terms varying according to the circumstances, between neighbouring libraries, whether they be county borough, municipal borough, urban district or county;
"(ii) the grouping of public libraries round regional centres, which will generally be the great urban libraries."[5]

This second proposal reflects the weakness of the county library service at this time: only in areas such as Dorset and Cornwall, where there was no pre-eminent urban library, was it thought possible that the county library could be the regional centre.[6]

To enter into the details of these schemes would not be specially profitable, but they did throw up various proposals, such as union catalogues and co-operative cataloguing, to which we shall make reference later.[7] All parties were agreed that the system must be a national one, with the Central Library for Students and its counterpart the Scottish Central Library serving as lending libraries of last resort. The Kenyon Report paid particular attention to this aspect of the matter, and this again is a matter to which we shall have occasion to return.[8]

On one point concerning co-operation the Kenyon Committee had to record a disagreement. This was the problem of the 28 metropolitan boroughs. The Committee, recognizing the wide variations in the quality of the service provided, proposed "fraternal co-operation", including a union catalogue, free interlending, and interchangeability of borrowers' tickets. Frank Pacy, speaking not only as Honorary Secretary of the Library Association but perhaps even more as City Librarian of Westminster, took the view that in the light of past history the possibility of any kind of effective co-operation was exceedingly remote. In a minority report he pointed out that not one of the

[1] Op. cit., p. 34.
[2] Mitchell Report, p. 42.
[3] County Library Conference Proceedings, 1924, pp. 90–99, 105–107.
[4] Op. cit., pp. 100–104.
[5] Kenyon Report, p. 151.   [6] Op. cit., p. 155.
[7] See below, pp. 320–323.   [8] See below, pp. 318–320.

boroughs had so far provided an adequate reference library, and that "the greatest commercial city in the world" was "virtually unprovided with special commercial and technical libraries". He therefore recommended the creation of a single metropolitan library authority, which would organize the service on the basis of six or eight districts.[1]

Lending Libraries

The most popular departments in all libraries were the lending library and the reading room. All except the smallest libraries commonly laid claim also to a reference department, and a library of any size would usually have also a separate children's department or departments, but it was the lending library and the reading room which were the backbone of the service.

Of the lending library the Kenyon Report remarks that "In most cases it provides the only point of contact between the library and the public, and by it the service is usually judged."[2] By this time a substantial majority of libraries in England and Wales had introduced the open access system,[3] and with the encouragement of the Carnegie Trust this had become standard in new and reconstructed buildings. "It is our view", declared the Kenyon Report judicially, "that the advantages of free access so far outweigh any disadvantage arising from extra wear and tear or loss by theft that the system should be universally adopted."[4] In Scotland, however, progress in this respect was still slow: at the beginning of the 'twenties open access was still exceptional.[5]

Sample figures compiled by the Kenyon Committee showed that fiction accounted for 37 per cent of the stock of lending libraries, and 78 per cent of the issues. The Committee took no exception to this: the question of the amount of fiction read, it commented, was "a matter of no particular moment." It did, however, draw attention to the librarian's need for guidance in the choice of books, and commended the preparation of lists of the type issued by the American Library Association and the New York State Library.[6] As far as the choice of fiction was concerned, it recommended the librarian not to be in too much of a hurry to buy. A few months' delay would help to sort out the wheat from the chaff, and in the meantime, "The needs of those who require the newest books while they are new are sufficiently catered for by the subscription libraries."[7] The notion that public libraries were for the poor died hard.

In this connection the Committee mentions the subscription libraries which, as we have seen, were organized in association with some public libraries. It does not specifically condemn this practice, but points out that it renders library premises liable to taxation.[8] The persistence of such arrangements reflects the continuing shortage of books. This particularly affected the

---

[1] *Kenyon Report*, pp. 154, 215–216.

[2] *Op.cit.*, p. 62.

[3] *Op. cit.*, p. 330.

[4] *Op. cit.*, p. 69.

[5] W. R. Aitken, *A History of the Public Library Movement in Scotland to 1955* (Glasgow 1971), p. 193.

[6] *Kenyon Report*, pp. 63, 194–196.

[7] *Op. cit.*, pp. 63–64.   [8] *Op. cit.*, p. 71.

small libraries—"No books have been bought since the War" was, according to the Mitchell Report, a common complaint.[1] Elsewhere the position was not usually quite so desperate, but by modern standards stocks were almost everywhere quite insufficient. Of Lincoln, where the splendid Carnegie library opened in 1914 housed ten years later some 25 000 volumes, we are told:

> "In those days books had to last a very long time. The junior members of the staff had their appointed days for repairing, for only when no amateur repair was possible was a book sent to the binders. Once a week a trip was made to Ruddocks' back door for sixpennyworth of bookbinders' paste and with the aid of this and many dusters to tie up the completed repairs until they had dried the stock was kept on the move."[2]

One way in which the Kenyon Committee tried to help was by pressing for an agreement between libraries and booksellers "whereby some concession could be allowed to libraries or groups of libraries making purchases exceeding some fixed amount in the year." This recommendation had reference to a long-standing controversy. In the nineteenth century booksellers were accustomed to offer libraries substantial discounts on the published prices, commonly of the order of 25 per cent. The net book agreement which came into force in 1900 put a stop to all this by stipulating that any book sold by the publishers as *net* could be resold only at the full price.

Repeated efforts by the Library Association in the early years of the century failed to secure any modification of this ruling, and the question lay dormant until it was revived in 1925, apparently at the initiative of the Kenyon Committee. A conference held in that year between representatives of the Library Association on the one hand and the Publishers' and Booksellers' Associations on the other still failed to resolve the problem, but eventually in 1929 it was agreed that public libraries spending £500 a year or more on books should be entitled to a 10 per cent discount, and those spending between £100 and £500 a year to a 5 per cent discount. To hard-pressed libraries this "library licence agreement" was a great boon.[3]

The book grants made by the Carnegie Trust from 1926 onwards were also of great assistance. A sum of £8000 a year for five years was allocated for this purpose, and by the end of 1927 grants had been made to forty libraries in Great Britain. Most of them were in England, but the list also included Dumfries, Elgin, Falkirk, and Peterhead in Scotland, and Newport in Monmouthshire. Usually the grants were of a few hundred pounds spread over three years, but grants of £1000 or more were made to Gateshead, Halifax, Middlesbrough, and Newport. Always conditions were laid down—reorganization, open access, increase in the book fund, collaboration with the county library—designed to bring the library concerned to a higher level of efficiency, and the results were often reflected, e.g. at Chesterfield, Stretford, King's Lynn, and Hereford, in a dramatic increase in issues.[4]

---

[1] *Mitchell Report*, pp. 12–13.

[2] *Lincoln City Libraries, 1914–1964* [Lincoln 1964], p. 12.

[3] *Kenyon Report*, pp. 201–202; J. Minto, *A History of the Public Library Movement* (1932), pp. 264–271. In 1932 the 10% discount was extended to purchases of £100 a year or more.

[4] Carnegie U.K. Trust, *Thirteenth Annual Report, 1926*, pp. 14–16; *Fourteenth Annual Report, 1927*, pp. 18–20.

The lending of music scores and of sets of plays was spreading rapidly at this time. Kenyon counts 157 out of 401 libraries with music collections and 71 with drama collections, and draws attention specially to the remarkable revival of interest in the drama in the last few years. The new county libraries, as we have noted, found themselves faced with the same demands. Kenyon points out that music scores present special problems of binding, classification and cataloguing, and argues that the provision of multiple copies both of music scores and of plays can hardly be satisfactorily undertaken without co-operation and the assistance of some kind of central library.[1]

The Kenyon Report also brought under review the special problem of the provision of books for the blind. This problem was also engaging the sympathetic consideration of the Carnegie Trust, which in 1915 gave £12 000 to purchase and equip premises for the National Library for the Blind at Westminster, and in 1925 gave a further £15 000 towards the enlargement of the building. The library now had 100 000 volumes and 10 000 readers, and was co-operating with over 100 public libraries. Only 41 public libraries (mostly large libraries) had their own special collections, and the Kenyon Report suggested that "any new scheme would probably best take the form of a subscription to the National Library and the delivery of books from the National Library direct to the blind reader or to the institution for the blind which the blind reader attends". This confirmed the trend we have already noted.[2]

Reading Rooms

The reading room or reading rooms (in some cases there were separate rooms for newspapers and periodicals) continued to absorb an inordinate proportion of library space and financial resources. Both Mitchell and Kenyon commented adversely on this. Mitchell noted that the reading room often occupied one-quarter to one-third of the total floor space, and that 148 out of 424 libraries in Great Britain spent more on newspapers and periodicals than on books. Kenyon produced tables showing that the smaller the library the larger was the amount, proportionately, spent on newspapers and periodicals; and that some libraries were devoting more than one-fifth of their total income to this purpose.[3] Here again Lincoln provides an apt reminiscence:

"In 1923 the staff consisted of the Librarian, six girls, a caretaker and an old age pensioner with a long white beard who looked after the newsroom in the afternoon. The 'twenties saw the hey-day of newsrooms and in its prime the Lincoln one was a fine room which then extended to the south end of the building. The Carnegie tablet was on the south wall and users of the room were presided over by portraits of city fathers and other local worthies. The newsroom was always

---

[1] *Kenyon Report*, pp. 140–141, 330.
[2] Carnegie U.K. Trust, *Twelfth Annual Report, 1925*, p. 36; *Kenyon Report*, pp. 141–144. Glasgow, however, had and still has special reading rooms for the blind at its Townhead and Elder Park branches. Provision at the former branch, which was close to the Blind Asylum, dated from 1910: at Elder Park provision began in 1925—information from Mr. C. W. Black, City Librarian.
[3] *Mitchell Report*, pp. 30–33; *Kenyon Report*, pp. 262, 264–265.

full, papers and magazines were worn to shreds and many a tramp had a nice nap on a cold day."[1]

Progressive librarians and library committees were now inclined to doubt the wisdom of such large expenditure on what was, in Mitchell's words, "often little more than a kind of public club-room or lounge",[2] and in some new or reconstructed libraries reading room space was either eliminated or drastically reduced.[3] In general, however, public demand prevented developments of this kind, and the Kenyon Report came down in favour of retaining reading room provision so long as the cost of newspapers and periodicals did not exceed about 5 per cent of total expenditure.[4]

Reference Libraries

Except in the largest libraries, the reference department tended to be weak and unsatisfactory—often, indeed, something of a white elephant. The Kenyon Report attributed this state of affairs to four main causes: (a) lack of funds; (b) lack of a systematic acquisitions policy; (c) lack of systematic classification and cataloguing; and (d) lack of suitably trained staff. All these came back in the end to the first—lack of money. The Committee suggested that the smaller libraries should concentrate mainly on quick reference works and literature of strictly local interest, relying for more specialized and costly works on the Central Library for Students and the regional libraries, urban or county, which the Committee wished to see established.[5] To assist in a systematic acquisitions policy, the Committee also proposed a central organization to provide annotated lists of new books for the guidance of librarians. It was hoped that this task might be undertaken by the Central Library for Students, and supported initially by Carnegie funds.[6]

In order to assist in the building up of these regional collections, the Committee urged the resumption of a more liberal policy in relation to the distribution of Government publications. In the nineteenth century, as we have seen, these had been freely available to public libraries on request, but in 1917, on grounds of economy, the free distribution had been ended, and the price to subscribers sharply increased. Under pressure from the Library Association, the Government at length agreed in 1924 to supply all Government publications at half price to public and university libraries, but this concession was largely nullified by the very large price increase which had already taken place. The Kenyon Committee recommended the renewal of free distribution to the Central Library and selected libraries—not more than about twenty in all—which would undertake to act as regional centres. Other public libraries

---

[1] *Lincoln City Libraries, 1914–1964* [Lincoln 1964], p. 12.

[2] *Mitchell Report*, p. 32.

[3] E.g. at Norwich (1920); Westminster (Great Smith Street 1922, and South Audley Street 1923–24); St. Marylebone (1923); and Liverpool, where in 1926 the reading room was removed to other premises to make way for a new central lending library. At Westminster the reading rooms had been closed during the war in the interests of economy.

[4] *Kenyon Report*, pp. 64–66.

[5] *Op. cit.*, pp. 60–62. Cf. above, p. 238.

[6] *Op. cit.*, pp. 194–196.

would also be able, at the discretion of the Stationery Office, to secure free copies of any such publications in which they were specially interested.[1]

In suggesting that the smaller reference libraries should concentrate in large measure on material of local interest, the Kenyon Report was striking a welcome note, for local collections were popular everywhere, and in the major libraries had now attained considerable dimensions. Gloucester in 1926 received a special grant of £600 from the Carnegie Trust towards the cost of publishing a special catalogue of its Gloucestershire Collection.[2] In the same year the work of the larger libraries in this field received a great stimulus when a number of them were designated by the Master of the Rolls as repositories for manorial documents.[3] This frequently led to the development of special record offices, either as part of the library service or as separate organisations.

Technical and Commercial Libraries

The larger libraries were now becoming increasingly aware of the need to make special provision for the needs of commerce and industry. Following the pioneer efforts by Glasgow, Liverpool and Leeds during the first World War, special Commercial Libraries were established at Birmingham, Dundee, Manchester, and Wolverhampton in 1919, and at Bristol in 1920. Manchester's Technical Library followed in 1922. At Leicester a former ladies' reading room was converted in 1919 into a Commercial and Technical Library; and at Coventry the combined commercial and technical section formed by E. A. Savage as early as 1915 became a separate department in 1920. Birmingham's Technical Library was created in 1924. The Kenyon Report, which deals with this new development at considerable length,[4] was able to record special industrial collections in 70 libraries, and special commercial collections in 46, but it is clear that in most cases these were not separately organized sectors of the library service.

The Kenyon Report did a useful service in distinguishing clearly between commercial libraries, serving the day-to-day needs of commerce and preferably situated at the commercial centre of the community, and technical libraries, which the Committee thought of as essentially scientific and technological. "A technical library," says the Report, "must necessarily have an organisation very different from that of a commercial library, and no advantage attaches to combining the two collections."[5] The Report also stresses the need for

---

[1] *Op. cit.*, pp. 196–201. The arrangement proposed was similar to that already adopted for Patent Office publications. See above, p. 75.

[2] Published 1928: see Carnegie U.K. Trust, *Thirteenth Annual Report, 1926*, pp. 16–17; *Fourteenth Annual Report, 1927*, pp. 23–24.

[3] Under the Law of Property Amendment Act of 1924. Mr. Roger Ellis, Secretary to the Historical MSS. Commission, informs me that 25 out of the 53 repositories recognized during the year 1925–29 were public libraries. They were: Birmingham, Camberwell (Minet), Cardiff, Carlisle, Colchester, Croydon, Derby, Exeter, Gateshead, Gloucester, Hereford, Hove, Ipswich, Lancaster, Leyton, Lincoln, Maidstone, Middlesbrough, Newport (Mon.), Norwich, Nottingham, Sheffield, Shrewsbury, Southend, and Walthamstow.

[4] *Kenyon Report*, pp. 127–140. Cf. J. P. Lamb, *Commercial and Technical Libraries* (1955), Ch. i.

[5] *Kenyon Report*, 130.

co-operation with the numerous specialist libraries outside the public library service, and draws attention to the creation in 1924 of ASLIB, the Association of Special Libraries and Information Bureaux. This body sought to bring into association not only the special collections in national and municipal libraries, but also the specialized libraries and information bureaux provided by industry and commerce, government departments, research associations and learned societies. It defined its objectives as "to consider, promote, and organise the systematic utilisation of informational and library services."[1]

Children's Libraries

The position regarding children's libraries at the outset of this period is well summarized by W. E. Doubleday, Librarian of Hampstead:

> "Today few, if any but the most impecunious of libraries, fail to make special provision of this kind. In many instances a distinct and separate portion of the library building is set aside for young people. Much too rarely there is a separate children's librarian, invariably (I think) a lady. Where separate rooms or buildings are not available, children's 'corners' or sections are provided. Sometimes special courses of lectures are arranged for children, and the local Education Authority is usually willing to regard visits there, with teachers, as official school attendances."[2]

The figures for 1923–24 furnished by the Kenyon Report enable us to give more precision to Doubleday's impressions, showing, as we might expect, that it was mainly the libraries in towns of more than 20 000 population which were able to provide separate children's departments. Altogether 151 library authorities were providing a total of 275 children's lending libraries, and 87 authorities were providing a total of 151 children's reading rooms.[3]

The most interesting development in work for children during these years was at Manchester, where from 1919 L. S. Jast was creating what he called "young people's rooms". In these rooms, supervised by specially chosen assistants, an attempt was made to get away from the schoolroom atmosphere that still lingered in most children's reading rooms. There were small tables, separate chairs, books in gaily coloured jackets in low bookcases, a few flowers and pictures. Lectures, talks and story readings added to the attractions. This pioneering work proved immensely popular, and by 1926 there were eleven of the new young people's rooms in operation. Their only serious drawback was that they were reading rooms only, books for borrowing being available in the adult lending library.[4]

The question who should provide school libraries was still not fully resolved. The Mitchell Report noted that library opinion was sharply divided on this issue, some librarians taking the view that provision for children of school age was none of their business. In general, however, the trend was

[1] Op. cit., pp. 131–132.
[2] Carnegie U.K. Trust, Seventh Annual Report, 1920, p. 52.
[3] Kenyon Report, pp. 47–48, 243.
[4] G. Rees, Libraries for Children (1924), p. 25; G. C. Paterson, A Short History of the Manchester Public Libraries, 1852–1948 (unpublished F.L.A. essay 1949), pp. 37–38; M. Barnes, "Children's Libraries in Manchester", in Manchester Review, Vol. XI (Winter 1966–67), pp. 83–85. Cf. Jast's comments in 1917, quoted above, p. 199.

towards co-operation, and many large towns now held special stocks from which collections of books were sent to local schools, the education authority making a substantial contribution towards the cost. In some cases the library committee and the education committee were the same, in others a joint committee had been established. There was in fact a movement towards the kind of co-operation introduced a quarter of a century earlier by Ballinger at Cardiff, and Mitchell prints detailed proposals along these lines submitted by the librarian of Atherton in Lancashire.[1]

The Kenyon Committee recorded 113 library authorities (again mostly the larger authorities) actively co-operating in the provision of school libraries, serving in all 1440 schools or school departments. Cardiff was still the outstanding authority in this respect, but others receiving honourable mention were Blackburn, Coventry, Halifax, Nottingham, Tottenham and Willesden. The report recommended that the education committee should be responsible for school libraries and for the cost of provision, but should seek the assistance of the library committee and the expert guidance of the librarian. Everything possible should be done to link the work in the school with that of the public library, and every library should provide a juvenile department for young people of eleven or twelve to sixteen or seventeen.[2]

Branch Development

Branch development was at a low ebb in the years immediately after the war, but like other library activities began to revive in the mid-'twenties, and became increasingly important as resources grew and population spread from the old town centres to the new suburban housing estates. In this matter, of course, different libraries had different needs, and were at different stages of growth, so that generalization is specially difficult. Neither Birmingham nor Manchester, for example, had an extensive building programme at this time, but this was because their branch system was already fully articulated before the war: the next phase of branch building, to meet the needs of outer suburbs, came in Birmingham in the years 1928–39, and in Manchester only after the second World War.[3] But Liverpool, which had lagged behind in branch development, began to make improved provision from 1923;[4] Nottingham, with assistance from Carnegie, embarked on a second round of branches in 1924; Leeds, also with Carnegie help, erected three new branches in 1926–27 (the first since 1904);[5] and Halifax, which had formerly relied heavily on delivery stations, secured its first purpose-built branch in 1926.[6]

At a humbler level Norwich established its first branch in the Old Lazar House in 1923;[7] four years later Lincoln established *its* first branch in a wooden hut that had formerly served as a rate-collector's office;[8] and in 1926–27

---

[1] *Mitchell Report*, pp. 42–46, 52. [2] *Kenyon Report*, pp. 45–47, 243.
[3] See below, p. 364.
[4] *Liverpool Public Libraries Centenary, 1850–1950* (Liverpool 1950).
[5] As a result of earlier development (see above, p. 50) Leeds had the largest number of branches in the country. See the comparative table (for 1923–24) in *Kenyon Report*, p. 244.
[6] *Halifax Reader*, Vol. 4, No. 1, July 1950, p. 3.
[7] P. Hepworth and M. Alexander, *City of Norwich Libraries* (Norwich 1957), p 26.
[8] *Lincoln City Libraries, 1914–1964* [Lincoln 1964], p. 6.

Rawtenstall, a small Lancashire authority with a scattered area to serve, created three small branches—two in schools and the other in a former Co-operative Society shop at Crawshawbooth, which was presented for the purpose together with the Society's own library.[1]

Purpose-built branch libraries were now tending to follow a fairly uniform pattern, with the lending library always as the central feature, flanked on one side by a reading room and on the other by a juvenile room. Nottingham's first new branch, at Bulwell in 1924, was fairly typical of this kind of layout, though in this case the reading room was divided to provide separate news and magazine rooms. Glasgow, the only Scottish library to make substantial new branch provision at this time, provides further examples, the plans of which may be seen in Appendix C of the Kenyon Report. The radiating stacks in the lending library at Bulwell, reflecting a continuing nervousness about open access, were very characteristic of the period.

Delivery stations were still in use, but not extensively outside Lancashire, which had more than fifty. Kenyon was prepared to approve of them only as a temporary expedient until such time as a full branch service became possible.[2] The Kenyon Report also mentions the travelling bookbox as the most economical form of distribution for areas unevenly or thinly populated, but it does not appear that this system was much used in urban areas except for schools.

Library Administration

Much library administration remained very old-fashioned, but in most large and medium-sized libraries more modern methods were gradually making headway as more and more trained librarians came into service. In classification and cataloguing, especially, there was a considerable improvement consequent upon the extension of open access which has already been noted.[3] For classification the Dewey system was now the established favourite, being employed in more than half the urban libraries of England and Wales making returns to the Kenyon Committee. Brown's subject classification, or some modification of it, came next in popularity, being in use in about 16 per cent of libraries, and the remaining one-third of libraries were using a miscellany of systems or non-systems which did not lend themselves readily to tabulation.

The Kenyon Report concerns itself chiefly with two classifications— Dewey and the Library of Congress. This latter, dating from the turn of the century, was an adaptation to the special needs of the Library of Congress of the earlier American scheme by C. A. Cutter.[4] There is no need here to enter into details about it, for although it proved attractive to university and other learned libraries it was never much in favour with public libraries. Kenyon suggested that either Dewey or the Library of Congress classification should be adopted as the basis for all libraries, but since at this time only three

---

[1] *Rawtenstall Public Library, 1906–1956* (Rawtenstall 1956).

[2] *Kenyon Report*, pp. 66–68, 296–297, 300–301. In his fourth edition (1931) of J. D. Brown's *Manual of Library Economy*, pp. 372–374, W. C. Berwick Sayers makes a distinction not made in earlier editions between "delivery stations" with no stationary stock and "deposit stations" carrying a small stock of books changed at frequent intervals. The establishment of deposit stations may reflect the influence of the county library.

[3] See above, p. 239.   [4] See above, p. 184, note.

public libraries were reported as using the latter, as against 180 using the former, the ultimate outcome was hardly in doubt.[1]

Reclassification meant catalogue revision, and many libraries found it convenient at this stage to change from the old printed dictionary catalogue to a card or sheaf catalogue. It is not without significance that in the Kenyon returns the number of libraries reporting the use of card and/or sheaf catalogues (185) was almost identical with the number reporting the use of the Dewey classification. It should be noted, however, that this still left a substantial number of libraries (146) where catalogues in book form were used in at least some departments.[2]

In large libraries this business of reclassification and recataloguing represented an immense labour. Birmingham is a case in point. Here, as we have seen, only a single branch had been converted to open access before 1919. After the war the work was taken in hand at once, and by 1926 only six of the sytem's twenty-two branches were still unconverted. The central lending library, which had 40 000 volumes shelved on wall presses 26 feet high, was tackled in 1923, and had to be closed for five months. These operations threw into relief the need for a thorough revision of classification and cataloguing. In 1922 the librarian, Walter Powell, reported sadly:

> "In the Reference Library the system of classification and the catalogue are both very antiquated. With the exception of four branches, all the lending libraries need classifying and recataloguing on modern lines. The position here is far worse than in the Reference Library, as there is no attempt at classification beyond 'main classes' which mean practically nothing. The lending libraries have unfortunately never been properly catalogued, the system adopted having no merit beyond cheapness in printing."

Apart from the books in the new commercial and technical libraries the reclassification of the reference library had to wait until after the second World War, but the reclassification of the lending libraries on the Dewey system, and their recataloguing on sheaf or on cards, were completed by 1930. A special team travelled from branch to branch to carry out this change.[3]

An example on a small scale of the kind of improvement that was going on at this time is provided by the small Lancashire industrial town of Swinton and Pendlebury, at that time an urban district with upwards of 30 000 inhabitants. For the first quarter of the century the public library facilities here were exceedingly sketchy, consisting of a reading room taken over in 1897 from the Pendlebury Institute, and a small collection of books in charge of the town hall caretaker which were made available for borrowing on two nights a week.

The appointment of a full-time librarian in 1926 was thus a revolutionary departure. F. I. Cowles, who held the post until his death twenty-two years

---

[1] *Kenyon Report*, pp. 191–193, 329. The three libraries reported as using the L.C. classification were Edinburgh, Cardiff and Wigan (reference library only). The present City Librarian of Cardiff, Mr. J. E. Thomas, tells me that the L.C. classification there never got beyond the experimental stage.

[2] *Op. cit.*, p. 329.

[3] *Notes on the History of the Birmingham Public Libraries, 1861–1961* (Birmingham 1962), pp. 11–12, 19–20; information from Mr. W. A. Taylor, City Librarian. Cf. above, p. 140.

later, was not a trained librarian, but he was an educated man and a fellow of a number of learned societies, and he at once set about the reorganization of the library on modern lines. During the years we are now reviewing he was only able to make a beginning, but by 1928 he had already established daily opening, a reference library, the Dewey classification, and the first *Bulletin* for library readers. The next few years were to see the process of modernization completed by the introduction of open access, a separate children's department, and the first branch.[1]

The most dramatic reorganization of this period, however, was at Sheffield. Here the almost simultaneous retirement, in 1920-21, of a librarian who had held office for twenty-seven years and a chairman of committee who had held office for nearly forty-six years opened the way to long overdue reform. R. J. Gordon was brought from Rochdale to be the new chief librarian, and T. W. Hand, Chief Librarian of Leeds, was asked to prepare a report on what needed to be done. He found the reference library, though small, in good order, and the local collection was also satisfactory, but in the lending libraries the bookstock was poor and the administration hopelessly inefficient:

> "The recording of issues was archaic and cumbrous; a curious system of fine receipts, called forfeits, involving a considerable waste of staff time, was in operation, and what little money was available was wasted by bibliographical incompetence both in book selection and binding. Thousands of books needed re-binding and many of those which had been bound had been chosen without reference to their condition or their suitability for further service. The buildings were revoltingly dirty, both externally and internally. Outside lamps had not been cleaned for years, and the upper shelves in all the libraries were not merely dusty but in some cases were nearly an inch thick with the accumulated filth of years."[2]

Hand's recommendations read like a catalogue of all the reforms that progressive librarians were seeking to introduce in these post-war years:

> "Open access; centralisation of book purchase, cataloguing and binding; the abolition of printed catalogues and recataloguing on cards; the formation of a union catalogue; intercommunication between branches by telephone and van; the provision of children's libraries; the abolition of ladies' reading rooms; the appointment of a supervisor of branches; and the closing of delivery stations. And, of course, a new Central Library."

The new central library had to wait—it was opened only in 1934—but Gordon and his newly appointed deputy J. P. Lamb, who in 1927 succeeded him as chief librarian, at once put in hand the administrative reforms and set about the gigantic task of restocking the lending libraries and converting them to open access. The central lending library was completed first, re-opening in June 1922 with no more than a fraction of its former stock; and from 1923 to 1929 branch conversions were carried out at the rate of one a year. Two children's libraries were also provided, one as part of the Park

---

[1] "Libraries in Swinton and Pendlebury", in *Swinton and Pendlebury Public Libraries Bulletin* (Sept. 1959).

[2] For this and what follows see *City Libraries of Sheffield, 1856–1956* (Sheffield 1956), pp. 28–34. Cf. J. P. Lamb, "Reconstructing a City Library System", in *L.A.R.*, N.S. Vol. V (1927), pp. 19–26.

Branch, the other (at Walkley) as a separate library. The sheer physical labour involved in this reorganization was immense, for apart from the replanning of the layout every book had to be examined, and thousands of dirty and out-of-date volumes discarded. At the Upperthorpe Branch (where Thomas Greenwood had once worked) only 4000 volumes out of 23 000 were found fit to keep.

Extension Activities

On the subject of library extension activities there seems at this period to have been a certain ambivalence of attitude. Library lectures continued to be popular, and were promoted by a considerable number of libraries in spite of the doubtful legality of expenditure on such activities. The Kenyon Committee found 111 library authorities providing lectures, and in spite of the difficulties with the district auditor we note that this figure included most of the metropolitan boroughs.[1] "Lectures are a feature much developed during the last twenty years . . ." declared Doubleday of Hampstead. "I know of no library where lectures are not a success, either for children or adults."[2]

Most libraries were also keen on assisting adult education classes—mainly at this time those organized by the Workers' Educational Association. Though urban libraries, because of their different tradition, generally found it less easy than the new county libraries to supply such classes with books on long-term loan, they were often able to help with accommodation, publicity, special booklists, and loans to individual students.

In the immediate post-war years some library authorities caught a glimpse of a wider vision, and the notion gained currency that the public library should be the intellectual centre of the community it served. Berwick Sayers, in his revised third edition of Brown's *Manual* (1920), wrote (perhaps with some wishful thinking): "modern librarians increasingly adopt the point of view that it is part of their duty and privilege to create readers . . . the object is to make the library the intellectual centre of the town."[3]

The average practising librarian, still faced with desperate shortages of funds for basic library essentials, viewed such lofty claims with some scepticism. A more realistic attitude is reflected in a special report on *The Public Libraries and Adult Education*, prepared by a joint committee of the Library Association and the recently founded British Institute of Adult Education and published in 1923. The report devotes most of its attention to the problem of book supply to adult classes. On this matter it anticipated the conclusions of many subsequent inquiries by recommending (*a*) that basic textbooks should wherever possible be bought by the students; (*b*) that the public library should play a more important role in the provision of supplementary reading material, for

---

[1] *Kenyon Report*, p. 330. Cf. above, p. 200.

[2] Carnegie U.K. Trust, *Seventh Annual Report, 1920*, pp. 52–53. Cf. the comment of the Denbigh County Librarian, above, p. 226.

[3] J. D. Brown, *Manual of Library Economy* (3rd edn. by W. C. B. Sayers 1920), pp. 467–468. A similar idea is implicit in a much earlier plea by H. M. Thompson, Chairman of the Cardiff Education Committee, in a paper on "The Relations between Public Education and Public Libraries", that librarians "shall not only be distributors of books, but diffusers of literary knowledge and cultivation" (*L.A.R.*, Vol. V, 1903, pp. 452–466.).

which hitherto the students have been mainly dependent on bookboxes provided by a university or the Central Library for Students; and (c) that recourse should be had to the Central Library (or its Scottish counterpart) for scarce books and books only in occasional demand.[1]

On the subject of direct library provision of anything beyond "informal talks and lectures", the report is noticeably cool. It does indeed express the hope that the library "should come to be regarded with pride and affection by the general public as the centre of intellectual life in the district," but in the context this aspiration rings rather hollowly.[2] The same note of caution is struck a year later in the Mitchell Report, which records the general opinion of librarians that "the Public Library should not become in any sense a substitute for the ordinary recognized educational institution." One cannot resist quoting Mitchell's own comment on accommodation for adult classes:

> "Lastly, it is difficult to believe that the average Public Library could not provide a room for adult classes. The library, in fact, seems to be the natural place for such classes, and where no other room is available small classes could be held in the librarian's private room . . . . No librarian worth his salt would object to putting himself out of the way for such a purpose."[3]

This report also devoted a good deal of attention to the provision of books for adult classes, a problem which it noted was at that time engaging the attention of the Carnegie Trust. The Trust did indeed undertake a three-year experiment (1924–26) in the direct provision, from its Dunfermline repository, of sets of books to all W.E.A. classes in Scotland and in the Association's North-Western District. It came to the conclusion that the needs of these classes could be met at reasonable cost by the public libraries, working in conjunction with neighbouring libraries and the Central Library for Students.[4]

The Kenyon Report also went very fully into the question of book supply, not only for W.E.A. classes but for university extra-mural and other adult classes. It came to the conclusion that a special service was certainly needed, and noted the discrepancy between the attitude of the county libraries and that of their urban counterparts. After considering and rejecting the idea that provision for adult classes should be a national responsibility discharged through the Central Library for Students, the report recommended that the responsibility for procuring books should continue to rest with the organizing bodies, drawing (a) on their own resources, if any; (b) on the public libraries; and (c) as a last resort on the Central Library for Students.[5]

On the more general question of library extension activities the Kenyon Report again advanced the ideal that "the public library should be the intellec-

[1] Library Association and British Institute of Adult Education, *The Public Libraries and Adult Education* (1923), pp. 4–7.
[2] *Op. cit.*, p. 12.
[3] *Mitchell Report*, pp. 47–48.
[4] *Op. cit.*, pp. 46–47; Carnegie U.K. Trust, *Thirteenth Annual Report, 1926*, pp. 34–37.
[5] *Kenyon Report*, pp. 174–180. The only adult education bodies with their own library resources were some university extra-mural departments, which had long been accustomed to send boxes of books to University Extension courses and to the tutorial classes run jointly with the W.E.A. Classes in Wales were in the fortunate position of being able to draw on the resources of the National Library of Wales.

tual centre of the area which it serves." It went on to suggest "that it is the duty of a library authority not only to provide an adequate stock of books but also to induce a substantial proportion of the local population to make use of them." To this end it recommended new legislation to make it clear that a library authority was free to make use of its premises in whatever way it thought fit, and that it was entitled, if it so wished, to provide lectures either free or on payment of an admission fee.[1]

The year in which the Kenyon Report was published, 1927, saw also the appearance of Lionel McColvin's volume (the first of its kind) on library extension work. This included practical hints on the organization of lectures, book talks, readings, gramophone recitals, and even films, though it was admitted that these last were difficult and expensive to obtain.[2] As it turned out, however, the Kenyon proposals for new legislation were never implemented, and throughout the inter-war years legal difficulties and shortage of funds continued to impede, in most libraries, any large-scale development of extension activities.

Librarians and Librarianship

Librarianship continued its slow struggle towards professional status. As in earlier periods, the subject is one on which it is difficult to generalize because the gap between the best and the worst, in qualifications, status, salary, and conditions, is so enormous. On the one hand were the librarians of our great civic libraries—men of the calibre of S. A. Pitt in Glasgow, E. A. Savage in Edinburgh, L. S. Jast in Manchester, Walter Powell in Birmingham, Berwick Sayers in Croydon, Frank Pacy in Westminster. These were people who would have made their mark in any profession. Scarcely less distinguished, though much less well rewarded, were some of the new county librarians, such as Miss A. S. Cooke in Gloucestershire and Kent, J. D. Cowley in Lancashire, Richard Wright in Wiltshire and Middlesex, Owen Williams in Denbighshire, and Alfred Ogilvie in Midlothian and Lanarkshire. At the other end of the scale—almost in another world—were the librarians of the small libraries, who as Mitchell points out were often little more than caretakers.[3] Kenyon actually records one borough, unidentified, which employed "at a salary of £2 a week an official who acts as 'Cleaner, Caretaker, Stoker, Borough Librarian and Secretary to the Committee.' "[4]

The Kenyon Committee took considerable trouble to secure information about salaries and conditions of staff. Its report expressed the conviction "that, owing to the unsatisfactory conditions of the profession, there are too many librarians holding posts in the public library service for which they are unfitted;" and it noted particularly that "it had been a matter of common report that the profession is inadequately paid."[5] The salary figures for urban libraries are tabulated in the report according to the population served, and consequently do not admit ready comparison with the figures cited above for earlier periods,[6] but they show some interesting features.

[1] *Op. cit.*, pp. 39, 73–75.
[2] L. R. McColvin, *Library Extension Work and Publicity* (1927), espec. Ch. iii.
[3] *Mitchell Report*, p. 12.
[4] *Kenyon Report*, p. 224.
[5] *Op. cit.*, pp. 78, 88.
[6] See above, pp. 202–203.

The committee secured information regarding 265 chief librarians (261 men and 4 women) on salary scales rising to £150 or more. One London librarian was receiving £1,000 a year, and one librarian of a large provincial library £1,100 a year, but these were exceptional. In all only 33 librarians were receiving £600 a year or more; 31, including the four women, were receiving less than £200 a year; the remaining 201 were receiving between £200 and £600.[1] For 88 towns of 20 000–50 000 population the average salary was £279; for 50 towns of 50 000 to 100 000 population the average salary was £398.

The report also tabulates the salaries of 910 male assistants and 112 female assistants, but does not attempt to categorize them according to their duties. Only 47 of the men were earning £400 a year or more, and 199 were earning less than £200. All the women were earning less than £300, and 84 less than £200. Of the 711 male assistants earning £200 a year or more, the great majority (649) were employed either in London or in the larger provincial libraries (100 000 population and over).

The figures for county libraries show 41 chief librarians (men and women) averaging £311 a year, the highest salary being £480; 30 male assistants mostly under £150 a year, and 14 female assistants of whom one received £105 and the rest less than £100.[2]

By and large, and bearing in mind the increase of about fifty per cent in prices, these figures for 1923–24 do not suggest any substantial advance over the position in 1911. Kenyon quotes also the scales for graduate and non-graduate teachers, but these figures, varying according to qualifications, length of service, size of school and geographical area, present such a wide range that the comparison is not very helpful. The same may be said of the report's final recommendation on this matter, namely that "in general, the trained librarian should be paid no less than the trained teacher, and that the one profession should not be less attractive than the other."

Hours of work seem to have remained much the same as before the war, with some slight improvement in the larger libraries, where weekly hours now averaged 40-44. Mitchell points out, however, that even where working hours are reduced to eight a day the staff may be compelled to be at or near the library for twelve hours a day. Sunday opening of reading rooms and/or reference rooms, though still popular in some places, e.g. Birmingham and the industrial towns of the North of England, was now restricted according to Kenyon to 27 library authorities. In view of the general movement towards shorter working hours, Mitchell thought there was now less justification than formerly for Sunday opening. He also stressed that all staff should be entitled to a weekly half-holiday.[3]

The basic requirement for professional status was an adequate scheme of training, and in this respect the inauguration in 1919 of the School of Librarian-

---

[1] About 140 librarians are excluded from the figures either because they earned less than £150 or because no information was available. A considerable number of these were part-time.

[2] *Kenyon Report*, pp. 88–90, 245–247. Cf. *Mitchell Report*, pp. 28–29, which shows, as might be expected, that the position was worse in Scotland. In 25 out of 61 Scottish libraries the total salaries bill was less than £100 per annum.

[3] *Mitchell Report*, pp. 54–57; *Kenyon Report*, pp. 75–78.

ship at University College, London, marked the only substantial step forward during this period.[1] The original Carnegie grant which made this venture possible was renewed, though on a smaller scale, for a further five years from 1925 to 1929, and by the time this second quinquennium had reached its mid-point the trustees were happily reporting that the school now had 70 full-time and 56 part-time students. The courses of study offered for the College Diploma in Librarianship occupied two years full-time (one year for graduates), and could also be taken part-time in three to five years. Candidates were also required to have undertaken at least one year's full-time paid work in an approved library.

The arrangements for the certificate and diploma of the Library Association continued on much the same basis as before the war, except that from 1924 the preliminary test in general knowledge was abandoned and candidates were required instead to have reached the standard of university matriculation. The work of preparation for these qualifications had still to be undertaken mainly by private study with the help of correspondence courses, summer schools, and occasional local lecture series. A very successful series of summer schools organized by Ballinger at Aberystwyth from 1917 to 1922 and again from 1925 to 1928, and a series of courses inaugurated by the Manchester University Extra-Mural Department in 1927, made some contribution to this work and helped to lay the foundations of library schools in those centres in later years.[2]

The Scottish Library Association did not attempt to provide its own examinations and certificates, but wisely agreed to accept those organized by its English counterpart. Part-time training courses were held in Glasgow from 1919 to 1923, and autumn schools in librarianship in Glasgow and Edinburgh alternately from 1922. The possibility of a Scottish library school for full-time training was canvassed more than once, but the project was held over till a more propitious time.[3]

The Kenyon Report placed great stress on the value of training, but made the important point that a distinction should be drawn in training schemes between "those who are engaged in the mechanical and lower routine duties of the library, from the cleaning staff up to the minor clerical work," and those "who are concerned with cataloguing, classification, the selection and care of books, preparation of bibliographies, guidance of readers, and the general administration of library policy". The needs of these two grades were different, though there should be opportunity for promotion from the lower to the higher.[4]

The issue of the report coincided with the Jubilee of the Library Association, which was marked by an international conference in Edinburgh, and led to important policy decisions. In particular it was agreed that the Association should appoint a full-time paid secretary in place of the honorary secretary

---

[1] See above, p. 203.
[2] Carnegie U.K. Trust, *Twelfth Annual Report, 1925*, pp. 34–35; *Fourteenth Annual Report, 1927*, pp. 35–36; *Kenyon Report*, pp. 78–88; J. Minto, *A History of the Public Library Movement* (1932), Ch. xiii.
[3] W. R. Aitken, *A History of the Public Library Movement in Scotland to 1955* (Glasgow 1971), pp. 224–227, 231.
[4] *Kenyon Report*, p. 85.

who had served hitherto; that it should acquire its own permanent head-quarters building; and that every effort should be made to induce other library associations "to come within a single unit". The number of these other associa-tions, independent of the Library Association, was at this time distressingly large: the most important were the North Midland Library Association (dating from 1890); the Association of Assistant Librarians (1895); the Society of Public Librarians (1895); the Birmingham and District Library Association (1895); the Scottish Library Association (1907), and ASLIB (1924).

The existence of all these different organizations was an obvious source of weakness. The Carnegie Trust, anxious to create a strong and unified profession, came forward with generous grants in aid, and as a first step appealed to county librarians to join the Association. A special County Libraries Section was created from 1st January 1928 to cater for their special needs.[1]

Some years necessarily elapsed before the Library Association's new policy was fully implemented, but at least it had set its face firmly towards the future.

[1] Carnegie U.K. Trust, *Fourteenth Annual Report, 1927*, pp. 12–13; Library Association, *Annual Report of the Council, 1928*; J. Minto, *op. cit.*, pp. 199–206 and Ch. xiv.

CHAPTER X

From Kenyon to the Second World War: General Development

The Background

THE years from 1928 to 1939 bear, in retrospect, a sad and gloomy air. The brief economic revival of the mid-'twenties was quickly dissipated, to give way to the worst depression the nation had ever known. The depression was at its deepest in the years 1931–33, when between two and a half and three million people—more than one in five of the country's insured workers—were unemployed. The slump was due much more to general world conditions than to national policies, but this was small consolation, and Ramsay MacDonald's second Labour Government, which had taken office in 1929, resigned in 1931 to make way for a National Government which, in various guises and under various prime ministers (MacDonald, Baldwin, Neville Chamberlain, and Winston Churchill) was destined to last until 1945.

After 1933 the worst of the depression was over, and trade began to pick up a little, but the level of unemployment remained high, and in some areas—South Wales, South Lancashire, Tyneside, Clydeside—the cloud of depression scarcely lifted till the eve of the second World War. This was the Britain of Priestley's *English Journey*, Walter Greenwood's *Love on the Dole* (both published in 1933), George Orwell's *The Road to Wigan Pier* (1937), and Ellen Wilkinson's *Town that was Murdered: the life-story of Jarrow* (1939). As economic depression gradually lifted, moreover, the international situation became increasingly menacing. The Italian invasion of Abyssinia, the Spanish Civil War, the German occupation of Austria and the Sudetenland, the Munich agreement, all these were steps along a road that led only too clearly to a new world conflagration. The Left Book Club, which published the books just referred to by Orwell and Ellen Wilkinson, was established by Victor Gollancz in 1936, and reflected the current anxieties both foreign and domestic.

However, at the time all was by no means gloom and despondency. As far as public libraries are concerned the picture is exactly hit off in the passage already quoted from E. A. Savage, in which he speaks of the "rude check" resulting from the crisis of 1931, and the "little summer of prosperity before 1939."[1] This is borne out by the figures for local government expenditure in England and Wales, which show expenditure on libraries and museums rising slowly from £1.8 millions in 1928 to £2.2 millions in 1931, remaining unchanged until 1933, then rising fairly sharply to reach £3.2 millions in 1939. Since prices were low in the 'thirties and even in 1938 had not recovered to the level of ten years earlier, these figures represent a considerable advance.[2]

[1] See above, p. 233.
[2] B. R. Mitchell and P. Deane, *Abstract of British Historical Statistics* (Cambridge 1962), pp. 345, 418.

The mid 'thirties brought a publishing event of no little significance in the library world—the launching by Allen Lane of his sixpenny paperback series. Penguin Books, as they were called, were at first reprints of fiction and general literature, and in spite of much head-shaking by more conservative publishers were an immediate success. They were followed in 1937 first by the Pelican series, which was more specifically educational in purpose, and began with a new edition of Bernard Shaw's *Intelligent Woman's Guide to Socialism*, and later by the Penguin Specials, which were new and specially commissioned works dealing with urgent contemporary issues. This was not the first of the cheap book movements: going back no further than the beginning of the present century one can recall Nelson's Classics, the World's Classics, Collins's Pocket Classics, and Dent's Everyman Library. Penguin Books, however, caught the public imagination in a way none of the older series had done, and set a fashion which was to be widely followed after the second World War.

The Non-County Libraries

For the non-county libraries the check in 1931 came at a most unfortunate time, when they were just beginning, belatedly, to feel the benefits resulting from the abolition of the 1d. rate limitation. Many of them, feeling that they had outgrown both the ideas and the buildings of their founders, had embarked upon, or were about to embark upon, ambitious programmes of modernization, involving such changes as open access, overhaul and reclassification of stock, replacement or improvement of buildings, increased branch provision, and better service for children.

All these fine prospects were now blighted. Some libraries were actually forced to cut back their services. Manchester, for example, in order to save the cost of staff had to close several of its now renowned Young People's Rooms and substitute children's sections in the adult libraries.[1] At Sheffield the economy axe fell on extension services and the book fund, and issues fell by nearly one-third between 1931–32 and 1936–37.[2] In general, however, severe cuts were not insisted upon, for the simple reason that, as the chief librarian of Hendon sadly remarked,

> "our past economies have so bared the bone that, even in these hard times, there is very little meat for economy committees to carve from it."[3]

What did happen was that development programmes were held up, and urgently needed new buildings indefinitely postponed. York is a case in point. Here, when the first section of the new city library in Museum Street was opened in 1927, and open access introduced, the library became so popular that there were queues stretching far out into the square. It was not until

---

[1] M. Barnes, "Children's Libraries in Manchester", in *Manchester Review*, Vol. XI (Winter 1966–67), p. 85.

[2] *The City Libraries of Sheffield, 1856–1956* (Sheffield 1956), p. 40. For the economies at Manchester and Sheffield see also J. P. Lamb, "What of the Future?" in *Library World*, Vol. XXXIV (1931–32), p. 171.

[3] J. E. Walker, in *Year's Work in Librarianship, 1931*, p. 58.

1934 that the position was somewhat eased by the erection of a further portion of the building, and not until 1938 that the building was completed.[1]

Paradoxically, the depression was also responsible for a considerable increase in library use, mainly by the unemployed but also to some extent by people who had hitherto been patrons of subscription libraries and now found it necessary to economize.[2] In both cases the demand was mainly for light fiction, and the result is neatly illustrated by the following issue statistics for adult readers at the Greenock Public Library:

	1930	1934	1937
Fiction	210 000	237 000	219 000
Non-fiction	45 000	37 000	47 000
Total	255 000	274 000	266 000

It will be noted that between 1930 and 1934 the fiction issues increased and the non-fiction issues declined; between 1934 and 1937 the position was reversed.[3]

This development was not without its difficulties. J. D. Stewart, Librarian of Bermondsey, wrote in 1933:

> "Libraries provided with reading rooms for the display of newspapers and periodicals have suffered from an invasion of persons to whom these departments represent not sources of information and interest but places in which to kill time.... In some districts the misuse of library premises has been severe and has interfered with the proper work. As a result there has been a tendency to adopt and enforce bye-laws; and in some places the 'blacking-out' of betting news (to which most librarians thankfully believed they had said farewell) has had to be reintroduced."[4]

Over against this comment we have to set the statement of an unemployed reader from Wimbledon, that the public library had been to him "the means of holding on to sanity during months of despair."[5] It was in the conviction that there were others like this that most librarians did their utmost to help, and that the Library Association first collaborated in, and then in 1935 took over, the National Book Appeal for the Unemployed. Under this scheme, initiated by the British Institute of Adult Education in 1933, 120 000 books (given or purchased) were distributed by public libraries to centres for the unemployed throughout the country, and a further 66 000 by the National Central Library. The work faded out after 1936, the responsibility for the worst hit areas being taken over by the Commission for the Special Areas.[6]

---

[1] *City of York Public Libraries, 1893–1943* (York 1943), pp. 4–5.

[2] J. E. Walker, in *Y.W.L. 1931*, p. 57.

[3] J. T. Hamilton, *Greenock Libraries: a Development and Social History, 1635–1967* (Greenock [1969]), p. 118.

[4] *Y.W.L. 1932*, pp. 50–51.   [5] *L.A.R.*, 3rd Ser., Vol. III (1933), p. 357.

[6] See on this, in addition to the references already given, *L.A.R.*, 3rd Ser., Vol. III (1933) pp. 368–373; 4th Ser. Vol. I (1934), pp. 400–401; Vol. II (1935), pp. 471–473; Vol. III (1936), pp. 144–147; Vol. IV (1937), p. 5R; Carnegie U.K. Trust, *Nineteenth Annual Report, 1932*, pp. 14–15; British Institute of Adult Education, *Annual Reports*, 1932–33—1935–36; and for South Wales *Report of the Proceedings of the Eighth Conference of Libraries in Wales and Monmouthshire, 1933* (Aberystwyth 1933), p. 34, and *Report of the Proceedings of the Twelfth Conference ... 1938* (Aberystwyth 1939), pp. 19–25.

For England and Wales we have precise statistical information for the years of depression, prepared by the Board of Education for comparison with the statistics in the Kenyon Report. The latter related to the year 1923–24; the new figures related to the year 1931–32, and covered 478 authorities— 426 in England and 52 in Wales.[1] *Prima facie* they indicated a very substantial improvement as the following comparisons show:

	1923–24	1931–32	percentage increase
Total stock (mills.)	12.3	16.6	35
Volumes per head	0.52	0.64	23
Total expenditure (mills.)	£1.2	£1.7	31
Expenditure per head	12d.	16d.	33
Total borrowers (mills.)	2.5	4.3	72
Borrowers per 100 population	11	16.7	52
Total issues (mills.)	74	136	84
Issues per head	3.0	5.3	72

J. D. Stewart, reviewing progress since Kenyon at the 1934 Library Association Conference, took comfort from these figures, which he regarded as

"ample justification for those who believed that some extra money for the really vital services of books and staffs would result in bringing many libraries to life, and insuring in all cases a more proper return for the whole of the public funds expended."[2]

Stewart also found evidence of a great improvement in library organization:

"Any observer, however casual, must have been impressed by the rapid and general levelling up of library equipment and methods throughout the country. Old buildings have been extended or replaced; schemes of reorganisation have been completed in a large number of places; and the out-of-date, inefficient library is now one of the rarer sights of the countryside."[3]

Lionel McColvin, Chief Librarian of Hampstead, using the same statistics, was much less optimistic. He was of the opinion that a situation in which issues were increasing so much more rapidly than stock and expenditure was not in the long run a healthy one. He also pointed out that averages based on the national figures concealed, as always, disturbing variations between individual library authorities. Some libraries were spending more than 3s. per head per annum, others less than 1d.; some had enrolled as borrowers 50 per cent or more of the population, others less than 2 per cent. Taking an enrolment of 10 per cent of the population and an expenditure of 1s. per head as reasonable minima for an efficient library service, McColvin counted

---

[1] Board of Education, *Statistics of Urban Public Libraries in England and Wales (1931–32)* (1933).

[2] J. D. Stewart, "Developments since the Report of the Public Libraries Committee of the Board of Education, 1927", in *L.A.R.*, 4th Ser., Vol. I. (1934), p. 349.

[3] *Op. cit.*, p. 354.

sixty authorities which failed to reach the former standard, and more than 140 which failed to reach the latter.[1]

Thus the problem of the small library, which had been emphasized in the Kenyon Report, and on several occasions since, especially by J. M. Mitchell of the Carnegie Trust, was brought to the forefront once more. Mitchell, in an address to the Library Association in 1929, declared roundly that "there are at least 200 municipal libraries which, as cultural assets, are practically negligible, and which could not be made efficient without rates of 3d., 4d., or even in some cases 6d." The only hope for these libraries, he thought, was either co-operation with a larger unit or, better still, surrender of their powers to the county library, and to show the great advantages of this latter solution he quoted the example of Stroud in Gloucestershire. Here, as a result of reorganization and restocking, issues rose from about 10 000 to about 100 000 in the first year of county administration.[2]

This was a problem which was to cause concern throughout the 'thirties, and indeed is still with us today. The Board of Education commented, in its Annual Report for 1933:

> "The number of independent Urban Library areas with a population of under 20000 is as high as 216 out of a total of 478, and in the last seven years only ten areas have taken advantage of the powers conferred by Section 2 of the Public Libraries Act, 1919, to relinquish in favour of the county . . . . The populations of independent Urban Library areas show a very large range, and it is manifest from an examination of the statistics that some areas find it difficult to maintain a satisfactory service on the amount of money available from the rates."[3]

Up to 1936 the Carnegie Trust continued to assist many small libraries with grants towards the cost of books. Grants were initially made available to authorities with a population of between 10 000 and 50 000, but from 1931 the upper limit was extended to 70 000. It was, however, made plain that grants would not normally be made to authorities with populations under 20 000 except on condition of amalgamation with the county service. From 1931 it was laid down as a condition of grant that the authority must undertake to carry out, as far as financial conditions permitted, the main principles of modern library practice as set out in the Library Association's *Manual* of that year.[4]

---

[1] L. R. McColvin, "Urban Public Libraries", in *L.A.R.*, 3rd Ser., Vol. III (1933), pp. 373–375; 4th Ser., Vol. I (1934), pp. 14–15, 75–76.

[2] J. M. Mitchell, "The Small Town in Relation to the County Library System", in *L.A.R.*, N.S., Vol. VII (1929), Conference Supplement, pp. 1*–7*. Cf. for further comments *Small Municipal Libraries: a Manual of Modern Methods* (1931), edited by Mitchell for the Library Association; and with special reference to Wales, J. Warner," Library Economy of Small Libraries", in *Report of the Proceedings of the Eighth Conference of Libraries in Wales and Monmouthshire, 1933* (Aberystwyth 1933), pp. 31–41. For Stroud see C. A. Austin, "Library Development in an Urban District", in *L.A.R.*, 3rd Ser., Vol. II (1932), pp. 201–208.

[3] Board of Education, *Education in 1933* (1933), p. 54. The number of authorities relinquishing library powers seems to be understated—see below, p. 263.

[4] Carnegie U.K. Trust, *Eighteenth Annual Report, 1931*, p. 12. The *Manual* is that referred to above, note 2.

In 1935 the Trust terminated its book grants scheme, though still reserving a small sum (£5000) for general grants, not restricted to book purchase, for the improvement of libraries in places of under 20 000 population which decided during the next five years to amalgamate with the county. When the final book grants had been allocated in 1936, the accounts showed a total of £138 600 spent on this purpose since 1926. The Trustees were convinced that these grants, though small in themselves, had been the instruments for effecting a great improvement in service:

> "Better balanced and more liberal budgets, the weeding out of 'dead' or badly soiled books, the remodelling of old-fashioned premises, the substitution of trained for untrained staff, and co-operation with Regional and County services are among the more important of the specific results achieved."[1]

At the other end of the scale concern was again being expressed at this time regarding the poor quality of the library service commonly available in London. Though the five-yearly reports edited by James Stewart of Bermondsey for the London and Home Counties Branch of the Library Association were always able to record encouraging overall increases in stock and issues,[2] the more detailed figures made available by the Board of Education for 1931–32 revealed some disquieting features.

Lionel McColvin, in an address to the Branch, pointed out that the service was, in general, much inferior to that provided by provincial cities, and that there were, moreover, great divergences between the standards of individual authorities. He admitted that there were two or three libraries of very high standard, but he drew attention to the general inadequacy of reference services, the lack of separate children's rooms, the out-of-date technical and scientific sections, and the filthy and dilapidated condition of many of the books in circulation.[3]

McColvin's solution lay in the direction of greater inter-library co-operation and a measure of inter-library specialization. W. A. Munford, at this time Chief Assistant Librarian at Ilford, roundly declared that "the public library service of London is a chaos," and thought the basic fault lay in the existence of twenty-eight separate metropolitan authorities differing widely in their resources and responsibilities. Using the 1931–32 figures, he showed that the rich City of Westminster, on a $\frac{1}{2}$d. rate, was spending £23 000 a year on its library service, i.e. 3s. 8d. per head, the highest *per caput* expenditure in the country. Holborn, on a $\frac{1}{2}$d. rate, was spending only £3600 a year, and even Poplar, with a rate of 4.6d. (the highest in London) was spending only £13 900 a year. The only satisfactory solution, Munford argued, was to have the library service run as a single unit by the London County Council, which for a uniform rate not exceeding 2d. could provide first-class and equal facilities for all citizens.[4]

---

[1] Carnegie U.K. Trust, *Twenty-Second Annual Report, 1935*, p. 20. See also *Sixteenth Annual Report, 1929*, pp. 16–22; and *Twenty-Third Annual Report, 1936*, pp. 17–18.

[2] J. D. Stewart (ed.), *Report on the Municipal Library System of London and the Home Counties, 1924* (1925), and later reports for 1929, 1934, and 1939.

[3] *L.A.R.*, 3rd Ser., Vol. III (1933), p. 154–155.

[4] W. A. Munford, 'Replanning London's Library Service', in *Library Assistant*, Vol. XXVII (1934), pp. 117–122.

By 1934, in spite of the persistence of unemployment in some areas, the economy was beginning to recover, library finance was a little easier, and the Library Association was receiving news of new buildings and extensions in all parts of the country. The opening in that year of the new central libraries at Manchester, Sheffield, and Birkenhead was a sign that Savage's "little summer of prosperity" was on its way.

The middle year of the decade was a time of stocktaking. The Library Association produced a new set of statistics for non-county libraries to match (more or less) the statistics already available for county libraries;[1] and also devoted the greater part of its annual conference at Manchester to a discussion of standards of service. The statistics for non-county libraries in Great Britain for 1934–35, which it is of interest to compare with those given above for 1923–24 and 1931–32, are as follows:

Total stock (mills.)	21.1
Volumes per head	0.71
Total expenditure (mills.)	£2.1
Expenditure per head	17d.
Total borrowers (mills.)	5.0
Borrowers per 100 population	17.0
Total issues (mills.)	158.8
Issues per head	5.4

The figures for the eight largest libraries (in terms of stock) are given as follows:

	Population (000s)	Volumes (000s)	Volumes per head	Issues (000s)	Issues per head
Birmingham	1,033	925	0.9	4,601	4.5
Glasgow	1,113	856	0.76	4,655	4.2
Manchester	755	735	0.97	4,591	6.1
Liverpool	866	589	0.67	6,841	7.9
Edinburgh	461	442	0.96	3,220	7.0
Cardiff	221	416	1.88	2,493	11.3
Bradford	294	384	1.3	2,987	10.2
Leeds	485	373	0.77	3,670	7.6

The outstanding position of Cardiff and Bradford, in relation to population, is very noticeable here. At the other end of the scale we have yet another analysis, this time by Luxmoore Newcombe, of the deplorable position of the 189 libraries (out of a total for England and Wales of 454) still serving populations of less than 20 000. He gives not only statistics, of which we have already had more than enough, but also a number of detailed examples, a few of which we cannot resist quoting:

> "We find that in one case the library is open one hour each week for the issue of books. The books are described as 'very out-of-date and in bad repair'. The library rate is almost entirely absorbed by the upkeep of the building and the very

[1] Library Association, *Statistics of Urban Public Libraries in Great Britain and Northern Ireland* (*1935*) [1936], See for further details below, App. VI.

small wage paid to the caretaker. The balance of £1 a year is paid to the County Library in return for the loan of twenty books exchanged every six months . . ."

"A library which no doubt appeals to several of the inhabitants is one in which the income is spent 'on the maintenance, heating and caretaking of a small reading room containing a billiard table and a bookcase'. A few newspapers are taken and the balance of the small sum available is spent on the purchase of second hand books . . ."

"A library which is making steady, if rather slow, progress is one which was opened in 1908. It has a nice little building with the words 'Public Library' on its front, and during the past twenty-seven years it has amassed a stock of 150 volumes. As the library no longer issues any books, the total is, no doubt, adequate for a population of some 2500 persons."[1]

In the discussion on standards at the Manchester conference,[2] only one speaker attempted to translate standards into monetary terms. This was Duncan Gray, City Librarian of Nottingham, who worked out a desirable level of expenditure (exclusive of fabric charges) of 1s. 10.4d. per head of population. This figure included 4d. per head for books. It was at once denounced as impossibly high by a councillor from Newcastle upon Tyne, and as dangerously low by an alderman from Bournemouth.[3]

The remaining speakers dealt with the question in more general terms, and reveal in an interesting way the special problems facing the librarian of a great city (Charles Nowell, Jast's successor at Manchester), a medium-sized industrial town (F. J. Boardman of Rotherham), an outer London suburb (Edward Sydney of Leyton), and a seaside resort (W. H. Smettem of Scarborough). All were, of course, agreed on the need for a comprehensive library service, administered by qualified staff and embracing reference, lending, and children's services. All were agreed, too, on the need to pay special attention to the needs of students, and to provide appropriate facilities for cultural societies and adult education groups.

Beyond this, however, there was a considerable difference of emphasis. Nowell stressed the needs of the student, "the real reader," "the reader who wants a particular book to read, not the man who merely wants to read a book."[4] He also urged careful book selection to cater for the wider interests now being fostered by the cinema and the radio. He was on the whole disposed to think that the 2d. "shop libraries", which became widespread in the 'thirties and were causing concern to some librarians, were a good thing in that they helped to relieve the public libraries of demands for purely recreational reading.[5]

Boardman of Rotherham also called for a high standard of service in the reference department, especially in relation to the requirements of local industry. As librarian of a town with a considerable working-class population, however, he was naturally inclined to be more sympathetic to the reader of popular fiction. "If", he argued, "we refuse to supply, within reason, works of popular fiction we lose the only contact we have with readers of this type."[6]

---

[1] L. Newcombe, "The Smaller Urban Libraries of England and Wales", in *L.A.R.*, 4th Ser., Vol. II (1935), pp. 508–509.

[2] These papers are printed in full in *L.A.R.*, 4th Ser., Vol. II (1935), pp. 363–402.

[3] *Op. cit.*, pp. 387, 401–402.   [4] *Op. cit.*, p. 368.

[5] *Op. cit.*, p. 365.   [6] *Op. cit.*, p. 389.

Smettem in Scarborough took a similar view, but Sydney at Leyton, though regretting the loss of potential readers, thought it was no part of the business of a public library to compete at the level of the "tuppenny library."[1]

Sydney and Smettem were, however, at one in believing that for their particular areas "pride of place should be given to the lending library and not to the reference library." Smettem, to meet the needs of holiday-makers and retired people, thought there was also much value in a good reading room, but Sydney expressed a not uncommon view when he declared that "The news-cum-illustrated-paper room is a survival from another age and should be smothered quietly and quickly."[2]

It is interesting to note here the emergence, in a new guise, of the perennial problem about the reading of fiction. Nowell and Boardman, however, also drew attention to a new problem. Boardman put it in a nutshell:

> "During recent years there has been, and still is in operation a disintegration of the old grim compactness of works, streets, shops and houses. Regional planning, housing developments and improved transport facilities have made it possible for large numbers of people to remove themselves from the shadows of their work-places."[3]

Hence arose problems regarding branch distribution, and the location of children's services, which are referred to below. The Carnegie Trust, even though it was running down its assistance to libraries, recognized the problem of service to new housing estates as far as the county libraries were concerned,[4] but declined to make comparable grants to urban authorities—a form of discrimination which one urban librarian at least bitterly resented.[5]

In concluding this brief general account of the non-county libraries it may be as well to point out that the pattern of library authorities was much less static in the period between the wars than official publications suggest. Defective records make it difficult to establish precise figures, but in round figures about sixty authorities were absorbed by the counties on the inauguration of the county services between 1919 and 1925, and another sixty before the close of 1939, while a further twenty authorities joined forces with neighbouring urban libraries. About half the authorities absorbed by the counties, and three of those absorbed by urban libraries, had never provided a library service.

Nor is this the whole story. It must be mentioned also that during the same period, excluding the county authorities and new authorities arising from mergers such as those of Lytham and St. Annes in 1922 and Sandown and Shanklin in 1934, there came into service more than sixty new library authorities. Some of these, such as Crewe in 1936 and Rhondda in 1939, filled long standing gaps, but others, especially in the Home Counties, were in new or rapidly developing urban areas, often carved out of the county

---

[1] This view was strongly put later in the year in a paper by E. A. Savage, "The Rakes' Progress", *op. cit.*, pp. 548–554.

[2] *Op. cit.*, p. 393.   [3] *Op. cit.*, pp. 387–388. For Nowell's remarks see p. 365.

[4] See below, p. 271.

[5] See the article on "Library Provision in New Housing Estates", by J. G. O'Leary, Librarian of Dagenham, in *Library Assistant*, Vol. XXIX (1936), pp. 139–144; and on the same theme *L.A.R.*, 4th Ser., Vol. III (1936), pp. 567–568.

domain. Examples are Carshalton, Surbiton, and Sutton and Cheam, all of which gained independent powers in the 'thirties after being served for some years by Surrey County.

The net result, after allowing for amalgamations, is shown by the following figures for non-county authorities in Great Britain at the close of 1918 and the close of 1939 (with the proviso that the figures in the second column may not be entirely accurate):

	1918	1939
England	406	412
Wales	61	57
Scotland	82	63
Great Britain	549	532

This slight reduction in the number of non-county authorities was, however, more than offset by the advent of the 87 county authorities (45 in England, 12 in Wales, and 30 in Scotland) to the development of which we must now turn.

The County Libraries

For the county libraries the year 1928 was pleasantly marked by the introduction of the special county library sign, which was installed at the cost of the Carnegie Trust outside some 15 000 centres. The simple but effective design (illustrated on following page), by fifteen-year old Philip Colman of the Bradford College of Arts and Crafts, was long a familiar feature of village life: for Wales there was a special version with the inscription: LLYFRGELL Y SIR.[1]

Soon, however, came the depression, at a time when, as we have seen, the county libraries were just beginning to grapple seriously with the problem of the populous areas. The Carnegie Trust was particularly interested in this development, on which it decided to concentrate its grants to county libraries for the quinquennium 1931–35. As it turned out the restrictions on capital expenditure resulting from the economic crisis made it necessary to modify this policy, and the grants intended especially to encourage growth in the populous areas were made available also for the general support of the county library service, provided only that it was being developed "in accordance with the best canons of modern practice."[2]

Most authorities took advantage of this offer, and the allocation of £97 000 for 1931–35 was fully committed before the end of 1934. The money was used chiefly for improvement of headquarters accommodation; provision of branches in urban areas; and strengthening of bookstocks.[3] With this assistance the county libraries fared much better than might have been expected during the depression years, and the statistics for 1934–35 show a quite remarkable advance:

[1] Carnegie U.K. Trust, *County Libraries in Great Britain and Ireland: Report, 1927–28* (Dunfermline 1928), pp. 2–3.
[2] Carnegie U.K. Trust, *Eighteenth Annual Report, 1931*, p. 13.
[3] Carnegie U.K. Trust, *Twenty-second Annual Report, 1935*, p. 21.

THE COUNTY LIBRARY SIGN
Designed by Philip Colman of Bradford.

Bookstock (mills.)	2.3	5.4
Issues (mills.)	17.3	47.1
Centres	11,744	16,136
Under 100 volumes	7,377	3,767
Over 2,000 volumes	44	253[1]

The two sets of figures are closely comparable, for the only new county service begun during the intervening years was that for Carmarthenshire in 1932. The cost of the service in 1934–35 was 4d. per head for England (average rate 0.9d.); 3.4d. per head for Wales (average rate 1d.), and 6.5d. per head for Scotland.[2]

The largest library systems in 1934–35 were those of the populous English counties:

	Bookstock (000s)	Issues (000s)	Centres	Branches
Lancashire	264	2,864	280	19
West Riding	245	2,337	608	13
Kent	208	1,975	252	5
Durham	207	2,469	278	13
Surrey	199	2,075	221	15
Middlesex	190	1,947	246	5

[1] Library Association, County Libraries Section, *County Libraries in Great Britain and Ireland: Statistical Report, 1934–35* [1936]. Figures adjusted to exclude Ireland. Compare also the figures for 1926–27 given above, pp. 230–231.

[2] *Op. cit.* In this Report Monmouth is included with England.

No Welsh or Scottish county could approach these figures. The largest county libraries in Wales were Glamorgan and Denbigh; the largest in Scotland were Lanark and Ayr:

	Bookstock (000s)	Issues (000s)	Centres	Branches
Glamorgan	99	448	251	—
Denbigh	58	273	200	3
Lanark	89	828	197	—
Ayr	80	863	163	8

These figures, however, do not tell the whole story. Bookstocks and issues can be adequately considered only in relation to population, and when we look at the statistics from this angle we find that many of the smaller county authorities had better records than those just listed. This was particularly true in Scotland, where 15 authorities held bookstocks of over 50 per 100 population, compared with 5 authorities in England and 1 (Denbigh) in Wales. The following table of averages reflects the superiority of Scotland in this respect, and the issue figure especially indicates the weakness of the position in Wales:

	Average bookstock per 100 population	Average Issues per head
England	36	3.2
Wales	34	1.4
Scotland	54	3.4[1]

The establishment of branches in the urban areas was checked by the depression but by no means halted, and it is surprising to read that even in 1932 twelve new branches were opened. Five of them were in purpose-built premises, of which the most notable was the second "regional branch library" opened by Derbyshire at Staveley at a cost of over £6000. The others were in temporary or adapted premises, on which the *Record* comments that "The provision varies from rooms adequately altered, adapted and equipped to fulfil the main functions of a Branch Library to rooms equipped merely with shelving and tables, and worked by voluntary helpers."[2]

The figures for 1934–35 actually show a total of 64 full-time and 129 part-time branches—mainly, of course, in the heavily urbanised English counties, which accounted for all but 18 of the full-time branches and all but 13 of the part-time ones. It will be seen from the table already given, that

[1] In Wales the lead was taken by Denbigh, with 63 volumes per 100 population and 3 issues per head per annum; in England the list was headed by the East Riding (70 volumes, 6.9 issues); but in Scotland these figures were surpassed by Selkirk (120 volumes, 3 issues) Roxburgh (82.6 volumes, 6.8 issues) and several other counties. Cf. the table for 1934–35 in App. VI, below.

[2] *L.A.R.*, 3rd Ser., Vol. III (1933), pp. 36, 276–277. On the Derbyshire "regional branches" see below, pp. 282–283.

Lancashire, with 19 branches, was the leading county in this respect.[1] The effect of the establishment of branches in multiplying the number of readers and the number of issues was, as might be expected, often dramatic, and many libraries were also able to take satisfaction in an increased proportion of non-fiction issues—obviously because more non-fiction was available.[2]

This development of county branches was due partly to Carnegie grants and partly, in England, to the system of differential rating which has been described above, under which, as a general rule, the local authority levied a supplementary rate to cover the cost of buildings and maintenance.[3] In Scotland there was no differential rating, but there was from 1929 a system of "dual rating" which in practice came to resemble differential rating. Under the Education Act of 1918 the Scottish county library system was operated by the county education authorities and financed from the education rate, but a clause in the Act exempted existing burgh or parish library authorities from payment of that part of the county education rate which related to library services, except where this exceeded the local library rate (which never happened). The Local Government (Scotland) Act, which came into operation in May 1929,[4] made a number of important changes.

In the first place the Act abolished the *ad hoc* county education authorities, and transferred their powers, including library powers, to the county councils;[5] in the second place it deprived the parishes of library powers, and transferred the powers of the dozen remaining parish authorities (four of them in Aberdeenshire) to their respective counties; and in the third place it withdrew the exemption of the burghs, other than Edinburgh, Glasgow, Aberdeen and Dundee, from the education rate levied for library purposes. This last change meant that the inhabitants of burghs which were library authorities were in effect paying two rates—a local rate and a county rate.

The disappearance of the parish libraries seems to have passed with little comment, though a tear might well have been shed for Tarves in Aberdeenshire, the oldest rural parish library in Great Britain.[6] Double rating, however, caused great indignation, and was the principal subject of discussion at a special conference convened by the Carnegie Trust and the Scottish Library Association at Dunblane in 1931. This resulted in two somewhat contradictory resolutions on the subject, the first directed to making the best of the new situation, the second to restoring the *status quo*.

The resolutions read:

(1) "That, pending future legislation with the object of regulating co-operation between Burgh and County Library Authorities, where money is raised as part of the Education rate by the County Authority for library purposes, some reasonable

---

[1] See above, p. 265. One county not included in this table but notable for its branch provision was Essex, which had at this time 12 branches.
[2] *County Libraries Statistical Report, 1934–35*, p.23.
[3] *Ibid.* Cf. above, pp. 227–228.   [4] 19 and 20 Geo. V, c. 25.
[5] The counties of Perth and Kinross were merged at this time for administrative purposes, and library provision became the responsibility of the education committee of the joint council. In Moray and Nairn, however, where a similar merger took place, the two county libraries retained their separate identity, under the aegis of a single committee, until 1960.
[6] See above, p. 65.

return should be given to the Burgh Authority, such return to be determined after consultation with the Burgh Authority."

(2) "That in order to facilitate and encourage co-operation between County and Burgh Authorities, the principle involved in the proviso in Section 5 of the Education Act of 1918 (i.e. avoidance of double rating) be restored."[1]

In the event the proviso never was restored, and the burghs had to make the best bargain they could with their respective counties. In this they were assisted by the example of the scores of small burghs which had already, before 1929, come to terms with the county authorities for their mutual advantage. Thurso and Wick, for example, as we have seen, entered into close co-operation with the County of Caithness from the first. Bonnyrigg, from 1921, allowed Midlothian County to provide its lending library service, under an arrangement similar to the English differential rating. The four Aberdeenshire burghs[2] paid the county rate from the beginning of the county service in 1926 in return for a supplementary supply of books, and from the same date four burghs of Angus and Kincardineshire[3] subscribed £7 10s. each annually for the loan of 600 volumes. Lockerbie in 1927 made a similar arrangement with Dumfriesshire. In Kirkcudbrightshire, Castle Douglas from 1926 received full service in return for allowing the use of its building as the county repository. By the date of the Dunblane Conference the counties of East Lothian, Fife, Lanark, Roxburgh and Stirling had already made agreements, or were negotiating agreements, for a return in money or in kind for the rate contributions made by their respective burghs.[4]

Other counties followed this lead, and in three instances it was possible to achieve something approaching a merger of county and burgh services. Thus in Dumfriesshire, in 1932, the county established a joint service with the burghs of Dumfries (with Maxwelltown) and Lockerbie, to be administered at the cost of the county through a library committee on which the burghs were represented. The burgh buildings were made available to the county on free lease, the building at Dumfries (the Ewart Library) becoming the county headquarters. Annan, the only remaining burgh, joined the scheme only in 1943.[5]

In Inverness-shire, where the county and burgh of Inverness were the only library authorities, agreement was reached in 1933 on a joint service to be administered by a joint library committee comprising ten representatives from each authority. Unfortunately this agreement, which lasted till 1962, did not work out very well, for it provided for the appointment of joint librarians of equal status, and this led, it was reported in 1948, to "virtually separate systems neither of which gains any advantage from the existence of the other."[6]

[1] Carnegie U.K. Trust and Scottish Library Association, *Proceedings of the Scottish Library Conference ... 1931* (Dunfermline 1931), pp. 42–57; Carnegie U.K. Trust, *Eighteenth Annual Report, 1931*, pp. 28–30.

[2] Peterhead, Fraserburgh, Inverurie, and Oldmeldrum.

[3] Arbroath, Brechin, Forfar and Montrose.

[4] For details of all these arrangements see the Conference Report already cited, pp. 19–22.

[5] The agreement between the county and burgh of Dumfries is given in W. R. Aitken, *A History of the Public Library Movement in Scotland to 1955* (Glasgow 1971), App. III.

[6] C. S. Minto, *Public Library Services in the North of Scotland* [Minto Report] (1948), p. 12, and also App. I, where the agreement is printed.

More successful was the arrangement made in 1936 by Clackmannan County library and the burgh of Alloa, which following the disappearance of three parish library authorities was the sole surviving non-county authority. This was similar to the arrangement in Dumfriesshire, with the Alloa Museum building becoming the county headquarters.[1]

A more limited measure of co-operation was achieved in Orkney in 1932, under which the county took over responsibility for the lending library services only of the two burghs, Kirkwall and Stromness.[2]

By 1934 it was possible to claim that "counties have now on the whole covered their areas, if only with a skeleton service,"[3] but in some areas the service was very much a skeleton one, with a strong emphasis on the lending of fiction, and very inadequate provision, either by way of lending or by way of reference books, for the serious student. The differential rating system was also a weakness, in that it stood in the way of a uniform county service.

For the county libraries as for the non-county libraries the year 1935 was something of a landmark. It saw the end, substantially, of the Carnegie grants (totalling some £500 000) which had nurtured the county service since its beginnings twenty years earlier; and the beginning of the end of differential rating, which had made possible the first county branches. It saw the publication of the Library Association's *County Libraries Manual*—the first attempt since the very early years to provide a comprehensive guide to policy and organization; and it saw also important discussions on standards of services and on the increasingly important problem of provision for the new housing estates.

Of the differential rating system it may be said that it was a necessary step in catering for the urban areas. Once it became widespread, it was relatively easy to abolish it in favour of a uniform rate. In the discussion on standards which took place at the Manchester conference in September 1935, Miss A. S. Cooke, County Librarian of Kent, explained that in order to secure reasonable efficiency and uniformity of provision it was necessary to have an overall plan, and that such planning was inconsistent with the kind of local option implicit in differential rating. "It is not satisfactory," she pointed out, "to have to wait until a local authority is willing to agree to the levying of a special rate before a Branch Library can be established."[4]

Actually before these words were spoken Kent had already taken the decisive step of abolishing differential rating, as from 1st April 1935, except for rent and loan charges. Lancashire, the West Riding, Warwickshire, and Herefordshire all introduced equal rating before the end of 1936, and by 1939 the differential rating system was rapidly disappearing.[5] The counties with a high rateable value were naturally the first to make the change.

Miss Cooke's survey of standards in other parts of the county service, i.e. in villages and small towns, reveals clearly the problems of the existing situation. Many village centres, she admitted, still had fewer than 100 volumes;

[1] Aitken, *op. cit.*, pp. 125–126.
[2] Minto, *op. cit.*, pp. 13–14, and App. II, where the agreement is printed.
[3] E. Cockerlyne (Lancashire County) in *Y.W.L. 1934*, p. 26.
[4] *L.A.R.*, 4th Ser., Vol. II (1935), p. 374.
[5] *Y.W.L. 1935*, p. 63; *1936*, p. 53; Library Association, County Libraries Section, *County Libraries in Great Britain and Northern Ireland: Statistical Report, 1938–39* [1940], p. 19.

and dependence on voluntary assistance made it difficult to insist that the centre should be open at least twice a week. The absence of reference facilities was also a grave weakness:

> "It is a serious criticism of our service that at present in order to consult, shall we say an atlas, *Whitaker's Almanac*, or the *Encyclopaedia Britannica*, a reader has in most counties to spend half a day in getting to a library where such books are kept."[1]

Miss Cooke suggested that the ideal solution might be a regional library in each market town, acting as a distributing centre to the surrounding villages and housing a small reference collection. This kind of arrangement might help also with the provision of adequate library facilities in the smaller towns, i.e. those with a population under 15 000, and especially under 10 000. Such towns needed larger collections than the villages, but they could not support a full-time branch, and it was difficult to organize the rota of voluntary workers needed to open the library three to four times a week.[2]

Edgar Osborne, Derbyshire County Librarian, tried at the same conference to translate county library standards into figures,[3] and both he and Miss Cooke accepted the figure of 4d. per head on books which had previously been put forward by Duncan Gray in respect of urban libraries.[4] A more detailed study, based on the 1934–35 statistics, is embodied in a *Memorandum on County Libraries* prepared by the County Libraries Section of the Library Association in 1936. This included a series of recommendations regarding minimum standards for various aspects of county library work. The figure here suggested for annual book expenditure was 5d. per head (plus 1½d. per head on binding) out of a total recommended annual expenditure of 1s. 7½d. per head. These proposals were, of course, far above the current levels of expenditure, but they set a useful objective.

A special County Library Conference called by the Carnegie Trust in London in November 1935 (the last such conference to be called under the Trust's auspices) further underlined the unevenness of the county library service, and Osborne of Derbyshire pointed to the differential rating system as an important contributory factor, because of the very large variations in the rateable value of the local authorities concerned. From the 1934–35 figures he calculated that the abolition of differential rating would increase the general county rate, on the average, only by $\frac{1}{10}$d.[5]

Raymond Irwin, who had recently succeeded J. D. Cowley as County Librarian of Lancashire, was able to tell the conference that in his county, which had 34 areas specially rated, the introduction of a uniform rate from 1st April 1936 would increase the general library rate from 1.4d. to just over 2d. He also made the important point that the change would make it very much easier for the small independent authorities to amalgamate with the county service. Hitherto the inhabitants of the specially rated areas had been paying

[1] *L.A.R.*, 4th Ser., Vol. II (1935), p. 373.
[2] *Ibid.*
[3] *Op. cit.*, pp. 436–40.
[4] See above, p. 262.
[5] Carnegie U.K. Trust, *Report of the Proceedings of the County Library Conference . . . 1935* (Dunfermline 1936), p. 9.

up to 2s. 3d. per head, compared with the flat rate of 1s. per head which would now be levied.[1]

By the same token, the differential rating system made it tempting for newly developed urban areas to contract out of the county system and set up their own library service. This was a particular problem in the home counties, where, to cope with London's overspill, roads and housing estates were spreading rapidly across the green fields. In Surrey, for example, though considerable progress was made with special rating schemes, seven boroughs and urban districts contracted out during the years 1930–35.[2] These places, at the beginning of the century, had been little more than villages: now they were sizeable towns, most of them with populations in excess of 50 000.

These withdrawals were naturally a matter of concern to the county authority. Miss M. J. Powell, the County Librarian, did not refer specifically to this point when she addressed the London conference, but she did speak feelingly about the problems of the new housing estates: their uniformity, their lack of social amenities, and the material and intellectual poverty of their inhabitants. Library provision for such areas, she thought, could best be developed in association with community centres where these existed. Not everyone agreed with these views. Other county librarians present feared that the independence of the library would be endangered if it formed part of a community centre; and J. G. O'Leary, Librarian of Dagenham, which had to provide for half of "the largest housing estate in England," thought she greatly underestimated the library potential of the working-class housing estates.[3]

Following the conference the Carnegie Trust decided to allocate £25 000 over the next five years for library development in new housing estates. In the event virtually the whole of this amount was allocated in 1936 to eleven counties. Essex and Middlesex, whose combined population increase amounted to about a quarter of a million, received the largest grants, £5000 and £4000; Kent received £3500, the West Riding £2500, Lancashire £2200; the remainder received grants between £500 and £1500.[4]

With this modest help, the provision of branch libraries, which had been resumed in 1934, went on apace during the years up to 1939; and good progress was also made in replacing the inadequate county library headquarters which had characterized the early years by more commodious premises.[5] During these

[1] Op. cit., p. 13. Pp. 7–27 of this Report offer a particularly good discussion of differential rating. On the financial difficulties of amalgamation see also D. F. Warren, "In the Wilderness", in Library Assistant, Vol. XXV (1932), pp. 27–32.

[2] The authorities were: Mitcham, Surbiton, Beddington and Wallington, Barnes, Carshalton, Coulsdon and Purley, Sutton and Cheam. The circumstances leading to the withdrawal of these authorities are described in R. G. Bird, A Short History of the Surrey County Library (unpublished F.L.A. essay 1950), pp. 8–16.

[3] Proceedings of the County Library Conference, 1935, pp. 1–6; J. G. O'Leary, "Library Provision in New Housing Estates", in Library Assistant, Vol. XXIX (1936), pp. 139–144. On O'Leary's attitude see also above, p. 263 and note.

[4] Carnegie U.K. Trust, Twenty-Third Annual Report, 1936, pp. 15–17; Twenty-Fifth Annual Report, 1938, p. 17.

[5] For details see Y.W.L. 1934, p. 27–28; 1935, p. 64; 1936, p. 54; 1938, pp. 82–84, and references there given.

years two of the remaining county areas unprovided for commenced service, Holland (jointly with Lindsey) in 1936, and the Scilly Isles in 1937. Only tiny Rutlandshire, and the islands and peninsulas of Argyllshire, had to wait for a library service until after the war.

Unfortunately amid all this busy activity the persisting problems of the rural areas tended to be neglected. This is seen in the statistics for 1938–39. In many respects these show, as we would expect, a general advance compared with those for 1934–35; bookstocks had increased from 5.4 to 7.3 millions, issues from 47.1 to 56.7 millions; the largest systems (the West Riding and Lancashire) now held more than 400 000 volumes each, and the issues for Lancashire had topped the 4 million mark; the number of branches had increased, the number of small centres had decreased; but there still remained nearly 2200 centres with fewer than 100 volumes, and of course there were in the rural counties many remote hamlets and farmsteads where even this modest provision was impossible.[1]

The difficulties of organizing a library service in such counties are feelingly described in an address delivered in 1937 by B. Oliph Smith, County Librarian of Hereford. Because of the lower standards of education, intelligence and environment, he thought, progress in the rural areas was bound to be slower than in urban areas, but he was driven to the conclusion that "the service provided in most counties is still grossly unsatisfactory, even regarded as a stage in a process of evolution."[2]

The Library Association Survey

For the years 1936–37 we are fortunate in having a general survey of British libraries, urban and county, undertaken by members of the Library Association as part of a wider survey which embraced also Europe and North America, and was financially assisted by the Rockefeller Foundation.[3] The British section comprised twelve chapters, each by a different expert, and each dealing with a specific geographical area. Unfortunately the time allowed for visiting libraries was very short—approximately a month for each area— so the resulting reports are bound to be a little impressionistic, but they are none the less of great value as indicating the broad characteristics of particular geographical areas.

Duncan Gray of Nottingham, who surveyed Edinburgh and points north, found "libraries and librarianship in every stage of development from the completely ineffective to the well-nigh perfect."[4] This latter adjective he would probably have applied to the Edinburgh City Library, once so backward, but now completely reorganized by E. A. Savage. Gray comments admiringly on the variety and efficiency of its central library, with its lending,

[1] Library Association, County Libraries Section, *County Libraries in Great Britain and Northern Ireland: Statistical Report 1938–39* [1940]. Figures adjusted to exclude Northern Ireland.

[2] B. O. Smith, "Policy in the Rural County", in *L.A.R.*, 4th Ser., Vol. V (1938), p. 507.

[3] L. R. McColvin (ed.), *A Survey of Libraries: Reports on a Survey made by the Library Association during 1936–37* (1938). Quoted henceforth as *Survey*.

[4] *Op. cit.*, p. 11.

reference and information services, its junior library, and its many special collections. In the other two major city systems, those of Aberdeen and Dundee, he finds little to remark, though he does draw attention to the particularly large and well stocked newsroom at Aberdeen, and to the surprising success of a new branch library in a high class residential area—the Dundee suburb of Broughty Ferry.

At the other end of the scale were the small burgh libraries, many of them, Gray was surprised to find, one-man libraries whose librarians, devoted as they sometimes were, were almost completely isolated from the rest of the library world. Even where operations were on a larger scale, bookstocks were often poor, and had to be made up with the help of book clubs, circulating libraries, and loans from the county. These last were often "relatively so large that it is difficult to see any valid reason for some of these small libraries preserving the empty form of their independent status."[1]

Many burgh libraries suffered from overlarge buildings. Of one such Gray notes that the Carnegie library lecture room had been converted into a billiard saloon, "and this was the only department of the building which showed any sign of life."[2] At another, "in a small county town with a full-time 'librarian' who had been formerly a lawyer's clerk, and whose salary was 24/- a week, the Reference Library and Reading Room had been 'closed for economy'."[3]

A few burgh libraries do qualify for favourable comment. Falkirk and Fraserburgh are praised for the excellence of their bookstocks; Kirkcaldy for its new central and branch libraries;[4] and Buckhaven for a new library "very tastefully decorated in light and pleasing colours."[5] Stirling, on the other hand, is castigated (though not by name) for clinging to its Cotgreave indicator, and refusing the public access to its shelves.[6]

Even some of the county libraries were so small that it was not easy to provide an independent service, and three had part-time librarians. Those in the north suffered acutely from difficulties of distances and transport, and some librarians never saw the centres to which the books were being despatched. In many cases, too, headquarters were inadequate. Only Fife and Clackmannanshire were shortly to have new buildings, the latter providing not only county headquarters but also, under the recently completed agreement for joint services, an open access library for the town of Alloa.[7]

Miss A. S. Cooke, County Librarian of Kent, wrote a devastating report on the South-West Scotland/North-West England area, which extended from Glasgow to Barrow in Furness. Both these towns came in for favourable comment—Glasgow for its Mitchell Library and the admirable work being done, often in depressing surroundings, by its branches; and Barrow as being

[1] *Op. cit.*, p. 19.
[2] *Op. cit.*, p. 14.
[3] *Op. cit.*, p. 16.
[4] For details see P. K. Livingstone, *Kirkcaldy and its Libraries* (Kirkcaldy 1950), pp. 25–31.
[5] *Survey*, p. 13.
[6] *Op. cit.*, p. 16. Open access was actually introduced in 1937, but the indicator remained in use for recording loans until 1946—information from Mr. John Robertson, Chief Librarian.
[7] Cf. above, p. 269.

above the average of the area in attractiveness and practical value. Glasgow, Barrow, and Kendal also received a word of praise for their children's rooms. Carlisle was awarded a good mark for its local collection, Lanark County for its new headquarters, Renfrew County for a new branch at Johnstone, and Kilmarnock for being "adequately cleaned and properly looked after."[1] Otherwise the picture was one of almost unrelieved gloom:

> "There was a dreary sameness about all the buildings. A stuffy staleness and an odious smell of scented disinfectant pervaded nearly all of them. One had the feeling that air and sunlight were never admitted . . ."[2]
> "Dark olive green shelving was in use in the majority of libraries and hardly anywhere was any attempt made to brighten up the library by pictures, posters, displays or flowers . . ."[3]
> "The book stocks throughout the area were in a woeful condition—dirty, out of date, laden with germs, dog-eared, and without any attraction whatsoever. That people borrow the books at all shows what a real desire for reading there must be. Perhaps the most distressing factor was that so many librarians were quite complacent about it . . ."[4]
> "Generally the 'reference library' consisted of a bookcase containing an old edition of an encyclopaedia and a few old tattered copies of dictionaries. Where there was a room set aside for the purpose it was stocked with large aged books for which there was no room and no use in the lending library."[5]

This report aroused bitter resentment among the librarians concerned and it seems clear that it painted too black a picture. Following an official protest the Library Association agreed to publish a new survey to be prepared by the Scottish Library Association, but owing to the war this never materialized.[6]

R. W. Lynn, Librarian of Birkenhead, reported on the rural area of South-East Scotland and the distressed counties of North-East England. In the former area, as in the rest of Scotland, he found too many libraries with large buildings and small incomes. A few small places managed to maintain a tolerable service: Peebles, for example, because its rate income was supplemented by endowments, and Bo'ness, Hawick and Kelso because of favourable arrangements with their county authorities as a result of the double rating system—but most did not approach the minimum standards for a modern library service. The staffing situation was everywhere bad: many urban libraries were still in the charge of librarian-caretaker-cleaners, and more than one county library was conducted by a part-time librarian.

In North-East England, i.e. Durham, Northumberland and the North and East Ridings, some of the small libraries were also very poor, but many of the public libraries of this region had proved their worth during the years of depression, and were encouraged to expand their provision as far as resources permitted. During the 'thirties Hull and Darlington enlarged their central premises; Gateshead made a beginning with branch provision, and Newcastle

---

[1] *Survey*, p. 25.
[2] *Op. cit.*, p. 24.
[3] *Op. cit.*, p. 25.
[4] *Op. cit.*, p. 28–29.
[5] *Op. cit.*, p. 29.
[6] For all this see *L.A.R.*, 4th Ser., Vol. V (1938), pp. 519–523; Vol. VI (1939) pp. 12–19.

upon Tyne enlarged its existing provision; new library services were opened at Blyth and Scarborough in 1930, and at Wallsend in 1933. At Scarborough, where a beginning was made in the converted mechanics' institute, public demand was so heavy that within a few years it was necessary almost to treble the size of the building, the reconstructed library, opened in 1936, being regarded as an outstanding example of new ideas in library design.[1]

The survey of the Lancashire area (excluding Furness) was allocated to William Pollitt, Librarian of Southend on Sea. This area was distinguished by the possession of some sixty independent library authorities, and Pollitt had to average three a day to complete his survey in the specified time. Just because the Lancashire towns had been pioneers in the adoption of the Public Libraries Acts many of them were saddled with out-of-date buildings which were not readily adaptable to the needs of a modern library service, and Pollitt found four examples of lending libraries—two of them in large towns—in which open access had not yet been introduced[2]. Unemployment, too, had hit the county hard, and fifteen libraries were still supplying books to centres for the unemployed. At Swinton weekly classes for the unemployed were held at the library, and visits were arranged to places of interest.

In spite of all these difficulties there were welcome signs of progress. New central library buildings were opened at Burnley in 1930, at Lancaster in 1932, and at Bolton in 1938, and Manchester's new central reference library, opened in 1934, was the most notable public library building in Britain during the inter-war years. Lancashire County Library, in the same year, occupied splendid new headquarters in the new County Hall.[3] Elsewhere, extensions had been completed or were on hand, and in a number of the larger towns, and some others, library systems were being modernized and remodelled. In many places branch services were being developed to meet the needs of new housing estates.

It was, as always, the smaller libraries which were the least satisfactory. Some, e.g. Orrell, Waterloo, and Ince in Makerfield, had attached themselves to neighbouring boroughs;[4] a few had surrendered powers to the county; others supplemented their stocks by hiring books from the county, or by subscribing to a commercial circulating library; but others again just remained inadequate, with out-of-date stocks, and ill-paid and ill-qualified staffs.[5]

[1] Survey, pp. 33–35; for the details see also A Short History of the Newcastle upon Tyne Public Libraries, 1854–1950 (Newcastle 1950); and Borough of Scarborough Public Libraries: a Brief Description of the New Building . . . 1936 (Scarborough 1936).

[2] No names are given, but one of the large towns must have been Oldham, where a branch (Northmoor) had open access from 1920 onwards, but owing to structural difficulties readers at the central library were denied this privilege until after the second World War —W. H. Berry, Oldham Public Libraries, Art Gallery and Museum, 1883–1923 (Oldham 1933), p. 22, and information from Mr. J. Hoyle, Deputy Director.

[3] I have here supplemented Pollitt's account with details from later sources, viz: R. Caulfield, "How we got our Public Libraries", in Burnley Express and News, 26 and 30 August 1950; Lancaster Public Library Service, Diamond Jubilee, 1893–1953 (Lancaster 1953) p. 4; The Centenary of the Bolton Public Libraries, 1853–1953 (Bolton 1953), p. 13; S. W. Davis, The History of Lancashire County Library (unpublished F.L.A. thesis 1968), p. 195.

[4] For details see below, App. III, s.v. Lancashire Co. (Orrell), Ashton under Lyne (Waterloo), Ince in Makerfield.

[5] For all this see Survey, pp. 46–59.

Similar comments are made by Edward Sydney, Librarian of Leyton, in his admirable report upon the West Riding of Yorkshire, where 25 out of 45 non-county library authorities served populations of less than 20 000 and 10 served populations of less than 10 000. Only two of these ten, he points out, had trained librarians; most of them were giving little more than newsroom provision.[1] The five authorities with populations between 20 000 and 30 000, though still seriously restricted by shortage of money for books, were in better shape, and one of them attracted Sydney's special notice:

> ". . . one library in particular (Todmorden), housed in a building the gift of the local Co-operative Society, is a sheer pleasure to visit, for despite the obvious structural limitations of premises far too small, the whole place and service is alive with evidences of a virile and thoughtful attempt to supply and create intellectual needs. The extension work of this service is quite unusually extensive and successful."[2]

For the remaining fifteen non-county authorities, all with populations over 30 000, Sydney has nothing but praise, and he also speaks well of the county system. Looking back over the events of the period since 1919, he selects as especially significant the establishment and extension of the county service, the reorganization of the two largest city systems, Leeds and Sheffield, and the opening of the magnificent new central library at Sheffield in 1934. He has little to say regarding Bradford, the third great city system and the largest in terms of bookstocks; and concerning Huddersfield he notes only that the building of a fine new central library has begun—it was opened in 1940. Other new central buildings which he commends are those opened in 1930 at Spenborough (a new library authority) and in 1931 at Rotherham (replacing the Victorian building which had been burnt down in 1925).[3]

Sydney's final verdict on the West Riding library services was one that could be applied to most parts of the country:

> "The advance guards are well out in front, the main body is in touch yet a little slow, but there are far too many stragglers in the rear slowing down the pace of the whole column."[4]

F. Seymour Smith, Deputy Librarian of Hornsey, who surveyed Cheshire (except N.E. Cheshire), Shropshire, and North Wales, found that fifty out of the fifty-six libraries visited fell into the category of small libraries, in which "there was little information to be obtained from those in charge, who were usually caretakers." Even the county libraries (which are apparently omitted from the above reckoning) were sadly lacking in funds, staff, and accommodation. One county (unnamed but presumably Anglesey) had a part-time librarian and an annual book fund of £165 to supply sixty-four centres. The only sizeable libraries in the area were Birkenhead and Wallasey (part of the Merseyside complex), Altrincham (part of the Manchester complex) and the county towns of Chester and Shrewsbury; and the only new building of note was the central library at Birkenhead, opened in 1934 to replace a Carnegie library which had been removed to make way for the entrance to the Mersey Tunnel.[5]

---

[1] *Op. cit.*, pp. 62–63.　　　　　　　　[2] *Op. cit.*, p. 65.
[3] *Op. cit.*, p. 61 (I have added some details from other sources).　　　　[4] *Op. cit.*, p. 74.
[5] *Op. cit.*, pp. 75–82; *Birkenhead Public Libraries Centenary, 1856–1956* (Birkenhead 1956), pp. 9–11.

Very different in character was the West Midlands area, which was defined as including Worcestershire, Warwickshire, Staffordshire, Derbyshire and North-East Cheshire, and which therefore embraced not only Birmingham, which with close on a million books was now the largest municipal library in Great Britain, but also such substantial libraries as Coventry, Stoke on Trent, Derby, Wolverhampton, Worcester and Smethwick. In the survey of this area by J. W. Forsyth, Librarian of Dunfermline, the problem of the small library is not specifically mentioned, though he does refer to some of the characteristic signs of inadequate funds—the large number of dirty and out-of-date books in many libraries; the scarcity of really good reference collections; the persistence in a few places of subscription libraries.

In the main, however, Forsyth's concern is with the problems of expansion, and especially with the problems arising in Birmingham, Wolverhampton, Walsall and other places from the rapid growth of new housing estates. Even at Halesowen in Worcestershire, which had assumed library powers only in 1931 and had opened its central library only in 1933, it had already become necessary to provide two branch libraries. Except for Derbyshire, which had developed a regional system for the service of its many rural centres, the county libraries were also mainly pre-occupied with provision for the populous areas within their boundaries.[1]

J. E. Walker, Librarian of Hendon, who visited fifty-one urban libraries and twelve county libraries in the East Midlands, pointed out that there were small and uneconomic county libraries as well as urban libraries, and that the inefficiency of the county service could sometimes stand in the way of the transfer of powers by smaller authorities. He probably had in mind the counties of Huntingdon and the Isle of Ely, where bookstocks at this time were very small.[2]

Walker describes in some detail the situation at Bury St. Edmunds, which provides a good example of the absurd position that sometimes arose from the existence of too many independent authorities. This little market town of some 17 000 inhabitants, county town for West Suffolk, had adopted the Libraries Acts in 1897 for the purpose of maintaining the Moyses Hall Museum, which was devoted to the history and biology of the region. From 1924, as the result of a bequest, the corporation also supported a free reference library of local materials (the Cullum Library), in the school of art, and paid the salary of a librarian. In 1931 a rate-aided public lending library was opened in the Athenaeum, with a stock of 3 500 volumes hired at £300 a year from the county library, and a part-time woman librarian. In addition Bury St. Edmunds housed the headquarters of the West Suffolk County Library itself, with a bookstock at this time of some 40 000 volumes, mostly on loan. This small town thus had three separate public libraries within a stone's throw of each other.[3]

Herbert Woodbine, Chief Assistant Librarian at Birmingham, surveying the mainly rural area of South Wales and South-West England, comments

[1] *Survey*, pp. 83–96.

[2] Huntingdon had 20 000 in 1938–39, the Isle of Ely 21 500—Library Association, County Libraries Section, *County Libraries in Great Britain and Northern Ireland: Statistical Report, 1938–39* [1940].

[3] *Survey*, p. 98; and information from Mr. Frank Fordham, Borough Librarian.

first and foremost on the "pitiful inadequacy" of the accommodation and staffing available to the county libraries:

> "One county library is housed in the disused cells of a prison; one in old army huts; one in a temporary wooden structure; four in houses, or parts of houses, converted to library use; three only in suitable premises; and of these three, two have outgrown their present accommodation . . . . In three cases the staff at head-quarters consisted of the librarian and his assistant."[1]

The difficulties of the small library again figure prominently in this report, and are analysed with penetration and with sympathy. Like Sydney in the West Riding, Woodbine found the medium-sized libraries (defined in this case as those serving populations between 20 000 and 60 000) giving a reason-ably efficient if somewhat unimaginative service; while the larger town and city libraries suffered mainly from lack of space. He points out that Cardiff, Newport and Bath all need new libraries, and that Exeter, which alone has a modern building, has all but outgrown its accommodation. Without having had time to examine these larger libraries adequately, he notes Exeter's splendid collection of county manuscripts; Cardiff's outstanding Welsh collections, and its continuing excellent work for schools; and Bath's particularly fine reference collection; but he refers critically to "Plymouth, spending all too little on its libraries and therefore short of the branches it needs."[2]

One important point made by Woodbine, and also by Duncan Gray in relation to the North of Scotland, is that the staff of libraries in rural areas were often terribly isolated and almost completely out of touch with modern library practice. This made training very difficult, since "there is practically no possibility of an assistant getting into touch with a reasonable sized collection of reference books."[3]

F. E. Sandry, Librarian of Edmonton, was called upon to survey the South Midlands and Central South Coast area, which reached from Bristol to Brighton and included a number of substantial libraries, but was still pre-dominantly rural in character. Not surprisingly, therefore, Sandry's report has many features in common with that on South Wales and the South-West. He too, though rarely mentioning names, comments on the weaknesses of the county and smaller non-county libraries, and on the overcrowded central libraries of the larger towns. In dealing with the small libraries he draws attention specially to the inadequacy of the non-fiction stocks, both reference and lending. Even where books were hired from the county these were com-monly fiction, and he cites one extreme example in which fiction accounted for 96 per cent of the annual issues. Like Edward Edwards long before him, Sandry points out that the proportion of non-fiction issues depends not only on demand but also on supply.[4]

Finally we come to South-East England, which was divided for the pur-poses of this survey into two sectors. London north of the Thames, with Hertfordshire and Essex, was reviewed by H. P. Marshall, Librarian of Smeth-wick, and London south of the Thames, with Middlesex, Kent and Surrey, by

---

[1] *Op. cit.*, pp. 108–109.
[2] *Op. cit.*, p. 113.
[3] *Op. cit.*, p. 107.
[4] *Op. cit.*, pp. 118–130. For Edwards see above, p. 45.

H. Fostall, Reference Librarian at Manchester. Each of these regions had its rural areas, served by the counties and small independent libraries, but each also included a considerable number of more substantial urban and metropolitan libraries; and Marshall was able to report that north of the river "The majority of libraries have more books than they can shelve and display adequately in the public rooms."[1]

Both he and Fostall commented at considerable length on buildings, and especially on the difficulties in the use of older buildings, "which were", says Fostall, "I have no doubt eminently suitable at the time of their erection, but are now unfortunately unsuitable for the modern methods of librarianship."[2] Both also drew special attention to the general neglect of provision for staff. "Generally," says Marshall, "the accommodation for the staff, dining, rest and cloakrooms, is poor. Administration, too, in some instances, is carried on in extraordinarily difficult conditions; routine work being executed in any odd corner, cramped for space, badly lighted and ill-ventilated."[3] This complaint, it may be noted, was a long-standing one, and figured in many reports.

Both writers allowed the existence of some good modern buildings, e.g. the new central library at Chelmsford (1935); and both mentioned particularly some of the new one-room branches, e.g. at Hampstead, Heston and Isleworth, and Coulsdon and Purley. Marshall commented also on the combination of public libraries with shops (as at Leyton) or with residential accommodation (as at Hackney) as a means of keeping down annual charges.

It was Marshall who underlined once more the special weakness of the London situation: the lack of technical and commercial libraries and of good reference libraries generally; the variations in administrative practice; and the lack of co-operative arrangements between adjoining library authorities. "Without the closest co-operation between all the boroughs," he wrote, "the vast and valuable book resources of London must fall short of their potential efficiency."[4] There were some, as we have seen, who thought that the fundamental weakness was the existence of too many metropolitan authorities.[5]

[1] Op. cit., p. 136.
[2] Op. cit., p. 148.
[3] Op. cit., p. 133.
[4] Op. cit., p. 141.
[5] See above, pp. 238–239, 260.

CHAPTER XI

From Kenyon to the Second World War: Organization and Use

Buildings

PUBLIC libraries now occupied such a variety of buildings, large and small, old and new, converted and purpose-built, that generalization on the subject may seem hazardous. If, however, we look at what was happening in the way of new building, extension, and conversion, especially in the mid and late 'thirties, the new trends in library building are clearly discernible.

One was towards simpler, more functional and more contemporary design, both external and internal. E. J. Carter, Librarian to the Royal Institute of British Architects, who for many years surveyed library building for *The Year's Work in Librarianship*, was particularly scornful of the borough engineers to whom the design of many small town libraries was entrusted. In 1930 he wrote that "the design of libraries tends to stand still in a worship of cliché and historical style," and in 1934 he made almost exactly the same complaint.[1] By 1937, however, though he still found library architecture unduly constrained by library tradition and public authority control, he was prepared to admit that

> "Libraries are now lighter, brighter places than they were and quite a good amount of progress has been made in shaking off the municipal glory idea and bringing library design, particularly branch library design, closer to the terms of ordinary living and reading."[2]

Wherever circumstances made it possible, for example in the case of a suburban branch library, it became increasingly common to set the building back from the road behind a small lawn or garden. This was also done, very effectively, with the Birkenhead Central Library, which was situated on a busy main road. The air of "quietness, dignity and detachment" which resulted can still be felt today.[3]

Interiors tended to be more open and flexible, with fewer separate rooms, or at least fewer permanent dividing walls. Rotherham and Wolverhampton are recorded as providing separate students' rooms,[4] but this was not common. Ladies' reading rooms, once so common, lingered now only in the older libraries, especially in working-class areas.[5] Because open access was now the order of the day, and required more space than the old closed lending library, the reading room for newspapers and magazines was often deposed from its

---

[1] *Y.W.L. 1930*, p. 111; *Y.W.L. 1934*, p. 95.

[2] *Y.W.L. 1937*, pp. 121–122.

[3] L. R. McColvin (ed.), *A Survey of Libraries: Reports on a Survey made by the Library Association during 1936–37* (1938), p. 78.

[4] *Op. cit.*, pp. 68, 85.   [5] *Op. cit.*, pp. 48, 68.

pride of place, and quite often, when old libraries were reconstructed, the reading room and lending library were interchanged.[1] Where this was done, the common but cumbersome practice of allotting to each periodical its special place at a table, and to each newspaper its separate stand or "slope", was dispensed with in favour of racks or shelves from which they were taken as required. Some new central libraries, e.g. Birkenhead, dispensed with newsroom provision altogether.

The radial arrangement of stacks in open access lending libraries, so wasteful but so long regarded as essential to security, persisted throughout the 'thirties, though in 1936 Edward Sydney was able to report from the West Riding that this fetish was at last breaking down, and that "an alcove arrangement which leaves the centre of the floor free for display fittings, tables and seats is the modern tendency."[2] Increasingly, too, it became customary to dispense with the barriers which had been regarded as an essential safeguard when open access was first introduced.

Book displays, or displays of book jackets, were now common form, old indicators or newspaper slopes often being used for this purpose. These were among many factors which contributed to brighter libraries. Others were the use of plants, flowers or pictures; light colours for paintwork in place of the customary drab greens and browns; new flooring materials such as rubber and linoleum; and increased window space. This last was made possible by new methods of building construction, though thin walls and larger windows, as E. J. Carter pointed out, brought problems of heating and ventilation unknown in older buildings. Heating was at this time still mainly by the traditional coke-fired low pressure hot water system, but experiments were being made here and there with gas and electrical heating. Air conditioning was still mistrusted.[3]

The development of electric lighting systems was enormously important, providing improved illumination in the public rooms and making it possible, as at the Manchester Central Library, for the bookstacks to be entirely independent of natural lighting. This gave to the architect, especially of the large library, a freedom of design he had never before known.[4]

All these comments, it should be made clear, refer to the non-county libraries. A final point worth mentioning is that now at long last attention was beginning to be paid to the need for adequate provision for staff and administration. On the former B. M. Headicar, Librarian of the London School of Economics, commented that local authorities had now become more humane than in his earlier days, when, apart from the chief librarian's office, staff rooms did not exist. "Even now," he added, "far less is done for the staff in this direction than they have a right to expect."[5]

The interesting thing about county library buildings at this period was their increasing variety and sophistication. Headquarters buildings, in the

---

[1] I have noted this interchange, between 1927 and 1933, at Abingdon, Dukinfield, Fulham, Hamilton, Harrogate, Hinckley, and Oxford, and there were doubtless other examples, though as we have seen this was a time when, owing to the depression, newsrooms were very heavily used in some areas.

[2] *Op. cit.*, p. 67.   [3] *Op. cit.*, pp. 70, 80, 87; *Y.W.L. 1932*, pp. 88–89.

[4] *Y.W.L. 1931*, pp. 145–146.

[5] B. M. Headicar, *A Manual of Library Organisation* (1935), p. 146.

early 'twenties mere distributing centres, often in a single room, were by the mid 'thirties accumulating a whole complex of functions. Raymond Irwin, of Lancashire County, estimated in 1936 that a large county library needed a headquarters building covering some 20 000 square feet, of which half would be occupied by a bookstore for 250 000 books—about fifty per cent of total stock. A smaller county library, with a total bookstock of, say, 100 000 books, would be able to manage with 5/8000 square feet, but even this was a large area compared with the 1000-1200 square feet which was regarded as normal when the county service began.

What about the half of the building not used for storage? In Irwin's view this was needed for administration (ordering, accessioning, cataloguing, dispatch and receipt of collections for centres); common rooms and other staff accommodation; a students' or reference library providing a personal service to those able to visit it and a postal service to others; a lecture and exhibition room; and rooms for special collections such as music and drama. If the headquarters should happen to be in a town which formed part of the county area, provision could also be made for a town branch.[1] These proposals, of course, represented at this time no more than an ideal. Even the recently opened Lanarkshire County Library headquarters at Hamilton, which it was claimed in the discussion on Irwin's paper could offer practically every facility to which he had referred, had a floor space of only 8500 square feet, with accommodation for 70/80 000 volumes.[2]

County branch libraries, provided initially, except in Scotland, under differential rating schemes, were commonly in converted premises, and the provision made to some extent reflected local wishes and local circumstances. The Kent County branch at Broadstairs, for example, converted from the former council offices, included all the facilities of a normal municipal branch—lending library, children's room, reading room and newspaper room. This, however, was unusual. Characteristically, the main feature of a county branch was the lending library. A small reference or study room equipped with a few quick reference works was often added, and sometimes a children's room, but a reading room or newspaper room was exceptional. A special report on county branch buildings published by the Library Association in 1930 summed up policy at that time as follows:

> "The lending department should be the first consideration; reference departments are important, but not strictly necessary in every district; children's and reading rooms should be regarded as luxuries."[3]

Five years later the *County Libraries Manual* reaffirmed these priorities, but made the point that when a branch served as a sub-centre for a county region it would be necessary also to provide accommodation for a regional store of books.[4] This is a reference to the scheme of regionalization which had

[1] R. Irwin, "Planning and Lay-out of County Library Headquarters Buildings", in *L.A.R.*, 4th Ser., Vol. III (1936), pp. 311–317. Cf. A. S. Cooke (ed.), *County Libraries Manual* (1935), Ch. viii; E. J. Carnell, *County Libraries* (1938), Ch. iv.

[2] *L.A.R.*, 4th Ser., Vol. I (1934), p. 45; Vol. III (1936), pp. 318, 396.

[3] Library Association, County Libraries Section, *County Libraries in Great Britain and Ireland: Report on Branch Library Buildings with Statistical Tables 1929–30* (1930), p. 22.

[4] A. S. Cooke (ed.), *County Libraries Manual* (1935), p. 93.

been devised by Edgar Osborne for Derby County Library, and which was the subject of much discussion at this time. Its purpose, as Osborne explained it in 1932, was "to provide a more adequate, flexible, and personal service to villages than is possible under present systems."[1]

To this end plans were prepared for administering the county library area through ten regional branches, each of which would serve not only the town in which it stood but also the surrounding villages, and would for this purpose carry an appropriate proportion of the stock which in a centralized system would be held at headquarters. Staff engaged in book distribution would likewise be located in the regions instead of at headquarters.

A beginning was made in 1929 at Heanor, where a regional branch was erected as part of a building shared with a technical school. Planned for a stock of 10 000 volumes, it served a population of 33 000, including some fifteen centres formerly served direct from headquarters. The second regional branch, opened at Staveley in 1932, was purpose-built and on a larger scale, being designed to meet the needs of a population of about 64 000, including twenty-six village centres and 15 children's centres. In addition to the usual lending department and study room, it had a regional store for 18 000 volumes.[2] A further three regional branches were established by 1939.[3]

Osborne's colleagues, though interested, were not convinced, and during these years his example was imitated only in Herefordshire, where regional branches were created at Kingston in 1937 and at Ross on Wye in 1938; and in North Lancashire, where in 1938 a scheme was inaugurated for the service of rural centres in North Lonsdale from the county branch at Ulverston.[4]

Travelling Library Services

The problem of serving isolated communities was still by no means completely solved. In the county libraries the use of library vans—either "delivery vans" carrying boxes or trays of books, or "exhibition vans" from which the rural centres made their own choice[5]—was soon well established, but there still remained scattered groups of homesteads remote from any sizeable village centre. Lancashire's scheme for North Lonsdale provided for a direct service to such groups by the exhibition van which was used to transport books to the centres. As a result of this development it became possible to close fifteen of the smaller centres.

[1] E. Osborne, "Decentralisation in County Library Administration", in *L.A.R.*, 3rd Ser., Vol. II (1932), p. 169.

[2] *L.A.R.*, 3rd Ser., Vol. III (1933), p. 36. Cf. the plan printed in the *Report on Branch Library Buildings* (just cited) p. 33.

[3] At Alfreton (1934), Chapel-en-le-Frith (1936), and Swadlincote (1938 in association with the Urban District library)—information from Mr. D. A. South, County Librarian.

[4] B. O. Smith, "Policy in the Rural County", in *L.A.R.*, 4th Ser., Vol. V (1938), pp. 496–507; J. Brindle, "North Lonsdale: an Experiment in Rural Distribution", in *L.A.R.*, 4th Ser., Vol. VI (1939), pp. 159–163; B. O. Smith, "Library Service in Rural Areas", *ibid.*, pp. 225–226. Cf. E. J. Carnell, *County Libraries* (1938), pp. 231–255, where the idea of the regional or district library is worked out in detail.

[5] See above, p. 222.

The county van now made its journey once a month, visiting twenty-five centres, and also making more than one hundred stops for service direct to readers. This was done on a family basis, without limit as to the number or character of the books borrowed. The van was fitted with an issue desk, and was thus in all essentials what would now be described as a mobile library.[1]

For Oliph Smith in Herefordshire, however, this kind of service was impossibly expensive. Smith had no library vans, and calculated that to make monthly visits on the North Lancashire plan (which he thought insufficient) five vans would be needed. As a cheaper alternative he began to develop what he called the "borrower-distributor" system, under which one person in each hamlet was authorized to borrow, from the nearest branch or centre, a small collection of books—perhaps twenty volumes—to be shared among his neighbours and himself for two to four weeks, and then exchanged for a fresh batch.[2]

Oddly enough the first library authority to make the mobile library a regular and recognized feature of its service was not a county but a city. In the years of depression Manchester, like many other large towns, was finding increasing difficulty in meeting the needs of the new housing estates on the fringes of the city. These estates desperately needed libraries but they were often remote from any existing branch and the money to create a ring of new branches was not forthcoming. Delivery and deposit stations, unsatisfactory as they were, continued in use in some towns, but in Manchester the answer was found in the mobile library, known at the time by the French name of "bibliobus". The idea owed its origin to Stanley Jast, and the first vehicle, a superannuated single-decker bus, took the road in 1931. In the *Record* it is thus described:

> "This is really a small Branch library on wheels. The van is of the largest size allowed upon the roads, and it is no disadvantage that it moves slowly on land, as we are told the ark did on the face of the waters, since the distances to be covered are small . . . . The Manchester van has a large central floor space (20 feet by 7 feet), lit by a skylight, and surrounded by the sixty fitted bookshelves, holding about 1200 books. In the free space is the assistant's charging-desk. Fiction is not placed together, but is distributed round the entire wall space, so as to avoid congestion of borrowers.
>
> "The use of the Bibliobus is primarily to bring the library service to the dwellers in the Corporation's new housing estates . . . . A pitch is selected and the Bibliobus encamps there for some hours, returning at night for supplies to the central library, and repeating the process the next day in another new suburb. Its weight makes a dry spot necessary; on its first day out (at New Moston) it was pitched on a piece of soft ground, and sank to the axles, and had to be towed out of the quagmire."[3]

This interesting experiment proved an immediate success, and was copied during the next few years by a number of authorities, the first being the urban district of Erith, on the eastern outskirts of London, in 1933.[4] The first county

---

[1] Brindle, *loc. cit.* Statistics of issues and cost are given by R. Irwin in *L.A.R.*, 4th Ser., Vol. VI (1939), p. 385, where it is also reported that a second van, based on branches at Garstang and Morecambe, is about to go into service for the Fylde and South Lonsdale areas.

[2] *L.A.R.*, 4th Ser., Vol. V (1938), pp. 37, 485, 503.

[3] *L.A.R.*, 3rd Ser., Vol. I (1931), pp. 318–319. Cf. W. G. Fry and W. A. Munford, *Louis Stanley Jast* (1966), p. 54.

[4] F. E. M. Young, "The Travelling Public Library Service in the Urban District of Erith", in *L.A.R.*, 4th Ser., Vol. II (1935), pp. 511–515.

mobile library was brought into use in Kent in 1935, to serve new housing estates in an urban area.[1]

Books and Readers

Of books and readers in general there is not a great deal more to be said at this point, beyond noting the growing concern of the more thoughtful libraries with the problems arising in this field. The old notion that public libraries were for the working classes was now at last disappearing, and many libraries were ready to proclaim, as did J. D. Reynolds, Chief Librarian of Blyth, that their potential *clientèle* was "the whole literate population".[2] It was recognized, however, that in practice the public library fell far short of this ideal. There was much heart searching about the reasons for this; much discussion as to whether book selection should be based primarily on public demand or should be related to some ideal concept of a "balanced collection"; and, inevitably, much rehearsing of the old arguments about the preponderance of fiction.[3]

A new and more constructive turn was given to these discussions by the growing demand for research into library use. E. A. Savage of Edinburgh had been one of the first to draw attention to the need for such inquiry, as long ago as 1924, in "A Plea for the Analytical Study of the Reading Habit",[4] and Berwick Sayers at Croydon made a contribution by a careful analysis of stock and issues.[5] In 1936 the need for research was again forcibly stated, and attention was drawn especially to the value of the work already accomplished by the Americans, e.g. in *The Reading Interests and Habits of Adults*, by W. S. Gray and Ruth Munroe (1930), and *Woodside does Read*, by Grace D. Kelley (1935).[6]

The same theme was taken up a year later by F. Seymour Smith, Deputy Librarian of Hornsey. Seymour Smith stood firmly by the idea of the librarian as educator: broadcasting, schools and universities, and the public libraries were, he declared, the three great educative forces of the modern world. "All three," he went on, "will fail to attain or maintain their ideal standards unless those who control them try to forget that there is such a thing as the general public."[7] The librarian, like other teachers, must forget the mere number of people he serves and think of them as individuals. On this basis Smith propounded a policy:

> "It will be seen, then, that the librarian's problems in relation to his public are threefold: first, to find out as accurately as possible the extent and nature of

---

[1] Information from Mr. D. Harrison, County Librarian.

[2] J. D. Reynolds, "Relations with Readers in the Small Library", in *L.A.R.*, 4th Ser., Vol. IV (1937), p. 363. L. R. McColvin, *Libraries and the Public* (1937), pp. 27–28, makes the same point.

[3] E.g. (to give just a few samples) in *Library World*, Vol. XXXIV (1931–32), pp. 227–228; in *L.A.R.*, 4th Ser., Vol. VI (1939), pp. 348–353; and in *Library Assistant*, Vol. XXIX (1936), pp. 83–91, 152–156, 181–184, 214.

[4] *L.A.R.*, N.S. Vol. II (1924), pp. 210–225 (reprinted in the author's *Special Librarianship in General Libraries* (1939)).

[5] See W. C. B. Sayers, *The Revision of the Stock of a Public Library* (1929), especially Ch. iii.

[6] See J. H. Wellard, "And What did I Learn?" in *L.A.R.*, 4th Ser., Vol. III (1936), pp.419–423; F. M. Gardner, "The Enquiring Librarian", *ibid.*, pp. 459–464; W. C. B. Sayers, "What People Read", in *Library World*, Vol. XXXVIII (1935–36), pp. 232–234.

[7] F. S. Smith, "The Librarian and his Public", in *L.A.R.*, 4th Ser., Vol. IV (1937), pp. 336.

that public: second, to try to discover why some use the library service and others do not; third, to estimate the value of the service he administers. As a corollary to these must be added a fourth: to think out a policy which will strengthen the weak points in the service and bring the full details of what is offered to as great a proportion of his public as he possibly can."[1]

Seymour Smith's paper was presented to the Library Association Conference at Scarborough in June, 1937. He makes reference only to one recent piece of research in this country, carried out at Fulham and Croydon. This was a simple popularity poll on readers' preferences in non-fiction books: predictably, travel, history, and literature were at or near the top of both lists, but other comparisons are difficult because the categories were not the same. At Fulham, where readers were also asked to indicate their favourite writers of fiction, P. G. Wodehouse and Edgar Wallace headed the list.[2]

It is odd that Seymour Smith did not mention E. A. Savage's recently published survey of "The Distribution of Book Borrowing in Edinburgh". This pioneering study, undertaken to discover which parts of the city were well or ill served, pointed to the surprising conclusion that two centrally situated libraries (a central library and a large branch) would serve the city more effectively than the existing thirteen libraries.[3] A similar survey in Falkirk two years later was equally revealing, showing that the new demand arising from the expansion of the burgh boundaries could be better met by an improvement of the existing central library than by the creation of branches in the suburbs.[4]

Among county librarians, too, there was a growing consciousness that their potential *clientèle* was larger and more varied than had been supposed when the service began. In 1929, when it was still a general axiom that rural reading tastes were very unsophisticated, Henry Wilson, County Librarian of East Sussex, was already claiming that the bookstock of a county library should not be inferior to that of a good urban library;[5] and in 1937 E. J. Coombe, County Librarian of the East Riding, was able to report a general rise in the level of demand. "The County Librarian", he declared, "has for some time past recognised the steady growth of a fairly large body of more discriminating readers whose demands indicate that the standard of taste of rural reading lags little behind that of the towns."[6]

Coombe goes on to analyse some of the elements in this new demand, including professional people, adult education students, people seeking to

[1] *Op. cit.*, p. 338.
[2] F. E. Hansford, "What Adults Read", in *Library World*, Vol. XXXVIII (1935-36), pp. 229-232. Sheffield later used the questionnaire method in its children's departments—see Sheffield City Libraries, *A Survey of Children's Reading* (1938).
[3] *L.A.R.*, 4th Ser., Vol. IV (1937), pp. 150-156.
[4] T. Brown, "Book Provision in A Small Town", in *L.A.R.*, 4th Ser., Vol. VI (1939), pp. 375-378.
[5] H. Wilson, "County Library Work in a Residential County", in *L.A.R.*, N.S. Vol. VII (1929), Suppl. pp. 12-15. For other contemporary views see Mrs. Read-Andrews, "Reading at the Local Centre", in *Library Review*, Vol. I (1927-29), pp. 290-293; E. Brooks, "Books Read in an Agricultural County", in *Library Review*, Vol. II (1929-30), pp. 32-34. Mrs. Read-Andrews was a voluntary librarian at a centre in Essex.
[6] E. J. Coombe, "Book Selection—What the County Libraries are Doing (i) Books for General Circulation", in *L.A.R.*, 4th Ser., Vol. IV (1937), p. 309.

equip themselves for a new career, and older readers who have discovered for themselves the pleasures of more serious literature. He concludes:

> "As each year passes, the older members of the library, whose tastes were often of the simplest, are being replaced by young people accustomed to making use of the libraries in the schools, where their reading has been unobtrusively guided by sympathetic teachers. The effect, already felt, is to diminish the ranks of those readers who see the library service only as a vehicle of light entertainment."[1]

Here, too, there was clearly scope for research and inquiry.

Special Collections

Turning back from theory to practice, we note the continued increase in special collections of various kinds. The big city libraries now had large numbers of these, some of deliberate policy and others, one would suppose, by the accident of gift or bequest. Here are a few sample entries from the *Libraries, Museums and Art Galleries Year Book*, 1937:

> *London, Guildhall*: "London (City); Libraries of Clockmakers Co.; Gardeners' Co.; Cooks' Co.; Playing Card Makers' Co.; Engraving, Cruikshank; Drama; Spain; Hebrew; Sir Thomas More; Dutch Church; Cookery."

> *Birmingham*: "Shakespeare Coll., 25 600; Local Coll., 50 000 vols.; Commercial Lib., Patents Lib., separate building; Technical Lib.; Photographs, 30 000 (Sir Benjamin Stone Coll.); Lantern slides (for loan), 29 000; Boulton and Watt Coll. of Manuscript drawings, letters, models, etc.; Byron, Milton and Cervantes Coll."

> *Cardiff*: "Welsh and Celtic; Welsh and other MSS.; Deeds and Documents, Maps and Prints."

> *Glasgow* [in addition to the Commercial Library]: "Scotland, Celtic, Music, Draughts, Scottish Poetry, Robert Burns, Genealogy, Ornithology, Foreign Literature."

> *Leeds* [in addition to the Law Library and the Commercial and Technical Library]: "Leeds and Yorkshire books and prints; Shakespeare; Ruskin; Angling; Music and Works on Music; illustrations."

Many smaller libraries, too, had similar collections though on a less ambitious scale, often merely as sections in their ordinary lending or reference stock. At Malvern, for instance, the lending library included a good collection of music scores and books on music, and Linguaphone records in French, German and Italian; while the reference library included a substantial local collection (books, MSS., maps, pictures, lantern slides), a Quaker collection, a genealogical collection, and an illustrations collection of about 8000 items for the use of teachers.[2]

---

[1] *Ibid.* Cf. the accompanying paper by Richard Wright of Middlesex on "Books for Students", *ibid.*, pp. 310–314; and the more personal comment by Mary C. Stanley-Smith of Oxfordshire, "Personal Contacts with Rural Readers", in *L.A.R.*, 4th Ser., Vol. III (1936), pp. 369–371.

[2] J. W. Lucas, *Malvern Public Library* (Malvern 1940), pp. 29–40. Other examples are cited in L. S. Jast, *The Library and the Community* (1939), pp. 93–94.

It is significant that after 1932 the *Year Book* abandoned the attempt to provide a comprehensive list of music collections. By this time every important municipal library had music available on loan—not only full scores but often vocal and orchestral parts for bands, orchestras, and choral societies. A few, for example Liverpool, had a separate music room, with a piano for trying over the music. Among the counties Warwickshire created a collection of piano-forte scores as early as 1921, and by the late 'thirties Aberdeen, Lanarkshire, Perthshire, Lancashire, Shropshire and the West Riding are all recorded as providing sheet music. The special problems of selecting, classifying, catalogu-ing, shelving, and issuing music were interestingly dealt with in an article by E. A. Savage in 1935, and more comprehensively in two volumes by L. R. McColvin and H. Reeves in 1937-38.[1]

J. D. Stewart noted in 1928 that "circulating collections of gramophone records have been instituted in a number of places", and that "some are now of long standing," but the only place he specifically mentions is Birmingham, and the reference is, in fact, to the subscription library there, not the public library.[2] Eight years later the Library Association survey recorded only one such collec-tion, for the use of schools in a county area; and in 1937 McColvin and Reeves still regarded gramophone record collections as a luxury. Savage disapproved of them, on the ground that "we cannot supervise a borrower's use of records—to prevent him from scraping the life out of them with steel needles or from blasting the grooves in one playing with a blunt needle."[3]

Few libraries now maintained a special collection of books for the blind, the general practice being to subscribe to the National Library for the Blind. The operations of this continued to expand, and the enlarged and reconstructed building in Westminster which was completed in 1935 had accommodation for over a quarter of a million volumes.[4]

Picture collections were becoming fairly common by the end of the 'thirties, and in 1939 more than half the municipal libraries in London and the Home Counties had such collections, ranging from a few hundred items to 75 000. The illustrations included prints and engravings, photographs, material cut from periodicals, and lantern slides. Wherever possible loose material was mounted to one of two standard sizes for protection and ease of storage. Such pictorial collections were often formed for educational purposes, for the use of teachers and lecturers—Hereford County Library, for example, which was a pioneer in the provision of lantern slides, had by 1926 sets of slides for forty-four lectures of which the subjects had been agreed with the Rural Community Council. Many libraries used them, too, in their work with children. Other

[1] E. A. Savage, "One Way to Form a Music Library", in *L.A.R.*, 4th Ser., Vol. II (1935), pp. 100–107; J. A. Carr, "Music and Libraries", in *L.A.R.*, 4th Ser., Vol. V (1938), pp. 595–599; E. J. Carnell, *County Libraries* (1938), p. 104; L. R. McColvin and H. Reeves, *Music Libraries*, 2v. (1937–38); *Survey*, pp. 18, 49.

[2] Information from Mr. W. A. Taylor, Birmingham City Librarian.

[3] J. D. Stewart in *Y.W.L. 1928*, p. 122; Savage, *loc. cit.*, p. 100; McColvin and Reeves, *op. cit.*, Vol. I, p. 49; *Survey*, p. 161. The county library referred to in the *Survey* was Middle-sex—see *L.A.R.*, 4th Ser., Vol. XVI (1949), p. 212; D. H. Harmer, *The Foundation and Growth of County Library Services around London, with special reference to Middlesex* (un-published F.L.A. essay 1964), p. 16.

[4] *L.A.R.*, 4th Ser., II (1935), pp. 569–571.

pictorial collections were formed primarily for record purposes, as part of a more general collection of local material.[1]

Local collections were to be found everywhere. Even the new county libraries were collecting local material, partly to meet the demands of their readers and partly because, once established, they tended to attract such material. They did not, of course, attempt to rival the major local collections already held in urban libraries. Norwich's long established Norwich and Norfolk Collection, and Gloucester's Gloucestershire Collection, just to name two examples, were far beyond anything their respective counties could hope to achieve.

Many of these local collections contained (and still contain) a great deal of manuscript and other archive material.[2] As long ago as 1902 a Local Records Committee appointed by the Treasury had expressed the view that public libraries were not suitable repositories for such material, on the grounds that they frequently lacked the necessary fireproof accommodation and that the custody of archives called for techniques different from those of libraries. The Committee accordingly recommended that county and borough councils should be constituted as the local record authorities for their respective areas, and should arrange suitable facilities under a competent custodian.[3]

No legislative action followed this Report and, with the recognition of many public libraries as repositories for manorial records in the late 'twenties, it seemed as though the position of the libraries was assured.[4] It remained true, however, that many libraries were ill-equipped to handle records, and as separate county and borough record offices began to be set up, slowly at first but more rapidly during the 'forties and 'fifties, the custody of new record deposits increasingly passed into their hands. The unfortunate result was that the care of archives became separated from the care of books, and the new profession of archivist was sundered from the old profession of librarian. The point of cleavage was marked by the foundation in 1932 of the British Records Association, which became the main professional organization and led to the development of special university training courses in London, Liverpool and

---

[1] J. D. Stewart, *loc. cit.*; J. D. Brown, *Manual of Library Economy* (5th edn., by W. C. B. Sayers, 1937), pp. 199–201, 504–506; Carnell, *loc. cit.*; *Survey*, pp. 49, 94, 112, 114, 129, 160; J. D. Stewart (ed.), *Report on the Municipal Library System of London and the Home Counties, 1939* (1940), p. 21.

[2] "Archives can be defined as 'all writings which accumulate naturally during the conduct of affairs of any kind and are preserved for reference either by the persons who compiled them, or by interested parties, or by their successors',—and records as 'archives which have been set aside for preservation in official custody, which must have been unbroken.'" —P. Hepworth in T. Landau (ed.), *Encyclopaedia of Librarianship* (1958, 3rd edn. 1966), p. 25.

[3] Committee appointed to enquire as to the Existing Arrangements for the Custody of Local Records, *Report* (1902), pp. 46–49. County record offices had been suggested, as early as 1889, by William Phillimore, founder of the British Record Society—P. Spufford, "The British Record Society—Eighty Years of an Index", in *The Indexer*, Vol. VI (1968–69), p. 20.

[4] See above, p. 243. More than a dozen additional libraries, including Liverpool and Manchester, were recognized later. See Historical MSS. Commission, *Record Repositories in Great Britain* (1964, 3rd edn. 1968).

Bangor. The Council for the Preservation of Business Archives was created a year later.[1]

The division of functions is now an accepted fact. Public libraries which have substantial record holdings commonly employ trained archivists to look after them and others with small collections often secure assistance from the nearest record office. In general the county and borough record offices are administratively separate from the public libraries, but liaison is often close, especially where, as at Exeter, Liverpool and Norwich, the two organizations share the same building.

Technical and Commercial Libraries

A similar narrowing of library functions took place in the field of technical literature. Up to this time, as we have seen, the public libraries in the larger provincial towns had attempted to meet the special needs of commerce and industry by establishing separate commercial and/or technical libraries. By the 'thirties many of these were giving a very competent and much appreciated service.

Liverpool's Commercial Library, situated in the main business quarter at some distance from the Central Library, was in 1931 so thronged with inquiries that larger premises were being sought.[2] A printed guide to the material obtainable—books, directories, periodicals, reports, gazetteers, maps, etc.—was much in demand, and special indexes were also maintained of articles in commercial periodicals; customs tariffs alterations; amendments to foreign commercial legislation; trade brands and names; variant spellings of place-names; telegraphic addresses not in the usual printed lists; and economic products capable of utilization in industry.[3]

Sheffield, to take another good example, had a combined Commercial and Technical Library which in 1934 (on the opening of the new Central Library) was divided into a Commercial Library and a Library of Science and Technology, the latter taking in pure science as well as technical material. There, two special indexes were maintained: one to the contents of books, and the other to the contents of scientific and technical periodicals not included in the American *Industrial Arts Index*. A close working relationship was also established with the Chamber of Commerce, and in 1933 there was launched, under the auspices of the city library and on the initiative of its librarian J. P. Lamb, a remarkable body known as the Organisation for the Interchange of Technical Books and

[1] On all this see J. L. Hobbs, *Libraries and the Materials of Local History* (1948), Ch. i, and *Local History and the Library* (1962), Ch. v; H. Jenkinson, *The English Archivist* (1948), pp. 12–14; G. B. Stephens, "Archives and Libraries", in *L.A. Conference Proceedings, 1953*, pp. 50–54. I am much indebted for information on these developments to Mr. Philip Hepworth, City Librarian of Norwich, whose "Archives and Manuscripts in Libraries, 1961", published in *L.A.R.*, 4th Ser., Vol. XXIX (1962), is the most recent examination of the position. It shows 11 public libraries (including one county library) with 75000 documents or more, and a further 19 (including 1 county library) with between 10000 and 75000 documents.

[2] Alas! they were never found, and eventually in 1960 the Commercial Library rejoined the main Central Library.

[3] *Y.W.L., 1931*, pp. 85–89.

Periodicals. This brought together the city library, the university library, and a variety of specialist libraries belonging to industrial firms and research organizations. Union catalogues were prepared, and an interlending scheme set on foot which resulted in 291 loans in the first year. By 1937 the number of organizations involved had risen to twenty-two and the number of loans to 318, and a co-operative plan was being operated for securing translations of foreign material.[1]

With their best endeavours, however, the public libraries found it difficult to cope with what was, even in the 'thirties, an ever-increasing flood of scientific and technical literature, most of it not in book form but in the form of periodical articles, reprints, duplicated reports and memoranda, and other often ephemeral material. The same was to become true, in the years after the second World War, in other fields of knowledge, such as social science and business administration. What was now needed was not a librarian in the traditional sense but a new type of worker, himself a subject specialist, who would keep the advance of knowledge in his own field constantly under review, collect information in whatever form it was available, and make it accessible by reproduction, abstracting, and bibliographical listing to all those interested either in its practical applications or in further research.

This new branch of library work came to be called by the name of documentation and its practitioners, eventually, by the rather clumsy name of documentalists. Its national organization in this country was ASLIB, founded as we have noted in 1924,[2] in which the public libraries took their place alongside the special libraries of government departments, learned societies, research organizations, and industrial and commercial concerns.

One of the overriding needs, as pointed out by Richard Haxby, Librarian of the Commercial and Technical Library at Leeds, was to secure an internationally agreed system of classification and cataloguing. At present, he pointed out, every library was ploughing its own furrow:

> "There are no standards; there is no co-ordination. In classification some follow Dewey, some Brown, some the Library of Congress, some Cutter, or even a scheme of their own. In cataloguing some follow the dictionary form, some the subject, and others the classified subject."[3]

Many looked for a lead in this matter to the International Institute of Bibliography which had been founded in 1895 by two Belgian lawyers, Paul Otlet and Henri la Fontaine, and had its first headquarters in Brussels. Its Secretary-General from 1928 to 1959 was Frits Donker Duyvis. It was the publications of the Institute which gave currency to the term "documentation",

---

[1] Op. cit., pp. 89–90. The commercial and technical libraries were brought together again in 1953—see The City Libraries of Sheffield, 1856–1956 (Sheffield 1956), p. 52. For the interchange scheme, still functioning under the name of Sheffield Interchange Organisation (SINTO), see "Interchange of Technical Publications in Sheffield", in L.A.R., 4th Ser., Vol. V (1938), p. 69. For descriptions of other comparable libraries about this time see R. Haxby, "The Leeds Commercial and Technical Library", in Librarian and Book World, Vol. XVIII (1928–29), pp. 218–222, 250–253, 289–290; and H. Fostall, "Manchester Commercial Library", in Manchester Librarian, Vol. V (1929), pp. 13–19.

[2] See above, p. 244.

[3] Y.W.L. 1931, p. 83.

and in 1931 the name of the organization was changed to International Institute for Documentation. A further change in 1938 substituted "Federation" for "Institute", thus recognizing the federal structure which had come into being since 1924. At this time also the headquarters were moved from Brussels to The Hague. An English section of the Institute, the British Society for International Bibliography, was established in 1927, with headquarters at the Science Museum Library.[1]

The Institute's primary concern was with world bibliography, which the founders regarded as a pressing need. For this purpose it developed a new Universal Decimal Classification (U.D.C.), in which the original Dewey system was modified, elaborated, and enriched to embrace all kinds of specialized subjects and all kinds of recorded information, pictorial as well as literary. The new system was first published in 1903. In this country it was first extensively used by the Science Museum Library for an ambitious subject-matter index of the world's scientific and technical literature, collected from all published documentation services.[2] In 1930 a committee of ASLIB recommended that U.D.C. should be adopted by the Association,[3] and it has in fact come to be extensively used by special libraries throughout the world.

Though public libraries have from the beginning been members of ASLIB, and have from time to time played no inconsiderable part in its proceedings, they have always been in a minority, and the work of documentation has never been central to their own activities. The science of documentation, like the science of archives, has thus developed as an independent discipline, largely outside the public library sphere.[4]

Children's Libraries

The development of services for children at this period, like that of services for adults, was not without its checks and difficulties. The depression, for example, brought a period of restraint and sometimes worse: at Manchester

[1] For the history see S. C. Bradford, *Documentation* (1948, 2nd edn. 1953), espec. Ch. viii; E. Scott, "IFLA and FID—History and Programs", in *Library Quarterly*, Vol. XXXII (1962), pp. 1–10.
[2] *Y.W.L. 1928*, p. 68; *L.A.R.*, N.S. Vol. VII (1929), Suppl. pp. 24–29; W. H. Spratt, *Libraries for Scientific Research in Europe and America* (1936), Ch. i. This great enterprise, the last serious attempt at a comprehensive catalogue of periodical articles on science, was closely identified with the name of Dr. S. C. Bradford. At the time of his retirement in 1938 the index numbered $2\frac{1}{2}$ million cards, and it went on accumulating for some years longer, but it was little used and eventually, like the more grandiose effort at a comprehensive world bibliography made in association with the Brussels Institute in its earlier years, it was abandoned: the costly cabinets were dispersed, and the cards, after having been kept in store for some years, were destroyed—H. T. Pledge in R. Irwin and R. Staveley (eds.), *The Libraries of London* (1949, 2nd edn. 1961), p. 50; and information from Dr. D. J. Urquhart, Director of the National Lending Library for Science and Technology, Boston Spa.
[3] See *Y.W.L., 1930*, p. 145, and references there cited.
[4] For the origins and effects of the split between librarians, archivists, and documentalists see the important introductory essay by J. H. Shera and M. E. Egan to the 2nd edition of S. C. Bradford's *Documentation* (1953).

the economies imposed in 1931 disrupted the work to such an extent that it did not recover till after the war.[1] Later, in some places, there were reports of a decline in issues of children's books, attributed variously to the decline of the birth-rate, the shift of population to suburban areas, the growth of traffic, and the improvement of provision in the schools.[2] The Library Association survey of 1936 commented on the inadequacy of the children's service in some areas,[3] and as late as 1942 McColvin found that "in more than 40 per cent of the main libraries visited (i.e. excluding branches) there was no separate department, children being served in the ordinary lending library."[4]

None the less the period as a whole did bring a substantial improvement, especially in the years immediately before the war. Separate children's rooms were now accepted as essential in all progressive libraries, and some of those provided in new buildings were most attractively furnished and equipped. Low bookcases and special chairs and tables were to be found everywhere, and we hear also of frescoes on the walls (at Sunderland and Darlington), a Children's Quiet Room (at Mile End), a paved garden (at Becontree Branch, Dagenham) and fireside seats round an electric fire (at Aspley Branch, Nottingham). Along with these comforts went all kinds of activities designed to interest and attract the children—story hours, play-readings, discussion groups, lantern lectures, even in some places films. Hendon, in 1928, led the way in organizing the first children's book week, during which, in addition to many other activities, an exhibition of new books was arranged in the children's library, and talks were given by well known children's authors.[5]

In London and the home counties work for children was more advanced than in most parts of the country. In 1939 only seven out of 102 urban authorities were making no provision. Of the rest, 82 had separate departments, 43 employed special staff, 42 organized lectures, 32 story-hours, and 6 films. Ten years earlier only 57 out of 71 libraries had possessed separate departments, and only 15 had special staff.[6]

In the county libraries books for children had been an important part of the provision from the beginning, and the rapid development of branch libraries now gave an opportunity for working with the children directly. Even in 1933 nearly every branch had a special children's collection, and the staff were alive to the possibilities of lectures, story-hours and the like. Of the home counties it was reported in 1939 that a number of the new branch library buildings had special children's rooms—once regarded as a luxury—and that

---

[1] See above, p. 256.

[2] *Y.W.L. 1936*, p. 72; L. R. McColvin (ed.), *A Survey of Libraries* (1938), p. 139.

[3] *Op. cit.*, pp. 30, 85–86, 129.

[4] L. R. McColvin, *The Public Library System of Great Britain* (1942), p. 73.

[5] See especially for these developments M. M. Kirby and others, "The Development of the Children's Library during 1937–38", in *Library World*, Vol. XLI (1938–39), pp. 83–88, 108–110. Contrast J. F. Halbert, "Libraries and Children: a survey of modern practice," in *L.A.R.*, 3rd Ser., Vol. II (1932), pp. 305–308. A recent general survey is A. Ellis, *Library Services for Young People in England and Wales, 1830–1970* (1971), Ch. v.

[6] J. D. Stewart (ed.), *Report on the Municipal Library System of London and the Home Counties, 1929* (1931), pp. 19–21; and *1939* (1940), pp. 15–16.

others usually provided a children's corner. Only one branch, however, at Gillingham in Kent, had a trained children's librarian.[1]

The new feature about children's work in the late 'thirties was the increasing attention paid to the needs of the adolescent. It was George E. Roebuck, Librarian of Walthamstow, who led the way in this field by establishing, in 1924, a separate "intermediate section" for readers between fourteen and seventeen, i.e. boys and girls who had left school but were not old enough to join the adult library. Here were placed books thought likely to be of special interest to readers of this age, books also which it was hoped would lead them on towards the wider interests appropriate to adult life. The readers were not restricted to the intermediate stock but could, if they wished, ask for books either from the junior library or from the adult library.[2]

This was an attempt to solve a very serious problem, an attempt, as Roebuck himself put it fifteen years later ,"to check the leakage in membership between the leaving of school and the re-awakening of interest in reading, which so often marks the opening years of maturity."[3] At that time he spoke in modest terms of what had been achieved:

> "The results have not been remarkable but they have been gratifying. We hold about a thousand young readers each year and carry most of them through until, at seventeen, they are eligible for the adult sections."[4]

For a long time Roebuck found few imitators. Charles Nowell at Coventry did indeed make a beginning with special displays of books for adolescents both in the junior library and in the adult library, but when he moved to Manchester in 1932 the experiment was abandoned. In the London area, however, the influence of Walthamstow evidently made itself felt, for five other libraries were reported as possessing intermediate sections in 1934. S. W. Anderson, of Croydon, reviewing the situation at this point, thought the provision of a separate entrance to the intermediate room at Walthamstow was a disadvantage, and that a better arrangement would be to place the room between the junior and adult rooms, with access from both.[5]

By 1936 an arrangement similar to that suggested by Anderson had actually been put into practice at Northampton, and special sections or departments for adolescents were reported also at Middlesbrough, Blyth, Burnley, Haslingden, and ten places (including Walthamstow) in the London area.[6] Unfortunately this promising development was cut short by the war.

---

[1] Stewart, op. cit., 1939, pp. 25–26. For the position in 1933 see B. O. Smith, "What the Counties are Doing: Children's and Reading Rooms", in Library Assistant, Vol. XXVI (1933), pp. 52–55.

[2] Walthamstow Public Libraries, A Year's Experiment in Intermediate Reading (1925); A Five Years' Experiment in Intermediate Reading (1929).

[3] G. E. Roebuck, "The Adolescent Reader", in L.A.R., 4th Ser., Vol. VI (1939), p. 577.

[4] Ibid.

[5] S. W. Anderson, "Catering for the Adolescent", in Library Assistant, Vol. XXVII (1934), pp. 192–195, 215–219, 254–259. Anderson was wrong in supposing that Walthamstow stood alone at this time—see Stewart, op. cit., 1934, p. 21.

[6] Survey, pp. 42, 50, 106; Stewart, op. cit., 1939, p. 16. E. Leyland, The Public Library and the Adolescent (1937), re-examines possible solutions to the problem, but adds little to our knowledge of the actual situation.

The importance of school libraries was emphasized at the beginning of this period by two Board of Education reports, the *Report of the Consultative Committee on Books in Public Elementary Schools*, and the *Memorandum on Libraries in State-Aided Secondary Schools in England*, both published in 1928.[1] In most cases the relationship between libraries and schools (especially elementary schools) was already close, and the Board's annual report for 1934 notes with approval a pamphlet on the subject issued by the Bermondsey Public Libraries:

> "The Junior Libraries in that borough are closed during school hours and at those times are available to any teacher wishing to conduct a lesson surrounded by the books dealing with the subject; again, the librarian is prepared to arrange for simple lessons on the use of books to be given to school classes; finally, in order that the older children may be familiarised with an important public provision for continued education after leaving school, classes of senior children are conducted around the Library departments and the time so spent is regarded as an educational visit for the purpose of school attendance."[2]

Relations with secondary schools were in general less close, but the same report notes "a surprising amount of co-operation between Public Libraries and secondary schools, ranging from advice by the librarian to the supply of volumes by the Public Library on payment by the education committee," and refers by way of illustration to "an experiment conducted in 1929 at Wigan Grammar School, whereby a selected form of boys spent one period each week on individual work under supervision in the Public Library." A special room was allocated for the purpose, and the boys were given preliminary instruction in the use of the library.[3]

The provision of school libraries was a different matter, and was often the responsibility of the education authority. Provision by municipal libraries continued to increase, however, at least until 1935: the Library Association statistics for that year show 138 English libraries providing libraries for 1997 schools, which represents a considerable advance on the position recorded in the Kenyon Report. Lancashire, with 29 authorities supplying 486 schools, was outstanding in this respect. In Wales, on the other hand, only five authorities provided, and the figure for Scotland was the same.[4] Most of the schools provided for were elementary schools: provision for secondary schools was still rather exceptional.

The variety of financial arrangements was bewildering. Sometimes the education authority met the entire cost, sometimes it contributed part of the cost, but quite often it gave nothing. At Cambridge, for example, where school libraries were inaugurated as long ago as 1900 following a request from

---

[1] See especially, in the first-named report, Ch. iv, and in the second, pp. 20–21.

[2] Board of Education, *Education in 1934* (1935), p. 56. Cf. Bermondsey Public Libraries, *Pictures for Schools and some other Facilities for Teachers and Students* (1928, 2nd. edn. 1932), pp. 10–11.

[3] Board of Education, *op. cit.*, pp. 56–57. This experiment is reported on in detail in the Wigan Public Library's *Annual Report* for 1929–30, pp. 9–10, but it does not appear that there was any follow-up—information from Mr. N. E. Willis, Director.

[4] Library Association, *Statistics of Urban Public Libraries in Great Britain and Ireland (1935)* [1936]. Cf. above, p. 245.

the teachers, the education authority did not contribute a penny until 1947.[1]
The Board of Education report for 1934 from which we have already quoted
comments rather plaintively that "it would be of considerable interest
if full details could be collected of the various methods of co-operation
which exist between the Public Libraries and the schools for the supply of
books."[2]

The most notable school library provision by a municipal library continued
to be that at Cardiff, but attention must also be drawn to the particularly comprehensive provision made by Edinburgh and Hull. In Edinburgh the school
library system was based on an agreement made in 1926 under which the
education authority undertook to provide accommodation and equipment, and
the library authority to provide the books and the staff. By 1936 four distinct
types of library were in operation:

> (i) *School libraries* (22 in number). A school library was a general collection
> for the use of a whole school, "usually located in a spare classroom, a hall, or other
> suitable place to which the children can go at convenient times to exchange their
> books."

> (ii) *Classroom libraries* (151 in number). These were small collections of books
> for the use of individual classes where a general school library was impracticable.

> (iii) *School branch libraries*, of which there were two, one at the Bellevue
> Technical and Commercial School and the other at the Leith Academy Secondary
> School. Each included a general children's collection, a selection of children's
> reference books, and a collection for the use of the staff.

> (iv) *School branch libraries for children and adults.* These were the latest develop-
> ment, and there were at this time four of them, all opened in the years 1934-36
> in elementary schools in new housing areas—Balgreen, Craigmillar, Granton, and
> Craigentinny. Each carried a stock of some 7000 volumes, of which about 1500
> were for children. Adults entered direct from the street, children during school
> hours from the school, but the children could also use the library, through the
> adult entrance, at times when the school was closed, and this was regarded as a
> great advantage. Libraries of this type were Edinburgh's answer to the problem of
> the new housing estates.[3]

The Hull scheme dated back to 1926, when a collection of 250 books was
provided for each of twelve school departments. The number of schools benefit-
ing by this service was increased each year, and from 1929–30 libraries were sent
also to evening institutes. By 1932–33 there were over a hundred such libraries,
with annual issues exceeding 400 000. Up to this date the cost, apart from
shelving, was borne by the public libraries committee, but the education
committee assumed responsibility from 1933.[4]

[1] W. A. Munford, *Cambridge City Libraries, 1855–1955* (Cambridge 1955), pp. 9–10. For
the very varied arrangements in the London area, see J. D. Stewart (ed.), *Report on the
Municipal Library System of London and the Home Counties, 1934* (1935), pp. 13–14, and
1939 (1940), pp. 11–12.
[2] Board of Education, *op. cit.*, p. 56.
[3] R. Butchart, "School Libraries in Edinburgh", in *L.A.R.*, 4th Ser., Vol. III (1936), pp.
410–413.
[4] Hull Public Libraries, *Annual Reports*, espec. for 1929–30 and 1932–33; and information from Mr. D. J. Bryant, Chief Librarian.

In the counties the problem was easier, because the county libraries were part of the education service. Practice varied, but by the mid-'thirties some counties were making extensive provision. The statistics for 1934–35 show 2755 county library service points in "school and other centres" compared with 13 381 in "adult and general centres". About 2000 of the former, it would appear, were serving elementary schools, the remainder being in secondary schools (186), evening schools (188), and a variety of other centres including factories, clubs, women's institutes, unemployed centres, hospitals, prisons and even lighthouses. The counties showing the largest number of "school and other centres" were Cumberland (220) and the East Riding (216), but Cambridgeshire, Derbyshire, Middlesex, East Suffolk, and the North Riding were also making substantial provision.[1]

By 1936 fourteen English county libraries were receiving grants from their education authorities for this work: Middlesex, for example, was receiving £5 per 100 children, and Derbyshire £1000 a year to provide libraries on the basis of one book for each school child aged nine or over.[2] In the 1938–39 statistics the figure for "school and other centres" shows an increase in almost every county over the figure for five years earlier, the lead being now taken by Cumberland (267), Northamptonshire (254), Derbyshire (235), Middlesex (229), the East Riding (220) and, surprisingly, Denbighshire (210), the first Welsh county to take up this work on an extensive scale.[3] In 1939, the County Libraries Section of the Library Association recommended the provision of books to elementary schools on the basis of three books for every two children over eight years of age.[4]

Hospitals, Prisons, Ships and Lighthouses

The remote beginnings of the hospital library service go back to the nineteenth century, but the problem did not really attract public attention until the time of the first World War, when the Red Cross and Order of St. John War Hospital Library was established to provide books for sick and wounded soldiers. This service was maintained after the war, and by 1930 the Library was supplying collections of books to over 2000 hospitals of all kinds. In more than 150 hospitals it was also able to arrange for voluntary helpers to distribute the books to patients. Other voluntary bodies were also active in the work, especially Toc H, but at this stage the participation of municipal libraries was exceptional. Only Worthing, in 1927, approached its local hospital with an offer of help; and Kidderminster, three years later, agreed to meet special requests for books from two neighbouring hospitals, each of which already had

---

[1] Library Association, County Libraries Section, *County Libraries in Great Britain and Ireland: Statistical Report, 1934–35* [1936].

[2] M. F. Austin, "Books for Children", in *L.A.R.*, 4th Ser., Vol. IV (1937), pp. 315–316. Cf. the work by A. Ellis cited at p. 293, note 5, above.

[3] Library Association, County Libraries Section, *County Libraries in Great Britain and Northern Ireland: Statistical Report, 1938–39* [1940]. On assistance by public libraries to secondary schools see Carnegie U.K. Trust, *Libraries in Secondary Schools* (1936), Ch. vi.

[4] Library Association, County Libraries Section, *Memorandum on the Provision of Libraries in Elementary Schools* (1939).

a small library.[1] The counties showed more interest, and by 1928–29 Buckinghamshire, Kent, Middlesex and Forfar were already making some kind of provision.[2]

It was not until the 'thirties, however, that there were real signs of a forward movement. Following discussion during the Library Association Conference at Cambridge in September, 1930, the Council of the Association appointed a Hospital Libraries Committee to look into the matter, with Marian Frost, Librarian of Worthing, as chairman, and Harry Farr, Librarian of Cardiff, as secretary. In its report, presented in the following year and duly approved by the Association, the Committee recommended:

> (1) That a hospital library service should be established in voluntary hospitals and council hospitals throughout the country, and that these should be a responsibility of the public library authorities.
> (2) That where the public supply of books is adequate the British Red Cross Hospital Library should confine itself to the supply of books to special hospitals not otherwise dealt with.
> (3) That in every hospital there should be, wherever possible, a distribution of books to patients individually, and this should be undertaken by, or under the supervision of, a competent librarian, who would be responsible not only for book selection and service, but also for the recruitment and training of the voluntary assistance that may be required.[3]

The Committee also suggested, in the course of its report, that public libraries should supply books to public assistance institutions.[4]

In spite of the depression many libraries were quick to respond to this new opportunity of service. By the end of 1931 Cardiff, East Ham, Hampstead, Heston and Isleworth, Kettering, Kingston upon Thames, Richmond on Thames, Sheffield, Stretford, and Watford all had the matter in hand, besides the counties of Clackmannan, Stirling and Worcester. Some of the larger authorities were rather slower to act, and it was only in 1933 that schemes were agreed for Birmingham and Manchester.

The Birmingham scheme provided for a central depot, staffed by the City Library, where books were assembled for distribution to hospitals, but the individual hospitals were responsible for collecting the books from the centre, organizing their distribution to patients, and ultimately returning them. The hospitals also contributed to the cost of the depot. For the supply of books the depot was dependent on donations: the public library supplied books only on special request. In Manchester, too, though the enterprise was much more firmly under public library control, many of the books came from dona-

---

[1] F. C. Pritchard, *The Development of Hospital Libraries in the United Kingdom* (unpublished L. A. Hons. Dipl. thesis, 1934). Mr. L. M. Bickerton, Chief Librarian of Worthing, confirms that bookboxes were supplied monthly to the Worthing Hospital from 1928, but Kidderminster has no record of hospital library provision at this early date.

[2] Library Association, *County Libraries in Great Britain and Ireland: Report, 1928–29* (1929), pp. 13–14. Pritchard also mentions Derbyshire as commencing service in 1928, but here again there is no local record.

[3] Library Association, *Memorandum and Recommendations of the Hospital Libraries Committee* (1931), p. 7. The "special hospitals" referred to in clause 2 were maternity hospitals, sanatoria, mental hospitals, hospitals for ex-servicemen, etc.

[4] *Op. cit.*, p. 6.

tions, and for financial reasons it was necessary to rely on voluntary helpers for the actual distribution to patients.[1]

For the county libraries, hospital service was in principle relatively easy: the hospital was scheduled as a library centre, and a supply of books arranged for, to be delivered by the library van and changed from time to time. As in other county centres, the distribution was done by voluntary helpers. It is not surprising, therefore, to find that by 1934–35 libraries were already being distributed to 53 hospitals (43 in England, 7 in Wales, and 3 in Scotland) and to 62 public assistance institutions (46 in England and 16 in Wales).[2] In 1938 Miss Cooke of Kent was able to report that in England, "in almost every county, consideration was being given to the question of hospital library provision", though she felt compelled to add that in some cases the provision amounted to no more than the giving of discarded books to hospitals for infectious diseases. Miss Cooke drew attention to the magnitude of the problem in some counties (118 hospitals in the West Riding, 95 in Kent, 86 in Surrey) and to the administrative complexities arising, for example, from the location of outlier L.C.C. hospitals in the Kent County area.[3]

The library system that grew up in the hospitals during the 'thirties was thus a mixture, in varying proportions, of public and voluntary service. The variety is well illustrated by the report on the London and Home Counties library services for 1939. This shows 20 out of 102 municipal libraries providing a book service to hospitals and/or public assistance institutions. They were supplying, in all, fourteen voluntary hospitals, one mental hospital, two infectious diseases hospitals, and eight public assistance institutions. In many hospitals provision was made, not only for the patients, but also for the medical and nursing staff. The library authority was normally responsible for the cost of the operation, and bore a major share in the provision of books and staff, but there was still scope for assistance from the Red Cross, Toc H, and other voluntary societies. It was the local Chamber of Trade which presented the book trolley at Watford, and the Rotary Club which made a similar gift at Colchester.[4]

Of the ten county libraries it is reported that all recognized the supply of books to hospitals as part of the normal service, but that in many the work was still only partly developed. In one county, however, the service was at a more advanced stage and a trained hospital librarian had been appointed to organize the scheme in collaboration with the voluntary workers.[5]

[1] C. Nowell, "Hospital Libraries as a Public Service", in *L.A.R.*, 4th Ser., Vol. IV (1937), pp. 365–369.

[2] Library Association, County Libraries Section, *County Libraries in Great Britain and Ireland: Statistical Report, 1934–35* [1936], p. 12. For the position in Wales at this time see *Report of the Proceedings of the Eleventh Conference of Libraries in Wales and Monmouthshire, 1936* (Aberystwyth 1936), pp. 51–64.

[3] A. S. Cooke, "The Problem of Hospital Library Service for the County Library Authority" in *L.A.R.*, 4th Ser., Vol. V, pp. 345–349.

[4] J. D. Stewart (ed.), *Report on the Municipal Library System of London and the Home Counties, 1939* (1940), pp. 16–18. The special hospital book trolley designed by George Bolton, Librarian of Watford, is illustrated in *L.A.R.*, 3rd Ser., Vol. I (1931) p. 359.

[5] Stewart, *op. cit.*, p. 26. The county with an advanced service is not identified, but is presumably Kent.

In considering all these developments, and the extent of public library participation, we must bear in mind not only that public library resources were severely limited but also that many large hospitals, such as the Middlesex, Guy's and Bartholomew's, already had patients' libraries of their own; and that many hospitals which did not possess such a service were on medical or disciplinary grounds opposed to its introduction. The public libraries were by no means always knocking at an open door.[1]

Prison libraries in the 'thirties were still operated under regulations laid down following a Home Office committee in 1911.[2] Each prison had its library, with a stock of recreational and educational books purchased from a grant of 1s. 3d. per head of the average prison population per annum. There was also in each prison a small collection of books for use in educational classes. These collections came into existence in the mid 'twenties as a result of the joint efforts of the Carnegie Trust and the British Institute of Adult Education.[3]

A considerable step forward was taken when in 1934 the Prison Commissioners created at each prison the new post of Librarian Officer. These officers were not trained librarians, but some of them underwent a course of training at a local public library. In 1936 the Library Association appointed a committee to consider what assistance could be given in respect of prison library provision. This Committee recommended that the capitation grant should be increased to 3s., that the Library Association should appoint a panel of librarians to advise on suitable books, and that a professional librarian should be put in charge of the whole prison library service.[4] These recommendations were accepted only in part: the advisory panel was agreed to, and the capitation grant was raised to 1s. 9d., but no action was taken on the appointment of a professional librarian. Looking back, we can see that these events represent the beginning of public library participation in prison library work, but prior to the war contacts between the prisons and their local libraries were still few and rather tenuous.[5]

Libraries for ships of the Royal Navy were provided, from the late nineteenth century onwards, by the Director of Victualling. Libraries for merchant ships were provided by a variety of voluntary bodies, of which the chief were the British Sailors' Society, which traced its origins back to 1828, and the Seafarers' Education Service, which had been founded in 1919 on the initiative

[1] On all this see, in addition to the works cited, M. E. Going (ed.) *Hospital Libraries and Work with the Disabled* (1963), Ch. iii; and for a fuller account Pritchard, *The Development of Hospital Libraries in the United Kingdom.*

[2] Home Office, Prison Libraries Committee, *Report of the Departmental Committee on the Supply of Books to the Prisoners in H.M. Prisons and to the Inmates of H.M. Borstal Institutions* (Cd 5588, 1911).

[3] *Y.W.L. 1930*, pp. 189–190; F. Banks, *Teach them to Live* (1958), pp. 218–219.

[4] *L.A.R.*, 4th Ser., Vol. IV (1937), pp. 565–566; Vol. V (1938), pp. 4–6.

[5] *Survey*, p. 57, reports that Bootle Public Libraries were maintaining prison libraries as early as 1936, but Mr. A. R. Hardman, the present Director, tells me that the service never amounted to more than the sending of discarded books to Walton Gaol. For prison library services by East Suffolk County and Portsmouth in 1938 see *L.A.R.*, 4th Ser., Vol. V (1938), p. 88; and R. F. Watson, *Prison Libraries* (1951), p. 17. This latter work, pp. 9–17, provides a brief general historical account.

of Albert Mansbridge. Both bodies received assistance from the owners, and in the 'twenties from the Carnegie Trust. The British Sailors' Society was responsible also for the provision of books to lightships and rock lighthouses. In all this work the public libraries played very little part, but the city libraries of Glasgow and Cardiff acted as sub-depots for the Seafarers' Education Service (which had its main headquarters in London) and the shore-based lighthouses were served by the appropriate county libraries.[1]

Library Organization

We have had occasion to refer more than once to the process of modernization and reorganization that was taking place in many public libraries at this time, and we have noted that this process, starting very often with conversion to open access, might involve a quite drastic reconstruction of library premises, re-allocation of rooms, relighting and redecoration. A great deal of administrative lumber—what W. A. Munford calls "neolithic readers' registers, methods of filing, stocktaking and accessioning"—was swept away at the same time, though much of the old routine lingered here and there, especially in the smaller libraries.[2]

Apart from this continuing open access revolution (virtually complete, except in Scotland, by 1939), innovations in library organization were relatively few.[3] A new system of book issue, the Dickman charging system, was imported from the United States in the mid 'thirties, and was adopted by West Ham and a few other authorities in the London area, but its use never became widespread. Its key feature was the issue to each reader of a metal ticket with his number embossed upon it: when a book was issued, this ticket was used to stamp the reader's number on the book card, thus making a permanent record of the loan. On the other hand, since the reader retained his ticket, there was no control over the return of the book, or over the number of books the reader might borrow.[4] Most librarians, therefore, preferred to keep to the traditional "pocket-

---

[1] See *Y.W.L. 1928*, pp. 198–201; S. K. Reynolds, "Libraries Afloat", in *L.A.R.*, 4th Ser., Vol. III (1936), pp. 150–153; H. M. Butt, "Naval Library Services", in *L.A.R.*, 4th Ser., Vol. IV (1937), pp. 479–481. H. K. Cook, *In the Watch Below* (1937), is a fascinating study of merchant seamen's reading. For the arrangements made for service to Scottish lighthouses see Carnegie U.K. Trust, *County Libraries in Great Britain and Ireland: Report 1927–28* (Dunfermline 1928), p. 15.

[2] W. A. Munford, "Some Opinions on Modern Library Organisation", in *Library Assistant*, Vol. XXIX (1936), p. 90.

[3] In Scotland, at least four indicators were still in use after the war, the last to go being at Dumbarton in 1951 (the others were at Lossiemouth, Stirling and Stornoway)—W. R. Aitken, *A History of the Public Library Movement in Scotland to 1951* (Glasgow 1971), p. 194. London's last indicator was removed from the Holborn Central Library in 1946—J. Swift, "Holborn Public Library", in *L.A.R.*, 4th Ser., Vol. XIV (1947), pp. 64–65.

[4] L. M. Harrod, "The Dickman Charging System in England", in *Library World*, Vol. XXXVIII (1935–36), pp. 107–109; H. G. Christopher, "The Dickman Bookcharging System", in *Library World*, Vol. XXXIX (1936–37), pp. 231–336; D. McDougall, "Lending Library Technique with Special Reference to the Dickman System", in *L.A.R.*, 4th Ser., Vol. IV (1937), pp. 165–169.

card charging", which by this time was customarily known as the Browne system.[1]

Librarians were now becoming increasingly conscious of the problem of bringing under control, and making available for the use of readers, the ever-swelling mass of books and documentary material. Techniques such as the photostat and the microfilm, at this time beginning to be used in the larger libraries, were eventually to make an important contribution to this problem,[2] but in the meantime attention was focused mainly on the tasks of classification and cataloguing. R. Haxby, of the Leeds Commercial and Technical Library, wrote in 1931: "The two main problems of all libraries, apart from finance, are classification and cataloguing, and they tend to increase in importance from year to year."[3] This concern showed itself in a number of different ways: in the elaboration of specialized classifications for special purposes; in the development of completely new and comprehensive classification schemes; and in proposals for the centralization or co-ordination of both classification and cataloguing.

The specialized classifications were commonly developed within the framework of Dewey or the Universal Decimal Classification.[4] They included special subjects such as business information or oriental literature, and special types of material such as music, films, microfilms and gramophone records.[5] A classification was also devised for school libraries;[6] and attempts were made, not very successfully, to classify fiction.[7]

[1] For the nineteenth-century English origins of this system see above, p. 89. The later name appears to derive from an American librarian, Miss Nina E. Browne, who introduced a similar system in 1895. See her own account in *Library Journal*, Vol. XX (1895), p. 168; the series of articles on Charging Systems by J. D. Brown in *Library World*, Vols. I–III (1898–1901), especially Vol. I (1898–99), pp. 244–245; and correspondence in *L.A.R.*, 4th Ser., Vol. XXII (1955), pp. 162, 234–235.

[2] Neither of these techniques was new. The microphotograph, invented by an Englishman, J. B. Dancer, as early as 1839, was effectively used during the siege of Paris in 1870. Paul Otlet of the International Institute of Bibliography invented a microfilm reader of which he published a description in 1906. The Americans discovered the value of the technique for the storing of newsprint in the 'thirties and in this country it came to the fore shortly before the war as a means of recording material threatened with destruction. For the early history see F. Luther, *Microfilm: a History, 1839–1900* (Annapolis 1959); and L. L. Ardern, *John Benjamin Dancer* (1960).

The photostat apparatus was first marketed in 1910 and was used by the Library of Congress and other large American libraries from 1912 onwards. In this country it was in use in the British Museum, the Birmingham Public Library, and apparently some other libraries, by 1937.

[3] *Y.W.L. 1931*, p. 82.

[4] ASLIB and the British Society for International Bibliography combined to publish in 1936 Vol. I of the first English edition of the U.D.C. In the same year the 3rd edition of the Science Museum's *Classification for Works on Pure and Applied Science in the Science Museum Library* provided an abridgement of the relevant U.D.C. classes.

[5] See for examples *Y.W.L. 1928*, pp. 126–127; *1929*, pp. 161–162; *1935*, p. 162; *1937*, p. 157; *1938*, pp. 172–174.

[6] E. S. Fegan and M. Cant, *The Cheltenham Classification: a Library Classification for Schools* (1937).

[7] Elaborate schemes for the classification of fiction, such as that described in L. A. Burgess, "A System for the Classification and Evaluation of Fiction", in *Library World*, Vol. XXXVIII (1935–36), pp. 179–182, which identified 92 different categories, did not find

Of the two completely new classification schemes that came into existence at this time, the Colon Classification (1933), and the Bibliographic Classification (1935), it is not necessary to write at length since neither has ever been adopted to any significant extent for public library work. This is fortunate, because they are both very difficult to describe in brief compass. They were, however, monumental achievements.

The Bibliographic Classification, devised by H. E. Bliss, Associate Librarian of the City College of New York, is based on a searching re-examination of the classification of knowledge, and on the "educational and scientific consensus" as to the way in which the various areas of knowledge are related to one another. His system has many useful features, and might well have won adherents had not the Dewey system already been so firmly established. The Colon Classification, devised by S. R. Ranganathan, Librarian of the University of Madras, is distinguished by the subtlety of its subject analysis and the complexity of its notation. By focussing attention, not on the philosophical divisions and subdivisions of which the subject to be classified forms part, but rather on the various aspects or "facets" of the subject itself, Ranganathan has produced a classification which is more adaptable than most to areas of knowledge undergoing rapid change, and which has been the parent, in the post-war years, of "faceted classifications" in many special fields. The symbols (letters and numbers) representing the various facets are used to make up descriptive classmarks, and the use of the colon to separate the various elements in the classmark gives the system its name.[1]

There was much discussion during these years about the centralized production and distribution of catalogue cards, but little was achieved. The fact is that the problems involved in producing a generally acceptable form of card, and producing it quickly enough to be useful, were more serious than the Kenyon Committee supposed when it recommended central cataloguing by the British Museum Library, and the economies the Committee foresaw tended to melt away in actual practice.[2] Eventually in November, 1936, the Government announced that it had not proved practicable to adopt the Committee's suggestions on this point.[3] Following this decision there were suggestions that the cental cataloguing function should be carried out by the recently established National Central Library,[4] but the resources of this institution were so patently inadequate to such a task that the idea was stillborn.

There were some in the public library world who looked on all this

favour with librarians, most of whom, if they classified fiction at all, were content to do so under the broad headings used in many libraries today—Romances, Adventure Stories, Detective Stories, etc. See the discussion in L.A.R., 4th Ser., Vol. V (1938), pp. 167–168, 235, 279, 382–383, 401.

[1] The layman interested in these classifications will find an introduction to them in W. C. B. Sayers, A Manual of Classification for Librarians (1926, 4th edn. 1967), Chs. xvi–xvii; and especially J. Mills, A Modern Outline of Library Classification (1960), Chs. ii–iv and xi–xii.

[2] See for some of the difficulties J. E. Walker, "Central Cataloguing", in L.A.R., N.S., Vol. VI (1928), pp. 1–7.

[3] Y.W.L. 1936, p. 138; Hansard, Parliamentary Debates, 5th Ser., Vol. CCCXVII, cols. 889–890.

[4] J. Powell, "Central Cataloguing: Two Projects", in L.A.R., 4th Ser., Vol. IV (1937), pp. 261–262; J. L. Thornton, Cataloguing in Special Libraries (1938), Ch. xxiii.

bibliographical activity with distrust, if not dismay.[1] James Cranshaw, Deputy City Librarian of Sheffield, very sensibly urged that a distinction should be made between bibliographical cataloguing and the kind of cataloguing needed by the ordinary public library reader. He suggested that in an age of open access catalogues of fiction and juvenile books were quite unnecessary and should be abolished; and that the entries in the catalogue of adult non-fiction should be drastically pruned and simplified.[2]

By the mid 'thirties the card or sheaf catalogue was becoming standard practice in the municipal libraries, and R. J. Gordon, City Librarian of Leeds, was able to declare his belief that "the day of the full printed catalogue is past, or very quickly passing, despite the few libraries that still cling to them."[3] To provide the guidance needed by the common reader, the emphasis now was upon the printing of subject lists, lists of recent additions, books of topical interest, books of the year, and so forth. Even in the county libraries, where at the outset the complete printed catalogue had seemed quite indispensable, considerations of expense were giving rise to serious doubts, and most county librarians grasped eagerly at the solution offered by the publication from 1937 onwards of monthly Readers' Guides, prepared by the County Libraries Section Committee of the Library Association. These valuable guides, each covering a single subject, provided over the course of the years a substitute for a basic catalogue, which individual counties could supplement with their own special lists. The first, the *Readers' Guide to Books on Religion*, was a 48-page booklet listing some 1200 carefully selected titles, and was good value at 1s. a dozen.[4]

It was E. A. Savage of Edinburgh who saw most clearly the significance for the public library service of the immense build-up of literary and other material, and the rapid development of subject specialisms. Public libraries, even large ones, were general libraries, not specialist libraries, but Savage argued that if they were to remain efficient they must have the services of specialists at their command. Without such specialists it was impossible even to make a proper selection from the flood of books and periodicals issuing from the presses, and he produced evidence to show that already, except perhaps in the relatively familiar fields of literature and history, the process of selection left very much to be desired.

The moral Savage drew was twofold. First, in every large public library system there must be a team of subject specialists, each in charge of a main subject throughout the system. Second, large central libraries must be depart-

---

[1] For a shrewd and amusing attack on the idols of classification and cataloguing see Sir Frederic Kenyon, "Testamentum Bibliotecarii", in *Bulletin of the John Rylands Library*, Vol. XXV (1941), pp. 67–82.

[2] J. Cranshaw, "Economies in Cataloguing Methods", in *Library Assistant*, Vol. XXVII (1934), pp. 32–41; and "Cutting Cataloguing Costs", in *Library World*, Vol. XXXIX (1936–37), pp. 179–184.

[3] *Library Review*, Vol. VI (1937–38), p. 22.

[4] See the two symposia on "Catalogues and other Printed Aids" in *Library Review*, Vol. V (1935–36), pp. 354–358, and Vol. VI (1937–38), pp. 22–25; and for an earlier view A. Henderson, "County Library Cataloguing", in *Library World*, Vol. XXIII (1930–31), pp. 117–122. Publication of the Readers' Guides, suspended in 1940, was resumed in 1948, and guide No. 100 in the new series was issued in 1968.

mentalized on a subject basis, with the reference library and the lending library for each subject brought together under specialist guidance. Thus in the Edinburgh central library he envisaged in 1937 nine departments. Three of these—music, fine arts, and economics and commerce—already existed as separate departments, and a new subject department of history would take in the existing local collection. The other five would be science and useful arts, government and social welfare, general and English literature, foreign languages and literatures, and philosophy and theology. He laid down no hard and fast rule as to the size of a subject department, save only that it must be large enough and busy enough to require the services of two assistants, so that it might be kept open all day. The revolutionary proposal that reference and lending sections should be combined, which ran contrary to all the accepted canons of library organization at this time, was based not only on convenience in use but also on the need to use specialist staff as economically as possible.

This idea of subject specialization, inspired, it must be said, largely by American practice, was one of the great creative ideas to emerge in librarianship in the inter-war years. Savage had, at this time, few imitators, and because of the exigencies of his Carnegie building he was unable to carry the process any further during his lifetime, but the idea remained, to germinate in some of our larger libraries after the war.[1]

Extension Activities

Library extension activities continued during these years at a modest level, mainly along familiar lines: lectures, exhibitions, story hours for the children, encouragement to local cultural societies, loan of books to adult classes.

The continuing popularity of lectures is attested by the fact that (in the absence of any follow-up to the Kenyon Committee recommendations) many library authorities, including the London County Council, secured legislative powers to spend money for this purpose, usually up to a limit of two or three hundred pounds a year.[2] There is, however, evidence of some decline in attendance at lectures of the general interest type which had once been so common, and in a few places, e.g. West Bromwich in 1936 and Lincoln in 1937, lecture halls were converted to other uses.[3]

The development of radio and the cinema no doubt had much to do with this trend. From 1927 onwards the British Broadcasting Corporation was earnest in its attempts to promote educational broadcasting, and many librarians co-operated eagerly in the formation of "wireless listening groups", meeting on library premises to hear and discuss radio talks. The results of these endeavours

---

[1] See Savage's Presidential Address to the Library Association in *L.A.R.*, 4th Ser., Vol. III (1936), pp. 271–280; his two articles on "Special Librarianship in General Libraries" in *L.A.R.*, 4th Ser., Vol. IV (1937), pp. 570–574, 615–621 (afterwards reprinted in his book of the same title, 1939); and M. A. Overington, *The Subject Departmentalised Public Library* (1969), pp. 95–97. Cf. Edinburgh Libraries and Museums Committee, *Historical Guide and Handbook to the Libraries* (Edinburgh 1958), pp. 8–10. The disadvantages of "departmentalitis" were pointed out by L. S. Jast, *The Library and the Community* (1939), pp. 82–86.

[2] *Y.W.L. 1930*, pp. 171–172; *1931*, p. 207; *1936*, p. 137.

[3] *Lincoln City Libraries, 1914–1964* [Lincoln, 1964], p. 7; information from Mr. R. B. Ludgate, West Bromwich Borough Librarian.

were, however, rather disappointing, chiefly because of the difficulty of finding really competent leaders.[1]

The provision of books to adult education classes was the subject of a special inquiry by a sub-committee of the Central Joint Advisory Committee on Tutorial Classes, which reported in 1937. The sub-committee noted that the National Central Library now preferred to issue books to classes not directly but through the local library, in order to make better use of existing supplies; and that this was one of the factors contributing to delay in book provision. Attention was also drawn to the difficulty of securing adequate supplies of certain categories of books, e.g. government reports, and the cheaper books not stocked by the National Central Library; and especially to the perennial problem of securing duplicate copies of textbooks. The sub-committee's recommendations, though well meant, did little to improve the position. The basic weakness lay in the fact that most urban libraries were unable or unwilling to lend books on the scale required, and that any system of co-operation designed to alleviate this difficulty was too slow to be effective.[2] Inquiries made on behalf of the sub-committee showed that during the session 1934–35, 144 urban libraries supplied 5109 books to adult classes, while 45 county libraries supplied 30 376 books.[3]

A very good general impression of the types of extension work going on at this time may be gained from the London and Home Counties Report for 1939, though it should be borne in mind that the public libraries in and around London were more prosperous and more active than most. The report shows that of 102 urban libraries, thirty-six were organizing weekly, fortnightly, or monthly lectures. At one library, lectures had been stopped for lack of support. A "library club" met weekly in two systems for literary talks and discussions on books.[4] Twenty-eight libraries were now able to finance lectures from their own funds, but the lectures were usually given free.

Forty urban libraries reported the holding of exhibitions, other than normal book displays. These exhibitions were usually concerned with such subjects as local history, painting, prints, pottery, photographs, and early printed books and manuscripts. Forty-five libraries provided meeting places, usually at nominal rates, for adult classes and local societies, but only six organized B.B.C. discussion groups. Forty-four libraries lent collections of books, usually to adult classes. The county libraries were particularly active in the

---

[1] For the general development of this experiment (which was terminated in 1946), see T. Kelly, *History of Adult Education in Great Britain* (Liverpool 1962, 2nd edn. 1970), pp. 318–320, and references there cited. For the public library aspect see C. A. Siepmann, "Group Listening to Broadcast Talks", in *L.A.R.*, N.S. Vol. VII (1929), Suppl. pp. 55–58; C. Nowell, "Broadcasting and Public Libraries", in *L.A.R.*, N.S. Vol. VIII (1930), pp. 81–92; C. Jackson, "Broadcasting and the Library", in *Library Assistant*, Vol. XXX (1937), pp. 180–184; *The City Libraries of Sheffield, 1856–1956* (Sheffield 1956), p. 39.

[2] This difficulty is brought out very clearly in Board of Education, Adult Education Committee, Paper No. 11, *Adult Education and the Local Education Authority* (1933), Ch. vi.

[3] The report is printed in *L.A.R.*, 4th Ser., Vol. IV (1937), pp. 431–434. Cf. E. Green, "Book Supplies to Adult Classes", in H. V. Usill (ed.), *Year Book of Education, 1938*, pp. 452–459.

[4] For a description of such a club, at Dover, see W. A. Munford, "An Experiment in Extension Work", in *L.A.R.*, 4th Ser., Vol. V (1938), pp. 464–465.

IXa. THE BRITISH MUSEUM READING ROOM

Though not accurate in every detail (the book-trolley, for example, seems an unlikely intrusion) this artist's impression gives a good idea of what Panizzi's great reading room must have looked like about the year 1902.

IXb. REFERENCE LIBRARY, WIGAN

In this library designed by Alfred Waterhouse, and opened in 1878, the influence of the Oxford and Cambridge collegiate libraries is clearly visible.

Xa. GORBALS BRANCH, GLASGOW: GENERAL READING ROOM
A library in a working-class district, pictured in a *Descriptive Handbook* of 1907.

Xb. WOODSIDE BRANCH, GLASGOW: LADIES' READING ROOM
Another early picture from the same source.

provision of books for adult classes and sets of plays for dramatic societies, but less active in other forms of extension work, though some county branches did organize lectures and provide accommodation for cultural societies.[1]

The year 1938 brought two interesting contributions on the subject of library extension. Edward Sydney, Borough Librarian of Leyton, writing in the *Year Book of Education* on "The Public Library and Adult Education", declared that the library should be "the headquarters of all local cultural activities", and should be equipped for this purpose:

> "The main aim of all libraries is to acquire and maintain an efficient stock of books, but that is a means not an end. Librarianship to-day must go further and must interest itself in any movement which promotes the development of thought and study, the circulation of ideas and the creation of intellectual needs. It must see these movements clearly, co-operate with them closely, and never allow any mass demand for less desirable purposes to hinder or retard the assistance which these movements so urgently require from the library."[2]

Eric Leyland, whom we have already had occasion to notice as the author of a book on *The Public Library and the Adolescent*, now produced a further volume on *The Wider Public Library*, which started from the proposition that, in spite of recent advances, less than one-third of the population were making use of public library services, and that something must be done to interest the remainder. In this task extension activities could play a valuable role, but first it was necessary to analyse carefully the various groups involved.

Leaving on one side young children, aged people, and illiterates, Leyland divides the non-users into two main groups: those who seek good literature and those who seek only newspapers and light fiction. In the first group are those upper middle-class people who consider the public library beneath them, and are unwilling to mix with working-class readers; and those who do not appreciate the facilities available. In the second group are those who are incapable of appreciating anything more demanding than light literature; and those who simply lack the time for serious reading. For each of these categories a separate approach needs to be worked out.[3]

This analysis of group needs is the keynote of Leyland's treatment of extension activities. He argues, for example, that general lectures, designed primarily as entertainment, are now of little value: they cannot compete with the radio and the cinema. Attention must therefore be focussed on more specialized needs, for example on hobbies such as gardening, philately or photography. Such work, of course, would link closely with the activities of local societies, and it might well be that it would be best to drop public lectures altogether and concentrate on assistance to societies, and where appropriate the formation of new ones. A similar attention to group interests should govern library policy in relation to booklists, exhibitions, and where appropriate, museum work.[4]

---

[1] J. D. Stewart, *Report on the Municipal Library System of London and the Home Counties, 1939* (1940), pp. 15–16, 18–20, 25–26. Cf. L. S. Jast, *The Library and the Community* (1939), Ch. ix. For extension activities for children see above, p. 239.

[2] H. V. Usill (ed.), *Year Book of Education, 1938*, pp. 476, 478.

[3] E. Leyland, *The Wider Public Library* (1938), Ch. i.

[4] *Op. cit.*, Chs. ii, iv, v, and vi. Specialization on lecture work had been recommended ten years earlier by J. G. O'Leary, "On Public Lectures", in *Library World*, Vol. XXXI (1928–29), pp. 139–141.

It will be fitting to conclude this section with a quotation from Leyland's final chapter, in which, like Sydney, he envisages the possibility that the library may evolve into a cultural centre:

"Built up with the Public Library as a nucleus, a Cultural Centre would include a library, which would undoubtedly be the most important department of the institution, but other facilities would also be available . . . . The facilities offered would include meeting rooms, lounges and reading rooms for the citizens of the town, lecture-rooms equipped with projection facilities, a central bureau for the dissemination of local information, a publicity department and a local collection or museum."[1]

One library which came very near this ideal was Sydney's branch library at Leytonstone, opened in 1934 to provide for the needs of a predominantly working-class area of East London. The accommodation included (in addition to the usual library rooms) a lecture hall and two classrooms, and equipment included showcases and exhibition screens, blackboard, piano, lantern, epidiascope, film unit, radio and gramophone. The library was used for local authority classes, and as the meeting place for about two dozen cultural and educational societies. Library-sponsored activities included a music club, discussion groups and lectures, play-reading and dramatic performances, and art exhibitions.[2]

Librarianship

A report prepared in 1931 for the Association of Assistant Librarians was able to record a considerable improvement in most aspects of library service. Referring to the change since 1911, when the first such report was issued, and especially since 1918, the report comments:

"Salaries and status have improved, the hours of work have lessened, a high standard of professional education is demanded by most authorities, a definite standard of general education for entrants to the profession is almost universal, and the conditions under which assistant librarians work have improved with better organisation and the better planning of library buildings."[3]

Hours of work, which had averaged 45.2 per week in 1911, now averaged 41.2. Split duties were still a nuisance, but most lending departments and a considerable number of reference departments now closed for at least one half day per week, and the report commends the "increasing number of libraries where two evenings off duty are allowed in addition to the half day". Only 22 libraries were now recorded as opening on Sundays.[4]

Salaries showed some improvement, not only over the figures for 1911, but also over those collected for the Kenyon Committee.[5] Direct comparisons are impossible because the statistics are not presented in the same form, but a

---

[1] Leyland, op. cit., p. 184.

[2] E. Sydney, "Adult Education and the Public Library", in L.A.R., 4th Ser., Vol. XIII (1946), pp. 275–279.

[3] F. Seymour Smith (ed.), Report on the Hours, Salaries, Training and Conditions of Service in British Municipal Libraries, 1931 (1932), p. 8. The report is based on returns from 242 libraries, out of a total of 506 to which the questionnaire was addressed. Cf. above, p. 203.

[4] Op. cit., pp. 10–14.   [5] See above, pp. 251–252.

maximum salary of £800 a year for a chief librarian was now by no means uncommon in authorities with a population of 50 000 upwards, and a salary of £1000 a year or more was no longer the rarity it had once been. Deputies were still relatively underpaid, with a maximum not usually in excess of £500 a year. The tabulation of salaries of assistants below this level is not very helpful, but we note that even junior assistants in many authorities (not the largest or the smallest) could hope to rise eventually to £300 a year.[1]

Concerning county libraries the 1931 report was less informative. In the 28 English county libraries (out of 44) for which particulars were available, nearly half the staff worked at headquarters, and most of these worked the customary office hours, with a half day on Saturday. The longest hours were worked by the staff of full-time branches.[2] The Statistical Report for 1934-35 provides more information, and reveals that county library staffs were still, in comparison with their municipal brethren, a depressed class. Four-fifths of the county librarians in Great Britain and Ireland were at this date earning less than £450 a year, and only one more than £650. The salaries of assistant staff were correspondingly low. Many smaller centres still employed untrained part-time staff, and the smallest villages were often still dependent on voluntary workers.[3]

One of the biggest changes between 1911 and 1931 was the growth in the employment of women. In the municipal libraries, in the latter year, 58.3 per cent of the 3606 professional staff recorded were female, though it is significant that in the table of salaries not one woman is shown as occupying a position above that of branch librarian. The figures for county libraries are not given, but the proportion of women here was certainly higher, and in 1934-35 no fewer than thirty-two authorities in Great Britain had women chief librarians.[4]

As the depression of the early 'thirties lifted, conditions continued to improve, and Lionel McColvin as honorary secretary of the Library Association was able to claim in 1937 that "salaries, hours, holidays, the number of staff employed, grading—all those elements concerning the personal well-being of library workers—are now very much better on the whole throughout the country than they were in 1930."[5] One way in which the status of librarians had improved is indicated by a casual remark of L. Stanley Jast in 1939. "There is a growing tendency," he says, "towards leaving book selection entirely to the librarian". Up to this time, except in the largest library systems, book selection had still been in a very real sense the responsibility of the library committee.[6]

---

[1] *Op. cit.*, p. 30. In Wales, where the position in 1932 is described as "positively appalling", there were still chief librarians earning as little as £85 a year, and deputies as little as £30. See G. Poole, "Salaries and Service Conditions in Wales", in *Report of the Proceedings of the Tenth Conference of Libraries in Wales and Monmouthshire, 1935* (Aberystwyth 1935), pp. 39–51.

[2] *Op. cit.*, pp. 26–27.

[3] Library Association, County Libraries Section, *County Libraries in Great Britain and Ireland: Statistical Report, 1934–35* [1936], pp. 15–18.

[4] F. Seymour Smith, *op. cit.*, pp. 10, 31; Library Association, *op. cit.*, pp. 28–29.

[5] L. R. McColvin, "The Library Association since 1930", in *Library World*, Vol. XXXIX (1936–37), p. 132.   [6] L. S. Jast, *The Library and the Community* (1939), p. 132.

McColvin naturally, and rightly, attributed some of the improvement to the Library Association, which had now become a much more effective body and, through its publications and its negotiations with employing bodies, was exerting a steady pressure in the direction of higher standards.

The development policy embarked upon by the Association following the Jubilee Conference of 1927 has already been commented on. This brought added strength in two ways—first, by union with other library associations hitherto independent—the Scottish Association, the Birmingham and District Association, the North Midland Association, and the Association of Assistant Librarians; and second, by the formation of sections to represent special interests: the County Libraries Section, the University and Research Section, and the School Libraries Section. Only the special librarians, represented by ASLIB, and the archivists, represented by the British Records Association, remained outside the new organization, which derived further strength from the establishment in 1928 of an International Federation of Library Associations. A decision taken in 1929 that only members of the Association could take its examinations brought a dramatic rise in individual membership.[1] The opening in 1933 of the new Library Association headquarters at Chaucer House, Malet Place, made possible by generous assistance from the Carnegie Trust, aptly symbolized the Association's new prestige and authority.

It would be wrong, however, to paint too rosy a picture, for there were still many authorities which, in staffing as in other library matters, were exceedingly backward. There were serious problems, too, in the field of professional training. The Library School at University College, London, offering its diploma and an easy route to the fellowship to graduates with relatively little library experience, gave rise to a good deal of jealousy and dissatisfaction, and in self-defence the Library Association from 1929 dropped the requirement of a thesis for its own diploma, except for those seeking a diploma with honours. The result was that the Association began to award even more diplomas than the Library School, and the market was flooded with diplomates unable to secure posts corresponding to their qualifications.[2]

It now at last became clear, as the Kenyon Report had observed, that to create an effective career structure in librarianship it was necessary to provide for different grades of work and different levels of salary, and that in large libraries at least there were some duties of a clerical kind which could be quite adequately carried out by people without any kind of professional qualification. As Lionel McColvin remarked, it was absurd to say to a new entrant to the profession: "qualify to command an army or we won't even make you a lance-corporal."[3] As a first step in this direction the Library Association from 1933 abolished its six professional certificates, which could be taken in any order, in favour of a graduated system which began with an Elementary Examination and proceeded by way of an Intermediate Examination to a Final Examination, which was in three parts and included certain options designed to meet the needs of specialist librarians. A revised version

---

[1] R. F. Vollans (ed.), *Libraries for the People* (1968), p. 56.
[2] W. Pollitt, "Library Staffs", in *L.A.R.*, 4th Ser., Vol. III (1936), pp. 290–295. See also the symposium on the School of Librarianship in the same volume, pp. 5–9.
[3] L. R. McColvin, "Salaries and Conditions of Service", in *L.A.R.*, 4th Ser., Vol. I (1934), p. 303. For the Kenyon Report see above, p. 253.

of this new system, planned to come into operation in 1938, was postponed to allow for further consideration and because of the war never took effect at all.

The appointment of J. D. Cowley, formerly librarian of Lancashire County, as Director of the University College School of Librarianship, in 1934, in succession to E. A. Baker, did something to improve relations between the School and the public library world, but a degree of jealousy persisted, and the new regulations for the fellowship proposed for 1938 were heavily loaded against the graduate entrant.[1] No new full-time library course was established, and outside London the only teaching available continued to be through correspondence courses (managed by the Association of Assistant Librarians from 1930), summer schools, and local classes. The Aberystwyth Summer School, which came to an end in 1928, was replaced by a school at Birmingham in collaboration with the university and the public libraries; and the Scottish school, which had alternated at Glasgow and Edinburgh since 1922, became from 1937 a residential course at Newbattle Abbey. A feature of the immediate post-war years was the rapid development of classes for the new elementary and intermediate examinations in local education authority technical colleges and colleges of commerce. From 1934 onwards such classes are reported from Manchester, Birmingham, Liverpool, Leeds, Glasgow, and several centres in and around the metropolis. This development pointed the way to the extensive collaboration with the local education authorities which was to be a feature of the post-war years.[2]

[1] See *Library Association Year Book*, *1937*, p. 114, and the letters by Philip Hepworth and J. D. Cowley in *L.A.R.*, 4th Ser., Vol. IV (1937), pp. 84–85, 191.

[2] A brief account of these developments is to be found in G. Bramley, *A History of Library Education* (1969), Chs. iii and iv. See also J. Minto, *A History of the Public Library Movement* (1932), Ch. xiii; W. R. Aitken, *A History of the Public Library Movement in Scotland to 1955* (Glasgow, 1971), Ch. viii; and for the local classes the periodical announcements in the *Library Association Record* for the years concerned.

CHAPTER XII

The National Libraries and the Beginnings of Inter-Library Co-operation

The National Libraries before Kenyon

WHEN library resources were limited it was natural that people's minds should turn to thoughts of inter-library co-operation as a means of economizing funds and at the same time improving the service to readers. Proposals and experiments to this end were already common before the first World War, and as early as 1903 J. D. Brown developed proposals for the inter-library lending of non-fiction works which in many respects antici-pated the present regional library bureaux. Brown was also a great believer in co-operative cataloguing, a first and unsuccessful attempt at which was made in 1901 through his journal the *Library World*.[1] Later, as we have seen, both Adams and Mitchell were enthusiastic in their advocacy of inter-library co-operation.

Ad hoc experiments on a local basis were also common, ranging from simple agreements regarding interavailability of readers' tickets in the libraries of neighbouring authorities to comprehensive regional schemes of the kind developed after the war in Leicestershire.[2] At the national level the initiative taken by the Carnegie Trust in fostering the development of the Central Library for Students and its Scottish counterpart was of crucial importance.[3] It is, however, to the Kenyon Report that we must turn for the first really comprehensive scheme for inter-library co-operation, a scheme which embraced not only the public libraries and the two central students' libraries but also the great national libraries and the special collections created by industrial, com-mercial and professional bodies. The national libraries have not hitherto figured more than incidentally in this narrative, and must now be briefly described.

The British Museum Library

The national libraries may be defined as those libraries which are supported by national funds and which meet national rather than local or sectional needs. At this stage the most important were the British Museum Library, the National Library of Wales, the National Library of Scotland, the Science Museum Library at South Kensington, the Victoria and Albert Museum Library, and the Patent Office Library.

---

[1] J. D. Brown, *Manual of Library Economy* (1903), pp. 290–293, 412–413.
[2] An interesting early example of inter-library lending was promoted by A. J. Philip, Librarian of Gravesend, among libraries in the London region in 1907. For this and other projects see L. Newcombe, *Library Co-operation in the British Isles* (1937), Ch. ii.
[3] See above, pp. 225–226.

The origins and early history of the British Museum Library have been recounted elsewhere, and need be only briefly indicated here.[1] The Museum was founded in 1753, when on the death of Sir Hans Sloane the Government purchased for £20 000 the unrivalled collections of natural history, art, antiquities, books and manuscripts which this well-known physician had accumulated. Along with the rest of the Museum, the library was opened to the public in 1759, in Montagu House, Great Russell Street.

It was from the beginning for reference only, "chiefly designed," as the trustees stated in 1757, "for the use of learned and studious men."[2] It comprised not only the Sloane books and manuscripts but also the Harleian MSS., purchased by the Government at the same time; the Cottonian collection of material on English history and antiquities, assembled by Sir Robert Cotton and acquired by the Crown in 1706; and the splendid Royal Library, collected by successive English monarchs since the days of Edward IV, and presented to the Museum by George II in 1757—all in all a precious and unrivalled collection of some 50 000 books and 15 000 manuscripts.

Unfortunately, the Government did not follow up the good work by providing adequately for the maintenance of the new institution, and for the first fifty years progress was very slow. In the nineteenth century the position began to improve. Government grants were gradually but substantially increased, and the trustees were thus able to purchase a number of important collections and to fill some of the gaps left by the rather haphazard way in which the library had been built up. There were also valuable gifts and bequests, notably the second royal library, the King's Library as it was called, which had been formed by George II after the original Royal Library was given to the Museum in 1757. Comprising over 65 000 printed books, 19 000 pamphlets, and about 450 MSS., it was transferred by George IV in 1828.

In the meantime rebuilding had begun, the original Montagu House being replaced, from 1823 onwards, by a new building in the Greek style (the present building) designed by Robert Smirke. Owing to the steadily increasing public demand, the reading room had four times to be moved to larger accommodation, until by 1838 there was accommodation for 168 readers.

The man who more than any other transformed the library from a museum of books into an efficient working collection was an Italian refugee named Antonio Panizzi, who joined the staff in a part-time capacity in 1831, became Keeper of Printed Books in 1837, served as Principal Librarian from 1856 to 1866, and was afterwards knighted for his services as Sir Anthony Panizzi. He brought to the work a clear conception of the special function of a national library, which must, he declared, possess not only "common modern books", but also "rare, ephemeral, voluminous and costly publications, which cannot be found anywhere else, by persons not having access to great private collections".[3]

With the help of larger government grants, and by a rigorous enforcement

[1] The standard work is A. Esdaile, *The British Museum Library* (1946). See also the same author's *National Libraries of the World* (1934), Ch. i. For a short account see T. Kelly, *Early Public Libraries* (1966), Ch. vii.

[2] Esdaile, *op. cit.*, p. 37.

[3] See his evidence in *Report from the Select Committee on the Condition, Management and Affairs of the British Museum* (1836), p. 391.

of the law of copyright deposit, Panizzi succeeded in increasing the stock of the Library from less than a quarter of a million books to nearly a million.[1] To provide room for these accessions, and also to meet the steadily growing demand for accommodation for readers, he procured the erection of the great circular reading room in the vacant central quadrangle of the new Greek building. This addition, opened in 1857, included seats for 300 readers, and the "iron library" which was constructed in the corners of the quadrangle provided shelving for a million volumes.

For the time being the problem of accommodation was thus solved. It should be mentioned, however, that at this time the Museum Library, in common with many other libraries, had no artificial lighting, so that the reading room had to close at dusk if not before. Gas lighting was available, but was regarded as dangerous, and harmful to the books. It was not until 1879 that electric lighting was introduced.

For such a large library an official catalogue was of crucial importance. When Panizzi became Keeper in 1837 the printed author catalogue originally produced in 1813–19 had been expanded by manuscript additions until it had become quite unmanageable, and acrimonious discussions were going on as to how a new catalogue could best be compiled, and what form it should take. The solution ultimately adopted, at Panizzi's insistence, was an alphabetical author catalogue made up of individual manuscript entries pasted into folio volumes, and capable of being rearranged when necessary.

Panizzi also played a leading part in compiling, in 1839, the famous Ninety-One Rules for cataloguing, which for the first time dealt comprehensively with the cataloguing of anonymous and pseudonymous works, works by joint authors, encyclopaedias, periodicals, publications of learned societies, and the like, and with all the other problems which arise in the preparation of an alphabetical list. These Rules provided a systematic cataloguing code for the British Museum for the next half-century, and in essentials still operate today.[2]

Panizzi was such a forceful and dynamic personality, and has such great and obvious achievements to his credit, that he has inevitably tended to over-shadow his successors. Men such as Sir Edward Bond (Principal Librarian 1878–88), Sir Edward Maunde Thompson (1888–1909), and Sir Frederic Kenyon (1909–31), all able scholars and administrators, had the unspectacular task of building on the foundations Panizzi had already laid.

Their principal administrative problems arose from the ever increasing flow of books and manuscripts. The great reading room, and the iron library surrounding it, which had seemed so commodious in 1857, soon began to be uncomfortably full, and various expedients were resorted to in order to ease

---

[1] The law of copyright deposit went back to the Licensing Act of 1662, which prescribed that three copies of every book published should be deposited with the Stationers' Company: one for the Royal Library, one for the Bodleian, and one for the University of Cambridge. By the beginning of the nineteenth century the number of libraries entitled to free copies had risen to eleven, but in 1836 the number was reduced to five: the British Museum (which had inherited the claim of the old Royal Library), the Bodleian, the University Library of Cambridge, the Advocates' Library in Edinburgh, and Trinity College Library, Dublin. Until Panizzi's time the rule had been persistently evaded.

[2] The latest and best biography of Panizzi as librarian is E. Miller, *Prince of Librarians: the Life and Times of Antonio Panizzi of the British Museum* (1967).

the pressure. A small additional wing to the south-east of the main building (the White Wing), erected on what had once been part of the Principal Librarian's garden, provided *inter alia* reading rooms for manuscripts and for newspapers. In 1887 the accommodation of the iron library was substantially increased by the introduction of additional "sliding presses" suspended on rollers from the iron ceilings. In 1902 a special newspaper repository was established at Hendon. In 1914 the erection of the King Edward VII Gallery made extra reading space available in the new North Library which linked the Gallery with the main buildings to the south. In 1920 a plan was prepared for adding another storey to the iron library, but this proved possible only in one of the four quadrants. By 1925 practically all available accommodation both at Bloomsbury and at Hendon was full, and books were continuing to accumulate at a rate which required about a mile of new shelving every year.

The pressure on space brought one incidental but immense advantage, namely the printing of the library catalogue. Panizzi had opposed a printed catalogue, arguing that it must always be hopelessly out of date, but by 1875 his catalogue of movable manuscript slips had swollen to 2250 folio volumes and was threatening to occupy the entire reading room. To save space it became absolutely necessary to use printed slips, and a printed catalogue, complete to the year 1900, was published in 1881-1905.

Panizzi was also opposed to a subject catalogue, on the not very convincing ground that no two people could ever agree on the classification. The library still lacks such a catalogue, but it now has an alphabetical subject index covering accessions since 1880. The first volume, dealing with the years 1880-85, was published in 1886, and the series has been continued ever since.

Such, then, was the position of the Museum Library at the time of the Kenyon Report. Thanks to the work of Panizzi and his successors, it now had the resources to take its place at the apex of the public library system, but its needs in the way of accommodation were desperate and becoming worse with every day that passed.[1]

Other National Libraries

The National Library of Wales, like the University of Wales, is a reflection of Welsh national pride and zeal for learning. It was in 1872 that the first Welsh University College was established in Aberystwyth, and in the following year a special meeting held in connection with the National Eisteddfod at Mold resolved "that it is desirable on many grounds that a National Library be formed, consisting chiefly of rare books and manuscripts in the Welsh Language, and in other languages, where they relate to Wales or its people."[2] A committee was formed, the University College offered temporary accommodation, and a

---

[1] See, in addition to the works already cited, G. F. Barwick, The *Reading Room of the British Museum* (1929), and for an intimate personal impression of the work of the library in the second half of the nineteenth century R. Garnett, *Essays in Librarianship and Bibliography* (1899). The position in 1927 is admirably set out in Sir Frederic Kenyon's memorandum of that year to the Royal Commission on National Museums and Galleries, which is printed in *Oral Evidence, Memoranda, and Appendices to the Interim Report* (1928), pp. 51-62.

[2] W. Ll. Davies, *The National Library of Wales: a Survey of its History, its Contents, and its Activities* (Aberystwyth 1937), p. 1.

collection of Welsh books and manuscripts began to be assembled. Before the end of the century a site had been secured on a hillside overlooking Aberystwyth, and in 1903 a successful appeal was launched for £20 000 towards the cost of building.

In 1907 a charter was granted for the formation of the National Library of Wales, which opened in the Old Assembly Rooms in Aberystwyth in 1909 with John Ballinger, formerly of Cardiff, as its first librarian. The library moved to its permanent home in 1916 but because of the war the building long remained unfinished, and the central hall which completed the original design was opened only in 1955.

It is interesting to note that the scope of the library as defined in the charter was wider than had originally been envisaged at Mold, including the collection not only of works of all kinds related to Wales but also of literary works in any language on any subject which might help to attain the purposes for which the educational institutions of Wales were created, and "duplicate and multiplicate" copies of works required for exhibition or instruction in connection with these institutions.[1] This provision made it possible for the library to serve, in due course, as a central library for loans to students.

The main task of the library, however, was to create a great national record and reference collection of Welsh material. In this task a splendid beginning was made. To the original "Welsh Library" assembled at the University College there was immediately added the magnificent library of the Welsh surgeon Sir John Williams, comprising about 25 000 books and 1200 manuscripts, and collected over a period of thirty years expressly for presentation to the Welsh nation. The valuable library of Edward Humphreys Owen of Caernarvon was purchased in the following year, and the library of Principal J. H. Davies was acquired in 1926. These four "foundation collections" included practically every important printed work in Welsh since 1546, besides rich treasures in manuscript. The acquisition of modern literature was satisfactorily provided for by the Copyright Act of 1911, under which the National Library of Wales became (with certain limitations) a copyright deposit library.[2]

In Scotland before the first World War there was no national library, but the library of the Faculty of Advocates, founded in Edinburgh in 1680, had in considerable measure assumed this role. The Advocates' Library was intended as "ane Bibliothecq whereto many Lawers and others may leave their Books,"[3] and was financed from the fees of new entrants to the Faculty. From the beginning, however, the curators seem to have thought in terms of a general rather than a merely professional collection, and although the library was technically a private one it was freely accessible for reference to all scholars. Its outstanding position was recognized by its inclusion as a deposit library in the Copyright Act of 1709. By 1742 there were already 25 000 volumes; and by the end of the century the library had become a recognized place of deposit for material relating to the history and literature of Scotland.

[1] The National Library of Wales: a Brief Summary of its History and its Activities (Aberystwyth 1962), p. 5. For details of this last provision see National Library of Wales, Charter of Incorporation [etc.] (Aberystwyth 1930), pp. 18–19.

[2] See in addition to the works cited A. Esdaile, National Libraries of the World (1934), pp. 48–55.

[3] W. K. Dickson, "The Advocates' Library", in Juridical Review, Vol. XIV (1902), p. 2.

In the early nineteenth century the library continued to grow, and more than once had to enlarge its premises in Parliament Square. By 1849 the number of printed works was returned as 148 000, besides 2000 MSS., and the Solicitor General for Scotland, Sir Thomas Maitland, boasted that there was no library in Great Britain where the access given to the public generally was more liberal than in the Advocates' Library.[1]

By this date, however, the flood of copyright material was already great, and it became clear that the Faculty could not indefinitely maintain a library for the use of the public on such a scale. Numerous attempts were made to obtain public support, but it was not until 1925 that the National Library of Scotland Act provided for the transfer of the library to the nation. At the date of the transfer, in 1926, the library comprised about three-quarters of a million books and pamphlets, besides music, maps, and invaluable manuscript collections.[2]

The libraries attached to the Science Museum and the Victoria and Albert Museum both traced their history back to the early nineteenth century, the former originating in 1843 in connection with the Geological Survey and the latter in 1837 in connection with the Government School of Design. The Science Museum Library eventually found a home in 1908 in the buildings of the Royal College of Science (one of the constituent colleges of the recently established Imperial College of Science and Technology). By 1927 it comprised 170 000 volumes, covering all branches of science and technology except medicine, and including the most complete collection of scientific periodicals in the country. It was open freely for reference, and books and periodicals were lent to other institutions.[3] The Victoria and Albert Museum Library (now the British Library of Art) was housed at the Museum, and was described in 1927 as "probably the finest special library devoted to the literature of art in the world."[4] At this date it included 150 000 books and a quarter of a million photographs.

The Act of 1852 which established the British Patent Office permitted the Commissioners of Patents to present copies of their publications to public libraries, but made no provision for a library in the Patent Office itself. That such a library came into existence (it was made available to the public on open access in 1855) was due in large measure to Bennet Woodcroft, Superintendent of Specifications, whose energy and enthusiasm we have already had occasion to notice. The library included not only patent material, English and foreign, but also a large range of relevant scientific and technical books and periodicals, so that its scope and importance are better indicated by its present title, the National Reference Library of Science and Invention. In 1927 it comprised some 220 000 volumes, mainly non-patent material.[5]

---

[1] Select Committee on Public Libraries, *Report* (1849) p. 93.

[2] W. K. Dickson, "The Advocates' Library", in *L.A.R.*, N.S. Vol. V (1927), p. 177.

[3] *Kenyon Report*, pp. 132–133; R. A. Rye, *The Students' Guide to the Libraries of London* (1908, 3rd edn. 1927), pp. 410–412; R. Irwin and R. Staveley (eds.), *The Libraries of London* (1949 and also 2nd edn. 1961), Chs. iii and iv; J. A. Chaldecott, "The Science Library", in *Technical Book Review* (Sept. 1964) pp. 8–9.

[4] Rye, *op. cit.*, p. 266.

[5] *Kenyon Report*, pp. 133–134; Rye, *op. cit.*, pp. 407–409. On Bennet Woodcroft see above, p. 75.

The Concept of a National Service

The remit of the Kenyon Committee was, of course, restricted to England and Wales. Within these limits its report outlined proposals for a single comprehensive national service embracing all types of libraries. At the base of the pyramid would be the public libraries, voluntarily co-operating among themselves at the local level, and seeking assistance from a regional centre (usually one of the great civic libraries) in meeting demands beyond their own immediate resources. Demands which could not be met at the regional level would be passed to a central library to be developed from the existing Central Library for Students. Through this library it would be possible to draw, not only on the resources of other regions, but also, it was hoped, on the resources of university libraries and the many specialist libraries of various kinds recently brought together in ASLIB—even, perhaps, those maintained by industrial and commercial organizations. There was precedent for an arrangement of this kind, for more than a score of university and special libraries, in return for grants from the Carnegie Trust, were already functioning as "outliers" of the Central Library for Students.[1] The Science Museum Library would, it was thought, be the main source of supply for works of science.

It was not thought that the obligations placed on the new Central Library would prevent it from continuing to discharge the duties for which the Central Library for Students had originally been created, but it was recognized that a different kind of institution would be called for. In the committee's recommendations the matter is summed up as follows:

> "The Central Library will have these main functions:—(i) to aid directly, and also through the responsible bodies, groups of organised students throughout the country; (ii) to aid through public libraries, and to a slight extent directly, the individual readers whose wants cannot be met from local sources; (iii) to serve as a link between the special libraries for the purpose of making their books available under proper conditions for students in all parts of the country. The proper performance of these functions implies a library on a national scale and on the footing of a public institution."[2]

It was accordingly recommended

(a) That the Central Library for Students be reconstituted as a special department of the British Museum, but with separate stock and administration.

(b) That the government make an interim grant of £5000 a year.

(c) That in the light of experience consideration be given to other central functions which such a library could usefully discharge, e.g. acting as a central bureau of information on all library matters.

(d) That the British Museum be asked to establish a Central Cataloguing Agency, associated with the work of the new Central Library, to supply catalogue cards for new publications to libraries throughout the country.[3]

---

[1] For the development of these arrangements, which continued till 1935, see especially the Annual Reports of the Carnegie U.K. Trust from 1925 onwards.

[2] *Kenyon Report*, p. 210.

[3] For the details of all this see Chs. iv and v of the Report. The recommendations are summarized at pp. 208–211. Cf. also above, p. 238.

Public Libraries and the Central Government

In propounding this modest scheme for a national library service the Kenyon Committee was naturally led to consider the relationship between public libraries and the central government. The possibility of government assistance to the libraries, and as a corollary a measure of government inspection and control, had often been canvassed. Ewart, as we have seen, thought in terms of government aid as early as 1848, and a recommendation to this effect was included in the report of the 1849 Committee[1]. The case for government inspection had later been argued by Edwards and Greenwood,[2] and Adams had urged the establishment of a central Library Advisory Committee.[3] There had even been an attempt, in an abortive Act of 1881, to secure legislative approval for inspection by the Education Department.[4] The latest proposal of the kind came from the 1919 Committee on Adult Education, which had taken the view that libraries and museums should be administered by local education authorities and thus have their share of the grants paid by the Board of Education.[5]

In spite of all these proposals, the connection between the public libraries and the central government was still exceedingly tenuous. Under the original 1850 Act the Treasury had to approve applications for loans. The 1887 Act transferred this power to the Local Government Board, and in 1901 it was enacted that the Board must be notified when a local authority adopted the Public Libraries Acts. In 1919 the functions of the Board were taken over by its successor the Ministry of Health, but in the following year powers in relation to public libraries were transferred to the Board of Education, with the proviso that both bodies would be notified of adoptions. By this provision, and by the Public Libraries Act of 1919 which placed the county libraries under education committees, the Board of Education was for the first time brought into association with public libraries.

On these issues the Kenyon Committee expressed its views with clarity and firmness. In view of past history, it believed that the transfer of public libraries to local education authorities would involve more loss than gain, and it was even more emphatic in resisting government grant and control:

> "We believe an atmosphere of freedom to be an essential condition of healthy library progress. Compulsion can only lead to resistance, to grudging compliance, to resentment, which will ensure unpopularity for the very idea of a library. Persuasion and example are the stimuli on which we should rely."[6]

Since recommendations to do nothing are always more readily acceptable than recommendations that call for action, this pronouncement settled the issue for a generation.

---

[1] See above, p. 13.

[2] E. Edwards, *Memoirs of Libraries* (1859), Vol. II, pp. 944–945; T. Greenwood, *Public Libraries* (rev. 4th edn. 1894), pp. xviii, 14.   [3] *Adams Report* (1915), p. 23.

[4] This was the Free Libraries Bill, introduced by Sir John Lubbock. For the second reading debate, in which the proposal for inspection was opposed by A. J. Mundella, Vice-President of the Committee of Council on Education, see Hansard, *Parliamentary Debates*, 3rd Ser., Vol. CCLVIII, cols. 1598–1603. Cf. J. J. Ogle, *The Free Library* (1897), pp. 49–50.

[5] See above, p. 216.

[6] *Kenyon Report*, p. 38. On relations with education authorities see pp. 40–44.

Inter-Library Co-operation after Kenyon

The Kenyon Report's proposal for a structure of library co-operation based on the local units and topped by a Central Library for Students functioning as a special department of the British Museum was referred by the Government to the Royal Commission on National Museums and Galleries, which accepted the view of the Museum Trustees that the Museum was not a suitable body to undertake such a responsibility. The Commission recommended that the Central Library should reconstitute itself under its own board of trustees, with representation of the Museum, and that the Exchequer should make an annual grant of £3000 to enable the Library to function as a central bureau of library information.[1] This recommendation the Government accepted, and in 1931 the Central Library for Students was reconstituted as the National Central Library. A royal charter was granted in the following year, and in 1933 the library moved into the splendid new accommodation in Malet Place which had been provided for the purpose by the Carnegie Trust, in a building shared with the Library Association.

In its new guise the library still maintained its old functions of supplying books to adult classes and to individual students not within reach of a public library service. The latter function, however, had dwindled almost to vanishing point by the end of the inter-war period, and even the supply of books to adult classes, though still important, became quite insignificant in relation to what was now the main function of the library, namely to act as a clearing-house for library interlending and a source of supplementary supply. In this work it was supported not only by the system of outlier libraries which, as we have seen, had begun in the 'twenties, but also by a network of eight regional library bureaux which came into existence in the years 1931–37, absorbing a number of earlier and more local co-operative schemes.

The creation of these regional bureaux, broadly on the lines suggested in the Kenyon Report, was one of the great library achievements of the inter-war years.[2] They brought together not only the major public libraries but also the university libraries and often a number of special libraries. Each bureau was thus able to act as a clearing-house for local interlending, passing to the National Central Library only requests which could not be met from within the region. With the single exception of the Yorkshire Region, the bureaux at once set to work to compile for each region a "union catalogue" of non-fiction works in member libraries: this was used to locate books for local lending, and a copy was also supplied to the National Central Library. In Yorkshire a union catalogue was thought unnecessary as it was believed that most of the books requested could be provided by one or other of the four large municipal libraries—Leeds, Bradford, Sheffield and Hull. In the West Midlands accessions to the Birmingham Public Libraries (which provided accom-

---

[1] Royal Commission on National Museums and Galleries, *Final Report*, Part I, Cmd. 3401 (1929), pp. 63–67, 77–78.

[2] Cf. above, p. 318. A more elaborate, three-tier, scheme was proposed by the County Libraries Section in 1928, and is described in *L.A.R.*, N.S. Vol. VI (1928), pp. 243–251.

REGIONAL LIBRARY AREAS IN 1936

modation for the Bureau and supplied most of the books) were excluded from the union catalogue after 1938.[1]

Much of the initiative in these developments came from the Carnegie Trust. The running costs of the bureaux were met from small subscriptions, commonly on a population basis, by member libraries, but the heavy cost of preparing the union catalogues was covered by generous grants by the Trust— amounting in all to over £260 000.[2] When war broke out in 1939 the task was still incomplete, but even the incomplete catalogues made the work both at the centre and in the regions immensely easier. The compilation of the catalogues, incidentally, revealed the surprising fact that in most regions more than half the books recorded (in Wales 84 per cent) existed only in single copies.[3] This confirmed Savage's belief that book selection without the help of subject specialists was a somewhat random affair.[4]

The regional library bureaux, with their dates of commencement, were as follows:

> *Northern Region* (1931), housed at the Newcastle upon Tyne Literary and Philosophical Society.
> *West Midland Region* (1931), housed at the Birmingham Public Library.
> *Wales* (1932), housed at the National Library of Wales, with a Sub-Bureau for Glamorgan and Monmouthshire housed at Cardiff Public Library.
> *South-Eastern Region* (1933), housed at the National Central Library.
> *East Midland Region* (1935), housed at the Leicester Public Library.
> *North-Western Region* (1935), housed at the Manchester Public Library.
> *Yorkshire Region* (1935). Zonal centres at Bradford, Hull, Leeds and Sheffield Public Libraries.
> *South-Western Region* (1937), housed at the Bristol Public Library.[5]

London was outside the regional system, but a union catalogue for the Guildhall and metropolitan borough libraries, financed by the Carnegie Trust, was begun in 1930. In 1934 the control and financial responsibility were assumed by the Metropolitan Boroughs Standing Joint Committee. A system of inter-lending was now introduced, covering initially 25 of the 29 libraries concerned, but loans were restricted for the most part to the member libraries. The union catalogue was housed at the National Central Library.

In Scotland legal technicalities deferred the establishment of a regional library bureau until 1945, but in practice the function of such a bureau was discharged by the Scottish Central Library for Students, and a union catalogue (housed at the Mitchell Library, Glasgow) was begun in 1939.[6]

The bureaux were supported in the main by the public libraries. In 1937 the list included the majority of urban libraries, all the county libraries but one (the Isle of Wight), and sixteen university libraries, but only forty-three

---

[1] The best account of the history of the bureaux is P. H. Sewell, *The Regional Library Systems* (1950). See also L. Newcombe, *Library Co-operation in the British Isles* (1937), espec. Chs. vi and ix.

[2] R. F. Vollans, *Library Co-operation in Great Britain* (1952), p. 96; W. Robertson, *Welfare in Trust* (Dunfermline 1964), pp. 68–69.

[3] Newcombe, *op. cit.*, Ch. ix.

[4] See above, pp. 304–305.

[5] Newcombe, *op. cit.*, pp. 89–90.

[6] Sewell, *op. cit.*, pp. 26–27; Vollans, *op. cit.*, pp. 92–93.

special libraries. Most of these last preferred to be outlier libraries, which meant that they were willing to lend to the N.C.L. but were not involved in local interlending schemes. At this time the list of outliers included 95 special libraries, 51 urban libraries, and 15 county libraries. Some libraries, both public and special, belonged to both systems.[1]

A special interlending system for the universities, established by the Association of University Teachers in 1925, and originally centred at Birmingham, was operated by the National Central Library from 1931. One valuable result of this inter-university co-operation was a union catalogue of periodicals, published in 1937.[2] From 1931 the Library also became the recognized centre for international loans, requests for which were usually channelled through an appropriate national centre. International lending was still on a small scale, but 1141 books were lent by British libraries to libraries abroad (mainly in Europe) during the years 1931–36, and 479 books were borrowed.[3]

Whenever possible the National Central Library met requests from its own stock. This comprised, in 1936, 140 000 volumes, and was constantly being added to. Lack of funds was always a difficulty, however, as the government grant of £3000 per annum was not intended to cover book purchase. Certain categories of books were excluded: cheap books currently in print; modern fiction, poetry and drama; dictionaries and other works of reference; examination texts and teachers' handbooks; popular travel and biography; books of sports and pastimes; guidebooks; and music. It was only under considerable pressure from the Carnegie Trust (which was contributing £4000 a year) that the Treasury at length agreed to increase its grant by £2000 a year for the five years 1936–41, provided that within two years the user libraries increased their contribution by the same amount, i.e. to about £3500 a year. This condition was, somewhat belatedly, fulfilled, and the library was thus assured for the time being of an income which, if not lavish, was at least tolerable. In 1938–39, though much of the work of interlending was now being undertaken within the regions, issues through the centre totalled close on 60 000.[4]

The National Libraries after Kenyon

Among the national libraries only the National Library of Wales and the Science Museum Library played any significant role in this national interlending scheme. The former, as we have noted, housed the headquarters of the Welsh Regional Bureau, and in fact it provided initially most of the books lent. The growth of the Library at this time was impressive. By 1939, enriched by a steady stream of gifts, purchases, and copyright deposits, and handsomely accommodated in a fine range of buildings on the hillside overlooking Aberystwyth, it had become a real intellectual powerhouse for the Welsh people,

[1] Newcombe, op. cit., Ch. v.
[2] J. H. P. Pafford, Library Co-operation in Europe (1935), pp. 101–102, 274–276.
[3] Newcombe, op. cit., Ch. viii. The International Institute of Intellectual Co-operation, founded under League of Nations auspices in 1922, did much to stimulate the formation of national library centres—Pafford, op. cit., pp. 322–323.
[4] On all this see the annual reports of the Carnegie U.K. Trust, 1935–38, and of the National Central Library, 1935–39; and Robertson, op. cit., pp. 60–68.

making its knowledge available not only within its own walls but also, by its loans to adult classes and to other libraries, throughout the Principality.

The Science Museum Library fulfilled an important national role as an outlier of the National Central Library, but the proposal of the Kenyon Committee that it should be assisted to become a complete central lending library for science was never implemented, and its formidable resources in periodicals and bibliographical references were at this time sadly underused.[1]

Of the other national libraries we need refer here only to the British Museum Library and the National Library of Scotland, both of which faced serious problems. The British Museum Library added year by year to its treasures—the Luttrell Psalter, the Bedford Psalter, and the Codex Sinaiticus were only the most spectacular of the acquisitions of this period—while struggling at the same time to cope with the ever-swelling flood of copyright material. The Royal Commission on National Museums and Galleries recommended in 1928 a number of measures, including a complete reconstruction of the iron library surrounding the reading room, and the conversion of the newspaper repository at Hendon into a newspaper library and reading room. This latter proposal was implemented by 1932, and afforded some relief, but the reconstruction of the iron library took longer, and only two of the four quadrants had been completed when war broke out.[2] The production of a new catalogue of printed books, begun in 1931, also proved a slow business: by the end of 1939 it had reached its twenty-ninth volume but had still not got beyond the letter B.[3]

The difficulties with which the National Library of Scotland had to contend were similar but even more severe. The generous gifts called forth by the transfer of the Advocates' Library to the nation in 1926 merely increased the embarrassment arising from inadequate premises, inadequate staff, inadequate facilities for readers, and a constant stream of copyright accessions. The cataloguing problem which was especially urgent (the latest catalogue available to the public was a printed catalogue of accessions prior to 1872) was dealt with expeditiously by the compilation of a provisional card catalogue of later accessions.[4] A solution of the building problem also seemed in sight when in 1928 Sir Alexander Grant, who had already provided for the library an endowment of £100 000, made a further gift of the same amount towards the cost of a new building. Because of delay in clearing the site, however, another ten years went by before a beginning could be made, and in 1940, before the building was far advanced, the war brought operations to a halt.[5]

[1] *Kenyon Report*, pp. 137–139; Board of Education, *Report of the Advisory Council of the Science Museum, 1935* (1936), pp. 51–53.

[2] Royal Commission on National Museums and Galleries, *Interim Report* (Cmd. 3192, 1928), pp. 32–34; A. Esdaile, *The British Museum Library* (1946), pp. 164–167.

[3] With the help of photolithography, the catalogue was eventually brought to completion, in 263 volumes, in 1966.

[4] Standing Commission on Museums and Galleries, *First Report* (1933), p. 17; National Library of Scotland, *Report . . . for the Year 1933* (1933), pp. 3–4.

[5] Standing Commission on Museums and Galleries, *Second Report* (1938), pp. 11, 22–23; *L.A.R.*, 4th Ser., Vol. VII (1940), p. 60.

BOOK IV
THE SECOND WORLD WAR AND AFTER
1939-1965

CHAPTER XIII

The Second World War

The Wartime Scene

D URING the second World War, which began in September, 1939, and came to an end five years later, the public libraries found themselves called upon to undertake additional services with resources which were restricted if not actually curtailed.

The restriction of resources was not due, this time, as it was during the first World War, to deliberate government policy. On the contrary, as early as June, 1939, the Lord Privy Seal, Sir John Anderson, expressed his conviction that in the event of war public libraries would "render useful service to the nation by maintaining, so far as circumstances permit, their recreational and educational facilities."[1] A year later the Board of Education issued a special circular drawing the attention of all authorities concerned to "the importance of maintaining and, where necessary, extending the Public Library service as part of the measures which the Minister of Labour is anxious to secure for the welfare of industrial workers." The public libraries, the circular went on to point out, afforded recreation and instruction to vast numbers of readers, and in addition they could often provide centres for the organization of study circles, listening groups, play reading circles, and similar activities. All these services could materially assist the national effort.[2]

This circular undoubtedly did much to create a favourable climate for public library work, and additional encouragement came from the government decision, later in the same year, to exempt books from the special wartime "purchase tax". At this period of the war many library authorities were increasing their book funds, and even library building was allowed to continue in some areas. The badly needed new central libraries at Birmingham and Norwich were indeed postponed—as time was to show, for twenty years or more—but splendid new central libraries were opened at Huddersfield and St. Marylebone in 1940, and in the same year some thirty branch libraries were opened in new or converted premises in various parts of the country— seven of them in the Lancashire County Library area.[3]

As time went on, however, pressure on resources increased. By 1942 book prices had risen by about thirty per cent over the pre-war level, and binding costs by about fifty per cent, and library funds were being stretched to the limit.[4] By that date, too, new library building had been completely halted, and even extensions and conversions had practically ceased. The list

---

[1] *L.A.R.*, Vol. XLI (1939), p. 463.
[2] Board of Education, *Administrative Memorandum No. 242*, Aug. 1940.
[3] The new Norwich Central Library was opened in 1962; at the time of writing the opening of the Birmingham Central Library is expected in 1973.
[4] *L.A.R.*, Vol. XLV (1943), p. 112; cf. Vol. XLVI (1944), p. 152, for increases in library expenditure.

of urgent building schemes held up included 14 urban central libraries, 12 urban branches, 4 county headquarters and about 30 county branches.[1]

The problem of maintaining book supplies was aggravated by an actual physical shortage of books (due to shortage of paper and other materials) and by a serious bottleneck in binding. We must take into account, too, the destruction of books by enemy action. Altogether, during the five years of the war, about fifty central and branch libraries were destroyed or very seriously damaged, and some 750 000 books perished.

Most of this damage was inflicted during the intensive bombing raids which marked the winter of 1940–41: the destruction during this period of the central libraries at Coventry and Plymouth and the central lending library at Liverpool were major disasters which alone accounted for the loss of some 400 000 volumes. The greater part of the National Central Library was also destroyed at this time (April, 1941), including the whole of the adult class department. The British Museum, too, was seriously damaged, losing about 200 000 volumes in the main building and 30 000 volumes of newspapers in the Hendon Repository. Damage during the later years of the war was more spasmodic, but Exeter's beautiful central library was almost completely destroyed in 1942, and some of the London boroughs suffered heavily in the flying bomb attacks of 1944.[2]

The loss of the buildings was, of course, also very serious, and caused grave difficulties to the library authorities concerned. Other authorities faced similar though less enduring difficulties owing to the take-over of library accommodation for war purposes. This does not seem to have happened as frequently as it did in the first World War, but individual library histories throw up some interesting examples. At Birkenhead the children's library in the basement was converted to a dormitory air-raid shelter; at Torquay part of the children's library was taken over as a food office. At Islington reference and reading rooms were taken over for essential war purposes; at York the newsroom and magazine room were similarly appropriated; at Lincoln the library housed the headquarters of the Civil Defence ambulance service; at Colchester the fine new central library, completed in 1939 but not yet opened, was occupied by government departments until long after the war. At Sheffield, for many weeks after the heavy air raids of December, 1941, the newsroom, reference library and offices of the central library were all occupied by one or other of the eleven local and national departments dealing with the emergency, and the public assistance department remained in possession until the war ended.[3] No public library, however, had quite such a frustrating experience as the Bingham Library at Cirencester, which at that time was still a private

[1] L. R. McColvin, *The Public Library System of Great Britain* (1942), p. 217.

[2] For details of these events see *L.A.R.* and *Library World*, *passim*, especially the series of articles on "Books in the Battle" by Frank Hickman in *Library World*, Vol. XLIII (1940–41); also L. R. McColvin, *op. cit.*, pp. 215-216.

[3] *Birkenhead Public Libraries Centenary, 1856–1956* (Birkenhead 1956), p. 11; *Torquay Public Library: Fifty Years of Service, 1907–1957* [Torquay 1957]; *Islington Public Libraries: Golden Jubilee, 1906–1956* [1956], p. 4; *City of York Public Libraries, 1893–1943* (York 1943), p. 5; *Lincoln City Libraries, 1914–1964* [Lincoln 1964], p. 8; A. T. Austing, "New Central Public Library, Colchester", in *L.A.R.*, Vol. LI (1949), pp. 11-12; *City Libraries of Sheffield, 1856–1956* (Sheffield 1956), pp. 47-48.

institution. Immediately war was declared a zealous Office of Works official requisitioned the library and gave notice to quit within twenty-four hours. The building them remained empty for three years before it was eventually brought into use as a service canteen.[1]

Lastly, in recording these wartime difficulties, we must refer to shortage of staff, which was a persistent and increasing problem. By 1942 most male librarians under 41, unless medically unfit, had been called into the armed forces or some other form of wartime service, and special steps had to be taken by the Library Association to ensure that a reasonable proportion of women staff was permitted to remain. The position was made worse by the fact that those who were not called up for full-time service were often heavily involved in part-time duties as food officers, fuel controllers, A.R.P. officers and the like. W. A. Munford, at the close of the war, made an interesting comment:

> "The Librarians left at home to run services, many of which experienced unprecedented demand, found themselves compelled to use temporary assistants of every age, every quality, nay even of every shape and size, often for part-time work only. The situation compelled new thought on rationalisation of routine methods and has probably done much to necessitate a more rigid distinction, in English public libraries at all events, between technical and service staff than was at all common before the war . . . ."[2]

It was in such circumstances, then, that the public libraries struggled to meet the new needs arising from the war. Greatest of these was the "unprecedented demand" just referred to, which made itself felt almost everywhere as soon as people had recovered from the immediate impact of hostilities. The blacking out of street lighting, the reduction in transport facilities, and the long hours of waiting involved in civil defence duties, all favoured the habit of reading, and the libraries assisted by adjusting their opening hours to match as far as possible the hours of daylight, and by creating temporary branch libraries or service points wherever necessary. St. Pancras brought a mobile library into service to meet the needs of those prevented by wartime conditions from visiting the ordinary libraries, and enrolled over 2000 new readers in the first month.[3] In its report for 1940 the Library Association records:

> "In reception, evacuation and neutral areas alike, in industrial and urban centres and in small towns and villages, there are libraries reporting an increase in issues of more than 20 per cent as compared with the previous year, as well as big increases in the number of readers. Remarkable figures have come from counties and towns in the Midlands, where, towards the end of the year, monthly issues in some cases showed a 50 per cent increase over the corresponding period in the previous year, and one or two instances of doubled issues. With a very few exceptions, the tale is one of record use of the public libraries in all parts of the country."[4]

[1] G. P. Jackson, *The Bingham Public Library Golden Jubilee*, repr. from *Wilts. and Gloucestershire Standard*, 17 Sept. 1955. For the later history of this library, now served by Gloucester County, see below, App. III.
[2] *Y.W.L. 1939–1945*, p. 230.
[3] F. Sinclair, "London's First Mobile Library", in *L.A.R.*, Vol. XLIII (1941), pp. 85–87. The van was lent by Hastings for the duration of the war.
[4] *L.A.R.*, Vol. XLIII (1941), p. 123. For further detail see McColvin, *op. cit.*, p. 200.

This passage hints at the considerable shift of population from the high risk areas—London, the ports, and the big industrial centres—to the relative safety of the county areas and the country towns. This movement, of course, was one of the factors leading to increased demand in the reception areas. Of one such, Bedford, we read:

> "The War brought a flood of evacuees to Bedford and an enormously increased volume of business to the Library . . . . The huge crowds, which packed the cramped Lending Department and fell over themselves and the reading-tables, turned the Library into bedlam, especially on Saturdays, when the queues usually stretched out into the street . . . . With the end of the War evacuees went home, and most of them appear to have taken Library books with them as souvenirs."[1]

What is more surprising is to find similar increases in the evacuation areas. Evidence of this comes from many areas, but the most interesting study is that made in the autumn of 1942 by Hilda McGill of the Manchester Public Libraries. Taking as an example a district library in one of the older suburbs, she points out that in spite of the disappearance into the Forces of many regular readers, the peak monthly issue has risen from 15 000 before the war to 20 000. The travelling library which used to serve one of the housing estates in the district, and which issued up to 4000 volumes a month, has had to be taken off the road, but has been replaced by a temporary "house library" which is issuing up to 10 000 volumes a month. These figures, she adds, are typical of Manchester's district libraries, and even the central lending library, after an initial drop in issues, has recovered almost to its pre-war record.

On the basis of her own experience, Miss McGill makes the important point that the increase in issues means not that everyone is reading more but rather that more people are reading. "Our issues", she says, "come from a great new public that is pouring into the library either for the first time, or for the first time since schooldays, and by the children who have never, to my knowledge, borrowed so keenly or in such great numbers." The new readers she identifies principally as the women whose husbands and sons are in the Forces or working long hours on munitions or some other wartime job; and she observes that such new or unaccustomed readers need more guidance than the depleted library staff is in a position to give them.

For the increase in children's reading (reported also from elsewhere) Miss McGill can find no obvious explanation, but she remarks with much prescience:

> "Something new is coming to birth during this war, and it is manifesting itself first in the children, the heirs of a new age, as is only right and proper that it should. More than at any time it occurs to me, the children want to *know*. They have been evacuated, blitzed and rationed out of the old security which their parents knew so well. No longer do the children take anything for granted . . . . In all this changing world, only the things of the mind cannot be touched: and this the child remotely realises."

[1] A. E. Baker, *The Library Story: a History of the Library Movement in Bedford* (Bedford 1958), p. 15.

Much of the demand, as might be expected, is for fiction, but there is an increased demand for technical books, for books about war-time activities such as first aid and gardening, and for books dealing with religious and philosophical topics.[1]

The provision of books for evacuated children was a serious problem which the Library Association had foreseen and for which contingency plans had been drawn up. In the early months of the war the movement of children to safer areas was on a large scale, and with the Association acting as co-ordinator nearly a quarter of a million books were transferred to the receiving library authorities. After a time many of these children began to trickle back home, but the heavy bombing of 1940–41 brought further evacuations and further considerable transfers of books.[2] In the meantime, as the case of Manchester illustrates, issues in the evacuated areas remained at least as high as ever.[3]

A valuable by-product of these events was greater co-operation across library boundaries. Special arrangements were made in a number of areas, e.g. between libraries in the London and Home Counties Branch, between Salford and Lancashire, and between Leeds and the West Riding; and arrangements for interavailability of library tickets, which had already made good progress before the war, received a further stimulus.[4]

The provision of books for H.M. Forces was naturally a matter of concern. In the early months of the war, many libraries supplied books to local units;[5] and the Library Association was only too happy to collaborate in the Service Libraries and Books Fund set up in November, 1939, on the initiative of the Lord Mayor of London. Public appeals for books met with a generous response, and by the end of 1942 about eight million books and the same number of magazines had been distributed to units of H.M. Forces at home and abroad for free circulation. Most of this literature, of course, was of a recreational character. The Library Association wanted to go further, and to set up in all the larger units organized libraries under the supervision of qualified librarians, but this plan met with considerable resistance from the Forces side. The most that could be done was to send to selected units small but balanced collections of 500–1000 books, including fiction, non-fiction, and some quick reference

---

[1] H. M. McGill, "Reading Tastes in Wartime", in *L.A.R.*, Vol. XLV (1943), pp. 23-9. Cf. McColvin, *op. cit.*, p. 201, and for other reading surveys see D. D. Nichols, *Twenty Years' Development: Stockport Public Libraries, 1936–1956* (Stockport 1957), pp. 7-8; J. T. Hamilton, *Greenock Libraries: a Development and Social History, 1635–1967* (Greenock [1969]), pp. 128-131.

[2] *L.A.R.*, Vol. XLI (1939), pp. 460-465; Vol. XLII (1940), p. 196; Vol. XLIII (1941), p.122. For a detailed treatment of the problems of the reception areas, see McColvin, *op. cit.*, pp. 202-210.

[3] In the London and Home Counties area, which was the worst affected, the issues of books for adult home reading in the municipal libraries increased from 44.9 millions to 48.4 millions between 1939 and 1944, but there was some falling off in issues of children's books, and the use of reference departments was sharply curtailed—J. D. Stewart (ed.), *Report on the Municipal Library System of London and the Home Counties, 1944* (1946).

[4] *L.A.R.*, Vol. XLI (1939), pp. 257-258, 509-510.

[5] *L.A.R.*, Vol. XLII (1940), p. 14.

works. A total of 657 such collections is reported to have been distributed by
the end of 1941, though most of the earlier ones were lost in the Dunkirk
withdrawal.[1]

In this country much was done also by direct contact between units and
local public libraries. Boxes of books were lent, arrangements were made for
troops to borrow individually from nearby library branches or centres, and
sometimes special centres were set up within units. Public libraries in the
ports supplied books to visiting ships. On Merseyside seven library vans,
provided by public subscription, distributed books from a stock of 20 000
to some 7000 readers in units scattered throughout the area. Such local arrangements became easier for the smaller libraries when in February, 1942, the
War Office approved a scheme for the hire of books by units at the rate of
£70 a year for 1000 volumes changed three times a year.

By this time provision was being made, in some areas, on a substantial
scale. In Norfolk, in 1942, borrowing facilities for troops were available
at 575 library centres, including 25 in units. In Kent the County Library
had 27 000 volumes in circulation among 189 centres. Manchester sent over
3000 volumes to troops in the Orkneys.

In the meantime the Services Central Book Depot set up to meet the needs
of the Service Libraries and Books Fund was still mainly preoccupied with the
collection and distribution of recreational literature, but as time went on
it devoted increasing attention to the provision of books requested to supplement existing unit libraries, and books required in connection with the various
Forces educational schemes—especially the vocational correspondence courses
begun in the autumn of 1941. This paved the way for the educational scheme
planned for the period immediately after the war, while the men and women
in the Forces were awaiting release. Textbooks to a total of nearly three million
volumes, many specially printed, were ordered for this great enterprise, a
special unit being established for the purpose in March, 1944, under the direction of Major J. H. P. Pafford, afterwards Goldsmiths' Librarian in the University of London. This was a self-contained scheme in which the public libraries
gave only peripheral assistance.[2]

A very considerable contribution to the provision of books for the Services
was made by the campaigns for paper salvage that were launched in various
parts of the country. Here the Library Association played a most useful role,
drawing attention to the dangers of indiscriminate pulping of books,[3] and
enlisting the aid of local librarians to ensure that all books collected were
carefully sorted before any decision was taken. On this basis a National Book

[1] J. D. Cowley, Director of the University College School of Librarianship, who had
been appointed Principal Librarian to the Fund, was so unhappy about the situation
that he resigned in October, 1940, and two librarian colleagues resigned with him.
Cowley gave expression to his disenchantment in an article on "The Services Central
Book Depot", in *Library World*, Vol. XLIII (1940–41), pp. 21–23.

[2] The best account of all this is in N. S. Wilson, *Education in the Forces, 1939–46: the Civilian
Contribution* [1949], Ch. ix. See also the articles and reports in *L.A.R.*, Vol. XLII (1940),
p. 196; Vol. XLIII (1941), p. 123; Vol. XLIV (1942), pp. 14–16, 106; Vol. XLV (1943),
p. 113; Vol. XLVII (1945), pp. 25–26, 134–136; and for the release period J. H. P. Pafford,
Books and Army Education, 1944–1946: Preparation and Supply (1947).

[3] See the statement by W. C. Berwick Sayers in *L.A.R.*, Vol. XLIII (1941), p. 179.

Recovery Campaign was launched in the autumn of 1942.[1] The results were astonishing. At Bristol alone, in a period of one month, 764 000 books were collected, and although most of these were sent for pulping, 68 000 were made available to H.M. Forces, and 26 000 (including some works of considerable bibliographical interest) were set aside for the reconstruction of damaged libraries.[2]

By the time the war ended the scheme had produced some millions of books for the Forces, and about 650 000 books and a very large number of periodicals for the replacement of stocks in war damaged libraries at home and abroad.[3] These latter books were at first retained at scattered storage points throughout the country, but in 1944 an Inter-Allied Books Centre was established in London, under the direction of B. M. Headicar, formerly librarian of the London School of Economics. Here were brought together not only the salvaged books but also books contributed as the result of an appeal to British universities, professional bodies, and learned societies, and books and periodicals purchased by a special Books Commission of the Allied Governments.[4] In the final distribution 24 000 volumes went to the British Museum, about 100 000 to other libraries in Great Britain, and the balance to libraries in allied countries.[5]

Provision for the civil defence services was a task in which public libraries were even more deeply involved than in provision for the armed forces, which always found co-operation with civilian organizations rather difficult. The Library Association records, in its annual report for 1940:

> "From the first days of the war, authorities had made special arrangements for supplying books to the civil defence services. Collections of books were sent by many borough and county libraries to Wardens' Posts, First Aid Posts, Auxiliary Fire Service Stations, Report Centres and other points at which civil defence personnel were engaged. There is no doubt whatever that this service has been keenly appreciated."[6]

In London books were even provided, during the winter of 1940–41, for the thousands of people who crowded nightly into the underground shelters. St. Marylebone, at this period, had collections of 50–550 books—mostly paperbacks—in forty-nine shelters, including two underground railway stations. These "libraries" were staffed by shelter wardens and volunteers, and special requests were met from central library stock.[7] Similar provision was made at Shoreditch,[8] and Bethnal Green, at an unused underground station, had a library of 4000 volumes serving a nightly clientèle of 6000 people.[9]

Finally, in this list of additional wartime tasks, reference should be made to the role of public libraries as information centres. This was a natural func-

[1] L.A.R., Vol. XLV (1943), p. 111.
[2] J. Ross, "Book Salvage Drive at Bristol", ibid., pp. 6–8.
[3] Library Association, The Restoration of Libraries: a brief account of Book Recovery and the Inter-Allied Book Centre (1946), p. 9.
[4] L.A.R., Vol. XLVI (1944), p. 178.
[5] Library Association, The Restoration of Libraries (1946), p. 9.
[6] L.A.R., Vol. XLIII (1941), p. 122.
[7] Ibid., pp. 46–47.
[8] Ibid., pp. 70–71.
[9] S. Snaith, "A Tube Shelter Lending Library", in Library Review, Vol. VIII (1941–42), pp. 154–158.

tion for them to fulfil, and many librarians acted as Information Officers, or played a leading role on Information Committees, under the nationwide scheme established at the outset of the war by the Ministry of Information. In addition the libraries acted as centres for the collection and distribution of information, for meetings, and for the often admirable lectures, displays and film shows which the Ministry arranged. Within the limits set by the needs of wartime, the Ministry during these years did an excellent educational job, and its activities were reinforced on the cultural side by those of the newly formed Council for the Encouragement of Music and the Arts (now the Arts Council). W.E.A. classes and other normal adult education activities were also booming, and many public libraries found themselves acting as cultural centres to a degree which they had never previously envisaged, and with resources which they had never hitherto been able to command.

This reference to library extension work leads us on to mention the establishment, during the war, of a new library authority which was in after years to be well known for its work in this field. The little railway town of Swindon was one of only three authorities which both adopted and implemented the Public Libraries Acts during the years 1939–45.[1] Hitherto it had been content with the service provided by the Great Western Railway Mechanics' Institution, but the influx of new residents as a consequence of the war led to the decision to establish a public library. The Acts were adopted in 1942, and the library opened, in temporary premises in a department store, in the following year. It was at once an immense success, and in spite of restricted accommodation the librarian, James Swift, made an early start in those cultural activities which were to be so strikingly developed by his successor Harold Jolliffe.[2]

The McColvin Report

In 1941, in the darkest days of the war, the Library Association took its courage in both hands and commissioned its Honorary Secretary, Lionel R. McColvin, City Librarian of Westminster, to undertake a survey of the present condition and future needs of the public library service. The City of Westminster generously released him for six months on full salary; and the Carnegie Trust, which was anxious for information concerning wartime problems, met the cost of the investigation. By the spring of 1942 McColvin had completed his survey, and in the autumn he presented his report.

McColvin has been described by a younger contemporary as "the outstanding librarian of his generation and one of the great figures produced by Public Libraries since 1850",[3] and the McColvin Report, as it was immediately

---

[1] The others were Henley on Thames (now a branch of Oxford County) and Crieff (now a branch of Perth and Kinross County). There were six other authorities which commenced service during these years, but all these had adopted before the war. See below, Apps. III and IV.

[2] J. Swift, "Swindon Public Library", in *L.A.R.*, Vol. XLV (1943), pp. 178–181; *21 Years of Public Library Service in Swindon, 1943–1964* [Swindon 1964]. Jolliffe was librarian from 1946 until his death in 1969.

[3] W. A. Munford, *Penny Rate* (1951), p. 54. For personal assessments by his son, K. R. McColvin, and by R. F. Vollans, see the volume of international studies edited by Vollans in McColvin's honour, *Libraries for the People* (1968), pp. 3–36.

christened,[1] still impresses after thirty years as an astonishing *tour de force*, especially when one remembers the difficult conditions under which it was carried out. It was, as F. M. Gardner remarked at the time, "an achievement of sustained brilliance which no one, even in a critical mood, can but admire".[2] To summarize it adequately in a brief space is impossible: we can only attempt to indicate some of its salient features.

The Report begins with some general statistics about coverage, showing that, on the basis of pre-war figures, only 326 000 people in Great Britain now inhabited areas for which the Public Libraries Acts had not been adopted.[3] The counties of Rutland and Argyll accounted for 73 000 of these, and the remainder lived in areas which had been excluded from the operation of their respective counties but had not yet developed their own service. All but two of these (Mountain Ash in Glamorganshire and Rothesay in Bute) were in England.[4] They included Swindon, which as we have seen adopted in the Acts in the year in which the Report was published;[5] Cirencester, where service comparable to that of a public library was provided by the Bingham Library;[6] Harwich in Essex; Banbury and Henley on Thames in Oxfordshire; and Berwick upon Tweed and five other urban areas in Northumberland. Actually Cirencester and Berwick upon Tweed should not have been included in this list: they should have been included, instead, in a further list which McColvin provides of authorities which had adopted the Acts but done nothing effective to implement them. In this list he includes Weymouth in Dorset (which had adopted as long ago as 1893), Newburn in Northumberland, Whitby in Yorkshire North Riding, and Barnes in Surrey (now part of Richmond upon Thames).[7] Making these minor adjustments we can say that in round figures 300 000 people were living in areas which had not adopted the Acts, and a further 100 000 in areas where the Acts had been adopted but not effectively implemented.

In general (allowing for wartime developments of the kind we have already described) McColvin's picture of the condition of the library service is not significantly different from that presented in the Library Association *Survey* published four years earlier,[8] but his analysis is more thorough, more incisive, and, because it is the work of one man and not of a team, more consistent in its observation. He emphasizes, as the earlier survey had done, the inequalities in the service, the enormous disparity between the best and the worst. He gives us the now sadly familiar horror stories about the smaller urban libraries, and points out that county libraries also can be small and

---

[1] L. R. McColvin, *The Public Library System of Great Britain* (1942).

[2] F. M. Gardner, "The Practical Isolationist", in *Library Assistant*, Vol. XXXV (1942), p. 136.

[3] The Report actually covers Northern Ireland as well as Great Britain. In this summary the figures for Northern Ireland are wherever possible excluded.

[4] McColvin seems to have been unaware that the County Library service in Bute was suspended in 1939. When service was eventually resumed in 1951, Rothesay became the county headquarters. See below p. 346.

[5] See previous page.

[6] See below, App. III, *s.v.* Gloucestershire.

[7] On all these see below, App. III, *s.v.*

[8] See above, pp. 272–279

inefficient.[1] He is severely critical of reference library work ("the outstanding failure of British librarianship")[2] and of services for children, both in the libraries and in the schools.[3] "A majority of the books seen in children's departments", he comments, "were shabby and unattractive and a scandalously large number were positively filthy." The adult fiction is not much better, and "at least 50 per cent of the non-fiction stocks are completely useless—at any rate where they are."[4] Staffing standards he found lamentable, pointing particularly to the almost complete absence of qualified staff in those urban libraries (still about 40 per cent of the total) which served populations of less than 20 000. Salaries, both in urban and county libraries, were for the most part correspondingly low.[5]

Though McColvin's critique is sharper and better documented than that of his predecessors, all this is fairly predictable. So, too, is his attitude on a number of current issues. Thus in dealing with the county library service it is no surprise to find him in favour of regionalization,[6] against the subordination of the library committee to the education committee,[7] and against differential rating.[8] In dealing with urban libraries he is against the provision of newsrooms,[9] against joint management of libraries and museums,[10] and, inevitably, in favour of open access: he notes with dismay that six of the hundred central or main lending libraries he visited had not yet achieved this essential reform.[11] He comments favourably on the Scottish library service, but is at one with Scottish librarians in urging a reform of the law to secure, amongst other things, the abolition of rate limitation and dual rating, and the separation of the county libraries from the education service.[12] On library extension activities he is cautious, fearing that any large-scale extension of these activities could lead the library "to neglect its chief work, which is service to the individual."[13]

Even in this descriptive and analytical section of the Report, however, there are some points which are new or are given quite a new emphasis. With his eye evidently on South Wales, the author is severe in his strictures on those libraries (urban and county) which delegate a large part of their responsibility to "poverty stricken miners' institutes."[14] The recently established Rhondda authority is specifically referred to in this connection—one of the few authorities mentioned in the Report by name.[15] He also draws attention more than once to the wasteful overlap of service where, as happens in fifty-four instances, a municipal library and the county library headquarters are in the same town.[16] At the administrative level, too, he has a number of shrewd

[1] *McColvin Report*, p. 39.
[2] *Op. cit.*, pp. 63–67.
[3] *Op. cit.*, pp. 72–80.
[4] *Op. cit.*, pp. 56–57.
[5] *Op. cit.*, pp. 35–37; 87–93.
[6] *Op. cit.*, pp. 25–26.
[7] *Op. cit.*, pp. 37–39.
[8] *Op. cit.*, pp. 29–30.
[9] *Op. cit.*, p. 28.
[10] *Op. Cit.*, pp. 70–71.
[11] *Op. cit.*, p. 83.
[12] *Op. cit.*, Ch. v.
[13] *Op. cit.*, pp. 69–70.
[14] *Op. cit.*, p. 24.
[15] *Op. cit.*, pp. 48–49. For another "horrid example" see p. 45. The Rhondda service was established in 1939, but only after protracted negotiations with the nineteen workmen's institutes in the area—see *Report of the Proceedings of the Twelfth Conference of Libraries in Wales and Monmouthshire, 1938* (Aberystwyth 1939), pp. 24–25.
[16] *McColvin Report*, p. 109. Cf. pp. 26, 43.

comments. County library methods, he considers, need a complete overhaul, in order to avoid the keeping of unnecessary records and to ensure a reasonable measure of uniformity in such matters as the recording of loans.[1] Dealing with subject classification, he notes that twelve out of a hundred urban lending libraries have no classification beyond a rough grouping of books under broad subject headings; and that though most librarians use Dewey or Brown there are many confusing local variations.[2] Catalogues, in both urban and county libraries, are in general poor:

> "Some catalogues are dirty and shabby; few are properly guided. All types are found—card, sheaf, printed, guard books; sometimes more than one type was used in the same system. Classified catalogues with author lists, alphabetical subject lists with author lists, and dictionary catalogues were found variously in use, with no marked preference."[3]

Some of McColvin's severest criticism is reserved for the Regional Library Bureaux. He admits that librarians everywhere "spoke most warmly of the importance of the services they received from their Regional Bureaux." He points out, however, that in 1939–40 the total number of books lent by all the 491 libraries in the regional systems of England and Wales, either to libraries in their own regional systems or through the National Central Library to libraries in other regional systems, was only 54 635—less than one-eighth of the number of non-fiction books issued from the Manchester Central Lending Library alone. Even if allowance is made for books borrowed through the National Central Library from outlier libraries outside the regional systems, the total would still only reach 70 000 or 80 000.

The interlending system was, moreover, slow, cumbersome, and expensive: "study the balance sheets of the various components, add the costs of postages and of the time spent by non-bureau staff and you will find that, viewed nationally, it would be much cheaper to *buy* every book handled that one *could* buy." Where books could not be bought, it would be more efficient to use a single national centre without the interposition of the regional bureaux.[4]

This kind of argument is not uncommon nowadays, but in those days it was revolutionary. The same iconoclastic spirit is carried forward into the sections of the Report which outline proposals for the future. It is these sections which mark off the McColvin Report so distinctively from all previous reports on the public library service (and indeed all subsequent ones). For generations librarians had been lamenting the inadequacy of library organization and library resources: McColvin for the first time followed these criticisms to their logical conclusion, and produced practical proposals for a national, co-ordinated, adequately financed library system designed to provide complete coverage throughout the country.

The essential features of his scheme were two. The first was the creation of larger and more efficient library units; the second was the establishment of an appropriate national authority to stimulate and co-ordinate local effort and to provide financial assistance.

[1] *Op. cit.*, pp. 34–35.
[2] *Op. cit.*, p. 84.
[3] *Op. cit.*, p. 83.
[4] *Op. cit.*, pp. 103–105.

His proposals for new library units involved a complete re-drawing of the library map, and the abolition of the distinction between urban and county library systems.[1] The 604 existing authorities in the United Kingdom would give way to 93. The City of London and the 28 metropolitan boroughs were grouped into 9 units; the rest of England was divided into 69 units; Wales made 5 units, Scotland 9, and Northern Ireland 1. His ideal unit was one which embraced "a normal natural congregation of people" and which had a sufficient population and sufficient resources to justify "the full normal range of book supply and related services", but in practice he placed the main emphasis on population and resources, and this led him into serious difficulties in dealing with the more thinly populated areas. The 60 library authorities of Lancashire (excluding Furness) could reasonably be grouped into 8 units based on the towns of Preston, Blackburn, Rochdale, Bolton, Wigan, Liverpool, Warrington and Manchester; but it seemed much less practicable to constitute a single unit embracing the whole of the northern half of Scotland, and another embracing three-quarters of Wales.[2]

Local government reform has been so much discussed since 1942 that the problems McColvin faced have become familiar, and the solutions he proposed no longer seem as shocking as they did to his contemporaries. Even in those days, however, local government reform was in the air, and McColvin was not without hope that the reorganization expected after the war would bring new local government areas "which, while not necessarily ideal, are practicable library areas." If not, he was prepared to go ahead with *ad hoc* library authorities, to be created either by legislation or by voluntary amalgamation in return for government grant in aid. Each of the new units would be managed by a joint committee exercising delegated powers and raising funds by precept from the constituent authorities. This committee would appoint a chief librarian, and take over all the powers, properties and liabilities of the existing libraries.

The central authority, McColvin thought, should be a government department responsible to Parliament for the promotion and maintenance of a nation-wide library service.[3] It could be a department of the Board of Education, but would more appropriately be placed under a Ministry of Fine Arts should such a ministry come into being. It would consider the development schemes submitted by the units, including proposals for buildings and loans; formulate minimum standards concerning book supply, qualifications and salaries of staff, and other aspects of the library service; conduct inquiries and issue reports; and maintain a staff of regional officers to ensure that government grant was properly spent. This grant would be the same as that applying in the case of higher education, i.e. at that time a grant equivalent to 50 per cent of total authorized expenditure.

Here then we have for the first time a fully worked out scheme for state assistance to, and state inspection of, the library service. The Kenyon Report, it will be remembered, had emphatically rejected this idea,[4] and subsequent

---

[1] *Op. cit.*, Chs. xiv–xv.
[2] The units are listed in *McColvin Report*, pp. 150–156, and those in England and Wales are mapped on p. 157. For a map of the Scottish units see W. R. Aitken, *A History of the Public Library Movement in Scotland to 1955* (Glasgow 1971), p. 182.
[3] *Op. cit.*, Ch. xiv., espec. pp. 129–132.
[4] See above, pp. 319.

XIa. LENDING LIBRARY, READING

This photograph, reproduced in Alfred Cotgreave's *Views and Memoranda of Public Libraries* (1901) is typical of the old-style lending library, in which the reader selected his books with the help of a printed catalogue and an indicator, and was served by an assistant over a counter.

XIb. THE MITCHELL LIBRARY, GLASGOW: MAIN HALL

The Mitchell Library, originally a private foundation, is now the city's main central reference library. This photograph taken in the 'sixties illustrates the main hall of the imposing building designed by W. B. Whitie and opened in 1911.

XIIa. KIRKBY BRANCH, LANCASHIRE COUNTY LIBRARY
A good impression of the interior of a modern open-plan library, designed by R. Booth and opened in 1964. The view is from the reference library across the entrance hall to the lending library. The quick reference section is in the immediate foreground, the entrance to the children's library on the left. The stairs give access to the library offices and a lecture room.

XIIb. EAGLESHAM BRANCH, RENFREWSHIRE COUNTY LIBRARY
A browsing area in a corner of the lending library in a county branch, designed by J. M. Whalley and T. W. Hepburn and opened in 1963.

attempts by the Welsh librarians to re-open the issue had met with a blank negative from the Board of Education.[1] In 1936, at a conference in Margate, the Library Association had pressed for state grants for certain limited purposes (including assistance to impoverished areas) to be administered by a joint advisory committee functioning on much the same lines as the University Grants Committee, but this proposal does not seem to have been pressed and McColvin now regarded it as inadequate.[2]

In addition to the two central proposals already described, the Report also elaborates proposals concerning inter-library co-operation and concerning the training, employment and salaries of staff. On the first of these subjects McColvin proposes[3]

(i) That each of the new library authorities be allocated an area of specialisation—preferably a subject of local interest, e.g. steel at Sheffield, pottery at Stoke on Trent, naval history at Portsmouth, fishing at Aberdeen; and that each of these authorities be required to keep a reserve stock of books in its special field, withdrawn from circulation.

(ii) That each of the new library authorities be expected to acquire, as a matter of course, all general standard works, i.e. everything except highly specialised or very expensive material, and that systematic arrangements be made for building up a national reserve stock of this material, in triplicate, when the time comes for it to be withdrawn from circulation. This reserve stock would also be held at local libraries on an agreed subject basis.

(iii) That eleven libraries, namely Newcastle upon Tyne, Leeds, Sheffield, Liverpool, Manchester, Birmingham, Bristol, Central London,[4] Cardiff, Glasgow and Edinburgh, be established as regional reference libraries for the purposes of research and scholarship. These libraries would attract special grant from the central authority. They would not only be freely available to all wishing to use them, but would also supply advice, information, and where appropriate photocopies of library material, to other units.

(iv) That should a reader ask for a book which is not held by his local library unit, then "(a) If it is a general, obtainable book not in the unit's stock the unit buys it; (b) if it is a general but non-obtainable book, the reader's unit applies to the unit with the appropriate allocated reserve; (c) if it is non-general, application may be made either direct to the N.C.L. or first to the appropriate special library."

(v) That the Regional Library Bureaux be discontinued, and that the responsibilities of the National Central Library in this matter be restricted to the maintenance of union catalogues of non-general material, and to arrangements for the loan of such material between libraries.

McColvin goes on to suggest that the National Central Library, thus relieved of some of its present responsibilities, would have more time to devote to other national concerns. In particular he would like to see it become a national centre of bibliographical information, and a central cataloguing agency. It should, in his view, be financed entirely by the central authority.

---

[1] *Report of the Proceedings of the Third Conference of Libraries in Wales and Monmouthshire, 1928* (Aberystwyth 1928), pp. 12, 19. See also the Reports of the Fourth Conference, 1929, p. 8, and of the Sixth Conference, 1931, pp. 8–16.

[2] The proposals are printed in *L.A.R.*, Vol. XXXIX (1937), p. 99. For McColvin's introductory address see *ibid.*, pp. 435–437.   [3] *McColvin Report*, Ch. xvi.

[4] The Central London unit comprises the City, Finsbury, Holborn, and McColvin's own library of Westminster.

McColvin's proposals concerning the training and remuneration of staff are detailed and precise.[1] He envisages that each of the new library authorities will require a staff of at least seventy, perhaps up to three or four hundred. As far as possible the routine duties—counter work, book processing, typing, packing, and the like—will be carried out by non-professional staff. Professional staff will fall into three grades: higher administrative and executive officers, subject specialists, and staff occupied in general professional duties. All these will have the same basic training leading, as hitherto, to the Associateship or Fellowship of the Library Association, but the normal mode of entry will in future be through a library school. The basic professional salary should be comparable with that for elementary school teachers. In order to cater for the training of staff on such a scale there should be five or six additional schools in large provincial centres such as Glasgow, Edinburgh, Manchester, Liverpool, Birmingham, Bristol, and Cardiff.

Proposals for Post-War Reconstruction

It was not to be expected that so far reaching a Report, and one which cut across so many vested interests, would command ready acceptance. As the Scottish Library Association Council put it, "the project as a whole was on too ambitious a scale and too revolutionary in principle to gain for it the approval of the authorities by whom the necessary decisions would be made."[2] Indeed when in September, 1942, the Report was first presented to the Council of the Library Association of Great Britain, some members were so alarmed by the proposals concerning new library areas that it was only at McColvin's insistence that it was eventually agreed to publish the document in its entirety. When it appeared it bore on its title-page the legend: "The Council of the Library Association, in publishing this report, do not commit themselves to the policy or the recommendations which have been submitted for their consideration."[3]

None the less when the Association came to publish its own statement a year later, it accepted in principle every one of McColvin's major proposals, even the proposal for larger library units.[4] On this latter point it suggested that "in general the population of the library area should lie between one-quarter and three-quarters of a million"—a figure only slightly less than the 300–800 000 proposed by McColvin.[5] One can, however, detect in these *Proposals* two signs of response to pressure from the Association's members.

In the first place, it is suggested that central government grant should be accompanied by some form of rate equalization in order to ease the position

[1] *Op. cit.*, Ch. xvii.

[2] W. R. Aitken, *A History of the Public Library Movement in Scotland to 1955* (Glasgow 1971), p. 184, citing Scottish Library Association, *Annual Report, 1943*, p. 15.

[3] *L.A.R.*, Vol. XLIV (1942), pp. 142–143, 159. An unsuccessful attempt was made to have the Report published by the Carnegie U.K. Trust.

[4] Library Association, *Proposals for the Post-War Reorganisation and Development of the Public Library Service* (1943), p. 7.

[5] This figure does not appear in the McColvin Report, but in the official summary published in *L.A.R.*, Vol. XLIV (1942), p. 164.

of the poorer areas.[1] In the second place, it is made clear that the creation of *ad hoc* library authorities is regarded as a last resort: "the creation of suitable library authorities," it is declared, "should be secured by such reform of local government areas and functions in general as will provide areas suitable not only for libraries but for education, public health and most, if not, indeed, all other local government purposes." Only in default of such comprehensive reorganization should the central library authority be empowered, as a condition of grant, to require "the formation by amalgamation of suitable library areas."[2]

In practice, as we know, the expected drastic overhaul of local government structure never took place, and since no action was taken by the government to establish a central grant-distributing library authority, the McColvin Report must have seemed at the time a useless exercise. This, however, was not so. By his rigorous and ruthless examination of the existing situation he made librarians more conscious than ever before of the deficiencies of the service, and by his proposals for reconstruction he set them a target towards which they have ever since been slowly but inexorably moving.[3]

One immediate practical outcome of the Report was that the Library Association set to work once more on the long-delayed revision of its training arrangements, and new proposals were agreed to come into effect in January, 1946. This, however, is a matter which can be more conveniently dealt with in the next chapter. In the meantime we conclude the present chapter with a quotation from the opening paragraphs of the Library Association's *Proposals*:

> "Any hopes we may entertain for post-war social and economic reconstruction, for sound democratic government, the improvement of educational standards, the fullness of individual living and the more fruitful employment of leisure presuppose free and full access to books and information. Without this opportunity none of these hopes can be realized. The necessities of both individual and communal life make the public library an essential part of the equipment of modern society."[4]

[1] *Proposals*, pp. 9–10.
[2] *Op. cit.*, pp. 8, 10.
[3] For a tribute by F. M. Gardner to the significance of the Report see R. F. Vollans (ed.), *Libraries for the People* (1968), pp. 107–109.
[4] *Op. cit.*, p. 3.

CHAPTER XIV

The Post-War Years

The Affluent Society

DURING the years 1944–46, as war changed to peace, a great series of parliamentary enactments completed the edifice of the welfare state—an edifice whose foundations, like those of the public libraries, had been laid far back in the nineteenth century. The Education Act, the National Health Act, the National Insurance Act, the National Assistance Act, the Children's Act: all these combined to create for ordinary people a world of better oppotunity and greater social security. The creation of the welfare state proved, also, to be the starting-point for what the American economist J. K. Galbraith has taught us to call "the affluent society", a society in which, in spite of continuing political and economic uncertainties, the advance of technology brought to people of all classes a great increase in material prosperity. The results are familiar to us all—higher wages, shorter hours, longer holidays, better houses, more cars, washing-machines, refrigerators, television sets and the like. How far this emphasis on purely material things is responsible for the decline in traditional moral standards which has been so marked in recent years is a question into which, fortunately, we do not need to enter here.

It is, however, worth while to seek to identify those aspects of this affluent welfare society which were of particular significance for public library work. One of them, undoubtedly, was the general increase in leisure—an increase due not only to shorter hours and longer holidays but also to smaller families, longer expectation of life, and earlier retirement. This change, however, must be recorded with some caution. Many more married women were working than before the war, and most weekly wage-earners preferred extra overtime pay to extra leisure.[1] It must be noted, too, that as leisure increased, so the facilities for employing it multiplied. With more than eight million private cars on the road by 1965, motoring now occupied an increasingly important part in people's lives, especially with the advent of the five-day week. Music, art, gardening, and sports and hobbies of all kinds competed for people's attention. Nothing, however, could compete in power and influence with the great new leisure-time occupation of television.

Before the war television scarcely existed, but by 1960 there were television sets in over 11 million homes, and it was estimated that at 8.30 in the evening, every evening, about one-third of the entire adult population was watching. By 1965 the number of licences exceeded 13 millions. For the public library, as for adult education, this astonishing development of television had possibilities both good and bad. At its best it could be a great stimulant to new interests,

---

[1] For statistics on this point, see T. Kelly, *History of Adult Education in Great Britain* (Liverpool 1962, 2nd. edn. 1970), p. 335.

but just because of its powerful appeal it could exercise a disruptive effect on other leisure-time activities, including reading.[1]

Undoubtedly the most important change of all, in the long run, was the enormous advance in education, which was initiated by the Education Act of 1944 (and the corresponding Scottish Act of the following year) and received new impetus from the publication of two major reports—the Crowther Report in 1959 on the education of the 15–18 year olds,[2] and the Robbins Report in 1963 on higher education.[3] In the twenty years following the war the number of primary school pupils rose from just under 4 million to over 5 million, the number of secondary school pupils from 1¾ millions to over 3 millions; the number of university students from 52 000 to 113 000; and the number of full-time and sandwich course students in other forms of further education (excluding teachers in training) from 54 000 to 202 000;[4] while the number of students in W.E.A. and university extra-mural classes more than doubled, and adult evening institute students trebled, in the same period.[5]

The direct implications of this growth for the public libraries were obvious: the call was for a big expansion of reference and study facilities. There were also indirect effects arising from the vast new market for educational books— a market which, thanks to developments abroad and to advances in publishing and marketing techniques, soon began to assume international dimensions. One such effect was that some publishers began to find it worth while to re-print, by photolithography, scholarly works such as the Rolls Series and the Parliamentary Papers, which had long been out of print but for which, at high prices, there was now a limited but sufficient market.

At the other end of the scale paperback publishing increased enormously after the war, extending not only to popular works but also to scholarly works and especially to every kind of textbook or prescribed text. This tended to keep book prices down for the private buyer, but not for the libraries, which could not satisfactorily make use of paperbacks.[6] Book production thus tended to become polarized, with paperback editions for the individual purchaser and limited hardback editions relying mainly on library purchase. Inevitably the prices of hardback books rose sharply but, thanks to the increased demand from the libraries of educational institutions (abroad as well as at home), the increase was on the whole kept within reasonable bounds. It has to be remembered that price levels generally were rising at this period at an average rate of between three and four per cent per annum.

It was rising prices, combined with competition from paperbacks, public libraries, and television that led in the 'sixties to the virtual extinction of the commercial circulating libraries. The oldest of the great national circulating

---

[1] *Op. cit.*, pp. 335–336. The figure for the number of licences in 1965 is taken from the B.B.C.'s *Annual Report, 1964–65*, App. I.

[2] Ministry of Education, Central Advisory Council (England) *15 to 18* (1959), 2v.

[3] *Higher Education: Report of the Committee appointed by the Prime Minister* (Cmnd. 2154, 1963).

[4] These figures are based on the Annual Reports of the Department of Education and Science and its predecessors, and of the Scottish Education Department.

[5] Kelly, *op. cit.*, pp. 336–337.

[6] Some publishers, especially Penguin Books, placed severe restrictions on the rebinding of paperbacks in hard covers for library use. See *Five Years' Work in Librarianship, 1961–1965*, p. 228 (cited henceforth as *F.Y.W.L. 1961–65*).

libraries, Mudie's, founded in 1842, had already disappeared, in 1937. Of its younger competitors, W. H. Smith's closed in 1961, the Times Book Club in 1962. In 1965 there remained only Boots' Booklovers' Library, destined to be closed in the following year. The old 2d. shop libraries, by this time commonly 4d. or 6d. libraries, faded out about the same time. The net result was an appreciable addition to the clientèle of the public libraries.[1]

There were many other changes in British life which made themselves noticeable at this period and which had their impact on public library development, though that impact is not always easy to measure. The immigration of considerable numbers of coloured people from the Commonwealth, for example, created quite precise problems for public libraries in those areas—certain parts of London, and of the midland and northern industrial areas—in which the immigrants tended to concentrate. The increase in the proportion of elderly people in the population is another change of which the results in the way of increased reading could reasonably be forecast. On the other hand it is much more difficult to assess the effect on library use of one of the most significant social changes of the post-war era, namely the growing affluence and independence of the younger generation.

For the present we must be content merely to mention changes such as these, and to close this introductory section by drawing attention to the economic uncertainty which hung like a cloud over most of this period. Neither the Labour Government of Clement Attlee which held office from 1945 to 1951, nor the successive Conservative Governments of Winston Churchill, Anthony Eden, and Harold Macmillan which ruled for the next thirteen years, nor the Labour Government of Harold Wilson which succeeded in 1964, could find any lasting solution to the country's underlying economic weakness. Rising wages and prices, combined with low productivity, inadequate exports, and heavy international commitments, repeatedly gave rise to balance of payments problems to which the only answer (short of devaluation) seemed to lie in raising bank interest rates and cutting back public expenditure—measures which, if persisted in too long, led to the opposite danger of unemployment. The resulting "stop-go" policy, in which economy campaigns alternated with bursts of carefully moderated generosity, made it very difficult for the library authorities to plan and carry through a consistent development policy. The remarkable thing is that they achieved as much as they did.

The Struggle for Reform

The history of public libraries since the Second World War can be interpreted as a record of steps taken towards the implementation of the McColvin Report of 1942. The major recommendation of that Report, however, namely

---

[1] See C. Barclay, "Tastes of the Book Borrower", in *Times Literary Supplement*, 17 Mar. 1960, and the anonymous article "Boots Stock and Branch", *ibid.*, 3 Feb. 1966. The story of Mudie's has recently been told in G. L. Griest, *Mudie's Circulating Library and the Victorian Novel* (1970). Harrods, which had bought up Mudie's stock in 1937 and taken over the Times Book Club in 1962, continued to provide a personal service in London and a postal service elsewhere.

These and other problems relating to the book trade are interestingly discussed in R. C. Benge, *Libraries and Cultural Change* (1970), Ch. vii.

that concerning the creation of larger library areas, was the subject of prolonged controversy, and time was to show that the libraries of their own
initiative were powerless to solve it. As we have seen, the Library Association
substantially approved this and other McColvin proposals in its post-war
policy statement of 1943,[1] but when this statement at length came to be debated
in the first post-war conference at Blackpool in 1946, the recommendations
regarding library areas and regarding a Ministry of Fine Arts came under serious
criticism, and were withdrawn for further consideration.[2]

During the years that followed, the debate continued, with the defenders
of the smaller authorities fighting a stubborn battle against the advocates of
efficiency.[3] In 1955, when a revision of local government areas was under
consideration, the Council of the Library Association again brought forward
proposals for far-reaching reform. They recommended (a) that as a first step
towards the creation of "suitable library authorities" the library powers of
authorities with a rateable value in 1953–54 of less than £300 000 should be
surrendered to the county authorities, or arrangements made for joint services
under the Public Libraries Act of 1893; (b) that library committees should be
directly responsible to their local authorities; (c) that consideration should be
given to the possibility of grant aid from the central government, especially
to reference libraries performing a regional function; and (d) that a suitable
government department should be charged with administering this grant and
otherwise promoting the efficiency of the library service.[4]

These proposals were rejected by the 1955 Annual General Meeting, and
subsequently approved by a postal ballot, but at the Annual General Meeting of
1956 the recommendations concerning the compulsory surrender of powers by
the smaller authorities, or compulsory participation in joint services, were
rescinded.[5]

There was indeed in these years, as in the years between the wars, some
voluntary surrender of powers by the smaller authorities, usually to the counties,
but this was still on a small scale. About a score of authorities relinquished
their powers in the years 1946–49, and about the same number—mostly in
Wales and Scotland—during the years 1950–59. In Wales a notable event was
the merger in 1947 of the Aberystwyth and Cardiganshire libraries under the
name of the Cardiganshire Joint Library, administered by a joint committee
established under the terms of the Local Government Act of 1933. In Scotland
collaboration between town and country was established on a somewhat different
basis in Selkirkshire, where in 1948 the Galashiels burgh library agreed to
take over the county stock and provide a service throughout the county as
agent for the County Council.[6]

[1] See above, pp. 340–341.   [2] L.A.R., Vol. XLVIII (1946), pp. 125–132, 139–140.
[3] The case for the defence is put by Arthur Smith of Newark, "Small Towns and Smaller
    Librarians," in Library World, Vol. XLIX (1946–147), pp. 110–112; and by Leslie Ranson
    of Accrington, "The Functions and Control of a Library in a Small Town", in L.A.R.,
    Vol. L (1948), pp. 233–237; the case for the prosecution by Miss F. E. Cook of
    Lancashire County, "A National Library Service: Voluntary or Compulsory?" in L.A.R.,
    Vol. LII (1950), pp. 260–268.   [4] L.A.R., Vol. LVII (1955), pp. 306–308, 314–315.
[5] L.A.R., Vol. LVII (1955), pp. 440–441; Vol. LVIII (1956), p. 314.
[6] W. R. Aitken, A History of the Public Library Movement in Scotland to 1955 (Glasgow 1971),
    p. 128.

New library authorities continued to come into existence at the rate of one or two a year. The creation of the Argyll County authority and the Rutland County authority in 1946 completed the circle of county provision, the Rutland library being serviced by Leicester County. In Bute, where the county service had been suspended on the outbreak of war, the Kilmarnock library made provision for the islands on an experimental basis from 1946–50, but in 1951 the county service was resumed from headquarters at the Norman Stewart Institute at Rothesay.[1] New urban authorities which came into existence at this time were either latecomers such as Banbury (1948) and Helensburgh (1950), or newly developed areas taken over from the counties, e.g. Solihull in Warwickshire (1947), and Gillingham in Kent (1952).

In England and Wales the vexed question of library areas was reopened when in September 1957 the Minister of Education appointed a committee under the chairmanship of Dr. S. C. Roberts to consider the structure of the public library service. Scotland, however, was excluded from this inquiry, and the position there, which was very different, must now claim our attention.

McColvin's recommendation that the whole of the North of Scotland should constitute a single library area had not surprisingly roused fierce local opposition, and after the war the Scottish Library Association appointed C. S. Minto, then Deputy Librarian of Edinburgh,[2] to undertake a new survey of this region and make fresh recommendations. His report, published in 1948, is a modest and unassuming document, which provides in brief compass a description of the work in the ten northern counties. The main impression one has is of scanty resources thinly spread over a vast area. The total population was only 656 000, and of this figure the City of Aberdeen accounted for 182 000, and the County of Aberdeen for another 144 000. The remaining 330 000 people were scattered over nine counties and about a dozen small boroughs. The smallest county, Nairn, had only 8300 inhabitants, the smallest burgh, Dornoch in Sutherland, only 800. Bookstocks ranged from 185 000 volumes in Aberdeen City and 77 000 in Aberdeen County to 2500 volumes in the burghs of Banff and Dornoch.

Minto was generous in his judgements, and he found the service in six of the ten counties—Aberdeen, Banff, Caithness, Ross and Cromarty, Orkney, and Shetland—either good or at least reasonable. Moray and Nairn, he thought, were both too small to give an adequate service, and as they already had a joint county council for several purposes he thought their library services also should be merged. Sutherland also, functioning spasmodically from a schoolroom in Brora, seemed to have no future as an independent authority, and should seek union with Ross and Cromarty. In Inverness the supply of books to the Outer Hebrides presented special problems to the county service, and the agreement of 1933 between the county and burgh of Inverness had in practice done little to improve the situation.[3]

The urban libraries, unlike the county libraries, still suffered under the limitation of a 3d. rate, and with the exception of the City of Aberdeen they were all pretty poor. Minto usually does his best to find something to praise,

[1] Op. cit., p. 113.
[2] Afterwards (1953–70) City Librarian.
[3] On this agreement see above, p. 268.

but it is not difficult to read between the lines, as in this account of Lossiemouth in Morayshire:

> "At *Lossiemouth* where a Cotgreave Indicator is still used for charging purposes although readers are admitted to the shelves, the library is in the charge of the caretaker of the Town Hall. Though both library and reading-room are kept in excellent physical condition the arrangement naturally works to the advantage only of the public purse. About £100 a year is spent on books by a teacher who puts in a little time on library work. The library is well patronised when open (on Saturday nights and one other week day). The reading room provides both newspapers and periodicals and is notable for the good design of the furniture."[1]

The general backwardness of these libraries is indicated by the fact that an indicator was also in use (without open access) at Stornoway in the Isle of Lewis, while at Elgin the burgh library was still operating a subscription section. At Tain in Ross and Cromarty even Minto had to describe the state of the library as "shocking", while of the burgh library at Banff he wrote:

> ". . . I suffered no greater disappointment during my tour than was occasioned by the condition of this library. . . . . Apart from that portion provided by the county service, the stock is moribund, unclassified, unlettered, unlabelled and without discernible shelf order. What good books there are bear no evidence of recent use . . . . . The former reference library and reading-room, closed on economy grounds some twenty or more years ago, was re-opened during the war as a services rest and reading room but is now once again closed to the public."[2]

Minto thought that all these small independent libraries should be merged with their respective counties, and in most cases this eventually happened. He also urged the recruitment of more qualified staff, and the use of mobile libraries in suitable areas. Since, however, it was plain that the indigenous resources of the region would never match up to the need, he recommended at the same time, on the one hand an expansion of the services of the Scottish Central Library, and on the other the creation of a Central Scottish Library Authority with power to make grants to local libraries on a sliding scale related to need—the more scattered the population the larger the grant.[3]

These last two recommendations (apart from the suggestion of a sliding scale) were based on proposals originally made by the Scottish Library Association early in 1942 in a *Memorandum on Post-War Development of Public Libraries in Scotland*, which set out what were deemed to be the essential changes needed in Scottish library legislation. The eleven points listed in the Memorandum were reaffirmed and amplified by the Association in a statement dated 3rd. September, 1947, which is printed as an appendix to the Minto Report. The other recommendations included, predictably, the abolition of the 3d. rate limitation, the abolition of dual rating, powers for libraries to enter into co-operative arrangements, and powers to organize and finance activities of a general cultural character. In 1947 the Association was prepared to recognize that a satisfactory library service could not as a rule be organized by a burgh with a population of less than 20 000 or by a county with a population of less than 50 000[4].

---

[1] C. S. Minto, *Public Library Services in the North of Scotland: a Report and Recommendations* (Scottish Library Association 1948), p. 13.

[2] *Op. cit.*, pp. 10–11.   [3] *Op. cit.*, p. 31.   [4] *Op. cit.*, pp. 36–40.

In January, 1947, before the Minto Report actually appeared, the Secretary of State for Scotland asked the Advisory Council on Education in Scotland, under the chairmanship of William McClelland, Professor of Education in the University of St. Andrews, to review the provision of public libraries, museums and art galleries throughout the country, and make recommendations. This was the first major Government inquiry into the Scottish library service, and the resulting report, published in 1951,[1] inevitably challenges comparison with its English counterpart, the Kenyon Report of 1927. It is indeed a well written document, and makes fascinating reading even to-day (not least for its frequent excursions into library history) but its account of the actual functioning of the library service is comparatively slight, and there is nothing to compare with the formidable array of statistical material assembled by the Kenyon Committee.

One suspects, indeed, that because it was working in an educational environment the Advisory Committee's mind was, in large measure, made up beforehand. Though the Report lays down the rule that "generally speaking, the larger libraries are also the more efficient libraries", it has in fact practically nothing to say about the four major city libraries (Edinburgh, Glasgow, Aberdeen and Dundee) and very little about the remaining seventeen burgh libraries serving populations of 20 000 upwards.[2] On the other hand the Report criticizes the smaller burgh libraries (i.e. those serving populations of less than 20 000) even more sharply than Minto had done, and one passage sums up the "various marks of inefficiency" which characterized such libraries:

> "unattractive bookstocks, insufficiency or absence of rebinding, out of date and inadequate books for serious study, insufficient funds for replacement, the absence of a proper supply of current ready-reference books, responsibility for a large but unendowed building, or a library staff that is frequently underpaid, sometimes unqualified and often inadequate."[3]

The conclusion reached is that an efficient library service cannot be economically provided for a population of less than 30 000.[4] The account given of the county library service is even more perfunctory, though it makes the important (and neglected) point that, owing to a recent recasting of the grant system to education authorities, the county authorities were now able to recover from the Education (Scotland) Fund sixty per cent of their approved net expenditure on education (including library expenditure).

Starting from the principle that "the library service cannot be regarded as other than an educational service",[5] the Report proposed a very simple solution to most of the difficulties facing the Scottish libraries, namely that library powers should be vested solely in education authorities, i.e. in the

---

[1] Scottish Education Department, *Libraries, Museums and Art Galleries: a Report of the Advisory Council on Education in Scotland* (Cmd. 8229, Edinburgh 1951), cited hereafter as *McClelland Report*.

[2] The details, extracted from the Library Association's *Statistics of Public (Rate-Supported) Libraries in Great Britain and Northern Ireland, 1952–3* (1954), are conveniently tabulated in W. R. Aitken, *A History of the Public Library Movement in Scotland to 1955* (Glasgow 1971), pp. 351–8.

[3] *McClelland Report*, p. 51.

[4] *Op. cit.*, p. 50.   [5] *Op. cit.*, p. 38.

counties and the four cities. This would at a stroke put an end to rate limitation and dual rating in the burghs, all of which would be merged, for library purposes, in their respective counties; it would make the library service everywhere eligible for government grant as part of the education service; and it would, the Committee thought, dispense with the need for special legislation to permit inter-library co-operation. To safeguard the position in the cities, it was also specifically recommended that rate limitation be abolished. Detailed recommendations were made as to the manner in which the service should be controlled—either by a separate library committee or by a sub-committee of the education committee—and each authority should be required to submit for approval a scheme showing the provision to be made in the various parts of its area.[1]

A further set of recommendations concerned the creation of a national library service embracing both central and local libraries. The Central Library for Students, at this time about to be transferred to Edinburgh, would function as the central lending library, and would be supported in part by government grants and in part by a levy on local library authorities. The National Library of Scotland, when adequately housed, staffed and financed, would be the central reference library. Specialist private libraries, if not already associated with the Central Library for Students, would be encouraged to participate in some kind of co-operative scheme. A Library Council for Scotland would act as a governing body for the central lending library, advise on general issues of library policy and on the schemes submitted by local authorities, and with the help of a full-time development officer ensure that an efficient service was being provided.[2]

Not surprisingly, many librarians objected to the abolition of the burgh libraries, and to the subordination of libraries to education. Discussions between the Secretary of State and the interested parties dragged out interminably, and it was only in 1955 that a private member, Sir William Darling, secured the passage of a short Act which (a) removed the 3d. rate limit; (b) provided for co-operation among library authorities and for contributions in support of the Scottish Central Library; (c) permitted authorities to relinquish their library powers; and (d) extended the lending powers of libraries to cover non-book materials.[3]

Clearly this Act was merely tinkering with the problem, leaving the basic weaknesses of the Scottish library structure untouched. It did not even remove the anomaly of double rating. Another four years were to pass before the Roberts Report on the library service in England and Wales provided a stimulus for fresh thinking.

[1] Op. cit., pp. 50–59.
[2] Op. cit., pp. 59–67.
[3] Public Libraries (Scotland) Act, 3 & 4 Eliz. 2, c. 27. See for the details Aitken, op. cit., pp. 264–274; and for a fuller treatment of this whole subject W. E. Tyler, The Development of the Scottish Public Libraries (unpublished M.A. thesis, Strathclyde Univ. 1967), Chs. ii–iii.

By the time this Act was passed, thirteen of the burgh libraries had already secured permission to increase or abolish the 3d. rate limitation, either by local legislation as at Glasgow (1946) or by taking advantage of clauses in the Local Government (Scotland) Acts of 1929 and 1947. See McClelland Report, p. 51; Aitken, op. cit., p. 259.

Recovery and Renewal

Throughout these long negotiations on policy matters the library service did not stand still. The early years after the war were occupied mainly in the tasks of renovation and recovery, and were hampered by persisting shortages of books, staff, building materials, even at times fuel. Replacement of damaged or worn-out stock proceeded only slowly, and new buildings, however desperately needed, were hard to come by. The only permanent new central library building opened during these years was that at Colchester, which had been completed before the war but was not occupied for library purposes till 1948.[1] The new central libraries at Eastbourne (1946) and Aberdare (1949), and the new central lending library at Westminster (1948) were all in converted premises, while Weymouth (1948) made do with temporary prefabricated buildings. Swindon in 1949 erected a prefabricated building for its central lending library, and adapted rooms in the town hall for its reference library. The hundred or so new urban branch libraries opened during the years 1946–48 were in either prefabricated or converted buildings, the latter including churches and chapels, schools, air-raid shelters, decontamination centres, mortuary huts, a civic restaurant, a police court, and a great many houses and shops.[2]

Somehow or other, however, by all kinds of shifts and improvisations, the work went on, and when the centenary of the public libraries came in 1950 they were able to present to the world a brave if not complacent front. The centenary year was marked by a splendid little history by W. A. Munford, City Librarian of Cambridge,[3] by a considerable crop of centenary articles and papers,[4] and by two special Library Association pamphlets. One of these, entitled *A Century of Public Library Service: Where do we Stand Today?* was critical in tone and intended for librarians and members of library committees, who were invited to consider a number of pertinent questions, e.g. as to the size and quality of their bookstocks, the amount they were spending and ought to be spending on books, the adequacy of their reference services, services to children, and special services of various kinds, the suitability of their premises, and the proportion of qualified staff. It was suggested that for a medium sized town the library stock should not be less than one "active" volume per head of population, and annual book expenditure should be about 2s. per head.

The other pamphlet, entitled *A Century of Public Libraries, 1850–1950*, was intended for the general public, and was mainly concerned to draw attention to

---

[1] See above, p. 328.

[2] J. C. Harrison, "Emergency Library Provision in Urban Areas (i) Temporary Buildings", in *L.A. Conference Papers, 1949*, pp. 92–97. Cf. R. G. C. Desmond, "Some Unquiet Thoughts on Public Library Architecture", in *L.A.R.*, Vol. LIX (1957), pp. 85–86.

[3] *Penny Rate: Aspects of British Public Library History, 1850–1950* (1951).

[4] E.g. J. D. Stewart, "The Progress of Librarianship: a Review of the Period 1919–1949", in *L.A. Conference Papers, 1949*, pp. 24–32; L. R. McColvin, "Public Libraries To-Day", in *L.A.R.*, Vol. LII (1950), pp. 330–337; C. Nowell, "The Last Hundred Years", in *L.A. Conference Proceedings, 1950*, pp. 33–43; and the special issue of the *Librarian and Book World*, Vol. XXXIX, No. 6 (June 1950).

the achievements of public libraries, and to the many and varied services they offered. Some of the basic statistics, from the late nineteenth century onwards, were presented both in tabular and in diagrammatic form, and revealed *inter alia* the following interesting comparisons between the position in 1939 and the position ten years later:

	1939	1949
Service points	18,000	23,000
Registered borrowers (lending libraries)	8,937,000	12,000,000
Volumes in stock	32,549,000	42,000,000
Issues	247,335,000	312,000,000
Library expenditure	£3,178,000	£7,705,000 [1]

It will be noted that with a total bookstock of 42 million volumes for a population, at that time, of some 50 millions, the library service was falling short of the minimum stock prescribed in the Association's advice to librarians. On the other hand, the Association could legitimately take pride in the fact that nearly a quarter of the total population were library members. The pamphlet ends with a warning that the public library service, which a hundred years earlier had been in advance of its time, was now falling behind other branches of the social services:

> "To bring the service nationally to a state of efficiency able to meet the needs of readers means more service points, more books, more trained staff, more skilled assistance to readers. Special services, to children, adolescents, to technicians and professional men, particularly, need improvement, but a general raising of standards is necessary first.
>
> "At present, variations of standards of service are a reproach to all concerned. One authority may spend 1s. 8d. per head of population on books, another thinks 3d. sufficient. One library may have one assistant for 2000 population, another one for 27 000. Progressive authorities are spending over 5s. per head of population a year on the library service, some spend a shilling, or even less . . .
>
> "The Library Association believes that three conditions are necessary for good future development. The provision of adequate services by library authorities should be made compulsory. There should be a Government department, preferably the Ministry of Education, responsible for guiding, encouraging, and co-ordinating the work of local authorities. All local authorities should be assisted financially to develop their library services."[2]

The process of reorganization and reconstruction which had its origins in the needs of the immediate post-war years gathered momentum in the 'fifties, with public libraries almost everywhere striving to improve their service and give themselves a new public image. Unfortunately although by 1950 many of the worst post-war shortages were over, building restrictions continued, and it was not until 1958 that the controls were removed. A great deal of building went on during this period, but it continued to be mainly by way of conversion, extension, adaptation, or the erection of prefabricated buildings.[3]

Almost the only major building projects of these years were in connection

---

[1] Both sets of figures include Northern Ireland, but this does not seriously distort the general picture.

[2] *A Century of Public Libraries*, p. 27.

[3] For details see *L.A.R.*, Vol. LIV (1952), pp. 234–235; *F.Y.W.L. 1951–55*, pp. 110, 154–155, 282–286; *F.Y.W.L. 1956–60*, pp. 150–151, 205–207, 275–280.

with the national libraries and a few large municipal libraries destroyed or badly damaged during the war. The restored National Central Library building in London was re-opened in 1952. In Edinburgh in 1953 the generosity of the Carnegie Trustees provided the Scottish Central Library, formerly at Dunfermline, with a new home in historic premises in the Lawnmarket; and the new National Library of Scotland, hard by, was at length brought to completion at the close of 1956. That same year saw the opening of the reconstructed central libraries at Plymouth and Shoreditch—the former completely rebuilt behind the original facade; and the following year brought the re-opening of the William Brown Central Library at Liverpool. A substantial extension to the Mitchell Library in Glasgow, opened in 1953, represented merely a further instalment of work which had originally begun in 1953 and was not to be completed until 1963.[1]

At the Library Association Conference at Brighton in 1958 G. A. Carter, Librarian of Warrington, launched an outright assault against building restrictions, which he claimed were being used by "half-hearted local authorities" as an excuse for inaction. He pointed out that although more than £10 000 millions had been spent on buildings since the war, less than £2 millions had been spent on library buildings, and that the consequence was to be seen in "unsuitable, outdated and woefully inadequate municipal central libraries" and "makeshift" county headquarters.[2] At the same conference S. G. Berriman, then County Librarian of Middlesex, emphasized the vast building backlog in the county library service, though he was able to point to some admirable new branch buildings which combined architectural beauty with functional efficiency.[3]

However, as librarians have so often pointed out, bricks and mortar are not the only thing, or even the main thing, in the library service, and in spite of all these difficulties and frustrations the service continued to improve. Some of the ways in which it improved will appear later, but even at the merely statistical level the number of library service points increased from 23 000 in 1949 to 34 000 (including more than 1300 full-time branches) in 1959; library membership from about 25 per cent to about 28 per cent of the population; volumes in stock from 42 millions to 71 millions; lending library issues from 312 millions to 397 millions; total library expenditure from £7.7 millions to £18.8 millions; expenditure on books from £1.9 millions (9½d. per head) to £4.5 millions (19¾d. per head); and full-time non-manual staff from 10 200 to 13 300.[4]

[1] Cf. *Glasgow Public Libraries, 1874–1966* (Glasgow 1966), pp. 30–31.

[2] G. A. Carter, "To Build or not to Build", in *L.A. Conference Proceedings, 1958*, pp. 81 sqq.

[3] S. G. Berriman, "The Provision and Design of County Library Buildings", *ibid.*, pp. 23–31.

[4] Library Association, *Statistics of Public (Rate-Supported) Libraries in Great Britain and Northern Ireland, 1952–53* (1954), pp. 2–3, and *1958–59* (1960), pp. 2–3. Both sets of figures include Northern Ireland. The 1959 figure for lending issues for the first time excludes issues to schools, which may have amounted to some 50 millions. The figure for service points excludes mobile libraries (235 in 1959). The Roberts Report of 1959 (Ministry of Education, *The Structure of the Public Library Service in England and Wales*, Cmnd. 660), p. 36, calculates library membership in England and Wales as 28.8 per cent of total population.

No satisfactory comparable statistics are available to show separately the development of Scotland and Wales, but it seems clear that though operating for the most part on a smaller scale, they shared in the general advance. Two reports from Wales enable us to assess some of the changes there between 1948 and 1955, indicating for example that book expenditure increased by 75 per cent, total expenditure by 94 per cent, bookstock by 70 per cent, and lending library issues by about 50 per cent.[1]

The removal of building restrictions in 1958 opened the way for a flood of new projects, many of which had been in cold storage for years, in some cases since before the war. By 1960 the work was in full swing, and in November of that year the *Library Association Record* was able to devote a special issue to reports and descriptions of new libraries, urban and county, recently completed or in active progress. Among the completed ones were handsome new central libraries for Kensington and Holborn; and three other major urban libraries, as well as five county library headquarters, were either being built or at an advanced stage of planning. Berriman was able to report with satisfaction that, since his paper of two years earlier, the county libraries alone had completed or put in hand buildings costing £2 500 000—more than the entire library building programme for the years 1945–58.[2]

The Significance of the Counties

It was in these post-war years—years as we have seen of rapid political, economic, social and educational change—that the public libraries moved decisively into the modern era. The last vestiges of the old working-class image now rapidly faded, and the library became in a real sense the possession of the community, even though it was still only a minority of the community that made regular use of its services. Many factors contributed to this change. Better designed buildings, more comfortable furnishings, improved display techniques, new and more attractive methods of binding, and a higher standard of professional service, all combined to make libraries more inviting places to visit; while on the other hand increased leisure, the widening range of people's interests, and the ever increasing pressure of higher education, brought a steady increase in demand.

These and other points will be dealt with in more detail below. In the meantime attention must be drawn to the dramatic change in the status of the county libraries. Between the wars they had been thought of very much as poor relations, purveyors of light reading to the ignorant country dwellers, and librarians in the larger urban systems were inclined to look down their noses

---

[1] See Library Association, Wales and Monmouthshire Branch, *Report on the Municipal, Urban District and County Libraries of Wales and Monmouthshire, 1948* (1950); and G. Davies, "Post-War Development in the Public Libraries of Wales and Monmouthshire", in *Report of the Proceedings of the Twenty-Fourth Conference of Library Authorities in Wales and Monmouthshire . . . 1957* (Swansea 1958), pp. 22–27. The figures for lending issues are somewhat obscure.

[2] *L.A.R.*, Vol. LXII (1960), pp. 345–378, 386. A bibliography of library buildings 1950–60 is appended to the article. J. D. Stewart (ed.), *Report on the Library System of London and the Home Counties, 1959* (1961), devotes eight pages to a record of new libraries completed or projected.

at the understaffed, underequipped, underpaid county service.[1] By the end of
the 'fifties all this was changed. If we look at the figures for 1958–59 to see
which libraries were spending most on books, we find that of the sixteen
authorities spending more than £50 000 per annum eleven were counties.
The list is as follows:

	£		£
Essex Co.	124 000	Middlesex Co.	c. 66 000
Lancashire Co.	118 000	Hertford Co.	65 000
Liverpool	90 000	Kent Co.	60 000
Buckingham Co.	84 000	Sheffield	60 000
Yorkshire West Riding Co.	84 000	Stafford Co.	60 000
Glasgow	78 000	Birmingham	55 000
Manchester	70 000	Durham Co.	55 000
Surrey Co.	66 000	Nottingham Co.	51 000 [2]

These figures by themselves, of course, would give a very misleading
impression. Counties differed enormously in size, geographical features,
population, and resources, and the disparities in the library service remained
very great. As H. D. Budge, County Librarian of Warwickshire, observed in
1958: "the differences between the highest and the lowest in expenditure and
effectiveness are so wide that, to anyone unacquainted with county libraries
in these countries, it would be incomprehensible that such differences continue
to exist."[3] An encouraging feature of this period, however, was that many of
the more backward counties were now making a serious attempt to bring their
services up to a more satisfactory level.

A very striking example is the advance made in Buckinghamshire under
the leadership of Miss Gwenda Jones, who was librarian from 1949 to 1969.
When she took office the county occupied a very lowly place in the library
hierarchy, "spending less", she tells us, "and providing less than almost any
other county" in England and Wales.[4] Comparative statistics collected by the
county treasurer at length shamed the authority into stepping up its expenditure,
and in 1951 a development plan was agreed on for the provision of branches
and mobile services. In 1957, because of sharply rising public demand, a
three-year programme was undertaken to improve the bookstock, and librarians
elsewhere rubbed their eyes on reading that the county's book fund had been

---

[1] Cf. L. V. Paulin in "County Libraries: Half a Century's Achievement", in *L.A.R.*,
Vol. LXXIII (1971), p. 349: "The attitude of the Library Association and of the profession
at large towards the establishment of county libraries varied from complete indifference
to actual antagonism". See also the correspondence in *L.A.R.*, Vol. XXXIX (1937),
pp. 50–51, 105–106, 182–183, 236–237. On the inadequacies of the county service
immediately after the war see R. Irwin, *The National Library Service* (1947), Ch. ii.

[2] Library Association, *Statistics of Public (Rate-Supported) Libraries in Great Britain and
Northern Ireland, 1958–59* (1960). The figure for Middlesex is approximate because the
published figure (£82 000) includes binding. It will be noted that no Welsh authority
appears in this list, and no Scottish authority other than Glasgow. The next largest
Scottish authorities were Edinburgh (£35 000) and Lanark Co. (£33 000); and the
largest Welsh authorities were Cardiff (£23 000), Swansea (£18 000), and Monmouth
Co. (£17 000).

[3] *F.Y.W.L. 1951–1955* (1958), p. 148.

[4] *Buckinghamshire . . . County Library, 1918–1968: Annual Report, 1967–68* (1968), pp. 6–7.

increased by more than 125 per cent. Buckingham's position in the table above reflects this campaign, which by 1959–60 had almost doubled the number of issues from the lending library.[1]

In Wales a similar transformation was begun in Cardiganshire by Ivor Davies, the young London Welshman who in 1947 was appointed first librarian of the new Joint Library with Aberystwyth. In two dynamic years, as his successor testified, he changed the service "from being one of the most backward of libraries to the most promising".[2] He built up new stock, introduced modern methods of administration, established a separate school library service, secured a travelling library, and laid plans for branch libraries at Cardigan and Lampeter. County library expenditure was increased from 1s. 1d. to over 5s. per head, and the library rate from 4½d. to 1s. 9d. Unfortunately this work was cut short by Davies's tragically early death in 1949.

Even in the poor counties of the North of Scotland there was some improvement following the publication of the Minto Report in 1948. Sutherland, for example, though it did not follow Minto's advice to unite with Ross and Cromarty, overhauled its service from 1952 onwards, absorbing the tiny burgh of Dornoch, and establishing part-time branches in several places for which up to this time little or no provision had been made. In spite of a decrease in population from 14 000 to 13 000, annual expenditure on books, which had been £190 at the time of Minto's visit, increased to £2200 by 1958–59, bookstocks were more than doubled, and loans trebled.[3]

Naturally, however, it was in the most populous counties that the most rapid progress was made. Some of these, for example the Home Counties, Lancashire and the West Riding, were now beginning to match the larger urban systems not only in the scale of their operations but in the quality of their service. The post-war population explosion was an important factor here, for as the population spread outward from the cities, first into distant suburbs and then into the adjoining county areas, the county libraries were forced to upgrade their provision. Village centres gave way to part-time branches, part-time branches to whole-time branches, whole-time branches, very often, to regional or district branches, which increasingly found themselves called upon to give an urban service, including reference facilities and where necessary a technical and commercial information service. In such a changing situation the old differential rating system was quite irrelevant, and though it lingered in a few areas for some years (in Cheshire until 1964) it was no longer a significant factor in county library administration.[4]

The urban responsibilities of the counties were increased by the New

---

[1] Buckinghamshire County Library, *Annual Reports*, 1956–57 to 1959–60. Bookstocks (including reference stock) increased from 344 000 to 591 000 in these three years, and loans from 2 496 000 to 4 872 000. Cf. *L.A.R.*, Vol. LIX (1957), p. 243; *F.Y.W.L. 1956–1960*, p. 243.

[2] A. R. Edwards, "The Joint Library in Practice", in *L.A.R.*, Vol. LII (1950), p. 286.

[3] *Minto Report* (1948), pp. 16–17, 23–25; Library Association, *Statistics of Public (Rate-Aided) Libraries in Great Britain and Northern Ireland, 1958–59* (1960); W. R. Aitken, *A History of the Public Library Movement in Scotland to 1955* (Glasgow 1971), p. 190.

[4] E. Osborne, "The County Libraries Statistical Report for 1945–1946", in *L.A.R.*, Vol. L (1948), p. 45, records ten libraries still using the differential rating system. On Cheshire see *Report of the County Librarian for the Years 1952–65*, pp. 8–9.

Towns Act of 1947, which led to the deliberate planting out in county areas of urban communities destined to grow in many cases to a population of 100 000 or more. Fifteen such projects were initiated in the late 'forties and the 'fifties, creating within a few years communities for which the county libraries concerned had to provide a complete library system—central library, branch libraries, mobile libraries, and a variety of specialized services.[1] By the end of the 'fifties the library service given by many counties was becoming more and more difficult to distinguish from that given by the larger urban authorities.

The Roberts Committee and After

The decision taken by the Government in 1957 to appoint a special committee to consider the structure of the library service has already been referred to.[2] This decision was taken in the context of a general reform of local government,[3] and the committee was appointed by the Minister of Education under the chairmanship of Dr. S. C. Roberts (afterwards Sir Sydney Roberts) Master of Pembroke College, Cambridge, and a one-time President of the Library Association. Its remit was

> "To consider the structure of the public library service in England and Wales, and to advise what changes, if any, should be made in the administrative arrangements, regard being had to the relation of public libraries to other libraries."[4]

The committee was thus invited to focus its attention on the long disputed question of the optimum local government unit for purposes of library administration. Many interested organizations were quick to give advice. The County Councils Association was in favour of large library authorities, and would have liked to see library powers restricted to counties and county boroughs; the Association of Municipal Corporations thought local opinion should be the decisive factor; and the Smaller Libraries Group, representing authorities serving populations between 5000 and 50 000, thought a satisfactory service could be provided for a population of 15 000 upwards. The Urban District Councils Association was prepared to go as low as 10 000. The Library Association, taking not surprisingly a middle position, fixed on 40 000 as a minimum population figure, and associated this with a minimum annual expenditure of £8000 on books, periodicals, binding, and non-book materials.[5]

---

[1] The counties affected were Berkshire (Bracknell); Durham (Aycliffe and Peterlee); Essex (Basildon and Harlow); Hertfordshire (Hatfield, Hemel Hempstead, Stevenage and Welwyn); Northamptonshire (Corby); West Sussex (Crawley); Monmouthshire (Cwmbran); Dunbartonshire (Cumbernauld); Fife (Glenrothes); and Lanarkshire (East Kilbride).

[2] See above, p. 346.

[3] See the White Paper on *Local Government: Functions of County Councils and County District Councils in England and Wales* (Cmd. 161, 1957).

[4] Ministry of Education, *The Structure of the Public Library Service in England and Wales* (Cmnd. 660, 1959), p. 1. This document is hereafter referred to as the *Roberts Report.*

[5] Library Association, *Memorandum of Evidence to be laid before the Committee appointed by the Minister of Education* . . . (1958), pp. 5–6. The whole of this interesting and well informed document deserves study.

The Roberts Report, in a prefatory historical review, pointed out that in the thirty-two years since the Kenyon Report the number of library authorities in England and Wales had fallen from 539 to 484, the biggest changes being a substantial increase in the number of non-county borough authorities and a substantial decrease in the number of urban district and parish authorities. There were, however, still 167 authorities serving populations of less than 30 000 (the minimum fixed by the 1951 Report of the Advisory Council on Education in Scotland[1]) and 123 authorities, including 16 out of the 17 parishes, serving populations of less than 20 000 (the minimum set by the Kenyon Committee[2]).

After a careful review of the problem the Report recommended:

(i) That counties, county boroughs, metropolitan boroughs, and the City of London, should continue to be library authorities;

(ii) That parishes should cease to be library authorities;

(iii) That other existing library authorities should be entitled to apply for a continuance of powers subject to a minimum annual expenditure on books of £5000 or 2s. per head of population, whichever was the greater;

(iv) That non-county boroughs and urban districts not at present library authorities should be eligible to apply for recognition subject to the same criteria of expenditure and subject also to a minimum population of 50 000.

The authorities referred to under the third of these proposals would have three years after the passing of the necessary legislation to reach the required standard, and it was suggested that even where non-county and urban district authorities were not able to establish their claim to library powers there might be some delegation of functions by the county authorities. The scheme of delegation adopted by Surrey in 1947 was commended for consideration in this connection.[3]

The Report also made recommendations for the improvement of staffing and premises, and for a statutory system of inter-library co-operation. All these will be referred to in their due place below. A special section on Wales pointed out that only seven of the fifty-two library authorities in that country were spending in 1957–58 as much as 2s. per head on books, and none was spending £5000 a year. None the less it was felt that the same standards should apply, and counties with small populations were recommended to consider a joint service with one or more neighbouring authorities. In view of the language problem, the establishment of a full-time school of librarianship in Wales would be helpful.[4]

Finally we must note a number of recommendations of a more general kind. Some of these were designed to fill gaps in the existing legislation, for example by giving powers to library authorities to co-operate with each other and with education and other authorities; to spend money on lectures and other cultural activities and charge for admission to such activities; and to provide and lend gramophone records, pictures and films.[5] Others, and these were the most important of all, proposed that the Minister of Education should

---

[1] See above, p. 348.
[2] See above, p. 238.
[3] *Roberts Report*, pp. 15–16. For the Surrey scheme see below, pp. 368–369.
[4] *Op. cit.*, pp. 23–25.   [5] *Op. cit.*, pp. 27–28.

be given "a general responsibility for the oversight of the public library service;" that he should appoint advisory bodies (one for England and one for
Wales) to assist him in this task; that it should be the statutory duty of every
library authority to provide an efficient service; and that county authorities
should be entitled to appoint independent library committees instead of
dealing with library matters through their education committees.[1]

The Report was published in 1959. The Minister of Education, after
consulting the local authorities, accepted most of the recommendations, but
varied the criterion for the recognition of library authorities by announcing
that existing non-county borough and urban district library authorities of
40 000 population and upwards would be allowed to retain their powers.
He also set up two working parties of librarians and other local authority
representatives, under Ministry chairmanship, to examine the technical implications of (a) the basic requirements for an efficient public library service and
(b) the recommendations concerning inter-library co-operation.

The first of these working parties, under the chairmanship of H. T. Bourdillon, made a detailed study of up-to-date library practice in a sample of
fifty-three authorities with a high annual expenditure on books. It found the
criteria of efficiency suggested by the Roberts Committee inadequate, and
suggested more sophisticated criteria related not to annual expenditure but
to number of books purchased. An annual provision of "not less than 250
volumes of all kinds and of not less than 90 adult non-fiction volumes for
lending and for reference purposes per thousand population" was proposed
as a standard of general application for libraries large and small, including
branches, but with the proviso that for an independent library service the
minimum must be 7200 volumes per annum in certain specified categories,
plus not less than 50 periodicals and up-to-date editions of basic works of
reference. It was pointed out that these figures implied a minimum population
of close on 30 000 for an independent authority. In Wales an appropriate
proportion of books and periodicals should be in Welsh.[2]

The Bourdillon Report also made recommendations, sometimes in
considerable detail, regarding standards for staffing and premises, lending and
reference services, children's services, and support for adult education and
cultural activities. The more important of these recommendations (and also
the recommendations of the working party on Inter-Library Co-operation
chaired by E. B. H. Baker[3]) will be dealt with under the appropriate headings
below. Naturally not all the proposals of the Bourdillon Report commended
themselves to everybody, but this was a notable attempt to define what was
meant by an efficient library service.

The Public Libraries and Museums Act of 1964, which replaced the Acts
of 1892, 1893, 1901, and 1919, was based on the recommendations of these
three committees. It placed upon the Secretary of State for Education and

---

[1] *Op. cit.*, pp. 15–16.

[2] Ministry of Education, *Standards of Public Library Service in England and Wales* [Bourdillon
Report] (1962), pp. 10–22, 37–40. The minimum of 7200 volumes was conditional upon
effective arrangements for giving readers access to wider resources, through schemes of
local as well as regional and national co-operation.

[3] Ministry of Education, *Inter-Library Co-operation in England and Wales* [Baker Report]
(1962).

Science[1] the duty "to superintend, and promote the improvement of, the public library service", and upon every library authority the duty to provide "a comprehensive and efficient service". Parish library authorities were deprived of their powers, and non-county borough and urban district library authorities of less than 40 000 population might be deprived of their powers if the Secretary of State deemed that this would result in an improvement of library facilities. Non-county and urban districts not library authorities but having a population over 40 000 might apply for library powers.

Library Advisory Councils were to be appointed for England and Wales, and the Secretary of State was to designate regions and prescribe arrangements for the purposes of inter-library co-operation. Library authorities were given powers to collaborate with other authorities; to create joint authorities; to provide pictures, gramophone records, films and other non-book materials; to use their premises for educational and cultural activities and make a charge therefor; and to charge for book reservations, overdue books, catalogues, and any facilities going "beyond those ordinarily provided by the authority as part of the library service".[2]

Even before the Act came into force on 1st April, 1965, the publication of the committee reports provided a stimulus for an improvement in library services. For the first time librarians and their committees were able to measure their achievements against more or less objective standards. For the better library authorities this was a chance to identify their shortcomings and endeavour to put them right; for the weaker authorities it was a revelation of the leeway they had to make up before their services could be regarded as satisfactory.

Willingly or reluctantly, library authorities everywhere tended to make money more readily available for library purposes. The result was most dramatically seen, as the next chapter will illustrate, in library buildings, but there was also an improvement in staffing and an upgrading of library services generally.[3] Between 1959 and 1965 sixteen small authorities decided in anticipation of the Act to surrender their powers to their respective counties; in addition, in 1965, the Isle of Ely merged with Cambridgeshire, and the Soke of Peterborough with Huntingdonshire. The urban district of Mountain Ash, in Glamorganshire, at long last adopted the Libraries Acts and in 1964 took over four miners' institute libraries as a basis for a public service.

By a coincidence the London Government Act of 1963 came into operation on the same day as the Public Libraries and Museums Act, involving a drastic reorganization of London's library authorities. The 29 authorities of London proper were reduced to 13—the City of London and 12 Inner London Boroughs—and the 40 authorities of Greater London, with parts of the counties of Hertfordshire, Essex, Surrey and Kent, were formed into 20 Outer London Boroughs. Among the casualties was the County of Middlesex, which completely disappeared. By the end of 1965, taking into account the disappearance of parish

---

[1] The Department of Education and Science, headed by a Secretary of State, took the place of the Ministry of Education in 1964.

[2] For a careful assessment of the Act, see R. L. Collison (ed.), *Progress in Library Science, 1965* (1965), pp. 111–124.

[3] Expenditure on books increased by 38 per cent between 1960–61 and 1964–65, and in the Smaller Libraries Group by 73 per cent—*F.Y.W.L. 1961–65*, p. 216.

library authorities, the number of authorities in England and Wales had been reduced from the 484 recorded by the Roberts Report to 419.[1]

All in all the prospects in 1965 seemed set fair for a rapid and substantial advance in the public library service. It was a cruel irony that less than four months after the Public Libraries and Museums Act came into force the Government once more imposed severe restrictions on local authority expenditure. Capital expenditure was sharply cut back, bringing new library building projects almost to a standstill, and hopes of improved staffing once more receded into the background.[2]

[1] Cf. *op. cit.*, p. 218; and for details below, App. III. Scotland, with fewer changes, had 93 library authorities at the close of 1965.

[2] Hansard, *Parliamentary Debates*, 5th Ser., Vol. 717 (1964–65), cols. 227–232.

CHAPTER XV

Patterns of Library Service

The Urban Library Service

BEFORE turning to consider matters of library organization and use during this period, it will be useful to note the great variety of patterns of service that the long historical evolution of the public libraries had created. That evolution had been painfully slow, and marked at every stage by a frustrating penury that led all too often to makeshift and inadequate accommodation. Even the accommodation provided by the generosity of Carnegie and others, excellent and well designed as it was, was apt to prove a snare and a delusion, eating up precious funds for its maintenance, and standing in the way of redevelopment to meet changing circumstances.

And circumstances were always changing, especially in the present century. Population grew and shifted, boundaries were altered, local authorities were merged or divided, and the library service had to adjust itself as best it could with such meagre resources as were placed at its disposal. All these difficulties were compounded by wartime population movements and building restrictions, and it was the resulting accumulation of inadequacies in many urban areas that led first to the feverish improvisations of the immediate post-war years and then to the more considered building activity of the late 'fifties and sixties'.

The outstanding feature of the urban library service at this period was the small scale on which most libraries continued to operate. There were indeed a few large city libraries with an elaborately articulated system of central and branch services. In 1956–57 the four giants were Glasgow with 37 full-time branches, Manchester with 33, Liverpool with 32, and Birmingham with 29; while in the second rank came a group of five cities—Bristol, Edinburgh, Leeds, Nottingham and Sheffield—with between 13 and 15 branches apiece. Cardiff, the largest urban library in Wales, had at this time 9 branches. Against figures of this order, however, we have to set the fact that more than one quarter of all the urban libraries in Great Britain had no branch organization at all, full-time or part-time, and that the average number of full-time branches per library authority was less than two.[1]

Development was going on both at central and at branch level. All over the country, alike in large cities such as Glasgow, Newcastle upon Tyne, and Stoke on Trent, and in small towns such as Stirling, Dukinfield and Camborne, operations were on foot to improve, modernize and enlarge central accom-

---

[1] These figures are calculated from Library Association, *Statistics of Public (Rate-Supported) Libraries in Great Britain and Northern Ireland, 1956–57* (1958). The figures relating to Northern Ireland have been excluded.

modation.[1] The large-scale extension to the Mitchell Library in Glasgow, which had been begun in 1939 and was not completed until 1963, was the biggest enterprise of this kind; but the reconstruction of the Passmore Edwards library at Camborne in 1951, involving as it did the now familiar exchange of reading room and lending library, and the creation of a separate juvenile library, was no doubt in its way just as significant.

All over the country, too, we find libraries engaged in creating or enlarging branch systems. Hastings, which had opened its first (part-time) branch in 1944, opened a second (also part-time) in 1949, supplementing this service with provision by its mobile library (returned by St. Pancras in 1946). A second mobile was put on the road in 1961.[2] Shrewsbury established its first branches, one part-time and two evening, in 1948–60.[3] West Bromwich, which had had only branch reading rooms before the war, created three full-time and two part-time branches between 1948 and 1956.[4] Swindon, which had commenced library service only in 1943, began to set up temporary branches in 1948, and opened its first permanent branch in 1957: by 1964 it had four permanent full-time branches, one temporary branch, and three sub-branches, as well as an Arts Centre.[5] Birkenhead, which had three full-time branches before the war, had by 1956 a development plan to provide for the entire county borough through six branches, so sited that every reader would be within a mile of a library.[6] Library authorities that were too small to develop branch activities often sought to cater for increasing demand in other ways. Bedford, for example, which like Swindon was a latecomer in the library field, made use from 1959 onwards of mobile libraries to provide for a population which had now risen to over 60 000.[7]

The examples of Hastings and Bedford illustrate one of the new features of this post-war period, namely the increasing use of mobile libraries as temporary provision for new housing areas. We have seen that this practice had been pioneered by Manchester and a few other authorities in the 'thirties. West Ham followed suit in 1942, and a number of others from 1946 onwards, especially in the Home Counties. By 1949 fourteen authorities were known to be using such vehicles, carrying a load of about 2000 books and usually visiting sites once a week.[8] This was a very poor substitute for a branch library, but it did show the flag, it helped to meet the needs of a still fluid situation, and it

---

[1] For details of some of the examples cited see *Glasgow Public Libraries, 1874–1966* (Glasgow 1966), pp. 30–31; *A Short History of the Newcastle upon Tyne Public Libraries, 1854–1950* (Newcastle upon Tyne 1950); *Stoke on Trent: Jubilee Report of the City Librarian* (1960), pp. 25–26; and J. F. Odgers, *Camborne Public (Free) Library, 1895–1963* (Camborne 1963), p. 24. The references to Stirling and Dukinfield are based on information supplied by the respective librarians.

[2] Information from Mrs. L. D. O'Nions, Borough Librarian. Cf. above p. 329.

[3] J. L. Hobbs, "Shrewsbury Public Library", in *Open Access*, Vol. IX, No. 2 (Jan. 1961), p. 2.

[4] Information from Mr. R. B. Ludgate, Borough Librarian.

[5] *21 Years of Public Library Service in Swindon, 1943–1964* [Swindon 1964].

[6] *Birkenhead Public Libraries Centenary, 1856–1956* (Birkenhead 1956), p. 21.

[7] Information from Mr. C. Hargreaves, Borough Librarian.

[8] For details see W. H. C. Lockwood, "Mobile Libraries: A Factual Report", in *L.A. Conference Papers, 1949*, pp. 98–105.

provided valuable information as to where, in due course, branches could most profitably be situated. By 1962, 70 urban libraries in the United Kingdom were using 79 mobile vehicles.[1]

The growth of population caused particular problems to the large city authorities, involving as it did not only the creation of new housing estates on the outskirts but also the clearance and rebuilding of the central slum areas in which the older branches were often situated. These changes made it very difficult to predict demand with any certainty, and the siting of new branches when these became possible was a hazardous business. None the less most of the large authorities reacted by extending their branch systems, in some cases very considerably, the commonly accepted ideal being that no reader should be more than a mile from a service point. At Glasgow the number of full-time branches rose from 27 in 1948 to 34 twenty years later; at Nottingham the increase in the same period was from 9 to 16; and at Liverpool from 22 to 29.[2] Birmingham, with a modest increase in the number of permanent branches, made considerable use of temporary libraries to cope with changing needs, while Edinburgh and Manchester built virtually no new libraries, preferring instead to serve the new suburbs by mobile library services. Manchester, which had suspended this type of service during the war,[3] resumed it in 1948; Edinburgh put its first mobile service on the road in the following year.

The idea of regional organization, which was already familiar in county libraries and had been brought into use in some American urban libraries before the war,[4] made little impact in the urban libraries of Great Britain. The first attempt to develop such an organization here was at Sheffield, where in 1945 the Library Committee was worried to discover that, although the city had 11 branches, 37 per cent of the population was not within reasonable distance of a permanent library. It was accordingly agreed that there should be built "in each large compact group of population a Divisional Library which would act as an area central library with reserve book stock, to supply and administer several small District Libraries serving populations of 10 000 to 20 000."[5] The librarian at this time, J. P. Lamb, hoped that the Manor Branch, which had been begun before the war and was opened in 1953, would be the first Divisional Library, but in fact this ambitious plan never materialized, and the city met its post-war needs as best it could, partly by building new branches, and partly by a mobile library service, which was introduced in 1962 to take the place of seventeen part-time libraries.[6]

One or two other major libraries took up the idea of regional organization in one form or another, but little progress was made towards its implementation during the period covered by this survey. Liverpool from 1951 brought a considerable number of branch libraries together into eight groups to facilitate interchange of staff, and steps were taken to build up stocks and services in some of the major branches. In 1956 a pioneer central library, intended to provide a full range of services, was established in the outlying suburb of

[1] C. R. Eastwood, *Mobile Libraries and other Public Library Transport* (1967), pp. 37–38.
[2] Figures from Annual Reports of the libraries concerned.
[3] See above, p. 284.
[4] B. M. Headicar, *A Manual of Library Organisation* (1935, 2nd edn. 1941), p. 151.
[5] *The City Libraries of Sheffield, 1856–1956* (Sheffield 1956), p. 50.
[6] Information from Mr. J. Bebbington, City Librarian.

Speke, but it was only after 1965 that plans were prepared for the creation of four regional libraries, of which Speke would be one. At Manchester, where mobile services were proving increasingly inadequate to meet the needs of the outer areas, a plan was at length approved in 1959 for a complete reorganization of the branch system, with eleven major district libraries and seven smaller libraries. Ten branches were promptly closed down, three branches were modernized and adapted as major libraries, and a new major library was built in Hulme, a slum clearance area which was just being redeveloped. This library, opened in 1965, included an adult lending library of 45 000 volumes, a reference library of 10 000 volumes with accommodation for 80 readers, a children's library of 19 000 volumes, and ample facilities for exhibitions, children's activities, and adult education activities. In the librarian's view it represented "the ideal in district library provision".[1]

The County Library Service

In the county library service the most remarkable change in pattern was the decline of the old-style village centres and their replacement either by full-time or part-time branches or, in rural areas, by mobile libraries. This change was due partly, as noted above,[2] to population changes, but partly also to the desire to provide a better service. The figures speak for themselves:

	1946	1951	1964–65
Full-time branches	246	391	745
Part-time branches	328	561	769
Mobile and travelling libraries	6	59	315
Centres	15 945	15 162	6380 [3]

As might be expected, this development was more noticeable in England than in the more rural countries of Wales and Scotland, as the following table for 1964–65 shows:

	Full-time Branches	Part-time Branches	Mobile and Travelling Libraries	Centres
England	613	607	259	4199
Wales	38	66	29	361
Scotland	94	96	27	1820
Total	745	769	315	6380 [4]

[1] Information from Mr. D. I. Colley, City Librarian. By this date four existing libraries, Crumpsall, Withington, Didsbury and Chorlton, had been upgraded to major district status—Manchester Public Libraries, *Annual Report, 1964–65*, pp. 5–6.

[2] See above, p. 355–356.

[3] Library Association, County Libraries Section, *Statistical and Policy Survey of the County Libraries of Great Britain and Northern Ireland, 1951* (1952); Institute of Municipal Treasurers and Accountants and Society of County Treasurers, *Public Library Statistics, 1964–65* (1966). The first two columns include Northern Ireland, the third column does not. A full-time branch for the purposes of these statistics is a branch giving service for not less than 30 hours per week; a part-time branch is one giving service for less than 30 but not less than 10 hours per week. The figures for "centres" include hospitals, prisons, borstals, etc., and sometimes school libraries, as well as the ordinary village centres in schools and institutions.   [4] *Public Library Statistics, 1964–65*.

Mobile library provision developed rapidly in the immediate post-war years, when building was restricted. The lead was given by the West Riding, where B. Oliph Smith, formerly of Herefordshire, was now County Librarian. Beginning in 1946, the county had 9 vehicles on the road by 1949, 20 by 1955, and 27 by 1965. From the beginning two types of mobile library were used to suit different sorts of terrain: a small library of some 1100 volumes giving a fortnightly service to farmers and isolated dwellings, and a large "mobile branch library" of 2500–3000 volumes providing a weekly service to more populous centres. Experiments were also made with articulated vehicles consisting of a tractor and trailer. These had proved very useful in some urban areas, the trailer being detached to form a temporary library while the tractor went off for service elsewhere, but they proved unsuitable to the conditions of the West Riding. In 1965 the operating fleet included 11 small libraries, 12 mobile branches, and 4 relief vehicles.[1]

Lancashire, Durham, Staffordshire, and Derbyshire, were also quick to see the advantages of mobile libraries, and by 1964–65 every Welsh county, and every English county except East Suffolk, the North Riding, and the Soke of Peterborough, had at least one. In Wales the greatest development was in Glamorganshire, which had six mobiles.[2] Many authorities, e.g. Derbyshire, Herefordshire, Nottinghamshire and Warwickshire, had indeed closed all their village centres, and arranged complete coverage for their rural areas by mobile services.[3] These services were much more efficient than the old static libraries. They covered not only the villages but many small hamlets and isolated farmsteads; they provided a much wider choice of books on the spot and a much improved service of books on request; and they made the assistance of qualified librarians available to all. Small wonder, therefore, that the mobile libraries were popular, and that the number of issues in the rural areas showed a tremendous increase.[4] The most notable exceptions to this general trend, at the end of the period, were Kent, which had only one mobile library, and the North Riding, which had none at all. In the latter case this was a matter of deliberate education committee policy: in Kent it was due simply to the fact that suitable volunteer centre librarians continued to be readily available.[5]

In the Scottish counties mobile services were slow to develop. Geographical reasons no doubt had much to do with this—the great distances to be covered in many counties, the difficult terrain, the narrow country roads, the severe winter weather—but one suspects that the poverty of many library authorities and the conservatism of their librarians were more important factors. Be this as it may, the early 'sixties brought a sudden surge of activity, and in 1964 C. S. Minto, after a second tour of the northern counties which he had visited sixteen years earlier, was able to report that all but two of the nine counties were now either operating or planning a mobile library service.[6]

[1] Information from Mr. W. J. Murison, County Librarian.
[2] *Public Library Statistics, 1964–65.*
[3] C. R. Eastwood, *Mobile Libraries and other Public Library Transport* (1967), pp. 38–40.
[4] K. A. Stockham, *British County Libraries, 1919–1969* (1969), p. 61.
[5] Information from Mr. Dean Harrison, County Librarian of Kent, and Miss D. M. Hudson, County Librarian of the North Riding.
[6] *S.L.A. News*, No. 66 (Sept.–Oct. 1964), p. 13 [the Second Minto Report].

Over the desolate moorlands of Sutherland, one of the two most northerly counties of the mainland, a "bookmobile" made its way to provide the scattered hamlets and farmsteads with a three-weekly service, returning only at weekends to its base at Brora on the west coast. Once, during a severe snowstorm, it had been stranded at an inn in the north-west for fourteen days.[1] Further north still, a mobile library was under construction to serve the mainland of Shetland, while on the mainland of Orkney a mobile had been operating since 1963 to supplement the full-time centres at Kirkwall and Stromness.

A special and well-known feature of the Orkney library was the Family Book Service, introduced by the librarian Evan MacGillivray in 1954 to serve the twenty-five smaller islands. A mobile library service was impracticable here, and book centres were of limited utility. The Family Service made available to each family, on request, a collection of 12–16 books which could be retained for up to two months. The books included both fiction and non-fiction, and more than half were sent in response to requests. Packed in tough fibre-board boxes, they were despatched twice weekly from headquarters at Kirkwall, ferried across to the islands by the local steamers, and delivered to the remote hamlets and farmsteads by local traders' vans. A very high proportion of the island families availed themselves of this service, and issues soared from less than 4000 a year to nearly 58 000.[2]

In the Scottish lowlands the pioneer in the development of mobile libraries (as in so many things) was Lanarkshire, which in 1964–65 had five mobile libraries in action, and six more planned. Midlothian at this date had three mobile libraries: no other Scottish county had more than two.

The county with the largest number of full-time branches was Lancashire, which in 1964–65 had 71 of which 26 were in new buildings opened since 1958. No other county came anywhere near this total, but Essex and Surrey had 42 each, Durham 40, and Staffordshire and the West Riding 38 each. In Middlesex, at the time of the dissolution of the county services in 1965, ten new branches were being built, to complete a total of 44 full-time branches which with four mobile libraries would completely replace the old voluntary library centres. In Scotland the leading counties in this respect were Lanarkshire with 26 full-time branches and Ayrshire with 16; in Wales the highest figures reached were in Monmouthshire, which had nine, and Glamorganshire, which had six.[3]

Closely related to this development, in many areas, was the introduction of a regional organization on the lines pioneered by Derbyshire before the war. Not all counties were suitable for development on these lines: some were too small, and some lacked sizeable towns where a regional library could suitably

---

[1] *S.L.A. News*, No. 65 (July–Aug. 1964), Suppl. p. 15.

[2] E. MacGillivray, "The Family Book Service in Orkney", in *County Newsletter*, No. 14 (May 1956), pp. 6–12; and the same author's "Library Services to Scattered Populations in a Remote Area", in Library Association, *Proceedings of the Public Libraries Conference . . . 1964* (1964), pp. 51–57; *S.L.A. News*, No. 66 (Sept.–Oct. 1964), pp. 9–10. The initial experiment, in North Ronaldsay, made use of the postal service.

[3] Institute of Municipal Treasurers and Accountants and Society of County Treasurers, *Public Library Statistics, 1964–65* (1966). For Middlesex see *Middlesex County Libraries, 1922–1965*, reprinted with additions from *Primary and Secondary Education in Middlesex, 1900–1965* (1964).

be located. Where regionalisation was possible, however, it had many advantages: it spread the administrative load; provided bases for the mobile libraries; brought lending stock and basic reference service within easier reach of readers in the rural areas; and facilitated the employment of qualified staff operating throughout the region.[1] In Warwickshire, which regionalised between 1950 and 1955, it was actually the mobile library which determined the limits of each region.[2]

In 1951 eight English counties were reported to be regionalised. Ten years later the number had risen to twenty, and eight more were considering the matter.[3] The first Welsh county to introduce a scheme of regional organization was Monmouthshire, in 1962.[4] There was still no example of the adoption of full regionalisation in any Scottish county, but Lanarkshire designated some of its larger branches as regional libraries, and arranged interchanges of staff on a regional basis.

One county in which regionalisation presented special problems was Lancashire. The sheer size and diversity of the area seemed to demand regional treatment, for the needs of the heavily industralised southern part of the county were very different from those of the mainly agricultural north, which was itself cut into two sections by the deep inlet of Morecambe Bay. The difficulty was that owing to the rapid development of public libraries during the nineteenth century nearly all the main centres of population, which would have been the natural centres for regional organization, were already independent library-authorities. In 1945 there were no fewer than 57 such authorities, 18 of them being county boroughs, and the remaining 39 municipal boroughs or urban districts within the county administrative area.

In these circumstances regionalisation was a gradual and *ad hoc* process, carried out as and when local circumstances suggested it. A beginning was made before the war in connection with the establishment of a mobile library service in North Lonsdale.[5] In the immediate post-war years the branches and centres began to be grouped together into what were first called "districts" and later "regions" or "areas".[6] This organization was later consolidated, as we have seen, by the development of the mobile library service and especially by the erection of branch libraries. The old-style village centres did not entirely disappear—there were still over a hundred of them in 1965—but every effort was made to upgrade the accommodation at these centres, and the creation of a link with a regional centre ensured improved staffing and book supplies. By 1962 the librarian was able to report:

---

[1] F. A. Sharr, "Decentralisation in County Library Administration", in *L.A.R.*, Vol. LII (1950), pp. 275–280; K. A. Stockham, "Regionalisation in Counties", in *L.A.R.*, Vol. LXII (1960), pp. 13–16.

[2] K. A. Stockham (ed.), *British County Libraries: 1919–1969* (1969), p. 24.

[3] Library Association, County Libraries Group, *A Policy Survey of the County Libraries of the United Kingdom, 1951–1961* (1963), pp. 5–6.

[4] Information from Mr. E. D. Pollard, County Librarian.

[5] See above, p. 283.

[6] The use of the terms "region" and "area" followed recommended Library Association practice. The regions were larger groupings, associated initially with mobile services. (From 1967 both terms were dropped in favour of the name "division".)

"Most of the County Library Regions . . . consist of full-time libraries in comparatively small urban districts, a number of part-time libraries and centres, a mobile service to the surrounding areas, school libraries, and sometimes special services to hospitals, old people's homes, etc. Their strength lies in the fact that they are large enough to be able to have an establishment of at least two, and usually more, qualified staff and a book stock which can meet at least the average day to day requests for books and information."[1]

This remarkable development was reflected in an increase of total issues from 6 millions in 1950 to 14 millions in 1965.[2]

Across the Mersey, in Cheshire, the problems were similar, but less acute. Here was a more compact county, basically rural, but with a scattering of industrial towns, mostly along its northern border, and a considerable amount of commuter settlement (some of it from Lancashire) in the same region. There were in 1945 four county boroughs and sixteen other independent library authorities. A development plan accepted by the county in 1949 and revised in 1960 provided for a division into nine regions, each with its "area library, or sub-headquarters". By 1965 area libraries had been provided at the county headquarters at Chester and two other centres, and another was being erected. Fourteen new branch library buildings, and one major extension, were brought into use between 1952 and 1965, and in the latter year twelve further new branches and one further major extension were projected. As in Lancashire, improvements were also made to the remaining village centres (64 in 1965). The first mobile library, based on headquarters, was introduced in 1962, to serve 98 villages and hamlets. Here too, there was a huge increase in issues, from just under two millions in 1952 to over five millions in 1965.[3]

In Surrey, the development of a regional organization covering the whole county area was impeded by the elaborate differential rating arrangements inherited from the pre-war period. In 1946 three municipal boroughs, eleven urban districts, and two rural districts (i.e. all except three of the local government districts in the county area) were operating under differential rates, with financial control from county library headquarters. In 1947 differential rating was abolished, and the district libraries were brought firmly under county control, but the local councils were still left considerable discretion within the broad lines of county policy and within the limits of approved estimates: they were, for example, responsible for the general supervision of the library service, and for the maintenance of buildings and grounds; they controlled the appointment of junior staff, and shared in the appointment of the district librarian.

The extensive consultation between county and district authorities which this system involved had many advantages, but it also added greatly to the complexities of county administration, and since village centres, service to hospitals, homes and schools, and mobile services, were excluded from local

[1] Lancashire County Library, *Report, 1960–62*, p. 8.
[2] For the preceding brief account of the Lancashire situation I am indebted to the Annual Reports of the library from 1950 to 1952, the Biennial Reports from 1954 to 1968, and information from the County Librarian, Mr. A. Longworth.
[3] *Report of the County Librarian for the Years 1962–65*, espec. pp. 1–4. The process of regionalisation involved the disappearance of differential rating (see above, p. 355).

control, a comprehensive regional service was rendered difficult. Following the changes in the county boundaries brought about by the London Government Act, the agreement was renewed in 1965, and the powers of the local authorities were spelt out in rather more detail.[1]

The New Look in Library Buildings

In 1947 the French fashion designer Christian Dior introduced "the New Look" for women's clothes. It was a gay and elegant style, which after the drab austerities of the war years was immensely appealing. Library architecture also underwent a change in style, but here, as we have seen, wartime austerity persisted longer, and it was only in the building boom of the late 'fifties and early 'sixties that the New Look was able to make its full impact.[2]

This boom was indeed a remarkable one, in spite of the reintroduction of capital restrictions in August, 1961.[3] An inquiry made in March, 1963, brought details of nearly 300 new public library buildings erected in the United Kingdom since 1960, and by 1965 there were many more. When Berriman and Harrison spoke of "the British library building renaissance" they were, if anything, understating the case.[4] Most of the new buildings were urban or county branch libraries, erected either to serve new areas or to replace buildings which had long since outlived their usefulness, but the list of buildings completed between 1960 and 1965 also includes a number of large urban central libraries and county headquarters. In the former category may be placed Holborn and Kensington (1960), Luton and Norwich (1962), Hampstead (1964), and Hornsey (1965), besides the major extensions at Hull (1962) and Sunderland (1963);[5] in the latter category we find the headquarters buildings for Staffordshire (at Stafford, 1961), Co. Durham (at Durham, 1963), Montgomeryshire (at Newtown, 1963), the West Riding (at Wakefield, 1964), and Kent (at Maidstone, 1964). The main activity was in England, but a considerable amount of building was also going on in Wales and Scotland—mainly in the way of branch libraries.[6] The Montgomeryshire building was Wales's first purpose-built county library headquarters.

The new look in the libraries of this period is to be seen both in their outward appearance and in their internal organization and equipment. Outward appearance before the war had still tended towards a conventional neo-Georgian

---

[1] The history of these developments is traced in an unpublished memorandum by Mr. R. F. Ashby, County Librarian, dated Aug. 1967. The original agreement of 1947 was printed as Appendix VI to the *Roberts Report*, and the agreement of 1965 was printed by the County Council (*County Library Service: Scheme of Delegation of Functions to County District Councils*, 1965).

[2] Cf. above, p. 353.

[3] *L.A.R.*, Vol. LXIII (1961), p. L95.

[4] S. G. Berriman and K. C. Harrison, *British Public Library Buildings* (1966), p. 18. The libraries described in this volume do in fact include some completed after 1963.

[5] Smaller urban central libraries included Swadlincote (1960), Great Yarmouth (1961), Guildford (1962), Nuneaton (1962), Aberdare (1963), and Eastbourne (1964).

[6] *F.Y.W.L. 1961–65*, pp. 252, 254–255; W. R. Aitken, *A History of the Public Library Movement in Scotland to 1955* (Glasgow 1971), App. 5 (report on a survey of new premises made by the Scottish Library Association in 1967).

or neo-classical, which was the formal dress expected of civic buildings. This was particularly true of the larger libraries. The last notable example of this civic style was the Kensington Central Library, opened in 1960 and designed by E. Vincent Harris, who nearly thirty years earlier had designed the monumental Manchester Central Library. Though in many ways a splendid building, the Kensington library came under severe criticism for being dressed up, as *The Times* architectural correspondent put it, "in the clothes of the past";[1] and it was contrasted unfavourably with the more contemporary style of the Holborn Central Library opened in the same year.

Henceforth library exteriors were uncompromisingly modern, relying for such beauty as they possessed on a functional arrangement of masses and materials, without the necessity for conforming to any conventional style. Not all were aesthetically pleasing, but some achieved real elegance and distinction— my personal choice among the larger libraries would be the Hampstead Central Library by Basil Spence and the Kent County Library headquarters by E. T. Ashley Smith, both opened in 1964.[2]

The extensive use of steel and concrete (often in combination with the more traditional brickwork), gave much greater freedom in construction, and in particular made possible the large "picture-windows" which now became a characteristic feature of library architecture. Even in large libraries, such as Holborn, an entire wall might be made of glass, often with dramatic effect, especially at night. Librarians were not slow to see the publicity value of this type of construction, and in at least one branch library, Kidbrooke in Greenwich, the main elevation was deliberately designed "as a shop window in order that passers-by will have a clear view of the books and be encouraged to enter the building and use the service."[3]

New building techniques also encouraged architects to experiment with unusual shapes—circular like the students' library at Kent County Headquarters, the Jesmond Branch at Newcastle upon Tyne (1963), and several other branch libraries;[4] octagonal as at the Selsey Branch, West Sussex County (1964); or even triangular as at the Eccleshill Branch, Bradford (1964). The Kent County building and the new Norwich City Library each incorporated a multi-storey tower block for purposes of storage. Thanks to development and redevelopment schemes, there were also some unusual combinations of libraries with other buildings. The erection of a branch library as part of a block of flats was by no means uncommon,[5] and the Newbold Branch at Chesterfield (1964) was part of a development which also included shops, a supermarket, flats and maisonettes.

The sheer size of the building programme in which some authorities were involved led inevitably to a measure of standardization, especially in

[1] *L.A.R.*, Vol. LXII (1960), p. L59. For a description see pp. 361-364; Berriman and Harrison, *op. cit.*, pp. 71-72.
[2] *L.A.R.*, Vol. LXVI (1964), pp. 502-509, 530-538; Berriman and Harrison, *op. cit.*, pp. 67-70, 93-96.
[3] *L.A.R.*, Vol. LXIV (1962), pp. 471-472.
[4] E.g. Bradmore Green Branch (Coulsdon and Purley 1963), Crawley Children's Library (West Sussex Co. 1963), and Swanage Branch (Dorset Co. 1965).
[5] E.g. Pimlico Children's Library (Westminster 1960), Roehampton Branch (Wandsworth 1961), Hangleton Branch (Hove 1962).

the smaller libraries. West Riding County, by 1963, had evolved a series of four prototype branch plans, ranging from Type A, 45 feet square, for populations between 4000 and 6000, to Type D, 65 feet square, for populations over 10 000. Lancashire County, about the same time, agreed on a series of three prototypes.[1] For speed and economy of building there was a trend also towards "modular construction", i.e. construction in units of uniform size. This method was pioneered in this country in the Manor Branch at Sheffield, completed in 1953, but it did not become popular till the 'sixties, when very large programmes of public building had to be undertaken.[2] Nottingham and Durham Counties made use of a modular system known as CLASP, which had been developed by a consortium of local authorities: this was based on prefabricated steel units, and was particularly suitable for areas liable to mining subsidence. A second consortium of local authorities produced the system known as SCOLA, which was used in branch libraries in Gloucester and West Sussex Counties.[3]

Modular construction was not without its effect upon internal organisation, for it helped to make possible the greater flexibility that was now generally felt to be desirable, especially at a time when, because of financial restrictions, buildings often had to be erected in two or more separate phases. Structural inside walls were replaced by columns, forming space units of standard size which could then be partitioned off as required; when needs changed, the partition walls could be moved to provide new space groupings. At the Sheffield branch just referred to the screens were of glass, giving a view through the whole interior from almost any point.

The internal structure of libraries at this period is particularly interesting because it reflects so clearly the changing views of librarians on users' needs. The basic elements were now the adult lending library, the adult reference library, and the children's library. To this nucleus were added such specialist rooms as might be appropriate to the size and situation of the library—a music and gramophone records room, a local history room, a technical and/or commercial room—together with the necessary rooms for staff and administration, and perhaps accommodation for cultural activities. Except in the older libraries, and some of the largest of the new libraries, e.g. Norwich and Hampstead, a separate reading room for newspapers and periodicals was now unusual: a few tables and chairs in a corner of the lending library or reference library, with newspapers and periodicals neatly accommodated in racks near by, were generally thought sufficient. As for ladies' reading rooms, they were looked upon as quite prehistoric, and it is with astonishment that one reads of provision for such a room in the reconstructed library at Stamford in 1961.[4]

A special feature of the post-war period, and especially of the 'fifties and 'sixties, was the enormously increased demand for reference and study books—a demand growing primarily out of the rapid expansion of secondary and higher education which was described in the last chapter. Even the smallest

[1] L.A.R., Vol. LXV (1963), pp. 463–464; Vol. LXVII (1965), p. 359; F.Y.W.L. 1961–65, pp. 238–239.
[2] A. Thompson, Library Buildings of Great Britain and Europe (1963), pp. 21–24, 114–117. On the Manor Branch see also above, p. 363.
[3] L.A.R., Vol. LXIV (1962), p. 198; F.Y.W.L. 1961–65, p. 239.
[4] Stamford Public Library and Museum, The Library Story: 60 Years of Public Service, 1906–1966 (1966), pp. 4–5.

branch now felt the need for at least a quick reference collection, and most new branches made provision for a reference room. The needs of schoolchildren, who because of television found it difficult to study at home, demanded special attention. The variety of responses to this situation by the smaller libraries is indicated by such titles as "Homework and Information Room", "Study and Information Room", "Magazine and Study Room", and "Children's Reference and Homework Room".[1] At Welwyn Garden City, Hertfordshire County found an effective solution by linking its new branch library (opened in 1960) to the technical college, the library of which served the reference needs of both town and college.[2] The major new civic libraries, of course, provided generous study space, including sometimes individual student "carrels".

Though many libraries continued to provide for their various departments in separate rooms, there was a distinct tendency towards a more open lay-out and a blurring of the distinction between departments. In some small libraries all departments were accommodated in a single room, separated, if at all, merely by an arrangement of bookcases. As far as small libraries were concerned, of course, there was nothing new in this. It had been suggested by the Carnegie Corporation of America as long ago as 1911, and between that date and 1939 there had been many examples of one-room libraries. The difference was that what had formerly been done perforce was now being done from choice.[3] American and Scandinavian influence was strong in this matter, and the fashion for open planning spread to many kinds of buildings, including department stores, schools, and private houses.

A good example among smaller libraries is the Bush Hill Branch at Edmonton, opened in 1963. This consisted of a single large L-shaped room comprising the following "areas":

> "a reference and study area adjacent to the staff desk; a children's area shelving 4000 volumes . . .; a music, gramophone record, and listening area with sound deck and head-phones; an adult fiction and browsing area (10 000 volumes) interspersed with table and chairs for reading books or periodicals; book selection areas for non-fiction works (14 500 volumes) also mingled with tables and chairs for periodicals, books, or news reading."[4]

Official staff rooms opened off a balcony, and a basement provided stacks for up to 60 000 volumes. (A reserve stack of this kind was by this time a standard feature of every sizeable library.)

There are a number of points of interest in this extract. One is the use of the term "area" instead of "room" or "department"; another is the provision of facilities for "browsing" as distinct from formal study; and yet another is the line drawn between fiction and non-fiction areas. All these represent

---

[1] Used respectively in the following libraries: Wood Avenue Branch (Folkestone 1960), Banstead Central Library (Surrey Co. 1961), Castlemilk Branch (Glasgow 1961), Hester's Way Branch (Cheltenham 1962).

[2] L.A.R., Vol. LXIV (1962), pp. 472–475; Berriman and Harrison, op. cit., pp. 208–210. For the links between county and technical college library services see below, p. 390.

[3] See above, p. 171. Cf. S. G. Berriman, "The Provision and Design of County Library Buildings", in L.A. Conference Proceedings, 1958, pp. 28–30.

[4] L.A.R., Vol. LXV (1963), p. 487.

fairly common trends, and the last hints at the increasingly sharp distinction between the recreational use of public libraries and their use for the purpose of serious study. This is a point we shall have to take up again in the next section.

For small and medium-sized libraries open planning had many advantages. It was attractive to the public, economical of space and staff, and gave maximum flexibility. The main problem was noise: it was difficult, where all departments shared a single room, to provide a really quiet place for study. Acoustic ceiling and wall surfaces helped, but there was much to be said for the kind of modified open plan adopted by Lancashire County in its largest branch, opened in 1964 to meet the needs of the 60 000 population of Kirkby, an overspill town on the outskirts of Liverpool. Miss F. E. Cook, County Librarian at this time, evidently believed that the more drab and unpromising the area was the more beautiful the library ought to be, and the Kirkby library was magnificent. On the ground floor a single large galleried room provided accommodation for the adult lending library, the children's library, the reference library and the quick reference section, but partial screening, combined with the careful positioning of bookcases and counters, provided some measure of separation and ensured a reasonable degree of quiet in the reference area.[1]

In large libraries the possibilities for open planning were, of course, more restricted, but the influence of the idea can be clearly seen in several of the new civic buildings, and the use of galleries (a device copied from Scandinavian practice) made it possible to house quite large collections compactly without losing the sense of openness and space. Frank Gardner, Librarian of Luton, acknowledged that the concept of the gallery library changed his whole thinking, and he made effective use of it in the new Luton Central Library, opened in 1962. This was a five-storey block of which the ground floor was occupied mainly by shops. The first floor housed the fiction library, which opened directly into a galleried general lending library. Here the books were housed in and under the galleries, the central area being left free for browsing and for the readers' advisory service. The galleries, reached by a broad open staircase, gave direct access to the reference collection.[2]

Galleries were also used in the lending libraries at the Holborn Central Library in 1960 (the pioneer in this type of building), the Hampstead Central Library in 1964, and the Hornsey Central Library in 1965. At Hampstead the galleried lending library at the semi-circular northern end of the long building was matched by a galleried reference library at the semi-circular southern end. At Norwich Central Library (1962), a gallery planned for the lending library was omitted on grounds of economy, at the insistence of the Ministry of Housing and Local Government.[3]

Lengthy as this section on new library buildings has been, there is still much that could be said. We must be content to pass over with no more than a

---

[1] *L.A.R.*, Vol. LXVII (1965), pp. 359–367; Berriman and Harrison, *op. cit.*, pp. 221–223.

[2] *L.A.R.*, Vol. LXII (1960), pp. 371–372; Vol. LXIV (1964), pp. 455–458; Berriman and Harrison, *op. cit.*, pp. 58–66; F. M. Gardner, "Planning of Central Libraries," in *L.A. Conference Proceedings, 1962*, pp. 12–20.

[3] For Hampstead see references at p. 370 note 3, above; for Holborn, Norwich and Hornsey, *L.A.R.*, Vol. LXII (1960), pp. 358–361, 373–374; Vol. LXVII (1965), pp. 117–123; Berriman and Harrison, *op. cit.*, pp. 52–55, 76–78, 243–244.

brief mention the offices, workshops, store-rooms and staffrooms which were so important in the functioning of all libraries and which in the larger libraries took up far more space than the public rooms. For the moment, too, we must leave on one side (though this is a subject we shall be able to return to later) the cultural facilities which were so generously provided by many libraries—the lecture-rooms, theatres, exhibition rooms and the like. We must, however, find space to comment on the transformation that took place at this time in library furnishings and equipment.

We have commented above on the movement towards lighter and brighter libraries which made itself evident in the 'thirties,[1] but few of the libraries built at that period could match the elegance and comfort of those which were being built in the 'sixties. The more open lay-out had something to do with it, and so had new techniques in lighting and heating. Fluorescent lighting, which began to be experimented with in libraries just after the war,[2] was now widely used, and the clumsy hot-water radiators of the pre-war years gave place to more modern and discreet forms of central heating, often operated by oil, gas, or electricity instead of by solid fuel. In open plan buildings under-floor heating became almost standard.

Although, moreover, library exteriors were apt to be severely functional, the interiors were often enlivened with enclosed gardens and courtyards, and adorned with sculptures, murals, indoor plants, even tanks of tropical fish. The bookcases themselves were attractively designed and grouped, with special displays to catch the eye at strategic points. Tables and chairs were scattered around for casual reading, and there might even be a carpeted area with low tables and comfortable armchairs.[3] Wallpapers, exotic African woods and plastic materials were freely used to give colour and variety. Of the adult and children's libraries at Knaresborough (a West Riding County regional library) we read:

"the floors are of jade green linoleum tiles and the decoration is pure white and quiet greys, broken by a brief splash of yellow."[4]

At the Fleetville Branch, St. Albans:

"The small entrance lobby is paved in grey terrazzo. One wall is painted in daffodil yellow with a fitted display case . . .

"Two silver-grey walls and the rich brown of the African hardwood floor and bookstacks provide a pleasing background for the book stock. Wallpaper in a modern French design on the remaining wall introduces a colourful note.

"The fibre glass chairs are in elephant grey and sea foam; the small tables and the counter top are finished with charcoal and white mottled perstorp. A walnut slatted window seat and two easy chairs upholstered in flame coloured vinyl fabric complete the furnishings of this room."[5]

---

[1] See above, pp. 280.

[2] The first recorded experiment in a public library was at Chesterfield in Derbyshire, and is described in *L.A.R.*, Vol. XLVIII (1946), pp. 60–62.

[3] Cf. S. G. Berriman, "The Provision and Design of County Library Buildings", in *L.A. Conference Proceedings, 1958*, p. 29: "I like to play with the idea that in this twentieth century we have created for our many readers the conditions we associate with a well-read gentleman's library of past centuries".

[4] *L.A.R.*, Vol. LXIII (1961), p. 132.   [5] *L.A.R.*, Vol. LXII (1960), p. 354.

And at the Airedale Branch, Castleford:

"All chairs are upholstered, some Scandinavian in origin, in shades of mustard, gold, blue and grey. Wallpaper is original in design and round the large window is white and maroon—the long window seat being upholstered in purple. The long wall stretching from the main lending library through to the junior library is in blue/green paper."[1]

The greatest transformation of all, however, was in the books themselves, and was due to the simple device of fitting a transparent plastic sheath over the book jacket in such a way as to hold the jacket in position and protect both it and the book cover from wear. This invention halved binding costs at a stroke, but it also enabled librarians, for the first time, to shelve the books in the brightly coloured jackets supplied by the publishers. The dull browns, red, blues and greens of traditional library bindings were gone for ever, for now by the time the cover was worn out the inside was usually worn out too. The idea was introduced in the United States soon after the war, and came into widespread use in this country during the 'fifties.[2] Many librarians regarded it as the greatest revolution of their working lives, and it certainly contributed much to making the modern library a gay and attractive place.

A final word must be said about county library headquarters, which were different from other libraries in that their main function was to act as a store and as a centre for distribution. This difference should not, however, be exaggerated. Of the five new headquarters buildings erected during these years, two, Staffordshire and Co. Durham, did indeed consist mainly of efficiently organized bookstacks and administrative areas, but the other three all included substantial public service areas. Montgomeryshire's headquarters at Newtown incorporated a complete branch library for the local population; the West Riding headquarters at Wakefield had a small lending and reference library of 12 600 volumes; and at the Kent headquarters at Maidstone the circular students' library accommodated just five times that number.[3]

Perhaps the most important point to be made about new county headquarters, however, is that they were still so few: even in 1965 there were still only about a dozen of them, out of a total of more than eighty county library authorities.

New Ideas in Departmental Organization

This brief survey of library buildings has hinted at the extent to which old ideas concerning library organization were coming under challenge at this time. There was indeed an impressive amount of new thinking and experimentation, especially in England.

In 1946, in an article in the *Library World*, the librarian of Folkestone explained how the great success of the one-room branch opened at Cheriton

---

[1] *L.A.R.*, Vol. LXIV (1962), p. 467.

[2] W. Stern, "Books, too, have that 'New Look' ", in *Library Journal*, Vol. LXXIII (1948), pp. 505–506; A. Glencross, "Plastic Jackets", in Library Association, *North-West Newsletter*, No. 15 (May 1952), pp. 2–3; H. E. Radford, "Some Observations on Plastic Jackets . . .", in *Library World*, Vol. LX (1958–59), pp. 116–118.

[3] *L.A.R.*, Vol. LXV (1963), pp. 514–517; Vol. LXVI (1964), pp. 522–538; Berriman and Harrison, *op. cit.*, pp. 85–96.

just before the war had led him to experiment with a more open lay-out for the central library. The result was a merging of lending library and reading room, which were made into one department. An alcove arrangement facilitated the grouping of the books under broad subject headings: Literature; Science and Technology; History and Sociology. Periodicals were made available alongside the appropriate books, and an alcove at one end was furnished with tables and chairs as a quiet room.[1]

A similar re-arrangement, also involving the merging of lending library and reading room, was carried out at Eccles in Lancashire in 1953. Here, too, alcoves were used to provide subject groups, in which reference books were shelved in close proximity to lending books and the relevant periodicals were also near at hand. Considerable liberties were taken with the Dewey arrangement in order to secure a grouping convenient to the reader. Language, for example, was grouped with literature, historical fiction with history. One alcove was occupied with "Recreational Reading" designed mainly for men—books on sports and hobbies, and stories of mystery and adventure. Adjoining it was a section of "Domestic Interests"—cookery, child care, dressmaking, and the like, with a selection of domestic and romantic fiction.[2]

There was about these experiments a strong flavour of those ideas of subject departmentalism which had been pioneered by Savage at Edinburgh before the war, and which he was still advocating in his retirement.[3] A. W. McClellan, Librarian of Tottenham, combined the idea of subject specialization with an original approach of his own which he called "service in depth", and which was based on the idea that the reader should be able to move easily from lighter to more serious literature. He expounded his views first in 1950, and again in 1955.[4] Recognizing that completely separate subject departments were neither possible nor appropriate in any except the largest libraries, he proposed an arrangement which in 1955 he described as follows:

> "The charging and discharging processes take place outside the main public room. The first portion of the room consists of an informal reading and smoking lounge in which small displays can be arranged. There follows an area in which the fiction and popular non-fiction sections are housed on straight-run wall shelving and occasional alcove shelving, together with display bookstands. Informal seating and tables are provided. The bookstocks are grouped under broad interest headings rather than by the straightforward Dewey classification. This part of the room is designed to give the appearance of a large but attractive bookshop. At the far end of the room are the remaining Lending and Reference books arranged in the same sequence and in the more or less customary class order.
>
> "The main feature of the arrangement, however, is the provision, at the junction of the popular section and the general Lending and Reference collections, of an information service counter. This forms the focal point of the room and from it will operate the subject specialist staffs."

---

[1] R. Howarth, "Open Planning", in *Library World*, Vol. XLIX (1946–47), pp. 43–45.

[2] J. F. W. Bryon, "Subject Arrangement in a Small Library", in *Librarian and Book World*, Vol. XLIV (1955), pp. 25–28.

[3] E. A. Savage, *A Librarian's Memories, Portraits and Reflections* (1952), pp. 76, 154–155.

[4] A. W. McClellan, "Service in Depth", in *Library World*, Vol. LII (1949–50), pp. 183–185; "The Organisation of a Public Library for Subject Specialisation", in *L.A.R.*, Vol. LVII (1955), pp. 296–303.

As it happened, it was not until 1964 that the enlargement and reconstruction of the central library made it possible to bring the new book arrangement here proposed to the test of reality. What McClellan was able to do, in the meantime, was to organize his staff on the basis of subject specialisms instead of, as was customary in smaller libraries, on the basis of administrative specialisms such as bibliography, reference, and lending. "I am more than ever convinced," he declared in 1955, "that subject specialisation is the key to a new level of service and to the fullest use of our professional staffs."

Up to 1960 there was still no example, even in the largest libraries, of the organization of an entire library in separate subject departments. Bradford had plans for such a library, but it was not built until 1967.[1] Birmingham also had in mind a considerable measure of departmental organization in its new central library, but this took even longer to materialise. Thus it came about that the first library in the country to achieve full subject specialization was Liverpool in 1961, following the rebuilding of the William Brown Central Library. Four years later J. D. Reynolds, editor of the *Library Association Record*, visited and described this immense library, totalling nearly one million volumes, and subdivided into more than a dozen separate but interlinked collections grouped in accordance with the Dewey classification. Bibliographies and reference works were shelved round the walls of the great circular Picton Reading Room, and the International Library occupied the tiered bookstacks in the former Picton Lecture Hall;[2] while on the six floors of the adjoining William Brown building were to be found (beginning with the uppermost storey) libraries covering Art; Local History; Biography; Science; Patents; Religion and Philosophy; Technical Subjects; America; British History, Topography and Literature; the Commonwealth; Commercial and Social Sciences; and Music. Wherever possible books were duplicated so as to provide copies, shelved side by side, both for lending and for reference; and each subject library included also pamphlets, periodicals, and where appropriate microfilms, tapes, gramophone records, maps, and pictorial material.[3]

Undoubtedly the exigencies of the Central Library buildings had something to do with the adoption of this kind of organization, but it was the firm conviction of the librarian, George Chandler, that for a large city library, serving a population of half a million or more, subject departmentalization was the only satisfactory management solution—the only solution which could make a large proportion of the stock available on open access, and provide the backing of the necessary specialist staff.[4]

The Liverpool reorganization made a tremendous impression, and led other large libraries to consider moves in the same direction, but the only other library in which subject departmentalization was fully operative before 1965 was Manchester. Here the Great Hall, which had once been a general reference library, was restricted to Bibliography, Religion, Philosophy,

[1] See for the details *L.A.R.*, Vol. LXII (1960), pp. 369–70.
[2] Cf. above, p. 46.
[3] *L.A.R.*, Vol. LXIII (1961), pp. 293–299; cf. Vol. LIX (1957), pp. 331–333. A small lending library of a more popular kind was provided in a separate building nearer the city centre.
[4] For a critical survey see M. A. Overington, *The Subject Departmentalised Public Library* (1969), pp. 97–112.

Social Science and History, and the Central Lending Library provided a lending service in the same subjects. Alongside these twin libraries were five subject departments—Technical, Arts, Music, Language and Literature, and Local History—in which reference and lending functions were combined. The new arrangement was completed by 1964.[1]

Edinburgh, which had pioneered subject specialization, made an interesting departure when in 1958 it removed all the fiction from its Central Home Reading Library to make a separate Central Fiction Library. The new library included classical as well as popular fiction, and accounted for 26 800 volumes compared with 84 600 remaining in the main lending library. It was claimed that as a result the issues from both sections increased and the quality of service was improved.[2]

This new approach fitted in with the growing feeling among many librarians of smaller libraries that the most important distinction in library use was between recreational reading (i.e. fiction and the lighter and more practical kinds of non-fiction), and what McColvin and others called "purposive reading". McClellan did not like this distinction and sought to minimize it, but others thought it should be frankly recognized and catered for. Bryon at Eccles, as we have seen, provided in 1953 separate sections for recreational and domestic reading, and S. H. Barlow, at Nuneaton, was experimenting about the same time on even more radical lines, involving the integration where practicable of lending and reference stock. When a new library was opened in 1962 provision was made for the following sections: (1) a General Library of fiction and popular non-fiction; (2) a Reference Library in which the main non-fiction stock, both lending and reference, was shelved under subjects; (3) a Study Room with twelve individual desks and shelf accommodation for special collections; and (4) a Children's Library.[3]

In the 'sixties many new library buildings were based on some such layout. Surrey County's Banstead Central Library, instead of having separate lending and reference departments, had a "general lending library" providing for leisure-time reading and a combined lending and reference department for "study and information".[4] Wandsworth's Roehampton Branch made a similar division in its open plan adult library;[5] and Finchley's Church End Branch, though it retained a separate reference library, had an open plan lending library in which fiction and recreational literature were grouped round two sides while the rest of the area was occupied by "informational" books and (in one corner) children's books.[6] The central library provided by Essex County at Harlow New Town was based on the principle of integrated reference and lending stocks in three broad subject divisions, with additional

[1] Manchester Public Libraries, *Annual Report, 1963–64*, pp. 3–4.
[2] C. S. Minto, "Action on Fiction", in *S.L.A. News*, No. 39 (Jan.–Feb. 1960), pp. 4–7, 10–11.
[3] S. H. Barlow, "A New Look at an Old Building", in *L.A.R.*, Vol. LXIII (1961), pp. 409–415; and the same on "Nuneaton's New Library", in *Library World*, Vol. LXV (1963–64), pp. 1–8.
[4] *L.A.R.*, Vol. LXIV (1962), p. 52.
[5] *Op. cit.*, pp. 52–54.
[6] *L.A.R.*, Vol. LXVI (1964), pp. 552–555.

sections for "general reading" (including fiction) and for young readers.[1] In the new Eastbourne Central Library, too, lending and reference books were shelved together, a quiet corner being furnished as a study area.[2]

These schemes differed in detail, but the starting-point of all of them was the idea that in the last resort the task of librarianship was to get books into the hands of readers, and that academic considerations of classification and library administration must be subordinated to that end.

[1] A. Bill, "Patterns of Public Library Service—a New Approach", in *Assistant Librarian*, Vol. LVIII (1965), pp. 172–174.

[2] *L.A.R.*, Vol. LXVI, (1964), pp. 517–521.

CHAPTER XVI

Library Organization and Use

Readers and Reading

BY 1950 Lionel McColvin was expressing the conviction that in future libraries would become more "active" and "purposive", and less concerned with "that kind of recreational demand for which other agencies provide adequate substitutes."[1] The ensuing years did indeed bring increasing emphasis on the function of the public library as a purveyor of serious literature. This was due mainly, as has already been pointed out, to the expansion of higher education. The lending and reference departments of urban central libraries overflowed with students, teachers and researchers, from universities, teacher training colleges, technical colleges and colleges of further education, and students on vacation carried the demand into remote corners of the country-side.

There were other factors, too. The rapid advance of technology, and the growing complexity of modern government, brought a steadily increasing demand for library services from industry and commerce, from councillors and civic officials, and from the great new army of social workers created by the welfare state. On the purely cultural side, increased demands arose from the expansion of adult education, from the new interests stimulated by television, and to some extent from the disappearance of the middle-class subscription libraries. The importance of this cultural element is emphasized by figures published in 1963 for a single day's issues from the Liverpool Central Lending Library. These showed that only in two of seven subject groupings did borrowings for "known non-professional use" form less than half the total. These were social sciences (21.5 per cent) and science and technology (18.3 per cent). In the other subject groupings, non-professional use ranged from 58.5 per cent in music to 77.8 per cent in fiction.[2]

On the whole, therefore, McColvin's prediction was justified. What he did not anticipate was that alongside the growth of demand for "purposive" literature (by which he meant mainly non-fiction) there would also be a growth in demand for fiction and other kinds of recreational literature—popular travel and biography, books about sports and handicrafts, and so forth. This, too, owed something to the disappearance of subscription libraries; it also reflected increased leisure, and a general raising of the level of literacy. Inevitably, it affected the branches most, the demand for serious literature tending to focus on the main libraries. Many librarians were worried by this development, and the 'fifties brought a revival of the old and sterile controversy about the provision of fiction.[3]

[1] L. McColvin, "Public Libraries in the Next Fifty Years", in *Librarian and Book World*, Vol. XXXIX (1950), p. 137.
[2] G. Chandler, "Provision of Special Services by Public Libraries", in Library Association, *Proceedings of the Public Libraries Conference . . . 1963* (1963), p. 16.
[3] The argument is summarized in *F.Y.W.L. 1951–55*, pp. 108, 189–190.

There was, inevitably, much discussion of the effect of radio and television on library reading. In 1953 Joseph Trenaman demonstrated conclusively that the effect of serialising a book on the radio was to stimulate library issues,[1] but television remained under suspicion. Reports from Radnorshire County Library, for example, tended to correlate every decline in issues between 1949 and 1969 with the advent or spread of television.[2] A more common assessment, however, was that represented in the Renfrewshire Report for 1963–64:

> "It is now possible to dismiss television as a threat to reading. The more serious and informative television and radio programmes send a large proportion of viewers and listeners to books for further study."

Research carried out by Bryan Luckham and J. M. Orr in the North-West of England in 1965 confirmed this empirical view, reaching the conclusion that "the effect of the broadcast programmes appears to have been consistent in stimulating a substantial increase in borrowing from public libraries of recommended titles, and arousing an interest in the subject generally."[3]

This particular piece of research was but one of many inquiries carried out during these years into various aspects of library use, for the constantly changing situation stimulated a desire among librarians to know more about their readers and their needs.[4] Altogether about a score of inquiries were made, concerned either with the characteristics of readers, or with the kind of books read, or both. Most of them were quite local, concerned with a single library or small group of libraries, and in many cases the results were never published, except in an annual report.

Reports of the first major inquiries to be undertaken after the war were produced by Middlesex County and by what was then the municipal borough of Tottenham, in the same county, in 1947. Middlesex's Survey of Reading was probably the most thorough and comprehensive ever carried out by any public library in Britain, covering as it did every book in the hands of the public throughout the county on a given day.[5] No fewer than 84 000 volumes were on loan out of a total stock of 173 000. The non-fiction issues, 39.3 per cent of the total, were analyzed under sixteen main subject headings, and issues in each of these subjects were analysed under appropriate subheadings. The favourite subjects were travel (with emphasis on England), applied science (with gardening as the most popular single topic), biography (especially the well-known classics), and fine arts and amusements (with out-

[1] J. Trenaman, "Reader Research, II, The B.B.C. Reading Enquiry", in Library Association, London and Home Counties Branch, *The Reader and his Needs* (Eastbourne 1953), pp. 20–29.

[2] *Radnorshire County Library: The Second Ten Years, 1949–1959* (1959), p. 12; *The Third Ten Years, 1959–1969* [1969], pp. 13–14.

[3] Public Libraries and Adult Education Committee for the North-West, Research Paper No. 4, *Educational Broadcasts and Book Borrowing* (1965).

[4] A. W. McClellan, "Reader Research, I, The Social Survey and Reading", in Library Association, London and Home Counties Branch, *The Reader and his Needs* (Eastbourne 1953), pp. 5–19, argues the case for readership inquiries and provides a useful bibliography.

[5] *Middlesex County Libraries Silver Jubilee, 1922–1947: a review of twenty-five years' work with a Survey of Reading carried out on 26th March, 1947* (1948).

door amusements, music, drawing and design, and architecture as the leading themes).

Fiction issues accounted for 60.7 per cent of the total (not an unduly high figure for a county library with many small branches). These issues also were analyzed in immense detail. A first rough grouping showed 12.6 per cent "acknowledged classics and modern novelists who are appreciated in particular for the power and style of their writing", and 33.2 per cent "light fiction which requires little mental effort to appreciate;" the rest, 54.1 per cent, represented the average competent novelist who could write well and tell a good story. A more detailed classification, into eleven types, showed romance heading the list (26.2 per cent) with sociological novels, detective stories, and psychological novels next in popularity; "westerns", surprisingly, rated only 2.8 per cent. Finally figures of stock and issues were provided for every individual novelist. The six most popular novelists, in order of issues, were Horace Walpole, Warwick Deeping, Jeffrey Farnol, P. G. Wodehouse, A. E. W. Mason, and John Buchan.

The Tottenham survey, wider in scope but less detailed, was carried out in 1946 by Mass Observation on behalf of the borough council, and covered a scientifically selected sample of 968 inhabitants.[1] Just over half of them, it appeared, read books, and just under a quarter were members of the public library. The readers were most numerous among the young, middle-class and well educated, and among library members this trend was even more marked. In no social group, however, were library members in a majority: in the middle class the figure was 49 per cent, in the skilled working class 28 per cent, and in the unskilled working class 16 per cent. Since the middle class represented only 5 per cent of the sample, they were still a minority of the users, but the trend represented by the figures was a notable one and was to be confirmed by later investigations. Another interesting finding was that library membership dropped sharply among people living more than half a mile from a library.

The part of the inquiry which dealt with reading tastes was not very revealing. It was carried out by asking people to make a choice among subjects and types of books that interested them. In all classes most people expressed a preference for fiction: even among middle-class readers only 28 per cent preferred non-fiction. The non-fiction subjects for which a preference was most frequently expressed were travel and adventure (12 per cent) and sport (10 per cent). In fiction the outstanding feature was the overwhelming popularity of detective and mystery stories; only among women readers did love stories achieve a comparable popularity.

A rather more sophisticated survey, embracing the South London boroughs of Bermondsey and Wandsworth as well as Tottenham, was undertaken in 1950 under the imposing auspices of the London School of Economics, the Government Social Survey and the British Institute of Public Opinion.[2] It was based on a selected sample of 506 people, and the results were not markedly different. The percentage of library members to total population was 23 in Tottenham,

[1] Tottenham Public Libraries and Museums, *Reading in Tottenham* (duplicated, 1947).
[2] A. Stuart, "Reading Habits in Three London Boroughs", in *Journal of Documentation*, Vol. VIII (1952), pp. 33–49.

20 in Wandsworth, and 17 in Bermondsey: all these figures were below the national average, which was estimated in 1949 as 25 per cent.

The most extensive survey in the London region was carried out in 1962–63 by the Research Institute for Consumer Affairs.[1] Using a sample of 1306 people from 7 of the 28 metropolitan boroughs and a sub-sample of 501 for more detailed analysis, this survey made a special study of public library membership and of attitudes to libraries among members, former members, and non-members. From the larger group it appeared that 30 per cent were library members, and a further 24 per cent were lapsed members, leaving 46 per cent who had never been in membership. The figure for membership tallies with the known average for all the London libraries except Holborn of 31.3 per cent in 1963: the libraries' own figures for registered members varied widely, ranging from 17.7 per cent in working-class Stepney to 48.1 per cent in Hampstead and (surprisingly in view of the figure given above for 1952) 51.2 per cent in Wandsworth.[2]

The most significant finding was the increasingly middle-class character of library membership. The percentages of members belonging to the various occupational groups were as follows (the national figure for each group is shown in brackets):

Groups 1 and 2 (professional and managerial)	22.6%	(7%)
Group 3 (lower managerial and executive)	23.2%	(10%)
Group 4 (highly skilled and senior clerical)	21.1%	(25%)
Group 5 (skilled and lower clerical)	16.1%	(20%)
Groups 6 and 7 (semi-skilled, unskilled, and unclassifiable)	17.0%	(38%) [3]

It will be observed that the first three groups, which constitute only 17 per cent of the population, account for 45.8 per cent of library membership. The statistics relating to education tell a similar story, 35 per cent of library members having stayed at school until at least 17 years of age.[4] At Esher in Surrey, a few years earlier, the same phenomenon had been illustrated in another way, when an inquiry revealed that library membership was positively correlated with the high rateable value of dwelling houses. The librarian rightly described this as "a minor social revolution when one considers the position twenty years ago."[5]

Readership surveys from the provinces confirmed the general picture presented by these surveys from the London area. In surveys of reading tastes fiction invariably came out at the top of the list, accounting for about two-thirds of all borrowing, with history, biography and travel as the next most

[1] B. Groombridge, *The Londoner and his Library* [1964].

[2] These figures illustrate the wide variations which are concealed in national averages of membership rates. Cf. the table for selected municipal and county libraries in Ministry of Education, *Standards of Public Library Service in England and Wales* [Bourdillon Report] (1962), p. 101.

[3] Groombridge, *op. cit.*, pp. 43, 110.

[4] *Op. cit.*, p. 35.

[5] H. R. J. Boulter, "Who Uses our Libraries?—A Survey of Coverage", in *Librarian and Book World*, Vol. XLIV (1955), p. 22.

popular category.[1] The few libraries which attempted a comparison over a period of years, however, all reported with satisfaction that the percentage of fiction issues was falling.

Stockport found that fiction issues had risen by 34 per cent over the period 1936–56, while non-fiction issues had increased by 164 per cent, the most dramatic increases being in science (222 per cent), fine arts (211 per cent), history (187 per cent), technology (173 per cent) and languages (142 per cent).[2] Folkestone, reviewing the years 1950–60, recorded that adult fiction issues had increased by 8 per cent whereas non-fiction issues had increased by 76 per cent, the largest increases under this heading being in the social sciences (192 per cent), history (158 per cent), and religion (110 per cent). This last is a surprising figure, and by no means typical. Among children, fiction issues had increased by 27 per cent, non-fiction issues by 440 per cent. The librarian commented:

"... there is a pronounced development of wider interests and clear evidence of reading of a much more purposive character. There is a growing and more persistent desire on the part of the general reader to understand the achievements of modern science and technology, and the demands of craftsmen, technicians and professional workers for textbooks and manuals have doubled. This may be surprising in a non-technical town, but it is not altogether unexpected to find an even more pressing interest in the wider aspects of living: in the arts, human speculation, and the intelligent use of leisure. Finally, there is an ever increasing call for books as tools: for that diversified class of simple, unpretentious, informative manuals, which help readers to play bowls, arrange flowers, decorate the house, keep tropical fish, and the like, more effectively."[3]

A table of issues for Greenock covering the years 1946 to 1966 shows no significant growth either in adult fiction issues or in junior issues, but a substantial growth in adult non-fiction (39 per cent) and a spectacular growth in reference issues (464 per cent), with the result that over the twenty-one year period adult fiction issues fell from 76 per cent to 66 per cent of the total. During these years history, travel and biography each averaged 10 per cent of the total non-fiction issues, and heavy demand from technical college and university students was reflected in the average figures for technology (22 per cent), fine arts (11 per cent), social sciences (11 per cent) and science (9 per cent).[4]

[1] For examples see County Borough of Reading, *Report of the Borough Librarian, 1948* (duplicated); the tables appended to Willesden Public Libraries, *The Willesden Library Service, 1894 to 1954: a Jubilee History and Annual Report, 1953–54* [Willesden 1954]; T. Cauter and J. S. Downham, *The Communication of Ideas: a Study of Contemporary Influences on Urban Life* (1954), p. 187, which gives comparative tables for Derby Public Libraries for 1938–39 and 1952–53; Plymouth Public Libraries, *Readership Survey, 1959* (duplicated, copy in Library Association library); Farnworth Public Library, *1911–1961, Golden Jubilee* (Farnworth 1961); B. Luckham, *The Library in Society* (1971), pp. 67–68.

[2] D. D. Nichols, *Twenty Years' Development: Stockport Public Libraries, 1936–1956* (Stockport 1957), pp. 9–10. During the years 1951–56 adult fiction issues had actually declined by 16 per cent.

[3] Borough of Folkestone Public Libraries, *Reading in Folkestone, 1950–1960* (Folkestone 1960, duplicated, copy in Library Association library).

[4] J. T. Hamilton, *Greenock Libraries: a Development and Social History, 1635–1967* (Greenock [1969]), Ch. xv. It should be observed that the tables in this chapter, which are accompanied by much detailed comment on particular categories of literature, show considerable variations from year to year, so that average figures must be treated with reserve.

Provincial surveys also confirmed the increasingly middle-class character of library membership, whether this was measured in terms of occupation or education. As early as 1953 a survey of 1200 people in Derby produced the following results:

	Class		Education		
	Middle	Working	Further	Secondary	Elementary
Total No.	351	849	78	218	891
No. borrowing from public library	137	170	39	89	89
Percentage borrowing	39	20	50	41	10

	Occupations			
	Non-manual	Skilled manual	Semi- and unskilled	Not in paid employment
Total No.	343	355	107	395
No. borrowing from public library	114	71	14	107
Percentage borrowing	33	20	13	27

The first set of figures shows the much higher percentage of borrowers among the middle class, even though there are in fact more working-class borrowers than middle-class borrowers. From the second and third sets of figures we see very clearly the low percentage of library use among those of elementary education and those engaged in semi-skilled or unskilled employments. Those not in paid employment, of course, include housewives.[1]

Later surveys, especially those undertaken by Bryan Luckham in the North-West of England, produced similar results.[2] In the great civic central libraries, which served a regional as well as a purely local function, the proportion of middle-class users was even greater, and of course such libraries inevitably attracted large numbers of students. A survey at the Manchester Central Library in 1964 showed that on a single day the 3681 users included 1450 students, 1854 other persons whose occupations were classifiable, and 377 others. In the second category 92 per cent were drawn from non-manual occupations.[3]

Both in the London area and in the provinces a number of libraries, following the example set by Edinburgh and Falkirk before the war, undertook surveys to ascertain the geographical distribution of their members. Since it had long been an article of faith among librarians that there should if possible be a library service point within a mile of every potential reader, it was no doubt

---

[1] Calculated from Cauter and Downham, *op. cit.*, p. 197. For the criteria used to determine social class see pp. 261 sqq.

[2] See especially B. Luckham, *The Library in Society* (1971), Ch. ii. Other surveys by the same author exist only in duplicated form: *Library Use in Leigh* (1965); Public Libraries and Adult Education Committee for the North-West, Research Paper No. 1, *Characteristics of Eccles Library Users* (1965); and Research Paper No. 3, *Preliminary Findings from Chester Library Survey* (1966). A pioneer survey at Chester made by the then City Librarian, J. G. McPeake, in 1960, is printed with notes by Luckham in *Research in Librarianship*, Vol. I, No. 2 (Feb. 1966), pp. 26–40.

[3] Luckham, *The Library in Society*, p. 56. Cf. the similar Liverpool survey reported by G. Chandler, "Provision of Special Services by Public Libraries", in Library Association, *Proceedings of the Public Libraries Conference . . . 1963* (1963), pp. 16–17.

satisfying that these surveys again showed a sharp falling off in library membership among people living beyond this distance from a library. This remained
true even in the 'sixties, in spite of the growing use of private cars. Here again
the big civic libraries were exceptional. In the Manchester Central Library
survey of 1964, 56 per cent of the 3500 users who stated their place of residence
came from outside Manchester—over 100 of them from outside the United
Kingdom.[1]

The great value of surveys such as these was that in a period of rapid
population changes they helped library authorities to ensure that adequate
coverage was maintained throughout their areas. This was particularly so where,
as at Manchester and Southampton, the survey was repeated after an interval of
some years.[2]

Reference Services and Advice to Readers

In spite of the new ideas in departmental organization described in the
last chapter, the great majority of libraries retained at least the traditional
distinctions between lending library, reference library, and children's library.
A feature of the post-war years was, as we have noted, the increasing emphasis,
both in urban libraries and in the counties, upon the importance of the reference
library. At the time of the McColvin Report this had been one of the weakest
aspects of library work,[3] but many urban libraries now improved their reference
service, and the more progressive counties, as well as providing a substantial
reference collection at headquarters, sought to ensure at least a basic service
at branch level. In London, which was particularly ill-served in this respect,
the Association of Metropolitan Chief Librarians agreed in 1956 on the establishment of nine regional reference libraries based on existing authorities, and
although this plan was never fully implemented some progress was made.[4]

As late as 1958 the position was still patchy. A Library Association report,
based on a survey made in that year, declared: "it is evident that reference
service is good in a few towns only, adequate in a few more, fair to poor in
many, and in some towns barely existent".[5] Judging from the text of the
report, however, this summing up seems rather severe, and certainly there was a
substantial improvement over the next seven years.

---

[1] Percentage calculated from information supplied by Mr. D. I. Colley, City Librarian.
A similar survey of 1954, printed in the *Annual Report, 1953–54*, showed a slight excess
of Manchester residents.

[2] See the article on Esher cited at p. 383, note 5; Southampton Public Libraries Committee, *Where do Readers Live?* (1963), and *Survey of Library Users* (1968); the *Census of
Library Use* prepared by the London Borough of Croydon (duplicated 1965); B. Luckham, *Library Use in Leigh* (duplicated 1965); the paper by the same author on *The Relation
of Distance to Library Membership and Use* (P.L.A.E.C. Research Paper No. 7, duplicated
1967); and his *Library in Society* (1971), pp. 33–35.

[3] See above, p. 336.

[4] *F.Y.W.L. 1951–55*, p. 249; *F.Y.W.L. 1961–65*, p. 338. The libraries concerned were
Battersea, Deptford, Hackney, Hammersmith, Islington, Lambeth, Westminster,
Woolwich, and the Guildhall.

[5] F. H. Fenton (ed.), *Reference Library Stocks: an enquiry into reference book provision in the
rate-supported libraries of England and Wales* (1960), p. 30.

A significant development was the increasingly important role of the "reader's adviser". Advice to readers had, of course, been a service given by the best librarians from the very beginning, but it was only in these post-war years that it came to be distinguished as a separate and specific professional function. Not surprisingly, it was the reference libraries which took the lead in this matter, but D. J. Foskett, in a well-argued little book published in 1952, urged that this was a mistake, since it was through the lending library that the majority of users made their first acquaintance with the public library.[1] It was in line with this thinking that A. W. McClellan in Tottenham and Frank Gardner at Luton planned the readers' advisory services for their new libraries in a central position accessible to both lending and reference collections.[2] By 1966 E. V. Corbett was able to report that: "In well administered libraries all advisory service is made the responsibility of qualified librarians who have the designation, 'Readers' Advisers',"[3] but one has the impression that this type of service was still restricted in the main to the larger libraries.[4]

Technical and Commercial Services

Increasing attention was also being paid to the development of commercial and technical library departments. By 1965, most towns with populations of 200 000 or more had either separate commercial and technical departments, or some kind of combined department; and the big city libraries were able to give a more and more sophisticated service to local commerce and industry—a service which complemented the detailed documentation provided by the special libraries attached to particular trades and industries. Here again it was the provinces that took the lead. Londoners had, of course, access to the resources of the great national libraries, including the splendid technical library at the Patent Office; but among local authority libraries only the commercial reference room at the Guildhall and the Commercial Economic and Technical Library at Westminster could match the information services available in the large provincial libraries.

In the early post-war years, because of rapid technological development during the war, the emphasis was on the building up of technical libraries, with the Library Association, the Department of Scientific and Industrial Research, and the Committee on Industrial Productivity all urging libraries to improve their facilities.[5] It was at this time that the Manchester Technical Library, which had had a somewhat chequered career since it was created in 1922, was re-established as a separate department (1947).[6] Liverpool's first Technical Library was established in 1952. Both of these quickly moved into the first rank. By the late 'fifties, as competition for world markets became sharper, and the improvement of commercial education became an urgent

[1] D. J. Foskett, *Assistance to Readers in Lending Libraries* (1952), pp. 38–39.

[2] See above, pp. 373, 376.

[3] E. V. Corbett, *An Introduction to Librarianship* (1963, 2nd edn. 1966), p. 207.

[4] Cf. J. D. Brown, *Manual of Library Economy* (7th edn., by R. N. Lock, 1961), pp. 39–40, 114, 149.

[5] *F.Y.W.L. 1951–55*, pp. 136–137.

[6] The story of the intervening years is told by G. E. Haslam in *Manchester Review*, Vol. IV (Autumn 1947), pp. 403–408.

objective of government policy,[1] commercial libraries also assumed a new importance. A sign of the times was the inclusion of a separate commercial library, with seating for 24 readers, in the new central library opened at Holborn in 1960.[2]

Three examples—Manchester, Glasgow and Hull—will illustrate the work of these new technical and commercial libraries. Manchester's Technical Library, after the re-opening in 1947, was so heavily used that within a few years it was necessary to increase the number of seats from 62 to 125. Even this was insufficient, and in 1958–59 the Technical Library exchanged accommodation with the Central Lending Library. This gave accommodation for over three hundred readers adjoining the main reference library in the Great Hall. The exchange was accompanied by the transfer of 15 000 volumes on science and technology from the Lending Library to the Technical Library, bringing the latter's total stock to 90 000 volumes, of which more than one-third were available on open access. The Library also subscribed to 1100 journals, and the current issues of nearly half of these were on display. The large collection of British and United States patents, much of it now on microfilm, was separately accommodated in a Patents and Microtexts Library. In the year 1959–60 the combined reference and lending issues (mainly the former) totalled nearly a million, over 14 000 inquiries were answered by telephone and over 400 by Telex, and over 6000 pages of photocopies were produced. In the 'sixties guides were published to technical translating dictionaries, abstracts and indexes, and non-book resources.[3]

It is interesting, in passing, to note the significance of new technical processes. Microphotography in a variety of forms—microfilm, microcard, microprint, microfiche—was now becoming absolutely essential as a means of handling and storing the vast amount of material, especially periodical and documentary material, being produced on both sides of the Atlantic.[4] Photo-copying became vastly easier, cheaper and clearer as a result of the introduction of the electromechanical process known as xerography, which did not require the use of sensitized paper. This process, invented by C. F. Carlson in the United States in 1938, and put on the market in 1950, had a revolutionary effect not only in technical libraries but in many other forms of library work. Among other uses it was particularly valuable as a cheap and easy method of reproducing periodical articles. The Post Office teleprinter system (Telex), which enabled typed messages to be transmitted telegraphically, was another invaluable means of communication, which was first introduced into the public library world by the Manchester Commercial Library in 1955. In spite of its high cost, its speed and accuracy made it increasingly popular, and within a few years it was in use in most leading public libraries.

[1] See Ministry of Education, *Report of the Advisory Committee on Further Education for Commerce* [McMeeking Report] (1959).
[2] Much useful information concerning the situation in the 'fifties is to be found in A. O. Hanson, "Commercial and Technical Library Service in Great Britain", in *Special Libraries*, Vol. XLVI (New York 1955), pp. 29–38.
[3] *F.Y.W.L. 1955–60*, pp. 179–181; and *1961–65*, p. 354.
[4] For technical details and post-war development see G. H. Davison, "Microcards and Microfiches: History and Possibilities", in *L.A.R.*, Vol. LXIII (1961), pp. 69–76.

Glasgow's Commercial Library was, as we have seen, the pioneer library of its kind in Great Britain.[1] On its establishment it was housed, along with Stirling's Library (the city's main lending library) in the Miller Street premises which had formerly been the home of the Mitchell Library (the main reference library). There it remained until 1954, when both libraries were transferred to the newly acquired Royal Exchange Building. The original accommodation available to the Commercial Library was very inadequate and for a long time its use was on a modest scale, but the move to new and more conveniently situated premises, coinciding with increased demand, soon transformed the situation. By 1965 the library was being extensively used both by business men and by business management students. It now had on open access a bookstock of 10 000 volumes and some 300 journals. It also had available more than 5000 trade catalogues; an index of United Kingdom manufacturers and agents; town, trade and telephone directories for the principal countries of the world; telegraphic addresses and cable codes; ordnance survey and other maps; and 5 000 000 British, colonial, and American patent specifications or abridgements.[2]

It may be mentioned by way of contrast that Edinburgh's Economics and Commerce Department, which had been established in 1932, proved unsuccessful, and in 1958 was re-integrated with the main lending and reference libraries. The result, we are told, was "a sharp increase in the use of books in the fields of economics, commerce, science and technology".[3] This quotation illustrates the fact that this department had to some extent been intended to serve the needs of industry as well as commerce. The same was long true of the Commercial Library at Glasgow: it was only in 1965 that a separate Library of Science and Technology was created as part of the Mitchell Library.[4]

In many of the large civic libraries new development was hampered by lack of space. This was the case whether the technical and commercial sections were separate, as at Birmingham, Liverpool and Manchester, or combined as at Leeds and Sheffield. Pressure on accommodation was especially acute at Birmingham, which in 1965 was still awaiting its long promised new central library building. Hull, thanks to the large extension opened in 1962, was more fortunate, and its Commercial and Technical Library, brought into being eleven years earlier and now enlarged and renamed the Library of Science, Technology and Commerce, was able to take over new quarters with seating for 80 readers and open access accommodation for 10 000 books and 620 periodicals. The coverage was necessarily wide rather than deep, but comprehensive collections were maintained in subjects of local importance such as paint, oils and fats, timber, and marine engineering, and information and lending services were provided for local firms.[5]

A remarkable and surprising feature of the 'fifties was the development of technical information services by the county libraries. A beginning was

[1] For its origins see above, pp. 143–144.
[2] *Glasgow Public Libraries, 1874–1966* (Glasgow 1966), pp. 36–7.
[3] Edinburgh Corporation, *Financial Review, 1968–69* (Edinburgh 1970), p. 143.
[4] *Glasgow Public Libraries, 1874–1966*, p. 32.
[5] *F.Y.W.L. 1951–55*, p. 138; and *1961–65*, p. 355; J. Binns, "Industry and the Public Library in Kingston-upon-Hull", in *ASLIB Proceedings*, Vol. V (1953), pp. 9–15; *L.A.R.* Vol. LXIV (1962), p. 466.

made in 1951 in Lancashire, when small collections of up-to-date technical books were provided at branches, together with subject lists and lists of new books. A larger collection of reference books, with bibliographies and indexes, was maintained at headquarters in Preston, and periodicals were available through inter-library loan.[1]

This was a valiant effort, but obviously limited in its possibilities. A more promising approach was adopted two years later by Hertfordshire, which, taking advantage of the fact that the county library was part of the county education system, made use of the technical colleges to provide a general technical library service. The time could not have been more appropriate, for in 1956 a Government White Paper urged the colleges to improve their libraries and make them centres for the supply of technical information and the exchange of technical ideas.[2] By this time Hertfordshire had already made the first move. When a new technical college was opened at Hatfield in 1953 the stock of the library was integrated with that of the county library. In 1956 Hatfield became the headquarters for a comprehensive county scheme known as HERTIS, embracing two other technical colleges (Watford and Letchworth), a college of art, an agricultural institute, and a number of colleges of further education, and linked through the county library with a group of special libraries attached to industrial and research organizations. A county technical librarian was appointed, and a union catalogue was compiled. Local firms were encouraged to use the college libraries both for borrowing and for reference, and in return for a modest annual subscription they received weekly information on new books and periodical articles relating to the subjects in which they were specially interested.[3]

Soon other counties began to follow Hertfordshire's example in seeking to link their nascent technical library services in one way or another with the libraries of their technical colleges. The Northamptonshire scheme, based on the Corby Technical College, embraced two other colleges and an agricultural institute as well as providing a service to commerce and industry. It began in 1957. The Nottinghamshire scheme, initiated in 1959, was centred on the technical colleges at Mansfield, Worksop and Beeston. By 1965 schemes were operating with varying success in Derbyshire, Essex, Gloucestershire, Herefordshire, Lindsey and Holland, Somerset, Staffordshire, West Sussex and Wiltshire. Lancashire County, although its main technical information centre was established at county headquarters, also took steps to form a link with the libraries of colleges of further education.[4] In Scotland the library of the Kirkcaldy Technical College was established in 1963 as the central technical library for Fife County.[5]

[1] H. Thompson, "Technical Library Services in the County", in *L.A. Conference Proceedings, 1955*, pp. 57–61.

[2] Ministry of Education, *Technical Education* (Cmd. 9703, 1956), p. 23; cf. the Ministry's Circular 322, *Libraries in Technical Colleges* (12 Apr. 1957).

[3] L. V. Paulin, "Technical Library Services", in *L.A. Conference Proceedings, 1960*, pp. 59–67; G. H. Wright, "Hertfordshire County Council Technical Library and Information Service", in *Journal of Documentation*, Vol. XVI (1960), pp. 190–202.

[4] *F.Y.W.L. 1956–60*, p. 187; and *1961–65*, pp. 243, 358; L. V. Paulin, *op. cit.;* "County Technical Library Services", in *L.A.R.*, Vol. LXIII (1961), pp. 119–125.

[5] Information from Mr. J. Brindle, County Librarian.

The county libraries did not, as a rule, attempt to provide a commercial library service, but Hertfordshire in 1965 created a commercial section based on its regional library at Stevenage—one of three libraries which housed major county reference collections.[1]

A great many libraries, both urban and county, created regional organizations to link together public and special libraries, academic and research libraries, and commercial and industrial concerns, for the more efficient dissemination and exploitation of technical information. Most of these regional organizations bore a family likeness to the scheme developed before the war by Sheffield and still flourishing under the name of SINTO (Sheffield Interchange Organisation).[2] After the war Manchester was first in the field in 1948 with MANTIS (Manchester Technical Information Service). Acton came next in 1951 with CICRIS (Co-operative Industrial and Commercial Reference and Information Service), and the 'fifties and early 'sixties brought a whole crop of unlovely acronyms, including such whimsical constructions as HATRICS (based at Southampton) and BRASTACS (based on Bradford). LADSIRLAC, which sounds like a character in the *Morte d'Arthur*, was the name given to the Liverpool scheme, inaugurated in 1955.[3]

The Liverpool Technical Library, since its opening in 1952, had already developed an inquiries service, a postal loans service to firms and other corporate bodies at an annual subscription of £1 per ticket, technical information lectures, and a monthly *Documents Bulletin* listing in U.D.C. order books, pamphlets, periodicals and patents. LADSIRLAC (the Liverpool and District Scientific, Industrial and Research Library Advisory Council) was created to facilitate consultation and encourage development of the service. In this scheme the loans were either from the library's own stock or (later) by arrangement from the National Lending Library, so that it was not necessary to compile a union catalogue. By 1965 there were 257 subscribers at a minimum of three guineas a year; loans totalled over 13 000; and the original bulletin had been divided into a *Technical Information Bulletin* and a *Commercial Information Bulletin*.[4]

Other Special Collections and Services

Special collections of many different kinds now abounded in the larger libraries, and in many smaller ones. Local history collections were almost universal; music libraries were common; art libraries, because of their cost, were restricted to a minority of libraries; other collections, e.g. related to particular writers or to particular industries, were random in their distribution, often depending on some local connection. Concerning most of these it is not

[1] *L.A.R.*, Vol. LXV (1963), p. 126; *F.Y.W.L. 1961–65*, pp. 242, 371.

[2] See above, pp. 290–291.

[3] Others included HERTIS, which has already been mentioned, CADIG (Coventry), HADIS (Huddersfield), HULTIS (Hull), LINOSCO (Stoke upon Trent), LIST (Teesside), MISLIC (Mid-Staffordshire), NANTIS (Nottingham and Nottingham Co.), NELTAS (Burnley), TALIC (Newcastle upon Tyne).

[4] G. Chandler, "Technical Information and Library Services", in *L.A.R.*, Vol. LXVI (1954), pp. 480–481; Liverpool Public Libraries, *Proceedings of the One-Day Technical Information Conference . . . 1955* (Liverpool 1955); LADSIRLAC, *Services to Industry and Commerce, 1964–65*. For the National Lending Library see below, 422–423.

necessary to say more than has already been said in earlier chapters, but the development of music libraries deserves brief comment.

In this field the Henry Watson Music Library at Manchester, with its great collection embracing in 1965 about 100 000 bound volumes and 250 000 unbound parts, was still outstanding. Next in size and importance came Liverpool, with some 77 000 bound volumes and 80 000 unbound parts, and Westminster, with 69 000 bound volumes and 18 000 unbound parts. The Westminster Central Music Library, founded and endowed by Mrs. Winifred Christie Moór, widow of the Hungarian pianist and composer Emanuel Moór, was placed in the care of the Westminster Public Libraries in 1948, and housed alongside their own music collection in their Buckingham Palace Road Branch. It quickly became widely known, and made its stock freely available to individual borrowers either directly or through other libraries.[1] Manchester and Liverpool also served a more than regional function, making sets of choral and orchestral parts available on subscription to societies and public libraries over a wide area.

In the county libraries the provision of sets of music for choirs, orchestras and schools was now almost a standard service, taking its place alongside the provision of sets of plays for dramatic societies and play-reading groups. The West Riding, in 1964, claimed that its new headquarters building housed "the finest collections of choral, orchestral, and brass band music and sets of plays in the country".[2] Across the Pennines Lancashire and Cheshire, from 1952, made sets of plays available on a subscription basis to all libraries in the North-West Region. This arrangement did not cover music, but within its own boundaries Lancashire supplied sets of music, hiring the orchestral scores where necessary from a commercial organization. Nottinghamshire, Staffordshire and Hertfordshire also held substantial music collections.[3]

A new feature was the provision in a number of libraries of collections of gramophone records. The origins of this went back, as we have noted, before the war, when Middlesex launched a record service for educational institutions.[4] Hereford County followed suit in 1940, and in 1945 became the first public library outside the United States to make records available on loan to the general public. Eric Leyland, in the following year, organized a lending service from Essex County's Chingford Branch, and in 1947 he made similar provision at Walthamstow—the first municipal library to engage in this activity.[5]

From this time provision gradually expanded, especially in London and the Home Counties. By 1949, 37 authorities were reported to have record collections and by 1954 about 50. Both Wales and Scotland were slow to venture

[1] J. Pemberton, "The Central Music Library", in Library World, Vol. LXIII (1961–62), pp. 318–322.

[2] L.A.R., Vol. LXVI (1964), p. 524.

[3] F.Y.W.L. 1951–55, p. 149; S. W. Davis, The History of Lancashire County Library (unpublished F.L.A. thesis 1967), pp. 338–339.

[4] See above, p. 288.

[5] L.A.R., Vol. LI (1949), p. 212; Vol. LVI (1954), p. 252; information from Mr. A. Shaw Wright, Director of Library Services, Herefordshire, and Mr. W. R. Maidment, Chief Librarian, Hampstead. Hampstead and Sutton Coldfield also made a beginning before the end of 1947.

into this field, and the McClelland Report in 1951 spoke of the need for "a carefully organised experiment" to see whether English practice in this matter could safely be imitated.[1] Motherwell and Wishaw, in 1953, was the first authority to take the plunge,[2] and Orkney County, in 1958, was the second (and the first to provide a mobile record library).[3] By 1964–65 expenditure on gramophone records (other than for educational institutions), was reported by 124 out of the 458 library authorities listed in *Public Library Statistics*. The extent of the provision is indicated by the following table:

Authorities incurring expenditure on gramophone records 1964–65
(Total of authorities listed shown in brackets)

	England	Wales	Scotland	Total
County boroughs	27 (81)	1 (4)	–	28 (85)
Metropolitan boroughs	15 (18)	–	–	15 (18)
Municipal boroughs	42 (159)	5 (11)	–	47 (170)
Urban districts	11 (70)	– (8)	–	11 (78)
Cities	–	–	– (4)	– (4)
Burghs	–	–	7 (19)	7 (19)
Counties	11 (46)	2 (13)	3 (25)	16 (84)
	106 (374)	8 (36)	10 (48)	124 (458) [4]

This table clearly indicates that at this stage the provision of gramophone records was an urban rather than a county function, even if we bear in mind that a number of counties are excluded from the figures because they provided only for schools or other educational institutions. Provision by the metropolitan boroughs was particularly good, and provision by the larger urban authorities was in general better than by the smaller authorities, but even among the larger authorities there were some surprising absentees, e.g. Birmingham, Manchester, Cardiff, and the four great Scottish cities. The most substantial collections, at this time, seem to have been those at Enfield, St. Pancras, and Westminster.

The reluctance of many library authorities to embark on provision of this kind was due not only to the expense (though this must have been a factor) but also to the fact that a gramophone record library brought with it a whole new range of administrative problems. New procedures had to be worked out (and very often additional staff appointed) for selection, purchase, accessioning, cataloguing, storage, handling and carriage; new types of equipment had to be purchased, and new forms and regulations provided. The greatest problem, as many librarians saw it, was to prevent damage through

[1] Scottish Education Department, Advisory Council on Education in Scotland, *Libraries Museums and Art Galleries* (Cmd. 8229, 1951), p. 69.
[2] W. R. Aitken, *A History of the Public Library Movement in Scotland to 1955* (Glasgow 1971), p. 201; *F.Y.W.L. 1961–65*, p. 255.
[3] *S.L.A. News*, No. 30 (Aug. 1958), p. 6.
[4] Calculated from Institute of Municipal Treasurers and Accountants and Society of County Treasurers, *Public Library Statistics, 1964–65* (1966). The list of authorities omits a number of counties and metropolitan boroughs, including some, such as Walthamstow and Westminster, which are known to have possessed record libraries.

careless use, or through the use of the wrong type of needle or instrument. So great was this fear that some libraries declined to lend to individuals at all, restricting loans to the accredited representatives of groups—e.g. musical societies. Where loans were made to individuals, borrowers had to choose their records, as they had once had to choose books, by means of an indicator, and were not permitted access to the storage racks. A deposit was commonly required, and sometimes, e.g. at Liverpool, an annual subscription. Jazz and popular dance music were not normally provided, but many collections did include Linguaphone and similar records for the learning of languages, and some also had records of poetry.

The advent in 1950 of long-playing records greatly reduced the risk of breakage, since these records were made of vinylite instead of the fragile shellac used for the traditional type of record, and were usually protected by stout "sleeves". The risk of damage remained, however, and some libraries e.g. Walthamstow, attempted to keep a check on this by providing with each record a circular chart of the same size, marked off into quadrants, on which any serious damage was indicated at the time of borrowing. A number of libraries reserved the right to check the record player the borrower intended to use, and Walthamstow purchased a special microscope to examine the pickup stylus needed for long-playing records.

These elaborate, time-consuming, and expensive precautions remind one of an earlier phase of library history. Before the end of the 'fifties a few libraries were using open access methods, but even in 1965, in something like half the libraries, the borrowers were still obliged to identify their needs from an indicator. In some cases, instead of the customary cards, the record sleeves were used to serve this purpose. Even in open access libraries the records were seldom classified on the shelves: as a rule they were arranged either under makers' numbers or under accession numbers. A catalogue was thus essential, and in the early years this was sometimes an ambitious affair, with entries under composers, conductors, and performers as well as under musical forms such as symphonies, overtures, and operas. As time went on, however, the tendency was towards greater simplicity, with catalogues based as far as possible on composers' names.

In 1965, in fact, the gramophone record library was still in a state of experiment and transition, and its future development was a little uncertain.[1]

Other non-book materials provided by libraries included maps, prints, photographs, slides, filmstrips, films, collections of illustrations, and original paintings. Both the McClelland Report[2] and the Bourdillon Report gave their

---

[1] The development of the service is well covered in the professional literature: see especially C. D. Overton, "A Gramophone Record Library Service", in *L.A.R.*, Vol. XLIX (1947), pp. 224–225; the special issue in *L.A.R.*, Vol. LI (1949), pp. 203–217; E. T. Bryant, "Long-Playing Records and the Gramophone Library", in *L.A.R.*, Vol. LIII (1951), pp. 76–78; L. G. Lovell, "Gramophone Record Provision in Public Libraries", in *L.A.R.*, Vol. LVI (1954), pp. 251–259; and J. W. Howes, "Gramophone Record Library Procedure", in *L.A.R.*, Vol. LXI (1959), pp. 289–294. An article by C. D. Overton in T. Landau, *Encyclopaedia of Librarianship* (1958, 3rd edn. 1966), pp. 193–197, gives a useful summary and bibliography.

[2] Scottish Education Department, Advisory Council on Education in Scotland, *Libraries Museums and Art Galleries* (Cmd. 8229, 1951), pp. 68–69.

blessing to such provision.[1] Maps, prints and photographs often formed an important part of local collections. Much of this material was not available on loan, but many libraries had collections of slides, photographs and the like illustrating local subjects which were readily available to schools and societies. Collections of illustrations, designed chiefly for educational use, might also include material on geography and natural history, and reproductions of works of art. Indeed the maintenance of such collections was much commoner than the scanty references in the professional literature would suggest— commoner than collections of gramophone records.[2] Birmingham's collection of over 200 000 mounted illustrations was outstanding.[3] The provision of films, on the other hand, did not become an important feature of the library service.

A particularly comprehensive Illustrative Aids Scheme was developed by Nottingham County from 1945. It embraced mounted illustrations, framed reproductions of paintings, models and museum cases, gramophone records, film projectors, film strips and filmstrip projectors. It was used by schools and societies, and became so popular that in 1949 it had to be separated from the county library and established as a separate department.[4]

Holborn, in 1954, pioneered a scheme for the loan of original paintings by local artists. The artists were invited to exhibit their works on library premises, and readers were invited to borrow. Loans were for a period of three months, at a charge of 10s. Hiring fees went to the artists but, if the picture was eventually sold (at a price not exceeding 20 guineas), the library claimed 15 per cent commission. After a slow start public interest gradually built up, and in the first four years more than 650 loans were made and 27 pictures were purchased.[5] Similar schemes were later developed by Aldershot,[6] and in Scotland by Motherwell.[7]

Concerning provision for blind readers there is by this date little to be said. For the most part such readers now secured their books direct from the National Library for the Blind. A few public libraries, mainly in the North of England and in Scotland, operated a service with bulk supplies from the National Library; fewer still now held their own stocks. For blind people who found difficulty in reading by touch an invaluable alternative was provided by the British Talking Book Service for the Blind, which was established in 1935 and operated under the aegis of the Royal National Institute for the Blind. It made use first of long-playing records (far in advance of their commercial use) and later of tapes.

---

[1] Ministry of Education, *Standards of Public Library Service in England and Wales* (1962), p. 26.

[2] *Op. cit.*, p. 108.

[3] *Notes on the History of the Birmingham Public Libraries, 1861–1961* (Birmingham 1962), p. 25.

[4] P. Dean, *The County Library Movement in England, 1938–48* (unpublished F.L.A. Essay, 1949), pp. 23–4.

[5] J. Davies, "Holborn's Picture Lending Scheme", in *L.A.R.*, Vol. LX (1958), pp. 193–194.

[6] S. M. Jarvis, "Public Library Picture Loans", in *Library World*, Vol. LIX (1957–58), pp. 83–84.

[7] W. E. G. Critchley, "Motherwell Picture Loan Collection", in *S.L.A. News*, No. 50 (Nov.-Dec. 1961).

In public library provision for hospital inmates there were some notable achievements, especially towards the close of the period. At Lincoln, for example, a new library wing at the County Hospital, opened in 1963, was provided not only with a general library for patients and staff but also with a full information and reference service, including periodicals, for medical and nursing staff.[1] Hertfordshire, in the same year, made comparable provision at the new Queen Elizabeth II Hospital at Welwyn Garden City.[2]

On the whole, however, progress was disappointingly slow and patchy. The National Health Service Act of 1946, though it created a co-ordinated hospital service, did nothing to clarify the confusion surrounding hospital libraries. Hospital management committees and boards of governors were free either to make their own arrangements for library service, or to approach a public library or voluntary organization. The St. John-Red Cross Hospital Library Department, which was still the leading voluntary body in the field,[3] had come into existence primarily to meet the needs of servicemen and ex-servicemen, and from 1950 was obliged to make a charge to civilian hospitals for its services (initially 5s. per annum per occupied bed, increased by 1961 to 13s. 6d.).[4] It took its work very seriously, and provided training and certification for its voluntary helpers, but of course they were not professional librarians, and this was for the Library Association a point of cardinal importance.

The Association did all it could to encourage the development of the work. It established a specialist certificate in hospital librarianship,[5] published manuals of guidance,[6] created a Hospital Library and Handicapped Readers Group,[7] and eventually produced a statement of recommended standards.[8]

An important report published by the King Edward's Hospital Fund for London in 1959 urged the need for higher standards of accommodation, equipment and book supply, and put the cost of an efficient service at £1 per bed per annum for a voluntary service and £3 per bed per annum where paid staff were to be employed. Drawing attention to the great variety of existing services, the report expressed the belief that "in the ideal hospital library

---

[1] *Lincoln City Libraries 1914–1964* [Lincoln 1964], pp. 10–11; D. G. Burgess, "The Hospital Library Service in Lincoln", in *Library World*, Vol. LXVII (1965–66), pp. 290–294.

[2] W. W. Partington, "The Queen Elizabeth II Hospital Library", in *Postgraduate Medical Journal*, Vol. LXII (1966), pp. 537–42. For accounts of some earlier developments see Ross, "Southmead Hospital Library, Bristol", in *L.A.R.*, Vol. LI (1949), pp. 345–347; K. M. Allsop, *A Mental Hospital Library: report of an experiment at Lancaster Moor Hospital in 1947–49* (1951); L. Aldrich, "Saxondale [Notts.]: a Mental Hospital Library", in *L.A.R.*, Vol. LXIII (1961), pp. 248–253; J. D. Stewart (ed.), *Report on the Library System of London and the Home Counties, 1959* (1961), pp. 25–28; and J. T. Hamilton, *Greenock Libraries: a Development and Social History* (Greenock [1969]), pp. 92–94.

[3] See above, pp. 297–299.

[4] G. W. Barker, "The St. John and British Red Cross Hospital Library", in *Libri*, Vol. IV (1954), pp. 393–400.

[5] This certificate, first offered in 1947, continued till the Association's new syllabus came into operation in 1964—see *F.Y.W.L. 1961–65*, p. 193.

[6] C. E. A. Bedwell, *Manual for Hospital Librarians* (1947); M. E. Going (ed.), *Hospital Libraries and Work with the Disabled* (1963).

[7] The origin of the Group, in 1961, is described in *F.Y.W.L. 1961–65*, pp. 190–192.

[8] Library Association, *Hospital Libraries: recommended standards for libraries in hospitals* (1965).

service of the future the public libraries would be the major source of the supply of books and that this would be a recognised function and duty of all such libraries"—a view that was afterwards endorsed by the Bourdillon Committee.[1]

In spite of this official encouragement, however, a Ministry of Health inquiry made in 1963 revealed that only 75 per cent of hospitals provided any kind of library service for their patients; nearly half those which had libraries were served by the St. John-Red Cross organization; and only 10 per cent were run solely by public libraries, though in some hospitals there was a combination of services.[2] Figures for the South-East Metropolitan Hospital Region illustrate the position in more detail. Of 128 hospitals which supplied information (about 75 per cent of the total), 105 had library services; and of these 50 were supplied by St. John-Red Cross, 39 by public libraries, 10 by the hospital authorities, 9 by public authorities and hospitals jointly, 8 by Toc H, 3 by the W.V.S., and 7 by other voluntary bodies.[3]

Clearly the hospital library service still had a long way to go. A related but administratively simpler problem was that of providing books for old people's homes and for readers housebound through sickness or infirmity. For the county libraries this kind of provision could easily be fitted into the normal routine, and in the 'fifties and 'sixties an increasing number of urban librarians were responding to this need, often again with assistance from the W.V.S. and other voluntary organizations. "Many authorities", noted the Report on London and the Home Counties for 1959, "report services to old and disabled people; these include mobile services and individual visits". Westminster, in the previous year, had lent over 20 000 books to the aged and infirm through their Personal Delivery Service.[4] In 1962 more than half the 53 county and municipal libraries studied by the Bourdillon Committee were providing a service for housebound readers.[5]

A serious attempt was made during the post-war years to improve the provision of books to the inmates of prisons and borstal institutions, and to link this provision more closely to the public library service. What the Prison Commissioners called "a new and fruitful departure" was initiated in 1942, when the East Suffolk County Library agreed to organize the library at the Hollesley Bay Borstal Institution as a county branch. In 1944 a similar plan was put into operation for Durham Prison, in collaboration with Durham County Library, and when in 1946 the prison authorities faced the task of rebuilding "the depleted and tattered libraries" which had survived the war, it became accepted policy to seek the assistance of the public libraries.[6]

---

[1] King Edward's Hospital Fund for London, *Hospital Library Services: a pilot survey* (1959), p. 48; *Bourdillon Report*, p. 25.   [2] *F.Y.W.L. 1961–65*, p. 192.
[3] B. M. Sanders, *Library Services in Hospitals* (1966), pp. 8–11. Many of the hospitals were receiving books from more than one source.
[4] J. D. Stewart (ed.), *Report on the Library System of London and the Home Counties, 1959* (1961), p. 27.
[5] *Bourdillon Report*, p. 107. For pioneer services for housebound readers at Edinburgh and Dumfries in 1963 see *S.L.A. News*, No. 62 (Jan.-Feb. 1964), p. 27, and No. 67 (Nov.-Dec. 1964), p. 10.
[6] Home Office, *Report of the Commissioners of Prisons . . . 1942–1944* (Cmd. 7010, 1947), pp. 45–46; *Report of the Commissioners of Prisons . . . 1946* (Cmd. 7271, 1947), p. 45.

By 1951, in England and Wales, 15 municipal libraries and 13 county libraries were providing some kind of service to a total of 31 prisons, and 1 municipal library and 10 county libraries were assisting borstal institutions. Fourteen prisons and five borstal institutions still relied on libraries provided by the Prison Commissioners, supported by the Central Education Library at Wakefield.[1] The service that public libraries were able to give, within the restrictions of prison discipline and within the limits of a capitation fee of 5s. per annum (10s. by 1965) was not particularly good. Usually the most that could be managed was a small loan collection, changed from time to time, and operated by a prisoner or prison officer.[2] None the less the libraries were well used and appreciated, and were felt by the prison authorities to be of great value:

> "The increased calls made upon the resources of the local authorities who are responsible for providing library services indicate that the importance of books in the day to day life of the inmate is greater than is generally supposed. The type of books most enjoyed varies very little: Westerns, crime mysteries and war narratives head the list, but many inmates develop from these to a degree of maturity in which they conceive books as tools of knowledge. With its thousands of books neatly arranged on shelves, the mere presence of the modern prison library suggests the outside world, with all the promise of interest and adventure, and, in consequence, books are handled better and with more than average care. There are few complaints of damage to books, and this in itself, shows the influence that they can, and do, have on the offender."[3]

Services for Young People

In spite of the disruption caused by bombing, evacuation, and the destruction or requisitioning of premises, the demand for library services for children continued to grow during the war years.[4] In 1945 a Youth Libraries Section was established in the Library Association, and in the following year special optional papers on work with children were introduced into the Fellowship examination.

Even before the war finished a special Work with Young People Group was considering future development. Its report was first published in 1946,[5] and was revised in 1949 and 1951.[6] All three versions draw attention to the weaknesses of the existing situation: the children's departments of many public libraries were ill-equipped, poorly stocked and badly staffed, and thousands of schools had no effective library. The first report sought to establish

---

[1] R. F. Watson, *Prison Libraries* (1951), pp. 16–18. In Scotland, in 1955, eleven prisons and borstals were being served by public libraries—W. R. Aitken, *A History of the Public Library Movement in Scotland to 1965* (Glasgow 1971), p. 207.

[2] See the acid comments in J. D. Stewart (ed.), *Report on the Library System of London and the Home Counties, 1959* (1961), pp. 28–29.

[3] Home Office, *Report of the Commissioners of Prisons . . . 1960* (Cmd. 1467, 1961), p. 19; cf. *F.Y.W.L. 1961–65*, pp. 201–202.

[4] See above, pp. 330–331.

[5] *L.A.R.*, Vol. XLVIII (1946), pp. 6–9.

[6] Library Association, *Work with Young People and School Libraries* (1949); *L.A.R.*, Vol. LIII (1951), pp. 111–114.

the position that the public libraries had a measure of responsibility for both sides of the work, but the final report, no doubt under pressure from the School Library Association,[1] took up a more realistic attitude:

> "The responsibility for the provision of a general library service outside the school to children and adolescents rests chiefly with the library authorities, although there are points at which the co-operation of the education authorities may be of great value . . . . The school library, on the other hand, should be a vital part of the school itself, developing organically from within it and planned and administered to serve its particular needs. The responsibility for the provision and control of school libraries therefore rests with the education authorities and with the individual schools, the staffs of which are trained and appointed to provide for the educational needs of their pupils. There are, however, points at which the schools can profitably seek the help and advice of the professional librarian. The assistance of the public library may also be sought in the loan of books, particularly in the initial stages of school library formation."

As in other branches of the library service, progress in the first decade after the war was slow. A survey carried out by the Youth Libraries Section in 1954 provides us with an outline picture at that date.[2] Particulars collected from 468 out of 581 library authorities in Great Britain showed, as might be expected, tremendous variety in the quality of the provision. Many smaller authorities were spending less than £100 per annum, while in large authorities the expenditure might be as high as £24 000. Stocks ranged from 140 volumes to nearly half a million; 160 authorities had no reference books, and 183 did not supply magazines. The figure of 365 authorities (78 per cent) which had separate children's rooms was at least a considerable improvement on the figure of less than 60 per cent reported in 1942 by McColvin.[3] Children's sections (as distinct from separate departments) were found in 310 authorities, and probably most authorities made some kind of provision. Only 84, however, maintained special sections for adolescents.

Extension activities were varied and widespread. The most popular were library lessons or class visits (recorded by 332 authorities), book displays (250), and story hours (164), but the list also included magazines, book weeks, lectures, film shows, reading circles and play-reading groups.

A surprising and encouraging feature of the report was the extent of the co-operation it revealed between the public libraries and the schools. Nearly all the county libraries which answered the inquiry, more than half the county borough libraries, and many borough and urban district libraries, were providing a school library service, usually at the cost of the education authority.[4]

Significantly, 255 library authorities had no designated children's librarians; and of the 213 authorities which had designated posts, only 181 had posts on professional grades. This shortage of professional staff was still being com-

---

[1] This Association was founded in 1936. A School Libraries Section of the Library Association, established in the same year, was wound up in 1946.

[2] Library Association, Youth Libraries Section, *Survey of Public Library Service for Children, 1954* [1955].

[3] Cf. above, p. 336.

[4] The term "County boroughs" here includes the four Scottish "Counties of Cities", and also, rather curiously, the Scottish "royal burghs".

mented on five years later, in the report of the London and Home Counties Branch:

> "Too much is made of 'suitable temperament' and 'desire to work with children': these are necessary attributes but equivalent 'suitabilities' and 'desires' must operate in the case of every other branch of librarianship. Recruitment to children's work appears to suffer because working with children is regarded as a form of dedication rather than a professional task of which every librarian must have some experience."[1]

A second survey of services to children was made by the Youth Libraries Section in 1958–59.[2] The figures, based this time on returns from 446 authorities, are not in a form easily comparable with those of the earlier survey, but such improvements as there were seem to have been little more than marginal. The total number of separate children's libraries, for example, increased from 829 to 910, and the number of authorities with designated posts from 213 to 227, but the number of authorities with designated professional posts fell from 181 to 178. This survey deals separately with Scotland, and it is of interest to note that the service there seems to have been somewhat more austere in character, with extension services "the exception rather than the rule":

> "No authority has yet promoted play-reading groups or reading circles. Clubs, book quizzes, film shows, book weeks and lectures are mentioned by one or two. Story hours, and the publication of some kind of magazine, are rather more frequent. The commonest extension activity is undoubtedly the organisation of library lessons or class visits."[3]

The number of authorities providing a service to schools showed some increase, from 180 to 202. In about two-thirds of the cases the service consisted of a deposit collection which was changed from time to time. The administrative position remained as confused as ever:

> "There is no uniformity of practice regarding grants from local education authorities nor apparently any consistency in the basis of calculation. In some county boroughs the school library service is administered either entirely or partly by the public library, in some cases independently, in others on behalf of the education committee. In the administrative areas of the county councils a number of independent library authorities receive grants from the education committee, although the more general practice is for the County Library to receive a grant to operate the service in the whole of the administrative area. In some cases a school library service is in operation with no financial assistance from the local education authority."[4]

One may suspect, however, that these surveys, which are mainly statistical in character, underestimate the improvement in the quality of the service that

---

[1] J. D. Stewart (ed.), *Report on the Library System of London and the Home Counties, 1959* (1961), pp. 19–20. This and the preceding Report (1954), include interesting details on children's work.

[2] Library Association, Youth Libraries Section, *Public Library Service for Children, 1958–1959* (1960).

[3] *Op. cit.*, p. 7.

[4] *Op. cit.*, p. 5. For a more detailed statement on the position in the counties, see Library Association, County Libraries Group, *A Policy Survey of the County Libraries of the United Kingdom, 1951–1961* (1963), pp. 24–26, 42–43, 55–56.

was gradually taking place throughout the post-war years as old buildings were replanned or replaced and old stocks renewed. In the 'sixties progress was accelerated by a number of factors. One was the impetus given both by the Roberts Report, which officially affirmed the importance of children's libraries "with adequate stocks and expert guidance,"[1] and by the Bourdillon Report, which stressed the need for "specially trained staff both at central and at major branch libraries."[2]

New buildings were another factor, making possible at long last the kind of provision many librarians had been dreaming of for years. Luton, for example, took advantage of its new central library in 1962 to create a special children's story-room, in the form of a fairy castle;[3] while Dover created a separate children's library, complete with its own study and reference room, in a park within a stone's throw of the central library.[4] Yet another factor was the enormous improvement in the quality of children's books. This was particularly noticeable in non-fiction books, and was reflected in figures for children's reading such as those cited above for Folkestone.[5] The Carnegie Medal, instituted by the Library Association in 1937 for an outstanding children's book of the year, and the Kate Greenaway Medal, established by the Association in 1955 as an annual award for the illustrator of a children's picture book, must have encouraged this trend, which to many librarians seemed one of the most important developments of the post-war years.[6]

In spite of continuing staff shortages (which did not ease until the late 'sixties) by 1965 some splendid and imaginative work was going on in both urban and county libraries, and many of the latter were within reach of their objective of a comprehensive service covering all children in and out of school. Lancashire County, for example, was in 1964 providing a service through 96 full-time and part-time branches, 125 centres, 11 mobile libraries, 265 secondary school libraries and 754 primary school libraries, and plans were in hand to supply libraries to the minority of primary schools still unprovided for. Issues of books to children (two-thirds of them through the schools) accounted for over $4\frac{1}{2}$ millions out of the County's total issues of nearly 12 millions. The only discouraging feature of the situation was that five out of fourteen posts for qualified children's librarians were vacant.[7]

Lancashire's record is specially impressive because its school library service was entirely a post-war creation. This is, however, only one of many success stories. Among county libraries which organized a particularly comprehensive service we may mention Wiltshire, whose schools service included not only books but also, for special projects, non-book materials such as films, photographs, and facsimiles of documents;[8] Nottinghamshire, which in 1958

---

[1] *Roberts Report*, p. 8.

[2] *Bourdillon Report*, p. 24.

[3] L.A.R., Vol. LXIV (1962), p. 456.

[4] L.A.R., Vol. LXVI (1964), pp. 550–551. For another separate children's library, in a block of flats in Pimlico, Westminster, see *L.A.R.*, Vol. LXII (1960), pp. 367–368.

[5] See above, p. 384.

[6] Cf. A. Ellis, *Library Services for Young People in England and Wales, 1830–1970* (1971), pp. 95–96, 127–132.

[7] Lancashire County Council, *Report of the County Librarian for the Years 1962–1964*.

[8] Ellis, *op. cit.*, p. 150.

pioneered "holiday mobiles" to meet the needs of children while the schools were closed;[1] and Hertfordshire, which in 1961 sponsored the first Children's Library Week. This last venture was on a much bigger scale than the "book weeks" which had frequently been organized in the past, mainly in the municipal libraries.[2] It was based on ten towns, each of which organized major book exhibitions, talks by children's authors, artists and publishers, and school visits. It was undoubtedly successful in stimulating interest (both among children and among adults) and in creating goodwill, but it involved the full-time work of more than forty members of staff, including fifteen children's librarians. Because of this, and because of the monetary outlay involved, it did not prove practicable to follow it up, as had been hoped, with a Children's Library Week on a national scale.[3]

As in the years between the wars, the libraries of London and the home counties continued to be in the forefront of children's work. Among outstanding municipal libraries were Hendon and St. Pancras. At Hendon the Children's Librarian was Eileen H. Colwell, who had been appointed as long ago as 1926 (actually before the library service was opened to the adult public), and who now had an international reputation as an expert on children's books and children's library activities. Story-telling was always a great feature here, and in 1963–64, in spite of the counter-attraction of television, story-hours for pre-school children and for two older age-groups were bringing record attendances. In book weeks Hendon was, as we have noted earlier, a pioneer,[4] and an annual parents' evening was another feature of the programme. There were exhibitions, book quizzes, puppet shows, indeed, as Miss Colwell herself reported, "every kind of extension work which introduces books".[5]

From the very beginning, the children themselves were encouraged to help with the work and to take a simple test of proficiency.[6] Close contact was also maintained with the schools: the school libraries were all administered by the public library, and special books were provided in connection with school projects.[7]

At St. Pancras both Frederick Sinclair, who was librarian from 1934 until his death in 1953, and W. A. Taylor who succeeded him, attached great importance to this side of the work. Taylor began his Annual Report for 1955–56 with an account of the junior libraries, to emphasize his belief that "the provision of books for children is the basis of all our work." He reported with pride that issues to children had reached a record figure of 188 000 (nearly 50 per cent non-fiction) and that more than half the children in the borough were registered readers. He attributed this happy position in large measure to the work of specialist staff—a children's librarian at each full-time branch and a

[1] Op. cit., p. 94.

[2] Op. cit., pp. 76–77, 102.

[3] L.A.R., Vol. LXIII (1961), p. L100. Details of organization are given in a duplicated report prepared by the County Library.

[4] See above, p. 293.

[5] Hendon Library Service, Annual Report, 1963–64, pp. 13–14.

[6] This practice was not uncommon: Ellis, op. cit., p. 51, notes that it was introduced by Berwick Sayers at Wallasey as early as 1915.

[7] Annual Report, 1963–64. This report was the last issued before Hendon's absorption into the new Borough of Barnet. Miss Colwell retired in 1967.

senior children's librarian with overall responsibility. Extension activities referred to included story hours, play-reading groups, puppetry, stamp clubs, music groups, talks, films, and an annual book week. School libraries were supplemented by bulk loans, and special classes were arranged at two branches to assist backward readers (many of them children of Cypriot immigrants).

The response of the children to efforts such as these was sometimes embarrassingly enthusiastic. The *Sunday Times* of 8th November, 1964, described the new Nine Elms Branch at Battersea as "reeling under an invasion of children":

> "They sweep through the glass doors after school into its warmth, polish, brightness, tropical fish and modern sculpture. They read, do their homework, meet their friends, change their books, chat with the library staff, put their feet up on the teak tables and generally treat the place as their club.
>
> "They took out the whole stock of 2000 children's books in the first week, and the council had to rush new orders. They so jammed their own section of the library that the council had to double its size. It is still not enough."[1]

The problem that still worried many librarians was that this enthusiasm so often vanished when the child left school. It was hoped that the raising of the school leaving age under the Education Act of 1944 would help to counteract this tendency, but the Crowther Committee reported in 1959 that only 16 per cent of the ex-secondary modern school pupils interviewed in connection with their inquiry were still in membership of a public library two years after leaving school.[2]

This situation led a number of libraries to focus renewed attention upon provision for the adolescent. In the London area, in 1959, most libraries had special collections of books for this group, housed usually in the junior library, sometimes in the adult library. Walthamstow, which had led the way in this kind of work before the war,[3] was unique in having a separate department, with 15 000 books and a staff of three. Shoreditch's large collection was in the junior library.[4]

Outside the London area only a minority of libraries maintained special collections for teenagers. One of them was Preston, which established a self-contained "youth library" in 1953. It had both reference and lending facilities, and operated with modest success for nearly twenty years.[5] Hertfordshire and Nottinghamshire demonstrated their interest by producing special annotated booklists, and in 1965 the County Libraries Group of the Library Association published *Attitudes and Adventure: a selection of books for young adults*, compiled by Colin and Sheila Ray. Nottinghamshire also created, in 1962, a special reference collection of books for teenagers for the use of teachers, librarians and youth leaders.[6]

[1] *L.A.R.*, Vol. LXVI (1964), p. 542.
[2] Ministry of Education, Central Advisory Council (England), *15 to 18* (1959), Vol. I, p. 112. Cf. the figures for Nottinghamshire given in M. F. Austin, "Library Service for Youth," in *L.A.R.*, Vol. XLIX (1947), p. 61.   [3] See above, p. 294.
[4] J. D. Stewart (ed.), *Report on the Library Systems of London and the Home Counties, 1959* (1961), p. 21.
[5] Harris Public Library, Preston, *Annual Reports, 1952–53* and *1953–54*, and information from Mr. J. Brown, Borough Librarian. The youth library was closed in 1972.
[6] *L.A.R.*, Vol. LXIV (1962), p. 180.

As early as 1945 the Library Association had urged that library authorities should establish close relationships with youth clubs, supply them with books, and assist them to build up libraries of their own.[1] The importance of this connection was re-emphasized in 1960 with the issue of the Albemarle Report on the youth service, which *inter alia* suggested that public libraries should remain open for use by teenagers, on at least some nights of the week, until 10 p.m.[2] The Library Association created a Service for Youth Sub-Committee in 1961, invited Stanley Rowe, honorary secretary of the National Association of Youth Leaders and Organisers, to address its 1962 annual conference, and organized a number of regional conferences to bring together librarians, teachers, youth leaders, and others concerned.[3] At the Public Libraries Conference held in 1963 the Mayor of Tottenham suggested that libraries should try to attract the "unclubbable" by setting aside part of their premises to form a coffee bar open till about 10.30 p.m. This would be "just a free and easy meeting place within the library", with "staff to serve coffee, keep an eye on the place, and act as hosts if required."[4]

All this activity was at least a token of good intent, and some positive steps did merge from it. In Leicestershire, for example, an experiment was begun in 1964 in the provision of collections of books for youth clubs, and mobile libraries visited some villages when clubs were in session.[5] On the whole, however, the effort to make contact with the youth clubs proved a difficult and unrewarding enterprise, and in 1965 the problem of the teenage non-reader seemed as far from solution as ever.

Library Administration

By 1945 library administration throughout Great Britain had achieved a substantial degree of uniformity, based on open access, the Dewey classification, the card or sheaf catalogue (usually author and subject), and the Browne system of "pocket-card charging". Twenty years later all these were still basic features of most library systems, but some libraries had already introduced quite drastic reforms, and nearly everywhere there was a disposition to look again at long-established routines. Office procedures were overhauled and modernized, unnecessary registration and accessioning procedures were eliminated, and wherever the scale of operations justified it a variety of sophisticated equipment was brought into play—electric typewriters, adding machines, duplicators and all kinds of other copying machines, punched cards and their accompanying sorting machines, intercom systems for internal communications, Telex for external communications, and so forth.[6]

---

[1] *L.A.R.*, Vol. XLVIII (1946), p. 9.

[2] Ministry of Education, *The Youth Service in England and Wales* (Cmnd. 929, 1960), p. 59.

[3] S. Rowe, "Libraries and Youth", in *L.A. Conference Proceedings, 1962*, pp. 21–26; H. K. G. Bearman, *"Literacy, Libraries and Youth,"* in Library Association, London and Home Counties Branch, *Book Provision for Special Needs* (1962), pp. 31–40; S. G. Bannister, "Libraries and Youth: a survey of progress", in *L.A.R.*, Vol. LXVI (1964), pp. 26–28.

[4] D. Clarke, "Library Services for Children and Young People", in Library Association, *Proceedings of the Public Libraries Conference . . . 1963* (1963), pp. 28–33.

[5] Ellis, *op. cit.*, p. 148.

[6] For a review of some obsolete procedures see W. B. Paton, "First Things First", in *L.A.R.*, Vol. LII (1950), pp. 2–7.

The basic cause of these changes lay in the growing pressure on the library service, combined with continuing financial stringency, but much was due also to increasing professionalization; to the development of management skills in the local authorities; to the example of the United States; and to the emergence of new techniques in special libraries and documentation centres. The influence of these last is particularly marked in the developments already noted in the facsimile reproduction of documents.[1]

It was in the central London boroughs that the pressure of peak issues first led to a radical reconsideration of the Browne charging system. Under this system the process of issuing, as most library users know from experience, is very quick: it is when the book is returned that delays are apt to occur, especially when there is a long queue of readers and several members of staff are trying to recover tickets from the issue trays. Some way of simplifying or speeding up the machinery was therefore very desirable. The most drastic simplification was that achieved by L. R. McColvin and his staff at Westminster, through the introduction in 1954 of the system known as token charging. Each reader was given a ticket valid for a year, and three tokens. In order to borrow a book he showed his ticket and surrendered a token, and when he returned the book he was given a token in its place. At the end of the year he was required to produce his three tokens or pay 10s. per token in default. The trouble about this system was that it left the library with absolutely no record of where individual books were at any given time; it was impossible to check on books retained for an undue period; and the identification of reserved books was more difficult. Although, therefore, a number of other libraries adopted the system within the next few years, sometimes in a modified form, most of them did so for fiction issues only, retaining the Browne system for non-fiction.[2]

More satisfactory from the point of view of book control were systems that operated on the principle of "delayed discharge", so that at peak periods the processes involved in discharging loans could be postponed until a more suitable time. One such system was punched card charging, introduced experimentally by Eric Leyland at Walthamstow in 1948,[3] and adopted at Holborn ten years later.[4] The Walthamstow system used two identically punched book cards—an orange card which was withdrawn at the time of lending and stamped with the reader's number, and a blue card which was withdrawn at the time of return and ultimately matched against its fellow by machine sorting.[5]

[1] See above, p. 388. The term "reprography" was coined in 1954 to cover the various processes involved. An Institute of Reprographic Technology was incorporated in 1960, and in the following year the Library Association sponsored the formation of a Council for Microphotography and Document Reproduction (later the Microfilm Association of Great Britain). See *F.Y.W.L., 1961–65*, pp. 546–547.

[2] L. R. McColvin, "Westminster Token Charging Scheme", in *L.A.R.*, Vol. LVI (1954), pp. 259–261. For other libraries using the system see *F.Y.W.L. 1956–60*, p. 151 and references there cited.

[3] E. Leyland, "Mechanized Book Charging", in *L.A.R.*, Vol. LII (1950), pp. 112–115.

[4] *L.A.R.*, Vol. LXII (1960), p. 359.

[5] On the uses of punched cards in public libraries see T. E. Callander, "Punched Card Systems", in *L.A.R.*, Vol. XLVIII (1946), pp. 171–4; J. R. Pike, "A Future for Mechanization", in *L.A.R.*, Vol. LVI (1954), pp. 47–49; E. G. Jones, "Mechanization of Accessions Records", *ibid.*, pp. 214–215.

This was an expensive system to operate. Much cheaper was "cheque book charging", introduced by W. R. Maidment at St. Marylebone in 1960. Under this plan the borrower, instead of surrendering a ticket for each loan as in the Browne system, surrended a numbered coupon which was eventually destroyed. The need to wait for a ticket when returning the book was thus eliminated.[1]

The best known of all the new systems, however, was photocharging, introduced by E. V. Corbett at Wandsworth in 1955. An essential feature of this system was a numbered and dated "transaction card". When a book was borrowed a microfilm camera photographed at one operation the particulars of the book (clearly written on the flyleaf), the reader's ticket, and the transaction card. A complete record of the loan having thus been made, the book and ticket were handed to the reader, with the transaction card in the book pocket. When the book was returned the transaction card was removed for subsequent sorting and the book was ready for reshelving. Missing books were detected in due course by gaps in the sequence of transaction card numbers and the developed microfilm could then be consulted to identify the borrower.[2]

This system, American in origin, attracted a good deal of attention, and by 1965, in spite of its cost (the microfilm camera normally used cost £400) it was in use in about fifty library authorities including several London authorities, Bath, Coatbridge, Coventry, Hull, Luton, Northampton, Norwich, Reading, Hertfordshire and West Sussex. Coatbridge, in 1957, was the pioneer in Scotland.[3] At Croydon from 1956, the system was operated with punched transaction cards for machine sorting.[4] A variant method, operating on the same principle, was audiocharging, in which the particulars, instead of being photographed, were read by an assistant into a tape recorder. This method proved slower and less accurate, but was a useful alternative to photocharging, e.g. in a mobile service, or if a machine was out of action.[5]

Another basically similar transaction card system, also American, was "Bookamatic" charging, introduced by W. A. Taylor at St. Pancras in 1961. This used an embossed reader's card, and an embossed book card, placed side by side in a machine, to imprint particulars of the loan on to a slip or card. At St. Pancras the method was adapted to the use of punched cards.[6]

By 1965 consideration was being given to the possibility of controlling issues by computer, but at this stage nothing definite had emerged.[7]

[1] W. R. Maidment, "The 'Cheque-Book' Charging System", in L.A.R., Vol. LXIII (1961), pp. 50–51. The name refers, of course, to the book of coupons issued to each reader. The system was adopted also by Kensington and Hornsey.

[2] E. V. Corbett, Photocharging (1957); E. V. Corbett, "Wandsworth's Experiment with Photocharging", in L.A.R., Vol. LXI (1959), pp. 248–251.

[3] S.L.A. News, No. 25 (Sept.-Oct. 1957), pp. 12–15.

[4] T. E. Callander, "Photo-punch Charging", in L.A.R., Vol. LX (1958), p. 337.

[5] E. V. Corbett, "Wandsworth's Experiment with Photocharging", in L.A.R., Vol. LXI (1959), pp. 250–251.

[6] W. A. Taylor, "Bookamatic comes to Britain", in Library World, Vol. LXIV (1962–63), pp. 42–45. Exeter also adopted this system.

[7] For a full study see F. N. Hogg, W. J. Mathews, and T. E. A. Verity, A Report on a Survey made of Book Charging Systems at present in use in England (duplicated, Library Association 1961); and for a study from the American angle H. T. Geer, Charging Systems (Chicago 1955).

This necessarily over-simplified account of new charging systems ignores many related problems of importance in library administration, e.g. overdues, book reservation, and the compilation of statistics, but it does at least reveal something of the ferment of new ideas which was characterisitic of public libraries at this period. In London the variety of methods in use when the London Government Act came into force in 1965 gave rise to serious problems.[1]

Classification continued to exercise its perennial fascination. The problems of the Bibliographic, Colon, and Universal Decimal Classifications gave rise to a mass of more and more esoteric literature, and there were even attempts at new classifications—an English scheme by J. E. L. Farradane[2] and an American scheme by Fremont Rider.[3] Of all these schemes the U.D.C. had the firmest foothold, and with the passage of time was becoming more and more divorced from its parent Dewey Classification. The Colon system was important less as a working scheme than for its seminal principle of faceted classification; and the Bibliographic system was finding it difficult to keep up with the advances in knowledge.

All these discussions were of great concern to special libraries, but of much less concern to the public libraries. These were still firmly wedded to the Dewey Classification, which appeared in its 17th edition in 1965. Time did indeed increasingly reveal the weaknesses of this system—"its procrustean outline, poor class order and overlong notation for modern developments in many subjects",[4] but time also made it increasingly difficult for libraries to change to any other system. Indeed Dewey strengthened its hold, as the few surviving libraries employing the Brown Subject Classification found it desirable to fall into line. As we have noticed, a few libraries did take liberties with Dewey shelf arrangements in order to achieve more popular groupings, and some libraries used U.D.C. for their technical literature.[5]

Another matter of great interest to special libraries, but of only marginal interest at this stage to most public libraries, was what came to be called "information retrieval". To industrial concerns and research organizations it was often enormously important to be able to lay hands quickly on the latest information on a particular subject, wherever it was published and in whatever form, and much ingenuity was expended, and is still being expended, on schemes for indexing and abstracting literature and making it available for selection by mechanized means, e.g. by punched cards or by computer. The development of the techniques of microphotography was a vital element in such schemes. Experience showed, however, that the creation of a really effective system of information retrieval called for classification and indexing of the literature

[1] *F.Y.W.L. 1961–65*, p. 219.
[2] J. E. L. Farradane, "A Scientific Theory of Classification and Indexing and its Practical Applications", in *Journal of Documentation*, Vol. VI (1950), pp. 83–99.
[3] F. Rider, *Rider's International Classification for the Arrangement of Books on the Shelves of General Libraries* (Middletown, Conn. 1961). The author died in the following year.
[4] W. C. B. Sayers in *Y.W.L. 1950*, p. 203.
[5] K. Davison, *Classification Practice in Britain* (1966), pp. 8, 19, records for 1964 twelve public libraries using the Brown classification, of which two were already changing. Two libraries (Edinburgh and Wigan) continued to use the Library of Congress Classification. Cf. above, p. 247 nate.

in far greater detail, and with far greater precision, than was practicable outside the limits of a specialized collection. As far as general libraries were concerned the American specialist's vision of the scholar of future seating himself at his desk, with a battery of sophisticated instruments at his disposal, for a question and answer session with a library computer, remained no more than a dream— many librarians would have said a bad dream.[1]

For their part, the public libraries were more interested in problems of bibliography and cataloguing. Because of the prodigious growth in the number of published books, bibliographical aids were more and more necessary, and both general and special bibliographies multiplied. A particularly valuable enterprise was the *British Union Catalogue of Periodicals*, which recorded the holdings in British libraries of the periodicals of the world from the seventeenth century to the present day, and incorporated material from the former *Union Catalogue of Periodicals in the University Libraries of the British Isles*.[2] The new catalogue, which had been begun in 1944, appeared in four volumes during the years 1955–58, with a supplement in 1962. From 1964 it began to appear quarterly under the auspices of the National Central Library and arrangements were made for a merger with the *World List of Scientific Periodicals*, of which the fourth edition appeared in 1963–65.[3]

Generous provision also continued to be made of bibliographical aids for the general reader. Many libraries issued periodical lists of additions to stock, or special subject lists drawn up with reference to their own stock, e.g. for drama, music, gramophone records, crafts and hobbies, local history, books for young people.[4] At the national level the County Libraries Section continued to publish its Readers' Guides, and the Library Association in 1956 embarked on a new series of Special Subject Lists, available monthly on subscription.

Despite occasional local variations, cataloguing practice was now pretty uniform throughout the country, and the reader, wherever he went, could be pretty sure of finding either a phalanx of wooden cabinets containing 5in. x 3in. cards or (less often) a range of shelves housing the miniature volumes of a sheaf catalogue. The problems in this field were of different kinds. In the large central library they were problems arising from the size and complexity of the operation, and the need to embrace new types of materials.[5] If such a library was divided, or partly divided, on a subject basis, should the catalogue also be divided, which because of the overlap of subjects would mean duplica-

---

[1] Cf. J. C. R. Licklider, *Libraries of the Future* (Cambridge, Mass., 1965), pp. 46 sqq.; B. C. Vickery, "The Future of Libraries in the Machine Age", in *L.A.R.*, Vol. LVIII (1966), pp. 252–260; R. C. Benge, *Libraries and Cultural Change* (1970), Ch. x; and Sean Kenny in D. E. Gerard (ed.), *Libraries and the Arts* (1970), p.145.

[2] See above, p. 323.

[3] For the history of these bibliographies see "Locating Periodicals", in *L.A.R.*, Vol. LV (1953), pp. 245–250. The *World List* was compiled at the British Museum, and its first edition appeared in 1925–27. *BUCOP* owed its existence to the initiative of Dr. Theodore Besterman, then of ASLIB, and it was this body which provided the secretariat.

[4] See for examples *F.Y.W.L. 1951–55*, pp. 151–152; *F.Y.W.L. 1956–60*, pp. 204–205.

[5] See on this R. L. Collison, *The Cataloguing, Arrangement and Filing of Special Materials in Special Libraries* (1950), which covers illustrations, slides, newspaper cuttings, gramophone records, trade catalogues, maps and films.

tion of entries, or should a single catalogue be maintained, which would mean a good deal of running about for the readers?[1]

At Liverpool where, exceptionally, the tradition of the printed catalogue still survived, the solution adopted for the central library after departmental-ization in 1952 was an unusual one. A union catalogue of all adult non-fiction works was provided in sheaf form in the Picton Reference Library, and sufficient copies were made to meet the needs both of branches and of service points within the central library. A sectional sheaf catalogue covering the appropriate Dewey classes was provided in each of the four principal departmental libraries. The catalogue was cumulated in book form every three or four years.

In smaller libraries, and especially in branch libraries, librarians were asking themselves, as they had begun to do before the war[2], whether in a small open access library a catalogue was really necessary, and if so, how such a catalogue could best be provided without limiting too much the possibili-ties of transfer within the library system. At Sheffield in the 'fifties a complete author catalogue of the entire city library service was placed in each branch and the branch classified catalogues withdrawn. In Tottenham, at the same period, the branch catalogues were abolished in favour of Desk-fax facsimile equipment at the central libraries and branches. Buckinghamshire County by 1962 had dispensed with branch catalogues and installed Telex throughout the system.[3] Liverpool was again exceptional in providing its branches with union catalogues in book form for adult fiction and for children's books respectively.

The mid 'sixties brought the first experiments in computer cataloguing. Dorset County led the way in 1964 with a computer produced catalogue of its drama holdings, and West Sussex set to work to put its entire catalogue into computer readable form.[4] The most remarkable opportunity for the new tech-nique, however, came in London, when following local government re-organization several of the new boroughs, bringing together as they did a number of formerly independent library authorities, found themselves faced with the task of conflating incompatible cataloguing systems. Barnet, Camden, Greenwich and Southwark all found the answer in computer printed union catalogues. If the result seemed at this stage crude and inadequate, it was at least a beginning.[5]

Undoubtedly, however, the most significant event in cataloguing history during these twenty years was the inauguration in January, 1950, of the British National Bibliography, which at long last provided a central cataloguing service for British publications. Created on the initiative of the Library Asso-ciation, and operating from the British Museum in order to have ready access to new publications, B.N.B. was placed under the control of an independent

[1] How Manchester tackled these problems is described in N. K. Firby, "The Manchester Reference Library and its Catalogues: some Problems of Growth", in *Manchester Review*, Vol. X (Spring 1963).   [2] See above, p. 304.

[3] *F.Y.W.L. 1956–60*, p. 231; G. Jones, "From Book-box to Telex", in *L.A. Conference Proceedings, 1962*, pp. 99–101.

[4] *F.Y.W.L. 1961–65*, pp. 236–237.

[5] See the specimen page of the Barnet catalogue printed in A. O. Meakin, "The Production of a Printed Union Catalogue by Computer", in *L.A.R.*, Vol. LXVII (1965), pp. 311–316. Cf. W. R. Maidment, "The Computer Catalogue in Camden", in *Library World*, Vol. LXVII (1965–66), p. 40.

Council representative of the British Museum, the Library Association, the National Central Library, the publishers' and booksellers' organizations, and certain other interested bodies. A. J. Wells, Deputy Librarian of Acton,was appointed as the first editor.

B.N.B. provided for its subscribers a weekly list of new books published in Great Britain, classified according to Dewey, catalogued according to the Anglo-American code, and arranged in subject order, with a monthly author index and an annual cumulative volume. Catalogue cards were not provided at this stage, but entries were printed on one side of the paper only so that they could be cut out and pasted up.[1] Inevitably improvements and modifications were made in the system as time went on. Catalogue cards, reproduced photographically from the main entries, were made available from January, 1956,[2] and in 1960 a number of supplementary classification schedules, constructed on faceted principles, were brought into operation to meet some of the inadequacies of the Dewey system.

As an authoritative bibliography of current publications B.N.B. was of immense value. A. J. Wells, initially, looked forward to a time when it would almost completely replace existing library catalogues,[3] but apart from the exclusion of books published before 1950, foreign books, and certain other categories such as music, there were practical difficulties which prevented more than a minority of libraries from using B.N.B. cards as a complete substitute for their own cataloguing.[4] A great many other libraries, however, used the cards in other ways, as an aid to classification and cataloguing. The *British Catalogue of Music*, launched under B.N.B. auspices in 1960, filled an important gap.

The results, published in 1965, of an inquiry conducted by the Research Committee of the Library Association, showed that of 353 subscribing public libraries fewer than 50 were using B.N.B. cards for cataloguing without modification, but about 240 more were either using the cards in a modified form or using the information provided by B.N.B. for cataloguing purposes.[5]

Extension Activities

At the outset of this period the attitude of most leading librarians towards extension work was still exceedingly cautious. McColvin, in 1942, had been unsympathetic: "We feel", he wrote, "that the library should stick to its

[1] F. C. Francis, "The British National Bibliography", in *ASLIB Proceedings*, Vol. II (1950), pp. 139–145.
[2] A centralized card cataloguing service on a commercial basis was begun by Harrods in 1949 but discontinued at the end of 1951—*Y.W.L. 1949*, p. 154; *F.Y.W.L. 1951–55*, p. 196.
[3] A. J. Wells, "The British National Bibliography: Some Thoughts for the Future", in *L.A.R.*, Vol. LI (1949), pp. 242–243.
[4] For their use in counties see *F.Y.W.L. 1956–60*, p. 204; for a municipal example S. F. Harper, "B.N.B. Cards at Willesden", in *L.A.R.*, Vol. LIX (1957), 269–271. One of the most serious difficulties was the delay which often occurred between the publication and the B.N.B. entry.
[5] "The British National Bibliography Questionnaire", in *L.A.R.*, Vol. LXVII (1965), pp. 52–57.

own job . . ."[1] The Library Association, in the following year, had reaffirmed this view:

> "It is the function of the public library to provide books; . . . The organisation of lectures and other adult educational activities, therefore, is not properly part of the library service, but the provision of books for these purposes should be the responsibility of the public library system."[2]

There were others, however, to whom the second World War proved a great stimulus, offering new opportunities for fruitful co-operation. Edward Sydney of Leyton was one of these:

> "As a result of war-time experiments we now have the Arts Council of Great Britain servicing and sponsoring the development and provision of art exhibitions, music and drama over the whole country; the Central Film Library lending films freely to all who care to ask; the Bureau of Current Affairs stimulating and servicing discussion groups of all kinds; the Central Council for Industrial Design supplying travelling exhibitions and portfolios of photographs; whilst the pre-war established British Drama League and British Film Institute are being compelled to enlarge their services to meet the ever-increasing demands upon them."[3]

It was developments of this kind that led to the formation in many places, either under public library sponsorship or in close association with the public library, of arts councils or similar bodies designed to bring together individuals and organizations interested in music, drama, the visual arts, and cultural activities generally. The first such council seems to have been the St. Pancras Arts and Civic Council, inaugurated in June, 1946.[4] Other similar bodies followed, before the year was out, at Swinton and Pendlebury, Dudley, Stoke Newington, and Deptford; while Manchester Public Library procured special legislation empowering it to hold exhibitions, lectures, educational film shows, and music recitals, to charge for admission, and to provide refreshments.[5]

Inevitably there were those who looked on these developments with a jaundiced eye, and for the next few years the debate waged furiously at conferences and in the professional press. At the Library Association's 1948 Conference at Scarborough, for example, we find George Chandler, then Librarian of Dudley, putting the case for arts clubs, and on the following day S. C. Holliday, Deputy Librarian of Kensington, denouncing "the librarian's morbid preoccupation with adult education".[6] One of the most downright opponents of extension activities was J. W. Forsyth, Librarian of Ayr, who wrote in 1948:

---

[1] L. R. McColvin, *The Public Library System of Great Britain* (1942), p. 70.
[2] Library Association, *Proposals for the Post-War Development of the Public Library Service* (1943), pp. 14–15.
[3] C. Thomsen, E. Sydney and M. D. Tompkins, *Adult Education Activities for Public Libraries* (1950), p. 26.
[4] *L.A.R.*, Vol. XLVIII (1946), pp. 169–170.
[5] *Y.W.L. 1946*, p. 70.
[6] *L.A. Conference Papers, 1948*, pp. 59–63, 105–113. See also the thoughtful and forward looking article by J. F. W. Bryon, "Shelving the Issue", in *L.A.R.*, Vol. XLIX (1947), pp. 116–122.

"I am not in favour of regarding the library as the cultural centre of the community. There is a grave danger here that a multiplicity of tails will wag the dog . . . . Only two things, in my opinion, will convert non-readers into readers—books; and the urgent need for books, whether this be created by the library or by outside agency. Converts will not be won, I maintain, by frittering away our time and energies on schemes of social service which clutter up the building and interfere with our legitimate work."[1]

This same year 1948, however, brought a new Local Government Act under which local authorities were empowered to spend up to a sixpenny rate on the promotion of entertainment and general cultural activities.[2] This Act enlarged and made general the powers which a number of authorities had already secured under local Acts, and thus did much to stimulate and facilitate some of the more spectacular developments in extension work. The Act applied to Scotland as well as to England and Wales. The McClelland Report of 1951, with its strong emphasis on education, naturally spoke with approval of the efforts of libraries "to increase the usefulness of their service by lecture courses, discussion clubs, and story hours for children", but as we have seen its recommendation that public libraries should become part of the educational system was not accepted.[3]

Many librarians on both sides of the border remained suspicious of too much involvement, and the statement drawn up by the Library Association for the Roberts Committee in 1958 opened with a firm declaration that "The first duty of the public library is to satisfy the reading needs of the individual". It did indeed go on to commend assistance to cultural and educational activities, but stressed that there should be "a recognisable limit to such work":

"It is not considered a proper extension of library functions for the librarian to initiate such activities as amateur dramatics, art exhibitions, pageants, concerts, formal instructional classes. In the small community he may well be called on to help in such activities, but his function is not that of a curator, concert manager, or entertainments manager."[4]

The Roberts Report itself was content to repeat the Kenyon Committee's recommendation that libraries should be empowered to spend money on lectures and "other external activities of a cultural character";[5] and the Bourdillon Report was vague on the subject of how such activities could best be promoted. The latter report, however, did make concrete recommendations for assistance to adult education:

"Since in many respects public libraries and adult education are complementary services, we consider that library authorities should provide suitable accommodation for an adult class wherever possible (e.g. a room holding 20 to 40 people with

---

[1] Scottish Library Association, *Annual Report, 1948*, p. 38, quoted W. R. Aitken, *A History of the Public Library Movement in Scotland to 1955* (Glasgow 1971), p. 202.

[2] 11 and 12 Geo. VI c. 26.

[3] *McClelland Report*, pp. 38–39, 117.

[4] Library Association, *Memorandum of Evidence to be laid before the Committee appointed by the Minister of Education to consider the Structure of the Public Library Service in England and Wales . . .* (1958), pp. 8–9.

[5] *Roberts Report*, pp. 27–28.

appropriate equipment) and should be willing to make this accommodation available either free of charge or for a nominal sum. It is also desirable that such accommodation should be available up to 9.00 or 9.30 p.m."[1]

These recommendations exerted a helpful influence, especially on the planning of new branch libraries. Most of the new central libraries built in the 'sixties made fairly generous provision for cultural activities.

Most of these discussions, it must be said, missed the point that public libraries can be and ought to be different things in different places. In practice the amount of extension work undertaken tended to be determined less by theoretical considerations than by the needs of the area and the extent of provision by other organizations. The historian of the Bedford Public Library declared bluntly:

> "The need for the library to act as impresario for plays, film shows, exhibitions and the other activities with which some libraries feel called upon to concern themselves, is not obvious in Bedford. They are well looked after by other organisations."[2]

This was no doubt true of the Bedford situation, but there were other places—especially medium-sized towns—where the need was great and the library felt called upon to respond.

If we look at the position as it was at the close of our period, we find that what may be called the traditional forms of library extension still continued very much as they had in the 'thirties.[3] A survey of work throughout the United Kingdom, undertaken in 1964, brought replies from some 380 library authorities, of which 276 engaged in some form of extension work.[4] Apart from talks given by members of the library staff to outside organizations, the most popular activity recorded was the holding of exhibitions. Book exhibitions were arranged both inside and outside libraries, often in association with book weeks; 135 libraries reported art exhibitions, and 137 "general exhibitions" (often with a local interest). Public lectures, though abandoned by some authorities, continued to figure high on the list, in spite of the competition of television, being reported by no fewer than 122 authorities. If we are to judge by the pattern in North-West England, these would mostly be of a rather popular kind—talks on local history and aspects of local government, illustrated travel talks, and so forth.[5] Gramophone recitals and film shows were also fairly common, concerts less frequent; discussion groups, poetry readings and play readings were well down the list.

Most libraries that had accommodation for meetings were willing to let it, usually at modest rates, to local societies and for adult classes. Quite often the librarian helped to organize such classes, or sponsored the formation of cultural societies. The Public Libraries and Adult Education Committee for the North West, whose investigations we have more than once had occasion to cite, was formed in 1960 with the deliberate purpose of fostering such co-

---

[1] *Bourdillon Report*, pp. 49–50.
[2] A. E. Baker, *The Library Story: a history of the library movement in Bedford* (Bedford 1958), p. 17.
[3] See above.
[4] H. Jolliffe, *Public Library Extension Activities* (1962, 2nd. edn. 1968), pp. 4–5.
[5] B. Luckham, *Libraries in the North-West as Cultural Centres* (Public Libraries and Adult Education Committee for the North-West [1965]).

operation. It brought together representatives of the North-West Branch of the Library Association, the Liverpool and Manchester University Extra-Mural Departments, and the corresponding Districts of the Workers' Educational Association.

The supply of books to adult classes remained a problem, especially in urban areas.[1] Many university extra-mural departments had by 1965 built up substantial libraries for the use of their own classes, but W.E.A. and other classes were for the most part entirely dependent on the local library and the National Central Library, and unless the class was in a county area the cry was apt to be "too little and too late". An inquiry into the position was made under N.C.L. auspices in 1954–56,[2] but neither this inquiry nor the Bourdillon inquiry was able to come forward with an effective solution.[3]

The most striking development in library extension during this period was the growth of activities in the arts, which as we have seen went back to the immediate post-war years. Only a minority of libraries was involved—the 1964 survey recorded 22 libraries with associated arts clubs or councils and 18 involved in the conduct of arts festivals—but many of these libraries really did succeed in making themselves, in the oft-quoted phrase, cultural centres of their communities.

An outstanding example was the railway town of Swindon (population in 1938, 60 000), where the long-delayed establishment of a public library in 1943[4] became the starting-point for a cultural advance on a wide front, embracing art, music, literature, theatre, and ballet. To cater for all these activities, a redundant Sunday school was converted in 1946 into a special Arts Centre; and in this same year, appropriately, the post of librarian passed to Harold Jolliffe, who was to become well known as the champion of library extension work.

By the time the library came of age in 1964, Jolliffe was directing a whole complex of institutions: a new and enlarged central library, a new and enlarged arts centre, half a dozen branch libraries, three museums and an art gallery. The extension work of the library, organized either directly or in collaboration with other bodies, included book weeks, exhibitions, concerts, theatrical performances, festivals, and adult education classes besides a wide variety of activities, all more or less subsidized, carried out under the auspices of a dozen or more sponsored societies. This great cultural enterprise was administered by the local authority through the Libraries, Museums and Arts Committee, exercising powers conferred by a local Act of 1947 and the Local Government Act of 1948.[5]

The nearest parallel to Swindon was Dudley, where the Arts Centre, sited at the Netherton Branch, was also directly controlled and financed by the local authority; but a similar range of activities, under a greater or lesser degree of library control or sponsorship, was carried on at a number of English libraries,

---

[1] Cf. above, p. 306, for the position in the 'thirties.
[2] See "The Provision of Books to Adult Classes", in *L.A.R.*, Vol. LVIII (1956), pp. 471–474.
[3] *Bourdillon Report*, pp. 25–26.
[4] Cf. above, p. 334.
[5] H. Jolliffe, *Arts Centre Adventure* (Swindon 1968). See also his *Public Library Extension Activities* (cited above), Ch. xi; and *21 Years of Public Library Service in Swindon, 1943–1964* [Swindon 1964].

amongst them Chesterfield, Dagenham, Folkestone, Holborn, Hornsey, Islington, Leyton, St. Pancras, and Sheffield.

Other libraries sponsored concerts or dramatic performances. Bradford was outstanding for its series of lunch-time concerts, begun in 1943. At Scarborough the concert hall in the central library provided a home, from 1955, for a theatrical company presenting "theatre in the round". Manchester alone ventured into professional theatre management. Its Library Theatre, housed in the basement of the central library, and managed from 1951 by the city librarian, quickly became well known, and its success was such that the Libraries Committee made plans for a second theatre at an outlying branch in Wythenshawe.[1]

Librarianship

It was only in these post-war years that librarianship really gained public recognition as a professional service. The growth of knowledge, the multiplication of books and periodicals, and the expansion of higher education, all combined to make expert guidance increasingly necessary, and the Library Association for its part took steps immediately the war was over to put its training arrangements on a new and better footing.

The new syllabus introduced by the Association as from January, 1946, provided for examinations at three levels—Entrance, Registration and Final. The Entrance Examination covered recent English literature and elementary library organization and procedures; candidates must be at least nineteen, must have a School Certificate including a foreign language, and must have worked for a year in an approved library.[2] The Registration Examination covered the essential professional training, in classification, cataloguing, bibliography, assistance to readers, library organization and the history of English literature. It was intended to be taken normally after one year's full-time study, and led after three years' approved library service to the Associateship of the Library Association (A.L.A.). This was the main career grade.

The Final Examination, leading to the Fellowship (F.L.A.), was planned as a more advanced examination and required a minimum of five years' approved service. It included a more detailed study of bibliography and library organization, together with the opportunity of specializing in some branch of literature, e.g. the literature of the social sciences, or music, or science and technology; and in some particular branch of library work, e.g. palaeography and archives or work with young people. An essay on an approved subject of the candidate's own choice provided further scope for specialization. Certain sections of the Final Examination might also be taken separately in order to provide Specialist Certificates, e.g. in Work with Young People and in Special Librarianship.

The term "Chartered Librarian" was introduced as a generic title to cover all fully qualified professional librarians, i.e. Associates and Fellows.[3]

This syllabus has been described in some detail because basically this was

---

[1] H. Jolliffe, *Public Library Extension Activities*, Chs. x and xi. Because of the reorganization of the London libraries, the first edition of 1962 must be consulted for this period.

[2] The age limit was dropped before it could come into force—see *L.A.R.*, Vol. XLVIII (1946), p. 102.

[3] *Library Association Year Book 1945* (1945), pp. 42–52; R. Irwin, "Professional Education", in *L.A.R.*, Vol. XLVII (1945), pp. 3–11.

the pattern of professional education until 1964. Progress towards full-time training at the Registration level remained slow, however. A number of technical colleges readily agreed to provide courses, and by 1950 there were nine new library schools, in addition to the long established school at University College, London, which re-opened, after four years' closure, in 1945.[1] These schools accounted, initially, for some 300 students, but the majority of candidates in 1955 still had to rely on part-time study at a local technical college or on a correspondence course conducted by the Association of Assistant Librarians, supplemented by the now traditional summer schools at Birmingham and in Wales and Scotland.[2] A variety of specialist courses was also to be had, for children's librarians, hospital librarians, teacher librarians, and so forth.

There were of course changes in the syllabus from time to time. The number of specialist options in the Final Examination was increased from 1950,[3] and the Entrance Examination, after several modifications to keep up with changes in the schools, was eventually replaced from 1956 by the First Professional Examination, the requirement of a preliminary year's library service being dropped.[4] Basically, however, the pattern remained the same.[5]

In 1951 the policy of increased professionalization received official approval in Scotland, when the McClelland Report recommended "that every public library in Scotland, large or small, accessible or remote, be directly or indirectly in charge of a fully-trained professional librarian".[6] For England and Wales, as we have seen, the Roberts and Bourdillon Reports spelled out the implications of this policy in detail.

The Roberts Report suggested a standard of one full-time assistant for 3000 population in urban areas, and a slightly reduced ratio for county areas. It also proposed that 40 per cent of non-manual staff should be qualified librarians. These standards would have involved an increase in non-manual staff from 11 600 to 15 000 and in qualified staff from 3700 to 6000.[7] The Bourdillon Report preferred an overall ratio of one full-time member of staff to 2500 population, but suggested that the proportion of qualified staff might be reduced from 40 per cent to 33 per cent, or perhaps even as low as 25 per cent, in urban libraries serving populations over 100 000.[8] Both reports called for an increase in the number of specialist posts.

The efforts of library authorities to comply with these standards (even though they were not mandatory) accentuated the already existing shortage of qualified librarians in the public library sector, especially in the county libraries. The library schools were quick to respond, and in 1965 there were four times as many students in the schools as in 1961. A post-graduate school of librarianship was established at the University of Sheffield in 1963; in 1964, in pursuance of the recommendation made in the Roberts Report, a residential College of Librarianship for Wales was established in Aberystwyth; and in the

[1] The new schools, opened 1946–50, were at technical colleges or colleges of commerce in Birmingham, Brighton, Cheltenham, Glasgow, Isleworth, Leeds, Loughborough, Manchester, and Newcastle upon Tyne.
[2] *F.Y.W.L. 1951–55*, p. 275.   [3] *Library Association Year Book 1950*, pp. 53–75.
[4] *Library Association Year Book 1956*, pp. 4–27.
[5] Interesting discussions of librarianship training at this period are to be found in *Library Review*, Vols. XIV–XVI (1953–58).   [6] *McClelland Report*, p. 45.
[7] *Roberts Report*, pp. 20–21.   [8] *Bourdillon Report*, pp. 26–31.

same year the Glasgow school became part of the new University of Strathclyde. In 1965 nearly 1600 students were in attendance at thirteen schools.[1] The number of chartered librarians, which had been 3011 in 1950 and 5200 in 1960, rose to 7173 by 1965.[2]

Unfortunately the public libraries were not getting their fair share of this increased output. This was partly because of the salary situation. The introduction of uniform salary scales for local government employees in 1946 had done something to remove the worst anomalies in library salaries, but the placing of staff on the various scales was still a matter for individual authorities and the decisions taken were not always in accordance with the Library Association's recommendations.[3] The Roberts Committee pointed out that parity with the teaching profession, which had been recommended by the Kenyon Report, had still not been achieved: at that time 60 per cent of qualified librarians were earning less than £725 a year, and only 5 per cent were earning more than £1325.[4] The consequence was a steady drain from public libraries to other and better paid branches of the library service.

Many other training and staffing problems came to the fore in these formative years of the early 'sixties—problems too complex to be adequately dealt with in a few brief paragraphs. We can do little more than note their existence.

One was the need to distinguish between professional and non-professional staff, and to provide appropriate in-service training and an appropriate career structure for the latter group. This distinction was one which the Library Association was long reluctant to accept, and which was indeed difficult to implement in small libraries, but it was implicit in the recommendation of the Roberts Committee that 40 per cent of non-manual staff should be qualified librarians. In 1965 a proposal for some form of Library Assistant's Certificate was still under discussion.[5]

Within the qualified sector there was the problem of providing adequate practical training facilities for the students from the schools, and adequate in-service training for the various specialist posts now deemed to be necessary—children's librarians, reference librarians, technical librarians, music librarians, readers' advisers, and so forth. Only the larger libraries could really offer very much in the way of training facilities, and there was talk about setting up "teaching libraries" on the model of the teaching hospitals established under the national health service.[6]

---

[1] *L.A.R.*, Vol. LXVII (1965), p. 203.

[2] *F.Y.W.L. 1956–60*, p. 413; *F.Y.W.L. 1961–65*, pp. 563, 604–605.

[3] R. F. Vollans (ed.), *Libraries for the People* (1968), p. 68. The Library Association's recommendations are printed in *L.A.R.*, Vol. XLVIII (1946), pp. 54–56.

[4] *Roberts Report*, p. 21.

[5] See above, p. 310; cf. *F.Y.W.L. 1951–55*, p. 273; *F.Y.W.L. 1961–65*, pp. 563, 616–617; and K. A. Mallaber, "The Division of Library Staffs into Professional and Non-Professional", in Library Association, London and Home Counties Branch, *The Changing Pattern of Librarianship* (1961), pp. 34–38; and Library Association, *Professional and Non-Professional Duties in Libraries* (1962).

[6] *F.Y.W.L. 1961–65*, pp. 223–224, 244. For the training of children's librarians see *ibid.*, pp. 377–378; and for the training of reference librarians *L.A.R.*, Vol. LX (1958), pp. 161–163; F. H. Fenton (ed.), *Reference Library Staffs* (1962).

A related problem was that of assimilating the graduate entrant to the profession, who was essential for many specialist and senior posts. A considerable number of graduates were now finding their way into the library schools, and by 1957 they already accounted for about 15 per cent of total Library Association membership.[1] They received, however, few examination concessions, and in the public libraries it was not always easy to find posts which could make use of their special qualifications. Among graduates especially, therefore, the drift to other branches of the library service was particularly marked. A great step forward was taken in 1964, when agreement was reached by the Library Association on a one-year post-graduate course to be offered by approved library schools.[2]

Then, too, there were tensions arising from the fact that the Library Association examinations, though catering mainly for public library personnel, served also to provide a general professional qualification for many working in other institutions, e.g. in universities, technical colleges, teacher training colleges, schools, government departments and industrial research establishments. More than a quarter of the Association's home based membership in employment in 1965 belonged to this category.[3] The needs of those working in special libraries were the subject of frequent discussions. One rather specialized group formed itself in 1958 into the Institute of Information Scientists, which devised its own syllabus and arranged with the Northampton College of Advanced Technology in London[4] for a post-graduate course to be provided from 1961. ASLIB, however, rejected the idea of a separate qualification, preferring to seek provision within the framework of the Library Association syllabus.[5]

Finally there was the problem of the multiplication of training institutions. In the 'twenties the Association had come to terms, not without difficulty, with the University College School of Librarianship, and after the war the new library schools had readily agreed to teach to the Association's syllabus; but in the mid 'sixties the position was changing. There were now additional university library schools at Sheffield and Strathclyde; Aberystwyth had a school under the auspices of the Cardiganshire Education Authority; and both through the universities and through the Council for National Academic Awards (established in 1964), the possibility of degree courses in librarianship began to be actively canvassed. The Library Association found itself faced, in fact, with a variety of courses, designed to meet a variety of needs, and provided by a variety of organizations, and the question inevitably arose whether the Association's examinations could continue to provide the major channel of recruitment to the profession.

In the meantime the new syllabus which came into operation in 1964 did something to widen the range of specialisms available and to bring library education into line with the changes in higher education generally. Though there were various transitional arrangements the general effect of the new

[1] F.Y.W.L. 1956–60, p. 413.
[2] L.A.R., Vol. LXVII (1965), pp. 16–18.
[3] F.Y.W.L. 1961–65, p. 562.
[4] Now the City University.
[5] F.Y.W.L. 1955–60, pp. 401–402; F.Y.W.L. 1961–65, pp. 605, 610.

regulations was to establish a two-year full-time course of professional training, leading to an Intermediate and then a Final Examination, and after a further year's approved library service to the Associateship (A.L.A.). The Intermediate Examination (Part I) comprised papers on the Library and the Community; the Government and Control of Libraries; the Organization of Knowledge; and Bibliographical Control and Service. The Final Examination (Part II) offered a wide variety of options, so that, as Miss L. V. Paulin put it, "each student may undertake a co-ordinated course of study with a bias towards his own particular interests".[1]

The former First Professional Examination disappeared, giving way to an entrance qualification based on the General Certificate of Education—passes in five subjects, of which one must be in English Language and two must be at Advanced level. The former Final Examination for the F.L.A. also disappeared, giving way to an arrangement under which admission to the Fellowship would be by thesis only.[2] By the close of 1965, twelve library schools were offering two-year courses.[3]

The growing diversification of library work was reflected in the formation within the Library Association, in 1950, of a Reference and Special Libraries Section (from 1959 Reference, Special and Information Section) and by the formation outside the Association of SCONUL (the Standing Conference of National and University Libraries). The most important event in the history of the Association during these years, however, was the decision taken in 1961 to convert it into a fully professional organization. The local authorities and other institutional members became affiliated members without voting rights, and it was agreed that from January, 1967, new individual members must be chartered librarians.[4] In October, 1965, after nearly thirty-three years at Chaucer House, the Association moved to a new, purpose-designed building in nearby Ridgmount Street.

Inter-Library Co-operation

As soon as the war ended international contacts and international lending were resumed, and before long the air was thick with plans for international bibliographies, international abstracting services, and international union catalogues. The efforts of the International Federation for Documentation and the International Federation of Library Associations were now reinforced by the work of UNESCO, which did much to stimulate and co-ordinate these activities. The strong position of the two federations at the close of our period owed, indeed, not a little to UNESCO support, financial and otherwise.[5]

Much of the pressure in this direction came from those who were specially concerned to secure complete coverage and immediate availability of current

---

[1] L.A.R., Vol. LXIII (1961), p. 166.
[2] The new regulations are printed in L.A.R., Vol. LXV (1963), pp. 109–121.
[3] On the profession of librarianship and on professional training see the interesting discussion in R. C. Benge, *Libraries and Cultural Change* (1970), Chs. viii and xii–xiv.
[4] L.A.R., Vol. LXII (1960), pp. 208–218; Vol. LXIII (1961), pp. 83–84.
[5] The British Society for International Bibliography, which had served as the British link with the International Federation for Documentation, merged with ASLIB in 1949 (see Y.W.L. 1949, p. 26; and Y.W.L. 1950, p. 40). On the support given by UNESCO see especially F.Y.W.L. 1961–65, Ch. xxxi.

scientific and technical literature—especially periodical literature. In Great Britain this interest was reflected in an ambitious scheme propounded in 1949 for complete coverage of all "useful English and foreign published material". It was devised by a working party established by the Library Association at the request of its University and Research Section, and proved in the event impossible to operate.[1] More practical, and from the public library angle more important, were co-operative schemes developed within the framework of the Regional Library Bureaux.

Inter-library lending recovered quickly after the war. In 1945 the system of regional library bureaux was completed by the creation of the Scottish Regional Library Bureau.[2] By 1949 the eleven bureaux[3] were lending a total of 163 000 volumes within their own systems, and a further 20 000 volumes to libraries in other regions, and to non-regional libraries, through the National Central Library. Total issues from the National Central Library (excluding adult classes) amounted to 76 000 volumes, and the Scottish Central Library was responsible for a further 16 000 issues. Of the applications received by the National Central Library (these, it should be remembered, were the difficult applications which could not be provided for at regional level) two-thirds were satisfactorily dealt with.[4] To complete the picture, it should be added that the National Central Library was now also operating the British National Book Centre, which was a clearinghouse through which public and other libraries could make unwanted books available to libraries which needed them. It was, of course, the lineal descendant of the Inter-Allied Books Centre which had operated during the war. In the first full year, 1948–49, the Centre distributed 5000 books and 7600 periodical parts.[5]

There were interesting developments, too, within the regions. In London in 1946 the metropolitan borough libraries agreed on a scheme for a joint fiction reserve to ensure the preservation of books which might otherwise disappear from circulation. Each of the co-operating libraries agreed to ensure the preservation of all works by certain authors, the distribution being made on an alphabetical basis.[6] To this was shortly added a scheme of subject specialization for non-fiction, each library taking responsibility for certain categories in the Dewey classification.[7] London's example in respect of subject specialization was followed in 1950 by the South-Eastern Region,[8] and subsequently by a number of other regions.[9]

[1] L.A.R., Vol. LI (1949), pp. 383–387; Vol. LVI (1954), pp. 16–17.
[2] Merged in 1953 with the Scottish Central Library—see W. R. Aitken, A History of the Public Library Movement in Scotland to 1955 (Glasgow 1971), Ch. vi.
[3] i.e. the seven English bureaux listed above, p. 322, together with the London system, the two Welsh bureaux (separated in 1948), and the Scottish bureau.
[4] National Central Library, Annual Report, 1949, pp. 8–9, 15–16.
[5] L.A.R., Vol. LI (1949), pp. 65–66. Cf. National Central Library, Annual Reports, 1947, p. 9; 1948, pp. 21–22; and 1949, pp. 22–23.
[6] L.A.R., Vol. XLVIII (1946), p. 153.
[7] L.A.R., Vol. LI (1949), p. 186.   [8] L.A.R., Vol. LII (1950), pp. 229–230.
[9] The Welsh Regions in 1953, the North-Western Region in 1954, and the South-Western Region in 1959. A number of libraries in the Northern Region also established in 1951 a joint fiction reserve. See P. H. Sewell, The Regional Library Systems (1950, 2nd edn. 1956), and the Addendum to this work in L.A.R., Vol. LXI (1959), pp. 254–257.

In spite of these encouraging facts, all was far from well. The burden of creating and maintaining union catalogues, on which the whole system was believed to depend, was becoming increasingly difficult to bear: both at the centre and in the regions the catalogues were far from complete, and the arrears were in many cases mounting rapidly. Doubts were beginning to be felt, too, regarding the value of much of the work, since such a large proportion of the entries were for books common to most libraries.

In January, 1949, "with a view to reducing the enormous and ever-growing post-war volume of loan requests", the National Central Library expressed the hope that all regions would aim at self-sufficiency through co-operative specialization.[1] In the same year a joint working party was set up with the National Committee on Regional Library Co-operation to examine the whole matter, and R. F. Vollans, Deputy City Librarian of Westminster, was commissioned to prepare a report. This document, published in 1952, was the most thorough examination of inter-library lending in this country ever undertaken, and revealed *inter alia* startling figures for the cost of this work. The cost of loans within regions ranged from 4s. 3d. to 8s. 7d. per loan; and the cost of loans through the National Central Library from 14s. 4d. to 19s. 1d. per loan. These figures represented a powerful argument in favour of purchasing books, wherever practicable, instead of lending them.[2]

The Vollans Report provided the starting-point for a series of recommendations published in 1954.[3] The first of these recommendations was that from a date to be fixed each region should be self-sufficient in current British material listed in the British National Bibliography; the existing union catalogues, both in the regions and at the centre, should be completed to that date; and thereafter records of current British material, notified by means of B.N.B. numbers, should be kept only at the regions.

The date was ultimately fixed as 1st January, 1959 and, in order to ensure that no current British material should be missed, an inter-regional subject specialization scheme, based on the Dewey classification, was introduced. From this date, therefore, the National Central Library was able to concentrate upon older publications and foreign literature. Later, as from 1st January, 1962, an inter-regional fiction reserve was established among the provincial regions to supplement the metropolitan scheme.[4]

In the meantime there had been important developments at the governmental level. In Scotland the Act of 1955 had provided for the statutory payment by library authorities of contributions to the Scottish Central Library,[5] and in England the Roberts Committee, following this lead, proposed that

[1] *Y.W.L. 1949*, p. 101; cf. National Central Library, *Annual Report, 1949*, pp. 4–5.
[2] R. F. Vollans, *Library Cooperation in Great Britain* (1952), pp. 99–103. See also his article, "Focus on Library Cooperation", in *L.A.R.*, Vol. LV (1953), pp. 152–157.
[3] National Central Library and National Committee on Regional Library Cooperation, *Recommendations on Library Cooperation* (1954).
[4] For these developments see *L.A.R.*, Vol. LXII (1960), pp. 254–255; Vol. LXIII (1963), pp. 349–351; and Vol. LXIV (1962), p. 329. The new fiction reserve absorbed that hitherto operated in the Northern Region. The National Central Library's *Annual Report, 1965*, records 232,000 loans by regional library bureaux to libraries within their own regions, 29,000 to other regions, 86,000 by the N.C.L., and 18,000 by the Scottish Central Library.
[5] See above, p. 349.

the regional committees should be given statutory recognition, and that the cost of maintaining these committees, and of providing a contribution from each region towards the cost of the National Central Library, should be met by a compulsory payment from each library authority.[1] The Baker Report of 1962 spelt out this proposal in more detail, recommending *inter alia* that public libraries should be responsible for 30 per cent of the expenditure of the National Central Library. This Report also suggested the reorganization of the union catalogues on more selective lines, and a reduction in the number of regions in England and Wales to four or five. The 1964 Act, as we have seen, made provision for the Secretary of State for Education to designate library regions and make schemes for their operation and finance.[2]

To many it seemed that this kind of thing did not touch the real problem, and that much more radical thinking was needed. In particular, it was argued, the time for regional organizations had gone by: a comprehensive national organization would be much more efficient and economical. Those who thought in this way derived much encouragement from the steps taken from the late 'fifties onwards to provide for the special needs of science and technology. One was the decision made in 1960 to create, under the auspices of the British Museum, a National Reference Library of Science and Invention which would bring together, for the benefit of research workers, the more recent scientific and technical material from the Patent Office and the British Museum, the older Patent Office material being passed to the Museum's main collections. Unfortunately because of accommodation difficulties the new library was not formally inaugurated till 1966. In the meantime all that could be done was to improve stock and amenities at the Patent Office.[3]

No such obstacle was allowed to impede the progress of the National Lending Library for Science and Technology, the establishment of which was recommended by the Advisory Council on Scientific Policy in 1954 to relieve pressure on the Science Museum Library. Planning began in 1956; by 1960 accommodation for the first million volumes had been prepared in a former ordnance factory at the village of Boston Spa in the West Riding; and by the time of the official opening in November, 1962, 600 tons of literature had been assembled, including about 20 per cent of the stock of the Science Museum Library.

The new library began its life under the auspices of the Department of Scientific and Industrial Research; when this organization was dissolved in 1965 control passed to the Department of Education and Science. It covered all fields of science and technology, including agriculture and medicine, with special attention to current periodical literature in all languages. Its services were available to industrial firms, research organizations, universities, colleges, hospitals and public libraries, but not to individuals. Its first director, D. J. Urquhart, came from the world of science and not from that of librarianship, and some features of his organization, e.g. the absence of a catalogue, the

[1] *Roberts Report*, pp. 18–19.
[2] See above, p. 359.
[3] See the symposium on the N.R.L.S.I. in *Journal of Documentation*, Vol. XVII (1961), pp. 1–39; and the article on the same subject by Maysie Webb, Librarian-Designate, *ibid.*, Vol. XXII (1966), pp. 1–12.

shelving of books by title instead of by subject and author, and the use of an overhead cradle conveyor for the transport of books and information, caused raised eyebrows in professional circles. This was not, however, an open access library, and the acid test of this novel management system was that it worked. By 1965 the library was handling as many loans as the National Central Library and the regional bureaux together, and was disposing of most requests within 24 hours of receipt. Its photocopying service was also in increasing demand.[1]

The success of this venture inevitably gave rise to thoughts of a parallel organization for the humanities—indeed Dr. Urquhart himself suggested such a possibility as early as 1960.[2] The parallel, however, was more apparent than real, and in 1965 the problem remained unsolved.[3]

National Libraries

The remaining pages of this long narrative must be devoted to a brief review of the position of the national libraries, in so far as they have not already been dealt with in the preceding section.

Of the new National Lending Library of Science and Technology enough has already been said. Concerning the National Central Library it may be well to recall that in addition to its central interlending function it was still responsible for loans to adult classes, for the production of the British Union Catalogue of Periodicals and for the operation of the British National Book Centre. By 1965 it had accumulated a stock of close on 300 000 books (including many American and other foreign works), and was in process of removing to new purpose-built premises in Store Street, adjoining the new headquarters of the Library Association. The cost of its work was still borne mainly by the Treasury, but as we have seen this was not expected to continue.

The Scottish Central Library, reorganized in 1952 under an independent board of trustees and a widely representative executive committee, had absorbed the Scottish Regional Library Bureau in 1953 and had now established itself, in its new premises in Edinburgh, as the recognized centre for Scottish interlending. It co-operated closely with the National Central Library and where appropriate with the National Lending Library of Science and Technology, and took its share in the national inter-regional scheme of subject specialization. Three-quarters of the cost was borne by the Treasury, the rest by the local authorities and other users.[4]

The creation of the National Lending Library of Science and Technology relieved the Science Museum Library of the responsibility it had formerly assumed for postal loans. It did, indeed, for some time continue to provide a supplementary loan and photocopy service to meet requests handed on from

---

[1] For a description see D. J. Urquhart, "Plain Man's Guide to the National Lending Library for Science and Technology", in *L.A.R.*, Vol. LXIV (1962), pp. 319–322.

[2] D. J. Urquhart, "The Needs of the Humanities: an Outside View", in *Journal of Documentation*, Vol. XVI (1960), pp. 121–131.

[3] Urquhart himself summarizes many of the difficulties in "The Ecology of Inter-Library Loans", *L.A.R.*, Vol. LXVII (1965), pp. 341–349. See also D. T. Richnell, "National Lending Library or National Lending Services for the Humanities", in *Journal of Documentation*, Vol. XVII (1961), pp. 197–214.

[4] Information from Mr. M. C. Pottinger, Librarian.

the N.L.L.S.T., but this was a diminishing commitment, and the Library was henceforth able to concentrate more and more on the needs of its immediate public—especially the staff of the Imperial College of Science and Technology and of the Science Museum itself. Despite transfers to Boston Spa, the Library's stock had by 1965 again been built up to 380 000 volumes, including 22 500 periodicals.[1]

Almost as large was the library of the Victoria and Albert Museum close by, a unique collection of books covering all branches of the fine and applied arts in all countries, and supported by an extensive collection of photographs.[2] This library, however, unlike its counterpart in the Science Museum, was for reference only.

The three major national libraries—the library of the British Museum, with something like seven million volumes in the Department of Printed Books alone, and the National Libraries of Wales and Scotland, with some two million printed volumes apiece—had one thing in common throughout the post-war years, namely a severe shortage of money and accommodation.[3] The amount of money made available for book purchase during the greater part of this period was indeed ludicrous: in 1962–63 it was £100 000 for the British Museum, £9000 for the National Library of Scotland, and £6000 for the National Library of Wales. It was not until the quinquennium beginning in 1964 that the grants were increased to a reasonable level.[4]

In the meantime, thanks less to purchase than to gifts, exchanges, and copyright deposits, stocks continued to grow, and so did pressure on accommodation. Because of the postponement of building operations the position was already serious when the war ended, and for some years it continued to deteriorate. In Edinburgh in 1948 the National Library was driven to storing books in the police cells and vaults of the Law Courts, and although cataloguing was seriously in arrears new staff could not be engaged because there was nowhere for them to sit. The opening of the long delayed new building in 1956 brought substantial relief, but within a few years more space was urgently needed for stack rooms, staff rooms and at least two new reading rooms. In Wales the central block which marked the completion of the original building planned in 1910 was completed in 1955, but books were still being stored in corridors, staircases, and any odd corners that were available. It was only in 1964 that the first of two planned bookstacks was completed and the second was not due to be commenced for another five years.

The British Museum Library was in the worst plight of all, for the possibilities of expansion on the existing site were exceedingly restricted. In 1953 it was reported that the main building had 75 miles of shelving, of which 73 were already occupied.[5] By the end of the 'fifties the war-damaged King's Library had been re-opened, the south-west quadrant of the Iron Library

[1] F.Y.W.L. 1961–65, p. 155.

[2] R. L. Collison, "Fine Arts Libraries and Collections in Britain", in Journal of Documentation, Vol. VI (1950), p. 59.

[3] See for details of development the periodical Reports of the Standing Commission on Museums and Galleries, 1948–69.

[4] Standing Commission on Museums and Galleries, Seventh Report, 1961–1964 (1965), p. 105. The new levels were: B.M.L. £262,000; N.L.S. £25,000; N.L.W. £18,000.

[5] Standing Commission on Museums and Galleries, Fourth Report, 1949–1953 (1954), p. 4.

(destroyed in 1941), had been rebuilt and enlarged in accordance with pre-war plans, and additional stack space had been provided for the rebuilt newspaper library at Hendon, but even so it was clear that within a few years all available storage space would be used up. The only possible answer was a new building, but plans for the acquisition of land to the south of Great Russell Street adjoining the Museum went ahead only slowly. At length in September, 1964, outline proposals for the use of the site were made public.

The imaginative design by Sir Leslie Martin and Colin St. John Wilson envisaged a complex of buildings grouped on either side of a central piazza which reached south from the portico of the old library to the fine eighteenth-century church of St. George's Bloomsbury, designed by Nicholas Hawksmoor. In order to make much more material available on open access, and to allow for some degree of subject specialization, the new library building to the east of the piazza provided seating for 1100 readers in several rooms, including a large public reference room and a number of reading rooms for special subjects. Provision was also made for one million square feet of storage space. A new lecture theatre, an exhibition building, and a restaurant would occupy the area west of the piazza.[1]

Even though it was not proposed to begin building until the early 'seventies, the Museum Trustees now felt that the future at last was secure, but time, alas, was to bring further cruel disappointments.

[1] British Museum, *Report of the Trustees, 1966* (1966), p. 22; J. M. Crook, *The British Museum* (1972), Ch. vi. The plans of the librarian, F. C. Francis, for "a system of de-centralization round a central core" are interestingly described in his paper, "The British Museum Looks towards the Future", in *Proceedings of the American Philosophical Society*, Vol. CIV (1960), pp. 408–412.

EPILOGUE

THIS narrative officially ends with the coming into force of the Public Libraries and Museums Act in 1965, but perhaps it may be of value to set down, in this brief epilogue, some of the things that have happened in the seven years that have passed since that event.

The Library Advisory Councils for England and for Wales have been formed, and have undertaken, with the assistance of the Government's small staff of library advisers, a series of studies of various aspects of librarianship. They have already produced two useful reports—one on training, which gave a salutary warning against over-production of qualified librarians, and the other on service points and staffing standards.[1] Both the Councils and the Secretary of State for Education have been handicapped by the knowledge that too firm an insistence on officially prescribed standards of efficiency would conflict with the severe restrictions imposed by the Government on public expenditure. None the less a considerable amount has been achieved. Total library expenditure in England and Wales (excluding services to schools) has increased by 72 per cent between 1965–66 and 1970–71, expenditure on books, periodicals and newspapers by 54 per cent, bookstocks by 41 per cent, and total staff by 14 per cent. In Scotland the figures have been similar—78, 51, 23, and 14 per cent respectively.[2] The parish authorities have disappeared, and more than a score of other small authorities in England and Wales have voluntarily surrendered their powers, besides half a dozen in Scotland.

One very remarkable development in England and Wales has been the introduction, from 1967–68 onwards, of central government grant in aid of public libraries. This had been the dream of librarians for three generations, and many had been disappointed that provision for it had not been made in the 1964 Act. In the event it arrived unheralded and unsung, in a paper defining new methods of rate-support grant by the Government in pursuance of the Local Government Act of 1966. Public libraries are not even mentioned in the body of the text, but a single line hidden away in an appendix indicates that library expenditure will in future qualify for grant.[3] It might be supposed that this change would have been one of the factors making for improvement, but in practice there is no evidence that this was the case.

In Scotland a working party on public library standards under the chairmanship of I. M. Robertson, appointed by the Secretary of State for Scotland in 1967, has not surprisingly come forward with recommendations almost

[1] Department of Education and Science, Library Advisory Councils, *A Report on the Supply and Training of Librarians* (1968); and *Public Library Service Points* (1971).
[2] Calculated from Institute of Municipal Treasurers and Accountants and Society of County Treasurers, *Public Library Statistics, 1965–66* (1967) and *1970–71* (1972).
[3] Ministry of Housing and Local Government, *Local Government Finance (England and Wales): the Rate-Support Grant Order, 1966* (1966), App. A, p. 11.

426

identical with those in the Bourdillon Report,[1] but legislation awaits final decisions on the reorganization of local government.

In this matter progress has been slow both north and south of the Border. The reconstruction of the Greater London area has been completed, and there has been extensive reorganization also (with a further reduction in the number of library authorities) in the West Midlands (1966) and on Teesside (1968), but the promised general reform is still round the corner. The main outlines, however, are now clearly visible. In England and Wales the new local government structure will come into force in 1974, and will result *inter alia* in a drastic simplification of the administration of the library service. In England the library authorities at present operating outside London will be reduced to 72, of which 38 will be counties and the remaining 34 will be districts within the six metropolitan areas.[2] In Wales the library authorities will be the eight counties, and possibly a few county districts which establish their right to library powers. Similar plans are in hand for Scotland,[3] where it is proposed to have ten regions, of which eight will be divided into districts and the other two (Orkney and Shetland) will be unitary authorities. The library authorities will be Orkney, Shetland, the Highlands, South-West and Borders regions, and the 31 districts in the other five regions. The number of library authorities will thus be reduced from 82 to 36.

Most of the new library authorities, especially in England and Wales, will be much larger and better endowed, and except in Inner London and Scotland (and any Welsh districts that may be accorded library powers) it should also be a source of strength that their boundaries will coincide with those of the education authorities.[4] It is difficult not to see the spirit of L. R. McColvin hovering over these proposals.

A sharp controversy arose in 1967 over a Government announcement that the site destined for the new British Museum Library would not be made available.[5] A special committee was appointed under the chairmanship of Dr. F. S. Dainton, Vice-Chancellor of the University of Nottingham, to re-examine the whole question of the national libraries, and especially to consider whether they should be brought into a unified framework. The committee recommended the creation of a new statutory and independent public body, to be known as the National Libraries Authority, which would take over responsibility for the British Museum Library (including the National Reference Library of Science and Invention), the National Central Library, the National Lending Library for Science and Technology, and the British National Bibliography. It also reaffirmed, to the satisfaction of the Museum trustees, the need for the Bloomsbury site.[6]

---

[1] Scottish Education Department, *Standards for the Public Library Service in Scotland* (Edinburgh 1969).

[2] Greater Manchester, Merseyside, South Yorkshire, Tyneside, West Midlands and West Yorkshire. Local Government Act, 1972, c.70.

[3] Secretary of State for Scotland, *Reform of Local Government in Scotland* (Cmnd. 4583, Edinburgh 1971).

[4] In Inner London the library authorities are the City and the 12 boroughs, but there is only one education authority.   [5] See *The Times*, 27 Oct. 1967.

[6] Secretary of State for Education and Science, *Report of the National Libraries Committee* [Dainton Report] (Cmnd. 4028, 1969).

In accepting these recommendations, the Government unhappily changed the name of the proposed new national authority to the Board of the British Library,[1] and in 1972 legislation was introduced to give effect to the proposals. The pattern for the future, therefore, seems to be set: a national reference library centred on the British Museum, with associated bibliographical services, and a national lending library (embracing both N.C.L. and N.L.L.S.T.) based at Boston Spa, the whole complex being related much more closely than hitherto to the public library service of the local authorities.

A final word may be devoted to what is somewhat confusingly called Public Lending Right, by which is meant the right of an author to receive some reward (over and above the initial royalty) when his books are lent by a library to the public. The matter was first brought into prominence in 1951, when Eric Leyland of Walthamstow wrote in W. H. Smith's *Trade Circular*:

> "it has always seemed to me most inequitable that an author must write a book, and spend large sums of money to produce it, only to find that thousands of copies, after being purchased by commercial lending libraries, are each read by hundreds of people—for the same royalty and profit return as though each copy were bought by a private individual."[2]

This put the problem in a nutshell, and in a subsequent letter Leyland suggested a levy of $\frac{1}{2}$d. per loan, for the benefit of the author.[3] It is not necessary to recount the details of the long controversy that followed.[4] The novelist John Brophy extended the argument to public libraries, and proposed a 1d. levy. The Society of Authors took the matter up, and enlisted the help of the publishers. When the Roberts Committee ignored the issue, Sir Alan Herbert headed a new campaign, but three attempts to secure legislation in 1960–61 failed to secure substantial support. The Library Association was hostile, the public indifferent, the Government nervous of any inroad on the free library principle. The Libraries Act of 1964 was silent on the question.

The recent change in the situation has been due in large measure to a study undertaken in 1965 by the Arts Council, which led in due course to the appointment of a Government working party which reported in 1972.[5] Even now the issue is not settled, but we could be moving towards a situation in which the Copyright Act of 1956 will be amended to make it a legal offence to lend copyright material to the public without a fee. The method of fixing and levying the fee remains a major difficulty, but the original idea of a levy on loans is now longer regarded as administratively practicable in this country, and the attention of the working party is focussed on finding a workable method of relating the payment to library purchases. There is no proposal to levy a charge on the borrower: the free library principle is still sacred.

There, for the moment, the matter rests.

---

[1] Secretary of State for Education and Science, *The British Library* (1971).
[2] *Trade Circular*, 3 Feb. 1951.
[3] *Ibid.*, 17 Feb. 1951.
[4] See W. J. Murison, *The Public Library: its Origins, Purpose, and Significance* (1955, 2nd edn. 1971), Ch. ix.
[5] Department of Education and Science, *Public Lending Right: Report of the Working Party appointed by the Paymaster General* (1972).

APPENDIX I

AN EARLY PROPOSAL FOR A PUBLIC LIBRARIES ACT

THE *Proposal* that follows is enclosed with a letter from H. B. Ker to Lord Brougham in the Brougham Papers at University College, London. The covering letter is printed above, p. 5 It is endorsed "6 February, 1831", but since the letter is headed "Sunday" the correct date should be probably 7th February.

For my knowledge of these documents I have to thank Mr. J. W. Scott, Librarian of University College, who when I embarked on the present work was kind enough to bring them to my attention. I am also indebted to Miss Margaret Skerl, Assistant Librarian at University College, who in sending me copies of the documents sent also, for good measure, copies of a number of related documents from the archives of the Society for the Diffusion of Useful Knowledge, which are housed in the same Library. Extracts from these also are printed below.

(1) *"Proposal for a bill to enable Towns of a given population to raise funds for the establishment of public reading and public lending libraries."*

"It is proposed to give *Towns*, or districts having a certain population, by a resolution of the inhabitants in vestry, a power to vote for the raising a sum (say £1000) this sum may increase and decrease according to a corresponding scale of inhabitants. The sum raised to be applied in founding a public library for the use of all the inhabitants to be used as a reading library: and rate payers are to have the power to borrow books to read at home: and when books are not returned or are lost their value to be recovered as the church rate is recoverable. The vestry to appoint a committee to superintend the library and a librarian—and a room to be hired or a room bought or built (as may be determined in vestry). In order to prevent improper selection of books the general control as to selection of books &c. to be in a board of Commissioners in London acting gratuitously in the same manner as the church commissioners act. Any rate payer may be responsible for any other parishioner not a rate payer, who may then borrow books as the rate payer might. This provision will give great circulation to the books and at the same time ensure the value of the books by the summary means to be furnished for recovering the price of cost. As however the inhabitants may not be induced to tax themselves with a sum necessary to found a library, the vestry are to have the power of borrowing the sum voted and charge it on the rates, to be repaid with interest by instalments of 1/20th of the principal each year. This is what is done under the Church acts when money is raised to rebuild or repair a church. There might be a power to borrow at 4 per cent from the saving Bank fund. Tho' this would not be absolutely necessary as there is never any difficulty in borrowing monies agreed to be raised in this way. The advantage of this plan is that it gives the parish the power of taxing themselves. And the whole machinery as to borrowing and charging the rates &c., may be adopted from the church building acts. And the board of general management for the selection &c. of books, will prevent improper books being had and all disputes &c. between the regular clergy and dissenters—there would be no difficulty in finding a few amateurs to act as commissioners, who would in fact have selections ready for the different classes of Libraries according to the amount raised. There are many small subscription libraries, Mechanics libraries &c. in different towns which have already given a taste and have shown the value of a public library.

"There is a statute little known the 7th of Anne for the better preservation of Parochial lending libraries in England founded for the benefit of the poor clergy, there is a charity called Dr. *Bray's associates* which since the reign of Queen Anne up to this time have founded different small parochial lending libraries principally in Wales for the benefit of the clergy only. There have been founded by this Charity 150 Libraries in England and about 30 in the North American Colonies. The number of books however in all these libraries only amounts to 13,000 owing to the funds being small but these libraries have been found extremely useful. In addition to the sums raised by rates there is every reason to suppose that in every Town when a library is established some individuals will add something to the sum raised, by donations.

"Assuming that £500 is the sum first laid out in books, this, at 4s/ a volume would give a library of 2500 volumes to which may be added Maps globes &c. A small annual stipend will be necessary for a librarian and lighting and warming— part of this may be defrayed by a small payment say ½d. on each volume borrowed &c.

H. B. Ker."

(2) *Extracts from S.D.U.K. Correspondence*

(a) H. B. Ker to Thomas Coates, S.D.U.K. Secretary, 1831:

". . . If you could write about Libraries to our local committees I will *give you a form*—perhaps you can call?"

(b) The same to the same, 1831:

". . . I send you the letter for Manchester and Nottingham, beg, that the information may be very *minute* as to the *working*."

(c) Memorandum in Ker's hand, 1831:

"Public Libraries

"enquire as to the establishment of public libraries at Nottingham and Man- chester, the rules, the facilities, the content—how maintained, how frequented. What are the good features and what the bad, if new books are added—if any other similar institutions are known?"[1]

(3) *Extracts from Minutes of S.D.U.K. General Committee.*

(a) 3 March, 1831:

"The Secretary stated that he had at the request of Mr. Ker written to all the members of the Local Committees of the Society requesting information concerning the public Libraries in their neighbourhoods . . ."

(b) 29 March, 1831:

"Mr. Ker stated that the Secretary had obtained very valuable information from some of the local Committees in answer to the circulars concerning Libraries, and he thought that these Committees might be rendered more useful than they now are.

---

[1] The inquiry in Manchester would almost certainly have reference to Chetham's Library; that to Nottingham may have been in connection with the Artizans' Library established there in 1824, though this institution was not unique.

"The matter was referred to Mr. Bingham Baring, Dr. Conolly, Mr. Ker, Mr. Loch, and Mr. Merivale as a Correspondence Committee, and they were instructed to report upon the measures to be adopted."

(c) 28 September 1832:

"It was resolved that Mr. Ker be requested to return the accounts of Libraries transmitted some time since to the Committee."

THE PUBLIC INSTITUTIONS BILL, 1835*

To facilitate the Formation and Establishment of Public Institutions for the diffusing of Literary and Scientific Information, including Libraries and Museums, with commodious Halls or Places of Public Meeting for Business or Entertainment, within such Cities, Boroughs and Towns as may require them for the use and accommodation of their Inhabitants.

WHEREAS it is expedient to encourage and promote the formation and establishment of Public Institutions for the diffusion of Literary and Scientific Information, including Libraries and Museums, with commodious Halls and Places of Public Meeting for Instruction and Entertainment, within such Cities, Boroughs and Towns as may require the same for the use and accommodation of their Inhabitants; BE it therefore Enacted, by the KING's most EXCELLENT MAJESTY, by and with the Advice and Consent of the Lords Spiritual and Temporal, and Commons, in this present Parliament assembled, and by the Authority of the same,

1 THAT in all cases in which Fifty Rate-payers of any City, Borough or Town, or of any Parish or Ward within the same, shall sign and send a Requisition to the Mayor or other chief civil authority of such Town, requesting him to call a Public Meeting of the Rate-payers of the same, for the purpose of considering the expediency of establishing within the Town such Public Institutions as are hereinbefore described, it shall be lawful for the said Mayor so to do; and in the event of his declining to accede to such Requisition, when duly signed, and presented to him by any Three or more of the Requisitionists, by whom the same may have been signed, or in case of his neglecting to comply with their request within Three clear Days after its delivery to him, it shall then be lawful for the said Three Requisitionists themselves to call such Public Meeting of the Rate-payers in any usual place of assembling within the Town, after giving Three clear Days' notice of the same to the Mayor.

2 And be it Enacted, That such Public Meeting being assembled, the question shall be publicly proposed by the Chairman of the same, and submitted to the open discussion of the Rate-payers then present, as to whether it is expedient that such Public Institutions for the diffusion of Literary and Scientific Information as aforesaid, should be formed and established within the Town in which such Public Meeting may be held; the costs of such undertaking to be chargeable, by way of assessment, on the rentals of the premises held and occupied by the inhabitants of the same.

---

*The version here printed, dated 6 August, 1835, incorporates the amendments made in Committee. The most notable changes were the substitution of "Committee of Public Institutions" for "Committee of Public Instruction", and the addition of Clauses 16, 17, 18 and 22.

3 And be it Enacted, That the decision of this question shall be submitted to the vote, at the close of such discussion, by a show of hands in the usual manner, and the declaration of the majority be publicly made on the spot by the Chairman of the Meeting; but in the event of a poll being demanded by any Three Rate-payers then present at the Meeting, such poll shall be taken on the spot by counting the numbers for, and the numbers against, the proposed Resolution.

4 And be it Enacted, That in the event of a majority of Two-thirds of the Rate-payers then present at such Meeting, who may vote on the question, being found, by such poll, to be in favour of the proposed resolution, the whole of the Rate-payers of the Town shall be bound by the act of such majority, and be liable to contribute, in the proportion of their respective rentals, to such assessments as may be subsequently levied by the proper authorities, to carry the resolution into effect, within the limited amount of rating, to be hereinafter prescribed.

5 And be it Enacted, That within Three clear Days after such decision of the majority as aforesaid, the Rate-payers shall proceed to elect, from among the resident householders of the Town, a Committee, to consist of Twenty-one persons, to be called "The Committee of Public Institutions:" to whom shall be confided the direction of all matters necessary for the execution and management of the Public Institutions to be formed and established under the powers of this Act; and in whom all Lands which may be purchased, with the Buildings erected upon the same for the purposes aforesaid, shall be vested, as Trustees *ex officio*, to hold and administer the same for the use and benefit of the Inhabitants generally.

6 And be it Enacted, That in the election of Members of the Committee, the mode followed shall be the same as that which is or may be in ordinary use in such Towns respectively for the election of Municipal or Parish Officers, as the case may be: Provided always, That no persons but those who are actually Rate-payers of such Towns shall be permitted to vote at such Elections, and that the poll for the whole of the Persons nominated for members of such Committee shall not be kept open longer than Six Hours, or from Ten o'clock in the Forenoon to Four o'clock in the Afternoon of one single Day; and provided also, that the Chairman of the public Meeting at which the original Resolution was carried, whether the Mayor or otherwise, or a Deputy appointed by the same, shall be the Returning Officer, to preside over and declare the result of such Election, by stating publicly the numbers voting for each of the several Persons nominated, and pronouncing the due return, as members of the Committee, of the Twenty-one who may have received the greatest number of votes in their favour.

7 And be it Enacted, That in order to encourage the wealthy Inhabitants of Towns, and of the neighbourhood, to come forward voluntarily to assist in the support of such Public Institutions for the diffusion of Literary and Scientific Information, the rank of Governor for Life shall be conferred (without election) on every person contributing the sum of One hundred Pounds as a donation, and the rank of Annual Governor shall be conferred (without election) on

every person contributing Ten Pounds per annum as subscription, so long as such annual subscription shall be continued; and such Life Governors and Annual Governors shall enjoy and exercise all the privileges of elected Members of the Committee.

8   And be it Enacted, That One-third of the Members of the Committee shall retire annually (in the first and second year, the Seven who were elected by the fewest number of votes, and in every succeeding year the Seven who have been longest members), and the filling up of the vacancies occasioned by such retirements, or by deaths, shall be by open election, in the same manner as that by which they were originally chosen: Provided always, That the members retiring by annual rotation may be eligible to be re-elected to the same office.

9   And be it Enacted, That the "Committee of Public Institutions," being thus formed, shall have power to procure designs and plans for the buildings required to form such Literary and Scientific Institutions, with Libraries, Museums, Halls, and other requisite accommodation, as aforesaid, with estimates of their cost, and to determine on the expediency of forming and establishing only a part or the whole of the several Works enumerated, as in their judgment may seem meet: Provided always, That the competition for such designs, plans and estimates shall be open to all persons offering to furnish the same, and that the selection or preference of any of those over others for actual adoption, shall be left entirely to the judgment of the Committee.

10   And be it Enacted, That the amount of the capital required for the completion of such Public Institutions as may be determined on, having been ascertained, it shall be lawful for the said Committee to borrow the requisite sum for that purpose, and such sum shall be charged upon the assessment hereby authorized to be levied for the repayment of the same: Provided always, That such sum shall in no case exceed, in its whole amount, the proportion of Ten Shillings to every inhabitant of such town, according to the last official census of the population of the same previous to the formation of such Institution therein.

11   And be it Enacted, That the annual payment of the Interest, and the gradual redemption of the Principal of such sum so borrowed, shall be provided for in manner following: a Public Stock or Fund shall be created, to be open for the investment of money, in the manner of other Public Funds, and transferrible by Shares of One hundred Pounds each, bearing interest at not more than Five Pounds per centum per annum, and redeemable in Twenty Years, by the paying off of Five Pounds per centum of the principal in every year, so that at the end of Twenty Years the whole of the Buildings forming the Public Institution may be free of any incumbrance or charge on the funds of the Town.

12   And be it Enacted, That for the payment of the said interest on such capital, and the annual redemption of Five Pounds per centum of the principal, as before described, the said "Committee of Public Institutions" shall be authorized to levy a half-yearly Assessment on the rental of all the dwellings

XIIIa. CATHAYS BRANCH, CARDIFF: CHILDREN'S READING ROOM

This picture, reproduced in the Library Association Conference Report for 1917, illustrates very clearly the formal atmosphere of the early children's libraries. In this instance an attempt has been made to relieve the formality by the use of pictures and flowers.

XIIIb. KINGSWOOD BRANCH, GLOUCESTER COUNTY: JUNIOR LIBRARY

The informal atmosphere of the modern children's library is well caught in this photograph taken in a new county branch in 1961.

XIVa. HOSPITAL LIBRARY SERVICE, EDINBURGH
Book service by the City Libraries in a hospital ward, 1946–47.

XIVb. PRISON LIBRARY SERVICE, PRESTON
Book service by the Public Libraries at H.M. Prison, 1950.

and other premises usually paying rates within the Town; such Assessment, however, not to exceed, in any case, the sum of Three-pence in the Pound on each Assessment, or Sixpence in the Pound on the rental within the entire year.

13 And be it Enacted, That the collection and recovery of the Sums assessed by order of the "Committee of Public Institutions" for the purposes aforesaid, shall be effected in the same manner in which the Rates for other local purposes are collected and recovered within such Towns respectively.

14 And be it Enacted, That the following shall be considered as primary objects, to be secured in all Public Institutions erected by the powers of this Act:—1. A spacious Hall, provided with fires, lights, tables and chairs as required, to serve as a Hall of Social Meeting for the Labouring Classes, at those periods of the year when recreation in the open air is impracticable: 2. A School Room, adapted for Infant teaching, with Class Rooms, for the studies of Youths of more advanced age: 3. Apartments for the meetings of Benefit Clubs, Sick Societies, Trade Committees or other Local Associations of mutual relief, and for the payment of wages, the sale of goods, or any other business for which such rooms are in constant requisition, but are now rarely to be procured, except at taverns and public-houses: 4. A Theatre, adapted for the delivery of Literary and Scientific Lectures, and for the exhibition of illustrative experiments, and containing the usual subdivision of seats, as in dramatic theatres, for the separate accommodation of different classes of Society: 5. A Library, Reading Rooms, Museum and Picture Gallery, adapted for the arrangement of such books, pictures, sculpture, specimens of natural history, and rare productions of nature and art, as may, by purchase or gift, be progressively accumulated in each: 6. That no Beer, Wine, Spirits or intoxicating drinks of any kind be permitted to be brought within the Public Institution, on pain of exclusion to the offending party for the period of a year at least; but that refreshments of every other description be permitted to be supplied to the Visitors by Persons appointed by the said Committee, and subject entirely to their direction.

15 And be it Enacted, That the said Committee may from time to time frame and pass such Rules and Regulations as they may deem necessary, for the preservation of order and decorum in every department of the Public Institution, and fix such moderate rates of payment for admission to the several parts of the same, as in their judgment may be sufficient to cover the current expenses of the Institution; keeping in view, however, the expediency of limiting such rates of admission to the lowest amount compatible with such maintenance, and with the comfort of the Persons frequenting the same.

16 And be it Enacted, That in any Cities, Boroughs or Towns in which the extent of the population may be such as to require more than one such Public Institution as hereinbefore described, it shall be lawful for the said "Committee of Public Institutions" to form and establish Auxiliary Institutions in such parts of the Town, or in such Wards or Parishes of the same, as may by them be deemed most eligible for the accommodation of the inhabitants thereof: Provided always, That the whole of the Capital to be expended in the forma-

tion and establishment of such Institutions shall not exceed the proportion of amount to population already prescribed, and that the whole of the assessments for the payment of the interest and redemption of the capital thus expended, shall not exceed the amount to which it is already limited by this Act: And provided also, That the management and regulation of all such Auxiliary Institutions, formed and established within the same City, Borough or Town, shall be under the direction of the "Committee of Public Institutions" as aforesaid, subject to such rules and provisions as are hereinbefore enacted, and to such other orders and regulations as the said Committee may from time to time think fit to issue for the government of the same.

17   And be it Enacted, That in any case in which particular spots of land may be deemed especially eligible for the erection of Buildings for such Public Institutions, but the same may belong to Corporate Bodies, or be under the management of Trustees, or be held by certain tenures which may prevent their being sold or exchanged, without special powers being given for this purpose, it shall be lawful for the Owners or Trustees of such lands, whether Bodies Corporate or otherwise, to sell, dispose of or exchange the same, on such terms as may be mutually agreed on by all the contracting parties: Provided always, That no such sale or exchange of lands shall be enforced or effected otherwise than by and with the full consent of all the parties having legal rights and interests in the same, and that the conveyances of such sale or exchange shall be made with all due form of law.

18   And be it Enacted, That in any case in which Public Institutions for the diffusion of Literary and Scientific Information already exist in any Town, or in any Parish or Ward of the same, and for the maintenance and support of which any funds have been bestowed or subscribed, and the same shall be found insufficient for the purposes required, it shall be lawful for the "Committee of Public Institutions," appointed in manner aforesaid, in any Town, Parish or Ward in which such case shall occur, to afford such aid, by way of loan, out of the funds raised by virtue of this Act, and within the limits fixed by the same, as the case may to them seem to require: Provided always, That the repayment of the Sums so advanced at the rate of Five per centum per annum of the principal, and the payment of interest on the same at the rate of not more than Five per centum per annum, be secured on the property of such Public Institutions, as well as on the assessment of the rate-payers of the Town, Parish or Ward in which the same may be situated, within the limited amount of rating already prescribed: And provided always, That in every such case the Public Institutions thus enlarged and improved by and from the funds as aforesaid, shall be placed under the direction and management of the "Committee of Public Institutions" for the Town in which the same may be situated, and be subject to all such rules and regulations as may by them be thought fit to be issued within the powers given to them by this Act.

19   And be it Enacted, That a Record shall be kept of all the Minutes of the said "Committee of Public Institutions," with Reports of their Proceedings at such Meetings as they may hold from time to time for purposes of business: and that such Minutes and Reports shall be signed by at least Seven of the members present at such Meetings, as forming the quorum of such Committee,

without the presence of which number no Resolutions shall be valid or binding upon the rest; and that an account shall be also kept of all receipts and disbursements connected with the Public Institutions authorized to be formed and established by this Act, and with the business of the said Committee within the year.

20 And be it Enacted, That for the purposes aforesaid, the said Committee shall be authorized to appoint and employ a Treasurer, Auditor, Clerks, Collectors, and such other Officers and Persons as may to them seem necessary to carry on the business of the Committee, with such salaries, and under such securities as may be proportioned to the responsibility vested in them respectively, and under full liability to such Rules and Orders as the Committee may think proper to frame for the regulation of their conduct, in the execution of their duties.

21 And be it Enacted, That within the month of January in every year, a Report of the past year's progress and proceedings shall be published, under the signature of the President or Chairman of the Committee for the time being, and countersigned by the Treasurer, Auditor and Clerk, containing detailed Accounts of all Receipts and Payments, as well as all Minutes of the Proceedings of the said Committee; and that a printed copy of such Report shall be supplied, free of expense, to every Rate-payer who may have been assessed for the purposes aforesaid, on his applying for the same.

22 And be it Enacted, That a Copy of such Annual Reports, well and strongly bound, in a separate volume, shall be forwarded, free of expense, to the Office of the Secretary of State for the Home Department, to the Library of the *British* Museum, and to the Libraries of the Houses of Lords and Commons, for the inspection of those who may desire to watch the progress and proceedings of such Institutions for the Diffusion of Literary and Scientific Information in different parts of the Kingdom.

23 And be it Enacted, That the expenses of all the preliminary proceedings, previous to the formation of the "Committee of Public Institutions," in manner before described, shall be borne by the requisitionists, and provided for by public subscriptions, or by such other means (not compulsory) as they may see fit; but in the event of the original Resolution submitted to the Public Meeting being carried in the affirmative, and the Committee being duly appointed, the expenses of such Meeting, and of all subsequent proceedings, shall then be defrayed out of the funds to be levied by the general assessment for which this Act provides.

24 And be it Enacted, That in the event of more than one-third of the Rate-payers of any Town assembled at a Public Meeting convened as aforesaid, voting against the original Resolution, by a poll taken at such Meeting, and thereby declaring it to be inexpedient to adopt, for the time being, any further proceedings as to the formation and establishment of any Public Institution for the diffusion of Literary and Scientific Information within the same, it shall not be lawful to make any other requisition for the purpose of calling

any Public Meeting to discuss the same question, within a period of less than One year from the time of such decision.

25   And be it Enacted, That in the construction of this Act, the word "Town" shall be construed to mean City, Borough, Town or any other Place usually understood by that term; and the word "Mayor" shall be construed to mean Mayor, Boroughreeve, Constable, Bailiff, Senior Magistrate or chief civil authority, by whatever title usually recognized, within the Town or Place in which his authority is exercised; that the words "Rate-payers" shall be construed to mean all Persons who have, for the period of One year at the least, paid the usual assessments levied on the Rate-payers of the Town or Parish in which they reside.

26   And be it Enacted, That this Act shall commence and take effect from and after the First day of October, in the year of our Lord One thousand eight hundred and Thirty-five.

27   And be it Enacted, That this Act shall extend to every part of *Great Britain* and *Ireland.*

PUBLIC LIBRARY AUTHORITIES 1847–1972

with dates of adoption and opening

IN the following list I have attempted, first, to present a complete and authoritative list of all library authorities that have existed in Great Britain since the passing of the Museums Act of 1845, with the dates of their establishment, and second, to show the stages by which the library authorities now existing have come into being. The list is complete to 1st April, 1972.

The names of existing authorities are shown in capitals, and are listed in order of counties.

The names of former library authorities are grouped under the authorities of which they now form part, and are shown either in small roman letters or (where there has been more than one stage in the process of amalgamation) in small italics.

The list deals only with library authorities, and does not attempt to record transfers of territory between library authorities, e.g. the absorption of county library branches by urban authorities.

For each authority I have endeavoured to establish

(a) *Date of adoption.* This usually means the date when the Libraries Acts were adopted, but a few early libraries operated under the Museums Act of 1845, and some others under local acts. In these cases the date of adoption is followed by an M or an L respectively.

(b) *Date of opening.* By this I mean the date at which a publicly maintained library service, or some part of it (e.g. a branch or reading room) was first made available to the public. I use the phrase "publicly maintained" because in certain boroughs libraries were maintained from public funds before adoption made rate-aid available. Where no library is known to have been opened during the independent life of the authority, the entry in the date column is NL.

(c) (*Where appropriate*) *Date of transfer to another library authority,* i.e. the date from which the transfer took effect. Where there has been more than one transfer the date given is that of the first, except where otherwise indicated.

The dates have been compiled in the first instance from library histories, Parliamentary Returns, reports of committees of inquiry, and library year books, and wherever possible have been checked by the libraries concerned. For England and Wales the files of correspondence preserved in the Public Record Office (Further Education, Public Library Files 1–307, Ed. 64, 1919–35) have also been helpful, and in cases of doubt I have, by courtesy of the Department of Education and Science, been able to use information from later files, which they still hold. Where, as with certain small and now defunct authorities, it has not been possible to achieve certainty, the best authenticated date is given in brackets, with a query where the evidence is doubtful.

The early history of library authorities in London has been studied in Mr. P. M. Whiteman's unpublished M.A. thesis on *The Establishment of Public Libraries and the Unit of Local Government in London to 1900* (Belfast 1969). For Wales I have derived much assistance from Mr. John Roe's recent work on *The Public Library in Wales*, which I had the privilege of reading and discussing with the author at the manuscript stage. In one or two instances, however, I have for what seems to me good reason ventured to differ from his dating.

Students of library history should be warned that the dates given in library year books, and even in many official reports, are not to be relied on without supporting evidence: this particularly applies to the date of "opening", since this word may be taken in a variety of senses.

It may be useful to summarise the abbreviations used:

M   : Library operated under Museums Act, 1845.
L   : Library operated under Local Act.
NL : No library recorded during the independent life of the authority.
( ) : Date probable but not confirmed.

ENGLAND

Name of Library Authority	Adoption (a)	Opening (b)	Transfer (c)	Remarks
Bedfordshire				
BEDFORD CO.	1924	1925		
BEDFORD	1889	1937		
LUTON	1894	1894		
Berkshire				
BERKSHIRE CO.	1923	1924[1]		[1] New Windsor M.B. excluded till 1933.
Abingdon	1892[2]	1896	1949	[2] Readopted 1922.
Letcombe Regis	1907	1907	1925	[3] Formerly in Oxfordshire.
MAIDENHEAD	1902	1904		
NEWBURY	1904	1906		
READING	1877	1883		
Caversham[3]	1905	1907	1911	
Buckinghamshire				
BUCKINGHAM CO.	1923	1923[1]		[1] Carnegie U.K. Trust Scheme from 1918.
East and Botolph				
Claydon	1897	1897	1965	NOTE: By 1900 East and
Grandborough	1896	1896	1923	Botolph Claydon, Grand-

Name of Library Authority	(a)	(b)	(c)	Remarks

Buckinghamshire, *continued*

Middle Claydon	1893	1893	1965	borough, and Water Eaton
Oakley	1905	1906	1936	were all operating in con-
Steeple Claydon	1901	1902	1965	junction with Middle Claydon
Water Eaton	1896	1896	1923	(*L.Y.B. 1900-01*). Steeple
HIGH WYCOMBE[2]	1920	1920		Claydon joined the scheme

later (*Adams Report*). Grand-
borough and Water Eaton had
ceased to operate by 1923.
[2] Earlier listed as Chepping
Wycombe.

Cambridgeshire and Isle of Ely

CAMBRIDGE AND ISLE OF ELY CO.				
Cambridgeshire Co.	1921	1922	1965	[1] Served by Cambridge.
Isle of Ely Co.	1925	1926	1965	[2] Cambridgeshire Co. area
Burwell	1895	1895	1965	1921–34.
CAMBRIDGE	1853	1855		
Chesterton	1897	[1]	1912	
Trumpington	1898	NL	1934[2]	

Cheshire

CHESHIRE CO.	1920[1]	1922		[1] Crewe and Congleton
Marple	1920	NL	1928	excluded till 1936, when
Middlewich	1889	1890	1967	Crewe established an
Nantwich	(1887)	(1889)	1967	independent service and the
Winsford	(1887)	(1888)	1939	Co. agreed to take
ALTRINCHAM[2]	1889	1892		responsibility for
BEBINGTON[3]	1894	1930[4]		Congleton.
BIRKENHEAD	1856	1856		[2] See also Bowdon and
BOWDON	1903	[5]		Hale below.
CHESTER	1874	1877		[3] Bebington and
CREWE	1936	1936		Bromborough till 1937.
DUKINFIELD	1894	1895		[4] Privately founded library
ELLESMERE PORT[6]	1907	1910		grant-aided from 1894.
HALE	1903	1907[7]		[5] Served by Altrincham
HYDE	1893	1893		since adoption.
KNUTSFORD	1903	1904		[6] Ellesmere Port and
MACCLESFIELD	1874	1876		Whitby till 1933.
NESTON	1901	1908		[7] Served by Altrincham
NORTHWICH	1883	1885		1903–07.
Winnington	1883	1885[8]	1936	[8] Joint service with
RUNCORN	1881	1882		Northwich 1885–1924.
SALE	1890	1891		[9] Joint service with Sale
Ashton on Mersey	1896	1896[9]	1930	1896–1930.
STALYBRIDGE	1888	1889		
STOCKPORT	1861	1875		
WALLASEY	1898	1899		

Name of Library Authority	(a)	(b)	(c)	Remarks
Cornwall				
CORNWALL CO.	1924	1925		[1] Ministry of Health, Isles of
Bodmin	(1895)	1897	1953	Scilly Order, 23 Aug. 1937.
Falmouth	1893	1894	1971	[2] Books supplied by Cornwall
Hayle	(1896)	NL	1924	Co.
Launceston	1897	1899	1947	
Liskeard	1895	1896	1949	
St. Austell	1895	NL	1924	
St. Ives	1895	1897	1970	
CAMBORNE-REDRUTH				
Camborne	(1893)	1895	1934	
Redruth	(1894)	1895	1934	
ISLES OF SCILLY	1937[1]	1940[2]		
PENZANCE	1893	1893		
TRURO	1885	1886		
Cumberland				
CUMBERLAND CO.	1920	1921		[1] Served by Cockermouth,
Arlecdon and Frizington	1891	1892	1937	since 1965 by arrangement
Aspatria	1902	1902	1940	with Co.
Cleator Moor	1892	1895	1962	[2] Served by Workington.
Millom	1887	1887	1948	
Papcastle	1902	[1]	1965	
Penrith	1881	1883	1965	
CARLISLE	1890	1893		
COCKERMOUTH	1899	1899		
WHITEHAVEN	1887	1888		
WORKINGTON	1889	1890		
Harrington	1899	1899	1934	
Stainburn	1908	[2]	1934	
Derbyshire				
DERBYSHIRE CO.	1923	1924		
Buxton	1886	1889	1967	
Glossop	1888	1889	1967	
New Mills	1893	1899	1967	
Pleasley	1906	1906	1933	
Shirebrook	1895	1895	1928	
South Normanton	1902	NL	1923	
Swadlincote	1904	1908	1967	
CHESTERFIELD	1875	1879		
DERBY	1870	1871		
ILKESTON	1901	1901		
LONG EATON	1903	1906		

Name of Library Authority	(a)	(b)	(c)	Remarks
Devonshire				
DEVON CO.	1924	1924		[1] No adoption: expense
Ilfracombe	1903	NL	1934	borne from Borough Fund.
Moretonhampstead	(1901)	1902	1962	[2] Amalgamation of Torquay
South Molton	[1]	(1889)	1940	and areas formerly served
BIDEFORD	1877	1877		by Co.
EXETER	1869	1870		
NEWTON ABBOT	1902	1904		
PLYMOUTH	1871	1876		
Devonport	1880	1882	1914	
TORBAY		1968[2]		
Torquay	1903	1907	1968	
Dorset				
DORSET CO.	1925	1925[1]		[1] In June, 1919, the County
POOLE	1885	1886		Education Committee took
WEYMOUTH AND				over responsibility for the
MELCOMBE REGIS	1893	1944		Dorset Schools and Village
				Booklending Association,
				then serving 106 centres,
				and launched its own
				scheme to serve 300 centres.
Durham				
DURHAM CO.	1923	1924		[1] By extension of Museums
Annfield Plain	1903	1908	1938	Act.
Boldon Colliery	1904	(1905)	1938	
Jarrow	(1902)	NL	1923	
Leadgate	(1896)	NL	1923	
Monk Hesledon	1899	(1899)	1929	
Trimdon	1896	(1896)	1954	
DARLINGTON	1883	1885		
GATESHEAD ON TYNE	1880	1885		
HARTLEPOOL	1891	1894		
West Hartlepool	1891	1895	1967	
SOUTH SHIELDS	1871	1873		
SUNDERLAND	1858[1]	1859		
Essex				
ESSEX CO.	1925[1]	1926		[1] Harwich excluded till 1946.
Brentwood	(1903)	NL	1925	[2] Formerly served by Co.
Halstead	1902	NL	1925	
Witham	1903	1904	1925	
CHELMSFORD	1902	1906		
CHIGWELL		1968[2]		
COLCHESTER	1891	1892		
SOUTHEND ON SEA	1903	1906		

Name of Library Authority	(a)	(b)	(c)	Remarks
Essex *continued*				
THURROCK		1936³		³ Amalgamation of Grays
Aveley	(1919)	(by 1923)	1936⁴	Thurrock and areas
Grays Thurrock	1893	1894	1936	formerly served by Co.
				⁴ Last reported in operation
				1923–24 (*Kenyon Report*).
Gloucestershire				
GLOUCESTER CO.	1922	1922¹		¹ Carnegie U.K. Trust
Stroud	1897	1897	1930	Scheme from 1917.
BRISTOL	1874	1876		Cirencester (*q.v.*) was
CHELTENHAM	1883	1884		excluded at the time of
CIRENCESTER	1935	1960²		adoption.
GLOUCESTER	1894	1897		² Grants by U.D. in aid of
				subscription library
				1944–60; service now
				provided by arrangement
				with Co.
Hampshire				
HAMPSHIRE CO.	1924	1925		¹ Last recorded, in Kenyon
Sheet	1896	1897	¹	Report, as in operation
ALDERSHOT	1953²	1954		1923–24.
ANDOVER	1896	1897		² Co. adopted in 1924, but
BOURNEMOUTH	1893	1895		provided little service.
GOSPORT³	1886	1890		³ Earlier listed as
PORTSMOUTH	1876	1883		Alverstoke, or Gosport
SOUTHAMPTON	1887	1889		and Alverstoke.
WINCHESTER	1851	1851		
Herefordshire				
HEREFORD CO.	1925	1926		¹ Serviced by Co. from 1941.
Colwall	1898	1899	1965	
Leominster	1890	1892¹	1951	
Ross on Wye	1906	1912	1938	
HEREFORD	1871	1871		
Hertfordshire				
HERTFORD CO.	1924	1925		¹ Co. branch 1926–36.
Bishop's Stortford	(1904)	NL	1924	
Hemel Hempstead	(1897)	NL	1924	
Hertford	1855	1856	1964	
Hitchin	1936¹	1937	1951	
CHESHUNT	1904	1907		
LETCHWORTH	1925	1936		
ST. ALBANS	1878	1882		
WATFORD	1871	1874		

Name of Library Authority	(a)	(b)	(c)	Remarks

Huntingdonshire and Peterborough

HUNTINGDON AND PETERBOROUGH CO.				[1] Act was used to maintain museum.
Huntingdon Co.	1924	1926	1965	[2] Service by Northampton
St. Neots	*1896*[1]	*NL*	*1925?*	Co.
Soke of Peterborough Co.	1925	1926[2]	1965	
PETERBOROUGH	1891	1892		

Isle of Wight

ISLE OF WIGHT CO.	1924	1924[1]		[1] Seely Library, controlled and in part maintained by
SANDOWN–SHANKLIN				Co. Education Committee
Sandown	1904	1905	1934	from 1904.
Shanklin	1935[2]	1933	1934	[2] Co. area 1924–33.

Kendal and Westmorland

KENDAL AND WESTMORLAND	1891[1]	1892		[1] Service for the Co. of Westmorland was
Kirkby Lonsdale	1903	1903	1949	originally provided by
WINDERMERE	1910	1926		Kendal only (see above p. 213). From 1948 to 1967 Co. representatives were co-opted to the Kendal Committee. Since 1967 this has been a Joint Committee under the Local Government Act, 1933.

Kent

KENT CO.	1920	1921		[1] *P.R. 1912* says supported
Northfleet	1903	NL	1920	from borough funds
Queenborough	1887	(1888)	1940[1]	without special rate. Co.
Tonbridge	1881	1882	1935	supplied books from 1927.
CANTERBURY	1847(M)	1847		[2] Co. area 1920–33.
CHATHAM	1893	1903		[3] Co. area 1920–23.
DARTFORD	1912	1916		[4] Co. area 1920–52.
DOVER	1933[2]	1935		[5] Co. area 1920–33. McColvin
FOLKESTONE	1878	1879		reports that service was
Cheriton	1923[3]	NL	1934	still being provided by
GILLINGHAM	(1902)	1952[4]		Co. 1942.
Rainham	(1896)	(1896)	1929	
GRAVESEND	1893	1894		
HYTHE	1933[5]	1933		
MAIDSTONE	1855	1858		
MARGATE	1923	1923		
RAMSGATE	1894	1895		

Name of Library Authority	(a)	(b)	(c)	Remarks
Kent *continued*				
ROCHESTER	1894	1894		[6] Until 1929 Sittingbourne
SEVENOAKS	1904	1905		only.
SITTINGBOURNE AND				
MILTON[6]	1887	1889		
TUNBRIDGE WELLS	1895	1921		

Lancashire

Name of Library Authority	(a)	(b)	(c)	Remarks
LANCASHIRE CO.	1924	1925		[1] Served by Ashton-under-
Audenshaw	1913	[1]	1929	Lyne till 1926.
Clayton-le-Moors	1915	1923	1969	[2] *Kenyon Report* 1920.
Dalton in Furness	(1900)[2]	(1905)	1950	[3] Served by Wigan 1920–37.
Great Harwood	1903	NL	1924	[4] Served by Union of
Horwich	(1906)	(1906)	1932	Lancashire and Cheshire
Leyland	(1887)	NL	1924	Institutes.
Littleborough	(1900)	(1902)	1959	[5] McColvin reports that
Milnrow	1908	1908	1969	service was already being
Orrell	(1918)	[3]	1937	provided by Co. in 1942.
Oswaldwistle	(1913)	(1915)	1962	[6] Tyldesley with Shakerley
Padiham	(1897)	[4]	1928	till 1933.
Rainford	(1905)	(1905)	1944[5]	[7] Supplied by Ashton to 1927.
Tyldesley[6]	1897	1909	1967	[8] Supplied by Ashton to 1936,
Upholland	1920	NL	1935	by Lancs. Co. 1936–54.
Wardle	(1904)	(1906)	1948	[9] "The Library was worked
Whitefield	(1895)	NL	1924	for twelve months under
Whitworth	(1904)	NL	1924	the scheme of the Union
Worsley	(1896)	NL	1924	of Lancashire and Cheshire
ACCRINGTON	1899	1900		Institutes, but has been
ASHTON IN				suspended until further
MAKERFIELD	1903	1906		arrangements can be made"
ASHTON UNDER LYNE	1880	1881		—*L.Y.B. 1910–11.*
Hurst	1901	[7]	1927	[10] Appears in some early lists
Waterloo	1908	[8]	1954	(incorrectly) as Shaw and
ATHERTON	1903	1905		Crompton.
BACUP	1924	1931		
BARROW IN FURNESS	1881	1882		
BLACKBURN	1853	1862		
BLACKPOOL	1879	1880		
Bispham with Norbreck	1906	1911[9]	1917	
BOLTON	1852	1853		
BOOTLE	1884	1887		
BURNLEY	1871(L)	1914		
BURY	1897	1901		
CHADDERTON	1902	1905		
CHORLEY	1897	1899		
CLITHEROE	1878	1879		
COLNE	1894	1895		
CROMPTON[10]	1903	1907		

Name of Library Authority	(a)	(b)	(c)	Remarks
Lancashire *continued*				
CROSBY	1903	1905		[11] Served by Wigan since
Waterloo with Seaforth	1892	1898	1937	1901.
DARWEN	1871	1871		[12] Acts adopted, and reading
DENTON	1887	1889		rooms opened, in or before
ECCLES	1905	1905		1902 (Carnegie U.K.
FAILSWORTH	1903	1909		Trust records).
FARNWORTH	1908	1911		[13] Or Newton in Makerfield.
FLEETWOOD	1887	1887		
HASLINGDEN	1900	1905		
HEYWOOD	1874	1874		
HINDLEY	1887	1887		
INCE IN MAKERFIELD	1898	[11]		
LANCASTER	1892	1893		
LEIGH	1892	1894		
LIVERPOOL	1852(L)	1852		
Much Woolton	1890	1890	1913	
LYTHAM ST. ANNES				
Lytham	1917	1917	1922	
St. Annes	1903	1906	1922	
MANCHESTER	1852	1852		
Gorton	1897	1901	1909	
Levenshulme	[12]	[12]	1909	
Moss Side	1887	1897	1904	
Newton Heath	1887	NL	1890	
MIDDLETON	1887	1889		
NELSON	1889	1889		
NEWTON-LE-WILLOWS[13]	1905	1909		
OLDHAM	1865(L)	1883		
PRESTON	1878	1879		
RADCLIFFE	1904	1907		
RAWSTENSTALL	1902	1906		
ROCHDALE	1870	1872		
ROYTON	1903	1907		
ST. HELENS	1869(L)	1872		
SALFORD	1849(M)	1850		
SOUTHPORT	1875	1876		
Birkdale	1902	1905	1912	
STRETFORD	1893	1893		
SWINTON AND PENDLEBURY	1897	1897		
WARRINGTON	1848(M)	1848		
WESTHOUGHTON	1903	1906		
WIDNES	1885	1887		
WIGAN	1876	1878		

Name of Library Authority	(a)	(b)	(c)	Remarks
Leicestershire				
LEICESTER CO.	1924	1924		[1] Monthly supply of books
Bottesford	1922	1922[1]	1929	from Grantham, made
Ibstock	1895	NL [2]	1927	available through local
Shepshed	1896	NL [3]	1934	subscription library; from
HINCKLEY	1888	1888		c.1924 assisted also by Co.
LEICESTER	1869[4]	1871		[2] Books supplied by Co.
LOUGHBOROUGH	1885	1886		from c.1924.
MELTON MOWBRAY	1903	1905		[3] Books supplied by Co.
OADBY	1900	1901		from c.1924.
				[4] By extension of Museums Act.
Lincolnshire—Kesteven				
KESTEVEN CO.	1924	1924		[1] For the Carnegie U.K.
GRANTHAM	1913	1922[1]		Trust scheme based on
STAMFORD	1903	1906		Grantham from 1920, see above, p. 214.
—Lindsey and Holland				
LINDSEY AND				[1] Service begun by Lindsey
HOLLAND CO.	1924	1925[1]		alone: joint service with
Cleethorpes with				Holland since 1936, though
Thrunscoe	(1900)	NL	1924	technically the two
Louth	(1898)	NL	1924	authorities remain
Spalding	(1904)	NL	1936	independent. The village
BOSTON	1904	1905		of Sturton, in Lindsey,
GAINSBOROUGH	1903	1905		adopted the Acts in 1918
GRIMSBY	1894	1901		under the scheme based on
LINCOLN	1892	1895		Worksop (see s.v.
SCUNTHORPE	1902	1904		Nottingham) but does not
Ashby	1905	1906	1919	appear ever to have made
Frodingham	1903	[2]	1919	independent provision.
				[2] Served by Scunthorpe.

London

Owing to successive amalgamations the library history of London is exceedingly complex. In 1900 the various districts and vestries of London outside the City were grouped into 28 metropolitan boroughs, constituting, with the City, the County of London. In 1965 the metropolitan boroughs were regrouped to form 12 Inner London Boroughs, and the various authorities of Greater London outside the boundaries of the County of London were grouped to form 20 Outer London Boroughs. Most of the present London Boroughs, therefore, represent amalgamations of library authorities, many of which were already amalgamations of earlier authorities. Some areas formerly served by county libraries have also been absorbed into the new Boroughs, and the County of Middlesex, which adopted the Libraries Acts in 1920 and provided service from 1922, has in the process entirely disappeared, being for the most part absorbed into the Boroughs of Hounslow, Hillingdon, Ealing, Harrow, Brent, Barnet, Havering and Enfield. In the list that follows the names of former metropolitan boroughs are distinguished by the prefix★

Name of Library Authority	Adoption (a)	Opening (b)	Transfer (c)	Remarks
Inner London				
CAMDEN				
★Hampstead	1893	1894	1965	[1] Remainder of Holborn
★Holborn			1965	District passed to Finsbury
Holborn District (part)	1891	1893	1900[1]	(see s.v. Islington)
St. Giles	1891	1892	1900	[2] Maintained till 1921 from
★St. Pancras	1904	1906	1965	the City's Privy Purse.
CITY	1921	1872[2]		[3] Adopted 1901 for part of
GREENWICH				borough which had not
★Greenwich	1902	1905	1965	adopted prior to
★Woolwich	[3]	1901	1965[4]	amalgamation 1900.
Woolwich	1895	NL	1900	[4] A small part of Woolwich,
Plumstead	1898	NL	1900	North of the Thames,
HACKNEY				passed to Newham.
★Hackney	1903	1908	1965	[5] No library in this part of
★Shoreditch	1891	1892	1965	Holborn before transfer
★Stoke Newington			1965	1900. See s.v. Camden.
Stoke Newington	1890	1890	1900	[6] Originally a joint library
South Hornsey	1898	1898	1900	of Lambeth and
HAMMERSMITH				Camberwell.
★Hammersmith	1887	1889	1965	[7] Remainder of Wandsworth
★Fulham	1886	1887	1965	passed to the London
ISLINGTON				Borough of that name, q.v.
★Islington	1904	1906	1965	[8] Jointly administered since
★Finsbury			1965	its establishment by
Clerkenwell	1887	1888	1900	Lambeth and Croydon.
Holborn District (part)	1891	1893[5]	1900	
KENSINGTON AND CHELSEA				
★Chelsea	1887	1887	1965	
★Kensington	1887	1888	1965	
LAMBETH				
★Lambeth	1886	1888	1965	
Minet Library		1890	1956[6]	
★Wandsworth (part)			1965[7]	
Clapham	1887	1889	1900	
Streatham	1889	1891	1900	
Upper Norwood		1900[8]		
LEWISHAM				
★Deptford	1904	1905	1965	
★Lewisham	1890	1891	1965	

Name of Library Authority	(a)	(b)	(c)	Remarks
Inner London *continued*				
SOUTHWARK				
★Southwark			1965	[9] Adopted 1901 for part of
Christchurch	*1888*	*1889*	*1900*	borough which had not
Newington	*1890*	*1893*	*1900*	adopted prior to
St. George the Martyr	*1896*	*1899*	*1900*	amalgamation 1900.
St. Saviour	*1891*	*1894*	*1900*	[10] Adopted 1901 for part of
★Bermondsey	[9]		1965	borough which had not
Bermondsey	*1887*	*1892*	*1900*	adopted prior to
Rotherhithe	*1887*	*1890*	*1900*	amalgamation 1900.
★Camberwell	1889	1890	1965	[11] Remainder of
TOWER HAMLETS				Wandsworth passed to
★Bethnal Green	1913	1922	1965	Lambeth, *q.v.*
★Poplar			1965	[12] Adopted 1900 for part of
Poplar	*1890*	*1892*	*1900*	borough which had not
Stratford-le-Bow	*1896*	*NL*	*1900*	adopted prior to
Bromley by Bow	*1891*	*1895*	*1900*	amalgamation 1900.
★Stepney			1965	[13] Served by St. Martin's.
Limehouse	*1898*	*NL*	*1900*	[14] Queen's Park Ward, taken
Mile End	*1896*	*NL*	*1900*	over from Chelsea 1901,
St. George in the East	*1896*	*1898*	*1900*	had a library opened in
Whitechapel	*1889*	*1892*	*1900*	1890.
WANDSWORTH				
★Wandsworth (part)	[10]		1965[11]	
Wandsworth	*1883*	*1885*	*1900*	
Putney	*1887*	*1888*	*1900*	
★Battersea	1887	1887	1965	
WESTMINSTER				
★Westminster	[12]		1965	
St. George, Hanover Square	*1890*	*1894*	*1900*	
St. Margaret and St. John	*1856*	*1857*	*1900*	
St. Martin in the Fields	*1887*	*1889*	*1900*	
St. Paul, Covent Garden	*1893*	*1893*[13]	*1900*	
★Paddington	1920	1920[14]	1965	
★St. Marylebone	1920	1923	1965	

Outer London

BARKING				
Barking	1888	1889	1965[1]	[1] A small part of Barking
Dagenham	1928[2]	1930	1965[3]	passed to Newham.
BARNET[4]				[2] 1926–28 Essex Co.
				[3] A small part of Dagenham
				passed to Redbridge.
				[4] Barnet itself, which forms
				part of the new London
				Borough, was served till
				1965 by Herts. Co.

Name of Library Authority	(a)	(b)	(c)	Remarks
Outer London *continued*				
Finchley	1930[5]	1933	1965	[5] Finchley had a small non-
Hendon	1919	1926[6]	1965	rate-supported library
BEXLEY				established in 1896, and
Bexley	1896	1899	1965	was excluded from the
Erith	1903	1906	1965	county service when
Sidcup	1958[7]	1958	1965	Middlesex adopted in 1920.
BRENT				[6] Children's service only till
Willesden	1891	1894	1965	1929.
BROMLEY				[7] Served by Kent Co. till
Beckenham	1936[8]	1938	1965	1958, when Chislehurst
Bromley	1892	1894	1965	and Sidcup became
Chislehurst	1958[9]	1958	1965	independent authority.
Orpington	1957[10]	1957	1965	Chislehurst passed 1965 to
St. Mary Cray	*1919*	*1919*	*1934*[11]	Bromley.
Penge	1891	1892	1965	[8] Kent Co. area 1920–36.
CROYDON[12]				[9] Chislehurst and Sidcup,
Croydon	1888	1890	1965	see *s.v.* Bexley.
Coulsdon and Purley	1935[13]	1936	1965	[10] Kent Co. branch 1936–57.
EALING				[11] Kent Co. provision 1935–
Acton	1898	1900	1965	57.
Ealing	1883	1883	1965	[12] For the Upper Norwood
Hanwell	1902	1905	1965	Joint Library see *s.v.*
Southall (Southall				Lambeth.
Norwood)	1903	1905	1965	[13] Surrey Co. service
ENFIELD				1920–35.
Edmonton	1891	1893	1965	[14] Formerly served by
Enfield	1892	1894	1965	Middlesex Co.
HARINGEY				[15] Comprising Hornchurch
Hornsey	1896	1899	1965	and Romford, formerly
Tottenham	1891	1892	1965	served by Essex Co.
Wood Green	1891	1892	1965	[16] Surrey Co. branch 1929–31.
HARROW			1965[14]	[17] Merton itself (part of
HAVERING			1965[15]	Merton and Morden) was
HOUNSLOW				served 1931–65 by Surrey
Brentford and Chiswick			1965	Co.
Brentford	*1889*	*1890*	*1927*	[18] Powers transferred to Surrey
Chiswick	*1890*	*1891*	*1927*	Co. 1924, resumed 1931.
Heston and Isleworth	1903	1905	1965	
KINGSTON UPON				[19] Small parts of Barking
THAMES				(*q.v.*) and Woolwich (see
Kingston On Thames	1881	1882	1965	*s.v.* Greenwich) were also
Surbiton	1931[16]	1931	1965	included in this new
MERTON[17]				Borough.
Mitcham	1922[18]	1933	1965	[20] A small part of Dagenham
Wimbledon	1883	1886	1965	also passed to this Authority
NEWHAM[19]				(see *s.v.* Barking).
East Ham	1895	1896	1965	
West Ham	1890	1892	1965	
REDBRIDGE[20]				
Ilford	1896	1909	1965	

Name of Library Authority	(a)	(b)	(c)	Remarks
Outer London *continued*				
RICHMOND UPON THAMES				
Barnes	1935[21]	1943	1965	[21] Surrey Co. service 1920–35.
Richmond	1879	1881	1965	[22] Surrey Co. service 1930–35.
Twickenham	1882	1882	1965	[23] Surrey Co. service 1930–35.
Hampton	*1900*	*1901*	*1937*	[24] Surrey Co. service 1927–36.
Teddington	*1895*	*1896*	*1937*	[25] Powers lapsed to Surrey Co.
SUTTON				1924; amalgamated with
Beddington and				Cheam 1928.
Wallington	1935[22]	1936	1965	
Carshalton	1935[23]	1935	1965	
Sutton and Cheam	1935[24]	1936	1965	
Sutton	1902	NL	[25]	
WALTHAM FOREST				
Leyton	1891	1893	1965	
Walthamstow	1892	1894	1965	

Norfolk

NORFOLK CO.	1924	1925		[1] Reported closed 1899—
Costessey	(1907)	(1907)	1927	*P.R. 1912.*
East Winch	(1909)	NL	1924	
North Walsham	(1901)	NL	1924	
Shouldham	(1895)	NL	1924	
Wells next the Sea	(1902)	NL	1924	
Wroxham	(1895)	(1895)[1]	1924	
GREAT YARMOUTH	1885	1886		
KING'S LYNN	1899	1899		
NORWICH	1850	1857		

Northamptonshire

NORTHAMPTON CO.	1924	1926		
Irchester	(1904)	(1909)	1965	
Rothwell	1894	1896	1972	
KETTERING	1895	1896		
NORTHAMPTON	1860	1876		
Kingsthorpe	(1896)	NL	1900	
RUSHDEN	(1902)	1905		
WELLINGBOROUGH	1894	1902		

Northumberland

NORTHUMBERLAND CO.	1924[1]	1925		[1] Wallsend and Morpeth M.B.s, and 15 U.D.s, were excluded from the original

Name of Library Authority	(a)	(b)	(c)	Remarks
Northumberland, *continued*				
Alnwick	1930	NL	1931	adoption. Wallsend and
Amble	1936	NL	1949	Gosforth U.D. later
Ashington	1945	NL	1947	became independent
Earsdon	1930	by 1931	1936	authorities, and the
BERWICK UPON				remaining areas were
TWEED	1920[2]	1948		brought within the county
BLYTH	1920	1930		area at various dates from
GOSFORTH	1949	1950		1929 to 1953.
NEWBURN	1937	1937		[2] This adoption was not
NEWCASTLE UPON				known to the Kenyon
TYNE	1874	1880		Committee, which counted
Benwell and Fenham	1903	NL	1904	Berwick as an excluded
TYNEMOUTH	1869	1869		area.
WALLSEND	1931	1933		[3] Whitley and Monkseaton
WHITLEY BAY[3]	1926	1940		till 1954.

Nottinghamshire

	(a)	(b)	(c)	Remarks
NOTTINGHAM CO.	1924	1924[1]		[1] Carnegie U.K. Trust
Mansfield Woodhouse	1919	NL	1929	Scheme from 1919.
East Retford	1923	1927	1934	Mansfield Woodhouse and
Stapleford	(1904)	1906	1935	five other urban districts
ARNOLD	1905	1906		excluded till 1929.
CARLTON	1888	(1888)		[2] Formerly Hucknall
HUCKNALL[2]	1884	1887		Torkard.
MANSFIELD	1890	1891		[3] Centre for Carnegie U.K.
NEWARK	1881	1883		Trust regional scheme
NOTTINGHAM	1867	1868		1916–18. Under this
SUTTON IN ASHFIELD	1898	1899		scheme ,taken over by the
Huthwaite	(1911)	1913	1934	County in 1919, the
WORKSOP	1895	1896[3]		following Nottinghamshire

villages are reported to
have adopted the Acts,
though it does not appear
that they ever provided an
independent service: in
1917, Babworth and
Ranby, Carlton in
Lindrick, Ollerton,
Tarworth; in 1918,
Barnby Moor, East
Markham, Eaton,
Edwinstowe, Gamston.

Oxfordshire

	(a)	(b)	(c)	Remarks
OXFORD CO.	1924	1924[1]		[1] Area of adoption excluded
Checkendon	(1895)	NL	1924	Banbury and Henley M.B.s.
Henley on Thames	1944	1944	1965	
Lower Heyford	1920	NL	1924	

Name of Library Authority	(a)	(b)	(c)	Remarks
Oxfordshire *continued*				
Woodstock	[2]	(1899)	1947	[2] Originally supported from
BANBURY	1945	1947		Borough funds without
OXFORD	1852	1854		adoption—*P.R. 1912.*
				Technically Woodstock
				was part of the Co. area
				from 1924.
Rutlandshire				
RUTLAND CO.	1946	1946[1]		[1] Books supplied by Leicester
Cottesmore	(1901)	(1903)	1946	Co.
Shropshire				
SHROPSHIRE CO.	1925	1925		
Oswestry	1890	1890	1967	
Wellington	1902	1904	1949	
Wem	1919	1919	1966	
Whitchurch	1900	1902	1965	
SHREWSBURY	1883	1885		
Somerset				
SOMERSET CO.	1923	1923[1]		[1] Carnegie U.K. Trust
Norton Radstock			1962	Scheme from 1918.
Midsomer Norton	*1903*	*1919*	*1934*	[2] Reference Library
Radstock	*1904*	*1907*	*1934*	maintained without
BATH	1900	1895[2]		adoption till 1900.
BRIDGWATER	1860	1860		
TAUNTON	1902	1905		
WESTON-SUPER-MARE	1886	1890		
YEOVIL	1920	1922		
Staffordshire				
STAFFORD CO.	1922	1922[1]		[1] Carnegie U.K. Trust
Audley	1903	NL	1931	Scheme from 1916.
Great Wyrley	(1898)	(1898)	1942	Seventeen urban districts
Kidsgrove	(1896)	(1898)	1933	excluded from Co. area
Rushall	(1903)	(1903)[2]	1922	initially were all absorbed
BURTON UPON				either into the County or
TRENT	1894	1897		into other library areas by
CANNOCK	1925	1925		1931.
LEEK	1887	1888		[2] Reported closed 1908—
LICHFIELD	1855	1859		*P.R. 1912.*
NEWCASTLE UNDER				
LYME	1884	1891		
STAFFORD	1879	1882		

Name of Library Authority	(a)	(b)	(c)	Remarks
Staffordshire *continued*				
STOKE ON TRENT				
Burslem	1863	1869	1910	
Fenton	(1902)	1906	1910	
Hanley	1884	1886	1910	
Longton	1891	1892	1910	
Stoke	1875	1878	1910	
Tunstall	1885	1885	1910	
TAMWORTH	1881	1882		
WALSALL	1857	1859		
Darlaston	1875	1876	1966	
Willenhall	1875	1875	1966	
WARLEY				
Oldbury	1888	1891	1966	
Rowley Regis	1904	1909	1966	
Smethwick	1876	1877	1966	
WEST BROMWICH	1870	1874		
Tipton	1887	(1890)	1966	
Wednesbury	1873	1878	1966	
WOLVERHAMPTON	1869	1869		
Bilston	1870	1873	1966	
Suffolk, East				
EAST SUFFOLK CO.	1925	1925		
Cratfield	1898	1898	1925	
Shotley	1896	1896	1925	
IPSWICH	1853	1853		
LOWESTOFT	1891	1905		
Suffolk, West				
WEST SUFFOLK CO.	1925	1927		[1] Non-rate-aided reference
BURY ST. EDMUNDS	1897	1924[1]		collection. Rate-aided lending library opened 1931.
Surrey				
SURREY CO.	1924	1925		[1] Co. area 1924–65.
Godalming	1923	1923	1948	
CHERTSEY	1918	1918		
EPSOM AND EWELL	1912	1965[1]		
GUILDFORD	1924	1924		
Sussex, East				
EAST SUSSEX CO.	1924	1924		
Bexhill	1924	1924	1949	
Cuckfield	1900	1900	1934	
Hailsham	(1919)	(by 1923)	1951	

Name of Library Authority	(a)	(b)	(c)	Remarks
Sussex, East *continued*				
Hayward's Heath	1906	NL	1924	[1] Maintained from borough
Slaugham	1904	1904	1948	funds till 1927.
BRIGHTON	1850(L)	1873		
EASTBOURNE	1896	1896		
HASTINGS	1927	1888[1]		
HOVE	1891	1891		
LEWES	1897	1898		
Sussex, West				
WEST SUSSEX CO.	1925	1925		
LITTLEHAMPTON	1905	1906		
WORTHING	1892	1896		
Warwickshire				
WARWICK CO.	1920	1920[1]		[1] Maintenance grant from
Atherstone	1895	1895[2]	1949	Carnegie U.K. Trust under
BIRMINGHAM	1860	1861		agreement negotiated
Aston Manor	1877	1878	1911	before 1919 Act. Area of
Erdington	(1904)	1907	1911	adoption excluded Sutton
Handsworth	1876	1880	1911	Coldfield (*q.v.*)
King's Norton	1903	1905	1911	[2] Reading Room only.
COVENTRY	1867	1868		[3] Transferred from Co.
LEAMINGTON SPA	1857	1857		
NUNEATON	1895	1895		
RUGBY	1890	1891		
SOLIHULL	[3]	1947		
STRATFORD UPON AVON	1902	1905		
SUTTON COLDFIELD	1931	1937		
WARWICK	1865	1866		
Wiltshire				
WILTSHIRE CO.	1923	1923[1]		[1] Carnegie U.K. Trust
Calne	(1904)[2]	1905	1949	Scheme from 1919. Area
SALISBURY	1890	1890		of adoption excluded
SWINDON	1942	1943		Swindon M.B. (*q.v.*)
				[2] *Kenyon Report* 1923.
Worcestershire				
WORCESTER CO.	1920	1923[1]		[1] Area of operation initially excluded the Urban Districts of Halesowen and Redditch (*q.v.*) two other urban districts and three parishes near Worcester City.

Name of Library Authority	(a)	(b)	(c)	Remarks

Worcestershire, *continued*

Name of Library Authority	(a)	(b)	(c)	Remarks
DUDLEY	1878	1884		[2] Staffordshire County, of
Brierley Hill	1875	1876	1966	which Coseley at this time
Quarry Bank	*(1902)*	*NL*	*1934*	formed part, also adopted
Coseley	1927	NL [2]	1933	in respect of Coseley in
EVESHAM	1897	1897		1930. Library service was
HALESOWEN	1931[3]	1933		provided by the County,
KIDDERMINSTER	1855	1855		by special agreement, from
MALVERN	1902	1903		1935 to 1948, when
REDDITCH	1930[4]	1930		Coseley relinquished its
STOURBRIDGE	1902	1905		powers to the County. In
WORCESTER	1879	1881		1966 most of Coseley was
				transferred to Dudley and
				Wolverhampton.
				[3] Worcs. Co. area 1920–31.
				[4] Worcs. Co. area 1920–29.

—Yorkshire

Name of Library Authority	(a)	(b)	(c)	Remarks
YORK	1891	1893		

East Riding

Name of Library Authority	(a)	(b)	(c)	Remarks
EAST RIDING CO.	1924	1925		[1] Reading Room only,
Norton	1898	1899[1]	1924	which Norton U.D.
BEVERLEY	1903	1906		continued to provide till
BRIDLINGTON	1925	1926		1939.
HULL	1892	1893		

—North Riding

Name of Library Authority	(a)	(b)	(c)	Remarks
NORTH RIDING CO.	1924	1925[1]		[1] Adoption excluded
Sowerby	1903	NL	1924	Scarborough M.B. (*q.v.*),
Whitby	1935	1944	1962	Redcar M.B. (see under
SCARBOROUGH	1925	1930		Teesside), and Eston and
TEESSIDE				Whitby U.D.s. Eston was
Middlesbrough	1870	1871	1968	included in 1935, when
Redcar	1935	1937	1968	Redcar and Whitby
Stockton on Tees	1874	1877	1968	became independent
Thornaby on Tees	1890[2]	1893	1968	authorities.
				[2] Adoption was by South
				Stockton, incorporated in
				Thornaby on Tees 1892.

—West Riding

Name of Library Authority	(a)	(b)	(c)	Remarks
WEST RIDING CO.	1921	1922		
Bolton Percy	1895	1895	1930	
Brampton-en-le-				
Morthen	(by 1921)	NL	1923	
Clayton	1905	1908	1923	

Name of Library Authority	(a)	(b)	(c)	Remarks
—West Riding *continued*				
Cudworth	1904	NL	1923	[1] In co-operation with Co. from 1931, now part of Pudsey M.B.
Farsley	(1900)	1901	[1]	
Featherstone	1899	NL	1923	
Halton	1895	NL	1923	[2] Served by Yorkshire Village Library— *Kenyon Report*
Harthill with Woodall	1917	[2]	c.1925	
Hebden Bridge	1902	NL	1932	[3] Periodicals only.
Mexborough	1899	1899	1966	[4] Amalgamation of Rawden (from Co.), Guiseley and Yeadon.
North and South Anston	1916	NL	1931	
Penistone	(1905)	1913	1965	
Silsden	1909	1911	1965	[5] New Central Library following amalgamation 1937 of Bolton upon Dearne with adjoining area.
Swinton	1903	1906	1965	
Thorne	1903	1906	1965	
Thorpe Salvin	(by 1921)	NL	1923	
Tickhill	1907	1908[3]	1967	[6] Libraries Acts adopted 1925.
AIREBOROUGH[4]				
Guiseley	1922	1923	1937	[7] To Co. 1921.
Yeadon	1923	1924	1937	[8] Service in co-operation with Co. 1935–37.
BARNSLEY	1890	1890		
BATLEY	1904	1907		
BINGLEY	1891	1892		
BRADFORD	1871	1872		
BRIGHOUSE	1898	1898		
CASTLEFORD	1902	1905		
DEARNE	1937	1938[5]		
Bolton upon Dearne	1903	1905	1937	
DEWSBURY	1887	1889		
DONCASTER	1868	1869		
ELLAND	1911	1912		
GOOLE	1903	1905		
HALIFAX	1881	1882		
HARROGATE	1886	1887		
HECKMONDWIKE	1904	1909		
HORBURY	1903	1906		
HORSFORTH	1917	1917?		
HUDDERSFIELD	1871[6](L)	1898		
ILKLEY	1902	1907		
KEIGHLEY	1899	1904		
Haworth	1901	NL	1938[7]	
LEEDS	1868	1870		
MORLEY	1904	1906		
NORMANTON	1905	1907		
OSSETT	1897	1898		
PONTEFRACT	(1903)	1905		
RAWMARSH	1893	1894		
ROTHERHAM	1876	1880		
Greasborough	1919	(by 1923)[8]	1937	
ROTHWELL	1903	1930		
SHEFFIELD	1853	1856		
Handsworth	1901	NL	1921	
Tinsley	1903	1905	1912	

Name of Library Authority	(a)	(b)	(c)	Remarks
—West Riding *continued*				
SHIPLEY	1903	1903		[9] The original adoption by
SKIPTON	1903	1910		Liversedge Parish (date
SOWERBY BRIDGE	1893	1893		unknown) was extended in
SPENBOROUGH	1929[9]	1930[10]		1915 to Spenborough U.D.
Birkenshaw	1923	1923[11]	1937	of which Liversedge at
TODMORDEN	1896	1897		that time became part.
WAKEFIELD	1902	1906		These powers were
WOMBWELL	1903	1907		allowed to lapse, however,

and from 1921–29 Spenborough was part of the County. Powers were resumed in 1929.

[10] At Cleckheaton, and often listed under that name.

[11] Books lent by Co. from 1925; Co. Branch 1932–37.

WALES

Name of Library Authority	Adoption (a)	Opening (b)	Transfer (c)	Remarks
Anglesey				
ANGLESEY CO.	1926	1926		
Beaumaris	1897	1897	1953	
Holyhead	1896	1896	1951	
Breconshire				
BRECON CO.	1924[1]	1924		[1] Carnegie U.K. Trust
Brynmawr	1897	1905	1936	Scheme from 1920; Joint Authority with Radnorshire till 1939.
Caernarvonshire				
CAERNARVON CO.	1923	1923[1]		[1] Carnegie U.K. Trust Scheme from 1918.
Llanberis	1895	1895	1954	[2] *P.R. 1912* reports closed
Llanddeiniolen	1910	1913	1962	1911, but *B. of E. Statistics*
Llanfair is Gaer	1908	NL	1923	*(1931–32)* show it
Penmachno	1895	1895[2]	1959	functioning as a newsroom.
Portmadoc	1899[3]	NL	1923	[3] Adopted by Ynyscynhaiarn,
BANGOR	1870(L)	1871		the Urban District which
CAERNARVON	1887	1887		included Portmadoc.
CONWY	1899	1899		
CRICCIETH	1902	1905		
LLANDUDNO	1907	1908		

Name of Library Authority	(a)	(b)	(c)	Remarks
Cardiganshire				
CARDIGANSHIRE JOINT LIBRARY[1]				[1] Joint Committee of
Aberystwyth	1871	1874	1947	Aberystwyth and Cardigan
Cardigan Co.	1923	1923[2]	1947	Co., 1947, under the Local
Aberaeron	*1899*	*(1900)[3]*	*1925*	Government Act, 1933.
Cyfoeth y Brenin	*1901*	*NL*	*1925*	[2] Carnegie U.K. Trust
Lampeter	*1907*	*(1912)[4]*	*1925*	Scheme from 1919.
				[3] Supported from public funds but no regular rate.
				[4] Not rate-aided.
Carmarthenshire				
CARMARTHEN CO.	1930[1]	1932		[1] Abortive adoption 1925.
Llanelli Rural Parish	1903	1907	1965	[2] The Pembrey Library was
BURRY PORT	1903	1903[2]		taken over in 1903, but it
Pembrey	1901	1901	1903	seems that from a very
LLANELLI	1897	1898		early stage it was necessary to have books from Llanelli. Since 1961 books have been provided by arrangement with the Co.
Denbighshire				
DENBIGH CO.	1921	1921[1]		[1] Maintenance grant from
Bersham[2]	1903	1904	1957	Carnegie U.K. Trust under
Broughton	1895	NL	1921	agreement negotiated
Chirk	1902	1903[3]	1949	before 1919 Act.
Denbigh	1922[4]	[5]	1949	[2] Also listed as Coedpoeth;
Esclusham Below	1919	[6]	1965	assisted by Co. from 1921.
Llangollen	1906	1906[7]	1960	[3] Assisted by Co. from 1922.
COLWYN BAY	1901	1905		[4] *L.Y.B. 1910–11* and *1914*
WREXHAM	1878	1879		say 1902. Part of Co. area 1921–22.
				[5] Served by Co. from 1923.
				[6] Served by Co. from 1925.
				[7] Assisted by Co. from 1925.
Flintshire				
FLINT CO.	1925	1925		
Buckley	1902	1904	1966	
Halkyn	1896	1898	1954	
Holywell	1902	1905	1965	
Mold	1902	1913	1965	
FLINT	1902	1903		
RHYL	1904	1907		
Glamorganshire				
GLAMORGAN CO.	1923	1923[1]		[1] Carnegie U.K. Trust

Name of Library Authority	(a)	(b)	(c)	Remarks
Glamorganshire, *continued*				
Bridgend	1901	1901	1927	Scheme from 1920. Area
Coedffranc	1903	1905	1965	of adoption 1923 excluded
Gorseinon	(1902)[2]	NL	1923	Urban Districts of
Higher Newcastle	1895	NL	1923	Mountain Ash and
Llantwitfardre	1904	1906	1965	Rhondda (*q.v.*)
Ogmore and Garw	(1895)	NL	1923	[2] Recorded only in *L.Y.B.*
Pencoed	(1901)	NL	1923	*1910–11* and *1914*. If
ABERDARE	1901	1904		adoption took place it
BARRY[3]	1891	1891		must have been by the
CARDIFF	1862	1862		parish of Llandeilo
Whitchurch	1903	1904	1967[4]	Talybont, to which
MERTHYR TYDFIL	1899	1900		Gorseinon belongs.
MOUNTAIN ASH	1963	1964		[3] Formerly Barry and
NEATH	1897	1899		Cadoxton.
Briton Ferry	1898	1902	1922	[4] Transferred to Co. 1965.
PENARTH	1894	1895		[5] Adoption by Margam,
PONTYPRIDD	1887	1887		which became part of
PORT TALBOT	1904[5]	1916		Port Talbot M.B. 1921.
RHONDDA	1933	1939		
SWANSEA	1870	1875		
Cockett	1903	1909	1918	

Merionethshire

MERIONETH CO.	1924	1927		[1] Sometimes listed as
Bala	1896	1898	1952	Festiniog. Reported closed
Blaenau Festiniog	1892	1893[1]	1952	1923 (*Mitchell Report*),
Corwen	1896	1896	1952	but excluded from
Dolgellau	1896	1896	1952	the Co. area under
Llandderfel	1897	(1897)	1924	resolution of 1926.
Llanfihangel y Pennant[2]	1896	1897	1939	[2] Abergynolwyn in this
Llanfor	1899	(1907)	1941	parish is also listed,
Llanuwchllyn	1895	1895	1952	erroneously, by Adams and
				Mitchell Reports as a
				separate authority.

Monmouthshire

MONMOUTH CO.	1925	1927		[1] Incorporated with
Abergavenny	1900	1901	1938	Pontypool 1935.
Abersychan[1]	1901	NL	1925	[2] Adoption by Llantarnam,
Cwmbran	1898[2]	1901	1950	which became part of
Pontypool	1906	1908	1961	Cwmbran U.D. 1935.
Rogerstone	1895	1896	1963	[3] Adoption by Upper
Bedwas and Machen	(1895)[3]	(1895)	1925	Machen, which became
NEWPORT	1870	1870		part of Bedwas and
				Machen U.D. in 1912.

Name of Library Authority	(a)	(b)	(c)	Remarks
Montgomeryshire				
MONTGOMERY CO.	1925	1925[1]		[1] Carnegie U.K. Trust
Llanidloes	1908	1908	1971	Scheme from 1920.
Machynlleth	1912[2]	1912	1971	[2] So *Kenyon Report*, but
Montgomery	1924	1924	1966	*L.Y.B. 1900–01* says 1897.
Newtown and				[3] Confused in some lists
Llanllwchaiarn[3]	1899	(1899)	1972	with Llanuwchllyn,
Welshpool	1887	1888	1966	Merionethshire.
Pembrokeshire				
PEMBROKE CO.	1920	1924		
Radnorshire				
RADNOR CO.	1924[1]	1924		[1] Carnegie U.K. Trust
Llandrindod Wells	1902	1912	1937	Scheme from 1919; Joint Authority with Breconshire till 1939.

SCOTLAND

Note. Date of adoption not given for County Libraries, which were not operated under the Libraries Acts.

Name of Library Authority	(a) Adoption	(b) Opening	(c) Transfer	Remarks
Aberdeenshire				
ABERDEEN CO.		1926		
Drumoak	1893	1894	1929	
Dyce	1906	1908	1929	
Oldmeldrum[1]	1900	1901	1930	[1] Burgh and parish.
Tarves	1883	1884	1929	
Udny	1911	1911[2]	1929	[2] Not rate-aided.
ABERDEEN	1884	1885		
FRASERBURGH	1903	1905		
INVERURIE	1903	1905		
PETERHEAD	1890	1894		
Angus and Kincardineshire				
ANGUS AND KINCARDINE CO.		1920[1]		[1] The joint authority (at that time Forfar and

Name of Library Authority	(a)	(b)	(c)	Remarks

Angus & Kincardineshire *continued*

ARBROATH	1896	1898		Kincardine) took over
BRECHIN	1890	1893		responsibility for the
CARNOUSTIE	1947	1947		Carnegie U.K. Trust
DUNDEE	1866	1869		Scheme based on
FORFAR	1870	1871		Montrose which had
MONTROSE	1902	1905[2]		operated since 1916.

[2] See above, *s.v.* Angus and Kincardine Co.

Argyllshire

ARGYLL CO.		1946		[1] Now in co-operation with
CAMPBELTOWN	1896	1898[1]		Co.
DUNOON	1914	1915[2]		[2] Now in co-operation with

Co.

Ayrshire

AYR CO.		1925	
AYR	1890	1893	
KILMARNOCK	1893	1895	
MAYBOLE	1903	1906	
NEWMILNS	1901	1901	

Banffshire

BANFF CO.		1926		[1] Co-operative arrangement
Banff	1899	1902	1967[1]	Co. from 1950.
Cullen	1903	NL [2]	1942	[2] Non-rate-aided library
Kirkmichael	1895	1895	[3]	only, used as Co. distributing centre by 1928-29.

[3] Co. service from 1927, date of transfer not known.

Berwickshire

BERWICK CO.		1920	

Bute

BUTE CO.		1926[1]		[1] Co. service suspended 1939–51; service from Kilmarnock (Ayrshire) 1946–50; Co. service resumed 1951 (see above p. 246).

Caithness

CAITHNESS CO.		1920		[1] Collaboration with Co. from 1920 (see above, p. 219).
Thurso	1872	1872	(1931)[1]	

Name of Library Authority	(a)	(b)	(c)	Remarks
Caithness *continued*				
Wick[2]	1887	1888	(1931)[3]	[2] Burgh and parish. [3] Collaboration with Co. from 1920 (see above, p. 219).
Clackmannanshire				
CLACKMANNAN CO.[1]		1921		[1] In addition to the libraries listed below, a library service was operated by the Town Council at Tillicoultry and probably at Alva, but there is no record of adoption. [2] Apparently non-rate-aided library only.
Alloa	1885	1889	1936	
Alloa Parish	1909	(1910)	1929	
Clackmannan Parish	(1901)	(1903)	1929	
Coalsnaughton	(1906)	NL [2]	1929	
Dumfriesshire				
DUMFRIES CO.		1924		[1] Including the parish of Dryfesdale of which the burgh of Lockerbie forms part.
Annan	1903	1906	1943	
Dumfries and Maxwelltown	1899(L)	1903	1932	
Lockerbie[1]	1900	1903	1932	
Dunbartonshire				
DUNBARTON CO.		1923		[1] Adoption by Alexandria parish, taken over by Vale of Leven 1930.
Vale of Leven	1907[1]	1907	1955	
CLYDEBANK	1910	1913		
DUMBARTON	1881	1883		
HELENSBURGH	1949	1950		
East Lothian				
EAST LOTHIAN CO.		1926		[1] Joint Committee with Co. from 1930.
Haddington	?	?	1970	
PRESTONPANS	1902	1905[1]		
Fife				
FIFE CO.		1921		[1] Burgh and Parish. [2] Libraries Acts adopted 1925, though not used for library purposes till 1928.
Burntisland[1]	1904	1907	1958	
Torryburn	1911	(1912?)	1929	
BUCKHAVEN AND METHIL	1919	1925		
DUNFERMLINE	1880	1883		
KIRKCALDY	1899(L)[2]	1899		

Name of Library Authority	(a)	(b)	(c)	Remarks
Fife, *continued*				
LEVEN	1938	1938		
NEWBURGH	1895	1895		
Inverness-shire				
INVERNESS CO.		1926		[1] Joint Committee with Co.
INVERNESS	1877	1883[1]		1933–62.
Kirkcudbrightshire				
KIRKCUDBRIGHT CO.		1920		[1] By arrangement with Co.
CASTLE DOUGLAS	1902	1904[1]		since 1926.
Lanarkshire				
LANARK CO.		1922		[1] Adoption by Motherwell,
AIRDRIE	1853	1856		which amalgamated with
COATBRIDGE	1901	1904		Wishaw 1920.
GLASGOW	1899(L)	1899		
Kinning Park	(1901)	1904	1905	
HAMILTON	1901	1907		
MOTHERWELL AND WISHAW	1902[1]	1906		
RUTHERGLEN	1901	1907		
Midlothian				
MIDLOTHIAN CO.		1920		[1] Adoption by Bonnyrigg,
West Calder	1902	1905	1929	now amalgamated with
BONNYRIGG AND LASSWADE	1907[1]	1909[2]		Lasswade.
EDINBURGH	1886	1890		[2] Service since 1921 by arrangement with Co.
Corstorphine	1901	1904	1920	
Moray and Nairn				.
MORAY AND NAIRN CO.				
Moray Co.		1924	1960	[1] Also listed by the name of
Fochabers[1]	*1904*	*1907*	*1929*	Bellie, the parish of which
Nairn Co.		1922	1960	Fochabers forms part.
Elgin	1891	1892	1960	
Lossiemouth	1901	1903	1962	
Orkney				
ORKNEY CO.		1923[1]		[1] Served by the Carnegie U. K. Trust North of Scotland scheme from 1916.

Name of Library Authority	(a)	(b)	(c)	Remarks
Orkney *continued*				
KIRKWALL[2]	1890	(1890)		[2] Though served by Orkney
STROMNESS[3]	1899	(1906)		Co. since about 1932, Kirkwall and Stromness remain independent authorities, controlling their library buildings and making some financial contribution.
				[3] Burgh and parish, see Kirkwall.
Peeblesshire				
PEEBLES CO.		1920		
INNERLEITHEN	1902	(1905)		
PEEBLES	1911	1912		
Perth and Kinross				
PERTH AND KINROSS CO.				
Perth Co.		1919[1]	1930	[1] Took over a voluntary
Kinross Co.		1924	1930	scheme, based on the
Crieff	1945	1945	1967	Sandeman Library, Perth,
BLAIRGOWRIE AND RATTRAY	1937	1937		which had operated since 1917.
KINROSS[2]	1905	1906[3]		[2] Burgh and parish.
PERTH	1896	1898		[3] Service since 1967 by arrangement with Co.
Renfrewshire				
RENFREW CO.		1920		
GREENOCK	1900	1902		
PAISLEY	1867	1871		
Ross and Cromarty				
ROSS AND CROMARTY CO.		1925		[1] Burgh and parish.
Cromarty[1]	(1903)	1905	1967	[2] Had probably ceased to
Dingwall	1902	1907	1948	function when powers
Edderton	1900	(1900)	1929[2]	transferred to Co. by Local
Stornoway	1897	1907	1964	Government Act 1929.
Tain[3]	1899	1900	1970	[3] Burgh and parish.
Tarbat[4]	(1898)	(1900)	[5]	[4] Or Portmahomack.
				[5] Co. Service from at least 1957.

XVa. PERTHSHIRE RURAL LIBRARY MOTOR VAN
The first motorized mobile library service, 1920.

XVb. LANCASHIRE COUNTY MOBILE LIBRARY
A modern mobile library in operation at Owlet Mill, Foulridge, Pendle, 1951–52.

XVIa. HENDON CENTRAL LIBRARY: CHILDREN'S LIBRARY

One of the most popular and widespread forms of extension activity for children is the story half-hour, glimpsed in this photograph at Hendon, 1962–63.

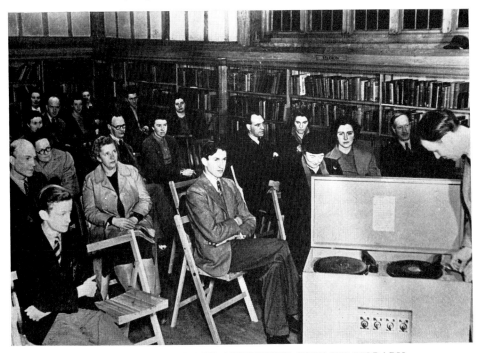

XVIb. RUISLIP BRANCH, MIDDLESEX COUNTY LIBRARY

Extension activities for adults include exhibitions, lectures, films, concerts and plays. This photograph from the Middlesex Silver Jubilee Report of 1947 shows a record recital in a branch library opened ten years earlier in a reconstructed fifteenth-century barn.

Name of Library Authority	(a)	(b)	(c)	Remarks
Roxburghshire				
ROXBURGH CO.		1925		
Maxton	1906	1908	1925	
HAWICK	1878	1879		
JEDBURGH	1892	1894		
KELSO	1906	1906		
Selkirkshire				
SELKIRK CO.		1923[1]		[1] Administered by
GALASHIELS	1872	1874		Galashiels since 1948.
SELKIRK	1888	1889		
Stirlingshire				
STIRLING CO.		1925		[1] *Libraries Yearbooks*
Denny and Dunipace	1924[1]	1924	1956	*1910/11–1933* refer to an
Larbert	1901	1904	1929	adoption 1902, but the
FALKIRK	1896	1896		library was not rate-
GRANGEMOUTH	1887	1887		supported before 1924.
STIRLING	1897	1904		
Sutherland				
SUTHERLAND CO.		1920		
Creich	(1899)	(1901)	1920?	
Dornoch	(1905)	1907	1952	
West Lothian				
WEST LOTHIAN CO.		1924		
Bo'ness	1901	1904	1967	
Wigtownshire				
WIGTOWN CO.		1922		
Zetland				
ZETLAND CO.		1923		

PUBLIC LIBRARY AUTHORITIES 1847–1972

in order of commencement of library service

(An (s) after the name of the adopting authority indicates service by another authority.

Authorities not known to have provided a service are excluded—see App. V).

Year and County	Adopting Authority	Present Authority (if different)
1847		
Kent	CANTERBURY	
1848		
Lancashire	WARRINGTON	
1850		
Lancashire	SALFORD	
1851		
Hampshire	WINCHESTER	
1852		
Lancashire	LIVERPOOL	
	MANCHESTER	
1853		
Lancashire	BOLTON	
East Suffolk	IPSWICH	
1854		
Oxfordshire	OXFORD	
1855		
Cambridgeshire	CAMBRIDGE	
Worcestershire	KIDDERMINSTER	
1856		
Lanarkshire	AIRDRIE	
Cheshire	BIRKENHEAD	
Hertfordshire	Hertford	HERTFORD CO.
Yorkshire W.R.	SHEFFIELD	
1857		
Worcestershire	LEAMINGTON SPA	
Norfolk	NORWICH	
London	St. Margaret and St. John, Westminster	WESTMINSTER
1858		
Kent	MAIDSTONE	

Year and County	Adopting Authority	Present Authority (if different)
1859		
Staffordshire	LICHFIELD	
Durham	SUNDERLAND	
Staffordshire	WALSALL	
1860		
Somerset	BRIDGWATER	
1861		
Warwickshire	BIRMINGHAM	
1862		
Lancashire	BLACKBURN	
Glamorganshire	CARDIFF	
1866		
Warwickshire	WARWICK	
1868		
Warwickshire	COVENTRY	
Nottinghamshire	NOTTINGHAM	
1869		
Staffordshire	Burslem	STOKE ON TRENT
Yorkshire W.R.	DONCASTER	
Angus	DUNDEE	
Northumberland	TYNEMOUTH	
Staffordshire	WOLVERHAMPTON	
1870		
Devon	EXETER	
Yorkshire W.R.	LEEDS	
1871		
Caernarvonshire	BANGOR	
Lancashire	DARWEN	
Derbyshire	DERBY	
Angus	FORFAR	
Herefordshire	HEREFORD	
Leicestershire	LEICESTER	
Yorkshire N.R.	Middlesbrough	TEESSIDE
Monmouthshire	NEWPORT	
Renfrewshire	PAISLEY	
1872		
Yorkshire W.R.	BRADFORD	
London	CITY OF LONDON	
Lancashire	ROCHDALE	
Lancashire	ST. HELENS	
Caithness	Thurso	CAITHNESS CO.
1873		
Staffordshire	Bilston	WOLVERHAMPTON
East Sussex	BRIGHTON	
Durham	SOUTH SHIELDS	

Year and County	Adopting Authority	Present Authority (if different)
1874		
Cardiganshire	Aberystwyth	CARDIGANSHIRE JOINT LIBRARY
Selkirkshire	GALASHIELS	
Lancashire	HEYWOOD	
Hertfordshire	WATFORD	
Staffordshire	WEST BROMWICH	
1875		
Cheshire	STOCKPORT	
Glamorganshire	SWANSEA	
Staffordshire	Willenhall	WALSALL
1876		
Worcestershire	Brierley Hill	DUDLEY
Gloucestershire	BRISTOL	
Staffordshire	Darlaston	WALSALL
Cheshire	MACCLESFIELD	
Northamptonshire	NORTHAMPTON	
Devon	PLYMOUTH	
Lancashire	SOUTHPORT	
1877		
Devon	BIDEFORD	
Cheshire	CHESTER	
Staffordshire	Smethwick	WARLEY
Yorkshire N.R.	Stockton on Tees	TEESSIDE
1878		
Warwickshire	Aston Manor	BIRMINGHAM
Staffordshire	Stoke	STOKE ON TRENT
Staffordshire	Wednesbury	WEST BROMWICH
Lancashire	WIGAN	
1879		
Derbyshire	CHESTERFIELD	
Lancashire	CLITHEROE	
Kent	FOLKESTONE	
Roxburghshire	HAWICK	
Lancashire	PRESTON	
Denbighshire	WREXHAM	
1880		
Lancashire	BLACKPOOL	
Warwickshire	Handsworth	BIRMINGHAM
Northumberland	NEWCASTLE UPON TYNE	
Yorkshire W.R.	ROTHERHAM	
1881		
Lancashire	ASHTON UNDER LYNE	
London	Richmond	RICHMOND UPON THAMES
Worcestershire	WORCESTER	

Year and County	Adopting Authority	Present Authority (if different)
1882		
Lancashire	BARROW IN FURNESS	
Devon	Devonport	PLYMOUTH
Yorkshire W.R.	HALIFAX	
London	KINGSTON UPON THAMES	
Cheshire	RUNCORN	
Hertfordshire	ST. ALBANS	
Staffordshire	STAFFORD	
Staffordshire	TAMWORTH	
Kent	Tonbridge	KENT CO.
London	Twickenham	RICHMOND UPON THAMES
1883		
Dunbartonshire	DUMBARTON	
Fife	DUNFERMLINE	
London	EALING	
Inverness-shire	INVERNESS	
Nottinghamshire	NEWARK	
Lancashire	OLDHAM	
Cumberland	Penrith	CUMBERLAND CO.
Hampshire	PORTSMOUTH	
Berkshire	READING	
1884		
Gloucestershire	CHELTENHAM	
Worcestershire	DUDLEY	
Aberdeenshire	Tarves	ABERDEEN CO.
1885		
Aberdeenshire	ABERDEEN	
Durham	DARLINGTON	
Durham	GATESHEAD ON TYNE	
Cheshire	NORTHWICH	
Shropshire	SHREWSBURY	
Staffordshire	Tunstall	STOKE ON TRENT
London	WANDSWORTH	
Cheshire	Winnington (s)	NORTHWICH
1886		
Norfolk	GREAT YARMOUTH	
Staffordshire	Hanley	STOKE ON TRENT
Leicestershire	LOUGHBOROUGH	
Dorset	POOLE	
Cornwall	TRURO	
London	Wimbledon	MERTON
1887		
London	Battersea	WANDSWORTH
Lancashire	BOOTLE	
Caernarvonshire	CAERNARVON	
London	Chelsea	KENSINGTON AND CHELSEA

Year and County	Adopting Authority	Present Authority (if different)
1887 *continued*		
Lancashire	FLEETWOOD	
London	Fulham	HAMMERSMITH
Stirlingshire	GRANGEMOUTH	
Yorkshire W.R.	HARROGATE	
Lancashire	HINDLEY	
Nottinghamshire	HUCKNALL	
Cumberland	Millom	CUMBERLAND CO.
Glamorgan	PONTYPRIDD	
Lancashire	WIDNES	
1888		
Nottinghamshire	CARLTON	
London	Clerkenwell	ISLINGTON
East Sussex	HASTINGS	
Leicestershire	HINCKLEY	
London	Kensington	KENSINGTON AND CHELSEA
London	LAMBETH	
Staffordshire	LEEK	
London	Putney	WANDSWORTH
Kent	Queenborough	KENT CO.
Montgomeryshire	Welshpool	MONTGOMERY CO.
Cumberland	WHITEHAVEN	
Caithness	Wick	CAITHNESS CO.
Cheshire	Winsford	CHESHIRE CO.
1889		
Clackmannanshire	Alloa	CLACKMANNAN CO.
London	BARKING	
Derbyshire	Buxton	DERBY CO.
London	Christchurch	SOUTHWARK
London	Clapham	LAMBETH
Lancashire	DENTON	
Yorkshire W.R.	DEWSBURY	
Derbyshire	Glossop	DERBY CO.
London	HAMMERSMITH	
Lancashire	MIDDLETON	
Cheshire	Nantwich	CHESHIRE CO.
Lancashire	NELSON	
London	St. Martin in the Fields	WESTMINSTER
Selkirkshire	SELKIRK	
Kent	Sittingbourne	SITTINGBOURNE AND MILTON
Hampshire	SOUTHAMPTON	
Devon	South Molton	DEVON CO.
Cheshire	STALYBRIDGE	
1890		
Yorkshire W.R.	BARNSLEY	
London	Brentford	HOUNSLOW
London	Camberwell	SOUTHWARK
London	CROYDON	

Year and County	Adopting Authority	Present Authority (if different)
1890 *continued*		
Midlothian	EDINBURGH	
Hampshire	GOSPORT	
Orkney	KIRKWALL	
Cheshire	Middlewich	CHESHIRE CO.
Lancashire	Much Woolton	LIVERPOOL
Shropshire	Oswestry	SHROPSHIRE CO.
London	Rotherhithe	SOUTHWARK
Wiltshire	SALISBURY	
London	Stoke Newington	HACKNEY
Staffordshire	Tipton	WEST BROMWICH
Somerset	WESTON-SUPER-MARE	
Cumberland	WORKINGTON	
1891		
Glamorgan	BARRY	
London	Chiswick	HOUNSLOW
East Sussex	HOVE	
London	LEWISHAM	
Nottinghamshire	MANSFIELD	
Staffordshire	NEWCASTLE UNDER LYME	
Staffordshire	Oldbury	WARLEY
Warwickshire	RUGBY	
Cheshire	SALE	
London	Streatham	LAMBETH
1892		
Cheshire	ALTRINCHAM	
Cumberland	Arlecdon and Frizington	CUMBERLAND CO.
London	Bermondsey	SOUTHWARK
Yorkshire W.R.	BINGLEY	
Essex	COLCHESTER	
Morayshire	Elgin	MORAY AND NAIRN CO.
Westmorland	Kendal	KENDAL AND WESTMORLAND
Herefordshire	Leominster	HEREFORD CO.
Staffordshire	Longton	STOKE ON TRENT
London	Penge	BROMLEY
Huntingdon and Peterborough	PETERBOROUGH	
London	Poplar	TOWER HAMLETS
London	St. Giles, Holborn	CAMDEN
London	Shoreditch	HACKNEY
London	Tottenham	HARINGEY
London	West Ham	NEWHAM
London	Whitechapel	TOWER HAMLETS
London	Wood Green	HARINGEY
1893		
Ayrshire	AYR	
Merionethshire	Blaenau Festiniog	MERIONETH CO.
Angus	BRECHIN	

Year and County	Adopting Authority	Present Authority (if different)
1893 *continued*		
Cumberland	CARLISLE	
London	Edmonton	ENFIELD
London	Holborn District	CAMDEN, ISLINGTON
Yorkshire E.R.	HULL	
Cheshire	HYDE	
Lancashire	LANCASTER	
London	Leyton	WALTHAM FOREST
Buckinghamshire	Middle Claydon	BUCKINGHAM CO.
London	Newington	SOUTHWARK
Cornwall	PENZANCE	
London	St. Paul, Covent Garden (s)	WESTMINSTER
Yorkshire W.R.	SOWERBY BRIDGE	
Lancashire	STRETFORD	
Yorkshire N.R.	Thornaby on Tees	TEESSIDE
Yorkshire	YORK	
1894		
London	BROMLEY	
Aberdeenshire	Drumoak	ABERDEEN CO.
London	ENFIELD	
Cornwall	Falmouth	CORNWALL CO.
Kent	GRAVESEND	
Essex	Grays Thurrock	THURROCK
London	Hampstead	CAMDEN
Durham	HARTLEPOOL	
Roxburghshire	JEDBURGH	
Lancashire	LEIGH	
Bedfordshire	LUTON	
Aberdeenshire	PETERHEAD	
Yorkshire W.R.	RAWMARSH	
Kent	ROCHESTER	
London	St. George, Hanover Square	WESTMINSTER
London	St. Saviour	SOUTHWARK
London	Walthamstow	WALTHAM FOREST
London	Willesden	BRENT
1895		
Warwickshire	Atherstone	WARWICK CO.
Somerset	BATH	
Monmouthshire	Bedwas and Machen	MONMOUTH CO.
Yorkshire W.R.	Bolton Percy	WEST RIDING CO.
Hampshire	BOURNEMOUTH	
London	Bromley by Bow	TOWER HAMLETS
Cambridgeshire	Burwell	CAMBRIDGE AND ISLE OF ELY CO.
Cornwall	Camborne	CAMBORNE-REDRUTH
Cumberland	Cleator Moor	CUMBERLAND CO.
Lancashire	COLNE	
Cheshire	DUKINFIELD	
Ayrshire	KILMARNOCK	
Banffshire	Kirkmichael	BANFF CO.

Year and County	Adopting Authority	Present Authority (if different)
1895 *continued*		
Lindsey, Lincs.	LINCOLN	
Caernarvonshire	Llanberis	CAERNARVON CO.
Merionethshire	Llanuwchllyn	MERIONETH CO.
Fife	NEWBURGH	
Warwickshire	NUNEATON	
Glamorgan	PENARTH	
Caernarvonshire	Penmachno	CAERNARVON CO.
Kent	RAMSGATE	
Cornwall	Redruth	CAMBORNE-REDRUTH
Derbyshire	Shirebrook	DERBY CO.
Durham	West Hartlepool	HARTLEPOOL
Norfolk	Wroxham	NORFOLK CO.
1896		
Berkshire	Abingdon	BERKSHIRE CO.
Cheshire	Ashton on Mersey	SALE
Merionethshire	Corwen	MERIONETH CO.
Merionethshire	Dolgellau	MERIONETH CO.
East Sussex	EASTBOURNE	
London	East Ham	NEWHAM
Stirlingshire	FALKIRK	
Buckinghamshire	Grandborough	BUCKINGHAM CO.
Anglesey	Holyhead	ANGLESEY CO.
Northamptonshire	KETTERING	
Cornwall	Liskeard	CORNWALL CO.
Kent	Rainham	GILLINGHAM
Monmouthshire	Rogerstone	MONMOUTH CO.
Northamptonshire	ROTHWELL	
East Suffolk	Shotley	EAST SUFFOLK CO.
London	Teddington	RICHMOND UPON THAMES
Durham	Trimdon	DURHAM CO.
Buckinghamshire	Water Eaton	BUCKINGHAM CO.
Nottinghamshire	WORKSOP	
West Sussex	WORTHING	
1897		
Hampshire	ANDOVER	
Anglesey	Beaumaris	ANGLESEY CO.
Cornwall	Bodmin	CORNWALL CO.
Staffordshire	BURTON UPON TRENT	
Cambridgeshire	Chesterton (s)	CAMBRIDGE
Buckinghamshire	East and Botolph Claydon	BUCKINGHAM CO.
Worcestershire	EVESHAM	
Gloucestershire	GLOUCESTER	
Merionethshire	Llandderfel	MERIONETH CO.
Merionethshire	Llanfihangel y Pennant	MERIONETH CO.
Lancashire	Moss Side	MANCHESTER
Cornwall	St. Ives	CORNWALL CO.
Hampshire	Sheet	HAMPSHIRE CO.
Gloucestershire	Stroud	GLOUCESTER CO.

Year and County	Adopting Authority	Present Authority (if different)
1897 *continued*		
Lancashire	SWINTON AND PENDLEBURY	
Yorkshire	TODMORDEN	
1898		
Angus	ARBROATH	
Merionethshire	Bala	MERIONETH CO.
Yorkshire W.R.	BRIGHOUSE	
Argyll	CAMPBELTOWN	
East Suffolk	Cratfield	EAST SUFFOLK CO.
Staffordshire	Great Wyrley	STAFFORD CO.
Flintshire	Halkyn	FLINT CO.
Yorkshire W.R.	HUDDERSFIELD	
Staffordshire	Kidsgrove	STAFFORD CO.
East Sussex	LEWES	
Carmarthenshire	LLANELLY	
Yorkshire W.R.	OSSETT	
Perthshire	PERTH	
London	St. George in the East	TOWER HAMLETS
London	South Hornsey	HACKNEY
Lancashire	Waterloo with Seaforth	CROSBY
1899		
London	BEXLEY	
Lancashire	CHORLEY	
Cumberland	COCKERMOUTH	
Herefordshire	Colwall	HEREFORD CO.
Caernarvonshire	CONWY	
Lanarkshire	GLASGOW	
Cumberland	Harrington	WORKINGTON
London	Hornsey	HARINGEY
Norfolk	KING'S LYNN	
Fife	KIRKCALDY	
Cornwall	Launceston	CORNWALL CO.
Yorkshire W.R.	Mexborough	WEST RIDING CO.
Durham	Monk Hesledon	DURHAM CO.
Glamorganshire	NEATH	
Derbyshire	New Mills	DERBY CO.
Montgomeryshire	Newtown and Llanllwchaiarn	MONTGOMERY CO.
Yorkshire E.R.	Norton	EAST RIDING CO.
London	St. George the Martyr	SOUTHWARK
Nottinghamshire	SUTTON IN ASHFIELD	
Cheshire	WALLASEY	
Oxfordshire	Woodstock	OXFORD CO.
1900		
Cardiganshire	Aberaeron	CARDIGANSHIRE JOINT LIBRARY
Lancashire	ACCRINGTON	
London	Acton	EALING
East Sussex	Cuckfield	EAST SUSSEX CO.

Year and County	Adopting Authority	Present Authority (if different)
1900 *continued*		
Ross and Cromarty	Edderton	ROSS AND CROMARTY CO.
Glamorganshire	MERTHYR TYDFIL	
Ross and Cromarty	Tain	ROSS AND CROMARTY CO.
Ross and Cromarty	Tarbat	ROSS AND CROMARTY CO.
1901		
Monmouthshire	Abergavenny	MONMOUTH CO.
Glamorganshire	Bridgend	GLAMORGAN CO.
Lancashire	BURY	
Sutherland	Creich	SUTHERLAND CO.
Monmouthshire	Cwmbran	MONMOUTH CO.
Yorkshire W.R.	Farsley	WEST RIDING CO.
Lancashire	Gorton	MANCHESTER
Lindsey, Lincs.	GRIMSBY	
London	Hampton	RICHMOND UPON THAMES
Lancashire	Hurst (s)	ASHTON UNDER LYNE
Derbyshire	ILKESTON	
Lancashire	INCE IN MAKERFIELD (s)	
Ayrshire	NEWMILNS	
Leicestershire	OADBY	
Aberdeenshire	Oldmeldrum	ABERDEEN CO.
Carmarthenshire	Pembrey	BURRY PORT
London	Woolwich	GREENWICH
By 1902		
Lancashire	Levenshulme	MANCHESTER
1902		
Cumberland	Aspatria	CUMBERLAND CO.
Banffshire	Banff	BANFF CO.
Glamorganshire	Briton Ferry	NEATH
Renfrewshire	GREENOCK	
Lancashire	Littleborough	LANCASHIRE CO.
Devon	Moretonhampstead	DEVON CO.
Cumberland	Papcastle (s)	CUMBERLAND CO.
Buckinghamshire	Steeple Claydon	BUCKINGHAM CO.
Northamptonshire	WELLINGBOROUGH	
Shropshire	Whitchurch	SHROPSHIRE CO.
1903		
Cheshire	BOWDON (s)	
Carmarthenshire	BURRY PORT	
Kent	CHATHAM	
Denbighshire	Chirk	DENBIGH CO.
Clackmannanshire	Clackmannan Parish	CLACKMANNAN CO.
Rutlandshire	Cottesmore	RUTLAND CO.
Dumfriesshire	Dumfries and Maxwelltown	DUMFRIES CO.

Year and County	Adopting Authority	Present Authority (if different)
1903 *continued*		
Flintshire	FLINT	
Westmorland	Kirkby Lonsdale	KENDAL AND WESTMORLAND
Dumfriesshire	Lockerbie	DUMFRIES CO.
Morayshire	Lossiemouth	MORAY AND NAIRN CO.
Worcestershire	MALVERN	
Staffordshire	Rushall	STAFFORD CO.
Yorkshire W.R.	SHIPLEY	
1904		
Glamorganshire	ABERDARE	
Denbighshire	Bersham	DENBIGH CO.
West Lothian	Bo'ness	WEST LOTHIAN CO.
Flintshire	Buckley	FLINT CO.
Kirkcudbrightshire	CASTLE DOUGLAS	
Lanarkshire	COATBRIDGE	
Midlothian	Corstorphine	EDINBURGH
Lindsey, Lincs.	Frodingham	SCUNTHORPE
Yorkshire W.R.	KEIGHLEY	
Lanarkshire	Kinning Park	GLASGOW
Cheshire	KNUTSFORD	
Stirlingshire	Larbert	STIRLING CO.
Berkshire	MAIDENHEAD	
Devon	NEWTON ABBOT	
Lindsey, Lincs.	SCUNTHORPE	
East Sussex	Slaugham	EAST SUSSEX CO.
Stirlingshire	STIRLING	
Glamorganshire	Whitchurch	CARDIFF
Shorpshire	Wellington	SHROPSHIRE CO.
Essex	Witham	ESSEX CO.
1905		
Lancashire	ATHERTON	
Lancashire	Birkdale	SOUTHPORT
Durham	Boldon Colliery	DURHAM CO.
Yorkshire W.R.	Bolton upon Dearne	DEARNE
Holland, Lincs.	BOSTON	
Breconshire	Brynmawr	BRECON CO.
Wiltshire	Calne	WILTSHIRE CO.
Yorkshire W.R.	CASTLEFORD	
Lancashire	CHADDERTON	
Glamorganshire	Coedffranc	GLAMORGAN CO.
Denbighshire	COLWYN BAY	
Caernarvonshire	CRICCIETH	
Ross and Cromarty	Cromarty	ROSS AND CROMARTY CO.
Lancashire	CROSBY	
Lancashire	Dalton in Furness	LANCASHIRE CO.
London	Deptford	LEWISHAM
Lancashire	ECCLES	
Aberdeenshire	FRASERBURGH	

Year and County	Adopting Authority	Present Authority (if different)
1905 *continued*		
Lindsey, Lincs.	GAINSBOROUGH	
Yorkshire W.R.	GOOLE	
London	GREENWICH	
London	Hanwell	EALING
Lancashire	HASLINGDEN	
London	Heston and Isleworth	HOUNSLOW
Flintshire	Holywell	FLINT CO.
Peeblesshire	INNERLEITHEN	
Aberdeenshire	INVERURIE	
Worcestershire	King's Norton	BIRMINGHAM
East Suffolk	LOWESTOFT	
Leicestershire	MELTON MOWBRAY	
Angus	MONTROSE	
Yorkshire W.R.	PONTEFRACT	
East Lothian	PRESTONPANS	
Lancashire	Rainford	LANCASHIRE CO.
Northamptonshire	RUSHDEN	
Isle of Wight	Sandown	SANDOWN–SHANKLIN
Kent	SEVENOAKS	
London	Southall	EALING
Worcestershire	STOURBRIDGE	
Warwickshire	STRATFORD UPON AVON	
Somerset	TAUNTON	
Yorkshire W.R.	Tinsley	SHEFFIELD
Midlothian	West Calder	MIDLOTHIAN CO.
1906		
Dumfriesshire	Annan	DUMFRIES CO.
Nottinghamshire	ARNOLD	
Lindsey, Lincs.	Ashby	SCUNTHORPE
Lancashire	ASHTON IN MAKERFIELD	
Yorkshire E.R.	BEVERLEY	
Essex	CHELMSFORD	
London	Erith	BEXLEY
Staffordshire	Fenton	STOKE ON TRENT
Yorkshire W.R.	HORBURY	
Lancashire	Horwich	LANCASHIRE CO.
London	ISLINGTON	
Roxburghshire	KELSO	
Kinross-shire	KINROSS	
West Sussex	LITTLEHAMPTON	
Denbighshire	Llangollen	DENBIGH CO.
Glamorganshire	Llantwitfardre	GLAMORGAN CO.
Derbyshire	LONG EATON	
Ayrshire	MAYBOLE	
Yorkshire W.R.	MORLEY	
Lanarkshire	Motherwell	MOTHERWELL AND WISHAW
Berkshire	NEWBURY	
Buckinghamshire	Oakley	BUCKINGHAM CO.

Year and County	Adopting Authority	Present Authority (if different)
1906 *continued*		
Derbyshire	Pleasley	DERBY CO.
Lancashire	RAWTENSTALL	
Lancashire	St. Annes	LYTHAM ST. ANNES
London	St. Pancras	CAMDEN
Essex	SOUTHEND ON SEA	
Kesteven, Lincs.	STAMFORD	
Nottinghamshire	Stapleford	NOTTINGHAM CO.
Orkney	STROMNESS	
Yorkshire W.R.	Swinton	WEST RIDING CO.
Yorkshire W.R.	Thorne	WEST RIDING CO.
Yorkshire W.R.	WAKEFIELD	
Lancashire	Wardle	LANCASHIRE CO.
Lancashire	WESTHOUGHTON	
1907		
Dunbartonshire	Alexandria	DUNBARTON CO.
Yorkshire W.R.	BATLEY	
Fife	Burntisland	FIFE CO.
Berkshire	Caversham	READING
Hertfordshire	CHESHUNT	
Norfolk	Costessey	NORFOLK CO.
Lancashire	CROMPTON	
Ross and Cromarty	Dingwall	ROSS AND CROMARTY CO.
Sutherland	Dornoch	SUTHERLAND CO.
Warwickshire	Erdington	BIRMINGHAM
Morayshire	Fochabers	MORAY AND NAIRN CO.
Cheshire	HALE	
Lanarkshire	HAMILTON	
Yorkshire W.R.	ILKLEY	
Berkshire	Letcombe Regis	BERKSHIRE CO.
Carmarthenshire	Llanelly Rural Parish	CARMARTHEN CO.
Merionethshire	Llanfor	MERIONETH CO.
Yorkshire W.R.	NORMANTON	
Lancashire	RADCLIFFE	
Somerset	Radstock	SOMERSET CO.
Flintshire	RHYL	
Lancashire	ROYTON	
Lanarkshire	RUTHERGLEN	
Ross and Cromarty	Stornoway	ROSS AND CROMARTY CO.
Devon	Torquay	TORBAY
Yorkshire W.R.	WOMBWELL	
1908		
Durham	Annfield Plain	DURHAM CO.
Yorkshire W.R.	Clayton	WEST RIDING CO.
Aberdeenshire	Dyce	ABERDEEN CO.
London	HACKNEY	
Caernarvonshire	LLANDUDNO	
Montgomeryshire	LLANIDLOES	

Year and County	Adopting Authority	Present Authority (if different)
1908 *continued*		
Roxburghshire	Maxton	ROXBURGH CO.
Lancashire	Milnrow	LANCASHIRE CO.
Cheshire	NESTON	
Monmouthshire	Pontypool	MONMOUTH CO.
Cumberland	Stainburn (s)	WORKINGTON
Derbyshire	Swadlincote	DERBY CO.
Yorkshire W.R.	Tickhill	WEST RIDING CO.
Lancashire	Waterloo	ASHTON UNDER LYNE
1909		
Midlothian	Bonnyrigg	BONNYRIGG AND LASSWADE
Glamorganshire	Cockett	SWANSEA
Lancashire	FAILSWORTH	
Yorkshire W.R.	HECKMONDWIKE	
London	Ilford	REDBRIDGE
Northamptonshire	Irchester	NORTHAMPTON CO.
Lancashire	NEWTON-LE-WILLOWS	
Staffordshire	Rowley Regis	WARLEY
Lancashire	Tyldesley	LANCASHIRE CO.
1910		
Clackmannanshire	Alloa Parish	CLACKMANNAN CO.
Cheshire	ELLESMERE PORT	
Yorkshire W.R.	SKIPTON	
Staffordshire	STOKE ON TRENT	
1911		
Lancashire	Bispham with Norbreck	BLACKPOOL
Lancashire	FARNWORTH	
Yorkshire W.R.	Silsden	WEST RIDING CO.
Aberdeenshire	Udny	ABERDEEN CO.
1912		
Yorkshire W.R.	ELLAND	
Cardiganshire	Lampeter	CARDIGANSHIRE JOINT LIBRARY
Radnorshire	Llandrindod Wells	RADNOR CO.
Montgomeryshire	Machynlleth	MONTGOMERY CO.
Peeblesshire	PEEBLES	
Herefordshire	Ross on Wye	HEREFORD CO.
Fife	Torryburn (?)	FIFE CO.
1913		
Lancashire	Audenshaw (s)	LANCASHIRE CO.
Dunbartonshire	CLYDEBANK	
Nottinghamshire	Huthwaite	SUTTON IN ASHFIELD
Caernarvonshire	Llandeiniolen	CAERNARVON CO.
Flintshire	Mold	FLINT CO.
Yorkshire W.R.	Penistone	WEST RIDING CO.
1914		
Lancashire	BURNLEY	

Year and County	Adopting Authority	Present Authority (if different)
1915		
Argyllshire	DUNOON	
Lancashire	Oswaldtwistle	LANCASHIRE CO.
1916		
Kent	DARTFORD	
Glamorganshire	Margam	PORT TALBOT
1917		
Yorkshire W.R.	Harthill with Woodall (?)	WEST RIDING CO.
Yorkshire	HORSFORTH (?)	
Lancashire	Lytham	LYTHAM ST. ANNES
1918		
Surrey	CHERTSEY	
1919		
Somerset	Midsomer Norton	SOMERSET CO.
Perthshire	Perth Co.	PERTH AND KINROSS CO.
London	St. Mary Cray	BROMLEY
Shropshire	Wem	SHROPSHIRE CO.
1920		
Angus and Kincardineshire	ANGUS AND KINCARDINE CO.	
Berwickshire	BERWICK CO.	
Caithness	CAITHNESS CO.	
Buckinghamshire	HIGH WYCOMBE	
Kirkcudbrightshire	KIRKCUDBRIGHT CO.	
Midlothian	MIDLOTHIAN CO.	
Lancashire	Orrell	LANCASHIRE CO.
London	Paddington	WESTMINSTER
Peeblesshire	PEEBLES CO.	
Renfrewshire	RENFREW CO.	
Sutherland	SUTHERLAND CO.	
Warwickshire	WARWICK CO.	
1921		
Clackmannanshire	CLACKMANNAN CO.	
Cumberland	CUMBERLAND CO.	
Denbighshire	DENBIGH CO.	
Fife	FIFE CO.	
Kent	KENT CO.	
Glamorganshire	PORT TALBOT	
Kent	TUNBRIDGE WELLS	
1922		
London	Bethnal Green	TOWER HAMLETS
Leicestershire	Bottesford (s)	LEICESTER CO.
Cambridgeshire	Cambridge Co.	CAMBRIDGE AND ISLE OF ELY CO.

Year and County	Adopting Authority	Present Authority (if different)
1922 *continued*		
Cheshire	CHESHIRE CO.	
Denbighshire	Denbigh (?) (s)	DENBIGH CO.
Gloucestershire	GLOUCESTER CO.	
Kesteven, Lincs.	GRANTHAM	
Lanarkshire	LANARK CO.	
Lancashire	LYTHAM ST. ANNES	
Middlesex	Middlesex Co.	LONDON BOROUGHS (see Appendix III)
Nairnshire	Nairn Co.	MORAY AND NAIRN CO.
Staffordshire	STAFFORD CO.	
Yorkshire W.R.	WEST RIDING CO.	
Wigtownshire	WIGTOWN CO.	
Somerset	YEOVIL	
By 1923		
Essex	Aveley	THURROCK
Yorkshire W.R.	Greasborough	ROTHERHAM
East Sussex	Hailsham	EAST SUSSEX CO.
1923		
Yorkshire W.R.	Birkenshaw	SPENBOROUGH
Buckinghamshire	BUCKINGHAM CO.	
Caernarvonshire	CAERNARVON CO.	
Cardiganshire	Cardigan Co.	CARDIGANSHIRE JOINT LIBRARY
Lancashire	Clayton-le-Moors	LANCASHIRE CO.
Dunbartonshire	DUNBARTON CO.	
Glamorganshire	GLAMORGAN CO.	
Surrey	Godalming	SURREY CO.
Yorkshire W.R.	Guiseley	AIREBOROUGH
Kent	MARGATE	
Orkney	ORKNEY CO.	
London	St Marylebone	WESTMINSTER
Selkirkshire	SELKIRK CO. (s)	
Somerset	SOMERSET CO.	
Wiltshire	WILTSHIRE CO.	
Worcestershire	WORCESTER CO.	
Zetland	ZETLAND CO.	
1924		
Berkshire	BERKSHIRE CO.	
East Sussex	Bexhill	EAST SUSSEX CO.
Breconshire and Radnorshire	Brecon and Radnor Co.	BRECON CO., RADNOR CO.
West Suffolk	BURY ST. EDMUNDS	
Stirlingshire	Denny and Dunipace	STIRLING CO.
Derbyshire	DERBY CO.	
Devonshire	DEVON CO.	
Dumfriesshire	DUMFRIES CO.	
Durham	DURHAM CO.	
East Sussex	EAST SUSSEX CO.	

Year and County	Adopting Authority	Present Authority (if different)
1924 *continued*		
Surrey	GUILDFORD	
Isle of Wight	ISLE OF WIGHT CO.	
Kesteven, Lincs.	KESTEVEN CO.	
Kinross-shire	Kinross Co.	PERTH AND KINROSS CO.
Leicestershire	LEICESTER CO.	
Montgomeryshire	Montgomery	MONTGOMERY CO.
Morayshire	Moray Co.	MORAY AND NAIRN CO.
Nottinghamshire	NOTTINGHAM CO.	
Oxfordshire	OXFORD CO.	
Pembrokeshire	PEMBROKE CO.	
West Lothian	WEST LOTHIAN CO.	
Yorkshire W.R.	Yeadon	AIREBOROUGH
1925		
Ayrshire	AYR CO.	
Bedfordshire	BEDFORD CO.	
Fife	BUCKHAVEN AND METHIL	
Staffordshire	CANNOCK	
Cornwall	CORNWALL CO.	
Dorset	DORSET CO.	
Yorkshire E.R.	EAST RIDING CO.	
East Suffolk	EAST SUFFOLK CO.	
Denbighshire	Esclusham Below (?) (s)	DENBIGH CO.
Flintshire	FLINT CO.	
Hampshire	HAMPSHIRE CO.	
Hertfordshire	HERTFORD CO.	
Lancashire	LANCASHIRE CO.	
Lindsey, Lincs.	Lindsey Co.	LINDSEY AND HOLLAND CO.
Montgomeryshire	MONTGOMERY CO.	
Norfolk	NORFOLK CO.	
Yorkshire N.R.	NORTH RIDING CO.	
Northumberland	NORTHUMBERLAND CO.	
Ross and Cromarty	ROSS AND CROMARTY CO.	
Roxburghshire	ROXBURGH CO.	
Shropshire	SHROPSHIRE CO.	
Stirlingshire	STIRLING CO.	
Surrey	SURREY CO.	
West Sussex	WEST SUSSEX CO.	
1926		
Aberdeenshire	ABERDEEN CO.	
Anglesey	ANGLESEY CO.	
Banffshire	BANFF CO.	
Yorkshire E.R.	BRIDLINGTON	
Bute	BUTE CO.	
East Lothian	EAST LOTHIAN CO.	
Essex	ESSEX CO.	

Year and County	Adopting Authority	Present Authority (if different)
1926 *continued*		
London	Hendon	BARNET
Herefordshire	HEREFORD CO.	
Huntingdon and Peterborough	Huntingdon Co.	HUNTINGDON AND PETERBOROUGH CO.
Inverness-shire	INVERNESS CO.	
Isle of Ely	Isle of Ely Co.	CAMBRIDGESHIRE AND ISLE OF ELY CO.
Northamptonshire	NORTHAMPTON CO.	
Huntingdon and Peterborough	Soke of Peterborough Co.	HUNTINGDON AND PETERBOROUGH CO.
Westmorland	WINDERMERE	
1927		
Nottinghamshire	East Retford	NOTTINGHAM CO.
Merionethshire	MERIONETH CO.	
Monmouthshire	MONMOUTH CO.	
West Suffolk	WEST SUFFOLK CO.	
1930		
Cheshire	BEBINGTON	
Northumberland	BLYTH	
London	Dagenham	BARKING
Worcestershire	REDDITCH	
Yorkshire W.R.	ROTHWELL	
Yorkshire N.R.	SCARBOROUGH	
Yorkshire W.R.	SPENBOROUGH	
Dunbartonshire	Vale of Leven	DUNBARTON CO.
1931		
Lancashire	BACUP	
London	Surbiton	KINGSTON UPON THAMES
1932		
Carmarthenshire	CARMARTHEN CO.	
1933		
London	Finchley	BARNET
Worcestershire	HALESOWEN	
Kent	HYTHE	
London	Mitcham	MERTON
Isle of Wight	Shanklin	SANDOWN-SHANKLIN
Northumberland	WALLSEND	
1934		
Cornwall	CAMBORNE–REDRUTH	
Somerset	Norton–Radstock	SOMERSET CO.
Isle of Wight	SANDOWN–SHANKLIN	
1935		
London	Carshalton	SUTTON
Kent	DOVER	

Year and County	Adopting Authority	Present Authority (if different)
1936		
London	Beddington and Wallington	SUTTON
London	Coulsdon and Purley	CROYDON
Cheshire	CREWE	
Hertfordshire	LETCHWORTH	
Lincolnshire	LINDSEY AND HOLLAND CO.	
London	Sutton and Cheam	SUTTON
Essex	THURROCK	
1937		
Yorkshire W.R.	AIREBOROUGH	
Bedfordshire	BEDFORD	
Perthshire	BLAIRGOWRIE AND RATTRAY	
Hertfordshire	Hitchin	HERTFORD CO.
Northumberland	NEWBURN	
Yorkshire N.R.	Redcar	TEESSIDE
Warwickshire	SUTTON COLDFIELD	
1938		
Fife	LEVEN	
1939		
Breconshire	BRECON CO.	
Radnorshire	RADNOR CO.	
Glamorganshire	RHONDDA	
1940		
Scilly Is.	ISLES OF SCILLY (s)	
Northumberland	Whitley and Monkseaton	WHITLEY BAY
1943		
London	Barnes	RICHMOND UPON THAMES
Wiltshire	SWINDON	
1944		
Oxfordshire	Henley on Thames	OXFORD CO.
Dorset	WEYMOUTH AND MELCOMBE REGIS	
Yorkshire N.R.	WHITBY	
1945		
Perthshire	Crieff	PERTH AND KINROSS CO.
1946		
Argyllshire	ARGYLL CO.	
Rutlandshire	RUTLAND CO. (s)	
1947		
Oxfordshire	BANBURY	
Cardiganshire	CARDIGANSHIRE JOINT LIBRARY	
Angus	CARNOUSTIE	
Warwickshire	SOLIHULL	

Year and County	Adopting Authority	Present Authority (if different)
1948 Northumberland	BERWICK UPON TWEED	
1950 Northumberland	GOSFORTH	
Dunbartonshire	HELENSBURGH	
1952 Kent	GILLINGHAM	
1954 Hampshire	ALDERSHOT	
1957 London	Orpington	BROMLEY
1958 London	Chislehurst and Sidcup	BEXLEY, BROMLEY
1960 Gloucestershire	CIRENCESTER	
1964 Glamorganshire	MOUNTAIN ASH	
1965 London	BARNET	
London	BRENT	
Cambridgeshire and Isle of Ely	CAMBRIDGESHIRE AND ISLE OF ELY CO.	
London	CAMDEN	
Surrey	EPSOM AND EWELL	
London	HARINGEY	
London	HARROW	
London	HAVERING	
London	HILLINGDON	
London	HOUNSLOW	
Huntingdon and Peterborough	HUNTINGDON AND PETERBOROUGH CO.	
London	KENSINGTON AND CHELSEA	
London	MERTON	
London	NEWHAM	
London	SUTTON	
London	TOWER HAMLETS	
London	WALTHAM FOREST	
1966 Staffordshire	WALSALL	
Staffordshire	WARLEY	
1967 Durham	HARTLEPOOL	
Westmorland	KENDAL AND WESTMORLAND	
1968 Essex	CHIGWELL	
Yorkshire N.R.	TEESSIDE	
Devon	TORBAY	

PUBLIC LIBRARY AUTHORITIES

not known to have provided a library service, in order of adoption

Year and Authority	Present Authority	Year and Authority	Present Authority
1887		*1901*	
Leyland	LANCASHIRE CO.	Abersychan	MONMOUTH CO.
Newton Heath	MANCHESTER	Cyfoeth y Brenin	CARDIGANSHIRE JOINT LIBRARY
1895		Handsworth	SHEFFIELD
Halton	WEST RIDING CO.	North Walsham	NORFOLK CO.
Higher Newcastle	GLAMORGAN CO.	Pencoed	GLAMORGAN CO.
Ibstock	LEICESTER CO.		
Ogmore and Garw	GLAMORGAN CO.	*1902*	
St. Austell	CORNWALL CO.	Halstead	ESSEX CO.
Shouldham	NORFOLK CO.	Hebden Bridge	WEST RIDING CO.
Whitefield	LANCASHIRE CO.	Jarrow	DURHAM CO.
		Quarry Bank	DUDLEY
1896		South Normanton	DERBY CO.
Hayle	CORNWALL CO.	Sutton	SUTTON
Kingsthorpe	NORTHAMPTON	Wells next the Sea	WEST RIDING CO.
Leadgate	DURHAM CO.		
Mile End	TOWER HAMLETS		
St. Neots	HUNTINGDON AND PETER-BOROUGH CO.	*1903*	
		Audley	STAFFORD CO.
Shepshed	LEICESTER CO.	Benwell and Fenham	NEWCASTLE UPON TYNE
Stratford-le-Bow	TOWER HAMLETS	Brentwood	ESSEX CO.
Worsley	LANCASHIRE CO.	Cullen	BANFF CO.
		Great Harwood	LANCASHIRE CO.
1897		Ilfracombe	DEVON CO.
Padiham	LANCASHIRE CO.	Northfleet	KENT
		Sowerby	NORTH RIDING CO.
1898			
Haworth	KEIGHLEY	Bishop's Stortford	HERTFORD CO.
Limehouse	TOWER HAMLETS	Cudworth	WEST RIDING CO.
Louth .	LINDSEY AND HOLLAND CO.	Hemel Hempstead	HERTFORD CO.
Trumpington	CAMBRIDGE	Spalding	LINDSEY AND HOLLAND CO.
		Whitworth	LANCASHIRE CO.
1899			
Featherstone	WEST RIDING CO.		
		1906	
1900		Coalsnaughton	CLACKMANNAN CO.
Cleethorpes with Thrunscoe	LINDSEY AND HOLLAND CO.	Hayward's Heath	EAST SUSSEX CO.
Ynyscynhaiarn (Portmadoc)	CARMARTHEN CO.		

Year and Authority	Present Authority	Year and Authority	Present Authority
1908 Llanfair is Gaer	CAERNARVON CO.	*1924* Checkendon	OXFORD CO.
1909 East Winch	NORFOLK CO.	*1927* Coseley	DUDLEY and WOLVERHAMP-TON
1916 North and South Anston	WEST RIDING CO.	*1930* Alnwick	NORTHUMBER-LAND CO.
1919 Mansfield Woodhouse	NOTTINGHAM CO.	*1936* Amble	NORTHUMBER-LAND CO.
1920 Lower Heyford Marple	OXFORD CO. CHESHIRE CO.	*1945* Ashington	NORTHUMBER-LAND CO.
by 1921 Brampton-en-le-Morthen Thorpe Salvin	WEST RIDING CO. WEST RIDING CO.		
1923 Cheriton	FOLKESTONE		

Note: For ten authorities reported to have adopted 1917-18 under the Carnegie Worksop scheme, see above, App. III, *s.v.* Lincolnshire and Nottinghamshire.

BOOKSTOCKS, ISSUES AND POPULATION
AT SELECTED DATES

1875–77

	England	Wales	Scotland	Total
Total population 1871 (000s)	21490	1222	3360	26072
Population of library areas 1871 (000s)	3912	145	201	4258
Population of library areas as percentage of total	18	12	6	16
Volumes in stock (000s)	996	12	54	1062
Volumes per head of total population	0.05	0.01	0.02	0.04
Volumes per head of library population	0.25	0.08	0.27	0.25
Annual lending issues (000s)	3619	38	248	3905
Issues per head of total population	0.17	0.03	0.07	0.15
Issues per head of library population	0.93	0.26	1.23	0.92

Figures for these years are calculated from *Parliamentary Returns of Public Libraries*, 1876 and 1877.

1884–85

	England	Wales	Scotland	Total
Total population, 1881 (000s)	24614	1360	3736	29710
Population of library areas, 1881 (000s)	6219	202	305	6726
Population of library areas as percentage of total	25	15	8	23
Volumes in stock (000s)	1811	45	105	1961
Volumes per head of total population	0.07	0.03	0.03	0.07
Volumes per head of population in library areas	0.29	0.22	0.34	0.29
Annual lending issues (000s)	Not recorded			

Figures for these years are calculated from *Parliamentary Return of Public Libraries*, 1885.

1913–14

	England	Wales	Scotland	Total
Total population, 1911 (000s)	34194	2025	4760	40979
Population of library areas, 1911 (000s)	21103	938	2403	24444
Population of library areas as percentage of total	62	46	50	60
Volumes in stock (000s)	9357	497	1551	11405
Volumes per head of total population	0.27	0.25	0.33	0.28
Volumes per head of population in library areas	0.44	0.53	0.65	0.47
Annual lending issues	47834	1340	5340	54514
Issues per head of total population	1.4	0.66	1.12	1.33
Issues per head of population in library areas	2.27	1.43	2.22	2.23

Figures for these years are calculated from W. G. S. Adams, *Report on Library Provision and Policy to the Carnegie United Kingdom Trustees* (Dunfermline 1915). The figures for issues probably include some reference issues.

1934–35

	England & Wales	Scotland	Total
Total population 1935 (estimated) (000s)	40645	4953	45598
Population of library areas (000s)	40049	4890	44939
Volumes in stock (000s)	22855	3576	26431
Volumes per head of library population	0.57	0.73	0.59
Annual lending issues (000s)	142875	22797	165672
Issues per head of library population	3.56	4.66	3.69

Figures for these years are calculated from Library Association, County Library Section, *County Libraries in Great Britain and Ireland: Statistical Report, 1934–35* [1936]; and Library Association, *Statistics of Urban Libraries in Great Britain and Northern Ireland* (1935) [1936]. By this date the difference between total population and the population in library areas is not significant enough to justify a separate calculation of percentages. The issue figures include some reference issues.

1961–62

	England	Wales	Scotland	Total
Total population 1961 (000s)	43431	2641	5178	51250
Volumes in stock (000s)	63316	5249	7440	76005
Volumes per head of population	1.46	2.00	1.44	1.49
Annual lending issues (000s)	391172	18277	36869	446318
Issues per head of population	9.00	6.92	7.12	8.90

Figures for these years are calculated from Library Association, *Statistics of Public (Rate Supported) Libraries in Great Britain and Northern Ireland 1961–62* (1963).

BOOKSTOCKS IN PUBLIC LIBRARIES
according to the Parliamentary Returns of 1876 and 1877

	Lending Libraries	Reference Libraries	Total
England and Wales (corporate towns)	532100	443800	975900
England and Wales (other authorities)	28700	3700	32400
England and Wales (total)	560800	447500	1008300
Scotland	44400	10000	54400
Total	605200	457500	1062700

PERCENTAGE OF BOOKS IN VARIOUS SUBJECTS
based on the Parliamentary Returns of 1876 and 1877

Subjects	Lending Libraries			Reference Libraries			Com-bined Total
	E. &W.	Scot-land	Total	E. &W.	Scot-land	Total	
Theology, Philosophy, Ecclesiastical History	4.8	7.5	5.0	5.9	9.8	5.9	5.4
Geography, History, Travels, Biography	24.5	24.2	24.5	22.2	19.9	22.2	23.5
Law, Politics, Commerce, Statistics	2.0	5.6	2.2	9.2	7.5	9.2	5.2
Art, Science, Education, Natural History, Geology	9.2	9.3	9.2	15.1	21.2	15.2	11.8
Books of Reference	0.2	0.06	0.2	1.6	10.7	1.8	0.9
Foreign Books	0.06	—	0.05	0.3	—	0.3	0.2
Fiction and Juvenile	25.2	26.4	25.3	6.6	—	6.5	17.2
Literature, Poetry, Drama, Miscellaneous	21.1	13.2	20.5	23.7	23.0	23.7	21.9
Magazines, Pamphlets	7.4	13.0	7.8	1.1	7.4	1.2	5.0
Patents	0.03	—	0.03	3.4	—	3.3	1.4
Books for the Blind	0.2	—	0.2	0.03	—	0.3	0.1
Not Classified	5.5	—	5.1	10.2	0.7	10.4	7.5

STATISTICS OF SELECTED PUBLIC LIBRARIES IN 1886

Except where otherwise stated, these figures have been supplied by librarians and are for the year 1886 or (where the year did not end on 31st December) for the year 1885–86.

	Population in thousands (1881)	Total Stocks	Reference		Central Lending		Branch Lending	
			Stock	Issues	Stock	Issues	Stock	Issues
Manchester	341	181095	81930	294444[1]	—	—	99165	726448
Leeds	309	146502	36865	103092	36158	398674	73479	333791
Birmingham	401	145349	88000	384124	25139	252470	32210	226433
Liverpool	553	134427	88671	675335	—	—	45756	383562
Salford	176	81431	41679	55193	12147	43414	27605	184492
Sheffield	285	80692	11251	29689	29518	125191	39993	274462
Bristol	207	66093	27569[2]	63285[2]			38524	366102
Nottingham	187	57277	19338	77081	23960	185655	13979	108873
Bolton	105	57246	29241	89438[3]	14209	48589	13796	38532
Newcastle upon Tyne	145	56205	28009	38149	28196	222866	—	—
Bradford	183	49034	15904	70045	14547	146581	18583	189085
Dundee	140	48548	14339	78529	34209	216632	—	—
Birkenhead	84	37378	8156	94848	29222	137876	—	—
Cambridge	35	31435	8670		18548	70771	4217	11553
Cardiff	83	20342	8722	9729	11620	109021	—	—
Westminster	60	19216	16610[4]	58158		68272	2606	13031
Warrington	41	18500	18500[4]	20986		18757	—	—
Norwich	88	14429	3223		11206	75116	—	—
Darlington	35	12859	12859[4]	1247		112340	—	—
Sunderland	117	12500[5]	300		12200	c.100000[6]	—	—
Leamington	23	11641[7]	3314	8298	8327	36860	—	—
Oxford	38	c.10000[8]						
Airdrie	16	c.7000[9]	(3828)		3172	19166	—	—
Aberystwyth	7	3093[5]	80		3013	c.2000[6]		
Winchester	18	c.3000[9]	(c.1350)		c.1650	27372	—	—
Canterbury	22	c.5000[9]	c.200		(c.4800)	14181	—	—

[1] Plus 440848 in Branch Reading Rooms.

[2] Combined figures for reference and central lending libraries. Greenwood (1887), gives total stock as 68000 v., and reference stock as 18000 v.

[3] Plus 28211 in Branch Reading Rooms.

[4] Combined reference and central lending stock. [5] Greenwood (1887).

[6] Combined reference and lending issues (Greenwood 1887).

[7] Plus 753 v. of patents and abridgments of specifications.

[8] P.R. 1885 gives reference stock Sept. 1884 as c. 7000 v., lending stock c. 3100 v.; Greenwood (1887) gives reference stock 6000 v., lending stock 3200 v.

[9] Greenwood (1887), figures for 1885. For Airdrie P.R. 1885 gives reference stock 139 v., lending stock 6723 v.

Appendix X

PASSMORE EDWARDS LIBRARIES

with dates of opening

(a) *In Cornwall*

1895	Camborne	1896	Truro
	Redruth	1897	Bodmin
1896	Falmouth		St. Ives
	Liskeard	1900	Launceston

(b) *In Devon*

1904   Newton Abbot

(c) *In or near London*

1892	Whitechapel, Stepney	1899	East Ham
1893	Haggerston, Shoreditch		St. George the Martyr, Southwark
1896	Nunhead, Camberwell	1900	Acton
	Shepherd's Bush, Hammersmith	1901	Bow Bridge, Poplar
1897	East Dulwich, Camberwell		Limehouse, Stepney
	Edmonton	1903	North Camberwell
1898	Hoxton, Shoreditch		Plaistow, West Ham
	St. George in the East, Stepney		

495

STATISTICS OF SELECTED PUBLIC LIBRARIES IN 1913–14

(Extracted from the *Adams Report*, 1915)

B.: Burgh; C.B. : County Borough; Met.B. : Metropolitan Borough; M.B. : Municipal Borough; P. : Parish; U.D. : Urban District.

Authority	Popula-tion in thousands (1911)	Total Stock	Annual Issues	No. of Branches	Remarks
Glasgow B.	784	468485	1732335[1]	17	[1] Excluding reading room issues
Birmingham C.B.	783	445675	2217563	22	
Manchester C.B.	714	434485	2764783	24	
Liverpool C.B.	747	349698	2268530	11	
Leeds C.B.	446	313196	1382237	14	
Cardiff C.B.	183	193099	458707	5	
Edinburgh C.B.	320	188271	832922	5	
Sheffield C.B.	455	186551	733488	8[2]	[2] And eight delivery stations
Bristol C.B.	357	177091	756560	9	
Bradford C.B.	289	174000	840000	12[3]	[3] And twelve travelling libraries
Newcastle-upon-Tyne C.B.	267	172000	592000	4	
Dundee B.	165	151268	417548	6	
Nottingham C.B.	260	145797	569146	6[4]	[4] And six branch reading rooms
Lambeth Met.B.	298	143913	723920	5	
Bolton C.B.	181	133525	500428	6	
Westminster Met.B.	160	127000	529000	[5]	[5] Four district libraries —no central library
Wandsworth Met.B.	313	123620	971185	3 [6]	[6] In addition to the four main district libraries —no central library
Hull C.B.	278	113630	791949	5	
Salford C.B.	231	95657	603254	6	
West Ham C.B.	289	85252	353865	3	
Aberdeen B.	163	79054	337187	[7]	[7] Four branch reading rooms
Kensington Met.B.	172	73902	243486	2	
Birkenhead C.B.	131	71112	321008	2	
Willesden U.D.	159	63100	353582	[8]	[8] Four district libraries —no central library

Authority	Popula-tion in thousands (1911)	Total Stock	Annual Issues	No. of Branches	Remarks
Swansea C.B.	115	62257	159787		
Cambridge M.B.	52	58878	168498	1	
Warrington C.B.	72	57896	110080	1	[1] Eight delivery stations
Sunderland C.B.	151	50740	351805	3	
Bournemouth C.B.	79	50348	344208	4	
Norwich C.B.	121	41200	113067	—	
Stockport C.B.	109	38296	157816	1	
York C.B.	82	37801	162351	—	
Stoke on Trent C.B.	235	34368[2]	299000	3	[2] Incomplete figure: see above, p. 160 note [3] Federation of six libraries
Aberdare U.D.	51	30000	63340	3[4]	[4] Workmen's institutes
Darlington M.B.	56	29000	183000	—	
Leamington M.B.	27	24847	59762	—	
Oxford C.B.	53	23997	105212	—	
Lincoln C.B.	57	15926	104229	—	
Dumfries B.	22	15873	35901	—	
Malvern U.D.	17	14670	67027	—	
Canterbury C.B.	25	12738	47077	—	
Bath C.B.	69	11600	[5]	—	[5] Reference library only
Whitehaven M.B.	19	11600	25030	—	
Winchester M.B.	23	10100[6]	32759[6]	—	[6] 1911 figures—*P.R. 1912*, p. 27
Airdrie B.	24	10000	63321	—	
Aberystwyth M.B.	8	7938	18201	—	
Tarves P.	2	6020	2960	1	
Camborne U.D.	16	5850	33050	—	
Hinckley U.D.	13	4300	10502	—	
Oakley P.	0.4	575[7]	996[7]	—	[7] 1911 figures—*P.R. 1912*, p.10

PERCENTAGE OF BOOKS IN VARIOUS SUBJECTS IN 1907
(from J. D. Brown, *Manual of Library Economy*, 2nd. edn. 1907, p. 411)

SUBJECT	*PERCENTAGE OF TOTAL STOCK*
Science	8
Useful Arts	7
Fine Arts	8
Social Science	8
Theology	6
History and Geography	15
Biography	8
Language and Literary History	5
Poetry	6
Fiction	20
Miscellaneous	10

SELECT BIBLIOGRAPHY

A. BIBLIOGRAPHIES AND ABSTRACTS

This is by no means a comprehensive list. I have merely attempted to bring together some of the more important references detailed in the footnotes, excluding for the most part references to articles in periodicals. For the sake of completeness I have included a few recent works (mostly unpublished theses) which I have not had the opportunity of examining in detail. These are marked with an asterisk. I have included the name of the publisher in the case of books published since 1945, and in a few other instances where it seemed likely to be useful. Entries in Sections A–C are in chronological order.

1. H. G. Cannons, *Bibliography of Library Economy, 1876–1920* (American Library Association, Chicago 1927). Continued as *Library Literature*, 1921–32 (1934), with supplementary volumes published by Wilson, New York. Now six times yearly with periodical cumulative volumes. A comprehensive guide to professional literature.

2. Margaret Burton and M. E. Vosburgh, *A Bibliography of Librarianship* (Library Association 1934).

3. Library Association, *Library Science Abstracts*, Vols. I–XIX (1950–68). Succeeded by

4. Library Association, *Library and Information Science Abstracts*, Vol. I (1969) (in progress).

5. Library Association, *Catalogue of the Library* (1958). An invaluable work of reference, covering accessions to 1956.

B. GENERAL HISTORY

1. *General Historical Surveys*

Surveys covering all or most of the period are few. The most significant are:

6. John Minto, *A History of the Public Library Movement in Great Britain and Ireland* (1932). Includes a summary of legislation.

7. W. A. Munford, *Penny Rate: Aspects of British Public Library History, 1850–1950* (Library Association 1951).

8. W. J. Murison, *The Public Library: its Origins, Purpose and Significance* (Harrap 1955, 2nd. edn. 1971).

Note also:

9. Albert Predeek, *A History of Libraries in Great Britain and North America* (American Library Association, Chicago 1947). Useful on certain limited aspects only.

10. J. L. Thornton, *Selected Readings in the History of Librarianship* (Library Association 1966). A useful companion throughout, including a 2nd edition of the author's *A Mirror for Librarians* (1st edn. 1948), and his *Classics of Librarianship* (1957).

11. Thomas Kelly, *History of Adult Education in Great Britain* (Liverpool University Press 1962, 2nd edn. 1970). For the general educational and cultural background.

12. J. G. Ollé, *Library History: an examination guidebook* (Bingley 1967, 2nd edn. 1971).

For library legislation it is essential to consult Hansard's *Parliamentary Debates* (3rd., 4th., and 5th. Series, from 1830) and the official text of the Acts, which may be found in the *Statutes at Large*.

2. *Special Periods*

(a) *Origins*

The key document for this period is:

13. Select Committee on Public Libraries, *Report* (1849). Note also the later Reports of 1850, 1851, and 1852.

Other government reports bearing on the subject are:

14. Select Committee on Inquiry into Drunkenness, *Report* (1834).
15. Select Committee on Arts and Manufactures, *Report* (1836).
16. Select Committee on the Condition, Management and Affairs of the British Museum, *Report* (1836).

The best narrative of events is to be found in two biographies:

17. W. A. Munford, *William Ewart, M.P.* (Grafton 1960).
18. W. A. Munford, *Edward Edwards, 1812–1886* (Library Association 1963).

For the precursors of the rate-aided libraries see:

19. Raymond Irwin, *The Origins of the English Library* (Allen and Unwin 1958). Enlarged edition, *The English Library: Sources and History* (1966).
20. Raymond Irwin, *The Heritage of the English Library* (Allen and Unwin 1964).
21. Thomas Kelly, *Early Public Libraries* (Library Association 1966).

(b) *1847–1918*

For narrative accounts see:

22. Edward Edwards, *Memoirs of Libraries* (2v. 1859, 2nd and incomplete edn. 1901).
23. Edward Edwards, *Free Town Libraries* (1869).
24. Thomas Greenwood, *Free Public Libraries* (1886, 2nd edn. 1887, 3rd edn., *Public Libraries*, 1890, 4th edn. 1891, 4th edn. revised 1894). Successive editions of this work repay careful study, providing an almost blow by blow account of library development at this period.
 5. J. J. Ogle, *The Free Library* (1887).

For the Carnegie benefactions see:

26. Carnegie United Kingdom Trust, *Annual Reports*, beginning with the *First Annual Report, 1913–14* (Dunfermline 1915).
27. W. G. S. Adams, *A Report on Library Provision and Policy to the Carnegie United Kingdom Trustees* [Adams Report] (Dunfermline 1915). The first great national report on public library policy. See also **123**.
28. Carnegie Endowment for International Peace, *A Manual of the Public Benefactions of Andrew Carnegie* (Washington 1919).
29. B. J. Hendrick, *The Life of Andrew Carnegie* (1933).
30. William Robertson, *Welfare in Trust: a History of the Carnegie United Kingdom Trust, 1939–1963* (Carnegie U.K. Trust, Dunfermline 1964).

For the contributions of Passmore Edwards see:

31. J. J. Macdonald, *Passmore Edwards Institutions* (1900).
32. E. H. Burrage, *J. Passmore Edwards, Philanthropist* (1902).
33. J. P. Edwards, *A Few Footprints* (1905).

Note also:

34. Alfred Cotgreave, *Views and Memoranda of Public Libraries* (1901).
35. Grace Carlton, *Spadework: the Story of Thomas Greenwood* (Hutchinson [1949]).

For non-rate-aided libraries at this period there is no general history, but see:

36. F. W. Naylor, *Popular Libraries in Rural Districts* [1885.]
37. F. W. Naylor, *Continuous Education* (1858).
38. Thomas Greenwood, *Sunday School and Village Libraries* (1882).
39. Lady John Manners, *Some of the Advantages of Easily Accessible Reading and Recreation Rooms and Free Libraries* (1885).
40. Lady John Manners, *Encouraging Experiences of Reading and Recreation Rooms* (1886).

(c) *1919–1965*

Library progress in this period is charted by a series of important reports and recommendations:

41. Ministry of Reconstruction, Adult Education Committee, *Third Interim Report: Libraries and Museums* (Cd. 9237, 1919); *Final Report* (Cmd. 321, 1919).
42. J. M. Mitchell, *The Public Library System of Great Britain and Ireland 1921–1923: a Report prepared for the Carnegie U.K. Trustees* [Mitchell Report] (Dunfermline 1924).
43. Board of Education, Public Libraries Committee, *Report on Public Libraries in England and Wales* [Kenyon Report] (Cmd. 2868, 1927). See also 127.
44. L. R. McColvin (ed.), *A Survey of Libraries: Reports on a Survey made by the Library Association during 1936–37* (1938).
45. L. R. McColvin, *The Public Library System of Great Britain* [McColvin Report] (Library Association 1942).
46. Library Association, *Proposals for the Post-War Reorganisation and Development of the Public Library Service* (1943).
47. C. S. Minto, *Public Library Services in the North of Scotland: a Report and Recommendations* [Minto Report] (Scottish Library Association, Edinburgh 1948).
48. Scottish Education Department, Advisory Council on Education in Scotland, *Libraries, Museums, and Art Galleries: a Report* [McClelland Report] (Cmd. 8229, Edinburgh 1951).
49. Library Association, *Memorandum of Evidence to be laid before the Committee appointed by the Minister of Education . . .* (1958).
50. Ministry of Education, *The Structure of the Public Library Service in England and Wales* [Roberts Report] (Cmnd. 660, 1959).
51. Ministry of Education, *Standards of Public Library Service in England and Wales* [Bourdillon Report] (1962).
52. Ministry of Education, *Inter-Library Co-operation in England and Wales* [Baker Report] (1962).

53. C. S. Minto, "Sixteen Years On: Impressions of a Tour of Public Libraries in the North of Scotland in 1964" [Second Minto Report], in *S.L.A. News*, No. 66 (Sept.–Oct. 1964).

For the years following the second World War it is necessary also to take account of a number of important Government reports on education, especially:

54. Ministry of Education, Central Advisory Council for Education (England), *15 to 18* [Crowther Report] (2v. 1959–60).

55. Ministry of Education, *The Youth Service in England and Wales* [Albemarle Report] (Cmnd. 929, 1960).

56. *Higher Education: Report of the Committee appointed by the Prime Minister* [Robbins Report] (Cmnd. 2154, 1963, with six volumes of Appendices).

57. Ministry of Education, Central Advisory Council for Education (England), *Half our Future* [Newsom Report] (1963).

Aspects of library work during the war years are described in:

58. Library Association, *The Restoration of Libraries: a brief account of Book Recovery and the Inter-Allied Book Centre* (1946).

59. J. H. P. Pafford, *Books and Army Education, 1944–1946: Preparation and Supply* (ASLIB 1947).

60. N. S. Wilson, *Education in the Forces, 1939–46: the Civilian Contribution* (Evans [1949]).

The centenary of the Public Libraries Act of 1850 was celebrated by two informative pamphlets:

61. Library Association, *A Century of Public Libraries, 1850–1950* (1950).

62. Library Association, *A Century of Public Library Service: Where do we Stand To-day?* (1950).

County Libraries

The advent of county libraries following the 1919 Act brought its own crop of literature. Note especially:

63. E. J. Carnell, *County Libraries: Retrospect and Forecast* (1938).

64. Phyllis Dean, *The County Library Movement in England, 1938–48* (unpublished F.L.A. essay 1949). Useful for some details.

65. Library Association, County Libraries Section, *Statistical and Policy Survey of the County Libraries of Great Britain and Northern Ireland, 1951* (1952).

66. Library Association, County Libraries Group, *A Policy Survey of the County Libraries of the United Kingdom, 1951–1961* (1963).

67. K. A. Stockham (ed.), *British County Libraries: 1919–1969* (Deutsch 1969).

68. *Library Association Record*, County Library Jubilee number, Vol. LXXI (Dec. 1969).

69. *Library World*, County Library Jubilee number, Vol. LXX (May 1969).

National Libraries

It is at this period also that the great national libraries begin to enter into a fruitful relationship with the local libraries. There is no general history of these libraries, but see below under Individual Libraries, and also:

70. Royal Commission on National Museums and Galleries, *Interim Report* (Cmnd. 3192, 1928); *Oral Evidence, Memoranda and Appendices to the Interim Report* (1928); *Final Report*, Part I (Cmnd. 3401, 1929).

71. Standing Commission on Museums and Galleries, *Reports* (1933–70). Eight reports were issued during these years.

72. A. J. K. Esdaile, *National Libraries of the World* (1934).

(*d*) *Since 1965*

Pending a more detailed treatment, it will suffice to cite a number important government reports:

73. Department of Education and Science, Library Advisory Councils, *A Report on the Supply and Training of Librarians* (1968).

74. Scottish Education Department, *Standards for the Public Library Service in Scotland* [Robertson Report] (Edinburgh 1969).

75. Department of Education and Science, *Report of the National Libraries Committee* [Dainton Report] (Cmnd. 4028, 1969).

76. Department of Education and Science, *The British Library* (1971). A sequel to the Dainton Report.

77. Department of Education and Science, Library Advisory Councils, *Public Library Service Points* (1971).

78. Department of Education and Science, *Public Lending Right: Report of the Working Party appointed by the Paymaster General* (1972).

3. Special Regions

(*a*) *London*

79. R. A. Rye, *The Students' Guide to the Libraries of London* (1908, 3rd edn. 1927). Includes useful historical notes.

80. Raymond Irwin (ed.), *The Libraries of London* (Library Association 1949, 2nd edn. by Raymond Irwin and Ronald Staveley, 1961).

81. D. H. Harmer, *The Foundation and Growth of County Library Services around London with special reference to Middlesex* (unpublished F.L.A. essay 1964).

82. *D. White, *The Public Libraries in the New Towns of the London Area* (unpublished F.L.A. thesis 1967).

83. P. M. Whiteman, *The Establishment of Public Libraries and the Unit of Local Government in London to 1900* (unpublished M.A. thesis, Belfast 1969).

See also **103, 124, 131.**

(*b*) *Wales*

84. John Roe, *The Public Library in Wales: its History and Development in the Context of Local Government* (unpublished M.A. thesis, Belfast University 1970).

See also **100, 132.**

(*c*) *Scotland*

85. G. H. Ballantyne, *Comparative Studies in Scottish County Library Organisation and Administration: an Historical and Critical Survey* (unpublished F.L.A. thesis 1965). Detailed studies of Angus and Kincardine; Bute; Dumfriesshire; and Fife.

86. W. E. Tyler, *The Development of the Scottish Public Libraries* (unpublished M.A. thesis, Strathclyde 1967). With special reference to the period since the McClelland Report.

87. W. R. Aitken, *A History of the Public Library Movement in Scotland to 1955* (Scottish Library Association, Glasgow 1971). The basic text for Scottish library history.

See also **47, 48, 53, 74, 102, 135, 143-4, 148**.

4. Biographies

Biographies of a number of library pioneers are listed above (**17, 18, 29, 32, 33, 35**). Biographies of librarians are few and far between.

88. E. A. Savage, *A Librarian's Memories, Portraits and Reflections* (Grafton 1952).

89. W. G. Fry and W. A. Munford, *Louis Stanley Jast: a Biographical Sketch* (Library Association 1966).

90. Edward Miller, *Prince of Librarians: the Life and Times of Antonio Panizzi of the British Museum* (Deutsch 1967).

91. W. A. Munford, *James Duff Brown, 1862–1914: Portrait of a Library Pioneer* (Library Association 1968).

5. Conference Proceedings

These are an important source of information, especially concerning developments in library practice. Published proceedings include:

92. *Transactions and Proceedings of the Conference of Librarians . . . 1877* (1878). Report of the international conference preceding the formation of the Library Association.

93. Library Association, *Transactions and Proceedings of the First Annual Meeting . . . 1878* (1879), and subsequent reports for various years and under varying titles, viz.,
    Transactions and Proceedings . . ., 1879–94.
    Proceedings . . ., 1885, 1893–94, 1919, 1924–28, 1950–62.
    Report . . ., 1892.
    Public Libraries: their Development and Future Organisation, 1917.
    Summary of Papers . . ., 1933–34.
    Papers . . ., 1935–39, 1946–49.

    Conference reports for 1886-91 and 1895-98 are printed in the *Library Chronicle*. From 1899 conference reports not separately published are printed in the *Library Association Record*. Superseded in part by

94. Library Association, *Proceedings of the Public Libraries Conference . . . 1963* (1963) (annually in progress).

95. *Transactions and Proceedings of the Second International Library Conference held in London . . . 1897* (Edinburgh 1898).

96. Carnegie U.K. Trust, *Rural Library Handbook: the Proceedings of the Carnegie Rural Library Conference . . . 1920* (Dunfermline 1921).

97. Carnegie U.K. Trust, *County Library Conference . . . 1924: Report of the Proceedings* (Dunfermline [1925]).

98. Carnegie U.K. Trust, *County Library Conference . . . 1926: Report of the Proceedings* (Dunfermline [1927]).

99. Carnegie U.K. Trust, *Report of the Proceedings of the County Library Conference . . . 1935* (Dunfermline 1936).

100. Library Authorities in Wales and Monmouthshire, *Report of the Proceedings of the Conference on Libraries in Wales and Monmouthshire, 1925* (Aberystwyth 1925), and subsequent reports, annually or biennually 1925–38, annually from 1946.

101. ASLIB, *Report of the Proceedings of the First Conference . . . 1924* (1925), and subsequent reports to 1947 (1948). See **150.**

102. Carnegie U.K. Trust and Scottish Library Association, *Proceedings of the Scottish Library Conference . . . 1931* [Dunfermline 1931].

103. Library Association, London and Home Counties Branch, *Papers read at the Week-end Conference . . . 1946* (1946), and subsequent reports, each with its own title (annually, in progress).

6. Year Books and Directories

104. *Library Association Year Book* (annually since 1891).

105. Thomas Greenwood (ed.), *Greenwood's Library Year Book, 1897* (1897). Succeeded by

106. Thomas Greenwood (ed.), *British Library Year Book, 1900–01* (1900). Succeeded by

107. (Various Editors), *Libraries, Museums and Art Galleries Year Book, 1910–11* (1910), with subsequent editions for 1914, 1923–24, 1928–29, 1932, 1933, 1935, 1937, 1948, 1954–55, 1964, etc. Now published by Clarke.

108. *Literary Year Book* (annually 1897–1923). The Libraries Section of this work provides much useful information. From 1923 this section was developed into a separate work under the title

109. *Librarians' Guide and Directory of Libraries* (Liverpool, annually 1923–32, except 1926 and 1929).

110. (Various Editors), *The Year's Work in Librarianship*, Vols. I–XVII, 1928–50 (Library Association 1929–54). Annually except that Vol. XII covers the years 1939–45. An essential commentary and guide to the literature. Succeeded by

111. P. H. Sewell (ed.), *Five Years' Work in Librarianship, 1951–1955* (Library Association 1958), with subsequent volumes for 1956–60 (1963) and 1961–65 (1968). Succeeded by

112. *H. A. Whatley (ed.), *British Librarianship and Information Science, 1966–1970* (Library Association 1972).

113. R. L. Collison (ed.), *Progress in Library Science, 1965* (Butterworth 1965), with subsequent volumes for 1966 (1966) and 1967 (1968).

7. Statistical Returns and Annual Reports

The earliest (and least used) source of library statistics is to be found in the great series of Parliamentary Returns of Public Libraries published in the Parliamentary Papers between 1853 and 1912. The information included in some of these returns is very detailed, covering not only such matters as bookstocks, issues, and costs, but also age, sex and occupation of readers. The list is as follows:

114. *Returns showing in what Boroughs in England and Wales Libraries and Museums have been formed . . .* (1853).

115. *Return from Places in which the Formation of Free Libraries has been proposed . . .* (1856).

116. *Returns of the Names . . . of all Places in which, according to a Return . . . in the last Session of Parliament, Free Public Libraries had then been agreed upon or established . . .* (1857).

117. *Return showing all the Boroughs and Places in the United Kingdom that have adopted the Act . . . for establishing Public Libraries and Museums and Schools of Science and Art . . .* (1870).

118. *Return from each Library Established under the 'Free Libraries Acts' . . .* (1876).

119. *Return from each Library Established under the 'Free Libraries Act' . . .* (1877).

120. *Return showing the Names of all Places in England, in Scotland, and in Ireland, that have adopted the Public Libraries Acts . . .* (1885).

121. *Return showing the Names of all Places in England, in Scotland, and in Ireland, in which the Public Libraries Acts had been adopted prior to the 25th day of March 1890 . . .* (1890).

122. *Return showing the Names of all Places in England, in Scotland, and in Ireland, in which the Public Libraries Acts had been adopted prior to the end of the last financial year . . .* (1912).

For the period prior to 1919 these returns may be supplemented from the statistical tables in the various editions of Greenwood's *Free Public Libraries* (**24**) and the *Year Books* inaugurated by him (**105-7**), and more reliably from the *Adams Report* (**27**). In connection with the latter see also:

123. Carnegie U.K. Trust, *Statistics relating to Public Libraries in the United Kingdom compiled from the Returns contained in Professor Adams' Report on Library Provision and Policy* (reprinted from the Trust's *Second Annual Report* (1916)).

For London at this period see:

124. London County Council, *Public Baths and Washhouses and Public Libraries: Return relating to (I) All Public Baths and Washhouses and (II) All Public Libraries and Museums . . .* (1899).

After 1919 much useful statistical material is to be found in the various major reports listed above, especially the Mitchell Report (**42**) and the Kenyon Report (**43**). Following the Mitchell Report the Carnegie Trust inaugurated regular statistical reports on the county libraries, afterwards continued by the Library Association:

125. Carnegie U.K. Trust, *County Libraries in Great Britain and Ireland: Reports, 1924* (Dunfermline 1925), with subsequent reports for 1925, 1926–27, and 1927–28. Continued in

126. Library Association, County Libraries Section, *County Libraries in Great Britain and Ireland: Report, 1928–29* (1929), with subsequent reports for 1929–30, 1930–31, 1931–32, 1934–35, and 1938–39. The title of the report for 1929–30 is *County Libraries in Great Britain and Ireland: Report on Branch Library Buildings with Statistical Tables 1929–30.* The report for 1938–39 covers Great Britain and Northern Ireland only.

The urban library service is less well documented:

127. Board of Education, *Statistics of Urban Public Libraries in England and Wales (1931–32)* (1933). An updating of some of the statistics in the Kenyon Report.

128. Library Association, *Statistics of Urban Public Libraries in Great Britain and Northern Ireland (1935)* [1936].

These periodical returns can sometimes be usefully supplemented from annual statistics published in the *Library Association Record*, but these are seldom complete enough to be satisfactory. For reasonably comprehensive statistics we have to wait until the 'fifties:

129. Library Association, *Statistics of Public (Rate-Supported) Libraries in Great Britain and Northern Ireland, 1952–53* (1954), with subsequent returns up to and including 1961–62 (1963), when they were replaced by

130. Institute of Municipal Treasurers and Accountants and Society of County Treasurers, *Public Library Statistics, 1961–62* (1963) (in progress).

For London see:

131. J. D. Stewart (ed.), *Report on the Municipal Library System of London and the Home Counties, 1924* (Library Association 1925), and subsequent reports at five-yearly intervals to 1959 (1961). The county library service is included; for 1954 the title is *Report on the Public Library System . . .*, and for 1959 *Report on the Library Systems . . .*

For Wales see:

132. Library Association, Wales and Monmouthshire Branch, *Report on the Municipal, Urban District, and County Libraries of Wales and Monmouthshire, 1948* (1950).

Among annual reports the most useful, till the mid 'thirties, are those of the Carnegie U.K. Trust, which are indispensable for the development of the county service. See also:

133. Library Association, *Annual Report of the Council, 1878* (1878) (in progress).

134. Board of Education, *Education in England and Wales . . . Report of the Board of Education and the Statistics of Public Education for the Year 1926–27* (1928) (annually, in progress, except for 1939–46). From 1927–28 the title is *Education in 1928* (etc.). The 1950 Report has the title *Education, 1900–1950*. From 1967 the title is *Education and Science in 1967* (etc.). From 1947 the Reports appear under the auspices of the Ministry of Education, from 1964 under those of the Department of Education and Science.

135. Scottish Education Department, *Education in Scotland in 1950* (etc.) (Edinburgh 1951, annually in progress).

8. Journals

The official journals of the Library Association are indispensable. Over the years these have been six in number:

136. *Library Journal*, Vol. I (1876 and annually, in progress). Vol. I was entitled *American Library Journal*, but the title was changed because from 1876 to 1882 (Vols. II–VII), the journal was jointly sponsored by the Library Association and the American Library Association. Since 1883 it has again been concerned mainly with American affairs.

137. *Monthly Notes of the Library Association*, Vols. I–IV (1880–83).

138. *Library Chronicle*, Vols. I–V (1884–88).

139. *The Library*, Vols. I–X (1889–98), N.S. Vols. I–X (1900–09), 3rd Ser. Vols. I–X (1910–19), since 1920 amalgamated with *Transactions of the Bibliographical Society*. From 1889 to 1898 this privately owned periodical served as the official journal of the Library Association.

140. *The Library Association Record*, Vol. I (1899 and annually, in progress). Vols. XXV–XXXII (1923–30) constitute N.S. Vols. I–VIII; Vols. XXXIII–XXXV

(1931–3), constitute 3rd Ser. Vols. I–III; and Vols. XXXVI onwards (1934–   ), constitute a 4th Ser. Between the wars volumes were commonly referred to by the Series number, and this convention has been followed here.

141. *Journal of Librarianship*, Vol. I (Library Association 1969, annually, in progress).

Note also the following publications of affiliated organizations:

142. *Library Assistant*, Vol. I (Library Assistants' Association 1898–99, annually or biennially till 1923, then annually, in progress). From Vol. XLV (1953), title is *Assistant Librarian*.

143. *S.L.A. News Sheet*, Nos. 1–15 (Scottish Library Association, Glasgow 1955). Succeeded by

144. *S.L.A. News*, beginning with No. 16 (1956, and thereafter six times yearly, in progress).

145. *Library History*, Vol. I (Library Association, Library History Group, 1967–69, in progress).

Other library journals published in this country include:

146. *Library World*, Vol. I (1898–99, and annually, in progress). Note that Vol. LIII covers two years (1951–53).

147. *Librarian and Book World*, Vol. I (1910–11, and annually, in progress). Vol. I is entitled *The Librarian*. Note that Vol. X covers two years (1919–21) and that from Vol. XXXVI (1947) each volume covers a calendar year.

148. *Library Review*, Vol. I (Dunfermline 1927–28, biennially, in progress). Now published from Glasgow.

149. *Journal of Documentation*, Vol. I (ASLIB 1945–46, annually, in progress). From Vol. VI (1950), each volume covers a calendar year.

150. *ASLIB Proceedings*, Vol. I (1949, and annually, in progress). Replaces Reports on ASLIB Conference (**101**).

151. *Research in Librarianship*, Vol. I (Oldham 1965, in progress).

English language journals abroad, which often contain material of British interest, include, in addition to the *Library Journal* (**136**):

152. *Library Quarterly*, Vol. I (Chicago University Press 1931, in progress).

153. *Libri: International Library Review*, Vol. I (Ejnar Munksgaard, Copenhagen 1950–51, in progress). Volume numbering erratic.

154. *Library Trends*, Vol. I (University of Illinois, Urbana, 1952–53, in progress).

C. HISTORY OF LIBRARY ADMINISTRATION AND SERVICES

Much concerning the history of libraries can be learnt from manuals, textbooks, and other works dealing with library administration and the various branches of the library service. The following is a selection of works I have found useful:

1. Administration

(a) General

155. J. D. Brown, *Manual of Library Economy* (1903, 2nd edn. 1907, 3rd edn., ed. W. C. B. Sayers, 1920, 4th edn. 1931, 5th edn. 1937, 6th edn. 1949, 7th edn., ed. R. N. Lock, Grafton 1961). The successive editions of this work form the best general guide to the development of library administration.

156. L. R. McColvin and E. R. McColvin, *Library Stock and Assistance to Readers: a Textbook* (1936).

157. B. M. Headicar, *A Manual of Library Organisation* (1935, 2nd edn. 1941).

158. E. A. Savage, *Special Librarianship in General Libraries* (1939).

159. R. Irwin, *The National Library Service* (Grafton 1947).

160. S. C. Bradford, *Documentation* (1948, 2nd edn. 1953).

161. E. V. Corbett, *An Introduction to Public Librarianship* (Clarke 1950, 2nd edn. 1952). see **164.**

162. D. J. Foskett, *Assistance to Readers in Lending Libraries* (Clarke 1952).

163. T. Landau (ed.), *Encyclopaedia of Librarianship* (Bowes and Bowes 1958, 3rd end. 1966).

164. E. V. Corbett, *An Introduction to Librarianship* (Clarke 1963, 2nd edn. 1966).

165. J. C. R. Licklider, *Libraries of the Future* (Massachusetts Institute of Technology, Cambridge, Mass. 1965).

166. Allen Kent and Harold Lancour (eds.), *Encyclopaedia of Library and Information Science* (Dekker, New York, Vols. I–VI, 1968, in progress).

167. R. F. Vollans (ed.), *Libraries for the People: International Studies in Librarianship in honour of L. R. McColvin* (Library Association 1968).

168. *K. H. Jones, *Problems of Public Library Provision for Towns between 20 000 and 100 000 population in England and Wales* (unpublished F.L.A. thesis 1969).

169. M. A. Overington, *The Subject Departmentalised Public Library* (Library Association 1969).

(b) *Municipal Libraries*

170. J. Macfarlane, *Library Administration* (1898).

171. J. M. Mitchell (ed.), *Small Municipal Libraries: a Manual of Modern Methods* (1931).

(c) *County Libraries*

172. R. D. Macleod, *County Rural Libraries* (1923).

173. A. S. Cooke (ed.), *County Libraries Manual* (1935).

2. *Special Aspects*

(a) *Buildings*

174. F. J. Burgoyne, *Library Construction, Architecture, Fittings and Furniture* (1897).

175. A. L. Champneys, *Public Libraries: a Treatise on their Design, Construction and Fittings* (1907).

176. J. L. Wheeler and A. M. Githens, *The American Public Library Building* (New York 1941).

177. Anthony Thompson, *Library Buildings of Britain and Europe* (Butterworth 1963).

178. S. G. Berriman and K. C. Harrison, *British Public Library Buildings* (Deutsch 1966).

See also the special features on new library buildings in *Library Association Record*, Vols. LXII–LXVII, 1960–65.

(b) *Branches and Mobile Libraries*

179. A. G. S. Enser, *Branch Library Practice* (Grafton 1950).

180. C. R. Eastwood, *Mobile Libraries and other Public Library Transport* (Association of Assistant Librarians 1967).

(c)   *Readership Surveys*

181.   Tottenham Public Libraries and Museums, *Reading in Tottenham* (duplicated 1947).

182.   Middlesex County Libraries, *Middlesex County Libraries Silver Jubilee 1922–1947: a review of twenty-five years' work, with a Survey of Reading carried out on 26th March*, 1947 (1948).

183.   A. Stuart, "Reading Habits in Three London Boroughs", in *Journal of Documentation*, Vol. VIII (1952).

184.   T. Cauter and J. S. Downham, *The Communication of Ideas: a Study of Contemporary Influences on Urban Life* (Chatto and Windus 1954). Includes a survey of library readership in Derby.

185.   Southampton Public Libraries Committee, *Where do Readers Live?* (1963). See **187.**

186.   B. Groombridge, *The Londoner and his Library* (Research Institute for Consumer Affairs [1964]).

187.   Southampton Public Libraries Committee, *Survey of Library Users* (1968). Sequel to **185.**

188.   Bryan Luckham, *The Library in Society* (Library Association 1971).

(d)   *Classification*

189.   J. D. Brown, *Manual of Library Classification and Shelf Arrangement* (1898). Ch. vi also published separately as *Adjustable Classification for Libraries, with Index* (1898).

190.   J. D. Brown, *Subject Classification* (1906, 2nd and 3rd edns. by J. D. Stewart, 1914 and 1939).

191.   W. C. B. Sayers, *Manual of Classification for Librarians* (1926, 4th edn. rev. by A. Maltby, Deutsch 1967).

192.   E. A. Savage, *Manual of Book Classification and Display for Public Libraries* (Allen and Unwin and Library Association 1946).

193.   Jack Mills, *A Modern Outline of Library Classification* (Chapman and Hall 1960).

194.   K. Davison, *Classification Practice in Britain* (Library Association 1966).

(e)   *Cataloguing*

195.   H. A. Sharp, *Cataloguing* (1935, 3rd edn. 1944).

196.   R. L. Collison, *The Cataloguing, Arrangement and Filing of Special Materials in Special Libraries* (1950).

(f)   *Charging Systems*

197.   Alfred Cotgreave, *Library Indicators* (1902).

198.   J. D. Brown (ed.), *Open Access Libraries: their Planning, Equipment and Organisation* (1915).

199.   H. T. Geer, *Charging Systems* (American Library Association, Chicago 1955).

200.   E. V. Corbett, *Photocharging* (Clarke 1957).

201.   F. N. Hogg, W. J. Mathews, and T. E. A. Verity, *Report on a Survey made of Book Charging Systems at present in use in England* (duplicated, Library Association 1961).

(g)   *Staffing*

202.   Library Assistants' Association, *Report on the Hours, Salaries, Training and Conditions of Service of Assistants in British Municipal Libraries* (1911).

203. F. Seymour Smith (ed.), *Report on the Hours, Salaries, Training and Conditions of Service in British Municipal Libraries, 1931* (Association of Assistant Librarians 1932).

204. Library Association, *Professional and Non-Professional Duties in Libraries* (1962).

205. G. Bramley, *A History of Library Education* (Bingley 1969).

206. *M. J. Ramsden, *A History of the Association of Assistant Librarians, 1895–1945* (unpublished F.L.A. thesis 1971). See also **217.**

(h) *Inter-Library Co-operation*

207. National Central Library, *Fifteenth Annual Report, 1930–31* (1931) (in progress). Earlier reports were from the Central Library for Students.

208. Luxmoore Newcombe, *Library Co-operation in the British Isles* (1937).

209. P. H. Sewell, *The Regional Library Systems* (Library Association 1950, 2nd edn. 1956, Addendum in *Library Association Record*, Vol. LXI (1959), pp. 254–7).

210. R. F. Vollans, *Library Co-operation in Great Britain: report of a survey of the National Central Library and the Regional Library Bureaux* [Vollans Report] (National Central Library 1952).

211. National Central Library and National Committee on Regional Library Co-operation, *Recommendations on Library Co-operation* (1954).

(j) *Other Aspects*

212. E. V. Corbett, *The Illustrations Collection: its Formation, Classification and Exploitation* (1941).

213. E. T. Bryant, *Music Librarianship: a Practical Guide* (Clarke 1959).

214. Frederic Luther, *Microfilm: a History, 1839–1900* (National Microfilm Association, Annapolis 1959).

215. *A. K. Campbell, *Non-book Materials and Non-Bibliographical Services in Public Libraries . . . 1850 to 1964* (unpublished F.L.A. thesis 1965).

3. *Special Services*

(a) *Reference*

216. F. H. Fenton (ed.), *Reference Library Stocks: an enquiry into reference book provision in the rate-supported libraries of England and Wales* (Library Association 1960).

217. F. H. Fenton (ed.), *Reference Library Staffs* (Library Association 1962).

(b) *Technical and Commercial*

218. J. P. Lamb, *Commercial and Technical Libraries* (Allen and Unwin and Library Association 1955).

(c) *Local History*

219. Committee appointed to enquire as to the Existing Arrangements for the Custody of Local Records, *Report* (1902).

220. W. C. B. Sayers, *Library Local Collections* (1939).

221. J. L. Hobbs, *Libraries and the Materials of Local History* (Grafton 1948).

222. [Sir] Charles H. Jenkinson, *The English Archivist* (Lewis 1948).

223. J. L. Hobbs, *Local History and the Library* (Deutsch 1962).

(d) *Children and Young People*

224. J. J. Ogle, "The Connection between the Public Library and the Public Elementary School," in *Special Reports on Educational Subjects*, Vol. II (Education Department 1898).

225. Library Association, *Report of the Committee on Public Education and Public Libraries* (1905).

226. W. C. B. Sayers, *The Children's Library: a practical manual for public, school and home libraries* (1912).

227. Gwendolen Rees, *Libraries for Children: a history and a bibliography* (1924).

228. Board of Education, *Memorandum on Libraries in State-Aided Secondary Schools in England* (1928).

229. Board of Education, *Report of the Consultative Committee on Books in Public Elementary Schools* (1928).

230. W. C. B. Sayers, *A Manual of Children's Libraries* (Allen and Unwin and Library Association 1932).

231. Eric Leyland, *The Public Library and the Adolescent* (1937).

232. Library Association, County Libraries Section, *Memorandum on the Provision of Libraries in Elementary Schools* (1939).

233. Library Association, *Work with Young People and School Libraries* (1949).

234. Library Association, Youth Libraries Section, *Survey of Public Library Service for Children, 1954* [1955].

235. Library Association, Youth Libraries Section, *Public Library Services for Children 1958–1959* (1960).

236. Alec Ellis, *Library Services for Young People in England and Wales, 1830–1970* (Pergamon 1971).

(e) *Blind Readers*

237. W. A. Munford, *A Short History of the National Library for the Blind* (first printed in the Library's *Annual Report, 1957–58*, 2nd edn. 1917).

238. *L. M. Cowburn, *The History and Development of the National Library for the Blind* (unpublished F.L.A. thesis 1966).

(f) *Hospitals*

239. Library Association, *Memorandum and Recommendations of the Hospital Libraries Committee* (1931).

240. C. E. A. Bedwell, *Manual for Hospital Librarians* (Library Association 1947).

241. K. M. Allsop, *A Mental Hospital Library: a report of an experiment at Lancaster Moor Hospital in 1947–49* (Library Association 1951).

242. King Edward's Hospital Fund for London, *Hospital Library Services: a pilot survey* (1959).

243. M. E. Going (ed.), *Hospital Libraries and Work with the Disabled* (Library Association 1963).

244. Library Association, *Hospital Libraries: recommended standards of libraries in hospitals* (1965).

245. B. M. Sanders, *Library Services in Hospitals* (Library Association 1966).

(g) *Prisons*

246. Home Office, Prison Libraries Committee, *Report of the Departmental Committee on the Supply of Books to the Prisoners in H.M. Prisons and to the Inmates of H.M. Borstal Institutions* (Cd. 5588, 1911).

247. Home Office, *Report of the Commissioners of Prisons . . . 1942–1944* (Cmd. 7010, 1947), and subsequent annual reports.

248. R. F. Watson, *Prison Libraries* (Library Association 1951).

249. Frances Banks, *Teach them to Live* (Parrish 1958).

(h) Libraries and the Community: Extension Activities

250. Library Association and British Institute of Adult Education, *The Public Libraries and Adult Education* (1923).

251. L. R. McColvin, *Library Extension Work and Publicity* (1927).

252. L. R. McColvin, *Libraries and the People* (1937).

253. Ernest Green, "Book Supplies to Adult Classes," in H. V. Usill (ed.), *Year Book of Education, 1938.*

254. Eric Leyland, *The Wider Public Library* (1938).

255. Edward Sydney, "The Public Library and Adult Education," in H. V. Usill (ed.), *Year Book of Education, 1938.*

256. L. S. Jast, *The Library and the Community* (1939).

257. Carl Thomsen, Edward Sydney, and M. D. Tompkins, *Adult Education Activities for Public Libraries* (UNESCO, Paris 1950).

258. Harold Jolliffe, *Public Library Extension Activities* (Library Association 1962, 2nd edn. 1968).

259. Harold Jolliffe, *Arts Centre Adventure* (Swindon Borough Council 1968).

260. G. Jefferson, *Libraries and Society* (Clarke 1969).

261. R. C. Benge, *Libraries and Cultural Change* (Bingley 1970).

261a D. E. Gerard (ed.), *Libraries and the Arts: a Symposium of Papers and Discussions held in the College of Librarianship Wales . . . 1969* (Bingley 1970).

D. HISTORY OF INDIVIDUAL LIBRARIES

1. National Libraries

British Museum Library

262. Richard Garnett, *Essays in Librarianship and Bibliography* (1899).

263. G. F. Barwick, *The Reading Room of the British Museum* (1929).

264. A. J. K. Esdaile, *The British Museum Library: a short history and survey* (Allen and Unwin 1946).

265. [Sir] Frank C. Francis, "The British Museum looks towards the Future," in *Proceedings of the American Philosophical Society*, Vol. CIV (1960).

266. J. M. Cook, *The British Museum* (Allen Lane 1972).

National Library of Wales

267. W. Llewellyn Davies, *The National Library of Wales: a Survey of its History, its Contents, and its Activities* (National Library of Wales, Aberystwyth 1937).

268. National Library of Wales, *The National Library of Wales: a Brief Summary of its History and its Activities* (Aberystwyth 1962).

National Library of Scotland

269. W. K. Dickson, "The Advocates' Library", in *Juridical Review*, Vol. XIV (1902).

270. W. K. Dickson, "The Advocates' Library", in *L.A.R.*, N.S. Vol. V (1927).

Science Museum

271. Board of Education, *Report of the Advisory Council of the Science Museum, 1920* (1921, and annually, under the Board and its successors).

2. Municipal Libraries

Detailed published histories of individual libraries are few, and mostly at least fifty years old. Only Norwich, Sheffield, and Greenock have substantial histories published within the last twenty years. For the rest we have to rely on annual reports and on articles and pamphlets, though in the last few years F.L.A. theses have begun to fill the gap. The following is a selection, published except where otherwise indicated by the public libraries concerned. They are listed in alphabetical order of libraries:

272. *Aberdare Central Public Library Golden Jubilee, 1904–1954* (1955).

273. [Aberystwyth]. N. Roberts, "A Town and its Library," in *Ceredigion*, Vol. III No. 2 (Aberystwyth 1956–59).

274. [W. Scobbie], *A Century of Reading: Airdrie Public Library, 1853–1953* (1953).

275. V. J. Kite, *Libraries in Bath, 1618–1964* (unpublished F.L.A. thesis 1966).

276. *Battersea Libraries: 1887–1890–1950* [1950].

277. *1866–1966: an Account of the Bebington Public Library Service* [1966].

278. A. E. Baker, *The Library Story: a history of the library movement in Bedford* (1958).

279. *Birkenhead Public Libraries Centenary, 1856–1956* (1956).

280. A. C. Shaw, "The Birmingham Free Libraries," in *L.A.R.*, Vol. IV (1902). Also published separately in book form (Aberdeen University Press 1902).

281. *Notes on the History of the Birmingham Public Libraries, 1861–1961* (1962).

282. *The Centenary of the Bolton Public Libraries, 1853–1953* (1953).

283. M. E. Hartley, "A Survey of the Public Library Movement in Bradford," in *L.A.R.*, Vol. VIII (1906). Also published in book form (Aberdeen University Press 1906).

284. Butler Wood, *A Brief Survey of the Bradford Public Libraries, 1874–1922* (1922).

285. H. D. Roberts, "The Brighton Public Library, Museums and Fine Art Galleries: a Retrospect", in *L.A.R.*, Vol. X (1908).

286. Charles Tovey, *A Free Library for Bristol, with a History of the City Library, its Founders and Benefactors* (Bristol and London 1855).

287. S. M. Booth, *Three Hundred and Fifty Years of Public Libraries in Bristol, 1613–1963* (1963).

288. J. F. Odgers, *Camborne Public (Free) Library, 1895–1963* (1963).

289. W. A. Munford, *The Cambridge City Libraries, 1855–1955* (1955).

290. [Sir] John Ballinger, *The Cardiff Free Libraries* (1895).

291. *Cardiff Public Libraries, 50th Anniversary Celebration of the Opening of the Central Library: a brief survey of the library movement in Cardiff* (1932).

292. *Chatham Public Libraries Jubilee, 1904–1964* (1964).

293. *Chelmsford Public Library Diamond Jubilee, 1906–1966* (1967).

294. *Allen Varley, A History of Libraries in Cheltenham from 1780 to 1900* (unpublished F.L.A. thesis 1968).

295. Frank Simpson, *Chester Free Public Library* [1931].

296. *Handbook to the Coventry Public Libraries: the Record of Sixty Years, 1868–1928* (1928).

297. [Darlington]. *Edward Pease Public Library: Fifty Years' Progress, 1885–1935* (1935).

298. *Dartford Public Libraries and Museum Jubilee, 1916–1966* (1966).

299. *Derby Borough Libraries, 1871–1971* (1971).

300. *J. L. Hannavy, *The Libraries of Dover and Folkestone* (unpublished F.L.A. thesis 1968).

301. *Dudley Public Libraries Diamond Jubilee, 1884–1959* (1959).

302. [Dumfries]. M. D. McLean, *Fifty Years a-Growing: the Ewart Library attains its Jubilee* (repr. from *Dumfries and Galloway Standard*, 8 Sept. 1954).

303. *Respice-Prospice: . . . the Ealing Public Library Service from . . . 1883 to 1964* (1964).

304. *Edinburgh Public Libraries and City Museums: Historical Guide and Handbook to the Libraries* (1958).

305. K. C. Harrison, *Sixty Years of Service: the Diamond Jubilee of the Eastbourne Public Libraries, 1896–1956* (1956).

306. H. Tapley-Soper, "Exeter Public Library: an Historical Essay", in *L.A.R.*, Vol XIII (1911).

307. *Farnworth Public Library 1911–1961* (1961).

308. [Folkestone]. See above under Dover.

309. [F. L. Hasker], *"To Commemorate the Approaching Jubilee of her Most Gracious Majesty": an outline of the evolution of the Fulham Public Libraries, 1887–1963* (1963).

310. T. Mason, *Public and Private Libraries of Glasgow* (privately published 1885).

311. T. Mason, *Account of Stirling's and Glasgow Public Library* (Stirling's and Glasgow Public Library, 1888)

312. *Descriptive Account of the Corporation Public Libraries of the City of Glasgow* (1924).

313. *Glasgow Public Libraries, 1874–1954* (1955), 2nd edn *1874–1966* (1966)

314. J. T. Hamilton, *Greenock Libraries: a Development and Social History, 1635–1967* [privately published 1969].

315. H. F Warren, *A History of the Hinckley Public Libraries, 1888–1938* (1938)

316. *Public Library Handbook: History of the Library Movement in Huddersfield* [1946].

317. J. F. Hooton, *Libraries in Hull in the Nineteenth Century and the Struggle for the Adoption of the Public Libraries Acts* (unpublished F.L.A. thesis 1967).

318. *Islington Public Libraries Golden Jubilee 1906–1956* [1956].

319. *The Public Library Service in Keighley, 1904–1954* (1954).

320. H. G. Massey, *Kensington Libraries Service* (1950).

321. *Raymond Wilson, *A History of King's Lynn Libraries, 1795–1905* (unpublished F.L.A. thesis 1971).

322. P. K. Livingstone, *Kirkcaldy and its Libraries* (1950).

323. *Lancaster Public Library Service Diamond Jubilee, 1893–1953* (1953).

324. T. W. Hand, "The Leeds Public Free Libraries," in *L.A.R.*, Vol. VI (1904). Also published in book form (Aberdeen University Press 1903).

325. T. W. Hand, *A Brief Account of the Public Libraries of the City of Leeds, 1870–1920* (1920).

326. *Letchworth: a Town Built on a Book* (Letchworth National Library Week Committee 1966).

327. *Lincoln City Libraries, 1914–1964* [1964].

328. P. Cowell, *Liverpool Public Libraries: a History of Fifty Years* (1903).

329. *Liverpool Public Libraries Centenary, 1850–1950* (1950).

330. F. Hope, *A History of the Liverpool Public Libraries, 1852–1952* (unpublished F.L.A. essay 1954).

331. J. W. Lucas, *Malvern Public Library* (1940).

332. W. R. Credland, *The Free Library Movement in Manchester* (1895).

333. W. R. Credland, *The Manchester Public Free Libraries* (1899).

334. G. C. Paterson, *A Short History of the Manchester Public Libraries, 1892–1948* (unpublished F.L.A. essay 1949).

335. Arthur Smith, *The Gilstrap Public Library, Newark* [1933].

336. ★John Morley, *Libraries of Newark on Trent, 1698–1960* (unpublished F.L.A. thesis 1969).

337. B. Anderton, "The Struggle for a Public Library in Newcastle upon Tyne", in *L.A.R.*, Vol. VII (1905).

338. *A Short History of the Newcastle upon Tyne Public Libraries, 1854–1950* (1950).

339. *Northampton Public Libraries, 1876–1926* (1926).

340. [Norwich]. G. A. Stephen, *Three Centuries of a City Library* (1917).

341. Philip Hepworth and Mary Alexander, *City of Norwich Libraries: History and Treasures* (1957, reprinted with other material in *City of Norwich Libraries*, 1965).

342. *Fifty Years: a Brief History of the Public Library Movement in Nottingham* (1918).

343. [Nottingham]. *The Public Libraries and Natural History Museum, 1868–1928* (1928).

344. *Nottingham Public Libraries Centenary: a Reading Public 1868–1968* (1968).

345. W. H. Berry, *Oldham Public Libraries, Art Gallery and Museum 1883–1933* (1933).

346. Henry Jones, *A History of Oswestry Public Library to 1963* [1963].

347. *Oxford City Libraries, 1854–1954* [1954].

348. A. C. Jones, *Paddington Public Libraries: a Short History* (1965).

349. J. B. Bowick, "Summary of the History of the Sandeman Public Library, Perth, from its Institution in 1898, to the Year 1908", in *L.A.R.*, Vol. XIII (1911).

350. City of Peterborough, *Fifty Years of Service, 1909–1955: Golden Jubilee of the Opening of the Central Library . . .* (1955).

351. *Rawtenstall Public Library, 1906–1956* (1956).

352. W. H. Greenough, *The County Borough of Reading: the Public Libraries: a retrospect of thirty years, 1882–1912* (1913).

353. *London Borough of Redbridge: Public Library Services, 1909–1969* (1969).

354. ★[St. Marylebone]. J. Cowell, *The Background of the Public Library Movement in Marylebone* (unpublished M.A. thesis, Loughborough 1970).

355. B. H. Mullen, *The Royal Museum and Libraries, Salford: their Inception and Development* (1899).

356. *The City Libraries of Sheffield, 1856–1956* (1956).

357. *Smethwick Public Libraries, 1877–1927* (1928).

358. *Stalybridge Public Library Diamond Jubilee, 1889–1949: Sixty Years—the Story of the Astley Cheetham Public Libraries and Art Gallery* (1949).

359. *The Library Story: 60 Years of Public Service 1906–1966. Compiled in the Diamond Jubilee Year of the Stamford Public Library and Museum* (1966).

360. R. E. G. Smith, *The First Fifty Years of Public Libraries in Stockport* (unpublished F.L.A. essay 1950).

361. D. D. Nichols, *Twenty Years' Development: Stockport Public Libraries 1936–1956* (1957).

362. *Stoke-on-Trent: Jubilee Report of the City Librarian* (1960).

363. *Public Libraries and Art Galleries in Stretford* (1946).

364. *21 Years of Public Library Service in Swindon, 1943–1964* [1964].

365. *Torquay Public Library: Fifty Years of Service, 1907–1957* [1957].

366. G. Hodges, *West Bromwich Public Library, 1874–1946* [1946].

367. Westminster Public Libraries, *Report of the Public Libraries Committee 1949–50* (Centenary Report 1950).

368. Westminster Public Libraries, *Great Smith Street Public Library, 1857–1957* (1957).

369. Westminster Public Libraries, *Public Library Service, 1900–1965: Report of the Public Libraries Committee* (1965).

370. *The Willesden Library Service: a Jubilee History and Annual Report, 1953–54* [1954].

371. Whitehaven Public Library and Museum, *Annual Reports*, 1951 and 1964. Both these reports include historical material.

372. W. Myson, *The Story of the Wimbledon Library Service* (duplicated 1965).

3. *County Libraries*

373. *Buckinghamshire County Library, 1918–1968: Annual Report 1967–68* (1968).

374. *Cheshire: Report of the County Librarian for the Years 1952–65* [1965].

375. A. Anderson, *The Old Libraries of Fife* (duplicated, Fife Co. Lib., Kirkcaldy 1953).

376. *Gloucestershire County Library, 1917–1967: Fifty Years of Public Service* [1967].

377. S. H. Davis, *The History of Lancashire County Library* (unpublished F.L.A. thesis 1968).

378. *Middlesex County Libraries, 1922–1965* (reprinted with additions from *Primary and Secondary Education in Middlesex, 1900–1965*, Middlesex Education Committee 1964). See also **81, 182.**

379. J. N. Taylor, *A Short History of the Nottinghamshire County Library* (unpublished F.L.A. essay 1953).

380. *Radnorshire County Library: The First Ten Years, 1939–1949* (1949). Followed by *The Second Ten Years, 1949–1959* (1959), and *The Third Ten Years, 1959–1969* [1969].

381. R. G. Bird, *A Short History of the Surrey County Library* (unpublished F.L.A. essay 1950).

GENERAL INDEX

Aberdeen, Mechanics' Institute, 67; Anderson Library, Woodside, 132

Aberystwyth, University College, 315; School of Librarianship, 357, 416, 418; National Library of Wales, *see separate entry*

Adams, Prof. W. G. S., 118; Adams Report, 118, 234; cited on various aspects of library service, 124–7, 144–5, 149, 158, 160, 165, 168, 203, 235, 319; recommendations concerning rural library provision, 211–12

Airdrie, Mechanics' Institute, 64

Albemarle Report, 404

Allington, village reading room, 136

Alyth, Ogilvy or Loyal Alyth Library, 132

Anderson, Sir John, benefactor at Aberdeen, 132n.

Anderson, Sir John, Lord Privy Seal, 327

Anderson, S. W., Librarian of Croydon, 294

Anderton, Basil, librarian of Newcastle upon Tyne, 148

Arbroath, subscription library, 134–5

Archer, William, librarian of the National Library of Ireland, 71

Archives, in local collections, 289–90; profession of archivist, 289–90, 292n.

Art galleries, in association with public libraries, 35, 47, 65, 140, 148–9, 164

Arts Council, 334, 428; local arts centres, in association with public libraries, 411, 414–15

Association of Assistant Librarians, formerly Library Assistants' Association, 203, 205, 254, 308, 310–11

Association of Metropolitan Chief Librarians, 386

Association of Special Libraries and Information Bureaux (ASLIB), origins, 244; other references, 254, 292, 310, 318, 408n., 418, 419n.

Association of University Teachers, 323

Atkins, Arthur, of Hinckley, 163

Atkinson, William, benefactor at Southport, 68

Atlay, Dr. [James], Vicar of Leeds, 28

Authors, and payment for library use of books, 428

Avebury, Lord, 98, 110–11, 113

Axon, W. E. A., of Salford, 76, 209

Aycliffe, new town, 356n.

Ayr, Mechanics' Institute, 134; public (subscription) library, 134

Baillie, George, benefactor at Glasgow, 142

Baker, E. A., librarian at Derby, later librarian of Woolwich and director, University College School of Librarianship, 195, 311

Baker, E. B. H., 358; Baker Report, 358, 422

Balfour, Sir Graham, Director of Education for Staffordshire, 214

Ballinger, Sir John, librarian of Cardiff and later of National Library of Wales, 144–5, 196, 198, 210, 234, 245, 253

Banbury, Sir Frederick, later 1st Lord, 216

Barlow, S. H., librarian of Nuneaton, 378

Barnett, Canon S. A., 121n.

Barrett, F. T., librarian of Glasgow, 142–3

Basildon, new town, 356n.

Bass, Michael T., benefactor at Derby, 61, 68

Bath, early libraries, 135n.

Beaney, Dr. J. G., benefactor at Canterbury, 157

Bebington, Mayer Library, 131–2, 135

Bentliff, G. A., 33n.; Bentliff, Samuel, benefactor at Maidstone, 33

Berriman, S. G., librarian of Middlesex Co., later of Cheshire Co., 352–3, 369, 374n.

Bertram, James, secretary to Andrew Carnegie, 117

Besterman, Dr. Theodore, 408n.

Bethnal Green, public (subscription) library, 134

Bevan, Mr. and Mrs., benefactors at Oakley, 164

Beveridge, Michael, benefactor at Kirkcaldy, 119

Bibliographic Classification, 303, 407

Biggs, Major B. G. D., of Darlington, 158

Birmingham, agitation for improvement of education, 19; Subscription Library, 47, 99, 288; University Library, 323; Birmingham and District Library Association, 254, 310

Birrell, William, joint librarian of Leicester Co., 230

Bishopwearmouth, Mechanics' Institute, 60

Blackwell, B. H., librarian of Oxford, 57, 99

Blaenavon, working men's institute library, 130–1

Blind, provision of books for, *see* Public Libraries, I (e) (xiv), Special Collections

Bliss, H. E., 303; his Bibliographic Classification, 303, 407

Board of Education, *see* Education Department

Boardman, F. J., librarian of Rotherham, 262–3

Bolton, Mechanics' Institute, 53, 66n.

Bolton, George, librarian of Watford, 299n.

Bond, Sir Edward, librarian of British Museum, 314

Books: cheap book movements, 256; paperback publishing, 343–4; public lending right, 428

Booth, Charles, 107

Boots Booklovers Library, 344

Borstals, library provision for, 397–8

Bourdillon, H. T., 358; Bourdillon Report, 358, 394–5, 397, 401, 412–14, 416, 427

Bracknell, new town, 356n.

Braddon, Mary Elizabeth, 193

INDEX OF PUBLIC LIBRARY AUTHORITIES

The authorities indexed here are those listed in Appendix III above. The names of authorities which are not known to have provided a library service are printed in italics. References to the tables in the Appendices are also given in italics. Branch libraries are not separately indexed.